ADULT DEVELOPMENT AND AGING

A D U L T
D E V E L O P M E N T
A N D
A G I N G

John W. Santrock
University of Texas-Dallas

wcb
Wm. C. Brown Publishers
Dubuque, Iowa

BOOK TEAM

T. Greg Bell *Editor*
Sandra E. Schmidt *Assistant Developmental Editor*
Catherine Dinsmore *Designer*
Laura Beaudoin *Senior Production Editor*
Faye M. Schilling *Visual Research Editor*
Vicki Krug *Permissions Editor*

wcb group

Wm. C. Brown *Chairman of the Board*
Mark C. Falb *Executive Vice-President*

wcb

WM. C. BROWN PUBLISHERS, COLLEGE DIVISION

Lawrence E. Cremer *President*
James L. Romig *Vice-President, Product Development*
David A. Corona *Vice-President, Production and Design*
E. F. Jogerst *Vice-President, Cost Analyst*
Marcia H. Stout *Marketing Manager*
Marilyn A. Phelps *Manager of Design*
William A. Moss *Production Editorial Manager*
Mary M. Heller *Visual Research Manager*

Cover photo by Gabe Palmer/The Image Bank

Printed in the United States of America
10 9 8 7 6 5 4 3 2 1

For . . . Marie Smith, Shauna Santrock,
Mary K. and Doc Jordan, and Freddie Kellmeyer

CONTENTS

Section **IV** SOCIAL PROCESSES, CONTEXTS, AND
DEVELOPMENT 233

Profile 234

PREFACE

TO THE STUDENT

The field of adult development and aging is an exciting one. For many years, the prevailing view of adult development suggested that the adult years were a time of little change. Many people believed that our thoughts and our feelings as adults were cast in stone before the end of adolescence. Some experts even maintained that our lives as adults were almost totally caused by what went on in the first five years of our lives. To be sure, what happens to us in childhood and adolescence constitutes important aspects of the life cycle. But the next five, six, or seven decades are just as complex and as important as the first two decades of life. They are important not just to those adults who are passing through them but also to their children, who must live with and understand parents and grandparents.

Many of you reading this book are just beginning your life as an adult. You will be motivated to think about what the rest of your adult years hold in store for you. What will you be like at mid-life, at age seventy? By the time you have completed this book, you should have a much clearer picture of the awesome, complex unfolding of development during the adult years. Not only will you learn important facts about the nature of this development, but you should be able to use some of these facts to interpret your own life as you grow older. Our hope is that this book becomes something special to you, something that you will want to take with you after this class is over so that you can refer to it the rest of your life.

TO THE INSTRUCTOR

The last several years have witnessed a prolific increase in the number of books available to instructors faced with the decision of which textbook to adopt for their course in adult development and aging. The book you are about to read is not an attempt to clutter the market with just another book. *Adult Development and Aging* presents a unique blend of sound research, issue-focused discussion, and a writing style and presentation that will motivate students. Virtually all authors say that they try to accomplish the difficult task of maintaining academic rigor while presenting material in a manner that will not turn off students because of academic stuffiness. How does *Adult Development and Aging* accomplish such a task better than the dozen or so adulthood and aging texts that have appeared within the last several years?

With regard to academic rigor, issue-focused discussion, and research orientation, *Adult Development and Aging* has a process orientation. By means of this orientation, your students will be able to see how developmental processes reflect fundamental changes that occur during the adult years. To this end, four of the six sections in the text focus on biological processes and physical development; cognitive processes and development; social processes, contexts, and development; and personality processes and development. In addition, the first section of the text provides the most comprehensive, comprehensible discussion of issues and methods available in any text on adult development and aging. The characterization of the chapters in this section as comprehensive and comprehensible means that instructors and their students will find that the material reflects a broad range of ideas about issues and methodology that are often either written in a manner too difficult for most students to understand or simply miss or misinterpret some of the important aspects of adult development and aging. We urge you to compare these two introductory chapters on issues and methods with our competitors in regard to scientific rigor, ease of understanding, manner in which the issues and methods are interpreted, and the completeness with which they are discussed. Our final section on death and dying gives special emphasis to the psychological meaning of death, the coping processes of both the dying individual and emotionally attached others, and attitudes about death.

The research included in the core of the text—research that is focused on biological, cognitive, social, and personality processes—includes basic ideas about adult development and aging, as well as "leading edge" research that helps students sense where the field is headed. For example, you will find the following up-to-date, intriguing discussion of important ideas and research:

Biological Processes and Physical Development
Evoked potentials
Use of PETT and CT scans
Difficulties in documenting how many neurons healthy adults lose as they age
Recent developments in the field of behavior genetics
Recent information about the role of exercise in slowing the aging process
Longitudinal data on physical health from early adolescence to mid-life
The role of life-style and personality in health
Developmental changes in basal metabolism rate and the preoccupation of
    women with weight
An in-depth look at various dimensions of sensorimotor development

Cognitive Processes and Development

Contextual view of cognitive stages

Why Piaget's model may be inappropriate for studying adult cognition

Converging agreement about the nature of possible changes in cognition
during the early adulthood years

Data from the California Longitudinal Study that address the issue of an
increase in crystallized intelligence and a decline in fluid intelligence

Nancy Denney's view on the importance of unexercised mental abilities

Treatment of the nature of change and decline in information processing and
memory during early, middle, and late adulthood, including provocative
conclusions about the nature of such changes and cognitive intervention

Stimulating discussion of attentional and perceptual changes in adulthood

Social Processes, Contexts, and Development

Interaction of marital relations, parenting, and the child's behavior

Recent conclusions about intergenerational relationships

Behavioral exchange view of marital relations

Detailed information about the effects of divorce on adults and children,
including developmental data about marital separation in middle and late
adulthood

Developmental course of attachment and love across the adulthood years

Social integration and isolation

Historical and cross-cultural views of aging

Recent data from the California Longitudinal Investigation that reveal
attributes that are likely to lead to upward occupational mobility

Characteristics of seventy-year-old workers in the United States

Intriguing relationship among intrinsic motivation, the work ethic, and worker
productivity

Personality Processes and Development

Erikson's life-span view, including conceptual and methodological evaluation

Critical evaluation of a number of adult stage views

Cognitive social learning perspective and importance of person $\times$ situation
interaction

Life-events framework

Stability and change, including data from the major longitudinal studies of
personality development

Recent longitudinal data on stability and change from early adolescence
through mid-life

Recent longitudinal data on stability and change from age thirty to age seventy

Contemporary ideas about coping and stress, including Richard Lazarus's
recent theory and research on adult development and aging

Material on androgyny from several different perspectives
Comparison of the moral perspectives of men and women
Margaret Gatz's comments about mental health services for the elderly
Stimulating thoughts about how the mental health needs of older people
    should be met

Now that you have seen how *Adult Development and Aging* achieves academic rigor by presenting a comprehensive, up-to-date treatment of research and issues in the field, we return to the matter of stimulating student enthusiasm and avoiding academic stuffiness. As stated earlier, the text is written at a level so that students can understand difficult concepts and complex research but still be stimulated to think deeply about provocative ideas and issues. How do we accomplish this difficult task? First, the writing level itself is purposely simple, direct, logical, and communicative. Second, a number of pedagogical devices make the book interesting as well as informative for students. Each section of the book opens with *Profile,* an easy-to-read description of one or two individuals whose aging through the adult years reflects some of the important points to be discussed in subsequent chapters in that section. Each chapter opens with a chapter outline, followed by a piece called *Imagine,* which stimulates students to think about what their life would be like if they experienced adulthood in a particular way. Each chapter also includes boxes that are designed to present supplementary and enrichment material beyond the primary text coverage. These are just some of the pedagogical and organizational features that make *Adult Development and Aging* not only the most informative text available but the most interesting and enjoyable one as well.

Audience

This text should be useful for students taking an introductory or advanced course in adult development and aging. Sometimes the course is titled adult development, sometimes it is labeled adult development and aging (or the psychology of adult development and aging), and sometimes it is referred to as adult psychology, psychology of the adult, or simply as aging. The typical student is most likely to be a sophomore, junior, or senior undergraduate who has had a general introduction to psychology course. However, the text requires no previous knowledge of the sort and is written at a level that allows the student to build a conceptual structure of the field from the ground up.

The text is also appropriate for instructors who teach a course in life-span development and want to use two books—one on child development or child psychology and another on adult development and aging.

Content and Organization

In *Adult Development and Aging,* the basic views, principles, research findings, and ideas about adults are presented from a psychological perspective. The text consists of six sections, which in turn are organized into thirteen chapters, each of which is concerned with a major theme or facet of adult development and aging. (See table of contents.)

Additional Textual Learning Aids

We already have mentioned the pedagogical aids *Profile,* chapter outlines, *Imagine,* and insert boxes. In addition, terms with specialized meanings are printed in boldface type to alert the reader to the fact that a definition can be found in the glossary at the back of the book. Graphs, tables, and charts illustrate and summarize the findings of important research studies. Photographs and line drawings give visual emphasis to concepts and events and to people present and past who have advanced our knowledge of adult development and aging. Finally, each chapter ends with a detailed summary, review questions, and suggestions for further reading. Separate indexes for authors and subjects appear at the end of the book. We hope you will agree that this text has been written with the student in mind.

Instructor's Manual

An Instructor's Manual, by Michael Walraven, will be available to adopters. In addition to an introductory essay to the instructor, it will contain an overview, six to eight essay questions, twenty-five multiple-choice questions, and a film list for each of the text's chapters. The multiple-choice questions will also be available on Testpak, **wcb**'s computerized testing service.

Acknowledgments

Special thanks go to my publisher, William C. Brown, for the special attention given this book. James Romig, Vice-President of Product Development, has an incredible sense of what is necessary to make a successful book. Greg Bell, Social Sciences Editor, has been an invaluable supporter. His advice and friendship are very special. Laura Beaudoin, Senior Production Editor, has cheerfully overseen the production of this book and has amended many errors on my part. Cathie Dinsmore, the designer, has made *Adult Development and Aging* a very attractive book. Faye Schilling deserves credit for her work on the photographs and Vicki Krug for her expedient effort in obtaining permissions.

I benefited considerably from the reviews of this text at different points during its development. Indeed, it was reviewer comments that persuaded me to change the format of this book from a chronological to a topical orientation. The following individuals deserve special mention for their insightful criticisms: Don C. Charles, Iowa State University; Elton C. Davis, Pasadena City College; Ernest Furchtgott, University of South Carolina; Bert Hayslip, Jr., North Texas State University; Mary W. Lawrence, University of Toronto; Robert Bruce McLaren, California State University–Fullerton; Mary Jane S. Van Meter, Wayne State University.

With 1,000 or more typed pages in the original manuscript and several revisions, typing was an arduous task. I owe special thanks to Florence Rowland for her typing expertise.

James Bartlett, whose name appears on four chapters in *Adult Development and Aging,* is an incredibly competent cognitive psychologist who has a keen sense of science and cognitive processes. I sincerely appreciate his willingness to contribute his wisdom to this project. His ideas and writing have made this book far better than my abilities alone could.

Michael Walraven deserves special thanks as well. He has prepared an instructor's manual that will greatly enhance the use of this text.

Finally, I would like to thank my wife, Mary Jo, for her patience and understanding while I prepared this manuscript.

ADULT DEVELOPMENT AND AGING

INTRODUCTION, ISSUES,
AND METHODS

PROFILE

Meet Steven and Cynthia Parke. They are but two of the more than a dozen adults we will introduce to you at the beginning of each of the sections in this text. In some ways they are like all adults, and yet there are ways in which they are different from each other and all other adults. Keep this point in mind as you read the "Profile" sections—we share certain commonalities with all other adults. For example, we were all born with a genetic code that came from two parents, we all have a brain, parents and peers are important to all of us, and experiences during our adult lives help to shape the kind of person we are. But the particular genetic code, the particular brain, the nature of our relationships with our parents and peers, and the particular experiences we have as adults often differ from one individual to the next. One of the goals of this text is to point to the commonalities, exceptions, and individual variation in adult development and aging.

When we enter the lives of Steven and Cynthia Parke, Steven is twenty-three years old and Cynthia is twenty-one. They have been married for six months, and last month Cynthia found out that she is pregnant. Cynthia is a senior at a state university, and Steven has just entered his first year of medical school. Cynthia is a psychology major and is taking a class this semester on adult development and aging. Her professor conducts research on adult development and has recently designed an investigation to study the lives of individuals during adulthood. Indeed, the professor is looking for subjects for his study of adult lives. The professor has decided to look at a number of different aspects of adult development. He is interested in studying physical development and will look at such matters as health and sexuality. He also wants to find out about the cognitive activities of adults, so he plans to study such subjects as attention, memory, how people process information about their world, and intelligence.

Cynthia's professor also wants to know something about the social aspects of adulthood, so he will investigate adults' relationships with their parents, the nature of their marital relationships, the nature of their relationships with their children, their social ties and relationships, such as friendships, and the role of work in their lives. He also has told the class that another important aspect of adult development and aging is personality. To this end, the professor plans to study the nature of personality development during the adult years by looking at such dimensions as introversion/extroversion, self-esteem, life satisfaction, and anxiety.

Cynthia's professor is a very ambitious individual—he will begin studying a group of adults at the start of their adult years and follow them for twenty years until they are middle-aged. Cynthia thinks her professor's investigation sounds intriguing, so she volunteers to become one of the subjects. Her husband, who is busy studying medicine, wasn't excited at first, but after the first session he became enthusiastic. Cynthia and Steven will be studied every two years, so they will be evaluated a total of eleven times (counting the first year) through their early adult lives.

Cynthia and Steven are among 500 married couples in this investigation. Cynthia's professor had to make some choices when he designed this investigation—he couldn't study everybody and everything. Indeed, one of the things Cynthia has learned in her adult development and aging class is that when research projects are designed, a number of decisions have to be made about what to include and exclude. Actually, the study she and Steven are involved in will look at many more aspects of adult development than do most investigations. For example, while this study will include a number of different aspects of physical, cognitive, social, and personality development, and a number of measures of each, Cynthia has learned that most of our knowledge about adult development and aging comes from studies that were much more focused. For example, last week her professor lectured about the controversy over whether memory begins to decline during the latter half of our adult years. The illustrations her professor used to make various points primarily involved specific experiments designed to evaluate only one or two aspects of memory development, for example, whether there is a decline in long-term memory and whether certain organizational strategies can be given to older adults to help reduce memory difficulties if they develop.

Cynthia's professor also believes that it is very important to study the contexts in which adults develop. He knows that adults function in many different contexts and that these contexts influence adult lives. While he can't study every context, he will study some of the most important ones—family and work, for example. And he will include both lower- and middle-class families so he can investigate whether adult development during the early adult years is different for people from different socioeconomic backgrounds. Something that bothers her professor, though, is that the historical context in which Cynthia and Steven live may make it difficult for him to generalize to people who have been born at other points in history and probably have experienced a different set of historical circumstances. If everything goes well in the first several years of this investigation, beginning in about eight to ten years, he plans to collect information on another set of young adults and follow them over time. In this way, he feels he can better determine whether being born at a different time and experiencing a different set of historical circumstances affects adults.

As you read this text, you will find that our knowledge about adult development and aging is made up of a vast array of focused studies of rather specific aspects of adult development and aging that usually involve adults only at one point in their lives. You will also find that while information on adult lives over a period as long as fifty years exists, as you might imagine, few of these lengthy studies have been conducted because of the time and expense involved. Nonetheless, you will find that long-term studies are invaluable in charting the lives of individuals as they age through the adult years.

1

ISSUES AND THE NATURE OF ADULT DEVELOPMENT AND AGING

John W. Santrock and James C. Bartlett

I MAGINE *that you are a healthy sixty-year-old faced with the*
possibility of early retirement from a position with a large
corporation.
Your career has been successful, and you have received steady increases in
pay. However, you have received no major promotion in the last ten years. You feel that
the company may have put you on a shelf and simply is waiting for you to retire to
make way for younger employees on their way up. Further, the company is offering
attractive early-retirement options that are beginning to look tempting. Indeed, the
company recently paid your way (and that of other employees in their late fifties and
early sixties) to a retirement seminar at a fancy ski resort. There were many group
discussions led by psychologists and counselors on the virtues of early retirement. You
were invited to think about the consequences for the company if you simply stopped
coming to work on Monday. Would the corporation fold? Would morale plummet?
Would production slow to zero? The answers all seemed to be no. Moreover, the
counselors spoke glowingly of all the possibilities opened up by early retirement
"while you still have your health and are able to travel and pursue new interests." The
sessions certainly were thought-provoking. What should you do?

On the one hand, you enjoy your work. You know that you are competent at your
job and do many fine things for the company (though it is not obvious that these are
noticed). You believe that you are every bit as sharp as the younger employees in your
department. Your greater experience has proven invaluable on countless occasions
where a truly critical decision had to be made. Finally, your health is excellent (aside
from a little arthritis), and you have never missed a day of work in over fifteen years. So
why should you retire?

On the other hand, it seems obvious that some of your superiors are ready to see
you leave (why else were you invited to attend that retirement seminar). Perhaps they
regard you as past your prime and slipping. Probably they regard you as less
imaginative or creative than some of the younger employees and are concerned that
you are standing in the way of new ideas and developments (little do they realize just
how silly and naive some of the creative ideas of your subordinates can be). Could
your superiors be right? Or is it just a stereotype that they are seeing instead of you?
You firmly believe it is the stereotype, and after thirty years of service it makes you
very angry indeed.

It is not that you believe you are exactly the same today as you were at thirty. The
changes you have gone through are many and obvious. But to characterize all of these
changes simply as slipping is as stupid as it is inhumane. Think of all the experience

Some individuals in their fifties and sixties may be forced into early retirement.

you have accumulated! Your knowledge of the company is vast, and your ability to get along with other employees is a constantly improving and an increasingly valuable asset. Further, the emotional maturity and self-discipline you possess today far exceed that which you had in earlier years. Why are these positive virtues—experience, maturity, indeed wisdom—so little appreciated by the youth-oriented management of your firm?

What *does* happen to people as they grow older? Is it true that they become less creative? (Assuming that some people do grow less creative with age, is this simply because they are *expected* to be less creative and begin to believe they are less creative as a result?) Is it true that people become wiser with age? Or is it that individual differences are so great that *no* cliché of this type can be justified? And what about qualitative change? Does it not seem likely that these less-versus-more questions are too simplistically posed? Cannot one change into a different *sort* of person as one gets older, making such questions meaningless? Finally, to what extent are changes in adulthood fixed and immutable, and to what extent are they reflective of culture, educational activities, and health?

INTRODUCTION

This chapter, indeed this text, is concerned with the questions raised in the first "Imagine" section. In the following pages, we introduce a life-span perspective of the changes in adulthood and consider several critical issues viewed from this perspective. Then we discuss metamodels of adult development and relate these metamodels to the issues.

A LIFE-SPAN PERSPECTIVE ON ADULTHOOD

A book entitled *Adult Development and Aging* obviously is based on a premise; the premise is that development is not restricted to children and adolescents but continues into adult life, perhaps all the way until death. Is this premise reasonable? Does it make sense to apply a single word—*development*—to the period between birth and twenty-one years of age, and also to the period between ages twenty-one and seventy, and even to that between seventy and ninety?

It is arguable, indeed it is widely believed, that the answers to these questions are no. After all, isn't it obvious that all of us begin to decline after reaching our prime at twenty or thirty years of age? Is it not clear that "aging" after these years is associated with deteriorating sensory capabilities (accompanied by bifocals, hearing aids, and so on), a loss in speed of reaction (or reflexes) and physical prowess, even deficits in intellectual capacities (Grandmother's memory is not what it used to be, is it?). Such supposed declines with aging would seem to stretch unduly the common meaning of development. So what could we mean by "adult development"?

Such common-sense arguments are not all supported by scientific research. Indeed, a major purpose of this text is to set aside preconceived notions about age-related declines and to replace such notions with objective observations and scientifically respectable theories based on these observations. Nonetheless, given the widespread belief in age-related decline, it is hardly surprising that until quite recently no explicit developmental psychology focused on themes of adult development (Havighurst, 1973). That is, before the middle of the twentieth century, there was no systematic set of information that covered even half of an individual's lifetime, and there were no theories or models of psychological development that focused on this part of the life cycle. By contrast, there is a much longer and richer history pertaining to the portion of the life cycle known as childhood.

Even today, experts on adult development do not agree on the degree to which change, particularly positive change (versus simple decline), characterizes our adult lives. Traditional approaches to human development have emphasized extreme change from birth to adolescence, stability in adulthood, and decline in old age (Baltes, 1973; Baltes, Reese, & Lipsitt, 1980). Figure 1.1 contrasts this traditional perspective of development with the life-span perspective

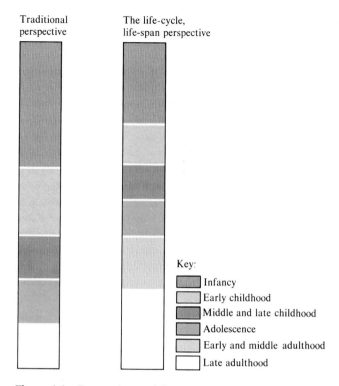

Traditional
perspective

The life-cycle,
life-span perspective

Key:

■ Infancy

□ Early childhood

■ Middle and late childhood

▨ Adolescence

▧ Early and middle adulthood

□ Late adulthood

Figure 1.1   Perspectives on life-span development reflecting points in the life cycle at which change and development are thought to occur.

adopted in this text. Note the powerful role allotted infancy and early childhood and the absence of change in early and middle adulthood in the traditional view. Also, notice the emphasis on change in adulthood in the life-cycle perspective, while still recognizing the importance of infancy as the building block of life-span development. A life-span perspective raises several important issues that are beginning to guide research in adult development and aging. These include the question of qualitative changes during adulthood; the issue of stages of adult development; the existence of differences among people in the progress and nature of development; the reversibility of undesired concomitants of development; the impact of biological, environmental, and cultural factors upon the course of development; and the relationship between development and differing conceptions of time.

Qualitative Changes During Adulthood

Jean Piaget, a great pioneer of developmental psychology, made many important claims about the development of intellectual functioning in children. Among these claims, perhaps none is more provocative than that a child's intelligence is not simply *less* than an adult's but that it is intelligence *of a qualitatively different kind.* For example, Piaget argued that very young children (one-year-olds) lack a fully developed *object concept* (Flavell, 1977) in that they do not conceive of objects as existing independently of themselves. According to Piaget, this object concept is something that must develop over the first two years of life and represents an outstanding intellectual achievement of this period. Before the object concept is fully developed, the child may not realize that an object continues to exist when one's back is turned or when the object itself has disappeared behind another object. Such inferences of *object permanence* appear intuitive and transparently obvious to adults and, indeed, to three-year-old children. Thus it is clearly arguable that a shift from one type of thinking to another, not simply an accumulation of mental power, has taken place. The development of the object concept represents a prototype of what qualitative change in development can mean.

Does development in adulthood involve qualitative changes of the sort that Piaget claimed for development in childhood? The answer is not obvious, but a life-span perspective suggests that qualitative changes are possible. For example, there may be qualitative changes in personality, although not necessarily for everyone, and not necessarily in intellectual or biological processes. These are empirical issues that must be resolved on the basis of intensive research in specific problem areas of adult development. The life-span perspective simply *raises* the question of qualitative change; it does not *answer* the question.

Stages of Adult Development

Piaget went further than simply to propose qualitative changes in childhood intelligence. He also proposed that there are identifiable **stages** of intellectual development in childhood. The notion of stages is a controversial one within psychology; not only do researchers disagree about the existence of developmental stages, they also argue about the characteristics of such stages.

Any conceptualization of developmental stages must incorporate the notion of qualitative change. Beyond this, the stages-of-development concept implies that qualitative changes must occur in certain sequences (stage 2 must be preceded by stage 1 and not vice versa). Many developmental psychologists (Flavell, 1977) would go still further to claim that the idea of stages implies (1) a certain degree of abruptness of transition from one stage to another and (2) concurrence in the appearance of behaviors or competencies that characterize a given stage.

That is, if an entire set of organized behaviors appeared rather suddenly in the course of development and did so for most if not all individuals at a certain point in the life span, we would have clear evidence for a developmental stage of some sort. Unfortunately, evidence for such occurrences is quite rare and unconvincing, leading some investigators to doubt the stage concept (Flavell, 1977) and others to redefine the concept (Wohlwill, 1973). Despite these problems, the concept of stages has an enduring appeal for developmental psychologists. We will return to this concept repeatedly throughout this text.

Continuity Versus Discontinuity of Change

To the degree that stage theories imply abruptness of change, they also imply a certain type of **discontinuity of change.** At another level, however, stage theories imply clear **continuity.** This is because such theories imply that psychological functioning at one developmental stage is contingent upon functioning at a prior stage. Put simply, stage theories imply that achievement of one stage is dependent upon achievement of all prior stages; one cannot achieve stage 3 without going through stage 2. Though change may be abrupt, stage theories assume a *connectivity* between functioning before and after the change (Kagan, 1980). Such connectivity is a type of continuity.

The type of continuity implicit in stage theories is stated succinctly by Piaget himself: "The ontogenetic formation of the intelligence includes a series of stages . . . each one of which has its origin in a reconstruction, on a new level, of structures built up during the preceding one. And this reconstruction is necessary to the later constructions which will advance beyond the former level" (Piaget, 1971, p. 147). Jerome Kagan has called attention to this passage from Piaget and has added that "the connection [between stages] is concretized as a process in which the structures or functions of one era are incorporated, completely or partially, into the present" (Kagan, 1980, p. 37). Thus, while developmental change can be qualitative and even abrupt—as stage theories suggest—there also can be a "necessary and contingent relation between phenotypically different structures or functions at two points in time due to the operation of specifiable processes" (Kagan, 1980, p. 32).

A life-span perspective on adult development recognizes the importance of continuous change but also raises the possibility of truly discontinuous change. Kagan (1980) has delineated two different types of discontinuous change, which he terms replacement and disappearance. *Replacement* refers to cases in which one process or behavior pattern is substituted for another, as when an infant's friendly approach to strangers suddenly is replaced with reactions of fear and avoidance at ages eleven to twenty months. *Disappearance* refers to cases in which a process or behavior pattern simply vanishes from a person's repertoire, as when an infant's babbling disappears at around six months of age. Kagan does not mention simple *appearance,* but presumably this, too, is possible, particularly in adulthood.

It is interesting to speculate about possible cases of replacement, disappearance, and appearance in adulthood. An obvious candidate for replacement is the change in daytime activities that accompanies retirement from a job. To be sure, postretirement activities may in some cases reflect simple increases in preretirement activities performed on weekends or at night (for example, one might have considerably more time for fishing after retirement). However, it is probable that a person develops entirely new behaviors that were not present before retirement. These may include new hobbies, volunteer work, and even a new career.

Disappearance may occur when societal expectations of people change. For example, in some segments of society, occasional states of high intoxication are quite acceptable (even encouraged) for a young person in college, but not for older people, particularly those with families. Thus, intensive drinking (in public at least) might disappear as changes in societal expectations occur. Cases of appearance might frequently be related to health (as might cases of disappearance and replacement as well). For example, a regimen of jogging or regular exercise might suddenly appear in a person's thirties, when it becomes obvious that these activities are needed to retain an attractive physique.

What are some of the factors that may lead to discontinuous change in adult development? Five such factors follow (Bee & Mitchell, 1980).

1. *Changes in broad expectations at different historical eras.* For instance, men may be more nurturant and women more assertive because of changes in sex roles linked with the women's movement. Further, historical changes in an individual's lifetime may produce discontinuous changes in personality, cognition, or even health (due for example to exercise).

2. *Changes in specific life experiences of the individual.* Social learning and contextual theorists argue that changes in behavior will occur whenever an adult's environment changes significantly.

3. *Regular changes in life tasks at different ages, consisting of different demands.* For example, is independence a crisis only in early adulthood?

4. *Biological changes, such as hormone changes, that affect both behavior and attitudes.* The hormone alterations that are related to menopause exemplify this kind of change.

5. *Hierarchical development.* An example of this type of change is Roger Gould's belief that it is important for adults to shed their childhood consciousness. For adults who cast off such consciousness through successive transformations, change rather than consistency is to be expected. From this perspective an introverted fifteen-year-old may become an extroverted thirty-eight-year-old by coming to understand herself.

In contrast, there are reasons why stability, or consistency, in adult development or between childhood and adulthood could occur.

1. *Biological processes.* An adult may inherit certain tendencies and characteristics. There is some indication, for example, that some forms of mental

illness, such as schizophrenia, are strongly influenced by inheritance. And intelligence as well as certain aspects of personality, such as introversion/extroversion, have genetic ties.

2. *The continuing influence of early experiences.* If early experience is more important in development than later experience, then the tendencies and characteristics we develop in childhood and adolescence may persist through adulthood. Both Freud and Piaget have taken this position.

3. *Early experience plus consistent adult experience.* Many of us choose life courses that are compatible with the way we think about ourselves. Consequently, we may continue to show consistency over our life course not necessarily because early experience predominates but because the early patterns continue to be rewarded in the circumstances we choose as adults. Social learning theory accepts this scenario as a major reason why some individuals show stability and consistency in their lives.

Individual Differences in Intraindividual Change

As discussed earlier, a life-span perspective implies a nonlinear view of development, that is, a view recognizing that declines in some types of functioning may accompany stability in other types of functioning and improvements in still others. Such **multidirectionality of change** may operate not only within individuals but also among individuals. That is, developmental changes in a given type of functioning (say, creative thought) may follow a declining course of development in some individuals, a stable course of development in others, and an increasing course of development in still others. This possibility is not inconsistent with impressions we form from everyday experience. We frequently are impressed that someone we knew as a young adult has developed remarkably by middle age, while someone else seems to have derailed somewhere along the line and has not developed or has even declined. Such everyday impressions do not constitute scientific evidence. However, a life-span perspective suggests that individual differences in the course of adult development—**intraindividual change**—may be critically important for an understanding of intellectual, personality, and biological functioning in adulthood.

Reversibility of Developmental Changes

There is little doubt that many aspects of adult development appear unattractive. No one wants to experience a decline in visual acuity, a loss in physical prowess, or a slowing in speed of reaction. Yet many people do experience these deficits as they grow older. As we will see, there is some evidence, albeit controversial, for age-related declines in certain types of intellectual performance such as memory. Surely no one wants memory to decline with age, yet there is a growing body of evidence that some types of memory do just that. What does a life-span perspective suggest about such age-related deficits?

An exciting implication of a life-span perspective is that undesirable aspects of adult development may sometimes be reversible. That is, certain age-related deficits may be removed through appropriate intervention, such as training and education programs, changes in diet or life-style, and altered expectations or stereotypes. Even purely biological deterioration may someday prove reversible as a result of scientific advances in our understanding of the physiological mechanisms underlying behavior.

Although the **reversibility** of certain aspects of adult development is an exciting possibility to explore, we have as yet very little scientific evidence on the extent to which such reversibility is possible. Moreover, it is important to consider many practical and ethical concerns that are involved in reversing various aspects of adult development. For example, is the reversal of a developmental function always useful?

Aside from this consideration, there are the related issues of value judgments and cost-benefit considerations. It may be possible to reverse an age-related decline but at such cost in terms of time, effort, and money that the whole enterprise might not be worthwhile. And not worthwhile for whom? When considering the costs and benefits of intervention, we must be wary of imposing our own priorities and value systems upon those we presumably are serving. A rigorous educational program to improve certain aspects of functioning in old age may simply fail to make sense within the context of an elderly person's life. These are issues that must be continuously examined and reexamined in our continuing research on the reversibility of developmental change.

Multiple Determinants of Adult Development

When we study children, particularly very young children, it may be possible to maintain that development is **normative,** that is, similar across individuals and even cultures. It may also be arguable that development is determined largely by **age-graded factors** that is, influences closely tied to time since birth (for example, cell growth in the brain, or marriage). However, it is clearly inappropriate to approach adult development in this way. In the first place, there are influences on adult development that are **nonnormative,** that is, not experienced by everyone but only by a small proportion of same-age individuals, indeed in some cases only a single individual. Who can doubt, for example, that the abduction of Patty Hearst was an event that profoundly influenced her subsequent development (at least for the next several months). In the second place, there are influences on development that are normative but more closely related to historical time than to age. These include such obviously potent factors as wars and economic depressions. Though such events occur only at certain times in history, they have obvious and profound effects on individuals, not only immediately but sometimes throughout their lives. Thus we can distinguish among three types of influence on adult development. These include normative age-graded influences, which have been emphasized in traditional developmental research; nonnormative life-event influences (such as the abduction of Patty Hearst); and normative history-graded influences (such as the Great Depression of the 1930s) (Baltes, Reese, & Lipsitt, 1980).

Nonnormative life-event factors can often be described as chance encounters, which Albert Bandura (1982) has defined as unintended meetings of people unfamiliar to one another. It is sobering to reflect that chance encounters may have been critically important determinants of many aspects of our life paths, including, for example, career choice and marriage. How many college students settle on their academic major because of an enthusiastic and inspiring professor they encounter by chance in a course taken as an elective? How many young men and women receive their first job offer through an unanticipated meeting at a party? These are interesting and important questions that have yet to be explored in the scientific literature. The role of scientific research in this area is probably not to predict the occurrence of chance encounters, but we can learn a great deal about the different types of chance encounters and about various factors that determine the long-term effects of such encounters on life paths. Some of these factors might be personal characteristics—personal values, for example—that might vary across the life span. Thus we must explore not only the occurrence of chance encounters but also the impact of such encounters in combination with age-graded influences on development.

Normative history-graded factors are known to be important in studies comparing individuals of different ages. For example, a classic study by John Nesselroade, K. Warner Schaie, and Paul Baltes (1972) examined intellectual performance in eight different age groups. On first testing, the groups ranged in age from twenty-four years to seventy years, and they differed dramatically in performance. For example, visualization performance dropped steadily from the youngest to the most elderly group. Taking these data by themselves, it might be concluded that visualization performance declines sharply with age. However, participants in all age groups were tested again seven years later (at that point the ages ranged from thirty-one to seventy-seven years), and there was no hint that visualization performance declined between the first and second testing in any age group. Indeed, performance at the second testing was generally better than at the first testing. These results strongly suggest that the differences among age groups were not the result of true age *changes* in visualization performance. Rather, it appears that these group differences reflected **cohort** effects, that is, differences in visualization ability among individuals born at different times in history. The importance of cohort effects in developmental research cannot be overemphasized. We will consider cohort effects further in the subsequent chapter on methodological issues. For the present, the point to note is that history-graded factors can contribute to intelligence test performance and doubtlessly to many other aspects of psychological functioning as well.

History-graded factors can do more than simply produce differences in psychological functioning at various points in the life span. Such factors can produce differences in the course of development itself. For example, it has been argued that intellectual performance might decline after a certain age in some cohorts and yet remain stable or even increase in others (Schaie & Geiwitz, 1982). Earlier we discussed the important problem of individual differences in intraindividual change. Here then is the related problem of cohort differences in intraindividual change.

Given the effects on development of nonnormative life-event influences and normative history-graded influences, how can these influences be characterized? Unfortunately, we have little evidence on which to base an answer to this question. It certainly seems plausible that events such as abduction, divorce, illness, and the death of a loved one are plausible candidates for nonnormative influences and that events such as war, epidemic, economic depression, and sociocultural change (for example, a change in sex roles) are good candidates for normative history-graded influences. Box 1.1 reveals how growing up during the depression and World War II may have influenced an individual's adult development.

Although it seems plausible that salient *life events* can alter development in adulthood, we have very little scientific evidence to substantiate their effects. Indeed, it is arguable that the major influences on developmental changes in adulthood are often not dramatic events such as divorces or wars but much less memorable occurrences such as daily hassles that pertain more to the microstructure of day-to-day existence than to the sorts of grand happenings that would be related in a history book or even one's autobiography. This approach differs from a life-events approach in its selective focus on daily experiences of a positive or negative nature. Such daily experiences may have at least as much influence on adult development as do major events of either a normative or nonnormative character (Lazarus & DeLongis, 1983).

Age As a Variable in the Study of Development

A final issue raised by a life-span perspective is how best to conceive of age. What is age? How is it best defined? Can it be considered a *cause* of development? These questions are considered by Jack Botwinick, who notes that there is widespread dissatisfaction with the concept of age. He reviews an interesting argument by Donald Baer (1970) that age *per se* is not relevant to an understanding of development. Botwinick (1978) continues:

> It is not difficult to argue for this extreme position. Age, as a concept, is synonymous with time, and time in itself cannot affect living function, behavior or otherwise. Time does not "cause" anything; it does not have physical dimensionality to impinge upon the sensorium, and it does not have psychological meaning independent of

related social and biological parameters. (It is this which underlies much of the philosophers' age-old concern with the meaning of time, and, it seems, the scientists' more recent concern with the definition of aging. From a research point of view, only the operational meaning of time and aging is possible.)

To continue the argument: Time is a crude index of many events and experiences, and it is these indexed events which are "causal." If we study these events and experiences, we need not be concerned with the crude index of time. We need not be concerned with age in order to understand that which has been "caused" by the time-indexed variables. These variables, unlike age itself, can be manipulated experimentally while holding related factors constant. Unlike age, the independent variable can be regarded as explanatory as well as descriptive.

While all the foregoing is correct, it is also correct that much of what we regard now as explanatory, or causal, is so only because our information is limited. Explanation and causality in science are matters of improving approximations, of determining better empirical associations. Age may be used as an explanation or predictor until better ones become available. For example, knowing the age of a person, we can predict his blood pressure levels within broad limits. Knowing about the state of arteriosclerosis, our prediction would be more accurate. Neither age nor arteriosclerosis would be as useful as information regarding the efficiency of the cardiac muscle. Knowing all these together, our predictions are best. Predictability, i.e., explanation based upon the degree of association, constitutes one definition of causality in science.

There is an important social reason, even if not a scientific one, for maintaining that age *per se* is germane to the purpose of studying developmental patterns. If age is regarded as irrelevant in studying developmental patterns, then focus will be only on function, not the person. If focus is not upon the person as well as the function, then we end up with a cadre of cardiovascular specialists, for example, but few geriatricians. The problems of childhood require special focus and receive it in pediatrics; the problems of old age are too extensive and too important to negate a geriatric specialty. Our present knowledge of aging processes is too meager, and our social needs too great, to insist upon study of only what appears to be the more immediate, causative variables. A working hypothesis here is that a specific focus upon age *per se* will not only be relevant to our social goals but will lead to a more precise delineation of the variables more immediately "causal." (pp. 390–91)

Botwinick argues that we should adopt a two-stage strategy for researching developmental issues (see also Baltes & Goulet, 1971). The first stage is that of description: scientific studies are performed to determine developmental functions relating age to some characteristic of interest (say, speed of reaction). The second stage is that of explanation: one conducts experiments to test specific hypotheses regarding causes of changes related to age (say, the hypothesis that age-related changes in speed of reaction are due to losses in sensory functioning).

Box 1.1
IF YOU WERE MIDDLE-AGED, HOW MIGHT HISTORICAL EVENTS AND LIFE EXPERIENCES HAVE INFLUENCED YOU?

One of the most elaborate longitudinal studies—the California Longitudinal Study—will be referred to frequently in this text because the investigation provides data on individual lives over a period of almost fifty years (e.g., Eichorn, Clausen, Haan, Honzik, & Mussen, 1981). The individuals in the California Longitudinal Study who are now in middle adulthood were born in 1920–21 and 1928–29, thus having birthdates that precede the depression. As Glenn Elder (1981) comments, the "forces set in motion by the swing of boom and bust—the economic growth and opportunity of the predepression era, the economic collapse of the 1930s, and recovery through wartime mobilization to unequaled prosperity during the 1940s and 1950s—influenced the life histories of these study members in ways that have yet to be fully understood" (p. 6).

Elder also describes how although it may seem that the two cohorts—those born in 1920–21 and those born in 1928–29—share the historical conditions of the 1920s and 1930s, on closer inspection there are some significant variations in the time of development at which these two groups of individuals experienced some important life events and circumstances. The earliest born subjects, those in the Oakland Growth Study, were children during the prospering 1920s, a time of unusual economic growth, particularly in the San Francisco area. They entered the depression after having a reasonably secure early childhood and avoided joblessness because of wartime mobilization. Most of them married and started families by the mid–1940s. This historical timetable minimized their exposure to the hardship of the depression.

For the group of middle-aged adults born in 1928–29, historical events and circumstances appeared at a different point in their development as children. Members of this group, who formed the Guidance Study, grew up in Berkeley, California. During their early childhood years, they and their parents experienced the hardship of the depression; then again, during the pressured period of adolescence, they encountered the unsettling experience of World War II. According to Elder, the hardships they experienced increased their feelings of inadequacy during the war years and reduced their chances for higher education. Nonetheless, when they were studied at mid-life, the disadvantage of deprivation had essentially disappeared, at least in terms of socioeconomic attainment. More differences were found between the men in these two cohorts than between the women, possibly because of the example and support of the mothers in Berkeley.

The following table shows the age of the Oakland and Berkeley subjects at the time of various historical events. How might some of these events and circumstances influence the lives of people—generational differences, the employment of women, and childbearing, for example? In considering such life events and circumstances, we can see how social history shapes the lives of adults.

AGE OF OAKLAND GROWTH AND GUIDANCE STUDY MEMBERS BY HISTORICAL EVENTS

		Age of study members	
Date	*Event*	*OGS*	*GS*
1880–1900	Birth years of OGS parents		
1890–1910	Birth years of GS parents		
1921–1922	Depression	Birth (1920–1921)	
1923	Great Berkeley Fire	2–3	
1923–1929	General economic boom; growth of "debt pattern" way of life; cultural change in sexual mores	1–9	Birth (1928–1929)
1929–1930	Onset of Great Depression	9–10	1–2
1932–1933	Depth of Great Depression	11–13	3–5
1933–1936	Partial recovery, increasing cost of living, labor strikes	12–16	4–8
1937–1938	Economic slump	16–18	8–10
1939–1940	Incipient stage of wartime mobilization	18–20	10–12
1941–1943	Major growth of war industries (shipyards, munitions plants, etc.) and of military forces	20–23	12–15
1945	End of World War II	24–25	16–17
1950–1953	Korean War	29–33	21–25

Source: Elder, 1981, p. 9. Copyright © 1981 Academic Press. Reprinted by permission.

Life for adults was very different in the 1920s than during the Great Depression.

Although acceptance of age as a purely descriptive variable is one approach to our conceptual problems, another approach is to refine our conceptualization of time since time is the foundation upon which any understanding of the age variable must be based. Some steps in this direction have been taken by Bernice Neugarten (Neugarten, 1980; Neugarten & Datan, 1973), who has distinguished three perspectives of time as they relate to the life cycle: life time, social time, and historical time.

Life Time, Social Time, and Historical Time

Life time is based heavily on the biological timetable that governs the sequence of changes in the process of growing up and growing old. However, as Neugarten (1980) suggests, chronological age is at best only a rough indicator of an individual's position on any one of numerous physical or psychological dimensions,

Events such as the Great Depression are called normative, history-graded influences.

because from early in infancy, individual differences are a known fact of development. Also, Neugarten and Datan (1973) argue that age is often not a very good index of many forms of social and psychological behavior, unless there is accompanying knowledge of the particular society as a frame of reference. They give an obvious example of a girl in the United States who is a schoolgirl, but the same-aged girl in a rural village in the Near East who may be the mother of two children. It is argued that the significance of a given chronological age, or a given marker of life time, when viewed from a sociological or anthropological perspective, is directly a function of the social definition of age, or social time.

Social time refers to the dimension that underlies the age-grade system of a particular society. It has been characteristic of preliterate societies to have rites of passage marking the transition from one age status to the next, such as the passage from youth to maturity and to marriage (Van Gennep, 1960). According to Neugarten and Datan (1973), however, only a rough parallel exists between social time and life time in most societies. There are different sets of age expectations and age statuses in different societies.

Historical time controls the social system, and the social system, in turn, creates a changing set of age norms and a changing age-grade system that shapes the individual life cycle. For example, childhood as a distinct phase of life did not emerge until the seventeenth and eighteenth centuries, and the concept of adolescence did not emerge until the twentieth century. Similarly, middle age as a stage is a recent concept, resulting from our increased longevity. Changes in industrialization, urbanization, and our educational institutions account for these changing concepts. Scientists in this area also recognize the importance of the timing of major historical events in the life of an individual. Wars and depressions often act as historical watersheds, that is, major turning points in the social system. Significant historical events often affect levels of education, fertility patterns, sexual mores, labor participation patterns, and so forth.

It is too early to judge whether Neugarten's perspectives on time might render age a truly explanatory variable in developmental research. It is clear, however, that our notion of age as "time by the clock since birth" is long overdue for revision.

PARADIGMS AND METAMODELS OF ADULT DEVELOPMENT

Throughout this chapter we have focused on the basic problem of how adults develop. It now is time to consider a different, though related, question: How can the science of adult development itself develop? The answer is not simple; specifically, it is *not* that we should simply collect facts about adult development, allowing these to accumulate until the truth about adult development emerges. Everything we know about the history and philosophy of science suggests that such a procedure would never work and, in any case, that it would not be followed. Rather, research in science is directed by paradigms, metamodels, or schools of thought that suggest important questions, define appropriate methodological approaches to answering these questions, and determine answers to these questions. In other words, scientific activity is not a random process of collecting infinite numbers of observations. Rather, scientific activity is guided by certain presuppositions regarding what is important to study, how it should be studied, and what kinds of theoretical ideas can be advanced on the basis of such study. A landmark book in the history and philosophy of science is Thomas Kuhn's *The Structure of Scientific Revolutions,* published in 1962. Kuhn argues forcefully that *mature science,* such as contemporary physics or chemistry, is guided by **paradigms,** which are "past scientific achievements, achievements that some scientific community acknowledges for a time as supplying the foundation for its further practice" (p. 10). A good example is Newtonian physics, based on Newton's achievements in *Principia* and *Opticks.* Another example is Benjamin Franklin's *Electricity.*

A very important aspect of paradigms is that they cannot be disproved or rejected on the basis of scientific evidence. They can only be rejected in favor of another paradigm that promises to serve as a better, or more encompassing, foundation for research. It is important to realize that paradigms are not to be equated with scientific theories. Theories make predictions that can be subjected to scientific test. Paradigms provide a framework in which to conduct and interpret research. They can be judged (though perhaps only in hindsight) by how well they serve this purpose, not by whether they are right or wrong.

There is no single achievement in adult development that the entire field acknowledges as an adequate foundation for all further work. However, we do have what might be called **metamodels** of adult development (Hultsch & Pentz, 1980; Reese, 1973), and these function as the foundation for research in selected areas. A **metamodel** is a grand model that transcends more specific, concrete, testable models. (Some adult developmentalists—Hultsch and Deutsch (1981), for example—prefer to call such models *world views.*) Like the paradigms of older sciences, metamodels are not directly testable; they incorporate assumptions that are highly abstract (for example, that the developing organism is active and not passive), too abstract to be objectively proved in the laboratory. Though metamodels themselves are not testable, they do serve to stimulate ideas, issues, and questions that can be tested. They also suggest the methodological approaches most adequate for addressing these ideas, issues, and questions. Three different metamodels are frequently distinguished: mechanistic, organismic, and contextual (Hultsch & Pentz, 1980).

The Mechanistic Metamodel

A natural way to contrast the mechanistic, organismic, and contextual metamodels is in terms of the assumptions they make about the nature of the developing individual. The **mechanistic metamodel** assumes a vision of the adult as a passive machine that reacts to events but does not actively anticipate events, formulate its own goals, or engage in complex internal activity of any kind. The mechanistic metamodel is rooted in the achievements of behaviorists and therefore focuses on simple relationships between observable stimuli and observable responses rather than upon the hypothetical internal processes and structures we associate with the concept of *mind.*

The Organismic Metamodel

The **organismic metamodel** assumes the adult is an active, *mindful* individual with goals and plans and who uses complex strategies to attain ends. The organismic metamodel is rooted in the achievements of cognitive developmental psychologists, including most notably Piaget, and also in the contemporary field of *cognitive science* (see Lindsay & Norman, 1977; Solso, 1979). Although the name *organismic* implies an image of the individual that is not machinelike, many cognitive psychologists argue that human cognition is very machinelike—indeed, that it has much in common with the operation of modern-day computers (Hunt, 1971). We need not dwell on the advantages and disadvantages of a computer metaphor for human cognition. The more important point is that all cognitive psychologists, and cognitive developmentalists, believe that human cognition is active, planful, and strategic (as is computer cognition). Emphasis is shifted from simple responses and observable stimuli to internal processes and structures. We should note that the organismic metamodel is not simply restricted to the topic of cognition. Many theoretical ideas regarding personality, social processes, and human action also derive from this metamodel.

The Contextual Metamodel

The **contextual metamodel** posits neither a purely active nor a purely passive view of the individual but rather an interactive view. The basic conception is that of an organism continuously responding to and acting on the context—there are both active and passive components of this interaction. It is important to understand that *context* is an open-ended term that can apply at different levels of analysis. For example, there is the environmental context, which pertains to one's physical environment. There is also the social, historical, or cultural context, which pertains to influences such as societal norms and expectations of friends and relatives. Further, there is the biological context, which pertains to an individual's health and physical skills. In all of these cases, we can speak not only of the context's having effects upon the individual, but also of the individual's having effects upon the context. To take a simple example, because the sun is hot, an individual either plants trees (altering the context) or moves to a cooler climate (changing the context). Alternatively, one's family might make unreasonable demands, and so one begins to refuse them more often, which might alter the family's subsequent behavior, which in turn alters one's own behavior, and so forth.

The roots of contextualism can be found in several achievements, including those of social learning theorists, who have demonstrated many ways in which social stimuli and reinforcements influence behavior and thought; those of cross-cultural psychologists, who have documented many important differences in behavior and thought among different societies; and those of the ecological theorists (Gibson, 1979), who have demonstrated the variety of ways in which the

The computer revolution has created a disequilibrium in some adult lives, as has the increased number of women in the world of work.

structure of the environment influences what we see, hear, and remember. Indeed, the *contextualist* view of perception described in box 1.2, provides a good illustration of what we have conveyed here.

Sometimes the contextual metamodel is referred to as a **dialectical view** rather than an interactive view. For example, Klaus Riegel (1977) believes that too much of our theorizing about development has consisted of efforts to portray the adult as striving for balance and equilibrium. By contrast, in Riegel's dialectical perspective, a better understanding of the adult will come about by studying disequilibrium and change. For Riegel, development is always in a state of flux. Balance and equilibrium, while strived for, are never attained. Riegel points out that adults are neither stable bundles of characteristics and traits nor passive reactors to environmental stimuli. Adults are changing beings in a changing world. He believes that at the very moment when completion or equilibrium seems to be reached, new questions and doubts arise in the individual and in society. From Riegel's view, then, the individual and society are never at rest. Riegel believes that contradiction and conflict are an inherent part of development and that no single goal or end point in development is ever reached. The dialectical perspective developed by Riegel is compatible with the interactionist position of Ulric Neisser described in box 1.2.

Box 1.2
ULRIC NEISSER'S CONTEXTUAL METAMODEL

The figures in this box present three approaches to perception—a **behaviorist approach,** according to which perception is based on differential responding to different stimuli; an **information-processing approach,** according to which environment is analyzed through a number of processing stages; and an **ecological approach,** which has been developed by Ulric Neisser (1976). The behaviorist approach is consistent with the mechanistic metamodel in that there is no role for active cognitive functioning. The information-processing approach fits the organismic metamodel in that great emphasis is placed on active transformations of stimulus information at different stages, or levels, of processing. Such active processing is also preserved in the ecological approach, but the latter places much greater emphasis on the information in the environment and on interactions between this information and the processes of perception.

A critical concept employed by Neisser is that of **schema,** which is an organized structure of knowledge. The schema is the part of Neisser's model that is internal to the individual. Many models of the organismic type also include *schemata.* However, organismic models emphasize the tendency of schemata to transform information from the environment. In contrast, Neisser emphasizes the role of schemata in directing exploration of the environment. For Neisser, perception is a never-ending cycle in which schemata direct exploration of the environment and in which schemata themselves are being continually modified by information picked up in the course of exploration. A good example is that of discovering and exploring a city. One begins with a schema that includes information about cities in general and that serves to guide one's exploratory activities (because we know that cities have museums, we may first be interested in visiting some of these, then moving along to major shopping centers, parks, and so on). As one explores and picks up information about a particular city, the general *city schema* is modified and becomes more specific. If one stays in a city for an extended period of time, this cyclic process may never end. One will continue to learn more about the city (knowledge of shortcuts and good restaurants may be picked up over quite extended periods of time), and the city itself will change (new buildings, new people, and so forth). In the process, the explorer will also change. Exploratory activities will continue to modify one's city schema (and many other schemata). Further, the perceptual cycle will be affected by other aspects of one's changing life. Changes in interests, resources (for example, money, a car), and social contacts all will influence the city schema and the exploratory activities that modify this schema. Thus Neisser's cyclic model of perception is also a cyclic model of development. It is one interesting model within the general class of contextual metamodels.

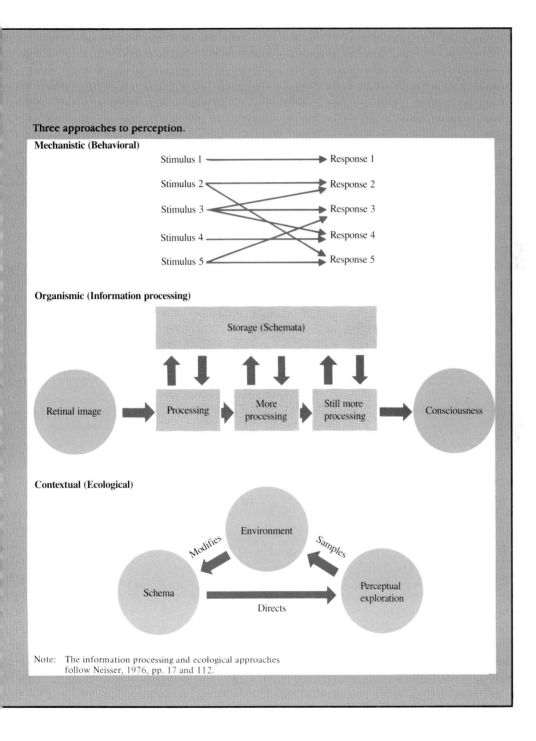

Three approaches to perception.

Mechanistic (Behavioral)

Stimulus 1 ⟶ Response 1
Stimulus 2 ⟶ Response 2
Stimulus 3 ⟶ Response 3
Stimulus 4 ⟶ Response 4
Stimulus 5 ⟶ Response 5

Organismic (Information processing)

Storage (Schemata)

Retinal image ⟶ Processing ⟶ More processing ⟶ Still more processing ⟶ Consciousness

Contextual (Ecological)

Environment

Modifies　　*Samples*

Schema ⟶ *Directs* ⟶ Perceptual exploration

Note:　The information processing and ecological approaches
　　　follow Neisser, 1976, pp. 17 and 112.

Table 1.1

METAMODELS AND ISSUES IN ADULT DEVELOPMENT

Metamodel **View of the Organism**	*Mechanistic* **Reactive**	*Organismic* **Active**	*Contextual* **Interactive**
Degree of Emphasis on Different Issues in Development			
Qualitative change	Low	High	Medium
Stages of change	Low	High	Medium
Continuity of change	Low	High	Medium
Individual differences in change	Medium	Low	High
Reversibility of change	Medium	Low	Medium
Multiple determinants of change			
Nonnormative life-events factors	High	Low	High
Normative age-graded factors	Low	High	Medium
Normative history-graded factors	Low	Low	High
Age as a useful variable	Low	High	Medium

Metamodels and Issues in Adult Development

It is useful to compare the mechanistic, organismic, and contextual metamodels with respect to the issues considered earlier in this chapter. Though this comparison is instructive, it is important to realize that each of the metamodels is abstract and subsumes a number of more specific ideas. Thus we compare the models with respect to their emphases, not with respect to black-and-white claims.

As shown in table 1.1, the organismic metamodel is distinguished by the emphasis it places on qualitative change, distinctive stages of development, and continuity of change. It also is unique in emphasizing the importance of age-graded influences on development and in accepting the importance of age as a variable in research (at least for purposes of describing change). The mechanistic and contextual models appear more similar to each other than either is to the organismic metamodel. However, there are some very important differences. One of these is the great emphasis placed on individual differences (in intraindividual change) by the contextual metamodel but not by the mechanistic metamodel. Another difference is the great importance of history-graded influences on development within the contextual metamodel but not within the mechanistic metamodel. Put simply, the mechanistic metamodel emphasizes nonnormative life-event influences at the expense of all other aspects of development. The contextual metamodel also emphasizes nonnormative influences but not exclusively. History-graded influences also are stressed, as are individual differences. Indeed, we have indicated in table 1.1 that no aspect of development receives low emphasis by the contextual metamodel. The thrust of this metamodel is the multifaceted and multidetermined nature of adult development. In a real sense, it incorporates the mechanistic and organismic metamodels, but it goes further in its recognition of factors specific to individual people, individual cultures, and individual times in history.

PROCESSES, PHASES, AND DEVELOPMENT

In this introductory chapter we have seen that there is disagreement about whether we should view adult development and aging from a stage perspective. Nonetheless, theorists and researchers often use the labels of early, middle, and late adulthood to describe three different developmental periods.

Early adulthood usually signifies the time frame from the late teens or early twenties through the thirties. You will see that this time period often involves the establishment of personal and economic independence. Career development takes on an even more important role than it did in late adolescence. For many young adults, selecting a mate, learning to live with someone else in an intimate way, and starting a family and rearing children take up a great deal of time.

Middle adulthood characterizes the phase of the life cycle from between thirty-five and forty-five years to between fifty-five and sixty-five years of age. It is a time for expanding personal and social involvement and responsibility, for assisting teenagers to become responsible and happy adults, for adjusting to the physiological changes of middle age, and for reaching and maintaining satisfaction in one's career.

Late adulthood extends from approximately sixty to seventy years of age until death. It is a time of adjustment to decreasing strength and health and to retirement and reduced income. Establishing affiliations with members of one's own age group and adapting to social roles are important during this period.

All individuals are not characterized in the manner sketched here. As you read this text, you will find many more aspects of adult development and aging that characterize individuals in early, middle, and late adulthood, and you will see that not everyone agrees that these characteristics are universal.

After you read about methods of studying adults in the next chapter, a number of processes of adult development and aging will be discussed—biological processes and physical development, cognitive processes and development, social processes and development, and personality processes and development.

Biological processes and physical development refer to changes that range from simple alterations in size, weight, and other anatomical features that can be charted to the genetic blueprint that places constraints on our development from conception to death. Patterns of growth are important; we have learned much about them and can use them as clinical instruments to determine whether an adult is healthy and developing normally. If an adult deviates substantially from the average for a particular age, say, in regard to cholesterol level or blood sugar, then a physician will want to examine the adult's diet and check for other possible abnormalities. The genes we were born with still influence our development as an adult. Scientists are looking closely at the role genetics plays in such adult mental disorders as schizophrenia and depression. And robust debate continues about the degree to which our intelligence is genetically determined.

Hormones are yet another aspect of biological makeup that are important in understanding adult development. At some point in adult life, for example, the onset of menopause occurs in women, accompanied by significant hormonal changes. These are but a few of the many aspects of biological and physical development we will explore as we describe development in adulthood.

Cognitive processes and development refer to the age-related series of changes that occur in mental activity—thought, memory, perception, and attention. As part of our study of cognitive development, we explore how adults process information, look carefully at the issue of whether there is a decline in memory during adulthood, and examine ways to improve the intellectual functioning of adults.

Social processes and development refer to the individual's interactions with other individuals in the environment. Two elderly people consoling each other, a mother hugging her daughter for a good report card, two sisters arguing, and a boss smiling at a secretary are all aspects of the social world. Social development focuses on how these many different aspects unfold as the individual grows. We also have added contexts to the section in which we discuss social processes and development. As we have seen in this chapter, the contexts in which adult development occurs are a very important aspect of understanding what people are like. Some of the most important social contexts of adult development are families, relationships, and work.

Personality processes and development usually refer to a property of an individual that allows us to distinguish him or her from another individual. But as we will see, some experts believe that there are also commonalities that characterize individuals at particular points in their adult development. One's sexrole orientation, one's perception of self, one's moral values, and how sociable one is represent some of the aspects of personality we will discuss. You will find that it often is impossible to meaningfully present the aspects of personality development in adulthood without frequently referencing the individual's interactions with and thoughts about the social world.

Indeed, although it is helpful to study the different processes of adult development in separate sections and chapters, keep in mind while reading this text that you are an integrated human being—you have only one mind and one body. Biological, physical, cognitive, social, and personality development are inextricably woven together. In many chapters, you will read about how social experiences shape cognitive development, how cognitive development restricts or promotes social development, and how cognitive development is tied to physical development.

Summary

In this chapter we attempted to characterize and elaborate the life-span perspective of adult development. Beginning with a basic question—Do adults develop?—we presented a brief history and outline of the life-span developmental framework. The notion of multidirectional trends in development was emphasized, and we explicitly rejected the older, unidirectional view of development.

We next turned to a discussion of seven issues raised by the life-span perspective of development. The issue of qualitative change in adulthood derives from Piaget's basic insight that intelligence in children does not simply increase but changes from one type of intelligence to another. It is possible that similar sorts of qualitative change may occur during the adult years. Moreover, such changes need not be restricted to the intellectual sphere.

Though the issue of the existence of stages of adult development is an intriguing one, convincing evidence is sparse. Moreover, there is disagreement about the very nature of stages.

In regard to the issue of continuity versus discontinuity of change, though change may be qualitative, and even abrupt, it still may be continuous in the sense that later achievements depend upon earlier achievements. Three types of discontinuous change— replacement, disappearance, and appearance—may all occur in adulthood.

In terms of the issue of individual differences in change, such differences in adult development are widely acknowledged, and they clearly constitute a very important problem facing life-span developmental psychology. Nonetheless, the nature and causes of these differences remain obscure.

Although the issue of reversibility of change offers some exciting prospects, several practical and ethical issues have been raised concerning reversibility.

A life-span perspective recognizes not only the multifaceted nature of change but also multiple influences on the nature of such change. In addition to the normative age-graded influences emphasized by traditional developmental theory, there also exist non-normative life-event influences (for example, accidents and chance encounters) and normative history-graded influences (for example, wars and depressions). It is possible that many influences on adult development may be small, day-to-day events rather than the major events that pertain to history or autobiography.

The issue of the status of age as a concept in life-span developmental psychology deserves further investigation. Although age may not be useful as an explanation of change, age is an important descriptive variable in research. Conceptualizations such as Neugarten's work on three types of time—life, social, and historical—may ultimately strengthen the explanatory power of the age concept.

Though metamodels are not testable as scientific theories, they are useful for generating ideas, issues, and questions for research and for suggesting appropriate methodological approaches to these ideas, issues, and questions. The contextual metamodel is unique in its broad attention to all types of change and all determinants of change. Indeed, the contextual metamodel can be said to encompass the mechanistic and organismic metamodels.

Review Questions

1. Describe how a life-span perspective of adulthood contrasts with a traditional child perspective.
2. Discuss the issue of qualitative change in adulthood.
3. What are some reasons that we might find stability or change in adult development?
4. Explain what is meant by individual differences in intraindividual change.
5. Describe the controversy over reversibility in developmental change.
6. Discuss the importance of nonnormative life events, normative history-graded events, and normative age-graded events in understanding adult development.
7. Why is the controversy over age a variable in the study of adult development?
8. What is a paradigm? How is a paradigm distinguished from a metamodel?
9. Describe the mechanistic metamodel.
10. Discuss the organismic metamodel.
11. Provide an overview of the contextual metamodel.
12. Evaluate the linkages between the three metamodels and the issues discussed in this chapter.

Further Readings

Baltes, P. B., Reese, H. W., & Lipsitt, L. P. (1980). Life-span developmental psychology, *Annual Review of Psychology, 31,* 65–110.

> This overview of important issues and research in adult development by three leading figures includes information about many of the issues addressed in this chapter. Medium reading level.

Havighurst, R. J. (1973). History of developmental psychology: Socialization and personality development through the life span. In P. B. Baltes & K. W. Schaie (Eds.), *Life-span developmental psychology* (pp. 4–25). New York: Academic Press.

> Havighurst, a leading figure in the study of life-span development, presents a number of theoretical ideas that focus on life-span development. Reasonably easy to read.

Human Development, Journal of Gerontology, and *The Gerontologist*

> These three leading journals will be referred to frequently in this text. To get a feel for the kinds of questions that interest people who study adulthood and aging, go to your library and browse through some issues of these three journals published over the last four or five years. Reading level varies from medium to difficult.

Neugarten, B. L., & Datan, N. (1973). Sociological perspectives on the life cycle. In P. B. Baltes & K. W. Schaie (Eds.), *Life-span developmental psychology.* New York: Academic Press.

> Neugarten, one of the leading figures in the study of life-span development, describes her views of multiple-time perspectives and the changing rhythm of the life cycle. This well-written article stimulates thinking about the nature of life-span development.

2

METHODS

James C. Bartlett and John W. Santrock

Imagine That You Want to Find Out Whether Creativity Declines with Age—How Would You Do This?

INTRODUCTION
BASIC ISSUES OF MEASUREMENT
Reliability of Measures
Assessing Reliability
Improving Reliability
Validity of Measurement

BASIC TYPES OF MEASURES USED FOR COLLECTING INFORMATION
Interview and Questionnaire
Behavioral Research
Behavioral Research in Laboratory Versus Field
Laboratory Research with Animal Models
Standardized Tests
Physiological Research
Box 2.1 Physiological Arousal and Learning in the Elderly

BASIC STRATEGIES FOR SUMMARIZING MEASUREMENTS
Measures of Central Tendency
Measures of Variability
Correlation Between Variables
Factor Analysis
Box 2.2 The Use of Factors and Factor Analysis in the California Longitudinal Study

IMAGINE   *that you want to find out whether creativity declines with age—how would you do this?*

Although you are aware of many common-sense opinions on this issue and realize that they are often held with great conviction, you feel that there is reason to doubt the *conventional wisdom* of your culture. Indeed, you suspect that many opinions about aging and creativity are rooted in *ageist* prejudices and stereotypes or are based on socially accepted standards of appropriate behavior for people of different ages. You are interested in obtaining objective, scientific evidence on creativity across the life span, but how should you proceed?

One approach might be simply to ask people of different ages to rate their creativity (using a ten-point scale, for example). But the whole point of your project is to gather objective, scientific data on creativity, not subjective impressions that doubtlessly are influenced by conventional wisdom, not to mention the egos of your participants. Why not collect ratings on people's creativity from friends and relatives? This *might* solve the ego problem, but conventional wisdom would remain a troublesome factor. Moreover, just how well can friends and relatives judge a person's creativity? (Do *your* friends and relatives appreciate how creative *you* are?) Another approach might be that of a questionnaire or structured interview. Rather than simply asking people about their creativity, you might ask them about a variety of items such as their life-style (are they unconventional?), work habits (do they waste many idle hours until spurred by a creative burst?), motivations (do they enjoy following orders and being told what to do, or do they prefer to set their own tasks and goals?). Responses could be scored as *creative* or *noncreative,* and a total *creativity score* could be derived. Unfortunately, participants might guess the purpose of your study and produce "creative" answers simply to appear creative. Further, the questions we are using are not truly relevant to creativity. For example, an unconventional life-style is not necessarily predictive of creativity.

Perhaps it would be better not to ask people about creativity but rather to test them *behaviorally* on their ability to find creative solutions to problems. Indeed, it might be useful to find a *standardized test* of creative problem solving, on which many samples of people have been tested. This approach seems promising, but you must be concerned with the **reliability** and **validity** of your creativity test. Does the test give consistent estimates of creativity if the same individual is tested twice? (This is a reliability question.) Does the test truly measure creativity, or simply intelligence? (This is a validity question.) Even given high reliability and validity with young adults, the test might not have high reliability and validity with elderly people. Further, age differences in creative problem solving might not reflect age *per se* but rather *extraneous* factors such as educational background or health. Some of these factors might be controlled if you used a **longitudinal design,** testing the same individuals every seven years from ages twenty to seventy-six. But do you have fifty-six years to complete your study? And how many of the participants you test today will still be available fifty-six years from now? The problem of extraneous factors and the extreme difficulty of longitudinal designs might lead you to use **animal models** in your research. With animals, it is possible to control a great many factors (diet, experiences in infancy, and so forth) that cannot be controlled in humans. Also, many animals have a relatively brief life span, making longitudinal research more feasible. But how do you devise a creativity test that can be completed by animals? And can results obtained with animals be *generalized* to humans? Faced with all of these problems, you might elect to use *archival* or historical data. For example, you might investigate the typical ages at which great artistic or scientific achievements are produced. Unfortunately, the evidence provided by archival investigations is highly indirect; many factors in addition to creativity determine at what age someone produces a great artistic or scientific accomplishment. (Indeed, it is arguable that many social and cultural factors, including conventional wisdom about aging and creativity, may influence the time course of creative achievement in adults.) Further, we must always be concerned with the accuracy and completeness of archival data.

Then what should you do to investigate aging and creativity? There is no right answer, only alternative approaches with varying cost and benefits. Furthermore, there is ample room for your own creativity in selecting, combining, and even modifying approaches to suit your own research goals. Indeed, the need for creativity in science is an integral part of its challenge and appeal.

INTRODUCTION

A major task of science is measurement. We begin this chapter with a discussion of two basic issues involved in measurement: the reliability of measurements and the validity of measurements. Then we move to a discussion of several basic measures used for collecting observations: the structured interview and questionnaire, behavioral research—including observational studies in laboratory research—standardized tests, and physiological research. Next we consider three basic ways of characterizing or summarizing measurements: central tendency, dispersion or variability, and relationships between variables, that is, correlation. Then we discuss the topic of research design, considering first simple correlational designs and then more powerful experimental designs, which allow assessment of causal relationships between variables. We also describe quasi-experimental designs, mixed experimental-correlational designs, and finally the *sequential* designs that have many advantages for developmental research. Throughout our discussion of research design, we examine the respective advantages of longitudinal comparisons and cross-sectional comparisons for assessment of development and change. The chapter closes with a section on sampling, a critical problem in all psychological research but particularly important in research on adult development and aging.

BASIC ISSUES OF MEASUREMENT

It sounds simple to say that the major task of science is measurement. However, to make accurate and meaningful measurements is far from simple. Let us look at two basic issues that must be considered when measurements are made.

Reliability of Measures

Suppose that you are assisting on a research project focusing on age changes in health, and you are asked to determine the height of a research participant. Having no prior experience in accurate measurement of height, you simply find a tape measure, ask the participant to stand against a wall, and measure the distance from the floor to the top of the participant's head. Suppose that you determine with this procedure that the participant is 5 feet 8 inches tall. And suppose that you report this result to the principal investigator of the research project, who wonders aloud about the reliability of your measure. What exactly is the principal investigator wondering? How could she be reassured? More important, how could other investigators, who later might read reports of this project, be reassured?

Essentially, the principal investigator is questioning the degree to which your estimation of height was determined by (1) the *true* height of the participant versus (2) *measurement error.* Given your inexperience at measuring height, many possible sources of measurement error exist. Did you ask the participant to remove her shoes? Did you use some sort of straightedge to determine the point on the wall that corresponds to the highest point on the skull of the participant? If so, how did you determine that the straightedge was held in a perfectly horizontal orientation (if it tilted, this would alter the height estimation). Did you give any instructions or make any observations regarding the posture of the participant? How do you know that the tape measure has not been stretched through repeated use?

Of course height is a relatively easy thing to measure. Other types of measurement can pose much greater problems of reliability. Suppose, for example, that you were asked to determine a person's IQ on the Wechsler Adult Intelligence Scale or the hypnotizability of the person using some other instrument (standardized tests of hypnotizability do exist). How reliable would your estimations be in these cases? How many sources of measurement error would exist? Obviously, reliability of measurement can frequently be questioned in behavioral research.

Assessing Reliability

How can we assess the reliability of measures? There are a variety of techniques, but all are based on the assumption that *reliable observations are repeatable.* We assume that measurement error, whatever its causes, will tend to vary across time, situations, observers, and so forth. Hence large amounts of measurement error (that is, low reliability of measurement) will result in measurements that are difficult to repeat.

Test-retest reliability can be assessed by taking the same set of measurements on two different occasions. The question is whether measurements (frequently numerical scores of some kind) on occasion 2 are predictable from observations on occasion 1. Of course, test-retest reliability is meaningful only when what we are measuring is assumed to be stable over time. Were we observing the momentary moods of individuals, we probably would not wish to assess test-retest reliability. For example, if a person were judged to be happy on day 1 and sad on day 2, this need not imply low reliability. It could simply mean that the person's mood had changed.

Inter-rater reliability should be assessed whenever measurements involve a subjective, judgmental component. This is frequently the case in studies of social behavior because terms such as *aggression, play,* and so on are frequently difficult to define in physical terms. The technique is simply to use two or more observers, who make their observations independently. Then the agreement among these observers (corrected for agreement expected by chance) can be assessed. High agreement implies high reliability.

Inter-item reliability can be examined whenever measurements entail multiple *items,* as in an IQ test with multiple questions. A common procedure for assessing inter-item reliability is to divide the items into two halves (for instance, the odd-numbered items versus the even-numbered items) and to determine the extent to which measurements (average scores) on one half are predictable from measurements on the other half. High predictability implies high reliability so long as the two sets of items are presumed to measure the same thing (for example, intelligence). If the two sets measure different things (arithmetic ability versus vocabulary), high predictability would not be expected regardless of reliability.

Improving Reliability

How do we improve reliability of measurements? One method is to take many different measures of the same individual or behavior. (This is one reason that IQ tests have so many different items.) Although the individual measures may be highly susceptible to measurement error, the average of many measures may cancel out this error, at least partially. However, there is no substitute for refinement and standardization of the procedures and tools for measurement. To return to our initial example of measuring height, reliability might be improved by multiple assessments of height, particularly if these were made by different research assistants. However, it obviously would be helpful to use a carefully planned and standardized set of procedures together with high-precision equipment (such as the extendable precision rulers found in physicians' offices). Indeed, such procedures and equipment might make multiple observations unnecessary. Of course, often we *cannot* refine and standardize procedures for measurement because we do not know how this can be done. In these cases, we must rely on crude methods, multiple measurements (if possible), and various tests of reliability (having independent observers rate the "aggressiveness" of behavior, for example). We also hope that future scientific advances will ultimately provide the refinements and standardization upon which truly high levels of reliability depend.

Problems of reliability are present in all psychological research. However, they are particularly bothersome in developmental research, especially when individual differences are at issue. If a group of people are given an IQ test at age eighteen, and again at age forty-five, it is probable that some will show gains from the first test to the second, whereas others will show losses. Are there true differences between the gainers and the losers, or are we simply seeing the effects of measurement error? Although there are statistical methods that can be applied to this problem, it remains troublesome.

Validity of Measurement

In our example of measuring height, the principal investigator questioned the reliability (essentially, the repeatability) of your measurements. It might have been worse, however. She might have doubted that you measured height at all. Suppose she suspected that you did not know the difference between height and waist size and that what you measured was not the distance from the floor to the top of the head but rather the distance around the participant's waist. One would hope that the sheer magnitude of your measurement (5 feet 8 inches) would indicate that you were not as inexperienced and ignorant as all that. Indeed, we should hope that the question of validity is never at issue when measuring height. However, the validity question is often at issue when we are measuring psychological variables, such as intelligence, creativity, anxiety, self-esteem, and so forth. In these cases, we are often concerned with whether measurements reflect what they are intended to reflect and not something else.

Although there are many different types of validity (some discussed later in this chapter), the type we are currently addressing is **construct validity. Constructs** are abstract entities that cannot be directly observed but are presumed to influence observable phenomena. Intelligence is a construct, as are anxiety, creativity, memory, self-esteem, and other aspects of personality and cognition. We often attempt to observe phenomena that we believe might reflect these constructs. The issue of whether the observed phenomena actually *do* reflect the constructs is the issue of construct validity.

A critical point to keep in mind is that high reliability of observations need not imply high construct validity. Were we to devise a test of creativity, we might be able to demonstrate high test-retest reliability as well as high inter-item reliability. However, we would still be vulnerable to the charge that we really are measuring intelligence, not creativity, and even that creativity does not truly exist. (A characteristic of most psychological constructs is that their existence is unproved and therefore questionable.)

For students of adult development and aging, an important concern is that a given test or measurement might have reasonable construct validity for young adults but not for elderly people. For example, a test of long-term memory might be reasonably valid for college students, who are accustomed to memory tests, but might appear intimidating and irrelevant to elderly people, who might not have experienced a memory test for decades. Hence performance by elderly people might reflect anxiety or tolerance for irrelevancies more than memory *per se.*

Unfortunately, assessments of construct validity are arduous and, at best, only suggestive. A useful approach is to develop different measures of the same construct and to see if they are associated. For example, the construct of anxiety might be measured by subjective reports of anxiety as well as by physiological indices (heart rate, palm sweat, and so on). It is to be hoped that the subjective reports of anxiety will be closely associated with physiological indicants of anxiety.

BASIC TYPES OF MEASURES USED
FOR COLLECTING INFORMATION

Having discussed some basic issues involved in making measurements, we now move to a discussion of the basic types of measures used for collecting information about adult development and aging. We will see that the issues of measurement discussed earlier are often relevant to our choice of a type of measurement in a particular investigation.

Interview and Questionnaire

Many scientific inquiries that focus on adult development have been based on the techniques of interview and questionnaire. An **interview** is a set of questions put to someone and the responses that person makes. The interview can range from very structured to very unstructured. For example, a very unstructured interview might include questions such as, "Tell me about some of the things you do with your friends" or "Tell me about yourself." A very structured interview might question whether the respondent highly approves, moderately approves, moderately disapproves, or highly disapproves of his friends' use of drugs. Highly unstructured interviews, while often yielding valuable clinical insights, usually do not yield information suitable for research purposes. Open-ended interview questions usually produce a wide variety of answers that make attempts to categorize and analyze the data difficult. However, open-ended interview questions can be helpful in developing more focused interview questions for future efforts.

Researchers are also able to question adults through surveys or questionnaires. A **questionnaire** is similar to a highly structured interview except that adults read the questions and mark their answers on a sheet of paper rather than vocally responding to the interviewer.

One major advantage of questionnaires is that they can easily be given to a very large number of people. A sample of responses from 5,000 to 10,000 people is quite possible to obtain. However, questionnaires, or surveys, must be carefully constructed.

A number of experts who study development (e.g., Ausubel, Sullivan & Ives, 1979) have pointed out that surveys and questionnaires have been badly abused instruments of inquiry. Questions on surveys should be concrete, specific, and unambiguous; often they are not. Some assessment of the authenticity of the replies should be provided; often it is not. (Assessment may involve a spot check against available records or the inclusion of built-in questions that reveal insincere and careless responses.)

Structured interviews conducted by an experienced researcher can produce more detailed responses than are possible with a questionnaire, and interviews can help eliminate careless responses as well. The interviewer has the opportunity to ensure that he or she understands the interviewee's answers. A good

Interviews can range from very unstructured to very structured.

interviewer can encourage an adult to open up. But interviews are not without problems either. Perhaps the most critical of these problems involves the response set of social desirability mentioned earlier. In a face-to-face situation, where anonymity is impossible, a person's responses may reflect social desirability rather than actual feelings or actions. In other words, a person may respond to gain the approval of others rather than say what she or he actually thinks. When asked about her sexual relationships, for example, a female may not want to admit having had sexual intercourse on a casual basis. Skilled interviewing techniques and built-in questions to help eliminate such defenses are critical in obtaining accurate information in an interview.

Another problem with both interviews and surveys or questionnaires is that some questions may be retrospective in nature; that is, they may require the participant to recall events or feelings that occurred at some point in the past. It is not unusual, for example, to interview adults about experiences they had as children, adolescents, or younger adults. Unfortunately, retrospective interviews are seriously affected by distortions in memory. It is exceedingly difficult to glean accurate information about the past from verbal reports. However, because of the importance of understanding retrospective verbal reports, 1978 Nobel prize-winner Herbert Simon and others are investigating better ways to gain more accurate verbal assessments of the past (Ericsson & Simon, 1978). This study focuses on the information-processing aspects of cognition, such as short- and long-term memory and incomplete and inconsistent verbalized information.

Behavioral Research

Regardless of advances in our understanding of verbal reports, they probably will never be adequate, by themselves, as a basis for psychological research. Totally apart from problems of response set or memory, verbal reports obviously are dependent upon conscious awareness. Yet many aspects of cognition, personality, and social behavior apparently are inaccessible to awareness. Thus we must go beyond what people can tell us about themselves and examine how they behave.

The realm of behavior includes verbal behavior (speaking and writing) as well as nonverbal behavior (running, smiling, pressing buttons, and so forth). Behavioral research can, of course, involve verbalization by participants. However, unlike research using interviews or questionnaires, behavioral research does not depend upon participants' verbal reports *regarding the issue under study.* As an example, a questionnaire study might collect verbal reports of memory problems as experienced by the elderly. However, a behavioral study of memory might actually test the efficiency of verbal recall performance by the elderly. (For instance, a list of words might be presented, followed by a test of verbal recall for these words.) Both approaches involve verbalization on the part of participants, but only the questionnaire involves verbalization *about memory itself.* Interestingly, there is evidence that reports of memory problems are not strongly associated with true deficits in performance on memory tasks. Marion Perlmutter (Perlmutter, 1978; Perlmutter, Metzger, Nezworski, & Miller, 1981) has collected both questionnaire and performance data on memory in young and elderly adults. She has found that older adults report more memory problems on a questionnaire and that they also perform more poorly on some (but not all) memory tasks. However, reported memory problems have proved to be a poor basis for predicting actual memory performance in this research. A person reporting many memory problems might actually perform very well and vice versa.

Behavioral Research in Laboratory Versus Field
In behavioral research, it is frequently necessary to *control* certain factors that might determine behavior but are not the focus of inquiry. For example, if we are interested in long-term memory in different age groups, we might want to control motivation as well as the conditions of learning (study time, distracting noises, and so forth). Even extraneous factors such as temperature and time of day might be important. Laboratories are places that allow considerable control over many extraneous factors. For this reason, behavioral research is frequently conducted in laboratories.

However, costs are involved in conducting laboratory research, and some of these costs are especially high when developmental issues are being addressed. First, it is impossible to conduct research in a laboratory without participants' knowing that they are in an experiment. This creates problems of **reactivity.**

Second, the laboratory setting is unnatural and might cause unnatural behavior on the part of participants. This problem can be particularly severe with elderly participants, who may find the laboratory setting even more unnatural than young adults do. Finally, certain phenomena, particularly social phenomena, are difficult if not impossible to produce in the laboratory. Stress, for example, might be difficult (and unethical) to investigate in a laboratory setting.

Because of these problems with laboratory research, many psychologists are beginning to do *field* or *observational* research in real-world settings. Such settings can include job sites, parks, shopping malls, schools, or any other place where appropriate observations can be made. The main drawback of field research is limited control over extraneous factors. However, this drawback is frequently outweighed by the benefits of low reactivity, natural contexts, and access to interesting phenomena that are difficult to observe in the laboratory.

Though often presented as dichotomous, laboratory and field research are really two points on a continuum, a continuum that can be labeled *naturalism* or *control.* Many laboratory experiments employ conditions or tasks of a decidedly natural character, and these belong in some middle area of the continuum. For example, a laboratory study of memory might examine recall of autobiographical events from one's past. A laboratory study of social behavior might bring middle-aged parents and their adolescent offspring together to discuss problems in their family. Researchers have found that many benefits of field studies can be enjoyed in the laboratory, *if* the activities of the participants are to some degree natural. This is an important lesson for psychologists interested in adult development and aging. It is frequently necessary to conduct developmental research within some form of laboratory-like context (perhaps a simple room with few distracting stimuli) that is the same for participants in different age groups. This does not mean that the tasks performed by participants must be unnatural and uninteresting. Such tasks might put elderly people who are unaccustomed to performing artificial and irrelevant tasks at an unfair disadvantage. Rather, it is frequently useful to employ natural and meaningful tasks of interest to all age groups.

Laboratory Research with Animal Models

Although laboratory and field research can be thought of as two points on a continuum, laboratory research with human participants is not an endpoint on this continuum. The endpoint is laboratory research done with animal participants because such research allows considerably more control than that possible with humans. With animal participants, we can control genetic endowment, diet, experiences during infancy, and countless other factors that obviously can affect behavior but must be treated as *random variation* or *noise* when humans are studied. We can also investigate effects of treatments (brain implants, for example) that would be unethical to attempt with humans. Moreover, with some animals it is possible to track the entire life course in a very short period of time. (Laboratory mice live at most a few years.)

Research with animals has greatly benefited our knowledge about adult development and aging, but generalizations to humans are sometimes tenuous.

A major disadvantage of animal research is, of course, its questionable generalizability to humans. Indeed, many aspects of human development—language, for example—are simply impossible to study except with humans. (Although it is possible to teach simple "languages" to chimpanzees, few would argue that chimps should be used to study language development in human infancy or language deficits associated with brain damage in old age.) Nevertheless, some aspects of animal development do generalize to humans and promise to teach us much about development across the life span.

Standardized Tests

Standardized tests can be questionnaires or structured interviews or behavioral tests. Their distinctive characteristic is that they are developed to identify an individual's characteristics or abilities *relative* to those of a large group of similar individuals. In order to maximize reliability, a good test usually has a reasonably large number of items and is given in an objective, standardized manner. In order to be practically useful, a good test is also constructed so that administration time is reasonably brief and scoring is reasonably easy. The **standardization** of tests actually refers to two different things. First, it refers to the establishment of fixed or standard procedures for administration and scoring. Second, it refers to norms for age, grade, race, sex, and so on. **Norms** are patterns or representative values for a group. Hence the performance of an individual can be assessed *relative* to that of a comparison group (people of the same age, sex, and so on).

Although most frequently used tests have good *reliability*—assessments of both test-retest reliability and split-half reliability are common—their *construct validity* can be questioned. IQ tests, for example, show impressive reliability, but there is considerable uncertainty about what such tests measure. The problem is compounded by the possibility that a single test might measure different things at different ages. (For example, an IQ test might measure intellectual ability in young adulthood, anxiety in old age.) This possibility is critical in developmental research. For instance, it is crucial for interpreting the finding that IQ performance can change with age (Eichorn, Clausen, Haan, Honzik, & Mussen, 1981).

Standardized tests are of many different types. There are standardized tests for intellectual functioning, standardized tests for psychopathology or mental illness, standardized tests for hypnotizability, creativity, and many other aspects of personality and cognition. Thus they are used for a wide variety of purposes and are invaluable in developmental research. However, when using such tests, it is important to keep the notion of construct validity in mind. It is frequently questionable that a standardized test for X truly measures X, or that X even can serve as a scientifically useful concept (substitute intelligence, creativity, neuroticism, anxiety, self-concept, and so on for X).

Physiological Research

There is no question that a biological level of analysis offers a great deal of information about adult development and aging. This is not to say that psychological and sociocultural factors are unimportant; indeed, there is good reason to believe that there are multiple determinants of development in adulthood. Moreover, it is probable that physiological factors and psychological-sociocultural factors *interact* during the course of adult development. Thus biological

Box 2.1

PHYSIOLOGICAL AROUSAL AND LEARNING IN THE ELDERLY

Carl Eisdorfer and others established that young adults frequently outperform elderly subjects on some types of learning tasks and that slowing the pace of the learning task can reduce this age-related difference. Further, there is evidence suggesting that elderly subjects in learning experiments are more highly aroused physiologically than are younger subjects (Powell, Eisdorfer & Bogdonoff, 1964). Thus Eisdorfer and two colleagues, John Nowlin and Francis Wilkie, developed a hypothesis: Perhaps we could *improve* learning performance in elderly people by *reducing* their physiological arousal.

In order to test their hypothesis, Eisdorfer, Nowlin, and Wilkie (1970) examined learning performance by two groups of elderly men whose average age was 68.6. One group was administered a drug—propranolol—prior to the learning test. Propranolol is known to reduce most physiological indicants of arousal, including heart rate and free fatty acid in the blood. The other group received a placebo (isotonic saline) known not to reduce indicants of arousal. Though each individual subject received either propranolol or the placebo, he was not told which. Likewise, the experimenters conducting the learning experiment did not know whether any individual subject had received propranolol or the placebo. (Only the physician who injected the substances had this information.) This *double-blind* procedure was used for the sake of objectivity of observations.

The results of the experiment were clear; subjects in the propranolol group made fewer errors during learning. Further, three different measures—heart rate,

development and change are important for understanding behavioral development and change and vice versa. In addition, biological measures frequently suggest strategies to remove or reverse certain types of behavioral change, which is sometimes desirable. Box 2.1 describes a study that tested one such strategy, that of administering a drug (propranolol), which reduces physiological manifestations of arousal.

BASIC STRATEGIES FOR SUMMARIZING MEASUREMENTS

Most scientific reports present only summaries of results of research projects. These summaries characterize the results that were obtained, but they do not convey everything about the results. The task of the scientist is to report what is important about his or her findings and to omit what is not important.

free fatty acid in the blood, and galvanic skin response (GSR)—indicated that subjects in the propranolol group were physiologically less aroused. Thus the researchers' hypothesis was supported.

A single experiment like this is inadequate to support sweeping conclusions about arousal and learning in elderly people. There was no comparison group of young subjects, only one sort of learning task was employed, and it is always possible to speculate that a drug like propranolol affects many things besides arousal. Nonetheless, the Eisdorfer experiment is useful to include in a methods chapter, and this is for two reasons. First, the study is an excellent example of how physiological measures can stimulate productive research on adult development and aging. Second, the study illustrates the importance of blind procedures in research. Without the double-blind procedure of the Eisdorfer experiment, it would be possible to argue that subjects in the propranolol group performed better because they were *expected* to perform better, that is, that *demand characteristics* of the situation might have increased motivation in this group. (This is the basic problem of reactance.) Further, the experimenters might have let their biases and expectations get the better of them by making inaccurate observations in favor of the propranolol group. (This is the problem of objectivity of measures.) Fortunately, because double-blind procedures were used by Eisdorfer and his colleagues, explanations in terms of demand characteristics and biased observations are unlikely. Rather, the results have interesting implications for effects of arousal upon learning across the life span.

A typical research project produces a mass of results. There is no simple rule that tells us what in this mass is important and what is not. Importance is determined by the research question, by other research relevant to the question, by the methodology used to address the question, and by aspects of the results themselves. (Unexpected findings, simply by virtue of their unexpectedness, can become important and worthy of report.) However, there are three ways of summarizing findings that are so generally useful and so frequently reported that they merit special attention. These are (1) measures of central tendency, (2) measures of variability, and (3) measures of correlation between variables. We consider each of these in turn.

Measures of Central Tendency

Most people are familiar with the procedure of averaging. Given a set of *n* scores, we add their values and divide by *n*. The result is called the **mean,** which is by far the most common measure of **central tendency.** The mean, however, is not the *only* measure of central tendency. There is also the **median,** which is a value in the middle of the distribution of scores (as many scores fall above the median as fall below it). In addition, there is the **mode,** which is the most frequent of the scores in the set.

Modes are rarely reported in scientific articles. Medians are reported more frequently, especially in studies where extreme scores are found. For example, studies of reaction time (speed of response) typically produce a small number of very extreme scores (very long reaction times that result from inattention or other chance factors). Extreme scores have large effects on means but relatively small effects on medians.

Although modes are seldom reported, they are important for an investigator to examine because *one* set of scores can occasionally produce *more than one* mode. Such *bimodality* can suggest two different phenomena or two different types of individual. As an illustration, consider the possibility that a group of elderly individuals produces a bimodal distribution of scores on some sort of problem-solving test. Although the mean for the group might be lower than the mean for a group of young adults, the higher scoring elderly (who create the higher of the two modes) might do as well as the younger participants. Such a result would suggest an important type of individual difference in aging. However, it could not be detected unless modes were analyzed.

Measures of Variability

The mean is truly a *summary* statistic; it is a single score used to represent an entire set of scores. Although it is certainly necessary to summarize, it is also necessary not to summarize too much. To report only a mean is frequently to summarize too much. For this reason, we often need information on the **variability** of scores as well as their mean.

The simplest measure of variability is the **range,** which is given by the lowest score in the set and the highest score in the set. Involving only two scores from an entire set of scores, the range can be misleading as an index of variability. A much more common measure is the **variance,** which can be measured by (1) computing the difference between each score in a set and the mean of the set, (2) squaring these differences, and (3) taking the mean of the squared differences. The **standard deviation** is another common measure, and it is equal to the square root of the variance. Note that if all the scores in a set were equal, the differences from the mean would all be zero. Hence the variance and the standard deviation would be equal to zero. The more the scores vary, the greater the differences will be between the scores and the mean. Thus the more the scores vary, the greater the variance and standard deviations.

Variances and standard deviations are reported frequently in research on adult development. There are several reasons for this, but none is more important than the relevance of these measures to individual differences in the course of adult development. Such individual differences should produce large variances, particularly among the elderly. Unfortunately, large variances can result not only from individual differences but also from low reliability of measurement (that is, measurement error). For this reason, measures of variability must frequently be interpreted with caution.

Correlation Between Variables

In order to understand the concept of correlation, one must first understand the concept of variable. The concept of variable is just what its name implies. A **variable** is something that can vary, that is, take on different levels or values. Age, for example, is a variable because it can take on values between 0 and 100 years or more. Other common variables are IQ, height, weight, and years of education. Some variables can take only two different values (gender, for example, can take on values of only male and female). However, variables *must* take on at least two different values or else they are not truly variables. Though age is a variable, sixty-three years of age is not.

A **correlation** is a relationship or association between two variables. In children, for example, age is correlated with height—generally, the older the child, the greater his or her height.

Correlations can be either positive or negative. A *positive correlation* exists when high values of one variable are associated with high values of the other— age and height of children are positively correlated. A *negative correlation* exists when high values of one variable are associated with low values of the other— amount of food eaten is probably negatively associated with degree of hunger.

Whether positive or negative, correlations can vary from weak to strong. A correlation is strong to the extent that values of one variable are predictable from values of the other. A perfect correlation is one in which the values of one variable are perfectly predictable from values of the other. Imagine that we measured the height of a hundred children and that we did this twice, once in inches and once in centimeters. We could then determine the correlation between height in inches and height in centimeters. Obviously, the correlation would be extremely strong; given a child's height in inches, we could accurately predict the child's height in centimeters and vice versa. Indeed, such prediction should be perfect, save for measurement error.

The strength of a correlation—positive or negative—can be measured quantitatively by computing the **Pearson product moment correlation coefficient,** which is abbreviated as *r*. A perfect correlation will give a Pearson's *r* of either $+1.0$ or -1.0, depending upon the positive versus negative nature of the association. As the association becomes weaker the *r* scores drop in absolute value from ± 1.0 to $\pm .90$, $\pm .60$, $\pm .40$, and so on, all the way down to 0, which is a *non*correlation. Perfect correlations (± 1.0) are seldom obtained, but even moderate correlations (say, those with *r*'s of .30 to .60) can be very important.

An example should help illustrate the importance of correlations and how they can be interpreted. A recent study involved measurement of Wechsler IQ on individuals at two points in their lives, once in late adolescence and again in middle age (Eichorn et al., 1981). The striking result was that IQ in late adolescence and IQ in middle age were strongly correlated, with *r* scores of about .80. Despite these high correlations, it was also true that about half of the subjects showed changes in IQ of at least ten points between the two testings. These IQ changes are at least as important as the stability in IQ implied by the high correlations. To be sure, a strong correlation implies significant predictability of scores on one variable (IQ in adolescence) from scores on another (IQ in middle age). But significant predictability is not perfect predictability. Even strong correlations allow for interesting discrepancies between values on two variables.

One final point to make about correlations is that measures of correlation, such as Pearson's *r,* reflect the strength of the **linear** association between variables. This is fine in many cases, but sometimes there are **curvilinear** associations between variables. For example, it doubtlessly is true that most people have little personal income in childhood but that their income increases and then falls again as they grow older. Such a curvilinear association between age and income cannot be measured by Pearson's *r.*

Factor Analysis

In many studies of adult development, it is important to examine many variables and to assess correlations between each variable and every other variable. For example, we might be interested in examining the variables of age and mathematical ability and also creativity, health, income, occupational status, and life satisfaction (as indicated on a questionnaire). That would give us seven variables in all, among which there are twenty-one possible correlations. Now suppose we had two or three different math-ability measures, two or three different health measures, and so forth. We could easily end up with a dozen or more variables, which would mean sixty-six or more correlations. How do we make sense of so many correlations? How do we get a view of the forest, not just of the trees?

Factor analysis can be useful for producing a kind of summary of many correlations. The goal is simply to reduce a large number of correlations to a smaller number of independent *factors*. These factors are variables, but they differ from the original variables that were actually measured. The factors are hypothetical in nature, they are relatively few in number, and they are mathematically independent, that is, uncorrelated with one another. The analysis provides *loadings* of each original variable upon each factor. These loadings are correlations, and they are used to interpret the factors. For example, if health, exercise, life satisfaction, and income all loaded heavily on a factor, we might want to interpret this factor as one of general well-being or vigor. In the process, we would have replaced four original variables with a single derived factor. An example of how factor analysis was beneficial in one well-known longitudinal study of adults is described in box 2.2.

Once a factor analysis has been performed, it becomes possible to examine differences among people and groups in terms of a small number of factors. This is often much simpler than examining differences among people and groups in terms of a large number of measures. For example, we might be able to compare different groups of people (elderly who live with family versus elderly who live in nursing homes) on the well-being/vigor factor described above. We might also be able to examine changes in the well-being/vigor factor as a function of age.

A problem with factors is their reliability. There are cases in which similar studies produce dissimilar factors (that is, the loadings of variables on factors are discrepant). Another problem with factors is their validity. Once we interpret a factor as representing X (well-being/vigor, for example), there is a tendency to believe that X truly exists (that there is a "trait" of well-being/vigor and that people differ on this trait). In fact, however, a factor is only a summary of a pattern of correlations among variables. Our label for a factor is just that, a label. It could be wrong or misleading.

BASIC STRATEGIES FOR RESEARCH DESIGN

In preparing to conduct a research project, we may have considered the basic issues of measurement and settled upon a type of measure to employ. Yet we still must concern ourselves with the *design* of the research project. The design will determine the relationships we will assess and/or the comparisons we will make. It will also determine how valid our conclusions can be.

Correlational Versus Experimental Strategies

It often is said that the experiment is the principal tool of the research scientist. Yet the vast majority of studies on adult development and aging are *not* true experiments; rather, they are correlational studies. What is the difference between the two? Why are correlational strategies used to study development? Do developmental researchers pay a price for not performing true experiments?

Box 2.2
THE USE OF FACTORS AND FACTOR ANALYSIS IN THE CALIFORNIA LONGITUDINAL STUDY

We will at several points in this book refer to a completed study of personality, social, and intellectual development between adolescence and middle age. The results of this study, called the California Longitudinal Study, have been published in *Present and Past in Middle Life,* a book edited by Dorothy Eichorn, John Clausen, Norma Haan, Marjorie Honzik, and Paul Mussen, all experts in the science of human development. The book contains many exciting and thought-provoking findings that could never be adequately summarized in a few paragraphs. However, it is appropriate here to review the way in which factor analysis was used by the investigators to examine the development of individual personality over a period of life exceeding twenty-five years.

Eichorn and her colleagues faced a difficult task in that their study was actually a combination of three individual projects, begun independently in the late 1920s and early 1930s. All three projects produced data on personality beginning in the adolescent years or earlier, but the procedures for assessing personality were somewhat different. Consequently, it was necessary to use a *Q-sort procedure,* in which researchers reviewed the data collected from each individual subject at a particular time of life and then rated the extent to which various descriptions were characteristic of that individual. Eichorn describes the procedure as follows:

> A Q sort consists of a set of descriptive items, such as "favors conservative values in a variety of areas" and "seeks reassurance from others." The judge doing a Q sort places the items in a forced normal distribution of nine categories in which the lower scores, that is, 1–3, represent traits or behaviors *least* characteristic of the person being rated, the higher scores, that is, 7–9, those most characteristic, and the middle scores, that is, 4–6, those moderately characteristic. . . . Because the information on which judges base Q-sort ratings can be of various kinds—for example interviews, case records, observational notes—the method has the marked advantage for pooling across studies that identical information for each sample is not necessary, only source material of sufficient breadth and depth. (Eichorn et al., 1981, p. 45)

Considering only a single subject and a single time of life (say, late adolescence), the Q-sort procedure produced "representativeness" ratings for over one hundred different personality items. But there were hundreds of subjects, and four times of life were examined—early adolescence, late adolescence, young adulthood, and middle age. Thus there was an enormous amount of data to analyze and interpret. This is where factor analysis came in. Using factor analysis, Eichorn and her colleagues were able to reduce the Q-sort data to six factors. We will consider just two of these factors, *cognitively invested* and *emotionally under/overcontrolled.*

According to Norma Haan (one of the researchers on the project), the cognitively invested factor

> is positively defined by a pattern of items that indicates ease and skill in dealing with intellectual matters, deliberate reflectiveness, and concomitantly, interest in personal achievement. Persons with high scores value thinking; they are verbally fluent,

introspective, philosophically concerned, and appear intelligent. They are also unusually ambitious, productive, and dependable. Persons with low scores are apparently defensive, diversely and disjointedly, because they are not only undercontrolled and push limits, but they are simultaneously self-defensive, uncomfortable with uncertainty, and withdraw when frustrated. Together, these items define a dimension that represents on the high end, successful adaptation, achievement, and use of abilities, whereas the low end includes various defenses that probably hinder adaptation, achievement, and efficient use of abilities (p. 125)

The cognitively invested factor showed several interesting properties. First, it was *stable* across time in that individuals who were high on this factor at one time period were also likely to be high on the factor at subsequent time periods. Second, at the same time, there was a general trend for subjects to score higher on this factor as they grew older. Apparently, the subjects became more cognitively invested as they aged. As Haan concludes: "This pattern suggests that cognitively invested is an important, omnipresent dimension of development that comes systematically to play a more important role in personalities over the life span" (Eichorn et al., p. 140). Interestingly, cognitively invested was positively correlated with measures of socioeconomic status, particularly in males. That is, individuals high on the factor were likely to achieve more prestigious careers and higher incomes than individuals lower on the factor. None of the other five factors examined by Eichorn and her colleagues showed such correlations. Perhaps the most fascinating finding involving the cognitively invested factor is that it was positively correlated with IQ (intelligence) and, at least with men, with *gains* in IQ between adolescence and middle age. That is, adolescent males who were high on the factor were more likely than others to show improvements in IQ across the life span!

Norma Haan describes the emotionally under/overcontrolled factor as

positively defined by items that represent a pressured, dramatic, and aggressive approach to interpersonal exchanges (self-dramatizing, talkative, undercontrolled, pushes limits, assertive, rebellious, and unpredictable) and at the other end, a calm, dependable, and sympathetic approach that is, nevertheless, clearly restricted. Emotionally bland ("flattened affect"), overcontrolled, and submissive are also important aspects of the negative end. Both extremes represent ineffective approaches to conflict. Two different ways that some people react when they are stressed—erratically flaying out or guardedly pulling in—are indicated. Because this dimension is clearly bipolar, both extremes are indicted in the title. (pp. 125–126)

The emotionally under/overcontrolled factor behaved quite differently from the cognitively invested factor. It was less stable over time in that individuals who were high on this factor at one point in their life (for example, late adolescence) often might be low on it at another time (middle age). Moreover, scores on the emotionally under/overcontrolled factor showed no general trend to rise or fall with age. Apparently, according to Haan, "Emotionally under/overcontrolled is not a developmental dimension; it probably fluctuates with specific, non–age-related changes in life situations" (Eichorn et al., p. 140).

A **correlational study** is one in which associations among variables are assessed. An *experimental study* also assesses associations among variables, but a distinction is made between **dependent variables,** which are the measures, and **independent variables,** which create two or more *treatments* or *conditions.* The independent variables are not measured; they are *manipulated* by the experimenter. Thus manipulation of independent variables is the critical feature of experiments.

A concrete example may help to clarify what constitutes an experiment. Suppose it is believed that individuals learn to solve problems simply by observing other people solve them. This belief could be subjected to experimental test by means of the following procedure. Each person in one group is individually exposed to another person who repeatedly assembles a jigsaw puzzle that has thirty-five pieces. Each person in a second group is individually exposed to the same person and the same jigsaw puzzle but does not see that person assemble it. Each person in both groups is then asked individually to assemble the jigsaw puzzle, and a record is made of the time taken to do so.

The independent variable in this experiment would be the amount of exposure the individual has to the person solving the problem. There are two degrees of this—some exposure to the person assembling the puzzle and no exposure. The dependent variable is the amount of time a person takes to assemble the puzzle.

If the group of individuals who had some exposure assembled the puzzle more rapidly than the group who had no exposure, the initial hypothesis would be confirmed: the people learned something—rapid puzzle assembly—following an experience in which they saw someone else perform that action.

Other factors might explain the superior performance of the one group. Perhaps they were brighter or had more experience with jigsaw puzzles or had more experience watching people solve problems. How do we know that it actually was the exposure manipulation that produced the difference between groups?

One approach to this problem is to match the two groups on **extraneous variables** that are suspected to be important. For example, we could give IQ tests to all participants, making sure that the groups were matched with respect to IQ. Such matching can be useful, but **random assignment** is a much more powerful technique. Individuals can be assigned to one or the other exposure condition on a random basis (flipping a coin might do, but there are more advanced procedures). If assignment to groups is random and if the number of subjects is reasonably large, we can assume that *all* extraneous factors will be randomly distributed in the two groups. This includes extraneous factors that we could never have thought of in advance, as well as the more obvious factors that might be handled through matching.

Studying adults of different ages often requires matching on extraneous factors such as health and socioeconomic status.

Manipulations Between and Within Subjects

Random assignment of subjects to groups is one way of manipulating an independent variable. Such manipulations are **between-subjects manipulations.** There are also **within-subject manipulations,** which involve examination of each subject in an experiment under two or more conditions. For example, if we suspect that a certain drug improves puzzle-solving ability, we might examine puzzle-solving times after administration of this drug and also after administration of a placebo. Each individual subject could be examined under the drug condition as well as the placebo condition (given at different times) in order to determine the effect. **Counterbalancing** would be advisable in such an experiment—we would test one half of the subjects first in the drug condition and later in the placebo condition, and we would test the remaining subjects first in the placebo condition and later in the drug condition. Counterbalancing controls for effects of the time at which variables are manipulated within subjects.

Quasi-Experimental Strategies in Developmental Research

All true experiments involve manipulation of variables. Unfortunately, some variables are difficult if not impossible to manipulate. Age is one of these variables. Since we cannot manipulate a person's age, we cannot perform true experiments to examine effects of a person's age. Thus, as K. Warner Schaie has remarked, "Whenever age is to be treated as the independent variable, it becomes impracticable to utilize the more precise experimental paradigms. [Rather,] recourse needs to be taken to the quasi-experimental approaches" (Schaie, 1977, p. 39).

Let us consider just what is meant by the claim that a person's age cannot be manipulated. Suppose we are conducting a study on adult development and succeed in finding an individual who is willing to serve as a subject. We can examine this subject under a variety of conditions that are under our control. For example, we can give the subject one of several different types of instruction, we can administer to the subject one of several different types of drugs, we can test the subject in a group or individually, we can present the subject with visual stimuli or auditory stimuli, and so on. It is up to us, the experimenters, to decide what conditions or treatments our subject will receive. But the subject's age is not up to us; we are stuck with the age our subject is when he or she arrives to participate in our study.

Of course, we can assign our subject to a group of similarly aged individuals and compare this group to another group of younger or older individuals. We can also plan to test our subject not only today but again several years from now and once again several years after that. Using these strategies (which are the cross-sectional and longitudinal strategies discussed below), we can compare functioning at different ages and gather evidence about effects and phenomena that are *related* to age. But clearly these strategies do not entail actual *manipulation* of age. They simply involve our taking advantage of differences and changes of age that occur independently of our study and are beyond our control.

Despite the fact that most studies involving age are not true experiments, they often resemble true experiments in the ways in which they are designed or analyzed. Specifically, age is treated as an independent variable even though it is not actually manipulated. Thus we look for *effects of age*—actually, *effects related to age*—on one or more dependent variables (measures). Because of their similarity to true experiments, but also because the independent variable—age—is not truly manipulated, such studies are called **quasi experiments.**

The Problem of Internal Validity

Perhaps you feel that the difference between an experiment and quasi experiment is rather subtle and has no practical importance. If so, you are right about subtlety but wrong about importance. The difference is critical, and it is clarified by the concept of **internal validity.**

Recall the concept of validity of measures: a measure is valid if it reflects what it is intended to reflect (thus an IQ test is valid if it truly reflects intelligence). The concept of internal validity is similar, except we are concerned with the independent variable of an experiment (or quasi experiment), not a measure. An experiment is internally valid if the independent variables reflect what they are intended to reflect and not something else. Specifically, the question of internal validity is the question of whether experimental conditions differ in the ways intended and not in other ways.

Internal validity is a concept that was developed by Donald Campbell and Julian Stanley in their classic book *Experimental and Quasi-Experimental Designs for Research* (1963). In it, they enumerate several threats to internal validity and show that quasi-experimental studies, which include most studies of adult development and aging, are highly vulnerable to these threats.

One internal validity threat is that of *selection,* which is especially serious when different-aged groups are compared (for example, when a group of young adults in their twenties is compared with a group of elderly adults in their seventies). In such cases, the procedures we use to select our groups can result in many extraneous differences among these groups, *differences which do not pertain to age, per se.* A young-adult group and an elderly group might differ with respect to years of education, health, and anxiety about the study, and this is only a start. Because of extraneous differences, a difference between groups on some dependent measure (problem-solving ability) can be difficult to interpret.

A second internal validity threat is that of *history,* which is especially serious when we are testing the same individuals at different ages. The problem is that many things can happen to a person between one time of testing and another. Such things might include cultural changes (attitudes toward sex, for example), economic events (a depression), or knowledge of scientific advances (a link between smoking and lung cancer). Studies of people's attitudes are especially susceptible to the history threat. Suppose for example that a group of subjects expressed considerable acceptance of smokers twenty years ago but hostility toward smokers today. Would this mean that attitudes toward smokers must change as a function of age? Hardly.

A third internal validity threat is *testing,* which occurs because taking a test on one occasion can affect test performance on a subsequent occasion. Obviously, the testing threat can accompany the history threat whenever we test the same individuals at different ages. However, the testing threat is especially serious when we are measuring some type of behavior that can change as a function of practice. (Many types of intellectual performance can change with practice.)

Imagine that we were able to manipulate a person's age. Suppose for example that we had a machine that could make someone twenty years old, forty years old, or even ninety years old, all at the turn of a switch (and that we could bring the person back to his or her original age, with no harm done). Then we could solve the problems of internal validity by using true experimental designs. For example, we could take a sample of subjects and randomly assign half of these subjects to a twenty-year-old condition and the other half to a ninety-year-old condition, and then compare them on many different dependent measures (problem-solving ability, creativity, attitudes toward sex, self-concept, and so forth). Chance would take care of all extraneous differences between the two age groups (the selection threat). History would not be a factor because we could test all subjects on the same day. Further, we would be able to test each subject only once, avoiding the threat of testing. This might be an ideal situation, at least for purposes of scientific rigor, but it is not the situation we face. Thus we must live with threats to internal validity and compensate for them as best we can. Fortunately, it is possible to compensate for internal validity threats, albeit not perfectly and not with a single quasi-experimental design.

Next we consider several different types of quasi-experimental design that are used in research on adult development and aging. We will see that different designs compensate for different internal validity threats. Specifically, we will see that the time span of a research design is a critical factor in determining what kinds of threats it can handle.

QUASI-EXPERIMENTAL DESIGNS FOR THE STUDY OF ADULT DEVELOPMENT AND AGING

Discussion of research designs can be complicated, especially when issues of development are involved. Our approach here is to start with the simplest designs, which we actually introduced above. These are the simple cross-sectional and simple longitudinal designs, which are the basis for all developmental research. Next we discuss an elaborated version of each of these designs, the treatment-by-levels version of the cross-sectional design and the nonrepeated-measures version of the longitudinal design. Finally, we describe the sequential designs, which are the most complex, although they are actually only further elaborations of simple cross-sectional and simple longitudinal designs. We will discuss the advantages and disadvantages of each design, focusing specifically on the way in which each compensates, or fails to compensate, for various threats to internal validity. Table 2.5 provides a summary of these designs, their susceptibility to internal validity threats, and other distinguishing features. It may be useful to consult this figure throughout the discussion that follows.

Cross-Sectional and Longitudinal Designs

Consider two different ways in which we might attempt to examine effects related to age. First, we might perform a **cross-sectional study,** comparing groups of people in different age ranges. A typical cross-sectional study might include a group of eighteen- to twenty-year-olds and a group of sixty-five- to seventy-year-olds. A more comprehensive cross-sectional study might include groups for every decade of life from the twenties through the nineties. The different groups could be compared with respect to a variety of dependent variables, such as IQ performance, memory, and puzzle-solving ability. All of this could be accomplished in a very short time; even a large study can be completed within a month or so.

Second, we might perform a **longitudinal study** to examine effects related to age. In this case, we would take a single group of subjects, all of approximately the same age, and test them today and on one or more occasions in the future. For example, we might decide to examine puzzle-solving ability at ages fifty, fifty-seven, sixty-four, and seventy-one. In studies involving adults, it is rare that an interval of less than approximately seven years can be informative. Thus longitudinal studies take a long time to complete.

An advantage of cross-sectional designs, then, is that they are very efficient in terms of time. Further, they are virtually free of two important internal validity threats. There is no threat of history because all subjects are tested at the same time. There is no threat of testing because it is necessary to test each individual subject only once. For these reasons, cross-sectional designs are enormously popular. However, as mentioned earlier, cross-sectional designs are highly susceptible to the internal validity threat of selection. We often do not know the extent to which the results of a cross-sectional study reflect the effects of age versus the effects of countless extraneous factors.

Many extraneous factors that are involved in cross-sectional designs pertain to *cohort effects,* that is, effects that are due to a subject's time of birth or generation but not actually to her or his age. For example, cohorts can differ with respect to years of education, child-rearing practices, health, and attitudes on topics such as sex and religion. These cohort effects are important because they can powerfully affect the dependent measures in a study ostensibly concerned with age. The effects of cohort can look like age effects, but they are not.

A fine example of cohort effects is the study of *visualization* ability across the life span, which we discussed in chapter 1 (Nesselroade, Schaie & Baltes, 1972). Subjects in eight different age groups were tested for visualization twice, once in 1956 and a second time in 1963. Despite the fact that subjects in older groups did not perform as well as subjects in younger groups, there was *no* evidence for a decline in visualization performance between 1956 and 1963. Indeed, performance tended to rise between the first test and the second. This pattern suggests that the differences among the age groups (the cross-sectional comparison) were due to cohort effects, not aging.

Since cross-sectional designs do not allow random assignment of individuals to age groups, there is no way for chance to control for effects of cohort and other extraneous variables. Our only approach to controlling these variables is through *matching*. For example, if our young subjects all are college students, we might make sure that all of our elderly subjects are also college students. Unfortunately, matching for extraneous variables is sometimes impossible. (We may be unable to find an adequate number of elderly college students who are willing to participate in our study.) Further, we can only match for the extraneous variables whose importance we recognize. Finally, matching can have the unwanted side effect of producing unusual or *nonrepresentative* groups—elderly people in college may differ in many ways from the average person of their age. Thus the threat of selection is serious in cross-sectional studies, and the technique of matching is not truly adequate to remove it.

Although longitudinal studies are time-consuming, they are valuable in that they remove the threat of selection, that is, cohort effects. Further, they have the great advantage of allowing us to *track* changes in individual subjects over time. If one's concern is with individual differences in the course of development, longitudinal designs are indispensible.

Unfortunately, the threats of testing and history are especially troublesome in longitudinal studies. To illustrate, consider again the study of visualization ability by Nesselroade, Schaie, and Baltes (1972). The rise in performance between 1956 and 1963 might have reflected a true (though small) increase in visualization ability with age. Alternatively, it might have resulted from practice effects, because subjects in 1963 had the benefit of prior experience with the visualization test. Another possibility is that certain cultural events occurring between 1956 and 1963 had the effect of improving the subjects' visualization ability. Which alternative strikes you as most likely? Suppose a similar pattern had been produced in a study of attitudes toward smokers. Which alternative would strike you as most likely then?

Treatment × Levels Cross-Sectional Designs

Although cross-sectional studies face the threat of selection, they will always be popular. This is because they can be completed much more quickly than longitudinal studies and because they are relatively inexpensive in terms of money and resources. Unfortunately, the threat of selection is pervasive and serious. However, an elaborated type of cross-sectional study can help. This is a treatment × levels study, which adds to the cross-sectional comparison a true experimental variable, one that is manipulated by the experimenter.

A treatment × levels study includes age as a *levels* variable, together with one or more manipulated variables, which produce the *treatments*. For example, we might examine memory in young and elderly adults (our cross-sectional comparison) and also include both a recall-testing condition (subjects must write down words presented previously) and a recognition-testing condition (subjects get a list of words and simply pick out those they saw earlier). With such a design, we can look for *interactions* between the nonmanipulated age variable and the manipulated type-of-test variable. That is, we can determine if effects related to age are constant or if they depend upon the manipulated variable. Indeed, there is substantial evidence that age differences in recall memory are pronounced, whereas age differences in recognition memory are small and sometimes absent (see chapter 6). Thus there is an interaction between age and type of test, and this interaction has figured very prominently in theoretical discussions of adult development and cognition. It also has important practical implications.

Table 2.1

COMBINED LONGITUDINAL/INDEPENDENT-SAMPLES DESIGN THAT PROVIDES A LONGITUDINAL COMPARISON FROM TIME 1 TO TIME 2 AND AN INDEPENDENT-SAMPLES COMPARISON FROM THE FIRST TESTING OF EACH GROUP

| | *Age* | |
	60	70
Repeated Group	Test in 1970	Test in 1980
(Born in 1910)		
Nonrepeated Group	Do not test	Test in 1980
(Born in 1910)		

Independent Samples in Longitudinal Designs

Although longitudinal studies face the internal validity threats of testing and history, the former can be removed through a modification of procedure. The modification is that of randomly assigning subjects to two or more groups and then testing these groups at different times. For example, a sample of sixty subjects might be divided into three groups, one of which we test today, the second of which we test seven years from now, and the third of which we test fourteen years from now. Since each of our groups is tested only once, the threat of testing effects is abolished.

Although the **independent-samples design** resembles the cross-sectional design, the former is more powerful in that it more closely resembles a true experiment. Specifically, independent sampling allows random assignment of subjects to age groups. This random assignment removes the threat of selection (cohort effects) that plagues cross-sectional designs.

There are, however, two principal weaknesses of the independent-samples design. First, the threat of history remains unsolved, just as it does in standard longitudinal designs. This is one reason why simple cross-sectional designs are useful; they remove the history threat completely. The second weakness is that individual differences in adult development are impossible to examine with independent-samples designs, just as they are in cross-sectional designs. This is one reason why simple longitudinal designs are useful; they allow us to track changes in individual subjects over time. Fortunately, it is not difficult to combine a standard longitudinal design with an independent-samples design. For example, we could randomly divide a sample of subjects into two groups, test one of the groups today, and then test *both* of the groups at some time in the future. This provides a longitudinal comparison (from the first and second testing of the group tested twice), as well as an independent-samples comparison (from the first testing of each group). Table 2.1 illustrates a combined longitudinal/independent-samples design of this type.

Table 2.2

**COHORT-SEQUENTIAL DESIGN THAT INCLUDES TWO LONGITUDINAL
STUDIES, EACH COVERING THE SAME AGES BUT CONDUCTED OVER
DIFFERENT SPANS OF TIME**

| | | *Age* | |
		60	70
Cohort	1900	Test in 1960	Test in 1970
	1910	Test in 1970	Test in 1980

Cohort-Sequential Designs

Another alternative to a simple longitudinal design is a **cohort-sequential design,** which entails two or more longitudinal studies, each covering the same range of ages, conducted over differing spans of time. An example of a simple cohort-sequential design is shown in table 2.2. Two different cohorts are selected; a cohort born in 1900 and a second cohort born in 1910. A sample from each cohort is tested twice, once when the subjects are sixty years old and a second time when the subjects are seventy (independent samples can be used if desired).

A strength of the cohort-sequential design is that cohort effects can actually be measured in addition to age effects. That is, we can compare performance by the 1900 cohort and by the 1910 cohort. This tells us something about how cohort-related factors might influence our measure. We can also compare each cohort at age sixty and at age seventy. This tells us something about how age influences our measure independently of cohort. Further, the design allows us to assess *interactions* between cohort and age. We can see if the age effect is constant across the two cohorts, or if it varies between the cohorts. It can obviously be very important if there are different aging effects in different cohorts.

The main weakness of the cohort-sequential design is the same as that of simple longitudinal and independent-samples designs: the threat of history remains. The effects of "age" might actually be due to events occurring between the two testings of our subjects. Another weakness of the design is that it takes a great deal of time to complete. As you can see from table 2.2, in order to study aging and cohort effects over a ten-year span, we need twenty years to collect the data.

Table 2.3

TIME-SEQUENTIAL DESIGN THAT INVOLVES TWO CROSS-SECTIONAL STUDIES, EACH COVERING THE SAME AGE RANGES BUT CONDUCTED AT DIFFERENT TIMES

		Age	
		60	**70**
Time of Testing	**1970**	Cohort born in 1910	Cohort born in 1900
	1980	Cohort born in 1920	Cohort born in 1910

Note: The four cells must represent four different samples of subjects.

Time-Sequential Designs

Though also requiring a lengthy time commitment, **time-sequential designs** have more in common with cross-sectional designs than longitudinal designs. Time-sequential designs involve two or more cross-sectional studies, each covering the same range of ages, conducted at different times. An example is shown in table 2.3. In 1970, we examine performance of two age groups (cohorts), one aged sixty years and the other seventy years. In 1980, we again examine performance of sixty-year-olds and seventy-year-olds (these are entirely new samples of subjects).

The beauty of this design is that history effects—or time of measurement—can be examined explicitly, in addition to differences related to age. That is, we can examine differences between performance in 1970 and 1980; this tells us directly about history effects. Independently of history, we can examine differences between sixty-year-olds and seventy-year-olds; this gives us information relevant to aging. As with cohort-sequential designs, interactions between the two variables examined can be of great importance. If age differences in 1980 are smaller than age differences in 1970, some interesting conclusions about history-related changes in the course of adult development might be supported.

Another advantage of the time-sequential design is that it is more efficient in terms of time than the cohort-sequential design. In our example (table 2.3), age and history effects over a ten-year span can be studied over a ten-year span (compared to a twenty-year span for the cohort-sequential design).

The disadvantage of the time-sequential design is the same as that of simple cross-sectional designs: cohort effects are uncontrolled. At each time of measurement, we must be concerned with the possibility that differences between our age groups reflect differences in their respective cohorts.

Table 2.4

CROSS-SEQUENTIAL DESIGN, A HYBRID OF CROSS-SECTIONAL AND LONGITUDINAL DESIGNS, IN WHICH TWO COHORTS ARE TESTED AND WHICH COVERS DIFFERENT AGE RANGES AT TWO DIFFERENT TIMES

| | | *Time of Testing* | |
		1970	1980
Cohort	1900	Adults are 70	Adults are 80
	1910	Adults are 60	Adults are 70

Cross-Sequential Designs

Cross-sequential designs are a kind of hybrid combination of cross-sectional and longitudinal designs. Despite this fact, they are not fundamentally relevant to adult development and aging because they do not separate age effects from either cohort effects or history effects. Rather, cross-sequential designs separate cohort and history effects from each other.

The technique, illustrated in table 2.4, is to examine two or more cohorts, covering *different* age ranges, at each of two times of testing. Differences among cohorts can be examined independently of differences among times of measurement. Unfortunately, neither of these differences can be separated from age. The cohorts differ on an age dimension, and subjects must obviously be older at the second time of testing than at the first.

Perhaps this is a good time for you to stop and review the various quasi-experimental designs in adult development and aging. Going over them once or twice probably won't be enough. Take some time to study the material in table 2.5, which summarizes the main characteristics of quasi-experimental designs used in the study of adult development and aging.

Schaie's "Most Efficient" Design

We can summarize the preceding discussion by saying that the cohort-sequential design is a useful extension of simple longitudinal designs and that the time-sequential design is a useful extension of cross-sectional designs. However, these sequential designs do not solve the most serious shortcomings of the simpler designs from which they are derived. History effects threaten the internal validity of cohort-sequential designs just as they threaten that of longitudinal designs. Cohort effects threaten the internal validity of time-sequential designs just as they do that of cross-sectional designs. So what are we to do?

One answer is to use both the cohort-sequential and time-sequential designs, and even to add the cross-sequential design for good measure. Performing all of these designs at once is not that much more work than performing one of them alone. K. W. Schaie (1965, 1977), an authority on sequential designs, has developed the **"most efficient" design,** which accomplishes this.

Table 2.5

SUMMARY OF QUASI-EXPERIMENTAL DESIGNS
IN ADULT DEVELOPMENT AND AGING

Design	Description	Threats to Internal Validity	Other Properties
Simple Cross-Sectional	Two or more age groups compared at one time of testing	Selection, especially cohort effects; differences between groups might reflect differences in time of birth	Easy to conduct; can be useful as a pilot study
Treatment × Levels	A cross-sectional design with one or more *manipulated* variables	Cohort effects, as above	Easy to conduct; can be used to analyze the *nature* of age-related differences (this is very beneficial for both theory and practice even though cohort effects are problematic)
Time-Sequential	Two or more cross-sectional comparisons made at different times of testing	Cohort effects, since every cross-sectional comparison is possibly influenced by cohort as well as age	Time-consuming, but not as time-consuming as cohort-sequential designs; allows separate examination of age effects and time of testing (history) effects
Simple Longitudinal	A single group of subjects is tested repeatedly at different points in time	Time of testing (history) effects; historical changes might produce effects that appear to be age changes; repeated testing might influence measures (testing effects)	Time-consuming; subjects may drop out of study prior to completion—experimental mortality (this will threaten generalizability of findings); allows assessment of individual differences in developmental change
Longitudinal with Independent Samples	Some subjects are tested now, and other subjects are tested at some time in the future	Time of testing (history) effects, as above; testing effects are more controlled	Time-consuming and disallows assessment of individual differences in developmental change

Table 2.5 *(con't.)*

SUMMARY OF QUASI-EXPERIMENTAL DESIGNS
IN ADULT DEVELOPMENT AND AGING

Design	Description	Threats to Internal Validity	Other Properties
Cohort-Sequential	Two or more longitudinal comparisons are made on different cohorts	Time of testing and testing effects, as above (can remove testing effects with independent samples)	Extremely time-consuming; requires two time periods to examine change over one time period; allows separate examination of age effects and cohort effects
Cross-Sequential	Two or more cohorts are compared at two or more times of testing	Neither time of testing nor cohort effects are independent of age changes	Time-consuming; provides no clear information on age changes

A simple example of the "most efficient" design is illustrated in figure 2.1. Individuals in three different cohorts are examined: a cohort born in the 1900s, a cohort born in the 1910s, and a cohort born in the 1920s. Further, measurements are made at three different times: 1960, 1970, and 1980. Finally, it is necessary to collect data from new, independent samples of the cohorts at the second time of testing (though retesting of the original samples is also recommended). Having accomplished all this, it is possible to perform a cohort-sequential analysis, a time-sequential analysis, and a cross-sequential analysis, as shown in the figure.

Such analyses provide a wealth of interesting comparisons. Indeed, certain patterns can reveal strong evidence for age changes, cohort differences, and history effects. Consider the following possible outcome in a study of problem-solving ability: The cohort-sequential analysis suggests a strong effect of cohort but only a weak effect of age. The time-sequential analysis supports only weak effects of time and age. Finally, the cross-sequential analysis supports, again, a strong effect of cohort but only a weak effect of time of measurement. In this hypothetical case, we would have clear indications that cohort was an important variable but that age and time of measurement were not.

Unfortunately, it is possible that the cohort-sequential, time-sequential, and cross-sequential analyses will provide a much more complex pattern than that described above. For example, it is possible to find strong effects of both variables in each of the three analyses. In such a case, the sheer wealth of comparisons can make it difficult to draw firm conclusions about the relative importance

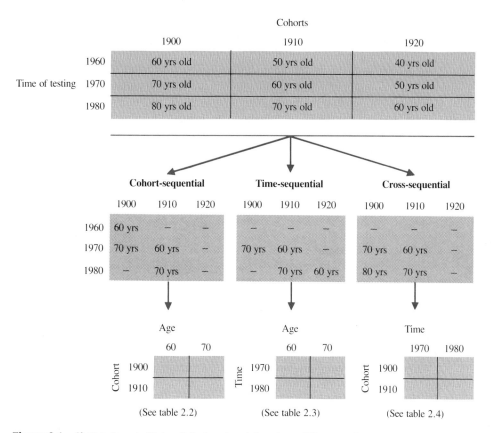

Figure 2.1   Shaie's "most efficient" design, involving three different cohorts tested at three different times plus new independent samples of cohorts.

of age, cohort, and history effects. Although cohort-sequential, time-sequential, and cross-sequential analyses are the most sophisticated available for dealing with the complexities of age comparisons, there is clearly room for future advances in methodology. Further, we must always be mindful of the tremendous difficulty of collecting the data that permit these analyses. Faced with this difficulty, it may frequently be advisable first to conduct simple cross-sectional studies, controlling as best we can for extraneous, cohort-related variables known to be important. Examining effects of different treatments in such designs can also be informative in isolating the particular ways in which younger groups differ from older groups at a particular time in history. Subsequently, once important differences between younger and older groups have been isolated, longitudinal and even sequential strategies can be carried out, allowing a much more complete understanding of the causes of these differences. This is a *practical viewpoint* on adult developmental research, one that has been ably summarized by Jack Botwinick (1978):

> If cross-sectional comparisons are oversimplified and considered as age effects only, or cohort effects only, if longitudinal comparisons are considered as either environmental or age effects but not both, then there is a problem with interpretation. But if the intrinsic confounding is recognized and kept in mind always, then meaningful interpretations are possible.
>
> Cross-sectional studies are very adequate for ascertaining age differences. Descriptive statements can be clear and meaningful. When explanation is desired, however, the relative contributions of the maturational and cultural determination must remain uncertain. The interpretation must involve a logical judgment as to which types of functions are more bound to the culture than others. Religious beliefs, for example, would be more likely a function of culture than would reaction time. There is no reason to maintain, however, that reaction time, or any other behavior, for that matter, is totally free from cultural impact.
>
> Longitudinal studies are preferable, but the cost is high, and it is important to weigh whether the cost is worth the potential results. . . . Longitudinal studies tell us much about how people change over time. Whether the change is due more to age than to the time-of-measurement factors is also a matter of what the measured behavior change is. Visual acuity is more likely to be related to age apart from time of measurement than is measured liberalism. Again, however, both may reflect the impact of time of testing.
>
> The three sequential designs above are the best strategies yet devised. They are difficult to arrange, costly to carry out, and imperfect, but they provide for the best approximations we can make at this time in tearing apart the confounded factors. However, because of the difficulty and expense, because they are relatively new, because of the inadequate interpretations that have been made, most of what is found in the aging literature is not the best. Although it seems likely that the number of studies using sequential strategies will increase, it also seems likely that cross-sectional studies will remain the bulwark of the data that are available. What was read in this book, therefore, and what probably will be read in future books, reflects this state of affairs. The bulk of the data in the study of aging involves the confounding of age and cohort—this should be kept in mind always. (pp. 377–378)

PROBLEMS OF SAMPLING IN DEVELOPMENTAL RESEARCH

When we decide to study a certain class of individuals (say, sixty-five-year-olds who have recently retired), we usually cannot collect measurements on everyone in that class. Rather, we must study a **sample** of the entire **population** of individuals in the class. Although we study only a sample, we wish to *generalize* our findings to the population. Thus the procedures for sampling comprise a very important aspect of research methodology.

Ideally, the sample of individuals we study should have the same characteristics as the population to which we want to generalize our findings. In such a case, we have what is called a **representative sample.** The best way to achieve a representative sample is through the technique of *random sampling,* a technique in which every member of the population has an equal chance of being in the sample that we study. For example, the ideal way to achieve a representative sample of recently retired sixty-five-year-olds would be to get a list of every such individual in the world, and then to randomly pick some of these individuals to be in our study. Obviously, the technique of random sampling can rarely be employed. Indeed, we often must struggle to find people with certain characteristics who are willing to participate in our studies. We simply use whatever resources we have to recruit such individuals and are happy if we get enough.

Because investigators of adult development seldom perform random sampling, they seldom can be sure that their samples are representative. This state of affairs produces two consequences, one pertaining primarily to cross-sectional designs and the other primarily to longitudinal designs.

Nonrepresentative Samples in Cross-Sectional Designs

In cross-sectional designs, the problem of nonrepresentative samples adds to problems of internal validity. Specifically, threats of selection to internal validity are due partially to nonrepresentative sampling. If we find differences between a group of young subjects and a group of elderly subjects but do not know whether either sample is representative, it is difficult to be sure that either age or cohort is responsible for the differences. Perhaps these differences occur because we selected one type of young person (say, one of average intelligence) and a different type of older person (say, one of very high intelligence). The solution to this problem is that of *matching*. We measure various extraneous variables (IQ, for example) that are suspected to be important. Then we assess the equivalence of our groups with respect to these factors. Though not the ideal, this approach is much better than nothing.

Nonrepresentative Samples in Longitudinal Designs

Longitudinal designs do not solve the problem of nonrepresentative samples. However, the issue in this case is not internal validity of age comparisons but rather external validity of these comparisons (Campbell & Stanley, 1963). That is, because of nonrepresentative samples, we often do not know whether age trends that are observed in one longitudinal study are representative of age trends that occur in the population at large.

The problem of sampling in longitudinal studies is not just a logical possibility; it has been shown to occur. It frequently takes the form of **experimental mortality,** which refers to the fact that subjects drop out of a longitudinal study before all of the testings are complete. Therefore, experimental mortality refers not simply to actual deaths among subjects but also to refusals by subjects to participate further in the study for reasons of health, loss of interest, and so forth.

The problem is that subjects who drop out of a study are likely to differ significantly from those who continue until the end. Indeed, it has been shown that people who return for testing in a longitudinal study have greater intellectual abilities than those who do not (Riegel & Riegel, 1972). Further, longitudinal declines in intellectual ability are more likely among those who drop out of a study after several testings than among those who do not (Eisdorfer & Wilkie, 1973; Wilkie & Eisdorfer, 1973). As a result, the data that are collected in a longitudinal study may reflect aging among adults of superior ability, not aging among adults of average or below-average ability.

Summary

Two basic problems of measurement are reliability of measurement and validity of measurement. Although the problem of reliability is serious, there are effective methods for assessing reliability (the test-retest method, for example) and methods for increasing reliability (collecting data on multiple items, for example). The problem of validity is more troublesome because many psychological concepts, such as creativity and self-concept, are highly abstract and difficult to see in behavior. When we attempt to evaluate such abstract concepts, it is often arguable that we are not truly measuring what we think we are measuring.

Among the basic measures used for collecting observations are the interview and questionnaire, behavioral research, standardized tests, and physiological research. Each has strengths and weaknesses. Interview and questionnaire studies can often be conducted when other sorts of study are impossible or at best impractical. However, they are especially susceptible to the problem of reactance, particularly the problem of response sets. Moreover, interviews and questionnaires are highly dependent upon subjects' conscious impressions of themselves, and these impressions can be at variance with actual behavior. Behavioral measures are many and varied. They can be collected in laboratory settings or in the field. Behavioral studies in the laboratory allow impressive control over many extraneous variables. However, they often can be artificial, even anxiety provoking, to subjects. Further, laboratory studies produce problems of reactivity and they cannot be used to study certain kinds of real-world phenomena. Field studies allow fewer controls, but they can be very naturalistic, they can reduce problems of reactivity, and they can reveal real-life phenomena that are not reproducible in the laboratory. Standardized tests are useful for comparing a particular sample of subjects to representative samples of subjects tested previously. However, the validity of such tests often can be questioned. Further, it is frequently the case that no previously developed test can measure exactly what we want to measure. Physiological measures can be invaluable for an increased understanding of behavioral data, and they can suggest ways to reduce or remove age-related differences in behavior when this is desirable.

Among the basic strategies for summarizing data are measures of central tendency (the mean, median, and mode), measures of variability (the range, variance, and standard deviation), and correlation between variables. Correlations are extremely important in research on adult development and aging. However, many studies produce so many correlations that interpretation is difficult. In these cases, factor analysis can be useful for reducing many correlations to a smaller number of factors.

In terms of research design, correlational studies must be distinguished from true experiments. Only the latter involve manipulation of independent variables and actually provide evidence for causal effects of independent variables upon dependent variables. Quasi experiments are similar to true experiments, but quasi experiments do not involve actual manipulation of independent variables. Since age cannot be manipulated, studies of this variable are typically quasi-experimental in nature. Three threats to internal validity, threats that are problematic in such quasi-experimental studies, are selection, history, and testing.

Several types of quasi experiments are frequently used to study adult development and aging. Simple cross-sectional and longitudinal designs are actually quite limited in their usefulness. Cross-sectional designs suffer from cohort effects, whereas longitudinal designs suffer from both testing and history effects. Treatments × levels cross-sectional designs are very useful for analyzing the nature of differences between age groups. Unfortunately, such designs suffer from cohort effects, as do simple cross-sectional designs. Longitudinal designs using independent samples are useful for removing testing effects but not history effects. Among the sequential designs, the cohort-sequential design allows independent assessment of age and cohort effects but does not solve the problem of history effects. The time-sequential design allows independent assessment of age and history effects but does not solve the problem of cohort effects. The use of both designs together, along with the cross-sequential design as well, can in principle allow us to distinguish age, cohort, and history effects. A substantial investment of time and resources is necessary in this case, however.

Researchers must frequently sample their subjects from different age groups (cohorts), and this sampling can introduce bias; samples can be nonrepresentative. The problem of sampling is unavoidable, but we must keep it in mind when we are interpreting the data from our own and other studies of adult development and aging. Particularly vexing is the problem of experimental mortality, which occurs when subjects drop out of a longitudinal study. Those who drop out are likely to differ systematically from those who remain. This can threaten the generalizability of longitudinal studies.

Review Questions

1. How can we assess reliability? How can we improve our assessment of reliability?
2. What are the issues involved in the validity of assessment?
3. Describe the basic types of measures used for collecting information about adults, including their advantages and disadvantages.
4. What are the basic strategies for summarizing measurements?
5. Explain how factor analysis was effectively used in the California Longitudinal Study.
6. Provide an overview of correlational and experimental strategies in research design. Include in your answer information about manipulations between and within subjects.
7. Discuss quasi-experimental designs and the problem of internal validity.
8. Discuss the various cross-sectional and longitudinal designs available in the study of adult development and aging, including combinations of such designs.
9. What are some of the main sampling problems to be aware of when conducting research with adults?

Further Readings

Eichorn, D. M., et al. (1981). *Present and past in middle life*. New York: Academic Press.
A longitudinal study that spans nearly fifty years. Includes information about physical, cognitive, emotional, social, and personality development. Reveals how a longitudinal study is conducted, as well as how factor analysis can be used effectively. Reading level: medium difficulty.

Neale, J. M., & Liebert, R. M. (1980). *Science and behavior: An introduction to methods of research* (2nd ed.). Englewood Cliffs, NJ: Prentice-Hall.
An excellent introduction to scientific methodology, particularly issues related to reliability, validity, basic types of measures, basic strategies for summarizing measurements, and basic strategies for research design. Reading level: undergraduate.

Nesselroade, J. R., & Reese, H. W. (1973). *Life-span developmental psychology: Methodological issues*. New York: Academic Press.
A series of articles by experts in life-span development. Articles focus on some of the issues discussed in this chapter, particularly the effective use of quasi-experimental designs in studying adult development and aging. Reading level: reasonably difficult.

PROFILE

Barbara Martin's mother died at the age of sixty-seven, and her father died when he was sixty-three. Her mother's death was due to cancer, whereas her father died of a heart attack. Barbara, herself, is now sixty-two years old. She is married to sixty-four-year-old Tom Martin. Barbara has watched her weight throughout her adult years and has been successful in keeping it within the prescribed range for a thin body. During her fifties, she jogged almost daily, but now she gets most of her exercise by going to a health spa, although she still takes a fast-paced walk nearly every day. Barbara admits that she has several weaknesses for food and drink. She can't seem to pass up Mexican food and a frozen margarita from time to time or pasta and several glasses of wine, although she has never been an excessive drinker. Although she smoked during her early twenties, she hasn't smoked since then. Barbara makes sure she gets eight hours of sleep almost every night, and she has had regular health checkups during her adult years. She characterizes her current health status as excellent, although she worries about the fact that her parents both died in their sixties.

Barbara is an extroverted person—she likes to be around people and is very outgoing. She says her mother was that way and so was her maternal grandmother. She reports that she has neurotic tendencies, which she swears also came from her maternal grandmother. Barbara has never worked full time, but she still gives piano lessons on a part-time basis.

During her fifties, Barbara's vision started to worsen; possibly because she reads extensively, she has to use bifocals. And within the last several years, she seems not to hear quite as well as she used to. Also, she says that she doesn't seem to hear the high-pitched notes on the piano quite as well as she did in earlier adulthood. Her hands don't seem to move as quickly across the piano keys now either.

With regard to her sexuality, Barbara never had much problem with her menstrual cycle during her early adult years, and when she went through menopause in her forties, it was only a minor annoyance. She and her husband still have an active sex life, having intercourse an average of once a week, an event that averaged several times a week during her forties. Barbara reports that sex has been a very enjoyable part of her marriage.

80

Tom Martin's mother is still alive at the age of eighty-four, but his father died several years ago at the age of seventy-eight. The health of Tom's mother has deteriorated rapidly in the last year, and for the past six months she has been in a nursing home. Her heart seems to be weakening, and an arteriogram performed last month revealed an aneurism that could be fatal at any time.

Tom has not been as careful about his health as his wife has. He just can't seem to pass up that double dish of vanilla ice cream while he watches the TV news before going to bed at night. Tom has also been known to be susceptible to the two-martini business lunch on too many occasions. He has a rotund body build and is about twenty-five pounds overweight. Tom is an achievement-oriented man, smokes on a regular basis, and has not been as conscientious as his wife about having regular medical checkups and exercising on a regular basis. Tom reports that he enjoys his sexual relationship with his wife.

Although Tom's father did not die until he was seventy-eight years old, the cause of his death was Alzheimer's disease, which first appeared when he was seventy-four and led to a progressive deterioration of his brain. Given Tom's disregard for his health, he may not have to worry about reaching the age of seventy-eight. Last year he suffered a heart attack, and although he initially stuck with a physical rehabilitation program, his persistence has slacked off considerably in the last few months.

3

BIOLOGICAL PROCESSES: GENETICS, LONGEVITY, AND AGING

I MAGINE *that you are 120 years old.*

Would you still be able to write your name? Could you think clearly? What would your body look like? Would you be able to walk? To run? Could you still have sex? Would you have an interest in sex? Would your eyes and ears still function? Could you work?

Has anyone ever lived to be 120 years old? Supposedly, one American, Charlie Smith (?1842–1979), lived to be 137 years old. In three areas of the world, not just a single person but many people have reportedly lived more than 130 years. These areas are the Republic of Georgia in Russia, the Vilcabamba valley in Ecuador, and the province of Hunza in Kashmir. Three people over 100 years old (centenarians) per 100,000 people is considered normal. But in the Russian region, approximately 400 centenarians per 100,000 people have been reported. Some of the Russians are said to be 120 to 170 years old (Benet, 1976).

However, there is reason to believe that some of these claims are false (Medvedev, 1974). Indeed, we really do not have sound documentation of anyone living more than approximately 115 to 120 years. In the case of the Russians, birth registrations, as well as other documents such as marriage certificates and military registrations, are not available. In most instances, the ages of the Russians have been based on the individuals' recall of important historical events and interviews with other members of the village (Benet, 1976). In the Russian villages where people have been reported to live a long life, the elderly experience unparalleled esteem and honor. Centenarians are often given special positions in the community, such as the leader of social celebrations. Thus there is a strong motivation to give one's age as older than one really is. One individual who claimed to be 130 years of age was found to have used his father's birth certificate during World War I to escape army duty. Later it was discovered that he only was seventy-eight years old (Hayflick, 1975).

What about Charlie Smith? Was he 137 years old when he died? Charlie was very, very old, but it cannot be documented that he was actually 137. In 1956 officials of the Social Security Administration began to collect information about American centenarians who were receiving benefits. Charlie Smith was visited in 1961. He gave his birthdate as July 4, 1842, and his place of birth as Liberia. On one occasion he said he had been bought at a slave auction in New Orleans in 1854. Charles Smith of Galveston, Texas, bought him and gave the young boy his own name. Charlie was twenty-one years of age in 1863 when he supposedly was freed under the Emancipation Proclamation, but he decided to stay with the Smiths. By the end of the nineteenth century Charlie had settled in Florida. He worked in turpentine camps, and at one point owned a turpentine farm in Homeland, Florida. Smith's records at the

How old the Abkhasians are has not been fully documented.

Social Security Administration do not provide evidence of his birthdate, but they do
mention that he began to earn benefits based on Social Security credits by picking
oranges at the age of 113 (Freeman, 1982).

Charlie Smith lived to be very old—exactly how old we will never know. He
seems to have lived a very active life even after the age of 100. Many other Americans
have lived to be 100 as well. In a recent book, *Living to Be 100: 1200 Who Did and
How They Did It* (Segerberg, 1982), 1,127 Social Security Administration interviews
from 1963 to 1972 were searched for physical, psychological, and social information.
Seventy-three other individuals were interviewed. Especially entertaining are the
bizarre reasons several of the centenarians gave as to why they were able to live to be
100: "because I slept with my head to the north," "because of eating a lot of fatty pork
and salt," and "because I don't believe in germs." While the impressions are those of a
journalist, not a scientist, the following conclusions based on what it takes to live a
long life seem to make sense. Organized purposeful behavior, discipline and hard
work, freedom and independence, balanced diet, family orientation, good peer and
friendship relations, and low ambition were among the most important factors related
to high self-esteem and low levels of stress, both of which are associated with
longevity.

INTRODUCTION

This is the first of two chapters that focus on the biological processes of development. The emphasis in this chapter is on underlying genetic foundations and influences on development. We describe how people study the effects of genetics on adults and attempt to come up with estimates of the degree to which various adult characteristics, such as intelligence and personality, are influenced by heredity. The topic of how long we are likely to live makes each of us curious. We evaluate various demographic characteristics of the population, emphasizing the changing age structure of America. Sex differences in longevity are discussed, and we take a fascinating journey through the reasons behind longevity, including a twenty-five-year longitudinal study that has attempted to pinpoint such reasons. We discuss a number of biological theories that have been developed to explain why people age, and we describe the possibility that humans have a biological clock that is identifiable and programmable, although scientists disagree about the location in the body of the biological clock of aging.

GENETICS

To appreciate the role of biological factors in development, it is necessary to know something about *genes,* the biological building blocks that still have strong effects on adults some twenty to one hundred years after conception.

Each adult still has the genetic code he or she inherited from his or her parents. Physically, this code is carried by biochemical agents called genes and chromosomes. The genes and chromosomes all adults have inherited are alike in one very important aspect: they all contain human genetic codes. A fertilized human egg cannot develop into a dog, a cat, or an aardvark.

Aside from the obvious physical similarity that the general hereditary code produces among adults (for example, in anatomy, brain structure, and organs), this code also accounts for much of the psychological sameness (or universality) among us. The particular kind of brain an adult inherits, however, is largely responsible for how the adult's thought processes develop.

The special arrangement of chromosomes and genes each person has inherited makes him or her unique; this arrangement or configuration is referred to as a person's **genotype.** On the other hand, all of the observed and measurable characteristics of the adult are referred to as his or her **phenotype.** Phenotypical characteristics may be physical, as in height, weight, eye color, and skin pigment, or they may be psychological, as in intelligence, creativity, identity, and moral character.

Identical phenotypical characteristics may be produced by different genotypes. For example, three unrelated adults may each have a measured IQ of 110 but vastly different genes for intelligence; in such a case, the adults have different genetic makeups but the same IQ. The opposite is also possible: differences in phenotypical characteristics may be produced by the same genotype. For example, identical twins may have different IQs (a not uncommon finding); thus different IQs may be produced by identical genetic makeups.

What is the relation between genotype and phenotype? In other words, how does heredity determine what each person becomes in life? Almost no characteristics of the adult are solely the result of a particular genetic code. Virtually all of the adult's psychological characteristics are the result of the interaction between the individual's inherited code and environmental influences. If someone asks whether we believe that some trait of an adult (for example, aggressiveness, shyness, activity level, intelligence, and so forth) is inherited or the product of environment, a safe answer is both.

Strategies for Determining Hereditary Influence

Several different methods are used to examine the influence of heredity on development. One of the most popular techniques is to compare identical (monozygotic, or MZ) twins with nonidentical (dyzygotic, or DZ) twins and determine the degree of similarity of the two groups on some characteristic. This strategy is related to a second type of investigation—**consanguinity** study. Related pairs, such as fathers and sons, siblings, or cousins, are compared with randomly paired individuals who are unrelated. The closer the blood relationship, the more similar the genetic makeup of the individuals. If some genetic mechanism influences the phenomenon under study, the scores of related individuals should be more alike than those of unrelated individuals. In fact, it should be possible to specify several different degrees of relatedness in such a study. For instance, parents and their children are more alike genetically than grandparents and grandchildren, who in turn are more similar than third-generation cousins. This type of genetic study is sometimes labeled a *kinship investigation.*

An assumption may be made in both kinds of inquiry that the environments are about the same for all individuals being studied. But such an assumption can be clearly unwarranted. Identical twins are genetically similar and are often treated alike because people perceive them to be similar. In many instances, this is a source of frustration and resentment by the twins, who want to be thought of as unique individuals. The same family might treat nonidentical twins very differently because they are perceived to be different. Thus studies that purport to measure genetic influence may in fact be measuring environmental influence as well.

In recent years there have been increases in the sophistication of designs and in sample sizes of the kinship groups studied. More care is also taken to determine the effects of similarity of environments. Furthermore, there is a tendency for newer studies to move away from point estimates of genetic and environmental parameters, providing instead ranges of heritability. For example, rather than saying intelligence has a heritability quotient of .50, such studies might give an estimate of between .30 to .60. In addition, there is an increasing tendency toward caution in the interpretation of heritability data (Henderson, 1982).

Of course, all genetic research with humans is correlational. Generally speaking, it is not possible to manipulate the genetics of the environment of humans directly and to have complete control over the significant independent variables. Consequently, researchers often turn to lower animals, with whom practical, ethical, and scientific considerations permit more tightly controlled research. It is possible to construct laboratory environments whose dimensions are well defined and well controlled and to breed many generations of animals over relatively short periods of time. Rats and mice are popular subjects because of the short time they require to produce a new generation.

Research is of two types. In **selective breeding,** animals are mated over successive generations on the basis of their similarities in a specific character- istic, such as speed of running or performance in a maze. It is assumed that these characteristics have a strong heredity component. Fast rats bred with other fast rats should produce a homogeneous strain of fast rats after several generations.

The second type of research involves **inbreeding.** Male and female animals of the same parent (brothers and sisters) are mated with each other. Their chil- dren, their children's children, and succeeding generations of children are mated in turn. When different families of animals are kept distinct and inbred over sev- eral generations, a number of specific genetic characteristics should appear. Each family will have a characteristic speed of running, level of activity, and perfor- mance in mazes.

What, then, is done with this evidence from experimentation with animal genetics? Of what value is it for understanding adult development and aging? It helps us to identify some characteristics that may be inherited by other animals, including humans. It suggests traits for us to look for in ourselves. It also im- proves our understanding of the mechanics of genetic transmission.

Genetic Influences on Development

What facets of development are influenced by genetics? From our earlier dis- cussion, one answer should pop out at you: They all are. A better question is, "What amount of variation in a characteristic among different people is ac- counted for by genetic differences?" If we know the tested intelligence of a group of adults and we know something about their genetic similarity or dissimilarity, we should be able to conclude something about the correlations between the two. Unfortunately, however, our ability to control other important variables— such as the similarity of the environments of the adults—is often weak, and sometimes we do not have precise enough measures of genetic similarity. Estimates often vary widely as to the heritability of a particular characteristic. **Heritability** is a mathematical estimate, which is often computed with a standard heritability quotient. Similarity is measured by use of the correlation coefficient *r*. The highest degree of heritability is 1.00. A heritability quotient of .80 suggests a strong genetic influence, one of .50 a moderate genetic influence, and one of .20 a much weaker, but nonetheless perceptible, genetic influence.

Although heritability values may vary considerably from one study to the next, it is often possible to determine the average magnitude of the quotient for a particular characteristic. For some kinds of physical characteristics and mental retardation, the heritability quotient approaches 1.00. That is, the environment makes almost no contribution to variation in the characteristic. This is not the same as saying the environment has *no* influence; the characteristic could not be expressed without it. Let's look at the heritability quotients for several aspects of development in adulthood—intelligence, personality, and disorders of aging.

Intelligence

One relatively new design, the **family-of-twins design,** has helped provide a more accurate estimate of the heritability of intelligence. It consists of adult monozygotic (MZ) twins, siblings, half-siblings, and parent–offspring. In one investigation that used this strategy, estimates of heritability for half-siblings were .40 whereas for parent–offspring they were .56 (Rose, Harris, & Christian, 1979).

Earlier studies of the heritability of intelligence placed the figure at approximately .80 (for example, Loehlin & Nichols, 1976), a figure that is now disputed and thought to be too high. In a recent review of human behavior genetics, Norman Henderson (1982) argues that a figure of .50 seems more appropriate. And in keeping with the trend of providing a range rather than a point estimate of heritability, intelligence is given a range of from .30 to .60. Clearly, then, adult intelligence is not totally malleable. By the same token, although genetic inheritance makes an important contribution to intelligence, environmental factors can modify intelligence substantially.

Personality

Two aspects of adult personality that have recently received attention by behavior geneticists are neuroticism and extraversion. The test used to assess these personality traits is usually either the Eysenck Personality Questionnaire or the California Psychological Inventory, both standardized, self-report measures (Eaves, 1978; Floderus-Myrhed, Pedersen, & Rasmussen, 1980; Koskenvuo et al., 1979). According to Eysenck, **neuroticism** is the opposite of emotional stability. **Extraversion** refers to a sociable, outgoing characteristic possessed by people who, when stress appears, lose themselves in people. The results of the twin studies that focused on the personality traits of neuroticism and extraversion are

Table 3.1

HERITABILITY ESTIMATES OF NEUROTICISM AND EXTRAVERSION FROM TWIN DATA

Study	Sample	N Pairs	Neuroticism	Extraversion
Eaves (1978)	English adults	542	.41	.50
Koskenvuo et al. (1979)	Finnish women	5,632	.59	.74
Koskenvuo et al. (1979)	Finnish women	5,044	.60	.72
Floderus-Myrhed et al. (1980)	Swedish men	6,793	.56	.61
Floderus-Myrhed et al. (1980)	Swedish men	5,934	.55	.59

Source: Reprinted, with permission, from the *Annual Review of Psychology,* vol. 33. © 1982 by Annual Reviews, Inc.

shown in table 3.1. As you can see, the heritability estimate for neuroticism ranged from .41 to .60 and for extraversion from .50 to .74, indicating a moderate to strong genetic influence on such personality traits.

Vocational Interests and Earnings

We usually do not think of genetics as playing a role in career choice or monetary earnings. Two studies of behavioral genetics, however, imply that even in these areas, adults seem to be influenced by their genetic heritage. People are not born into the world with genes that will make them a doctor, plumber, or composer when they grow up. But we have already seen that adults vary genetically in the degree to which they are intelligent, neurotic, and extraverted. Such genetically influenced predispositions may make adults better suited for some occupations than others. For example, in one investigation the interests of two kinds of families were compared. In one group the adolescents were adopted, whereas in the other group the adolescents lived with their biological parents. The families did not differ greatly in terms of income or educational level. Both the adolescents and their parents were questioned about such matters as whether they were oriented toward pursuits that were "rugged" or "scientific." There was extensive overlap in the interests of the biologically related adolescents and their parents, but there was virtually no correspondence between the interests of the adopted adolescents and their parents.

In the biologically related group of adolescents and parents, it appears that the adolescents were drawing some interests from one parent and some from the other. Was this due to genetic transmission alone? Not necessarily. It simply suggests that two people who are more alike biologically tend to have more similar interests. They not only share the same gene pool but the same environment as well.

Table 3.2

MORBIDITY RISK FOR RELATIVES OF SCHIZOPHRENICS

Relationship	N Pairs	Percent Morbidity[1]	Predicted Percent from Genetic Model[2]
Spouses	194	2.1	2.4
MZ twins	261	45.6	45.4
DZ twins	329	13.7	12.1
Siblings	8,817	8.4	8.3
Children	1,578	11.3	10.1
Half-siblings	499	3.4	3.6
Nieces and Nephews	3,966	2.7	3.1
Grandchildren	739	2.8	3.5
First cousins	1,600	1.6	1.7

[1]Based on Gottesman & Shields, 1982.
[2]Model of Rao, Morton, & Gottesman, 1981.
Source: Reproduced, with permission, from the *Annual Review of Psychology*, vol. 33. © 1982 by Annual Reviews, Inc.

In another investigation of several thousand adult male twins, there was evidence that genetic factors were strongly linked with earnings at maturity (Behrman, Hrubec, Tauban, & Wales, 1980). Thus, although we usually think only of social and cultural factors as determinants of vocational interests and earnings in adulthood, evidence from these investigations of behavior genetics suggests that we would be wise to consider the possibility of genetic influences as well.

In addition to the studies of genetic effects on intelligence and personality, there have been a number of efforts to document the role of genes in psychological disorders. One such disorder—**schizophrenia,** which involves disturbed, unrealistic thought processes—has been evaluated in a number of twin and kinship studies.

Schizophrenia

In a recent overview of the role of genetics in schizophrenia, data were compiled on the incidence of schizophrenia in a number of kinship positions—spouses, MZ twins, DZ twins, siblings, children, half-siblings, nieces and nephews, grandchildren, and first cousins. As suggested in table 3.2, the incidence of schizophrenia followed very closely along the lines predicted by a genetic model in that the closer the relative was in the kinship network, the more likely he or she was at risk for schizophrenia (Gottesman & Shields, 1982; Rao, Morton, Gottesman, & Sew, 1981).

Currently, it is believed that schizophrenia is not a homogeneous disorder. And some experts believe that future categorizations may be based on the origins of the disorder rather than the symptoms. For many years, psychologists spent long hours classifying mentally retarded individuals into morons, imbeciles, and idiots. Yet such symptomatic classifications told nothing about the origin of the mental retardation. At present, there are some meaningful subgroups of mental retardation, and the different genetic transmission is better understood; consequently, such subgroups of retarded individuals can be treated differently. The same strategy may prove fruitful with such psychological disorders as schizophrenia and depression. Although table 3.2 suggests that a child with a schizophrenic parent has approximately a 10- to 11-percent chance of becoming schizophrenic, as we become more adept at classifying subgroups of particular disorders, such heritability estimates may vary accordingly (Matthysse & Kidd, 1976).

One way in which schizophrenia can be meaningfully classified involves whether it initially appears in adolescence or adulthood. The early symptoms in adolescence not only are more blurred but the prognosis for successful treatment is not nearly as good as when the disorder first appears in the adult years (Weiner, 1980). However, at present there is no evidence as to whether one of these forms has a stronger genetic linkage than the other.

While schizophrenia has been the most widely studied mental disorder in adulthood in terms of genetic transmission, several disorders related to aging have also been scrutinized as possible gene-linked disorders.

Aging Disorders in Middle and Late Adulthood

One serious disorder that seems to appear often during middle adulthood is called Huntington's disease or **chorea,** sometimes also referred to as Woody Guthrie's disease after the folksinger who died from it. The disease produces involuntary movements and progressive mental deterioration, usually over a period of about fifteen years. Change in personality, irresponsibility, and dementia (a mental state involving severe deterioration of intellectual abilities such as memory and judgment) occur. It is generally agreed that the disease is caused by a dominant gene, and children have a 50 percent chance of inheriting this severe disorder. So Arlo Guthrie, Woody's son, has this risk.

It has been speculated that two other well-known disorders of middle and late adulthood—Alzheimer's disease and senile dementia—may be influenced by genetic factors as well (Omenn, 1978). **Alzheimer's disease** usually begins in the fifth or sixth decade of life and is sometimes thought of as a presenile dementia. Speech disturbance and a problem in gait are common symptoms. There is an atrophy of all areas of the brain in this disease. The main clinical features of **senile dementia** include a progressive disorganization of virtually all aspects of the mind, with personality being affected as much as memory, intelligence, and judgment. In one investigation of senile dementia, first-degree relatives had a 4.3 times greater risk for this disorder (Larsson, Sjogren, & Jacobson, 1963). However, it is important to keep in mind that whereas senile dementia has an organic (biological, physical tissue) base, environmental factors probably play a prominent role in its onset and development as well.

Table 3.3

COMPARATIVE INFLUENCE OF HERITABILITY ON ASPECTS OF DEVELOPMENT

Physical attributes (hair color, eye color, facial shape, skin pigment)
Huntington's chorea
Mental retardation
Intelligence
Temperament (activity level, neuroticism, introversion/extraversion)
Psychosis (schizophrenia)
Alzheimer's disease and senile dementia
Vocational interests and earnings

Source: Yussen & Santrock, 1978. All rights reserved. Reprinted by permission.

It should be clear by now that we cannot ignore the role of genetics in de-termining adult development. For a summary of our discussion, see table 3.3. While we are far from being able to understand accurately the manner in which genetic transmission and genetic-environmental interaction works, genes pro-vide an important foundation for adult development.

To end our section on genetic influence, a description of the almost ex-haustive physical, psychological, and biological data of fifteen twins is presented in box 3.1.

LONGEVITY

How long do you think you will live? Do you think you have a shot at Charlie Smith's purported 137 years? Unfortunately, probably not. In this section, we look first at life expectancy in different historical periods, including projections of the number of people likely to be in different age ranges in the year 2030. Then as part of an effort to decipher the cause of longevity, you will have the opportunity to get a sense of whether you have an opportunity to live to be 100. Finally, we explore sex differences in longevity.

Life Expectancy

One characteristic of contemporary life cycles that is very different from what it was several generations ago is that we are no longer a youthful society. As more and more people have lived to older ages, the proportion of people at different age levels has become increasingly similar. In the 1980 census, the number of people sixty-five and older climbed by 28 percent in the 1970s to 25.5 million. Population projections by the U.S. Bureau of the Census in 1977 suggest that by

Box 3.1
IDENTICAL TWINS WHO HAVE BEEN SEPARATED FOR MANY YEARS

We have seen that identical twins are very close genetically—they come from the same egg. And we have seen that it often is difficult, if not impossible, to separate genetic from environmental effects in studies of individuals of differing genetic relationships. One of the most promising strategies is to study identical twins who have been separated for many years and who have not experienced the same environments. This strategy has been followed by University of Minnesota psychologist Thomas Bouchard, who has intensively studied the physical, psychological, and biological makeup of fifteen identical twins and who is currently adding more identical twins to his data bank. All of these identical twins share something important: they all were reared apart. Bouchard originally expected far more differences than he has found.

Extensive personality testing, detailed medical histories (including diet and smoking and exercise habits), chest X rays, heart stress tests, pulmonary tests, allergic tendencies, and EEGs are all obtained. Each of the twin pairs is assessed for six days and asked more than 15,000 questions that focus on family and childhood environment, personal interests, vocational orientation, values, and aesthetic judgments. In addition, three ability tests, including the Wechsler Adult Intelligence Scale, are administered.

Although no scientific conclusions can yet be drawn from Bouchard's research, his research team has made a number of interesting observations.

Jim Springer and Jim Lewis were adopted as four-week-old infants into working-class Ohio families. They never met each other until they were thirty-nine years old. Both had law enforcement training and worked part time as deputy sheriffs. Both vacationed in Florida; both drove Chevrolets. Much has been made of the fact that their lives are marked by a trail of similar names. Both had dogs named Toy. They married and divorced women named Linda and remarried women named Betty. They named their sons James Allan and James Alan. While the laws of chance dictate against such an unlikely string of coincidences, Bouchard has noted that twins seem to be highly subject to such strange similarities.

Other similarities, however, are probably more than coincidental. In school both twins liked math but not spelling. They currently enjoy mechanical drawing and carpentry. They have almost identical drinking and smoking patterns, and they chew their fingernails down to the nubs. Investigators thought their similar medical histories were astounding. In addition to having hemorrhoids and identical pulse, blood pressure, and sleep patterns, both had inexplicably put on ten pounds at the same time in life. Each suffers from "mixed headache syndrome," a combination tension and migraine headache. Both first suffered headaches at the age of eighteen. They have these late-afternoon headaches with the same frequency and same degree of disability, and the two used the same terms to describe the pain they experienced.

The Coffman Gallery area of the Coffman Union Program Council is responsible for the visual arts programs and exhibitions which are presented in its three formal gallery spaces and other facilities

The Coffman Gallery area of the Coffman Union Program Council is responsible for the visual arts programs and exhibitions which are presented in its three formal gallery spaces and other facilities.

Though Barbara and Daphne were raised separately, their handwriting is remarkably similar.

The twins also have their differences. One wears his hair over his forehead; the other has it slicked back with sideburns. One expresses himself better orally, the other in writing. Even though the emotional environments in which they were brought up were different, still the profiles on their psychological inventories were much alike.

Another pair, Daphne and Barbara, are fondly remembered as the "giggle sisters," because they were always setting each other off. There are evidently no gigglers in their adoptive families. The sisters both handle stress by ignoring it. Both avoid conflict and controversy; neither has any interest in politics. This similarity is particularly provocative since avoidance of conflict is "classically regarded as learned behavior," says Bouchard.

Psychologist David Lykken finds that the brain waves of the twin pairs in the Minnesota study resemble each other in the same way as those of twins who have been raised together. Moreover, Lykken finds that tracings from each twin of a pair differ no more than tracings from the same person taken at different times.

To be sure, identical twins differ in myriad ways. One of the most common is in tendencies toward introversion and extraversion. Another common difference, according to the English researcher James Shields, is dominance and submissiveness. Bouchard and his colleagues note that one twin is likely to be more aggressive, outgoing, and confident.

Box 3.1 *(con't.)*

But they find twins reared together usually differ the most in that respect. In other words, dominance and submission seem to be traits that twins use to assert their individuality. Because twins brought up together often feel compelled to exaggerate their differences, David Lykken thinks it is possible that twins reared separately may actually have more in common with each other than those raised together.

Because of the comparatively small numbers of twins they have studied, the investigators face difficulties in proving that their results are more than a random collection of case histories. What they would like to do, according to Tellegen, is "invent methods for analyzing traits in an objective manner, so we can get statistically cogent conclusions from a single case." This will require first establishing what is to be expected on the basis of chance alone. For example, how likely are two randomly selected IQ scores to be as similar as those of two identical twins? This method of analysis will be crucial in weeding out similarities between twins that may be no more common than coincidences that occur between randomly paired people.

Of all the members of the Bouchard team, Lykken is the most willing to entertain ideas that so far are only supported by subjective impressions. He says, "Looking at these fifteen pairs of identical twins, I have an enhanced sense of the importance of the genes in determining all aspects of behavior." But he acknowledges the importance of the environment as well. "What is emerging in my mind," Lykken concludes, "is that the most important thing to come out of this study is a strong sense that vastly more of human behavior is genetically determined or influenced than we ever supposed." (Holden, 1980)

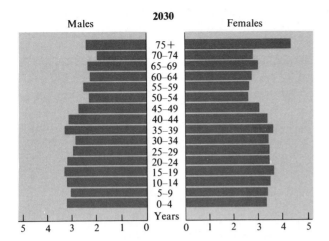

Figure 3.1   Percent of total population projected at each age group in the year 2030.

the year 2030, the number of Americans in different periods of the life cycle will indeed be approximately equal (see figure 3.1). Until about 1970, most of the change in life expectancy came from improved health care in infancy and early childhood. Life expectancy at age fifty, by contrast, remained virtually unchanged for 150 years (Tanner, 1966). Longevity at age fifty has witnessed some change in the last decade as fewer males seem to be dying in middle adulthood and the early part of late adulthood because of heart attack or stroke. Two of the major reasons for recent age changes and projected age changes in future populations are that fewer children are being born now than in past years, possibly due to improved contraceptive methods and the fact that improved health care has increased the life span of many older individuals.

Since 1900 the percentage of the American population aged sixty-five and over has increased substantially. The actual number has increased more than eightfold from 3 million to 25.5 million. A child born in 1900 had an average life expectancy of forty-eight years, whereas two of every three of you reading this book are likely to live to be seventy or older. Projections suggest that between 1970 and the year 2000, people seventy-five to eighty-four years old will increase by 65 percent and those eighty-five and over by 52 percent.

Nonetheless, it is intriguing that the life span has remained virtually unchanged since the beginning of recorded history. What has changed is *life expectancy*—the number of people anticipated to reach what seems to be an unbudging end point. This means that although improved medicine and nutrition have provided us with an additional twenty-two years of life on the average since 1900, there are still very few of us who will live to be 100. When we reach the age of seventy, we are likely to live approximately twelve more years, a figure not much different from that in 1900. If we become terminally ill during this period of time, we can have our life prolonged by medical science—we can be fed intravenously, we can be placed on machines that help us breathe and eliminate our wastes, and we can have our hearts stimulated electrically. But while we can be kept alive much longer than would have been possible eighty years ago, eventually we die. Most of us will make it to seventy, but very few of us will make it to 100.

What factors are responsible for longevity? We noted several at the beginning of the chapter when we discussed the reasons centenarians gave for their longevity. Contrary to the belief of one centenarian, sleeping while facing north is not one of the valid ones.

Predicting Longevity

What about you? What chance do you have of living to be 100? By taking the test in box 3.2, you not only can get a rough estimate of your chances but you will also see what some of the most important contributors to longevity are. According to the longevity questionnaire, heredity and family, health (weight, dietary habits, smoking, and exercise for example), education, personality characteristics, and life-style are important ingredients in longevity.

The Duke Longitudinal Study

Just as actuaries predict longevity for the purpose of insurance risk on the basis of age, sex, and race, several investigations have revealed that certain physical, mental, and social factors can be used to predict longevity (Palmore, 1980, 1982; Palmore & Jeffers, 1971; Rose & Bell, 1971). Referred to as the Duke Longitudinal Study of Aging, these data analyses have focused on the same group of adults over a period of twenty-five years. In the early analysis of these individuals, the strongest predictors of longevity (when age, sex, and race were controlled) were physical function, nonsmoking, work satisfaction, and happiness (e.g., Palmore 1969, 1974). The most recent analysis of these individuals (Palmore, 1982) allowed more precise determination of longevity because (1) some of the individuals have now died, so their exact life span is now known and (2) in addition to the original factors tested, a number of new ones were added to allow for more complex evaluation.

Erdman Palmore (1982) has developed a simplified model of possible predictors of what is called the *longevity difference.* This refers to the difference between the number of years individuals live after initial testing and the actuarially expected number of years remaining based on their age, sex, and race. Parents' longevity is believed to have a direct effect through genetic transmission and an indirect effect through environmental experience. Intelligence is thought

Longevity is influenced by a number of activities factors.

Box 3.2
CAN YOU LIVE TO BE 100?

The following test gives you a rough guide for predicting your longevity. The basic life expectancy for males is age sixty-seven, and for females it is age seventy-five. Write down your basic life expectancy. If you are in your fifties or sixties, you should add ten years to the basic figure because you have already proved yourself to be a durable individual. If you are over age sixty and active, you can even add another two years.

BASIC LIFE EXPECTANCY
Decide how each item below applies to you and add or subtract the appropriate number of years from your basic life expectancy.
1. Family history
   Add 5 years if two or more of your grandparents lived to eighty or beyond.   _____
   Subtract 4 years if any parent, grandparent, sister, or brother died of heart attack or stroke before fifty. Subtract 2 years if anyone died from these diseases before sixty.   _____
   Subtract 3 years for each case of diabetes, thyroid disorder, breast cancer, cancer of the digestive system, asthma, or chronic bronchitis among parents or grandparents.   _____
2. Marital status
   If you are married, add 4 years.   _____
   If you are over twenty-five and not married, subtract 1 year for every unwedded decade.   _____
3. Economic status
   Subtract 2 years if your family income is over $40,000 per year.   _____
   Subtract 3 years if you have been poor for the greater part of your life.   _____
4. Physique
   Subtract 1 year for every ten pounds you are overweight.   _____
   For each inch your girth measurement exceeds your chest measurement deduct 2 years.   _____
   Add 3 years if you are over forty and not overweight.   _____
5. Exercise
   Regular and moderate (jogging three times a week), add 3 years.   _____
   Regular and vigorous (long distance running three times a week), add 5 years.   _____
   Subtract 3 years if your job is sedentary.   _____
   Add 3 years if it is active.   _____

6. Alcohol
   Add 2 years if you are a light drinker (one to three drinks a day). _____
   Subtract 5 to 10 years if you are a heavy drinker (more than four
   drinks per day). _____
   Subtract 1 year if you are a teetotaler. _____
7. Smoking
   Two or more packs of cigarettes per day, subtract 8 years. _____
   One to two packs per day, subtract 2 years. _____
   Less than one pack, subtract 2 years. _____
   Subtract 2 years if you regularly smoke a pipe or cigars. _____
8. Disposition
   Add 2 years if you are a reasoned, practical person. _____
   Subtract 2 years if you are aggressive, intense, and competitive. _____
   Add 1–5 years if you are basically happy and content with life. _____
   Subtract 1–5 years if you are often unhappy, worried, and often feel
   guilty. _____
9. Education
   Less than high school, subtract 2 years. _____
   Four years of school beyond high school, add 1 year. _____
   Five or more years beyond high school, add 3 years. _____
10. Environment
    If you have lived most of your life in a rural environment, add 4
    years. _____
    Subtract 2 years if you have lived most of your life in an urban en-
    vironment. _____
11. Sleep
    More than nine hours a day, subtract 5 years. _____
12. Temperature
    Add 2 years if your home's thermostat is set at no more than 68°F. _____
13. Health care
    Regular medical checkups and regular dental care, add 3 years. _____
    Frequently ill, subtract 2 years. _____
                    Your Life Expectancy Total _____

Source: Schultz, 1978, pp. 97–98, table 5.1. Reprinted with permission.

to have a direct effect through problem-solving ability, which contributes to survival, and an indirect effect through its influence on other factors involved in longevity. Activities are said to have a direct effect through increased physical, mental, and social stimulation and an indirect effect by means of their contribution to more life satisfaction and improved health. Sexual relations may have a direct effect through psychosomatic processes as well as an indirect effect through their influence on life satisfaction and health. Tobacco and alcohol abuse are predicted to have a direct effect on longevity through their effects on lung cancer, cardiovascular diseases, and other health problems and indirect effects through a reduction of life satisfaction and general health. Satisfaction is also predicted to have a direct effect through psychosomatic processes and an indirect effect through its influence on general health. And health is believed to have a direct effect on longevity.

In the Duke Longitudinal Study, 270 volunteers were examined for the first time between 1955 and 1959 by means of a series of physical, mental, social, and laboratory tests (Palmore, 1970). At that time the adults ranged in age from sixty to ninety-four, with a median age of seventy. All were noninstitutionalized, and although they were not a random sample, there was a mixture of males and females, blacks and whites, and socioeconomic groups. Analysis of these individuals was undertaken again in 1981, some twenty-five years after their initial testing. Only twenty-six were still alive, and estimates of their longevity were made.

Of the various predictors of longevity, the following were the most powerful:

1. In terms of parents' longevity, only the father's age at death was significant.
2. Two intelligence predictors were significant—the performance part of the Wechsler Adult Intelligence Scale was the stronger, but the verbal part was also significant.
3. Three socioeconomic predictors were significant: education, finances, and occupation.
4. Five activity factors were significant in predicting longevity: *locomotor activities,* which referred to the number of activities involving physical mobility either in their performance or getting to the place to do them; *secondary activity,* which was based on the number of organizations the individual belonged to, number of meetings attended, time spent reading, and number of leisure activities mentioned (secondary activities contrast with primary activities, which involve activities engaged in with family and friends); *club activity,* which referred to the number of different organizations an individual belonged to; a secondary activity rating

obtained through an interview conducted by a social worker—this rating focused on the amount of formal group or specialized contacts in which the adult was involved; and a nongroup activity rating, which was also made by the social worker—this rating emphasized the adult's activities outside of groups and ranged from 0 (nothing to do) to 9 (time filled with daily activities and hobbies other than group activities).

5. Three indicators of sexual relations were significant predictors: frequency of intercourse per week, past enjoyment of intercourse in younger years, and present enjoyment of intercourse.

6. Tobacco use was scored by having the individual rate how much he or she smoked (cigarettes, cigars, or pipes) on a daily basis.

7. Four satisfaction factors predicted longevity: work satisfaction, religious satisfaction, usefulness, and happiness.

8. Three health predictors were significantly linked with longevity. A physical function rating was obtained by having an examining physician provide a score for the individual's level of physical function in everyday activities. This score was based on the individual's medical history, physical and neurological examination, audiogram, electroencephalogram, electrocardiogram, and laboratory evaluation of blood and urine. The health self-rating was the individual's own rating of his or her health, whereas the health satisfaction score relied on an individual's agreement or disagreement with six statements, including "I feel just miserable most of the time" and "I am perfectly satisfied with my health."

Table 3.4 presents a summary of these eight factors.

Of all the predictors of longevity, it is not surprising that the health group was the best. For men, the strongest predictor was the health self-rating, whereas for women it was the health satisfaction scale. In summary, health, nonsmoking, intelligence, education, work satisfaction, usefulness, secondary activities, and happiness were the best predictors of longevity in Palmore's earlier investigations, and his present work confirms the importance of these factors in the longevity equation. In the present study, several additional factors were also found to predict longevity: finances for men, locomotor activities for women, frequency of intercourse for men, and past enjoyment of intercourse for women.

Not only are some of the predictors for longevity different for men than for women, but the age structure of our population and longevity itself are characterized by sex differences.

Table 3.4

SIGNIFICANT PREDICTORS OF LONGEVITY DIFFERENCE[a]

Predictors	Women (N = 130) r	Men (N = 122) r
1. Father's Age at Death	—	.15
2. Intelligence		
Performance	.21	.29
Verbal	.19	.22
3. Socioeconomic Status		
Education	—	.14
Finances	—	.29
Occupation	—	.15
4. Activities		
Locomotor	.22	—
Secondary	.20	—
Clubs	.14	—
Secondary rating	.20	.19
Nongroup	.17	.22
5. Sexual Relations		
Frequency of intercourse	—	.15
Past enjoyment of intercourse	.22	—
Present enjoyment of intercourse	.14	—
6. Tobacco Use	−.17	−.15
7. Satisfaction		
Work	—	.28
Religious	—	.24
Usefulness	—	.16
Happiness	.17	.18
8. Health		
Physical function rating	.30	.31
Health self-rating	.21	.33
Health satisfaction	.36	—

[a]All values shown were statistically significant at the .05 level except for present enjoyment of intercourse, which had a *p* value of .12.

Sex Differences in Longevity

Beginning at the age of twenty-five (in the 1980 census data), females begin to outnumber males, a gap that widens through the remainder of the adult years, such that by the time people reach the age of seventy-five, slightly more than 61 percent of the population is female, and for those eighty-five and over, the figure is almost 70 percent female.

Why might this be so? It has been argued that the sex difference in longevity may be due to social factors or to biological factors. In regard to social factors, health attitudes, habits, life-styles, and occupational styles are said to be important. For example, among some of the major causes of death in the United States, such as cancer of the respiratory system, motor vehicle accidents, suicide, cirrhosis of the liver, emphysema, and coronary heart disease, men are more likely to die from such factors than are women (Waldron, 1976). Such causes of death are often associated with habits or life-styles. For example, the sex difference in deaths due to lung cancer and emphysema is probably linked with the fact that men are heavier smokers than women.

However, if life expectancy is influenced strongly by stress at work, we would expect the sex difference in longevity to be narrowing since so many more women have entered the work force, beginning with Rosie the Riveter in World War II, in the last forty years. But just the opposite has been occurring. Apparently the self-esteem and work satisfaction derived from work has actually outweighed the stress of juggling a family and work and of job-related stress when longevity is at issue.

There is good reason to believe that the sex difference in longevity is influenced by biological factors. In practically all animal species, females have a longer life span than males, even under laboratory conditions. Women have more resistance to infectious and degenerative diseases. For instance, the female's estrogen production helps to protect her from getting atherosclerosis (hardening of the arteries) (Retherford, 1975). Further, the X chromosome women carry may be linked with the production of more antibodies to fight off disease (Waldron, 1976).

In this section we have looked extensively at the topic of life expectancy and longevity. In our discussion of longevity we have found that most attempts to predict how long we will live take into account how long our relatives lived, particularly our parents. Thus it is believed that genetic factors play an important part in longevity. Next we look at the number of biological theories that have been proposed to explain the reasons behind the aging process.

BIOLOGICAL THEORIES OF AGING

Before we explore some of the different biological theories that have been developed to explain the aging process, it is important for us to define what we mean by **aging.** In introducing the *Handbook of Mental Health and Aging,* James Birren and Jan Renner (1980) indicate that aging refers to "processes of change in organisms that occur after maturity," as distinguished from *old age,* which refers to the last phase of life. Birren and Renner (1980) also believe that it is important to distinguish among biological age, psychological age, and social age. Not all aspects of the individual may be in close synchrony as he or she ages. For example, a person may show expansion in the psychological realm but decline in the physical realm. The authors define *biological age* as life expectancy, *psychological age* as the adaptive behavioral capacities of the individual, and *social age* as the social roles of the individual with regard to the expectations of the society in which he or she lives for someone of his or her age. In other words, one person may be old in body but young in spirit, whereas another may be young in body and old in spirit.

We have seen in the course of this text that there are clearly biological, psychological, and social aspects to the aging process. From a biological perspective, we have seen that genes are among the most important biological mechanisms that influence development. Let's look more closely at biological perspectives on aging, focusing first on genetic explanations of the aging process.

Virtually every biological theory of aging gives genes an important role. It is assumed that the life span of the individual is determined by a program wired into the genes of the species. Support for the genetic basis of aging comes from research demonstrating that certain cells of the body are able to divide only a limited number of times (Hayflick, 1965). Prior to this research it was believed that cells could divide an unlimited number of times. However, it was found that connective tissue cells extracted from human embryonic tissue double only about fifty times rather than an endless number of times. And cells taken from an older individual are likely to double fewer times than those obtained from a younger individual. Nonetheless, the cells of even elderly individuals are still likely to divide, suggesting that we rarely live to the end of our life-span capability. Based on the manner in which human cells divide, the upper limit on longevity is 110 to 120 years of age (Hayflick, 1977).

While virtually all biological theories indicate the importance of genes in aging, some biological theories give genetics a more central role than others. Scientists have debated whether the cause of aging is to be found within each cell or whether it is possibly housed within a particular part of the body, such as the hypothalamus. At a more macro level, some experts on aging believe that the concept of homeostatic balance is critical to understanding the aging process. First, we will look at several variations of a genetic view of aging called error theory.

Genetic Error Theories

Genetic error theories indicate that aging is caused by damage to the genetic information contained in the formation of cellular protein. The information stored in the genetic code is determined by the structure of a complex molecule called deoxyribonucleic acid (DNA). DNA is the control center that monitors the formation of life-sustaining proteins. In addition to DNA, a second complex molecule, ribonucleic acid (RNA), must be considered when we attempt to describe how aging occurs at the cellular level. The information contained in DNA must be transmitted to another location within a cell where the formation of proteins actually occurs—the molecule that does this work is RNA, sometimes called messenger-RNA because of its transportation function. Some scientists have argued that aging is caused by some type of breakdown, or error, that develops in the DNA-RNA cellular system.

There are a number of ways in which such errors could occur (Williamson, Munley, & Evans, 1980). According to the **mutation theory,** aging is due to changes, or mutations, in the DNA of the cells in vital organs of the body. In cells that continue to divide throughout the life cycle, these mutations are likely to be passed on to new cells. Eventually, a substantial number of cells in the organ decline to the point at which there is an observable reduction in its functioning. Possible sources for these mutations may be intrinsic factors in cell division, such as chance errors in DNA replication (Burnet, 1974) or genes that specifically cause mutations in other genes, which may be of benefit in evolutionary terms but might also hasten the aging process (Spiegel, 1977); or extrinsic factors such as toxins in the air, water, and food.

According to the **genetic switching theory,** certain genes switch off, which then causes aging. Information needed to produce DNA is no longer available, and so the cells age (Strehler, 1973). Eventually, genetic switching leads to cell death and the loss of organ functioning. According to this theory, the biological clock of aging is genetically programmed into each of the body's cells.

According to the **error catastrophe theory,** the focus is on damage to RNA, enzymes, and certain other proteins rather than on errors in DNA. For example, if an error occurs in the RNA responsible for the production of an enzyme essential to cell metabolism, the result will be a marked reduction in cell functioning and possibly cell death. The escalating impact of the original error in the RNA is the "error catastrophe" (Orgel, 1973).

Other genetic theories emphasize that aging is caused by changes that occur in cellular proteins after they already have been formed. Two such perspectives are the cross-linkage theory and the free-radical theory (Shock, 1977).

The Cross-Linkage and Free-Radical Theories

The **cross-linkage theory** stresses that aging occurs because of the formation of bonds, or cross-linkages, between various parts of the cell (Bjorksten, 1968, 1974). This theory was developed when Bjorksten detected that the protein gelatin used in early copying machines was irreversibly changed by certain chemicals. He indicated that proteins in our body may be altered in similar ways. Such alteration of proteins may cause us to age. The cross-linkages that may produce aging could be between RNA, DNA, other proteins, and enzymes. For example, cross-linkage between various DNA molecules may interfere with the production of RNA and with cell division. Why does cross-linkage occur? Possibly because of normal cell metabolism eventually breaking down, possibly because of radiation and possibly because of our diet. Another reason for cross-linkages are what have been called "free radicals."

The **free-radical theory** is a special application of the cross-linkage theory. Chemical components of the cells that exist only for one second or less before they react with other substances such as fats are called free radicals. They can damage cells through their reactions with other substances, and they can cause chromosome damage. It has been speculated that vitamins C and E reduce the collisions of free radicals with other cell substances and, as a consequence, may increase an individual's life span. Empirical evidence to support the vitamin hypothesis has not been developed, however.

Other biological theories indicate that aging occurs because some physiological coordinating system fails to function properly—two such systems are the immunological and hormonal systems.

Breakdown of Physiological Coordination

Each of us has an immune system that protects our body from foreign substances such as viruses, bacteria, and mutant cells (for example, cancer). The immune system may generate antibodies that react with the proteins of foreign organisms, and it may form cells that literally eat up the foreign cells. The peak of the immune system's ability seems to occur in adolescence, becoming gradually less efficient as the individual ages. It is also important to note that as an individual ages there is an increase in **autoimmunity** (meaning that the body actually attacks itself). Autoimmunity may occur because the immune mechanisms fail to detect that normal cells really are normal or because of mistakes in the formation of antibodies, such that antibodies react to normal cells as well as foreign ones (Walford, 1969).

We also may age because the efficiency of our hormonal system declines—this theory is called the **hormonal theory.** Hormonal changes are controlled by the brain, particularly the pituitary gland and the hypothalamus. One scientist (Finch, 1976) believes that aging pacemakers in these control centers of the brain stimulate a series of neurological and hormonal changes that cause us to age.

Another proponent of hormonal theory (Denckla, 1974) describes the developmental sequence of aging involving the hypothalamus and pituitary. The hypothalamus periodically stimulates the pituitary gland, located under the brain to release antithyroid hormones that travel in blood cells throughout the body. The "blocking hormones" begin to be released shortly after puberty. They keep the body's cells from absorbing an adequate supply of thyroxine, a hormone produced in the thyroid that is required for normal cell metabolism. A number of metabolic imbalances result when thyroxine is not available in adequate quantities. According to this view, it is these imbalances that produce an excess of free radicals, mutations, cross-linkages, the build-up of toxins within the cell, and autoimmunity (Rosenfeld, 1976).

A Macrobiological Theory—Homeostatic Imbalance

The biological theories outlined so far attempt to explain aging by looking at some part of the organism, either within a cell or a particular organ of the body. A theory that tells us to look within a cell when we try to explain the aging process is a microbiological theory. The label *micro* refers to the fact that a cell is a very small unit of analysis. By contrast, some scientists believe that we ought to be looking at a more molar, or macro, level when we attempt to explain the aging process. One such macrobiological perspective of aging is the **homeostatic imbalance theory.**

At the level of the organism, life may be defined as internal homeostasis. The internal milieu of the body is adjusted within strict limits by compensating mechanisms in many organs, including the heart, lungs, kidneys, and liver. Various neural and endocrine systems help monitor and maintain this balance in the body's internal environment. In young adult life, the functional capacity of human organs is four to ten times that required to sustain life. The existence of *organ reserve* enables the stressed organism to restore homeostasis, or balance, when it is damaged by external threat. Measurement of organ reserve over time shows an almost linear decline beginning at about the age of thirty (Shock, 1960). As organ reserve decreases, so does the ability to restore homeostasis, and eventually even the smallest perturbation prevents homeostasis from being restored. The inevitable result is natural death, even without disease. Although a disease process may seem to be the cause of death, the actual cause may be the body's inability to maintain homeostasis. Any small perturbation, without coexistent organ reserve, would have the same fatal result. After the age of thirty an individual's mortality rate doubles every eight years (Upton, 1977). Proponents of the homeostatic imbalance theory link the linear decline in organ function to the increase in mortality rate.

While there is a great deal of disagreement about the causes of aging, more and more scientists are acknowledging that there is a biological clock that is identifiable and programmable. We have seen that some scientists believe the clock resides in the cells of our bodies, others argue that it lies in the brain, still others are searching for it in genetic material, and yet others believe the ability to maintain homeostatic balance is a key to the aging process.

Summary

This chapter focused on the biological underpinnings of adult development. Some twenty to one hundred years after conception, genetic influences are still important. Physically, the genetic code is carried by biochemical agents called genes and chromosomes. The special arrangement of genes and chromosomes makes each person unique. This arrangement is called a person's genotype. All of the observed characteristics of the adult are referred to as her or his phenotype; these characteristics include skin color, intelligence, and personality. For obvious scientific, ethical, and practical reasons, manipulating the breeding of lower animals has allowed us to discover more precisely how genetic mechanisms work than would be possible with humans. Genetic strategies with humans have focused on twin and kinship patterns of characteristics. One of the most widely used methods is the twin study method in which identical and fraternal twins are compared on some characteristic. An increasing number of investigations of behavior genetics have relied on kinship studies. Further, there is a trend toward arriving at a heritability range rather than a specific heritability point in making genetic predictions. Heritability is a statistical concept that provides an estimate of the degree of inheritance of a characteristic.

The field of study that focuses on the heritability of various characteristics is called behavior genetics. Behavior geneticists, using the twin and kinship study methods, have estimated the genetic contribution to a number of adult characteristics. Though at one time the genetic contribution to intelligence was said to be as high as .80, more recent estimates suggest that the range is between .30 and .60. For such personality characteristics as neuroticism and extraversion, the figure is approximately .50 to .60, and for some disturbances in development, such as certain forms of mental retardation and Huntington's chorea, the estimate runs close to 1.00. Kinship studies of schizophrenia, a disorder involving serious disruptions in thought processes and orientation to reality, suggest that the child of a schizophrenic parent has approximately a 10 percent chance of becoming schizophrenic, an identical twin has a 45 percent chance, and a first cousin has only a 1.6 percent chance. It is important to keep in mind, however, that while some characteristics have a strong genetic link and involve biological, physical matters, environmental factors always play some role in the determination of an adult characteristic, for without an environment, a genetic characteristic cannot be displayed. For virtually all adult characteristics, it is wise to think in terms of the contribution of genetic-environmental interaction.

While our life expectancy has increased substantially in recent years, the maximum life span has remained remarkably stable over the last 150 years, seemingly being in the range of 110 to 120 years. Though there have been reports of individuals living more than 120 years, none has been documented empirically. Until 1970 much of the increased life expectancy was due to a reduction in deaths during infancy and early childhood, but in the last decade improved nutrition and health care have improved the likelihood that someone aged fifty or older will live longer.

In the most comprehensive investigation of what factors contribute to longevity, the Duke Longitudinal Study followed individuals aged fifty-five to ninety-four over a twenty-five-year period. Of all of the predictors, none surpassed health. For men, health self-rating was the best predictor of longevity, whereas for women it was satisfaction with their health. Nonsmoking, intelligence, education, work satisfaction, usefulness, secondary activities, and happiness contributed to the predictability of longevity. Other factors included finances and frequency of sexual intercourse for men and locomotor activities and past enjoyment of intercourse for women. Not only are some of the predictors of longevity different for men than for women, but women consistently live longer than men. Both social and biological reasons have been given for this difference, but there seems to be a particularly strong argument for a biological explanation of the sex difference.

A number of biological theories of aging have been proposed, several of which stress a central role for genes. There is considerable controversy about the biological causes of aging but general agreement that there is an identifiable biological clock. Scientists argue as to whether this clock resides in the cells of our body or the brain, in the biochemical nature of genes, or at a more macrobiological level, in homeostatic balance and physiological coordination.

Review Questions

1. What is a gene? Distinguish between genotype and phenotype.
2. Discuss the different strategies for determining the influence of genetics on adult development.
3. How strong is the genetic influence on intelligence, personality, and disorders?
4. Outline the changing age structure of our population.
5. What factors seem to contribute most to longevity?
6. How has the sex difference in longevity been explained?
7. Discuss the different biological theories of aging.

Further Readings

Fries, J. F. (1980). Aging, natural death, and the compression of morbidity. *The New England Journal of Medicine, 303,* 130–135.

Fries describes his provocative theory of aging and health care. Interesting reading.

Hayflick, L. (1975). Why grow old? *The Stanford Magazine, 3,* 36–43.

An easy-to-read overview of our aging population, biological theories of aging, and the limits of the life cycle.

Henderson, N. D. (1982). Human behavior genetics. *Annual Review of Psychology, 33,* 403–440.

A challenging chapter to read, but one that is an authoritative summary of the contribution of behavior genetics to our understanding of adult development. An accurate presentation of the hopes and limitations of genetic research, including details about recent advances in genetic kinship studies of adult development.

Palmore, E. B. (1982). Predictors of the longevity difference: A 25-year follow-up. *The Gerontologist, 22,* 513–518.

The full report of Palmore's recent data analysis focused on the twenty-five-year longitudinal study of aging. Includes a detailed discussion of the factors that contribute to longevity. Moderately easy to read.

Segerberg, O. (1982). *Living to be 100: 1200 who did and how they did it.* New York: Charles Scribner's Sons.

An easy-to-read, entertaining account of 1,200 people who became centenarians. Though written by a journalist, the conclusions seem intuitively on target. Easy reading.

4

BIOLOGICAL PROCESSES, PHYSICAL DEVELOPMENT, HEALTH, AND SEXUALITY

THE REPRODUCTIVE SYSTEM AND SEXUALITY

I **MAGINE** *that you are a seventy-two-year-old competitive runner.*
You have just awakened from ten hours of restful sleep. You fix yourself a
yogurt shake for breakfast and then put on your Nike running shoes and shorts.
You drive to the stadium early to loosen up. The race, a two-mile Senior
Olympics event, will begin in thirty minutes. You see some of the friendly competitors
you run with on a regular basis and chat with them for a few minutes. Then the gun
sounds, and the race begins. You finish third behind a sixty-five-year-old and a seventy-
one-year-old, but you are pleased by your performance because it is only ten seconds
off your best time in the last year. You pushed yourself; you are still breathing hard and
your heart is still beating fast, but you feel good.

The majority of individuals in late adulthood do not exercise regularly. Major
reasons are the negative attitudes they, their relatives, and some health professionals
have about exercise and its possible risks. Such attitudes include the following:

1. The need for exercise decreases and eventually may even disappear at some point
    in late adulthood.
2. The risks involved in vigorous exercise after middle adulthood are grossly
    overexaggerated.
3. The benefits of light, sporadic exercise is overrated.
4. The abilities and capacities of individuals in late adulthood are underestimated.

Robert Wiswell (1980) discusses such barriers to exercise in late adulthood. Many
older people simply feel that they do not need to exercise, but many experts suggest
that the single most effective method of accelerating the aging process is to do nothing.
The perception of risks continues to be a major barrier. The news media have helped to
promote such attitudes by dramatizing the occasional cardiac problem that occurs
during exercise. In practical terms, we can expect that in an exercise class of fifty
people meeting three times per week, a cardiac fatality will occur only once in 6.5
years.

Jogging hogs have become a part of scientists' attempts to determine whether an
outpouring of sweat helps adults become healthier. At the University of California at
San Diego, Colin Bloor and Frank White trained a group of hogs to run approximately
100 miles a week. Then the scientists narrowed the hogs' arteries that supplied blood
to their hearts. The hearts of the jogging hogs developed extensive alternative pathways
for blood supply, and 42 percent of the threatened heart tissue was salvaged
(compared to only 17 percent in hogs who did not jog).

Competitive runners in late adulthood—recognizing the benefits of exercise.

Though exercise does seem to have some demonstrable positive effects on our physical health status, we know much less about its possible effects on our mental health. It is generally accepted that exercise is beneficial to emotional well-being, but the existing scientific literature is at best contradictory and incomplete (Wiswell, 1980).

Those who argue for the positive mental benefits believe that exercise increases stamina and thus the tolerance for work, builds confidence, and promotes group participation. However, there may be a more direct link. It has been suggested that exercise raises the level of a natural morphinelike substance (called beta-endorphin) in the blood, and this chemical may elevate mood. Researchers argue over whether it is this chemical that produces the so-called runner's high.

More about the role of exercise in late adulthood appears later in the chapter. Indeed, one of the most intriguing issues in the study of aging is the extent to which such factors as vigorous exercise can possibly delay the aging process and insulate an individual from serious disease.

INTRODUCTION

Our second chapter on biological processes and physical development focuses on sensorimotor development, the brain and nervous system, health and health care, and the reproductive system and sexuality. We describe the developmental course of vision, hearing, and the other senses in adulthood and evaluate the question of when decline in the senses occurs. Next we describe the developmental pattern of motor performance. Our discussion of the brain emphasizes its awesome complexity, power, and mystery. The issue of whether we lose neurons as we age is carefully investigated, and we go inside a neuron in search of substances that may be linked to the aging process. Then we discuss the electrical activity of the brain and evaluate its link to behavioral slowing. We give attention to the peaking of health and physical performance in early adulthood and how easy it is to develop bad health habits when we are physically competent. Our focus on health in the middle adult years emphasizes weight problems and cardiovascular disease. We describe the decline of health status in late adulthood but stress the possible role of exercise and nutrition in slowing down the aging process. The final section focuses on the biological aspects of sexuality, including the menstrual cycle, menopause, and the male climacteric, and stresses the behavioral and attitudinal aspects of sexuality.

SENSORIMOTOR DEVELOPMENT

We make contact with the world around us through our five primary senses—hearing, touch, taste, smell, and sight. Psychologists distinguish between sensation and perception. *Sensation* is the picking up of information by our sensory receptors—for example, the ears, skin, tongue, nostrils, and eyes. In hearing, sensation occurs when waves of pulsating air are collected by the outer ear and transmitted through the bones of the middle ear to the cochlear nerve. In vision, sensation results when rays of light are collected by the eyes and focused on the retina. *Perception,* on the other hand, is the interpretation of what is sensed. The physical events picked up by the ear may be interpreted as musical sounds, a human voice, noise, and so forth. The physical energy transmitted to the retina may be interpreted as a particular color, pattern, or shape. In this chapter we will describe sensory development in adulthood, and in chapter 6 we will discuss perceptual development.

Not only do we take in information from our environment through our five senses, but we also perform actions in our environment. We move about, walk, run, write, talk, swim, play tennis, and eat. How motor actions unfold through the life cycle is called *motor development.* The combination of the sensory and motor aspects of the nervous system is described as *sensorimotor development.* The incoming sensory information is carried to the brain through **sensory pathways,** and signals for motor performance are carried from the brain and spinal cord to various parts of the body—muscles and glands—through **motor pathways.**

Sensation

What is the nature of the various sensory processes, and how well do they continue to function as we grow through the adult years? Does our vision begin to decline during the middle adult years? Does our hearing often fail us in late adulthood?

Vision

Sensory systems seem to show little change during the early adult years, although the lens of the eye may lose some of its elasticity and be less able to change shape and focus on near objects (Marshall, 1973). In the middle adult years, however, difficulties in vision become a problem for many people. **Accommodation** of the eye (the ability to focus and maintain an image on the retina) experiences its sharpest decline between forty and fifty-nine years of age (Bruckner, 1967). In particular, it becomes difficult for individuals in middle adulthood to view close objects. There also appears to be a reduced blood supply to the eye, although this does not usually occur until the fifties or sixties. The reduced blood supply may decrease the size of the visual field and account for an increase in the size of the blind spot.

There is also some evidence that the retina becomes less sensitive to low levels of illumination (the amount of light reaching the retina steadily declines with age) as the individual goes through the middle and late adulthood years. This means that the middle-aged adult will likely have trouble seeing in the dark and may need brighter lighting to read. In one investigation, the effects of illumination level on the productivity of workers in early and middle adulthood were studied (Hughes, 1978). The workers were asked to look for ten target numbers printed on sheets that had a total of 420 numbers printed on them. Each of the workers performed the task under three different levels of illumination. While increased levels of illumination enhanced the proficiency of both the young and middle-aged adults, the performance of the middle-aged adults improved more.

As we go through the late adult years the decline in vision that usually begins in the latter part of early adulthood or in middle adulthood becomes more pronounced. Night driving becomes very difficult for many individuals in the late adult years, to some extent because their tolerance of glare diminishes. Similarly, dark adaptation is slower, meaning that old people take longer to recover their vision when going from a well-lighted room to semidarkness (McFarland, Domey, Warren, & Ward, 1960). Further, the area of the effective visual field becomes smaller in that the size or intensity of stimuli presented in the peripheral area of the visual field needs to be increased if the stimuli are to be seen, and events occurring away from the center of the visual field may not be detected (Welford, 1980).

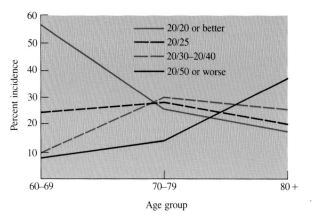

Figure 4.1   Corrected best distance vision in the better eye.

Such visual decline can usually be traced to reductions in the quality or intensity of light reaching the retina. In extreme old age, such changes are often accompanied by degenerative changes in the retina, which can cause severe difficulties in seeing. In such instances, large-print books and magnifiers may be needed. Indeed, investigations of the incidence of blindness and visual acuity are associated with age. Legal blindness is defined as corrected distance vision of 20/200 in the better eye or a visual field restricted to 20 degrees as the largest diameter. Legal blindness occurs in less than 100 out of every 100,000 people under the age of twenty-one, but in people over the age of sixty-nine, it occurs in more than 1400 cases per 100,000. Visual acuity also becomes less efficient as we age (Anderson & Palmore, 1974). If one's visual acuity is 20/50 or worse, such important activities as driving and reading are likely to be impaired. As suggested in figure 4.1, from the ages of sixty to sixty-nine, more than half of the 213 individuals tested in the Duke Longitudinal Study had good visual acuity, but for those aged seventy to seventy-nine, the figure dropped to almost one fourth. Although we can correct vision by means of glasses for a majority of people until they are approximately seventy, as they pass this age, the task becomes much more difficult.

Hearing
Hearing is usually at its peak in adolescence, remains fairly constant during much of early adulthood, and starts to decline toward the end of early adulthood and the beginning of middle adulthood. By the age of forty, a perceptible decline in hearing can sometimes be detected. At about the age of fifty, we are likely to have problems hearing sounds above the pitch of a "silent" dog whistle. Why? The failure to hear high-pitched sounds seems to be caused by a breakdown of

cells in the **corti,** the organ in the inner ear that transforms the vibrations picked up by the outer ear into nerve impulses, as well as deteriorating nerve fibers. Sensitivity to high pitch seems to decline first, whereas the ability to hear low-pitched sounds does not decline very much in middle adulthood. Men are more likely than women to lose their auditory acuity for high-pitched sounds (Farnsworth, McNemar, & McNemar, 1965), although this sex difference may be due to the greater exposure of men to noise in occupations such as mining, automobile work, and so forth.

Although hearing impairment may begin to occur during middle adulthood, it usually does not become much of an impediment until late adulthood. Even then, some but not all hearing problems may be corrected by the use of hearing aids. Only 19 percent of people from forty-five to fifty-four experience some hearing difficulty, but for those between seventy-five and seventy-nine, the percentage is 75 (Harris, 1975). It has been estimated that 15 percent of the population over sixty-five are legally deaf (Corso, 1977). Such hearing loss is usually due to degeneration of the *cochlea,* the primary neural receptor for hearing.

Wearing two hearing aids that are balanced to correct for each ear separately can sometimes help hearing-impaired adults. If the aids are not balanced or if only one is used, the subtle differences in phase and intensity at the two ears, which enable sounds to be localized and identified, are lost. Location of sounds helps us to attend to one conversation while ignoring another. When we don't do this well, both wanted and unwanted sounds seem to become combined and produce noise or confusion. Some adults who wear a single hearing aid complain that all it does is bring in noise. Other attempts to help with hearing such as placing a hand to the ear or turning toward a speaker may also help (Welford, 1980).

The Other Senses

Not only do we experience declines in vision and hearing as we age, but we may also become less sensitive in our ability to taste and smell (Schiffman, 1977). Sensitivity to bitter and sour tastes seems to persist longer in life than sensitivity to sweet and salty tastes (Schiffman & Pasternak, 1979). However, when the study of such sensory experiences is confined to healthy individuals in late adulthood, there is some indication that the decrease in sensitivity to tastes and smells may be slight or even nonexistent (Engen, 1977).

One loss of sensory sensitivity as we age may have an advantage. For the most part, it has been found that old people are less sensitive to and suffer less from pain than do their younger counterparts (e.g., Harkins & Chapman, 1976; Kenshalo, 1977). Of course, although decreased sensitivity to pain may help the elderly cope with disease and injury, it can be harmful if it masks injuries and illness that need to be treated.

Motor Development

The physical skills of an individual usually peak between the ages of eighteen and thirty. As an example of this peaking, J. M. Tanner, an expert on physical growth and development, reviewed the age strata of Olympic athletes. Of the 137 athletes Tanner studied, only twenty-one were over thirty years of age, and only one was under eighteen. All of the athletes competing in events that demand extreme speed or agility, such as the 100-meter dash and broad (long) jump, were under thirty years of age. Think about the college and professional football and basketball players in the United States who are the best in the world at their sports. By far the majority of these athletes are in the eighteen–thirty age bracket. It always is heartening, though, when someone like George Blanda throws two touchdown passes in the last two minutes to win the game. Some of Blanda's heroics for the Oakland Raiders in the early 1970s were accomplished in his middle 40s.

Reaction time has been among the most widely studied aspects of motor development during adulthood. **Reaction time tasks** measure the time elapsed between the appearance of a signal and a person's responding movement. A simple reaction time task involves having an adult push a button when she or he detects that a light has come on.

There is good reason to believe that reaction time peaks in the late teens and early twenties and then becomes gradually slower through the remainder of adult life. In one investigation, more than 400 females between the ages of six and eighty-four were instructed to release a key when they detected that a light had come on (Hodgkins, 1962). Reaction time improved from childhood until about the age of nineteen or twenty, remained constant until approximately the age of twenty-six, and then began a gradual decline. Between the twenties and fifties there was a 25 percent decrease in reaction time, and between the twenties and seventies there was a 43 percent decrease.

Muscular strength and the ability to maintain maximum muscular effort both decline steadily during middle adulthood. At age thirty, about seventy of a man's 175 pounds are muscle. Over the next forty years, he loses ten pounds of that muscle as cells stop producing and die. By the age of forty-five, the strength of a man's back muscles has declined to approximately 96 percent of its maximum value, and by age fifty, it has declined to 92 percent. Most men in their late fifties can only do physical work at about 60 percent of the rate achieved by men who are forty. Much of this decline appears to be linked with such physiological changes as the thickening of the wall of the air sacs in the lungs, which hinders breathing, and the hardening of connective sheaths that surround muscles, which is linked with both a decrease in oxygen and blood supply (Marshall, 1973).

In this section we have seen that sensorimotor development usually peaks during late adolescence or early adulthood. By middle adulthood there is perceptible slowing or decline in many aspects of sensorimotor development, and by the time old age is reached, the slowdown and decline are easily detected. As we see next, the slowing of behavior that accompanies aging is often traced to the brain.

THE BRAIN AND NERVOUS SYSTEM

Thus far in our discussion of aging and the slowing of behavior, we have focused primarily on the peripheral aspects of the nervous system. We have talked about how information comes in through the senses and how physical actions occur in the form of motor responses. We have also talked about some of the connections of the brain to sensory and motor parts of the body, such as the retina and the cochlea, the most important neural receptors in the eye and ear, respectively. But our discussion of biological processes, physical development, and aging would be incomplete without a discussion of the important role of the brain itself.

Our remarkable psychological accomplishments as human beings would not be possible without the human brain and the workings of the central nervous system. This is truly the most complex, intricate, and elegant system imaginable. Although substantial advances are being made almost daily in the computer sciences, the human brain can easily be said to be the most advanced computer we know. The *central nervous system* (CNS) consists of the major structures of the brain, the spinal cord connected to it, and their various fluids, blood vessels, and membranes. The average adult brain weighs about three pounds (1400 g) and is approximately the size of a clenched fist.

Aging and Neuron Loss

It has generally been reported that as we age we lose a large number of neurons. Some researchers estimate that the loss may be as high as 50 percent over the adult years, although other researchers believe there is little or no such loss of neurons (Bondareff, 1977). Perhaps a reasonable estimate is the atrophy of about 5 to 10 percent of our neurons until we reach the seventies. After that, neuronal loss may accelerate (Leaf, 1973). Nonetheless, some biologists believe that we really do not have evidence for neuronal loss with age (Diamond, 1978). We know that nerve fibers are not replaced by new ones once the old ones die, so the loss of significant numbers of nerve fibers may be important. However, it is generally believed that the brain has remarkable recovery and repair capability such that even though neuronal loss may occur, the brain may lose only a slight ability to function (Labouvie-Vief, 1982).

The CT Scan and the Brain

Going inside a human skull and actually observing the brain, of course is usually not done. However, recent advances in the field of computer technology allow us to "look" at the brain by means of the combination of a computer and an X ray; the result is the **CT scan.** Even more recently the **PETT scan** has been

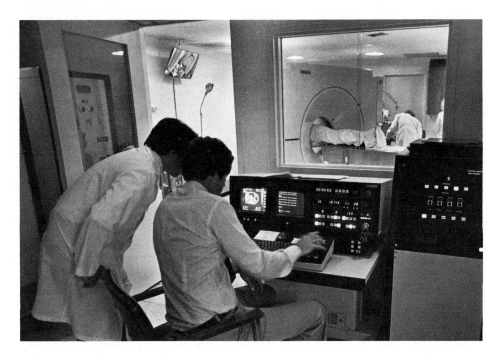

The CT scan has helped us to "look" inside the brain.

developed. Unlike the CT scan, which reveals only brain anatomy, the PETT (positron emission transaxial tomography) records the brain's actual metabolism. PETT measures the radioactive emissions from the brain and produces an image revealing which regions are metabolizing the most sugar (in other words, which are the most active). Of course, there is much more to know than what the CT and PETT scans tell us. Much of the research conducted on the elderly has taken place because an autopsy was called for after an individual's death (Bondareff, 1977). Other research on the brain takes place during operations that are being conducted because of some neurological problem. But, for ethical, practical, and scientific reasons, the majority of research on the brain uses animals as subjects.

The CT scan is a remarkable breakthrough in our ability to look into the brain. However, it cannot be used to either confirm or reject a diagnosis of senile dementia unless a specific lesion is discovered to account for the symptoms. The inability of the CT scan to make this diagnosis may be due to the fact that it cannot measure the density of plaques and tangles in the hippocampus or cortex, neuronal changes that accompany the aging process. More is described about these plaques and tangles within neurons in the next section.

The enlargement of *ventricles*—the four cavities within the skull that surround the brain and contain cerebrospinal fluid—has been linked with age. CT scans reveal that from the first through the seventh decades of life there is a gradual increase in the size of the ventricles and, importantly, that in the eighth and ninth decades there is a sharper increase (Barron, Jacobs, & Kirkei, 1976). Whether such cortical changes are related to cognitive performance among the elderly is a matter of debate, however (LaRue & Jarvik, 1982).

Inside Nerve Fibers

While the brain loses about 7 percent of its weight when we are old compared to its weight when we are middle-aged and we probably lose a substantial number of neurons as we age, more important changes may be going on in the brain to help explain the aging process. Some of these changes are microscopic and involve a proliferation of abnormal blobs, tangles, and intracellular garbage. The blobs are *plaques* that contain an abnormal protein called amyloid. By the time we reach late adulthood it is believed that we have some plaques in our brain cells, but their role in the aging process still remains unclear. The tangles are called *neurofibrillary.* They, too, are inside nerve cells, as well as other cells, and are no better understood than plaques. These tangles resemble an old, snarled fishing line. The garbage is a mysterious brown pigment called *lipofuscin,* or age pigment. The accumulation of lipofuscin in cells seems to accompany aging, but we do not know whether the material is a by-product of cellular activity or whether it is harmful. This material apparently resists the cleansing process in cells that is accomplished by enzymes.

Brain Waves and Electrical Activity

We can measure the electrical activity of the brain by means of an **electroencephalogram (EEG).** Although four different patterns of electrical activity are detected in the brain, one in particular has been the focus of considerable research on aging. The **alpha rhythm** is the dominant rhythm displayed by the brain and is linked with relaxed yet awake behavior. The dominant alpha rhythm contrasts with the faster **beta rhythm,** which characterizes an adult in an attentive, alert state.

Research on the alpha activity of the brain suggests that it peaks during adolescence. Some investigators have argued that the alpha rhythm begins to slow gradually in the late part of early adulthood (e.g., Wang & Busse, 1969), although more recently it has been argued that the slowing does not occur until the late fifties or early sixties (e.g., Obrist, 1980; Woodruff, 1978).

What causes the slowing of the alpha rhythm in late adulthood? One explanation has focused on neuronal loss and a reduction of cerebral blood flow (Obrist, 1972). The argument is that because of reduced blood flow and subsequent reduction in oxygen a loss of neurons occurs. Indeed, when adults with and without arteriosclerosis are compared, differences in cerebral blood flow and alpha frequency are usually detected, with the diseased adults showing a slowing in these areas (Obrist & Bissell, 1955).

There have also been attempts to link the slowing of the alpha rhythm with the slowing of behavior. Adults with slower alpha rhythms do respond more slowly on reaction time tasks (Surwielo, 1963), but this does not mean that slower electrical activity causes slower reaction time. An alternative explanation offered by Diana Woodruff (1978) is that the older adult's nervous system is in a state of underarousal when compared to that of a younger adult's and that lowered arousal is behind both lowered alpha levels and slower reaction time. Thus although we don't have an answer about the precise manner in which electrical activity in the brain and behavior work, we do know that alpha rhythm does slow down for most individuals by the time they reach sixty years of age.

There has been an upsurge of interest in what are called event-related electrophysiological responses in relation to both normal and pathological aging. In contrast to the EEG, **event-related responses (ERPs),** or **evoked potentials (EPs),** are linked with the processing of specific stimuli and are thought to represent a limited set of cognitive operations, usually sensory discrimination and decision making (John et al., 1977; Regan, 1979). A typical ERP experiment involves embedding an infrequent stimulus in a series of common stimuli and determining the extent of electrical change in the brain when the infrequent stimulus is detected. An example would be presenting an individual with a series of tones that are within a particular frequency range. Say, 85 percent of the tones are within this dominant range, whereas 15 percent are not. The person is asked to count the irregular tones.

A late-occurring brain wave called P300 is thought to be elicited when the irregular stimuli appear. A number of investigations have shown a shift toward longer latency (the amount of time it takes a person to respond) of the P300 brain wave with advancing age, from a mean of 300 milliseconds for adolescents to 400 milliseconds or more for those in their seventies (e.g., Brent, Smith, Michaelewski, & Thompson, 1976; Ford et al., 1979). The investigators suggest that the longer latencies of cognitive-processing operations may underlie some of the observed age-linked changes that occur in motor behavior, although they did not directly investigate this link.

We have seen that significant changes in sensorimotor development and the brain characterize the aging process. Next we look at the general health conditions of individuals at different points in adult development and at some further specific aspects of physical condition such as the cardiovascular system.

HEALTH, HEALTH CARE, AND AGING

What is your health like now? How well do you care for your body? In this section we focus on how healthy individuals are during early, middle, and late adulthood.

Table 4.1

CHANGES IN USAGE RATES FOR CIGARETTES, ALCOHOL, MARIJUANA, AND OTHER DRUGS

	Percentage of Respondents Reporting Usage During the Period		
	1968–69	1969–70	1973–74
Daily use of cigarettes	35	40	44
Weekly use of alcohol	31	44	58
Any use of marijuana	21	35	52
Any use of amphetamines, barbiturates, hallucinogens	12	18	24

Source: Bachman, O'Malley, & Johnson, 1978.

Health in Early Adulthood

Not only do most people reach their peak physical performance during early adulthood, but during this time they are the healthiest as well. According to data accumulated by the U.S. Department of Health, Education, and Welfare, more than nine out of ten people between the ages of seventeen and forty-four view their health as good or excellent (1976). Few young adults have chronic health problems, and young adults have fewer colds and respiratory problems than do children. The most frequent reasons young adults have to be hospitalized are childbirth, accidents, and digestive and genitourinary system problems (U.S. Department of Health, Education, and Welfare, 1976).

Physical Competence and Bad Health Habits

Young adults rarely recognize how much bad eating habits, heavy drinking, and extensive smoking can influence their physical status when they reach middle adulthood. For example, despite the warnings on cigarette packages and in cigarette advertisements that cigarettes are hazardous to health, evidence suggests that as adolescents grow into early adulthood, there is actually an increase in their cigarette usage. In a longitudinal study conducted by Jerald Bachman, Patrick O'Malley, and Jerome Johnson (1978), as individuals went from their senior year of high school to the fifth year following high school, they increased their use of cigarettes. As suggested by table 4.1, they also increased their weekly use of alcohol, any use of marijuana, and any use of amphetamines, barbiturates, and hallucinogens.

Experts on health care suggest that during early adulthood it is important to begin preventive health care (Carroll & Nash, 1976). Recommended practices include proper nutrition, sleep, rest, and exercise. During early adulthood few individuals take the time to think about how their present life-styles will affect their health in middle and late adulthood. As young adults, many of us develop a pattern of not eating breakfast, not eating regular meals but relying on snacks as our main food source during the day, eating excessively to the point that we exceed a normal weight for our age, smoking moderately or excessively, drinking moderately or excessively, failing to exercise, and getting by with only a few hours of sleep each night. Such poor practices were linked with poor health in one investigation of 7,000 individuals ranging in age from twenty to seventy (Belloc & Breslow, 1972). In the California Longitudinal Study, in which individuals were evaluated periodically over a period of forty years, physical health at age thirty was a significant predictor of life satisfaction at age seventy, more so for men than for women (Mussen, Howzik, & Eichorn, 1982).

There are some hidden dangers in the fact that physical performance and health are at their peak in early adulthood. Though young adults can draw on their physical resources for a great deal of pleasure, the fact that they can bounce back so easily from physical stress, exertion, and abuse may lead young adults to push their bodies too far. If this pushing does not indicate harm in early adulthood, its negative effects are bound to appear in middle or late adulthood.

An increasing health problem in adulthood is the number of overweight individuals. Next we look at one of the factors that contributes to the increase in obesity during the adult years and the decline that also appears in some aspects of physical development in early adulthood.

BMR, Fatty Tissue, Muscle Tone, and Strength

There are relatively more overweight and obese young adults than adolescents or children. **Obesity** may be defined as weighing more than 20 percent over normal skeletal and physical requirements. For the most part, this is indicated by an excess of fat content in the body. Obesity is influenced by a number of factors, including diet, hormones, and exercise. One factor that we often fail to recognize when we consider weight gain is the biological mechanism known as the basal metabolism rate. The **basal metabolism rate (BMR)** is defined as the minimum amount of energy a person uses in a state of rest. To a considerable extent, BMR is genetically determined (although it can be regulated, within limits, through exercise or drugs, including nicotine). Young adults with a high basal metabolism rate can eat almost anything and not get fat, whereas those with a low BMR must constantly monitor their food intake to keep from gaining weight.

As indicated in figure 4.2, an individual's BMR continuously drops from ages eleven to twenty. From ages twenty to thirty-five, BMR levels out and then begins a gradual decline. Males usually have a slightly higher BMR than do females. If young adults do not reduce their food intake or exercise more, they are likely to gain weight because of the slowdown in BMR. In the middle to late twenties there is also an increase in the body's fatty tissue. Early adulthood can be a particularly problematic time for individuals who exercised vigorously during adolescence and/or the first part of early adulthood and then took sedentary jobs that require them to sit for long hours at a time. Individuals who were in athletic programs in high school or college are particularly prone to such problems.

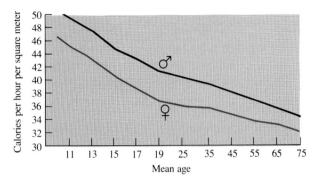

BMR varies with age and sex. Rates are usually higher for males and decline proportionally with age for both sexes.

Figure 4.2   The decline of basal metabolism rate through the life cycle.

Around the age of thirty, muscle tone and strength often begin to show signs of decline—sagging chins and protruding abdomens may appear. And it is not unusual for a gray hair (or hairs) to signal aging in the latter part of early adulthood. Thus although health peaks in early adulthood, in the latter part of early adulthood signs of decline in some aspects of health and physical development often begin to appear.

Health in Middle Adulthood

As people age through the adult years, they get shorter—their bodies can't hold off gravity forever. As muscles weaken, an adult's back slumps. And as the disks between the bones of the spine deteriorate, the bones move closer to one another. For example, a man who is 5 feet 10 inches tall at age thirty will likely be 5 feet 7⅞ inches by age forty, 5 feet 9⅝ inches by age fifty, and 5 feet 9¼ inches by age sixty.

Health status becomes a major concern in middle adulthood, whereas in young adulthood it usually gets much less attention. Middle adulthood is characterized by a general decline in physical fitness, and some deterioration in health is to be expected. The three health concerns that have received the greatest attention in middle adulthood are heart disease, cancer, and weight. Cardiovascular disease is the number one killer in the United States, followed by cancer (U.S. Department of Health, Education, and Welfare, 1979). Smoking-related cancer often surfaces for the first time in middle adulthood.

The Harvard Medical School health letter indicates that about 20 million Americans are on a "serious" diet at any particular moment. Being overweight is a critical health problem in middle adulthood. For people who are 30 percent or more overweight, the probability of dying in middle adulthood increases by 40 percent. Furthermore, obesity increases the likelihood that an individual will suffer a number of other ailments, including hypertension and digestive disorders. In box 4.1, we explore further the weight consciousness of our nation.

Box 4.1
Women and Weight Consciousness

Kim Chernin (1981) describes how we have become a nation acutely concerned about weight and suggests why women are more concerned about their weight than men are:

A tall woman enters the locker room of the tennis club. She removes her towel, throws it across a bench, faces herself squarely in the mirror, climbs on the scale, and looks down.

"I knew it," she mutters. "Two pounds. Two pounds!!"

Then she turns, grabs the towel, and wings out at the mirror. The towel splatters water over the glass.

"Fat pig!" she shouts at her image in the mirror. "You fat, fat pig!"

Two facts make the current obsession with weight extraordinary. One is the scope of it. Throughout history, there have been dieters, including Roman matrons who were willing to starve themselves. But there never has been a period when such large numbers of people have spent so much time, money, and emotional energy on their weight. Weight Watchers, for example, holds more than 12,000 individual classes every week and has enrolled 13 million members since it began in 1963.

The other extraordinary aspect of today's diet phenomenon is the degree to which it is focused on women. Of course, the nation has its share of fat men who want to lose weight. But interviews with physicians and psychologists make it clear that the truly obsessive dieter is almost inevitably female.

Representatives of diet organizations acknowledge that 95 percent of their members are women. According to Dr. Hilde Bruch, professor emeritus of psychiatry at Houston's Baylor College of Medicine and an expert on eating disorders, women make up more than 90 percent of the people suffering from anorexia nervosa, a personality disorder that leads to self-starvation. Bulimia, a condition in which periods of heavy eating are followed by self-induced vomiting, is almost entirely limited to women.

Why have so many millions of American women, in the last decade, become so concerned about their weight? The subject has not received much attention, except on a superficial level. It deserves better.

There is, for example, the medical explanation: Women diet because of the long-proclaimed correlation between obesity and ill health. Yet that fails to explain the intense upset many women experience because of two or three pounds of excess weight. And in any event, medical opinion has changed dramatically in recent years. Dr. Reubin Andres, clinical director of Baltimore's National Institute on Aging, has found, for example, that "there's something about being moderately overweight that's good for you." He bases his opinion on forty worldwide studies involving 6 million people.

Most Americans define their degree of "overweight" on the basis of the charts that hang on doctors' walls. Since 1969, when the Metropolitan Life Insurance Co. began publishing one of the most widely used charts today, it has become routine for physicians to tell their patients to take off those ten or fifteen pounds that exceed the appropriate figure on the chart. "You'll look better," they say. "You'll feel better, and it's healthier."

Today, experts have their doubts. In fact, the insurance companies will be bringing out new charts within the next few months. The companies acknowledge that the weight guidelines will shift upward, but they won't say by how much.

Weight consciousness has become a profile feature of our culture, particularly for adult women.

This does not mean, however, that obesity is a desirable state, nor should it suggest that the medical world understands all the effects of being overweight.

But this much seems clear: By and large, an extra ten pounds beyond the figure on the old insurance-company chart is not harmful, and it may even be good for you. The weight obsession of the modern American woman cannot be dismissed as simply a medical issue.

The woman who lies in bed in the morning—counting the number of calories she ate the night before, wondering whether her body has added substance to itself at the expense of her will—actually is pursuing a line of philosophical inquiry.

In our culture we have strong, ambivalent feelings about the relationship between a woman's power and her size, and they are reflected in our dislike for large, fleshy women.

The male-dominated culture calls for slender women; unconsciously, society seeks to limit the symbolic physical expression of women's power. And women themselves accept this tyranny of slenderness not only in submission to the male but because of their own ambivalence about their bodies.

As long as this culture maintains its traditional, male-centered balance, there may be some limited variation in the acceptable weight of women. At the turn of the

Box 4.1 *(con't.)*

century, for example, the prevailing mood favored some excess weight, and the fashions in clothing were—as usual—a clear reflection of the psychological state of the culture. Women at the time were permitted to wear flowing clothes, cut on the bias, to complement their ample hips.

In the 1920s, a shift in fashion signified the arrival of a major cultural change. The suffragist movement was approaching the culmination of its efforts to obtain the vote for women. Suddenly, women were supposed to look like boys. They bound their breasts and bobbed their hair.

When women are clearly subordinate, when they don't seek to change their social status, men seem free to delight in them as physical beings. At such a time, voluptuous women may be welcome. But in an age when women assert their claim to power and autonomy, men have a different response. The culture calls for fashions that reflect a distinct male fear of a mature woman's power, particularly as it expresses itself through a woman's large body, with its capacity to remind men of a time when they depended upon a woman for their very survival.

In the last two decades, society's standards for the size of women have undergone an amazing change. In 1959, when Marilyn Monroe made the film *Some Like It Hot,* she was voluptuous, as large as a woman in a Renoir painting. For those of us who fell in love with her then and yearned as adolescent girls, to look like her, that film today is a revelation. She was, by modern standards, fat.

Now fashion model Kristine Oulman sets the standard for women's beauty. A recent television program showed Kristine behind the scenes. She is in a room filled with people who are combing her, making her up, preparing her to wear the latest in sophisticated clothing. When their labors are done, this is the result: a preadolescent girl, with slender arms and shoulders, undeveloped breasts and hips and thighs, whose body has been covered in sexy clothes, whose face has been painted with a false allure and whose eyes imitate a sexuality she has, by her own confession, never experienced. Kristine is thirteen years old.

This is the message that fashion conveys and society teaches. This is what a mature woman should attempt to look like. A woman who wishes to conform to her culture's ideal, in this age of feminist assertion, will not be large, mature, voluptuous, strong, or powerful. She, who has the knowledge of life and birth, is to make herself look like an adolescent girl if she wishes to appease her culture's anxiety about female power.

During the last two decades, this society has witnessed the emergence of two significant movements among women. Because of the women's liberation movement and the weight-watcher's movement, the question of how large a woman is permitted to be has come to occupy Americans' lives in both a literal and a metaphorical form. Much has been said about the metaphorical side; now serious attention must be given to the implications of society's very literal obsession with women's weight and size.

This social malaise, this tyranny of slenderness, is expressed in unhealthy dieting, in ever-more-widespread eating disorders, in the dictates of fashion. For millions of women it is a cause of unremitting pain and shame. And it cannot be obliterated unless we begin to address ourselves to resolving some of the most basic conflicts of this culture.

Women seem to show a much greater concern about weight than do men. Since a youthful appearance is stressed in our culture, many individuals whose hair is graying, whose skin is wrinkling, whose body is sagging, and whose teeth are yellowing strive to make themselves look younger. Undergoing cosmetic surgery, dying the hair, purchasing a wig, enrolling in a weight reduction program, participating in an exercise regimen, and taking heavy doses of vitamins are frequent excursions of those in middle age. One investigation found that middle-aged women focus more attention on their facial attractiveness than do older or younger women, and middle-aged women are more likely to perceive that the signs of aging have a negative effect on their physical appearance (Nowak, 1977).

In our culture some aspects of aging in middle adulthood are taken as signs of attractiveness in men, whereas similar signs are viewed as disasters in women. Facial wrinkles and gray hair may symbolize strength and maturity in men and be seen as unattractive in women.

How people deal with physical change and decline varies greatly from one person to another. One person may be able to function well under severe physical problems or deteriorating health, whereas another with the same problems may become hospitalized and bedridden. Some people call a doctor at the slightest indication that something is wrong and worry extraordinarily about their health. Other people ignore serious signs of physical dangers that might indicate the imminence of a heart attack or cancer.

The Role of Emotional Stability and Coping with Stress in Determining Health Status

In the California Longitudinal Study (Livson & Peskin, 1981; Peskin & Livson, 1981), goodness-of-health ratings at ages thirty-four to fifty were significantly and positively associated with several personality measures that reflect emotional stability and controlled response to stress. The strongest association of health at middle age was with a calm, self-controlled, and responsible personality, a pattern that appeared at least by early adolescence. Not only was health at mid-life linked with this personality pattern, but it also was associated with a number of similar personality characteristics during mid-life. As we see next, life-style has been specifically linked to cardiovascular problems as well.

The Cardiovascular System

The heart and coronary arteries undergo change in middle adulthood. The heart of a forty-year-old can pump only twenty-three liters of blood per minute in times of stress, while the heart of a twenty-year-old can pump forty liters under comparable conditions. Just as the coronary arteries that supply blood to the heart narrow during middle adulthood, the level of cholesterol in the blood increases with age (age twenty: 180 milligrams; age forty: 220 mg; age sixty: 230 mg) and begins to accumulate on the artery walls, which are themselves thickening. The net result is that arteries are more likely to become clogged, increasing the pressure on the arterial walls, which in turn pushes the heart to work harder to pump blood, thus making a stroke or heart attack more likely. Blood pressure, too, usually rises in the forties and fifties. At menopause, the blood pressure of women rises sharply and usually remains above that of men through the later years of life.

Life-style seems to be associated with the incidence of cardiovascular disease in middle adulthood. One intriguing theory that has been developed classifies individuals as having either a high risk of heart disease (Type A) or a low one (Type B) on the basis of behavioral patterns (Friedman & Rosenman, 1974). The **Type A** person is excessively competitive, has an accelerated pace of ordinary activities, is impatient with the rate at which most events occur, often thinks about doing several things at the same time, shows hostility, and cannot hide the fact that time is a struggle in his or her life. By contrast, the **Type B** person is typified by the absence of these behavioral tendencies. About 10 percent of the subjects studied were clearly Type A or Type B.

The main investigation of the link between behavioral patterns and coronary risk consisted of data collected from more than 3,500 men between the ages of thirty-five and fifty-nine (Rosenman et al., 1970). At the beginning of the study none of the men had any sign of coronary disease. At that time behavioral patterns were noted and physiological checks were made. Then the men were assessed two and a half, four and a half, and eight and a half years later. Coronary disease was much more likely to occur among the Type A men than the Type B men. More than 70 percent of the thirty- to forty-nine-year-old men who developed coronary problems were Type A; whereas less than 30 percent were Type B. The percentages for the older group were similar. Clearly, coronary disease is influenced by many other factors, such as diet, smoking, obesity, and genetic tendencies as well. However, these data suggest that personal life-style is one of the factors associated with the incidence of coronary problems.

Health in Late Adulthood

As we age, the probability that we will have some disease or illness increases. A majority of individuals who reach the age of eighty will likely have some type of impairment; indeed, it is very rare to find anyone over the age of eighty who is free from disease or illness.

Perhaps the most significant change in late adulthood is that the entire circulatory system is less efficient. There is less *elastin,* the molecules that determine the elasticity of heart and blood vessels, and more *collagen,* the stiff protein that comprises about one third of the body's protein. An individual's heart rate does not rise as predictably in response to stress as was true during middle adulthood. Further, the heart muscle cannot contract and relax as fast, and the arteries are more resistant to the flow of blood. Heart output—about five quarts a minute at age fifty—subsequently drops about 1 percent a year. With the heart muscle less efficient and the vessels more resistant, heart rate and blood pressure both rise—and are both related to heart disease. Even for a healthy old person, blood pressure that was 100/75 at age twenty-five is likely to be about 160/90 in late adulthood. The blood also carries less oxygen to the brain and lungs. If elderly people rise too quickly from a chair, they may get dizzy; if they climb a set of stairs too speedily, they may get out of breath.

Illness and Impairment

Many of the chronic diseases of the elderly, such as cancer and heart disease, lead to long-term illness and impairment. Other chronic conditions, such as arthritis and hypertension, do not directly cause death but usually leave the afflicted person with some kind of physical impairment such as lameness or blindness. Almost two of every five people between the ages of sixty-five and seventy-five have some impairment of physical functioning. After age seventy-five, the rate rises to three of five (Riley & Foner, 1968). The four most prevalent chronic conditions that impair the health of the elderly are arthritis (38 percent), hearing impairment (29 percent), vision impairment (20 percent), and heart condition (20 percent) (Harris, 1978). Sex differences in health indicate that elderly women are more likely to have higher incidences of arthritis and hypertension, be more likely to have visual problems, and have less difficulty with hearing than men do (Harris, 1978).

Although adults over the age of sixty-five often have a physical impairment, many of them can still carry on their everyday activities or work. Chronic conditions linked with the greatest limitation of activity or work are heart condition (52 percent), diabetes (34 percent), asthma (27 percent), and arthritis (27 percent) (Harris, 1978).

Low income is also strongly related to health problems in late adulthood (and at other points in the life cycle as well). Approximately three times as many poor as nonpoor people report that their activities are limited by chronic diseases. In the elderly population, the health gap between low and middle income seems to continue (Wilson & White, 1977).

Health Treatment

An important aspect of health is the interaction between people who seek health care and those who provide it. Unfortunately, it has been revealed that physicians and other health-care personnel share society's general stereotypes and negative attitudes toward the elderly. In a medical setting, such attitudes can take the form of avoidance, dislike, and pained tolerance rather than positive types of treatment. Slower, less spectacular preventive medicine and chronic care are often perceived as boring, tedious, uninteresting, and unproductive by health-care personnel who too frequently are more stimulated by acute cases and greater chances of successful treatment with younger individuals (Butler, 1975). It is not uncommon for physicians to diagnose an elderly person's problems with some catchall diagnosis—"age," "hardening of the arteries," "senility," and so on.

One of the most promising alternatives for the infirm elderly is geriatric day care. Patterned after the British day hospitals, geriatric day care offers part-time supervision for even the severely impaired. Such care may allow harried relatives an opportunity to catch up on work and rest. Only fifteen geriatric day-care centers were available in the United States in 1969. Now approximately 800 dispense medical treatment, rehabilitation, counseling, and custodial care.

One of the most widely discussed issues in the medical treatment of the elderly focuses on drugs. Though drugs can often relieve suffering and pain and delay death, there is increasing realization that many health-care personnel do not exercise very much caution in dispensing drugs. The elderly clearly take a lot of drugs; whereas they make up approximately 10 percent of the U.S. population, they take 25 percent of the nation's prescription drugs (Basen, 1977). Tranquilizers and sedatives are used more frequently than any other drug in late adulthood. Although these particular drugs can help to reduce anxiety, depression, and insomnia, some health experts believe that their usage is often excessive (Butler, 1975).

The Role of Exercise

Table 4.2 presents a summary of the major physiological changes that occur as a result of the aging process and that most likely affect the individual's ability to perform physical exercise. Also included in the table is information about possible physiological benefits of regular exercise. *Physical exercise* is here defined as an activity that would require a relatively high percentage of maximal aerobic capacity over a prolonged period of time (Wiswell, 1980).

While such changes suggest the need for a decrease in exercise intensity as an individual ages, people often vary extensively in the degree to which such reduction is necessary. The body's capacity for exercise in late adulthood is probably influenced by the extent to which the individual has kept his or her body physically fit at earlier points in the life cycle. It is not uncommon to find individuals in late adulthood who participate in the Senior Olympics to have a greater capacity for exercise than some individuals in early adulthood.

One investigation designed to demonstrate the physical benefits of exercise on men (deVries, 1970) and another on women (Adams & deVries, 1973) were successful. By getting adults aged fifty to eighty-seven to do calisthenics, run, walk, and engage in stretching exercises or swim for forty-two weeks, researchers observed dramatic changes in the oxygen-transport capabilities of the adults' bodies. The improvements occurred regardless of the age of the individuals or their prior exercise history. Clearly, then, exercise and physical activity in late adulthood seem capable of slowing down the deterioration of an aging body.

Table 4.2

PHYSIOLOGICAL DECLINE ASSOCIATED WITH AGING AND THE POSSIBLE BENEFIT OF REGULAR STRENGTH AND ENDURANCE EXERCISE

Structural Change	*Functional Effects*	*Effects of Exercise*
Musculoskeletal System		
1. Muscular atrophy with decrease in both number and size of muscle fibers 2. Neuro-muscular weakness 3. Demineralization of bones 4. Decline in joint function—loss of elasticity in ligaments and cartilage 5. Degeneration and calcification on articulating surface of joint	1. Loss of muscle size 2. Decline of strength 3. Reduced range of motion 4. Reduced speed of movement 5. Joint stiffness 6. Declining neuromotor performance 7. Changes in posture 8. Frequent cramping 9. Gait characteristics affected: 　a. Center of gravity 　b. Span (height/arm length) 　c. Stride length, speed 　d. Width of stance 10. Shrinkage in height 11. Increased flexion at joints due to connective tissue change	1. Increased strength of bone 2. Increased thickness of articular cartilage 3. Muscle hypertrophy 4. Increased muscle strength 5. Increased muscle capillary density 6. Increased strength of ligaments and tendons
Respiratory System		
1. Hardening of airways and support tissue 2. Degeneration of bronchi 3. Reduced elasticity and mobility of the intercostal cartilage	1. Reduced vital capacity with increased residual volume 2. O_2 diffusing capacity is reduced 3. Spinal changes lead to increased rigidity of the chest wall 4. Declining functional reserve capacity	1. Exercise has no chronic effect on lung volumes but may improve maximal ventilation during exercise and breathing mechanics
Cardiovascular System		
1. Elastic changes in aorta and heart 2. Valvular degeneration and calcification 3. Changes in myocardium 　a. Delayed contractility and irritability 　b. Decline in oxygen consumption 　c. Increased fibrosis 　d. Appearance of lipofuscin 4. Increase in vagal control	1. A diminished cardiac reserve 2. Increased peripheral resistance 3. Reduced exercise capacity 4. Decrease in maximum coronary blood flow 5. Elevated blood pressure 6. Decreased maximal heart rate	1. Increased heart volume and heart weight 2. Increased blood volume 3. Increase in maximal stroke volume and cardiac output 4. Decreased arterial blood pressure 5. Increase in maximal oxygen consumption 6. Myocardial effects increased: 　a. Mitochondrial size 　b. Nuclei 　c. Protein synthesis 　d. Myosin synthesis 　e. Capillary density 7. Decreased resting heart rate

Source: Robert A. Wiswell, "Relaxation, Exercise, and Aging" in *Handbook of Mental Health and Aging.* Edited by Birren/Sloan, © 1980, p. 945. Reprinted by permission of Prentice-Hall, Inc., Englewood Cliffs, N.J.

Health Care

In the mid-1970s the National Council on Aging conducted a survey to explore American attitudes toward aging and the elderly. Few of the people polled chose old age as the most desirable period of life; generally, it was viewed as the least desirable (Harris, 1975). Regardless of whether the respondent was over or under the age of sixty-five, poor health and physical impairment were listed as the biggest problems of aging. However, although the general public perceives that people over the age of sixty-five seem to have major health problems, a survey of noninstitutionalized people over the age of sixty-five found that two of every three respondents considered their health good or excellent. Furthermore, only 5 percent of Americans over sixty-five live in institutions, and only 20 percent of elderly individuals will ever be confined to a nursing home. For approximately 80 percent of the elderly, the only care they will ever require can be provided by their families.

The family is the number one caretaker of our elderly, but the pattern is changing. Today adult children are much more likely to live a long distance from their elderly parents than was true in the past. Only 15 percent of the aged actually lived with their children in 1980, compared with 30 percent in 1950. This change may be due in part, to the fact that the extended family household has become impractical. Low birthrates that occurred during the depression led to fewer offspring to care for the older generation. By the 1970s, spare bedrooms and full-time housewives no longer appeared in a majority of American homes.

Are the elderly healthier than the public thinks? Are the conclusions of the studies we have noted based on the same definition or perception of health? In order to define and recognize poor health, we have to define the standards of good health. Though physical criteria such as pulse rate, body temperature, and other indicators are clearly important in assessing a person's health, such indicators are interpreted subjectively by each individual. A person who has a rapid pulse and wheezes may often see these as symptoms of poor health, whereas another individual may not. Assessing health status, then, is a complex task.

Medicaid and Medicare

The attitudes of policymakers affect the health of people in late adulthood as do the attitudes and competencies of physicians and other health-care personnel. By deciding on the type of publicly funded medical care that is to be made available to the elderly, policymakers can have a powerful impact on the health of the elderly in our society. Health care is among the largest expenditures in the national budget, but public Medicare is not adequate for all who need it. There are gross inequalities in treatment of the rich and the poor, the young and the old. Although Medicare and Medicaid programs were implemented to help improve the quality of health of the aged and the poor, quality care has not reached a satisfactory level (Williamson, Munley, & Evans, 1980).

Next we look at one final aspect of biological processes and physical development in adulthood—the reproductive system and sexuality.

THE REPRODUCTIVE SYSTEM AND SEXUALITY

Perhaps the strongest interest in the biological aspects of sex in adulthood has focused on menopause. More recently has come the question of whether there is a corresponding change in men. Before we tackle these aspects of reproductive change in middle adulthood, we discuss the female's menstrual cycle and evaluate its relation to mood and personality. Finally, we describe changes in sexual attitudes and behavior as individuals go through early, middle, and late adulthood.

The Menstrual Cycle and Hormones

From early adolescence until some point in middle adulthood, a woman's body usually undergoes marked changes in hormone levels that seem to be linked with her menstrual cycle. The possibility that biological cycles (such as menstruation) may influence the psychological orientation of an individual is one of the most unexplored areas of development. In the past it was assumed that monthly biological cycles like menstruation occurred exclusively in the female. Males have no correspondingly obvious physical signs to signal monthly or other periodic biological changes. However, some biologists now believe that both males and females are influenced by cyclic biological changes called *circadian rhythms*. The menstrual cycle is but one example of such a biological rhythm.

Researchers are gradually beginning to show more interest in how the menstrual cycle is related to personality fluctuations in the female. Judith Bardwick (1971) reports that the latter part of the menstrual cycle, from about day 22 on, is associated with a greater incidence of depression, anxiety, and irritability than is the middle of the menstrual cycle, when ovulation is occurring. Bardwick reports that women show higher levels of self-esteem and confidence during ovulation in comparison to other parts of the cycle. Bardwick's study and most others have concentrated on females in young adulthood.

The weight of the research evidence shows that there are definite mood swings in the female, swings associated with the middle of the menstrual cycle and the later premenstrual phase. However, it is not entirely clear whether the mood changes are due to a positive upswing of mood during the middle phase, a downward swing during the premenstrual phase, or a combination of both. Moreover, some studies point out that as many as 25 percent of all women report no mood shifts at all during these two phases (e.g., Hyde and Rosenberg, 1976).

Nevertheless, 75 percent of all women do experience mood shifts during different menstrual phases. What causes the changes in mood that occur in about three out of every four women? Hormonal changes are clearly one important factor. Female hormones reach peak levels at about day 22 to day 24 of the menstrual cycle, just at the time when depression and irritability seem to be at their peak. On the other hand, the cause-effect relationship could be the direct opposite; in other words, it is possible that mood changes influence hormone levels. If this is true, intense feelings of irritability and depression may feed back to the endocrine system and produce more estrogen.

Menopause and the Male Climacteric Syndrome

Most of us know something about menopause. But is what we know accurate? Stop for a moment and think about your knowledge of menopause. What is it? When does it occur? Can it be treated? In this section we look at the nature of menopause, including myths and stereotypes that have been developed about it, and explore the nature of the male climacteric syndrome, which involves the decline of the male's sexual and reproductive powers.

Menopause

My first sign of menopause was the night sweat. Even though I knew why I was having the sweats, it was a little frightening to wake up in the middle of the night with my sheets all drenched. It was hard not to feel that something was very wrong with me. And I lost a lot of sleep changing sheets and wondering how long the sweats would go on. Sometimes I felt chilled after sweating and had trouble going back to sleep. It was a good thing I could absorb myself in a book at times like that.

I also had hot flashes several times a week for almost six months. I didn't get as embarrassed as some of my friends who also had hot flashes, but I found the "heat wave" sensation most uncomfortable.

I felt generally good around the time of menopause. My children were supportive and patient, particularly when I was irritable from lack of sleep. My husband, unfortunately, was quite insensitive and frequently accused me of "inventing" my "afflictions." Without the help of friends and children who did try to understand what I was going through, it might have been harder for me to be around him. . . .

I usually think of geriatric types: little old white-haired women in wheelchairs in nursing homes. It's such an ugly word and image. Dried-up womb—bloodless insides. I'll never forget a man's description of an elegant hotel in the Virgin Islands as "menopause manor"! It made me glad at that time that I was still menstruating and didn't qualify for his derogatory observation. Now, ten years (and Women's Liberation) later, I can see the folly of his remarks and his machismo. But the word by itself still gives me a chill. It seems so final—as if an important bodily function had ceased, and with it all the fun of youth—which, of course, isn't true. . . .

I am constantly amazed and delighted to discover new things about my body, something menstruation did not allow me to do. I have new responses, desires, sensations, freed and apart from the distraction of menses [periods]. . . .

I feel better and freer since menopause. I threw that diaphragm away. I love being free of possible pregnancy and birth control. It makes my sex life better. (Boston Women's Health Book Collective, 1976, pp. 327, 328)

These comments by four women suggest both negative and positive reactions to menopause. The popular stereotype of the menopausal woman has been negative; she is exhausted, irritable, unsexy, hard to live with, irrationally depressed, and unwillingly suffering a change that marks the end of her active reproductive life.

Biologically, **menopause** is defined as the end of menstruation, a marker that signals the cessation of childbearing capacity. A related term, **climacteric,** is often used to refer to menopause. However, while menstruation refers to the onset of irregular menses (periods) and their eventual total cessation as a result of ovarian degeneration and a decline of estrogen secretion, climacteric generally occurs over a more prolonged period of time, at least several years, and refers to the loss of the ability to reproduce. The term has been applied to such a loss in men as well as women.

The average age at menopause in the United States is fifty. Menopause is considered to have occurred when twelve consecutive months have passed without a period (Block, Davidson, & Grambs, 1981). A number of symptoms accompany menopause, but only two, hot flashes and the atrophy of the vagina, are believed to be directly related to decreased estrogen levels. Recent estimates indicate that approximately 20 percent of women have no symptoms at all, whereas 15 percent have symptoms that are sufficiently severe to warrant treatment (Women's Medical Center, 1977). The majority of women (65 percent) experience mild symptoms and can cope with them without undergoing medical intervention.

The **hot flash,** a feeling of extreme heat that is usually confined to the upper part of the body and often accompanied by a drenching sweat is the most commonly experienced symptom of menopause. Hot flashes gradually diminish in frequency and generally disappear completely within a year or two. A second symptom that often is associated with menopause is atrophy of the vagina. The inner lining of the vagina becomes drier, thinner, and less flexible—conditions that can make intercourse painful for some women.

Depression may also be associated with menopause, but menopause does not cause depression. Menopause comes at a time when some women are losing their full-time jobs as mothers and as wives, when some middle-aged men are attracted to younger women, and when other aspects of the aging process— wrinkles, a bulging figure, and so forth—also are occurring. Therefore, it is these factors, rather than menopause, that may cause depression. Indeed, many women handle menopause in very positive ways, as suggested by the comments of two of the four women at the beginning of this section.

Many women undergo a hysterectomy, a sort of artificial menopause. The uterus and cervix are removed in the case of a *simple hysterectomy,* whereas the ovaries and fallopian tubes are taken out as well in a *total hysterectomy.* Hysterectomy is the most common operation performed in the United States (Morgan, 1978). In 1977 the figure had reached some 800,000 women per year. A hysterectomy is performed for various reasons. The most common involves the improper positioning and slippage of the uterus, which happens most often in women who have had several children because pregnancy stretches the ligaments that hold the uterus in place. A hysterectomy also may be performed to eliminate fibroid tumors, which as many as 25 percent of all women experience. Such tumors are not cancerous, but they may cause abnormal bleeding. The third most common reason for a hysterectomy is cancer, which if detected early by a Pap test, is not necessarily life threatening (Block, Davidson, & Grambs, 1981).

One of the most controversial aspects of menopause involves the decrease in natural estrogen levels and the use of estrogen replacement therapy (ERT). *Estrogen replacement therapy* involves replacing the estrogen that a woman's body no longer produces; it is usually prescribed for severe cases.

Estrogen has been highly successful in relieving hot flashes and vaginal atrophy and, consequently, has been viewed as welcome relief by many women. However, there are some negative, as well as positive, aspects to the use of estrogen therapy.

Marilyn Block, Janice Davidson, and Jean Grambs (1981) state that the use of ERT is highly controversial because of the unknown relationship between estrogen and cancer. Despite reports that contend that ERT does not cause uterine or breast cancer, the FDA warns that the chances for uterine cancer increase five to seven times with ERT. Much of the danger of ERT is that the medication is taken for long periods of time. The average amount of time spent on ERT by most women is ten years. According to Block, Davidson, and Grambs:

> Even though ERT is effective in ameliorating hot flashes, women so affected must determine for themselves whether the condition is serious enough to warrant the use of a drug that causes cancer in animals and is associated with increased risk of cancer in women. (p. 28)

Do men experience biological changes related to their sexuality as they go through middle adulthood? We explore this intriguing possibility next.

The Male Climacteric Syndrome

The **male climacteric** differs in two important ways from menopause: it comes later, usually in the sixties or seventies, and it progresses at a much slower rate. During their fifties and sixties most men do not lose their capacity to father children, but there is usually a decline in sexual potency at this time. Men do experience hormonal changes in their fifties and sixties but not to the extent that women do. For example, testosterone production starts to decline about 1 percent a year during middle adulthood. Consequently, what has sometimes been referred to as male menopause has less to do with hormonal change than with the psychological adjustment men must make when they are faced with declining physical energy and business, social, and family pressures. The fact that testosterone therapy does not relieve such symptoms suggests that they are not induced by hormonal change.

Certain common characteristics indicate the beginning of a male climacteric in middle adulthood. First, sexual functioning changes. For example, the older a man gets, the longer it takes him to have an erection but the longer he is able to maintain it (Wagenwoord & Bailey, 1978). Although sexual potency may decrease, sexual desire does not necessarily decline. There also are some changes in secondary sexual characteristics during the climacteric: the voice may become higher pitched, facial hair may grow more slowly, and muscularity may give way to flabbiness.

Sexual Attitudes and Behavior

In addition to the biological aspects of reproductive capacity and sexuality, attitudes and behavior associated with sex need to be considered. Next we look at sexual attitudes and behavior in early, middle, and late adulthood.

Sexual Options for Adults

The importance of our body and our sexuality in establishing our identity as adults is captured in the comment that whether we attempt to ignore it or not, our skins present us as male or female (Lerbinger, 1972). Our sexual identification and our human sexuality are therefore an important part of our personality and can influence interpersonal perceptions and relations. And many different sexual activities are available to the adult.

Many adults have a number of misconceptions about sexuality, and sexual myths are prevalent in our culture. We live in an era of fluctuating and contradictory attitudes about sexuality. For instance, many adults and parents believe that we, as a nation, should be better informed about the realities and myths of sexuality, yet large percentages of the parents of high school students have never discussed sex with their offspring.

During the course of the life cycle, a person's sex drive fluctuates—a process that is independent of the amount of sexual activity the person engages in. Hormonal changes influence the sex drive as do cultural standards about sexual activity.

Some of the sex differences in sexuality are probably a consequence of the way we are socialized. Many of us are brought up to believe that premarital sex is acceptable for males but not females. Often, males are reared to dissociate the sexual act from a caring commitment to the other person. Males also are thought to have more sexual knowledge than females. Men, then, often enter into long-term sexual relationships and/or marriage with the belief that they are responsible for the satisfaction of the couple's sex life. In a sexual relationship, if either one or both of the partners do not have a climax, the blame usually rests with the male (Masters & Johnson, 1970). Such a perspective leads the male to think that his most important function is to get the job done rather than to spend more time in relating to his partner's sensual and emotional needs. Females who adopt a passive role in sexual relationships and who remain naive about sexual techniques may contribute to the difficulties many couples experience. In recent years it has become more culturally acceptable for females to express their sexuality and to be knowledgeable about sexual matters and techniques, a fact that may help decrease the burden on males to do everything in a sexual relationship. For sexual fulfillment, it is best that both partners be informed and active in exploring their own sexuality and in being able to communicate their needs to each other (Sarrell & Sarrell, 1974).

Today many middle-aged women, who spent their early adulthood years in a more sexually inhibited atmosphere, are showing a stronger interest in being active contributors and knowledgeable partners in sexual relationships. Whereas at earlier points in history it was unacceptable for females to achieve orgasm, this is no longer our cultural standard. Achieving orgasm on the part of both the male and the female is an important part of each individual's sexual makeup.

Type and Incidence of Sexual Activity

The data presented in the Kinsey reports suggest that most American males develop a pattern of orgasm and ejaculation during adolescence that continues into early adulthood and is, to some degree, independent of marital status. By contrast, for most individuals the outlet for their sexual drive is different in early adulthood from what it was during adolescence. Masturbation is the dominant form of male sexual behavior during adolescence, particularly during the early phases of adolescence, but sexual intercourse is more prevalent in early adulthood (Kinsey, Pomeroy, & Martin, 1948; Masters & Johnson, 1966).

Premarital Sex

Our cultural standards concerning premarital sex have changed substantially during the course of this century. In recent years, a climate suggesting that it is not morally wrong to engage in premarital sex has developed. For example, in a 1969 study of adults, 48 percent of the men under the age of thirty said that premarital sexual relations are not wrong, and by 1972 the figure had reached 65 percent. For women, the figures during the same period increased from 27 to 42 percent (Udry, 1974). Although earlier studies of premarital sex (e.g., Kinsey, 1948) indicated that males were more likely than females to have premarital sex, more recent data from a number of studies of the sex lives of college students suggest that women are often as likely as men to have had premarital sex (Luria & Rose, 1981).

In the United States, national surveys indicate that by the time they are twenty-five, 97 percent of males and 81 percent of females have engaged in premarital intercourse (Hunt, 1974). In West Germany, the incidence is 44 percent male and 33 percent female among twenty- to twenty-one-year-old unmarried students; among unmarried workers of the same age the figures rise dramatically to 81 percent male and 83 percent female (Sigusch & Schmidt, 1973). In France, the prevalence of premarital intercourse for those twenty to twenty-nine ranges from 75 percent for males to 55 percent for females (Condonneau, Mironer, Dourlin-Rollier, & Simon, 1972). Yet there are other countries and cultures in which premarital sex is unheard of.

Usually, as students go from the freshman to the senior year of college in the United States, an increase in premarital sex occurs. The range of premarital sex for men is between 28 percent at the beginning of college and 82 percent during the senior year; for women the corresponding figures are 29 and 86 percent, not much different than for men.

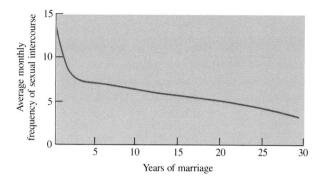

Figure 4.3   Average monthly frequency of sexual intercourse by duration of marriage.

Sexual Intercourse in Marriage

When we consider how long a couple has been married, it appears that sexual relations go better at first. For example, intercourse is practiced frequently in the early months of a marriage and then decreases over the length of the marriage. (Figure 4.3 traces the average monthly incidence of intercourse through thirty years of marriage.)

The famous sex researcher Alfred Kinsey reported that women reach their peak of sexual functioning in their middle years (Kinsey, Pomeroy, & Martin, 1953). However, there is little support for Kinsey's belief today. His impressions were probably influenced by the somewhat pristine attitudes toward female sexuality in the middle of the twentieth century. Possibly it took women some twenty years or so to overcome their sexual inhibitions. It seems likely that women in the 1970s and 1980s are much more sexually uninhibited at younger ages than was the case when Kinsey's data were collected.

Evidence that sexual intercourse in marriage is a highly satisfying physical experience, particularly for wives, comes from data reported by more than 2,000 middle-class American married women (Bell & Lobsenz, 1974). Married women in their twenties reported that they enjoyed the physical aspects of sexual intercourse more than their counterparts in their thirties, who were more inclined to enjoy its emotional aspects. Most of the women reported that they had orgasms, and those who had orgasms more frequently also were more likely to indicate they were happy. Further, married women in early adulthood were more likely than their adolescent or middle adulthood counterparts to take part in love-making experiments. Married women in their twenties and thirties said that they practiced oral-genital sex more than the other two age segments of married women did. The young adults also indicated that their husbands, rather than they, were more likely to initiate love-making sessions. However, because these data were collected in a cross-sectional manner, cohort effects may be involved.

The link between frequency of intercourse and marital satisfaction is not the same in every marriage and may not be the same for partners in the same marriage. Nonetheless, there is a substantial association between marital satisfaction and the incidence of intercourse when large numbers of couples are surveyed (Bell & Bell, 1972; Levinger, 1970). The most common reason given for sexual abstinence among married couples is marital conflict. Other reasons include physical illness, loss of interest, and emotional stress (Edwards & Booth, 1976).

Husbands usually show a stronger interest in sexual activity than do wives (Broderick, 1982). In one novel investigation, participants were asked to select from a list of more than ninety possibilities five most preferred leisure-time activities (Mancini & Orthner, 1978). The men ranked sexual and affectional activities among their top five choices more often than any of the other activities. The women ranked reading their first choice, and sex and affection were tied with sewing for second place. Nonetheless, whereas men on the average may show a stronger interest in sex, some investigators find that women indicate they are more sexually frustrated than men (Bell & Bell, 1972).

Extramarital sex, though considered appropriate by some individuals, still is not condoned as morally appropriate conduct by the majority of our society. Pollster Daniel Yankelovich (1981), writing in *New Rules in American Life,* found that 76 percent of adult Americans disapprove of men having extramarital affairs. And though the popular press has given a great deal of attention to mate swapping by marital couples, a maximum of 2 percent of married pairs are involved (Bartell, 1972; Hunt, 1974).

Sexual Attitudes and Behavior At Mid-Life

Although there is usually little biological decline in a man or a woman's ability to function sexually in middle adulthood, sexual activity usually occurs less frequently than in early adulthood. Career interest, family matters, and energy level may contribute to the decline in sexuality.

Still, a large percentage of individuals in middle adulthood continue to show a moderate or strong sexual interest and continue to engage in sexual activity on a reasonably frequent basis. For example, in one national survey of 502 men and women between forty-six and seventy-one years of age, approximately 68 percent of the fifty-one- to fifty-five-year-old respondents said that they had a moderate or strong interest in sex (Pfeiffer, Verwoerdt, & Davis, 1974), and approximately 52 percent said that they had sexual intercourse once a week or more.

Typically, surveys note sex differences in sexual interest and activity in middle adulthood. Men consistently report greater interest in sex and indicate that they engage in sexual activity more than women. For example, in the study just mentioned, 81 percent of the men and only 56 percent of the women between the ages of fifty-one and fifty-five said that they had a moderate or strong interest

Table 4.3

CURRENT LEVEL OF SEXUAL INTEREST (PERCENTAGE)

Age Group	Number	None	Mild	Moderate	Strong
Men					
46–50	43	0	9	63	28
51–55	41	0	19	71	10
56–60	61	5	26	57	12
61–65	54	11	37	48	4
66–71	62	10	32	48	10
Total	261	6	26	56	12
Women					
46–50	43	7	23	61	9
51–55	41	20	24	51	5
56–60	48	31	25	44	0
61–65	43	51	37	12	0
66–71	54	50	26	22	2
Total	229	33	27	37	3

Source: Pfeiffer, Verwoerdt, & Davis, 1974. Copyright 1974 by Duke University Press.

in sex; 66 percent of the men and only 39 percent of the women said that they had sexual intercourse one or more times per week (Pfeiffer, Verwoerdt, & Davis, 1974).

The data for current levels of sexual interest on the part of those between forty-six and seventy-one are shown in table 4.3. In addition to the points already mentioned about these data, note that as individuals reach the end of middle adulthood and the beginning of late adulthood, sexual interest and activity does decline.

One factor that seems to be particularly important in the sexual activity of women in middle adulthood is the availability of a sexual partner. Thus it is not surprising that women in middle adulthood who are married engage in sexual activity more frequently than women who are single.

We have seen that there are marked individual differences in the manner in which people in late adulthood show deterioration in different aspects of physical development. We have also seen that the quality of medical care in late adulthood shows a great deal of variation. Next we note the considerable variability of sexuality in late adulthood as well.

Sexuality in Late Adulthood

Alex Comfort (1976), a noted expert on the elderly, concludes that aging does induce some changes in human sexual performance, more so in the male than in the female. Orgasm becomes less frequent in males, occurring in every second or third act of intercourse rather than every time. More direct stimulation is usually needed to produce an erection. In the absence of two disabilities—actual disease and the belief that old people are or should be asexual—sexual requirement and capacity are lifelong. Even if and when actual intercourse is impaired by infirmity, other sexual needs persist, including closeness, sensuality, and being valued as a man or a woman.

Such a view, of course, is contrary to folklore, to the view of many individuals in our society, as well as to many physicians and health-care personnel. Fortunately, many elderly people have gone on having sex without talking about it, unabashed by the accepted and destructive social image of the dirty old man and the unsexual, undesirable older woman. Bear in mind that many individuals who are now in their eighties were reared when there was a Victorian attitude toward sex. In early surveys of sexual attitudes, older people were not asked about their sexuality, possibly because everyone thought they didn't have sex or because people thought it would be embarrassing to ask them about sex.

Most of the published work in the area of sexuality and aging suggests or concludes that there are no known age limits to sexual activity (e.g., Kaplan, 1974; Masters & Johnson, 1970). Healthy older people who want to have sexual activity are likely to be sexually active in late adulthood (Comfort, 1976, 1980; Pfeiffer & Davis, 1974). Various therapies for elderly people who report sexual difficulties have also been effective (White & Catania, 1981). For example, in one investigation sexual education (consisting largely of giving sexual information) led to increased sexual interest, knowledge, and activity in the elderly (White & Catania, 1981).

In reviewing the existing literature on sexuality and aging, Charles White (1981) concluded:

1. Males are more active than females, except for very old age groups (those eighty-five or older) in which males and females do not significantly differ.

2. When sexual interest or activity ceases or declines in the aging female, it is usually due to declining interest or illness in her male partner.

3. Males do show a gradual decline in sexual activity with advancing age, though this decline may be a cohort difference because some males actually show an increased interest in sex with age. In the absence of longitudinal data, a cohort explanation cannot be ruled out.

4. Physiological changes in the sexual organs in advanced age present some difficulties for some individuals but do not adequately explain decreased or nonexistent sexual activity in either sex.

5. It is difficult to find research on aging and sexuality that does not suffer from sample bias and methodological problems.

In a recent investigation of sexual activity and interest, White (1981) evaluated a group of elderly people whose sexuality rarely has been studied—those who are institutionalized in nursing homes. Eighty-four males (mean age of eighty-one) and 185 females (mean age of eighty-three) in fifteen nursing homes in Texas were asked about their sexuality. Attitudes and knowledge about sexuality were significantly related to sexual activity and sexual habits earlier in adult-hood. Seventeen percent of the sexually inactive residents indicated a desire to be sexually active, which conforms with other data collected from noninstitu-tionalized individuals in late adulthood and suggests that sexual interest exceeds sexual activity (e.g., Verwoerdt, Pfeiffer, & Wang, 1969).

In summarizing his ideas about sexuality in late adulthood, Alex Comfort (1980) made a number of suggestions about how health-care personnel can help the elderly with their sexual needs. Sexual responsiveness should be fostered but not preached. The elderly need to be reassured against their own false ex-pectations, the hostility of society, including children and potential heirs, and the interference of some health-care personnel who do not understand such needs. Comfort suggests that where a partner is not available, masturbation should be viewed as an enjoyable release of sexual tension and not looked at with a jaundiced eye. He believes that explicit discussion of masturbation with the el-derly may relieve anxiety caused by earlier prohibitions. Group discussion among elderly couples can be a valuable means of ventilating sexual anxieties and needs, needs that may not be sanctioned in conversations with others. Comfort believes that sexual dysfunction usually is produced by culture-based anxiety and that it is never too late to restructure sexual attitudes. He reports that many couples in their seventies have for the first time achieved communication and fulfillment that had been denied them earlier in their lives.

Our discussion of reproductive capacity and sexuality concludes the section on biological processes and physical development. In the next section we dis-cuss cognitive processes and development in the adult years.

Summary

Sensorimotor development pertains to the sensory systems whereby our five senses pick up information from the environment and the motor systems whereby we perform phys-ical actions in the environment. Vision and hearing are the two most important sensory systems in adulthood. Some decline in vision is characteristic in the middle adult years. Accommodation of the eye undergoes its sharpest decline between the ages of forty and fifty-nine, for example. Visual decline in late adulthood is characteristic of most individ-uals and can usually be traced to the quality and intensity of light reaching the retina. In extreme old age the retina itself may degenerate. While glasses may be used to correct vision, the older we get the more difficult corrective vision becomes. Hearing usually reaches its peak in adolescence, remains reasonably stable during early adulthood, but in middle adulthood may start to decline. Less than 20 percent of those between forty-five and fifty-four have a hearing problem, but for those between seventy-five and seventy-nine, the figure reaches 75 percent. Hearing impairment can be corrected in many cases through the use of two hearing aids, balanced to correct for each ear separately. We also become less sensitive to taste, smell, and pain as we age. Motor skills usually peak between eigh-teen and thirty and are often best between nineteen and twenty-six. Reaction time be-comes gradually slower through the remainder of the adult years.

The human brain is the most complex, elegant, intricate system imaginable. It is generally agreed that we lose a large number of neurons as we grow old, but there are few precise conclusions about just how important this phenomenon is in the aging process. Scientists believe that a more important concern is what goes on within nerve cells as we age. A number of intracellular changes have been detected during aging, but the precise function of such changes is not well known. At a more macrolevel of analysis, the electroencephalogram has been used to measure the electrical output of the brain. One brain rhythm is more dominant than others—the alpha rhythm; this is associated with a relaxed, yet awake state. Alpha activity definitely begins to slow by the time we reach our late fifties. Though the slowing of alpha activity has been linked with a slowing of behavior, some experts believe that reduced arousal rather than slower alpha activity accounts for the behavioral slowing.

Most people reach their peak of health in early adulthood. However, because young adults can bounce back so readily from physical abuse of their bodies, it is easy for them to develop bad health habits. Health status becomes a major concern in middle adulthood, whereas among young adults it gets much less attention. Heart disease, cancer, and weight are the greatest health concerns of middle-aged adults. A pattern of emotional stability and controlled response to stress is associated with good health at mid-life. While coronary disease is influenced by many factors such as diet, smoking, obesity, and genetic predisposition, there is reason to believe that individuals whose life-style is competitive, accelerated, and impatient are more likely to develop coronary problems than those with an absence of these behavioral tendencies. As we age the probability that we will have some disease or illness increases. At some point in late adulthood biological deterioration is inevitable. The age and swiftness of decline varies considerably from one individual to another. One of the most significant changes is that the circulatory system becomes less efficient. Another major problem is arthritis. Too often our research on individuals in late adulthood has not focused on healthy individuals. By studying healthy old people, researchers hope to discover how the body can optimally age and to determine the factors that cause disease-free or disease-reduced aging. In searching for factors that will slow the aging process, the role of exercise is prominent. The evidence suggests that a regular exercise program promotes good health. Information about the type of health care the elderly receive suggests that some health-care personnel share society's negative stereotypes about the elderly.

Sexuality consists of biological, behavioral, and attitudinal components. The menstrual cycle is a biological rhythm in women that is linked with psychological change. Sexual activity occurs frequently in early adulthood, and there are many sexual options available to young adults. Premarital sex is prevalent among young adults, and sexual activity seems to be a source of great pleasure among young married couples. Menopause—the end of menstruation—is surrounded by many myths. The majority of women cope with menopause without having to undergo medical intervention, and for some women, menopause can be a positive event. Although males do not experience the swiftness in decline of reproductive capacity that women do during middle age, men seem to undergo a climacteric, indicating gradual loss of reproduction capability and sexual functioning. Although there is usually little biological decline in the ability to function sexually in middle age, sexual activity usually is less frequent than in early adulthood. Sexual activity can and does occur for many individuals in late adulthood. Though there is a decline in sexual activity in late adulthood, many individuals still have strong sexual interests.

Review Questions

1. Discuss the development of sensory systems during the adult years, focusing heavily on vision and hearing.
2. What is the course of motor development during adulthood?
3. To what extent do scientists believe we lose neurons as we age? How strong is the evidence for neuron loss in late adulthood?
4. Discuss how scientists are interested in the brain at the microlevel in terms of neurons and intracellular functioning and at the macrolevel in terms of the electrical activity of the brain.
5. What is the nature of health during early adulthood? Include in your answer information about BMR, fatty tissue, and muscle tone and strength.
6. Why is it so easy to develop bad health habits in early adulthood?
7. What is the nature of health during middle adulthood? Include in your answer suggestions about the extent of illness and impairment, health care, and the role of exercise in reducing disease.
8. Discuss the biological aspects of sexuality in adulthood, including information about the menstrual cycle, menopause, and the male climacteric.
9. Narrate the behavioral and attitudinal components of sexuality through the adult years.

Further Readings

Birren, J. E., & Schaie, K. W. (1977). *Handbook of the psychology of aging.* New York: Van Nostrand Reinhold.
An authoritative volume containing thirty chapters by various contributors, including chapters on motor performance; vision; hearing; taste and smell; age changes in touch, vibration, temperature, kinesthesis, and pain sensitivity; and intervention, treatment, and rehabilitation of psychiatric disorders. Medium to difficult reading.

Busse, E. W., & Blazer, D. G. (1980). Disorders related to biological functioning. In E. W. Busse & D. G. Blazer (Eds.), *Handbook of geriatric psychiatry.* New York: Van Nostrand Reinhold.
Includes information about sleep disturbances, sexual problems, psychosomatic conditions, and drug abuse. Treatment strategies for geriatric problems are described as well. Moderately difficult reading.

Rossman, I. (1980). Bodily changes with aging. In E. W. Busse & D. G. Blazer (Eds.), *Handbook of geriatric psychiatry.* New York: Van Nostrand Reinhold.
Provides a comprehensive overview of bodily changes that occur during middle and late adulthood. Includes information about stature, contour, muscles, bones, joints and various organ systems, including the cardiovascular, pulmonary, renal excretory, reproductive, and digestive. Medium reading.

Wiswell, R. A. (1980). Relaxation, exercise, and aging. In J. E. Birren & R. B. Sloane (Eds.), *Handbook of mental health and aging.* Englewood Cliffs, NJ: Prentice-Hall.
A thorough overview of what we know and don't know about the role of exercise in adult development and aging. Moderately easy reading.

COGNITIVE PROCESSES
AND DEVELOPMENT

PROFILE

Sarah Chaffin was an idealistic thinker during her adolescent years. Her thoughts seemed to have a dreamlike quality. She believed that the world should be better than it was—too much poverty, too much discrimination, and too much hypocrisy. But Sarah's thoughts on how to go about changing the world were abstract; she really had not come up with a pragmatic system for viable change, and she really had not considered how realistic her thoughts were.

As she went through her college years, Sarah's thoughts retained some of their idealism and abstractness, but her logical thought processes seemed to improve. Compared to the way she was in junior high school, for example, she was now more likely to consider a more complete set of strategies for solving a difficult problem and then to choose among alternative strategies. After college, Sarah took a job as an elementary school teacher. When we look at her cognitive orientation several years into her work experience, we find that she has a more realistic, pragmatic view of the world than she did during her adolescent and college years. Her ability to solve problems, make inferences, and think in a logical manner all seem to have improved.

When we look at Sarah at the age of forty-five, we find that she still has a strong cognitive orientation. She has continued in the education system and has now moved up to the position of supervisor of elementary school mathematics in the county school system. She spends much of her spare time reading, and she still loves to solve complicated reasoning problems. Even with such a strong cognitive orientation, however, Sarah's long-term memory seems to be slipping just a little. At times she can't remember some of the things that she used to be able to retrieve in an instant, and sometimes it takes her a little longer to remember other things that she wants to remember. Nonetheless, Sarah is a very organized person, and her memory has been one of the targets of her organizational capabilities. Her verbal knowledge seems to be greater than it was in early adulthood—she knows the meaning of more words, and her practice with tough "mental teasers"—not to mention the tough questions and hard issues she has to deal with daily in her work—seems to have kept her reasoning skills finely tuned.

152

When we look at Sarah at the age of sixty-five, we find that she is still working as the supervisor of mathematics and that she still lives a very active, healthy life. She continues to play with the mental teasers she developed an interest in during early adulthood, and she remains a voracious reader. She feels that her long-term memory, however, has become noticeably poorer; to help her memory, she increasingly has to call on memory strategies and organizational techniques that help her to code and retrieve information. In some cases, the strategies don't work quite as well as they did in middle adulthood. She seems to be better at recognizing something from the past than having to recall some bit of information totally on her own. Nonetheless, Sarah's vocabulary remains strong, and she considers herself to be wiser than she was in her earlier years. She believes that her fifty years of experience as an adult make up for some of her physical and cognitive slowdown. That is, she feels that she can call on a broader base of information and experience when she has to make decisions than she did in early and middle adulthood.

When we follow Sarah into what has sometimes been referred to as late late adulthood, we look at her cognitive skills and activity at the age of seventy-eight. She has been retired from her job with the school system for twelve years now. For most of her adult life she has been very healthy, but in the last several years, her heart has given her problems, and there are times when her breathing is irregular. There seems to be more of an overall decline in her cognitive skills than was true when we saw her at the age of sixty-five. Sarah's long-term memory is often sketchy and her motivation for working seems to have slackened considerably in the last several years. But she still picks up a newspaper and tries to work crossword puzzles and is even able to solve some of the mind teasers she enjoyed so much during her earlier years. Sarah has lived a very productive, cognitively invested life that remained at a high level of competence until a very old age.

5

COGNITIVE STAGES, INTELLIGENCE, CREATIVITY, AND ADULT EDUCATION

John W. Santrock and James C. Bartlett

IMAGINE   *that you are sixty-seven years old and decide to learn to drive, play tennis, and play the piano.*
Could you learn to do these things? Or if you already knew how, are there certain cognitive strategies that could help keep your performance at its current level, or perhaps even improve it, even though you will be seventy years old in three years?

Your author is also a tennis professional. Three months ago, V. B. Harris came to me on his eighty-fifth birthday and asked if I would sign him up for a series of tennis lessons. I was somewhat surprised because Bucky, as he is called, was already a very accomplished player, so accomplished that when he was eighty he was ranked fourth in the United States in the eighty-and-over category. Even when he was eighty-four his ranking had only dropped to twelfth. In tennis, once you are thirty-five you enter a new age bracket every five years, so Bucky was getting ready to enter the eighty-five-and-over division. Bucky turned out to be one of the most enjoyable, attentive, and cognitively resourceful pupils I taught last summer. Would that some of the adolescents I teach had his motivation and organizational capabilities. When he came to his second lesson he told me that as soon as he got home after the first lesson he summarized and wrote down what he thought were the three most important things I had told him. Then he proceeded to rehearse those ideas and practice them, in front of a full-length mirror at his house, on the backboard at the club, and in practice matches with his compatriots. I should point out that Bucky has had two coronary operations, has a rotund body build, is overweight, and hits a tennis ball harder than most people I have seen. Indeed, one of the major problems Bucky had was that he invariably tried to hit the ball very hard and after doing so would stand too far back in the court. He quickly learned to vary the pace of his shots and when he hit hard to take several steps forward so that he would be in better position for short returns.

Marian Perlmutter (Perlmutter & Mitchell, 1983) recently summarized the findings from investigations that have attempted to train older adults in complex cognitive skills. Studies have shown that such complex skills as fluid intelligence can be modified and transferred to thinking on tasks other than the ones the older adults were trained in (e.g., Baltes & Willis, 1978). Nonetheless, when these older adults were retested six months later the effects were not as clear.

Older adults also have been successfully trained to perform better at tasks that require them to learn an efficient strategy for solving reasonably simple identification problems (Sanders & Sanders, 1978), a finding that generalized to improved performance on more complex cognitive tasks that were given one year later. Older adults also have been trained to improve their performance on Piagetian-type conservation tasks (e.g., Hornblum & Overton, 1976) and on perspective-taking tasks (e.g., Schultz & Hoyer, 1976) and role-taking tasks (Zaks & Labouvie-Vief, 1980). In one intriguing study that has direct application to helping individuals in late adulthood deal more effectively with their environment, the information-processing skills necessary for effective driving were significantly improved through a training program, with the effects lasting for at least six months (Sterns & Sanders, 1980).

In conclusion, the fact that cognitive skills in late adulthood can be improved through training is encouraging. However, there clearly are limitations on how much improvement can be made. The future should provide more precise information about how elastic various cognitive skills are in late adulthood and how easily they can be modified.

INTRODUCTION

This is the first of two chapters that focus on cognition in adulthood. Initially, we present the cognitive stages that have been proposed to describe the way adults think. We will see that many adult developmentalists believe that Piaget's view of cognitive development is an inappropriate model of adult cognition. In addition to describing several adult contextual views of cognitive development, we chart the course of social cognition. We will find that it is important to consider the manner in which adults reason about social matters. After examining the cognitive stage view, we discuss a second important perspective on adult cognition, the psychometric approach, a measurement-based view that has sparked debate on the nature of development and decline in cognition during the adult years. We also survey what is known about the role of physical health in cognition, the developmental course of creativity in the adult years, and reasons why adults do or do not initiate or continue their education.

COGNITIVE STAGES AND STRUCTURES IN ADULTHOOD

Piaget's theory of cognitive development suggests that adulthood is not characterized by the development of any new cognitive changes. Nonetheless, his theory of *how* people think has important implications for understanding adult cognition. In this section, we look at the extent to which adults think in formal operational ways and describe why many developmentalists believe that Piaget's model is inappropriate for interpreting adult cognition. From this perspective, we present several variations of the adult contextual view of cognitive development. We conclude by describing the increasing interest in the social cognition of adults, arguing that not only do adults think and reason about nonsocial matters, but they engage in cognitive activity about social matters as well.

Piaget's Stage of Formal Operational Thought

For Piaget, the manner in which the adult thinks is basically no different from the way in which most adolescents think. However, many cognitive structuralists believe that it is not until adulthood that many individuals who reach formal operations actually consolidate their **formal operational thinking.** It also seems certain that many adults do not think in formal operational ways (Keating, 1980). For example, only 17 to 67 percent of college students show this type of thinking (Elkind, 1961; Tomlinson-Keasey, 1972).

What is formal operational thinking like? Most significantly, it is abstract. The adolescent or adult is no longer limited to actual, concrete experience as an anchor for thought. Instead, she or he may conjure make-believe situations, events that are strictly hypothetical possibilities, or purely abstract propositions and proceed to reason logically with them.

The abstract quality of thought at the formal operational stage is evidenced primarily in the thinker's verbal problem solving. While the concrete thinker would need to see the concrete elements A, B, and C to be able to make the logical inference that if A>B and B>C, then A>C, the formal operational thinker can solve this problem merely through verbal presentation.

In the social realm, one important implication of this theory is that the formal thinker no longer needs to rely on concrete experiences with people to form complex judgments about them. He or she may make such judgments largely on the basis of verbal description, speculation, or gossip.

The make-believe nature of thought can be seen in a person's ability to propose and work with contrary-to-fact reasoning. Suppose, for example, that someone is asked to imagine that the room in which she is sitting suddenly has no walls and to describe what she now sees. Most adolescents and adults can easily perform such mental gymnastics (e.g., Elkind, 1976). The important point is that this mental feat involves representing an imaginary event that counters the concrete reality of the moment.

Many examples can be used to demonstrate how this thought influences the individual in his or her social sphere. The adolescent or young adult for the first time engages in extended speculation about ideal characteristics of people, himself as well as others. Ideals, which are contrary-to-fact representations, often preoccupy him. He may become impatient with his inability to make reality conform to these newfound ideals, and he is perplexed over which of the many available ideal selves to adopt.

The adolescent or young adult's ability to work with these conjured possibilities is easily seen in the way she or he approaches problem solving. The style of problem solving that the formal operational thinker uses has often been referred to as *deductive-hypothesis testing.* Jerome Bruner (1966) and his associates used a modification of the familiar game twenty questions in an extensive research project with individuals of varying ages. Each subject is shown a set of forty-two colorful pictures displayed in a rectangular array (six rows of seven pictures each) and is asked to determine which picture the experimenter has in mind by asking only yes or no questions. The object of the game is to select the "correct" picture by asking as few questions as possible. The person who is a deductive-hypothesis tester formulates a plan to propose and test a series of hypotheses, each of which narrows the field of choices considerably. The most effective plan consists of a halving strategy: for example, the subject asks, "Is it in the right half of the array?" "Is it in the top half?" And so on. Used correctly, the halving strategy guarantees the questioner the correct solution in seven questions or fewer, no matter where the correct picture is located in the array. Even if he or she is using a less effective strategy, the deductive-hypothesis tester understands that when the experimenter answers no to one of his or her guesses, several possibilities are immediately eliminated.

The person who uses **concrete thinking,** by contrast, may persist with questions that test some of the previously eliminated possibilities. For example, the individual may have asked whether the correct picture was in row 1 and received the answer no, but later asks whether the correct picture is X, a picture that is in row 1.

The social implications of deductive-hypothesis testing are clear. When the adolescent or young adult meets people, his or her abstract hypotheses about what they are like are more amenable to practical verification through the actions and attitudes the people convey. An individual's belief in the goodness of a friend may be quickly dispelled if he observes her being cruel to someone. A concrete thinker would be less open to disenchantment from practical experience.

A final property of formal thinking is the ability to appreciate metaphorical meaning. A *metaphor* is a figure of speech that compares two things of different classes. Thus snow may be a blanket, and a person may be a tiger. Concrete thinkers find it difficult to understand such metaphorical meanings. Consequently, many children are puzzled by the meanings of parables and fables whereas most adolescents and adults are not (Elkind, 1976).

Again, the social implications are obvious. Metaphor greatly extends the network of symbols that the adolescent and young adult can use in thinking about people. It makes possible a host of abstract comparisons between people and nonliving things, people and animals, and people and plants, among others.

Research on Formal Operational Thought in Adulthood

Several earlier investigations of cognitive structural change in late adulthood (e.g., Papalia & Bielby, 1974; Storck, Looft, & Hooper, 1972) implied that regression from formal operational thought to lower cognitive stages occurs in the elderly. However, more recent data suggest that such observations may be attributed to the fact that many older adults had never achieved formal operational thought in their younger years. Indeed, many adults think in concrete operational rather than formal operational ways (Protinsky & Hughston, 1978).

When we present the elderly with intellectual problem-solving tasks, such as those used to assess Piaget's stages, it is important that the tasks be relevant to the interests of the elderly. One researcher (Sinnott, 1975) has found that individuals in late adulthood perform better on adult relevant tasks that have more meaningful content for the elderly than on standard Piagetian tasks that were designed for use with children.

Next we see that from the adult contextual perspective the strategy of looking for regression and decay in Piaget's stages is inappropriate.

The Adult Contextual Perspective

The most comprehensive, detailed criticism of using Piaget's theory, as well as other child- or youth-centered models of development, to interpret adult development has been articulated by Gisela Labouvie-Vief (e.g., Labouvie-Vief, 1980a, 1980b). She argues that what actually may be a form of growth is often interpreted as regression and deficit when we use a child-centered model like Piaget's to interpret development and aging. Thought may be viewed as maladaptive from a traditional cognitive development model when formal logic diminishes and more pragmatic, reality-oriented thought increases. As we soon will see, however, from the **adult contextual model** much of the changing thought of individuals as they go through the adult years can be viewed as adaptive.

Even Piaget (1967) mentioned that formal operational thought may have its hazards:

> With the advent of formal intelligence, thinking takes wings and it is not surprising that at first this unexpected power is both used and abused . . . each new mental ability starts off by incorporating the world in a process of egocentric assimilation. Adolescent egocentricity is manifested by a belief in the omnipotence of reflection, as though the world should submit itself to idealistic schemes rather than to systems of reality. (pp. 63–64)

Formal thinking, then, may be a faulty choice because idealism may insulate the individual from pragmatic orientation to the real world. Piaget said that dreams should often be discarded or modified to accommodate reality.

As people go through their college years, there is some evidence that the absolute nature of adolescent logic begins to diminish. Some psychologists believe that the realization that there are multiple perspectives and alternative solutions to problems accounts for the diminishing use of formal thought during the transition from adolescence to adulthood. (Perry, Brown, & Perry, 1979). From Labouvie-Vief's perspective (1981), this cognitive realization indicates a new integration of thought, namely, that the pragmatic constraints of adulthood have to be accepted and that this adaptive strategy means the adult will rely less on the search for logical certainty in solving problems. As part of this change in cognition during early adulthood, people need to show more specialization in their thinking than absolutism and idealism.

From the perspective of Labouvie-Vief, then, different criteria of cognitive maturity need to be applied to adulthood—the criteria of formal operational thought are misleading. Commitment, specialization, and channeling energy into finding one's niche in the complex social system become mature concerns in adulthood, replacing the youth's fascination with the exercise of idealized logic.

If we were to assume that buoyant optimism and logical formal thought represented the criteria for cognitive maturity, we would have to admit that the cognitive activity of adults is overly concrete and pragmatic. But in the contextual

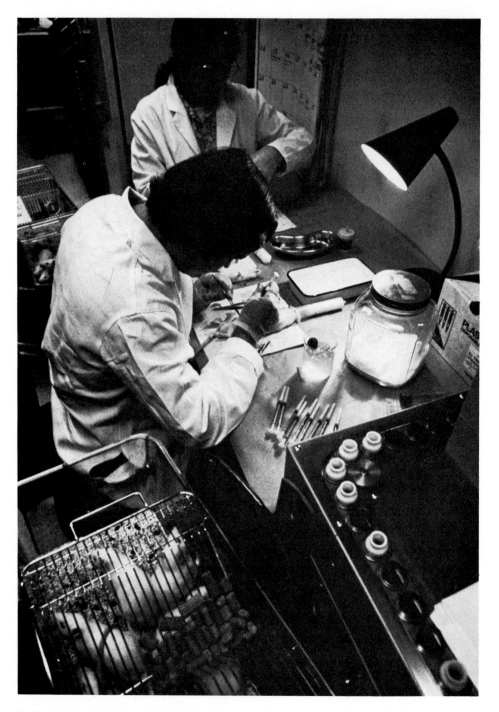

Early adulthood brings pragmatic constraints to the idealistic thought of adolescence.

perspective, rather than being a regressive change, understanding the constraints of reality in adult life indexes cognitive maturity and development, not regression (Labouvie-Vief, 1980).

Thus Labouvie-Vief's ideas (1980, 1981) suggest the possibility that a fifth cognitive stage emerges in the form of relativistic, pragmatic, contextual thinking. The characteristics of this stage are likely to begin to appear in the years just after high school, the period called youth by some theorists (e.g., Kenniston, 1970). During the early adult years, this type of thinking becomes consolidated and characterizes the young adult's cognitive activity. It is important to remember that while Piaget himself did not talk about a fifth stage, he did suggest that entering professional work may lead to accommodation in young adulthood.

Norma Haan (1981) agrees that a contextual perspective is necessary to explain the manner in which cognitive activity unfolds during the early adult years. She stresses that real-life adaptation (equilibration) is never final and that more than logical formal cognitive structures are involved in this adaptation. Whatever cognitive structures develop between adolescence and middle adulthood, adults increasingly make greater investments in cognitively solving problems and increasingly see their own thought as relevant to understanding the world in which they live (Haan, 1981). This may come about because such strategies are found to be adaptive and workable. Haan also believes that young adults successfully adapt not just by accommodating but by overaccommodating, a trend that may only diminish in middle age when a person is either an established success or has reconciled himself to whatever achievements he has accomplished (Clauson, 1981; Stroud, 1981). Besides formal logic (defined as holistic, organized, and logically consistent understanding), Haan speculates that other mental structures such as morality, an understanding of human embeddedness in social contexts and attachments, and affective attitudes probably characterize adult thought. In concluding, Haan stresses that the accommodative changes of young adults cannot be explained apart from the social contexts and life events they experience. Thus Haan's ideas are compatible with those of Labouvie-Vief. Another stage perspective that emphasizes the importance of social matters and contextual considerations is the stage view of K. Warner Schaie.

K. Warner Schaie (1977) has speculated about the possible existence of four stages of cognitive development: acquisitive, achieving, responsible, and reintegrative. The **acquisitive stage** refers to a period of childhood and adolescence during which the individual functions in a protected environment and his or her goal is the acquisition of knowledge. With the achievement of adult status, the individual is less protected from the consequences of failing at problem solving. At this stage, the goal is no longer the acquisition of knowledge but rather the achievement of potential. Schaie therefore calls this the **achieving stage.** The **responsible stage** corresponds with middle adulthood. At this stage, the individual has attained competence and independence and now has to assume responsibility for others. Schaie believes that this stage requires solutions to problems that focus on an individual's family and/or important other people in his or her life. The **reintegrative stage** corresponds with late adulthood. According to Schaie (1977), the three previous stages require the individual to integrate his or her intellectual abilities at higher levels of role complexity. However, during this final stage of cognitive development, the focus is on simplification. This does not mean that the individual stops performing intellectually but that his attention becomes focused more on those aspects of his life that are more meaningful to him. Schaie says that the reintegrative stage completes the transition from the "what should I know," through the "how should I use what I know," to the "why should I know" phases of life. Consequently, Schaie believes that in late adulthood, cognitive activity is influenced more by motivational factors than at any other stage. Clearly, the measures of adult intelligence we now use will have to be greatly modified if we believe that Schaie's stages have merit as a viable approach to the study of cognitive structural change in adulthood.

Although Lawrence Kohlberg is best known for his ideas about moral development, he has also proposed a general cognitive structural view of development (1976). He argues that young children reason from a **concrete-individualistic perspective** in which they see the world revolving around themselves. Older children and adolescents view themselves and their social world from a **member-of-society perspective.** The adolescent sees himself as a member of a larger social unit—family, school, city, culture, and so forth. His reasoning focuses on preserving the social order and fitting each member of society into it.

Adults reason from a **prior-to-society perspective** in Kohlberg's scheme. At this stage, adults reason about being a member of many different social units, each with an arbitrary membership determined by many uncontrollable factors. Social units are thought of as convenient and imperfect systems developed by people to assist them in getting along with one another.

Kurt Fischer (1980) believes that there are ten cognitive structural stages of development, the last three of which have important implications for our study of cognitive development in adults. Fischer delineates six levels of intellectual functioning in childhood. Level 7 marks the first appearance of abstract thought. At level 7 an individual can construct a "simple abstract set" in which two representational systems can be coordinated. For example, he or she can construct a single abstraction about his or her occupational identity. Level 8 of Fischer's view is called **abstract mapping,** which involves a person's ability to relate his or her abstract identity to that of another person in a rudimentary way. Level 9 is called **abstract system,** which entails the reciprocal coordination of one's own identities with those of significant others and with societal expectations. The most advanced level, level 10, is called **system of abstract systems.** The coordination of one's identities over the life cycle so that a meaningful whole can be achieved is involved at this level of thinking. It is possible that levels 8 through 10 in Fischer's theory can be attained by the end of early adulthood, but no developmental data have been collected that would support such an idea. A major point here, however, is that the kind of cognitive skills described by Fischer may be prerequisites for psychosocial stages of development. Thus, if the individual can reason at level 10 of Fischer's cognitive skills, she or he is more likely to be able to put together a cohesive account of the complexities of her or his life to form some meaningful pattern.

Fischer (1980) believes that most adults probably master some of the cognitive skills at levels 8 through 10. Identity concepts are the most plausible area in which cognitive skills are likely to involve some type of abstract mapping. Other skills that probably belong in the range of levels 8 through 10 are advanced moral judgments, the managerial skills required by a corporation or a school system, the skills required to write an effective essay or novel, and the skills involved in programming and operating a computer (Fischer & Lazerson, in press).

In Fischer's perspective, reasoning about social matters clearly comes into play in his attempt to develop levels or stages of adult thought. Indeed a characteristic of all of the Piagetian revisionists described here is that formal operational thought is not the dominant characteristic of adult cognition but rather that the development of cognitive stages in adulthood takes into account the interchange of the individual with his or her social world. From the contextual perspective, the adult constructs his or her cognitive activity by dynamically interacting with people in changing social and historical contexts. Piaget, of course, took such a constructivist position but placed less emphasis on the role of changing social and historical contexts. And Piaget did not believe that a new stage of thought was constructed during the adult years. An overview of the stages proposed by different contextual theorists is presented in table 5.1.

As we have seen, the adult contextual perspective of cognitive development gives a more central role to social factors than does the Piagetian approach. Not only has there been an increasing interest in how the social, historical context modifies the adult's cognitive activity, but there has also been an increased interest in the adult's reasoning about the social world. This latter perspective has been referred to as **social cognition.** Indeed in the description of adult cognitive stages set forth by Schaie, Fischer, Haan, Kohlberg, and Labouvie-Vief, we find a theme of social cognition as well as a contextual orientation. Let us look more closely at the study of social cognition in adulthood.

The majority of studies on social cognition have focused on moral development. This topic will be discussed in chapter 12. Two other important aspects of social cognition, which will be described in the next section, are impression formation and role taking or perspective taking. We begin our discussion of social cognition, however, with information about the adult's ability to monitor his or her social cognition, an idea that has important implications for our understanding of adult development.

Table 5.1

BEYOND PIAGET: THE DEVELOPMENT OF COGNITIVE STRUCTURES IN ADULTHOOD

Theorist	*Piaget*	*Labouvie-Vief*	*Schaie*	*Haan*	*Fischer*	*Kohlberg*
Adolescence	Formal operations	Formal operations	Acquisitive stage	Formal operations	Simple abstract set	Concrete-individual and member-of-society perspective
Early adulthood		Pragmatic orientation; specialization; adaptation to social, historical content	Achieving stage	Continuing equilibration and development of cognitive structures other than formal logical thought, such as affective attitudinal systems	Abstract mapping	Prior-to-society perspective
Middle adulthood			Responsible stage		Abstract systems	
Late adulthood			Reintegrative stage		System of abstract systems	

Social Cognition in Adulthood

Most theory and research on cognitive development has focused on how people think about impersonal objects and events, those that are inanimate and nonsocial. Piaget's ideas about cognitive development also downplay the role of social and environmental events in the development of cognitive structures. Recently, theory and research on cognitive development has begun to take into account people's reasoning about social matters as well. The field of social cognition focuses primarily on these matters.

According to cognitive developmentalist John Flavell (in press), social cognition, or *social cognitive enterprises,* should be defined broadly to include all intellectual endeavors in which the aim is to think or learn about social or psychological processes in the self, individual, others, or human groups of all sizes and kinds (including social organizations, nations, and people in general). Thus what is thought about during a social cognitive enterprise could be a perception, feeling, motive, ability, intention, purpose, interest, attitude, thought, belief,

In early adulthood we increase our ability to monitor our social thoughts.

personality structure, or another such process or property of self or other(s). It could also be the social interactions and relationships that obtain among individuals, groups, nations, or other social entities. A social cognitive enterprise can be very brief (e.g., "I sense that my last remark hurt your feelings") or very extended (e.g., "I feel I am still learning new things about the kind of person you are, even after all these years of trying to understand you)" (pp. 1–2).

An individual's ability to monitor his or her social thoughts and make sense of them seems to increase during adolescence and adulthood. An important aspect of social cognition is the individual's development of conscious self-awareness. Flavell (in press) believes that developing differentiated thoughts about oneself is a gradual process. Statements such as "I think I am not easily fooled by others" or "I tend to give people the benefit of the doubt" evidence the development of such self and social awareness. Although children may distinguish only between succeeding or failing to learn something they want to know about someone else, adolescents and young adults may understand the more complex notion that what they have learned may be either accurate or inaccurate. Acquiring this latter distinction can serve as the basis for still further development in monitoring social thought during adulthood. For example, during adulthood the individual may recognize that the accuracy of social thoughts is difficult to assess and that knowledge of certain aspects of the self or of others may actually decrease accuracy. For instance, prejudice, intense emotions, and mental and physical illness might produce inaccurate perceptions of oneself and others. Adults are more likely than adolescents to monitor such thoughts.

Flavell believes that the ability to monitor social cognition is an index of social maturity and competence:

"In many real-life situations, the monitoring problem is not to determine how well you understand what a message means but rather to determine how much you ought to believe it or do what it says to do. I am thinking of the persuasive appeals the young receive from all quarters to smoke, drink, commit aggressive or criminal acts, have casual sex without contraceptives, have or not have the casual babies that often result, quit school, and become unthinking followers of this year's flaky cults, sects, and movements. (Feel free to revise this list in accordance with *your* values and prejudices.) Perhaps it is stretching the meanings of . . . cognitive monitoring too far to include the critical appraisal of message source, quality of appeal, and probable consequences needed to cope with these inputs sensibly, but I do not think so. It is at least conceivable that the ideas currently brewing in this area could some day be parlayed into a method of teaching children (and adults) to make wise and thoughtful life decisions as well as to comprehend and learn better in formal educational settings. (Flavell, 1979, p. 910)

From Flavell's perspective, then, we become more competent as adults to the extent that we monitor our social thoughts. He suggests that as we make the transition from adolescence to adulthood there is an increase in such social monitoring. These views coincide with the ideas of Labouvie-Vief and other contextual theorists who argue that the pragmatic concerns of social interchange in different settings with different people modify our cognitive activity.

Our social cognitions are indeed a pervasive aspect of our lives. We make all sorts of decisions involving social matters in our adult life. We may weigh the pitfalls of giving up our independence versus the benefits of romance and love in a marriage; we have to make decisions about whether to take one job offer versus another; we have to choose whether to have children and if so, how many; and so forth. All of these decisions involve social cognition. Quite clearly much of our cognitive activity is enmeshed in our social, historical surroundings.

As one approaches and goes through middle adulthood, several aspects of social cognition become prevalent. Social cognition at mid-life often begins to focus on concerns about appearance, health, and sexual attractiveness; on the limits and boundaries in one's world, such that a feeling often develops that time is running out; and on retrospective glances at one's occupational history and the possibility that one is facing an occupational plateau (Steinberg, 1980). In middle adulthood, the individual's social cognition is bound up with the development of others. Middle-aged adults are not only confronted by their own developmental tasks but also by those that face their adolescent or young adult children and their aging parents. Consequently, social cognition that focuses on the development of control over one's own life must take into account the coordination of one's development with the development of others.

In late adulthood, social cognition probably takes an even stronger turn toward looking back and reminiscing about one's life and the myriad experiences that have occurred. The extent to which people feel satisfied with their lives seems to be an important part of social cognition in old age. Late adulthood is a time when extensive social adjustments have to be made. Changes in social networks may come about through the loss of a spouse, partner, or friend; retirement from work; and changes in family and community relationships. Studies of how the elderly reason about these changing social relationships and networks form the subject matter of social cognition.

In one recent investigation (Dolen & Bearison, 1982), it was predicted that the quality of elderly people's social interactions would be related to their social cognitive abilities. The study included 122 middle-class individuals ranging from sixty-five to eighty-nine years of age, most of whom were generally healthy and capable of maintaining themselves in the community. The social interaction measures included such factors as level of role participation (twelve different roles such as grandparent and church member) and participation in activities (twenty-two activities such as going to the movies). The social cognition measures included person perception, conceptualizing alternatives in interpersonal problem solving, and coordinating multiple perspectives.

In regard to person perception, the elderly were asked to select two people they knew well and to tell what kind of person each was (Peevers & Secord, 1973). Their responses, all confined to nonfamily members were scored as (1) *undifferentiating*—person described in terms of his or her environment, such as possession or social situations, e.g., Betty lives in a small apartment; (2) *simple differentiating*—person differentiated from his or her environment but in a superficial manner, such as appearance, global disposition, a like-dislike, and role category, e.g., Harry is sixty-nine years old; (3) *differentiating*—person described in terms of reasonably specific personality characteristics, such as interest, abilities or beliefs, or temporary stages, e.g., Bob is really a hard-working person; or (4) *dispositional*—person characterized in terms of traits that have implications for his or her behavior in multiple situations or that refer to his or her thoughts and feelings, e.g., Marla is very generous. The last two categories refer to inferences about the psychological attributes of others, whereas the first two categories refer to concrete or overt attributes. Thus those who described people in terms of the first and second categories were scored lower on person perception than those who characterized people in terms of the third and fourth categories.

Interpersonal problem solving involved reading the elderly stories simulating real-life problems in which a need is aroused in the protagonist at the beginning of the story but becomes satisfied by the end. The elderly were asked to fill in those events that might have occurred between the arousal and satisfaction of the protagonist's needs. Here is one story (Platt & Spivack, 1975):

> Mr./Mrs./Ms. A. was listening to people speak at a meeting about how to make things better in the neighborhood. He/she wanted to say something important and have a chance to be a leader too. The story ends with him/her being elected leader and presenting a speech. Please begin the story at the meeting where he/she wanted to have a chance to be a leader.

The adults' responses were scored in terms of how well the strategies they adopted were designed to reach the goal and overcome an obstacle and in terms of any alternative means of accomplishing relevant social goals they may have provided.

Coordinating perspectives, a projective task (Feffer, 1959), was used to assess the adults' ability to coordinate multiple perspectives. The adults were read two stories, each accompanied by a picture, and asked to retell each story from the perspective of the character in the picture. The adults were rated on how effectively they changed perspectives and elaborated on the perspective of the character.

We have taken some time to describe the measures of social cognition in order to give you a sense of how social cognition is studied in adult development. The results of the investigation just described revealed some strong associations between social interaction and social cognitive abilities. For example, total level of role participation was strongly associated with the adults' person perception, interpersonal problem solving, and coordinating perspective scores. The implications for our study of adult cognition are that the social interactions of the elderly are related to their cognitions about the social world and that it may be fruitful *not* to study the cognitive activity of the elderly in isolation from the social contexts in which they live and the manner in which they reason about social matters.

INTELLIGENCE AND THE PSYCHOMETRIC APPROACH

When we say that someone uses a **psychometric approach,** we mean that he or she emphasizes measurement-based tests. A professional who administers tests is sometimes referred to as a psychometrist or psychometrician. The psychometric approach that has received the greatest attention in our study of adult development is that of Raymond Cattell and John Horn.

Cattell proposed that two forms of intelligence act to influence the primary mental abilities described by Thurstone. Cattell labeled the two forms fluid and crystallized. **Fluid intelligence** focuses on the individual's adaptability and capacity to perceive things and integrate them mentally. It appears to be independent of formal education and experience. For instance, some adults seem intuitively to be able to think through problems with strategies that they have never been taught. By comparison, schooling and environment determine **crystallized intelligence,** which involves skills, abilities, and understanding gained through instruction and observation. For example, an adult may learn how to play a particular game only after he has seen someone else do it or has been given instructions on how to proceed.

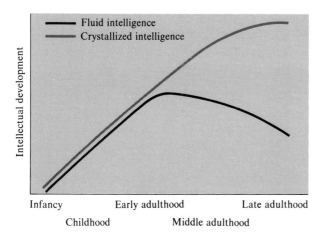

Infancy   Early adulthood   Late adulthood

Childhood   Middle adulthood

Figure 5.1   Fluid and crystallized intellectual development across the life span.

Cattell's theory of fluid and crystallized intelligence has served as the basis for a number of life-span developmental investigations of intelligence. Cattell's student, John Horn, has provided the impetus for much of the life-span work. Basically, as indicated in figure 5.1, Horn (e.g., Horn & Donaldson, 1980) believes that crystallized intelligence increases throughout the life span because it is based on cumulative learning experiences. By contrast, he states that fluid intelligence increases from infancy through adolescence, levels off during early adulthood, and then steadily declines in middle and late adulthood.

Prior to the work of Cattell and Horn, psychometric measures of intelligence in childhood and adulthood indicated that verbal abilities, such as scores on the Wechsler vocabulary and information subtests, tend to increase in adulthood, whereas perceptual-motor abilities, such as scores on the Wechsler incomplete pictures and block design subtests, are more likely to decline in adulthood (Wechsler, 1958). However, distinguished psychologist D. O. Hebb (1978), in reflecting on his own adult development, indicated that in his late forties he began to notice a loss in the effective use of vocabulary and that by his sixties he had to use a thesaurus in his writing.

Horn and Cattell (e.g., 1966, 1967) believe that the increase in verbal abilities found by Wechsler reflect the development of crystallized intelligence, whereas the decline in perceptual-motor abilities is explained by the concept of fluid intelligence. In conducting their own research with 279 adolescents, young adults, and middle-aged adults, Cattell and Horn found that fluid intelligence declines and crystallized intelligence increases across a large portion of the life span (see figure 5.2).

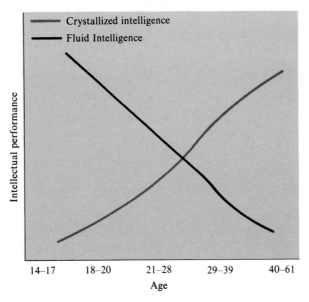

Figure 5.2   Fluid and crystallized intellectual performance across a portion of the life span.

By now you have had an opportunity to get some feel for the psychometric approach to adult intelligence. How does this approach differ from Piaget's approach? Read box 5.1 for the answer.

Cohort and Context in the Study of Intelligence

We have seen that some aspects of intelligence seem to increase over the life span while others decline. One group of life-span developmental psychologists, however, believe that much of the data on intelligence is flawed because it has been collected in a cross-sectional rather than a longitudinal manner. K. Warner Schaie, Paul Baltes, and Gisela Labouvie-Vief (e.g., Baltes & Labouvie, 1973; Schaie, 1970, 1979) argue that the nature of cohort effects and historical change restrict data collected on intelligence (and personality) to the culture and generation(s) being studied. (Note: Although Schaie and Labouvie-Vief were described in the cognitive structural section to illustrate the adult contextual view of cognitive structure, in their research they have primarily used standardized intelligence tests.)

These life-span developmentalists believe that many of the age-related changes we find in intelligence, such as those emphasized by John Horn, are cohort effects rather than actual age changes. (You may want to read again the part of chapter 2 on research strategies where we described cohort studies in the context of a combined cross-sectional longitudinal method.) In general, these

Box 5.1
COMPARISON OF PIAGETIAN COGNITIVE STRUCTURAL AND PSYCHOMETRIC APPROACHES TO INTELLIGENCE

By now you probably have guessed that Piaget's views about intelligence differ from the views of Cattell and Horn. Although there are differences, there are similarities as well.

Piaget began his career as a developmental psychologist by working in Binet's laboratory, but he was more intrigued by the errors individuals made on the tests than by their correct answers. Piaget and the psychometricians agree that intelligence has a genetic component and that the maturation of thought processes is critical to understanding intelligence. The two views also agree that the most important aspect of intelligence is reasoning.

The most obvious difference between Piaget and the psychometric theorists lies in their views on the course of mental growth. The psychometric theorists are interested in quantifying mental growth, which often produces a number to describe the person's general level of intellectual functioning and to predict intelligence from one age to other ages, since it is argued that IQ is reasonably stable. The psychometric approach, then, maximizes individual differences and seeks to measure them. The Piagetian approach essentially ignores individual differences. Piaget emphasizes the dynamic nature of intelligence and how it qualitatively changes. He is particularly concerned with how new cognitive structures emerge.

Another difference between the two approaches is evident in a comparison of their views on genetics. While both approaches stress the importance of genes in determining intelligence, the psychometric theorists are interested in differences across individuals—for example, they are very interested in how scores from a random sample of 5,000 individuals fall into place on a distribution of scores. Piaget, on the other hand, focuses more on changes within the individual that shape the organization of intelligence—for example, in how egocentrism constrains the way the individual organizes information about the world (Elkind, 1969).

researchers have conducted a number of large-scale studies in which they have shown that cross-sectional data support a number of age changes in intelligence, whereas longitudinal and combined cross-sectional longitudinal data do not.

For example, in 1956 Schaie administered two intelligence tests, Thurstone's Primary Mental Abilities and Schaie's Test of Behavioral Rigidity, to 500 adults ranging in age from twenty-one to seventy. Seven years later, 301 of the adults were retested with the same tests. In analyzing the intelligence test data, four main aspects of intelligence were revealed: (1) *crystallized intelligence,* formal reasoning and abstract thinking; (2) *cognitive flexibility,* the ability to shift from one way of thinking to another within a context of familiar intellectual operations; (3) *Visuomotor flexibility,* the skill to shift from familiar to unfamiliar patterns in tasks requiring coordination between visual and motor abilities (e.g., having to copy words but interchange capitals with lowercase letters); (4) *visualization,* the ability to organize and process visual materials (e.g., finding a simple figure contained in a complex one or identifying a picture that is incomplete).

When the test data were organized cross-sectionally, the traditional pattern of early decline in intellectual functioning appeared. However, when the data were analyzed longitudinally, a decline in only one of the four areas, visuomotor flexibility, was noted.

The Baltes and Schaie study found no strong age-related change in cognitive flexibility. On the important dimensions of crystallized intelligence and visualization, a systematic, steady increase in scores for the various age groups occurred through early and middle adulthood and into late adulthood.

John Horn (Horn & Donaldson, 1980), challenges the position of Baltes and Schaie, claiming it is oversimplified and overoptimistic. He believes that the longer a person lives the more likely it is that some important aspect of intellectual performance will decline. And he argues that more research is needed before questions on adult mental processes are satisfactorily answered.

Baltes and Schaie (1976) have countered that Horn and Donaldson do not understand their theoretical position, misrepresent their data, and are guilty of selectively quoting from their writings. Schaie (1979) summarized what he has learned from his research on psychometric intelligence: First, reliable decline in intellectual abilities does not occur until very old age (the late eighties for most people) and does not occur for all abilities or all individuals. Second, for most individuals, there is a decline in abilities involving speed of response. Third, a decline in intelligence is likely to be found in those people with severe cardiovascular disease at any age and for people in socially deprived environments beginning in the late fifties and early sixties.

Of these three conclusions, the first is perhaps the most important; it is directly counter to that of Horn and Donaldson and is of considerable practical significance. Fortunately, some recent ideas developed by Nancy Denney may point the way to clarifying the nature of intellectual changes in mid-life.

The Exercise of Mental Abilities

Nancy Denney (1981) believes that in order to better understand cognitive activity across the life span we should distinguish between **unexercised ability** (level of performance that can be expected if the individual has had no exercise and/or training on the ability in question) and **optimally exercised ability** (level of performance expected if optimal exercise and/or training has occurred). The proposed developmental levels for these two types of ability are

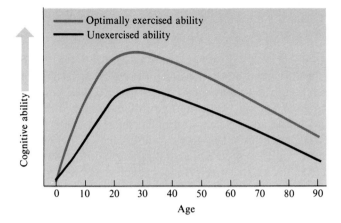

Figure 5.3   Hypothesized relationship between age and both unexercised ability and optimally exercised ability. (Nancy Wadsworth Denney, ''Aging and Cognitive Changes'' in *Handbook of Developmental Psychology,* edited by B. J. Wolman, © 1982, p. 819. Reprinted by permission of Prentice-Hall, Inc., Englewood Cliffs, N.J.)

shown in figure 5.3, which indicates that both ability groups increase up to early adulthood and decrease gradually thereafter. The curve for unexercised ability level has been drawn to decrease starting in early adulthood because abilities that are not exercised, such as those measured by performance subtests of intelligence tests and abstract problem-solving tasks, begin to decline in early adulthood.

The curve for optimally exercised ability also has been drawn to indicate a decrease starting early in adulthood because even in abilities that are the most resistant to age-change effects, such as verbal abilities and practical problem-solving abilities, there may be some decline. The region between the two types of abilities in the figure represents the degree to which exercise and/or training can affect abilities. Of course, exercise or training can accumulate over a long period of time, even years or decades. Thus some types of ability might be essentially unexercised for many young adults but optimally exercised for middle-aged adults. Such abilities should not decline from young adulthood to middle age. Indeed, they might even improve.

To illustrate the importance of distinguishing between unexercised and optimally exercised abilities, Denney (Denney & Palmer, in press; Denney & Pearce, 1981) conducted two investigations. In the first study adult performance on a traditional problem-solving task was compared with performance on a series of practical problems to determine whether different types of problem-solving abilities exhibit different developmental functions. Denney and Palmer found that adults between the ages of twenty and seventy-nine showed a linear decrease in performance on the traditional problem-solving task, whereas there was an increase in performance on the practical problems up until the forties and fifties and a decline thereafter.

In the second study, adults of different ages were compared on three types of practical problems—problems that young adults would be most likely to have to deal with, problems that middle-aged adults would most likely have to deal with, and problems that elderly adults would most likely have to deal with in their everyday lives. Performance on the traditional problem-solving task decreased linearly with age during the adult years, and performance on the practical problems increased from the twenties to the thirties and decreased thereafter. However, when the young adult, middle-aged adult, and elderly adult problems were analyzed separately, it was found that performance decreased linearly on the young adult problems, whereas performance increased up to the thirties, remained relatively stable through the fifties, and decreased thereafter on both the middle-aged adult problems and the elderly adult problems.

The results of these two studies are consistent with the proposed model of unexercised and optimally exercised cognitive abilities. The ability tested by the traditional problem-solving task is one that is not exercised very much during the adult years and, thus, it follows the unexercised ability curve rather closely. Practical problem-solving ability is exercised much more frequently by adults and, thus, is more likely to be maintained through the middle-adult years. The reason the twenty-year-olds' performance is lower than the thirty-, forty-, and fifty-year-olds' performance is, according to the model, that the twenty-year-olds have less frequently had to deal with the types of practical problems employed in the Denney and Palmer study and used for the middle-aged and elderly adult problems in the Denney and Pearce study. As a result, they do not approach their optimally exercised ability level with these types of problems. Only the middle-aged adults who have had more experience with such problems and yet who have a relatively high optimally exercised ability level perform better.

According to the model, the elderly adults do not perform well even on problems designed specifically to be the types of problems they would most likely have to deal with in their own lives because during the later adult years the declining level of optimally exercised ability actually limits their performance.

Denney (1981) suggests that there are undoubtedly limitations to this model of adult cognitive development. For example, the effects of experience on performance are described only in the most general sense. And the likelihood of sex and cohort differences would require further changes in the model. Contextual factors such as motivation, health, and the nature of the task used to study cognitive activity also need to be taken into account in the study of adult intelligence. Nonetheless, the idea that it is important to distinguish between unexercised and optimally exercised mental abilities is an intriguing addition to our conceptualization of adult intelligence.

Conclusions About Intellectual Decline

The group of researchers headed by Schaie, Baltes, and LaBouvie-Vief argue that there is a great deal of plasticity in the cognitive functioning of elderly individuals. Rather than evaluating such plasticity, our standardized tests of intelligence have been designed to measure stability. Furthermore, the majority of them have been developed for use with younger individuals. In the Imagine section that opened this chapter, we suggested that studies of cognitive intervention are important in understanding the nature of intelligence in late adulthood. The importance of plasticity in adult intelligence also supports the view of intellectual development proposed by Nancy Denney. Since some cognitive activities are underexercised in most individuals, using such abilities should improve performance based on them. However, Denney has speculated that unexercised and exercised abilities are closer together in childhood and old age and further apart during the young and middle adult years because of the data on both the structural changes in cognitive abilities across the life span and the relative effectiveness of training on various age groups (refer to figure 5.3). There seems to be a growing consensus that as the child develops, his or her cognitive abilities become more differentiated. That is, with increasing age during childhood, a larger number of factors appear to represent cognitive ability, with lower correlations between the factors and a weak general factor (e.g., Asch, 1936; Garrett, 1946). Although less research has been conducted on structural changes in adults, some evidence suggests that there is a reintegration of cognitive abilities during late adulthood—that is, there are fewer factors, higher correlations between the factors, and a much stronger general factor (e.g., Balinsky, 1941; Green & Berkowitz, 1964). Even though there are some methodological problems with the research conducted on this topic, the suggestion that cognitive abilities differentiate as the child develops and reintegrate in old age merits more attention. Denney (1981) points out that the training (cognitive intervention that attempts to improve cognitive functioning) research also indicates that there may be more room for experience to have an effect on cognitive ability in young and middle-aged adults than in either younger or older individuals.

Thus, while Nancy Denney (1981) agrees with Paul Baltes (1980) that we ought to be looking at unexercised mental abilities and their plasticity in late adulthood, she does not believe that there is as much room for change in late adulthood as in early and middle adulthood.

Psychometric theorists, then, disagree about the degree of plasticity in intellectual functioning during late adulthood, as well as the extent to which such functioning declines.

PHYSICAL HEALTH AND COGNITION

Clearly, at some point in late adulthood, biological processes begin to degenerate. In this section we evaluate the relationship between physical health/disease and cognition.

The scope of biological degeneration supports John Horn's claims that the decline of fluid intellectual abilities is due to physiological deterioration involving the brain and nervous system. However, it is important to distinguish whether such declines are genetically related or are more often due to life stress and disease.

Intellectual decline is more likely to be observed in individuals who are experiencing some pathology, such as a cardiovascular disease. A well-known study linking health and cognition was conducted by James Birren and his associates (Birren, Butler, Greenhouse, Sokoloff, & Yarrow, 1963). On the basis of health status, the men in the study were classified into two groups: group 1, those with only trivial incidences of diseases, such as partial deafness or varicose veins, and group 2, those who showed evidence of a potentially serious disease, such as arteriosclerosis. (Even though the individuals in group 2 showed these characteristics, they were not seriously ill at the time they were studied.)

The two groups performed differently on a number of cognitive measures. The scores of the "healthy" men on the verbal part of the Weschler Adult Intelligence Test were significantly higher than those of the "unhealthy" men. And a number of other correlations between health and cognitive activity appeared in the assessment of the group 2 men that did not emerge for the group 1 men.

Investigations that have focused on specific aspects of health have also shown that deteriorating health conditions influence cognitive activity. Individuals with various brain disorders, cardiovascular disease, and hypertension do not perform as well on measures of intellectual functioning as healthy individuals do (e.g., Spieth, 1965; Wang, 1973; Wilkie & Eisdorfer, 1971).

Adults not only think, but they can think creatively as well. Next we look at the course of creative thinking in the adult years.

CREATIVITY

Most of us would like to be creative. What is it about someone like Thomas Edison that made him able to invent so many things? Was he simply more intelligent than most people? Did he spend long hours toiling away in private? Surprisingly, when Edison was a young boy his teacher told him he was too dumb to learn anything! And there are other examples of famous individuals whose creative genius went unnoticed when they were younger (Larson, 1973): Walt Disney was fired from a newspaper job because he did not have any good ideas; Enrico Caruso's music teacher informed him that he could not sing and that his voice was terrible; Winston Churchill failed one year of secondary school.One of the reasons, as we shall soon see, that such creative genius is overlooked is the difficulty we have in defining and measuring creativity.

Table 5.2

GUILFORD'S COMPONENTS OF DIVERGENT (CREATIVE) THINKING

1. *Word Fluency:* How facile are you with words? For example, name as many words as possible and as fast as possible that contain the letter z.

2. *Ideational Fluency:* Here you have to name words that belong to a particular class. For example, name as many objects as you can that weigh less than one pound.

3. *Associational Fluency:* In this type of divergent thinking you have to name words that are associated with other words, such as by similarity of meaning. For example, name as many words as possible that mean "easy."

4. *Expressional Fluency:* Here you have to put words together to meet the requirements of sentence structure. For example, write as many sentences as you can that have four words, each word starting with these letters: *T, a, s, a.* (One sentence using these letters might be: *Tomorrow a salesman arrives.*)

5. *Spontaneous Flexibility:* Even when you are not asked to give divergent answers, do you give unique answers as well as common answers? For example, if you are asked what a paper clip can be used for, do you spontaneously generate different categories of use for the paper clip?

6. *Adaptive Flexibility:* In this type of divergent thinking you must be able to vary your ideas widely when this is called for. For example, if you are shown a series of matchsticks lined up on a table, you may be asked to put them together to form four triangles.

7. *Redefinition:* You might be asked to say how specific common objects can be used for new purposes.

8. *Originality:* This time you would be required to name some unique ways to use an object. For example, what are some unusual ways to use hairpins?

Source: Guilford, 1967. All Rights Reserved. Reprinted by permission.

Definition and Measurement of Creativity

The prevailing belief of experts who study creativity is that intelligence and creativity are not the same (e.g., Getzel, 1975; Richards, 1976; Wallach, 1973). And while intelligence has been defined in different ways, so has creativity. David Ausubel (1968) emphasized that *creativity* is one of the most ambiguous and confusing terms in psychology. He believes the term *creative* should not be applied to as many people as it is but should be reserved for describing people who make unique and original contributions to society.

J. P. Guilford's model of intelligence (1967) has important implications for creative thinking. The aspect of his theory of intelligence that is most closely related to creativity is what he calls **divergent thinking,** a type of thinking that produces many different answers to a single question. Divergent thinking is distinguished from **convergent thinking,** a type of thinking that moves toward one correct answer. For example, there is one correct answer to this question: "How many quarters can you get from sixty dimes?" It calls for convergent thinking. But there are many possible answers to this question: "What are some uses for a coat hanger?" This question requires divergent thinking. Going off in different directions may sometimes lead to more productive answers. Examples of what Guilford means by divergent thinking (his term for creativity) and ways of measuring it are shown in table 5.2.

Paul Torrance (1966) has given an even broader definition of creativity than Guilford's. He talks about creativity in much the same way that general intelligence has been described. That is, Torrance views creativity as problem solving that goes off in different directions. Creativity is the process of first identifying a problem and then carrying through until the results of the problem solving are communicated. In between, the person searches for answers, identifies difficulties, makes hunches, develops hypotheses, and then modifies and retests them.

Most of the work on creativity has been conducted in the psychometric tradition; that is, extensive efforts have been made to measure creativity. However, some efforts have been designed to develop ways to encourage creativity. Michael Wallach and Nathan Kogan (1965), for example, attempted to refine the ability to separate creativity from intelligence and specified how creative people in the arts and sciences think. People who are rated as highly creative are asked to probe introspectively into what it is that enables them to produce creative pieces of work. Two major conclusions evolved from this self-analysis by creative adults: (1) They have what is called *associative content* in their effort to attain novel solutions to problems. (2) They have the freedom to entertain a wide range of possible solutions in a playful manner. These responses led Wallach and Kogan to administer their creativity tests in a relaxed, nonthreatening, informal context and to remove time limits from the tests.

Most experts on creativity stress the importance of *flexibility,* a term referring to the replacement of a fixed set of ideas by a set of alternative views about a problem. The use of imagery seems to be linked to flexible thinking and creative problem solving (Durio, 1975). For example, compared with verbalization, imagery seems to lead to a more playful shifting from one solution to the next (Walkup, 1965). *Brainstorming* is another technique that has been effective in several programs developed to stimulate creativity. In brainstorming situations, a topic is presented for consideration and participants are encouraged to suggest ideas related to it. Criticism of the ideas contributed must be withheld initially so that the flow of ideas will not stop. The more freewheeling the ideas, the better. Participants are also encouraged to combine ideas that have already been suggested. In another useful technique, called *playing with improbabilities,* the individual is stimulated to think about what is likely to follow an unlikely occurrence. For example, what would happen if there were no jails or prisons? What would happen if computers were able to develop feelings? And so forth.

The Developmental Course of Creativity in Adulthood

Two studies on creativity in adulthood have been more widely quoted than others (Dennis, 1966; Lehman, 1953, 1960). In one investigation (Lehman, 1953), the creative products of recognized adults were chartered (see figure 5.4). The quality of productivity was highest in the decade of the thirties and then gradually declined. It was argued that approximately 80 percent of the most important creative contributions are completed by the age of fifty.

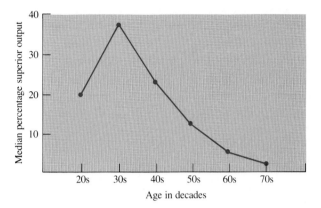

Figure 5.4   Percentage of superior output as a function of age. This generalized curve represents a combination of various fields of endeavor and various estimates of quality. Data are from Lehman, 1953, table 34.

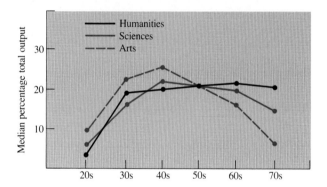

Figure 5.5   Percentage of total output as a function of age. The humanities, sciences, and arts are represented by the means of several specific disciplines. Data are from Dennis, 1966, table 1.

Wayne Dennis (1966) studied the total productivity, not just the superior works, of creative people in the arts, sciences, and humanities who had lived long lives. As can be seen in figure 5.5, the point in adult development at which creative production peaked varied from one discipline to another. In the humanities, the seventies was just as creative a decade as the forties. Artists and scientists, however, began to show a decline in creative productivity in their fifties. In all instances, the twenties was the least productive decade in terms of creativity. Nonetheless, there are exceptions: Benjamin Dugger discovered the antibotic aureomycin when he was 72. In a study of Nobel laureates in science, their first major paper was published at the average age of twenty-five. All laureates in this study who were past seventy, however, continued to publish scholarly papers in scientific journals. These facts support the belief that people who are bright and productive during their early adult years maintain their creativity in their later years.

Pablo Picasso was a highly creative artist in late adulthood.

Table 5.3

MEANS FOR FLUENCY, FLEXIBILITY, ORIGINALITY, AND SELF-ESTEEM IN ALL AGE GROUPS

Age Group	Fluency	Flexibility	Originality	Self-esteem
Young adults 18–25 years n = 70	30.9	19.1	18.9	34.1
Adults 26–39 years n = 58	30.2	18.4	18.6	36.5
Middle adults 40–60 years n = 51	36.2	21.1	19.9	38.2
Elderly 61–84 years n = 39	22.3	15.4	15.2	31.5

Source: Jaquish & Ripple, 1981, p. 115.

Table 5.4

THE RELATIONSHIP BETWEEN CREATIVITY AND SELF-ESTEEM IN EARLY, MIDDLE, AND LATE ADULTHOOD

Age Group	Fluency	Flexibility	Originality
Self-esteem and Divergent Thinking			
Young adults	−0.04	−0.01	−0.01
Adults	0.17	0.17	0.15
Middle adults	0.29*	0.30**	0.31**
Elderly	0.41***	0.43***	0.13

*$p \leq 0.05$
**$p \leq 0.01$
***$p \leq 0.001$

Source: Jaquish & Ripple, 1981, p. 116.

Clearly, it is inappropriate to conclude that there is a linear decrease in creativity during the adult years. One recent investigation suggests that it may be wise to consider factors such as self-esteem when we evaluate the creativity of adults (Jaquish & Ripple, 1981). Divergent thinking scores—fluency, flexibility, and originality—and self-esteem were assessed in 213 adults between the ages of eighteen and eighty-four. Divergent thinking scores did not decline as early or as precipitously as reported in previous work (e.g., Alpaugh & Birren, 1977). Actually, middle-aged adults—aged forty to sixty—scored highest on the measures of self-esteem and creativity, and when decline did appear, it seem to be more characteristic of quantity (fluency) than quality (flexibility) (see table 5.3). In middle and late adulthood, but not early adulthood, self-esteem and creativity were associated (see table 5.4, in which the data are Pearson *r* correlation coefficients).

Table 5.5

HYPOTHESIZED STAGE OF CREATIVITY IN ADULTHOOD

Type of Creativity	*Age Range*
Expressive spontaneity: Creativity that may have a biological base and may be suppressed by formal education; shows up in children's games, dance, drawings	Childhood, appearing again in the late thirties
Technical proficiency: Creativity that is a function of the refinement of skills, as in concert instrumental work, dance	Typical of the twenties and forties
Inventive ingenuity: Creativity as it is expressed in idealized drawing, gadgetry, tinkering	Typical of the thirites and fifties
Innovative flexibility: Creativity that allows one to modify and adapt basic ideas, systems, and organizations for new purposes	Ages twenty-five to fifty
Emergentive originality: Creation of totally new or original ideas	After fifty

Source: Taylor, 1974.

A contextual view of adulthood suggests that a number of psychological and social changes may influence creativity. In a discussion of life-span creativity, Jean and Michael Romaniuk (1981) provide an example from the academic world of how incentives for productivity may influence an individual. Tenure and attenuation of pressure to publish may have an effect on creative accomplishment. Shifts in career interests and activities, such as from research to administrative activity, revised views concerning career goals and job security, and attention to refining earlier creative accomplishments, may influence creativity. And the opening of new research fields and the saturation of existing fields may also influence creative accomplishments.

In addition to environmental circumstances that may influence creativity, one model of creativity attempts to delineate qualitatively different stages of development through the adult years (Taylor, 1974). Creative ability is said to undergo five sequential stages—expressive spontaneity, technical proficiency, inventive ingenuity, innovative flexibility, and emergentive originality. See table 5.5 for an explanation of these forms of creativity that may appear at different points in the adult years.

In summary, we have seen that creativity is an elusive concept, difficult to define and measure. We have also found that creativity does not develop in a fixed and stable manner through the adult years. Further, we have discovered that some types of creativity may appear at different points in development and that environmental experiences may modify the individual's creativity. For example, individuals who experience an education that encourages flexibility, alternative solutions to problems, and the use of imagery and brainstorming to solve problems may increase their creativity. Next we look at the role of education in the lives of adults; in particular, we will examine the factors that stimulate adults to initiate or continue their education.

ADULT EDUCATION

In recent years, there has been a tremendous increase in adult learning—both formal and informal. Adults today constitute more than half of all full-time and part-time college students and will make up well over half the total in the years to come. Millions more are learning at their places of employment, through private lessons, in local school districts, in their churches, through their professional associations, and in voluntary community organizations. Even more are learning on their own through television, libraries, museums, correspondence courses, and other sources (Aslanian & Brickell, 1980).

Why Adults Initiate or Continue Their Education

Cyril Houle (1961) suggested that five factors lead adults to lifelong learning: family background; teachers and schools; public libraries; occupation; and the exchange of friends. One investigation (Morstain & Smart, 1977) identified the following five distinct types of adult learners: (1) nondirected learners with no specific goals; (2) social learners who want to improve their social interests and personal associations; (3) stimulation-seeking learners who want to escape boredom and routine, (4) career-oriented learners who learn because of occupational interests, and (5) life change learners who want to improve multiple facets of their lives (e.g., career, intellectual, and social aspects).

Individuals who continue to show an interest in education and learning throughout adulthood are often already well educated. Individuals who are highly motivated, have had past success, have good information networks, and have adequate funds get more and better education. In contrast, those already dragging in the educational race when they reach early adulthood continue to fall farther and farther behind as they go through the adult years. For this latter group, the same things that led to relatively early exit from school contribute to a lack of interest in returning (Cross, 1978).

However, in one investigation undertaken by the College Entrance Examination Board (Brickell, 1979), it was found that economic barriers are not always at the heart of why adults do not initiate or continue their education. Information was collected from 3,500 workers in a truck plant to find out why 99.5 percent did not use the tuition reimbursement plan that their own union leaders negotiated into their current contract with the manufacturer. The tuition reimbursement plan is a method designed to remove economic barriers to learning by having the company pay for any job-related training—training that can include earning college degrees. The economic barriers were removed, but the workers themselves never become motivated to go to school, to take television or correspondence courses, or even to undertake independent study. Apparently, the economic barriers were less real than rationalization.

We do not have good information about why some adults do not continue their learning. In one analysis of an extensive amount of data on the characteristics of adults who discontinued their learning, it was concluded that 90 percent of whatever it is that leads adults to participate in and drop out from adult education has not been identified (Anderson & Darenwald, 1979). The strongest relationships among a generally weak set suggested that younger adults are more likely to drop out of a learning situation than older adults, that those with fewer years of schooling are more likely to drop out than those with more education, and those who are black are more likely not to continue their education than others.

Why Adults Do Not Initiate or Continue Their Education

Patricia Cross (1978) examined the results of a number of surveys that have asked adults not oriented toward education to indicate the possible barriers that have kept them from learning. She concluded that three such barriers exist:

1. *Situational barriers*—those that arise for the individual in a particular situation, such as a lack of time due to home or job responsibilities, lack of transportation, geographical isolation, lack of child care, and so forth.
2. *Dispositional barriers*—those referring to attitudes about learning and perceptions of oneself as a learner—feeling too old to learn, showing a lack of confidence, or being bored with school.
3. *Institutional barriers*—those erected by learning institutions or agencies that exclude or discourage certain groups of learners—included are such factors as inconvenient schedules, full-time fees for part-time study, or restrictive locations.

Transitions and Triggers as Instigators of Adult Education

In the book *Americans in Transition,* Carol Aslanian and Henry Brickell (1980) describe a number of life changes as possible reasons for adult learning. They indicate that many transitions occur and that information on current and prospective social and economic changes makes it apparent that more adults will experience life transitions in the future. Changes in population, mobility, technology, occupation, housing, income, inflation, government, family life, politics, minority affairs, and leisure will signal an even faster rate of change in adult life than ever before.

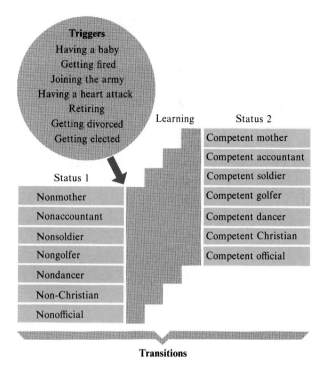

Figure 5.6   Examples of transitions and triggers.

In an investigation probing for reasons for career changes in adults, Aslanian and Brickell (1980) found significant transitions for many adults. Those transitions included entry, progression, and exit not only with respect to specific jobs but even with respect to career fields. They concluded that some 40 million adults in the United States anticipated making a job or career change.

Life transitions may be a reason for learning, and life events may trigger learning. Examples of these life transitions and triggers are presented in figure 5.6. Aslanian and Brickell (1980) end their important book on adult education with a number of questions which indicate that we need much more information about the nature of adult education.

Presumably a large number of adults experience important transitions in their lives. Why do some adults choose learning as a means to cope with these transitions while others do not? Do other adults fail at their transitions? Or do they have alternative ways of coping that make it unnecessary for them to learn?

Why do the advantaged learn more often than the disadvantaged? Do the disadvantaged not have as many transitions, or do they not see school as useful in making those transitions?

Is there some optimum match between a given type of transition and a given provider of learning? Are employers the best providers for those in career transition?

Adult participation in learning is increasing but at a slower rate than in earlier years. If social and economic changes are taking place at an ever-increasing rate, why isn't adult participation in learning taking place at an ever-increasing rate?

Is there some maximum proportion of adults in the society who can be engaged in learning at the same time? Is there some maximum proportion of all adult time that can be constructively dedicated to learning rather than to other activities needed to maintain society?

In the next chapter we further explore the cognitive world of adults as we provide an overview of memory development and information processing.

Summary

Important aspects of the study of adult cognition include cognitive stages and structures, intelligence and the psychometric approach, the relationship between physical health and intelligence, creativity, and adult education. According to Piaget's ideas about formal operational thought, adult thought is no different from adolescent thought. Formal thought is logical, idealized, and abstract. Modifications of Piaget's ideas have included attempts to discover a fifth stage of thought that characterizes adult thought, a form that is different from the formal thought of adolescence. One fifth-stage view suggests that thinking about formal thought, improvement in logic, and specialization in abstract educational disciplines represent adult thought. Perhaps the most provocative view of cognitive structure in adulthood is the adult contextual perspective, a view that has been stressed by Labouvie-Vief and others. In their view, the abstract, idealized, formal thought of adolescence is replaced in early adulthood by a more pragmatic orientation to the real world, an orientation that recognizes the importance of channeling one's energy into finding one's niche in a world of complex social systems. Viewed from a child-centered Piagetian perspective, such pragmatism may be interpreted as regression to concrete thought, but from the adult contextual view, this orientation to reality represents an adaptive developmental advance.

Not only has there been increasing interest in the contextual model of adult cognition, but there also has been increased interest in social cognition, which refers to reasoning about social matters. Reasoning about one's self, about others, and perspective taking are among the most frequently investigated aspects of social cognition. Many of the adult contextual stage theorists include ideas about social cognition in their description of how cognitive stages unfold during adulthood. For example, Norma Haan believes that we need to consider a number of cognitive structures that include moral reasoning and attachment to others. Lawrence Kohlberg agrees with Labouvie-Vief that adulthood is characterized by increased recognition of the relative nature of knowledge, uncertainty, and the arbitrary nature of the social units in which the adult lives. John Flavell believes that an important task for adults is the ability to monitor their social thoughts. As we go through the adult years, our social cognitions probably change—in middle adulthood a time perspective becomes more dominant, and in late adulthood changing social networks may dominate more of our cognitive activity. Evidence exists that the social interaction of the elderly is linked to their social cognitive knowledge.

The psychometric approach to intelligence emphasizes a measurement-based orientation, often the use of standardized tests of intelligence. Using psychometric tests to buttress his ideas, John Horn believes crystallized intelligence, based primarily on education and experience, increases in adulthood, while fluid intelligence, comprised of cognitive abilities like abstract thinking, declines with age. K. Warner Schaie, Paul Baltes, and Gisela Labouvie-Vief vehemently disagree with Horn. They believe that bias partly explains the lower scores of the elderly on intelligence tests. After all, most intelligence tests were designed for children and young adults, not the elderly. Further, they argue that the environment of the elderly is not culturally and educationally enriched. And they believe that because many younger people have a negative view of old age, the elderly face discrimination. In sum, they believe that there is a great deal of plasticity in intelligence during late adulthood. Although Nancy Denney agrees with Paul Baltes that we ought to be looking at unexercised mental abilities in late adulthood, she does not believe that there is as much room for change in late as in early and middle adulthood.

As adults we not only think, but we can think creatively as well. While definitional and measurement problems plague creativity research, creative thought is an important aspect of our development in adulthood. Research on developmental changes suggests that in the arts creative thought peaks in the thirties, whereas in the humanities creativity remains high even into the early part of late adulthood. Self-esteem may be important to consider in relation to creativity; in one investigation, both self-esteem and creativity peaked during mid-life, and during middle and late adulthood, self-esteem and creativity were associated. It is important to consider the context in which creativity occurs, particularly the use of strategies to increase creativity such as imagery, flexibility, brainstorming, and few constrictions on thought.

Adult education of all sorts has been increasing and will continue to do so for years to come. Adults initiate or continue their education for many reasons: love of learning, to improve social and personal associations, to avoid boredom, and to improve careers.

Review Questions

1. Discuss the Piagetian view of adult cognition and research on formal operational thought in adulthood.
2. Describe the various adult contextual views of cognitive structure in adulthood.
3. Why do the adult contextual theorists believe Piaget's view is an inappropriate model for conceptualizing adult cognition?
4. Discuss the nature of social cognition in adulthood.
5. Compare the Piagetian and psychometric perspectives on adult cognition.
6. What is the nature of the argument between John Horn and the Baltes/Schaie/Labouvie-Vief group?
7. Outline Nancy Denney's ideas on the exercise of mental abilities.
8. Discuss plasticity and cognitive intervention in late adulthood.
9. What is the relation between physical health and cognition in adulthood?
10. Try to define creativity and describe what you think is the best way to measure it.
11. What is the developmental course of creativity in adulthood?
12. What factors cause adults to initiate and continue their education, what causes them not to initiate or continue their education, and what are some of the transitions and triggers of adult education?

Further Readings

Aslanian, C. B., & Brickell, H. M. (1980). *Americans in transition: Life changes as reasons for adult learning.* Princeton, NJ: College Board Publications.

An excellent source of information about adult education. The authors incorporate current thinking about perspectives of adult development in their attempt to show how transitions and triggers stimulate adult learning. Easy reading.

Dolen, L. S., & Bearison, D. J. (1982). Social interaction and social cognition in aging. *Human Development, 25,* 430–442.

A good overview of different aspects of social cognition and how they are measured. Reveals links between social cognitive knowledge and social interaction. Medium reading difficulty.

Jaquish, G. A., & Ripple, R. E. (1981). Cognitive creative abilities and self-esteem across the adult life span. *Human Development, 24,* 110–119.

An overview of what is known about creativity in adulthood, including information about the relationship between creativity and self-esteem at different points in adult development. Reasonably easy reading.

Labouvie-Vief, G. (1982). Dynamic development and mature autonomy: A theoretical prologue. *Human Development, 25,* 161–191.

Labouvie-Vief's contextual perspective of adult development, in which she argues that there is considerable plasticity and change in adult development. Moderately difficult reading.

Willis, S. L., & Baltes, P. B. (1980). Intelligence in adulthood and aging: Contemporary issues. In L. W. Poon (Ed.), *Aging in the 1980s* (pp. 239–252). Washington, D.C.: American Psychological Association.

An overview of issues in the study of psychometric intelligence. Provides an optimistic picture of intellectual functioning in late adulthood. Moderately difficult reading.

6

INFORMATION PROCESSING

James C. Bartlett

I **MAGINE** *that we human beings are actually computers.*
Like other computers, we human computers may have input devices that take *analog signals* (patterns of auditory or visual energy) and convert these signals into *digital codes* (for example, sequences of ls and Os). These digital codes are stored briefly in *buffer memories,* but subsequently they are identified through comparison with digital codes stored permanently in a central or *long-term memory.* The identification process provides symbols for the digital codes, and the symbols are placed in a temporary or *short-term memory.* What we think of as consciousness is perhaps nothing more than the scanning of symbols in the short-term memory. By the way, it is not necessary to assume that the symbols held in short-term memory must correspond to words in spoken language. We human computers have our own internal languages, just as manufactured computers do.

Once symbols have been deposited in the short-term memory, they are available for use in *programs.* Such programs may include an executive program that calls up subsidiary programs. Programs involve the additional *processing* of the information (symbols) in short-term memory. The nature of this processing depends upon what the computer (you or I) is doing—reading, daydreaming, worrying about an exam, planning a romantic rendezvous, working arithmetic problems, and so on. Our attending to information corresponds to the processing of this information by the executive program or subsidiary programs. Our ignoring information corresponds to the executive or subsidiary program's *not* processing the information. If information in short-term memory is not processed by programs, it is soon lost from this memory. For example, it may be erased by new information entering the memory.

It is reasonable to assume that the computer (you or I) has a type of backup memory to support the short-term memory. When the computer is solving a complex problem, relevant information is placed in this backup memory so that it can be rapidly placed in the short-term memory when needed. This backup memory might be called intermediate-term memory (Hunt, 1971), since it is longer lasting than short-term memory but not so long lasting as long-term memory.

In many situations it may be useful for the computer to make a permanent record of information in short-term memory, that is, to make a new long-term memory *file.* Indeed, this is one way that the computer learns. An important problem in such cases is not so much in making the long-term memory files but in ensuring that these files will subsequently be *retrievable*. Long-term memory is vast, and retrieval of information can fail. Fortunately, the problem can be solved—to some extent—by means of programs that organize material in memory. Just as a library is organized in order to facilitate the finding of books, the computer's long-term memory can be organized by programs in order to facilitate the retrieval of files. There may be other important "trick" programs (those involving imagery, for example) for forming retrievable files in long-term memory. Differences between people (computers) with "good" and "poor" memories may reflect differences in the programs they use for processing information in short-term memory.

Having imagined that people are computers, let's also imagine how young adult computers might differ from elderly computers. Do young and elderly computers have different programs for perceiving, attending, problem solving, learning, and so on? This seems plausible and may very well explain why memory, for example, is sometimes deficient in older individuals. Or is it that young and older computers may have many of the same programs but differ with respect to processing speed? Timothy Salthouse and Benjamin Somberg (1982) ask us to "consider a contrast between an old, obsolete, slow computer and a modern, state-of-the-art, fast computer. The two machines might operate on the same types of information and even use the same programs . . . and yet the output would be produced much more quickly on the faster computer than on the slower one" (p. 203). Still another possibility is that intermediate-term memory (also called working memory by some investigators) is better in one type of computer than in the other. These and other possibilities have been considered by psychologists interested in information processing across the life span. They illustrate something about the information-processing approach to cognition, which is based, to a considerable extent, on a metaphor relating human beings to computers. This approach assumes that human cognition entails information processing and that information processing whether human or nonhuman can be described in the same kinds of terms (memories, programs, and so forth). We describe this approach more fully below.

INTRODUCTION

In chapter 5 we considered the cognitive stage and psychometric approaches to cognitive changes in adulthood. In this chapter we present the information-processing approach. We begin by briefly tracing its history and delineating its most essential characteristics. Then we consider specific areas of research within information-processing psychology and present information about age differences and changes within each of these areas, including perception, attention, memory, and thinking, which includes solving problems, acquiring concepts, comprehending language, and *metacognition,* that is, thinking about cognition. We should note at the outset that though the information-processing approach has many strengths, two limitations pertain to most of the research completed to date. First, the great majority of information-processing research is cross-sectional in nature, producing confoundings between age and cohort (see chapter 2). Second, most of this research involves comparisons between young adults and elderly adults, so that we know relatively little about information processing in middle adulthood. These limitations will doubtlessly be corrected; meanwhile, there has been tremendous progress in our understanding of information-processing differences between young adulthood and old age. The research we have available has been provocative for theory and has many exciting practical implications.

THE INFORMATION-PROCESSING APPROACH

According to the information-processing approach, mental activity is synonymous with the processing of information from the world. Such processing underlies **perception,** which is conceptualized as the encoding of information; **attention,** which controls what and how much information is encoded; **memory,** which allows access to knowledge needed for encoding and which also stores the products of encoding for later use; and **thinking,** which involves complex processes of organizing information, combining different types of information, selecting strategies for perceiving, remembering, attending to information, and so on. It should be stressed that perception, attention, memory and thinking are not considered as unitary processes; they are best considered as *functions* or *capacities,* each of which is based on many different processes. Thus many different processes presumably contribute to perception, memory, attention, and thought. The goal of scientists in this area is to study and understand the elementary processes that determine how perception works, how memory works, how attention works, and how thought works. Of course, all of these functions may work differently at different points of the life span. Such differences are the focus of the information-processing approach to adult development and aging.

The Roots of Information-Processing Theory

In the context of recent history, information processing has three clear influential sources (Siegler, 1982). The first is the field of **communications.** Beginning over a quarter of a century ago, communication scientists sought to develop a general model of how someone sends a message over a particular **channel** of communication to a specific **receiver** (e.g., Broadbent, 1958). In doing so, scientists developed ideas about how to define the information contained in a message, the capacity of different channels to transmit information, and the processes by which receivers pick up information. The theory was developed along physical science lines, drawing upon physics and electronics and treating radio and television transmissions as prototypical cases of communication phenomena to explain. However, the human was quickly added as a special case of communication phenomena to explain, with the different human sensory systems treated as the sources for information pickup (for example, seeing, hearing, feeling).

A second, closely related development was the growth of computer sciences and the interest in using the computer to model theories of artificial intelligence (e.g., Klahr & Wallace, 1975; Newell & Simon, 1972). Computers are essentially high-speed information systems that can be constructed and programmed. It was reasoned that computers offered a logical and concrete simplification of how information might be processed in the human mind. For example, both the computer and the mind employ *logic* and *rules* (Belmont & Butterfield, 1971; Wallace, 1977). Both have *limits* imposed on their capabilities to handle information and on what types of information can be processed. Some of these limitations have to do with the physical **hardware**—for the computer, the physical machinery; for the human, the limits of the brain and sensory systems. Other limitations are imposed by the **software**—for the computer, the programming; for the human, presumably, learning and development. Many experts believe that as progress is made in understanding computers, we will gain an increased understanding of how the human mind works. Some go so far as to claim that unless we have a working computer program that delineates the steps needed to complete human cognitive tasks, we really don't understand how the human mind might solve it (e.g., Simon, 1980). Thus some (but not all) of contemporary work on information processing is devoted to using the computer to model the steps involved in solving a variety of logical problems confronted by people in the everyday contexts of school (for example, reading and mathematics), work (for example, decision making), and leisure activities (for example, playing chess).

The third development that has influenced the information-processing field focuses on advances in the field of modern linguistics. From such scholars as Noam Chomsky (1965) have come brilliant models of how to describe the structure of language and the rules underlying linguistic productions. Since language is among the highest achievements of humans, it is a good candidate for building models of cognition. Information-processing psychologists have used models of language to understand how rules are organized in people's minds, how natural events are structured, and how people use rules to interpret events (e.g., Anderson, 1979; Schank & Abelson, 1977; Stein & Glenn, 1979; Yussen & Santrock, 1982).

PERCEPTION

A. T. Welford (1980) reviewed ideas about the nature of perceptual change in late adulthood and described some of the most important experiments that have been conducted. One aspect of perception that appears to show deficits as people get older is that of discriminating information that is relevant for some task from information that is irrelevant. For example, investigators have found that individuals in late adulthood have more difficulty than do young adults in detecting figures embedded in target designs (e.g., Crook et al., 1962). This difficulty may reflect age differences in attention, which we will consider subsequently.

Another perceptual problem that elderly individuals appear to have is perceiving information out of context. The process of listening to a conversation provides a relevant example. Older people often request repetition of what has been said, especially if there has been a sudden change in the topic being discussed. Thus one special technique for communicating with the elderly is to begin a conversation with an alerting remark, such as "I say," or "Listen to this." Any change in topic can be prefaced with a remark such as "Changing the subject. . . ."

A third sort of perceptual deficit that can occur in old age has been detected in laboratory experiments in which **masking** techniques are used. If a visual pattern is presented briefly and then, after a brief interval, another visual stimulus is given, the individual's perception of the first pattern may be impaired: the second stimulus has **masked** the first. Presumably it takes time for the data from the initial pattern to build up to a critical level at which they trigger a judgment and so become immune to interference by further stimulation. In the absence of a masking stimulus, data from the initial pattern can continue to be accumulated in some kind of **iconic** (sensory) image up to one-half second or so after the initial experience has stopped. It has been predicted that the time over which this can occur lengthens with age (e.g., Fozard, Wolf, Bell, McFarland, & Podolsky, 1977). It has been found that in order to see the pattern initially presented, individuals in their sixties required either a longer exposure or a longer interval before the masking stimulus than did individuals in their twenties (Kline & Szafran, 1975; Walsh, 1976).

A plausible interpretation of these results is that the rate of visual information processing becomes slower with age (Hoyer & Plude, 1980). This "perceptual slowing" may itself be due to stimulus-persistence; the visual system in elderly adults may be "slowed in rate of processing owing to the extended refractory period of aged neurons" (Hoyer & Plude, 1980, p. 231), a belief consistent with a large body of research (e.g., Botwinick, 1978). However, we still need to determine more precisely the mechanisms and locus of perceptual differences between young and elderly adults. Is age-related slowing due to changes in the photoreceptors of the retina (Pollack, 1978), a more peripheral explanation, or does slowing reflect changes in more central structures such as the visual cortex of the brain? Researchers are actively involved in attempting to answer such questions.

Practice Effects

Given that there are differences between young and elderly adults in various aspects of perception, to what extent can these differences be removed through practice? This was one of the questions raised by Timothy A. Salthouse and Benjamin L. Somberg (1982), who examined performance by young and elderly adults on a visual signal detection task over a period of fifty experimental sessions. Subjects taking the signal detection task viewed a display screen on which a pattern of sixty dots was presented. The dots were presented for a very short time period—one quarter of a second—and the subjects' task was to judge whether any of the dots were in motion. On half of the trials, a pattern of five dots was in motion (this was the signal), but on the remaining trials all of the dots were stationary.

The signal detection task devised by Salthouse and Somberg was difficult, and it was designed to demand very rapid perceptual processing. To the extent that there is perceptual slowing with age, we would expect young adults to outperform elderly adults on this task. Indeed, this is precisely what Salthouse and Somberg observed. Of greater interest, they found that the difference between young and elderly adults persisted over fifty days of practice.

The results of the Salthouse and Somberg experiment are shown in figure 6.1. Trials are shown along the horizontal axis of the graph (the fifty-first trial of the experiment was delayed by four weeks, accounting for the break on the horizontal axis just prior to trial 51). Performance level is shown along the vertical axis ("area under the ROC curve" is a common measure of the accuracy of signal detection performance). The graph shows clearly that performance improved with practice and that this practice effect was perhaps slightly larger among elderly subjects than among young subjects. However, the graph also shows a difference between young and elderly subjects, a difference that does not disappear at high levels of practice. In response to these data—as well as other data from their own and other experiments—Salthouse and Somberg suggest that "older adults go through essentially the same processing operations as young adults but merely at a slower rate" (p. 203). They attribute this reduced rate of processing to a "fundamental physiological change in the nervous system" (p. 203). Though other researchers doubtlessly will challenge these conclusions, they are consistent with much of the evidence we presently have in hand.

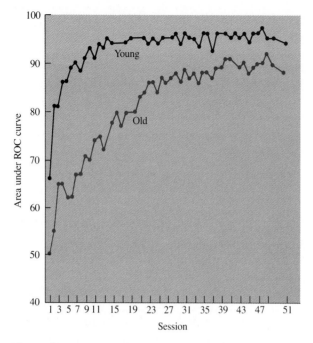

Figure 6.1   Mean signal-detection performance for young and old subjects as a function of practice. (ROC = receiver operating characteristic.)

ATTENTION

According to current perspectives on attention, there are two main ways in which our attention can fail us. First, there are failures of **divided attention.** These occur when we have problems processing all of the information that is present in a situation and is of importance to us (try listening to two or more conversations simultaneously). Second, there are failures of **selective attention.** These occur when we have difficulty ignoring material that is irrelevant to our interests or goals (try reading difficult material while ignoring a television set that is going full blast in the same room). Studies of aging and cognition have focused on both types of failure in order to characterize the nature of age-related differences in attention.

Although it is possible that elderly people show deficits in selectively attending, the available evidence has been mixed. Considering this mixed evidence, David Madden and Robert Nebes (1981) argue *against* the existence of important age differences in selective attention processes. This conclusion is supported by one of their own recent experiments in which a visual search task was used. Individuals held two target items (letters) in memory and on each trial responded yes or no as to whether one of these targets was contained in a visually presented display of six letters. The display was composed of three red and three

One way attention can fail us is through selective attention, such as when we ignore information irrelevant to our interests or goals.

Box 6.1
DIVIDED ATTENTION BY YOUNG AND ELDERLY ADULTS

In a recent research article, Somberg and Salthouse (1982) noted prior evidence for an age-related deficit in dividing attention. However, they argued that this prior evidence was questionable in light of several considerations. First, they pointed out that researchers have used a restricted number of experimental methodologies and that the most popular of these methodologies—the *dichotic listening* methodolgy—is poorly understood. The dichotic listening methodology involves simultaneous presentation of two auditory messages, one to each ear, via headphones. The task is to report both verbal messages, and generally young adults do better at this task than do elderly adults. Unfortunately, the age-related deficits may be due to perceptual difficulties and also to memory difficulties. They do not necessarily imply an age-related deficiency in divided attention, per se.

Another issue raised by Somberg and Salthouse is that researchers sometimes have examined **dual-task performance** (which entails dividing attention between two tasks) but not **single-task performance** (which does not entail dividing attention). This is important because age differences found in dividing attention may simply reflect age differences in performing each of two tasks individually.

Still a third issue raised by Somberg and Salthouse is that measures of dual-task performance have not adequately accounted for **resource allocation strategies.** That is, young and elderly adults in a dual-task situation may differ in their strategies for trading off one task against the other. For example, one may find that younger adults give equal attention to the two different tasks, whereas elderly adults simply concentrate on one task alone. An experiment by Broadbent and Heron (1962) supports this possibility.

In order to deal with these issues, Somberg and Salthouse devised a dual-task perceptual experiment in which single-task performance was controlled. In this experiment, subjects were asked to view a TV monitor. On each trial, a pattern

black letters. One half of the trials were cued: before each display, subjects were shown either a black dot or a red dot, which meant that the target (if present) could only be one of the three black or red items, respectively. The presence of this cue effectively partitioned the display into three relevant and three irrelevant items. Half of the trials were noncued (for example, preceded by a green dot that gave no information regarding the target item's potential color). On the noncued trials all six display items, therefore, were relevant.

In the first experiment, twenty-four young and twenty-four elderly subjects performed this visual search task. On each trial, the cue was presented for 100 msec, followed by a 900 msec delay, followed by the item display, which remained in view until the individual responded. Any presence of selective atten-

consisting of four *X*s (forming a rectangle) and four +s (forming a smaller rectangle) were presented briefly (for less than a second). The subjects' job was to judge whether one of the four *X*s contained a "target" (a small vertical or horizontal line extending from the *X*) and *also* to judge whether one of the four +s contained a target (a small diagonal line extending from the +). Since the *X*s and +s were presented simultaneously, the subjects' task was one of divided attention.

The experiment included two important innovations. First, Somberg and Salthouse controlled for single-task performance by young and elderly subjects. Prior to the divided attention trials, each subject was tested on his or her ability to perform under single-task conditions (with *X*s only and with +s only). The duration of the displays was set so that the performance of all subjects—young and elderly—was between 80 and 90 percent correct under single-task conditions. Second, the investigators systematically varied the resource allocation strategies of their subjects. They did this by rewarding their subjects financially for accurate performance and by making rewards greater for the *X* task than for the + task, by making rewards greater for the + task than for the *X* task, or by making rewards equal for the *X* task and the + task.

The results of the experiment were straightforward. Subjects in both age groups showed lower performance under dual-task (divided attention) conditions than under single-task conditions. Further, subjects in both age groups were able to trade off one task against the other in accordance with the rewards they were offered. Of greatest importance, having controlled for single-task performance, the authors found no evidence that elderly subjects performed more poorly in the dual-task conditions. As they stated, "It may thus be concluded that in these pairs of tasks, at least, no age-related divided attention effect was found" (Somberg & Salthouse, 1982, p. 661).

tion deficit in the elderly would then appear as greater age differences on the cued trials than on the noncued trials. Analysis of reaction times suggested no selective attention deficit in the elderly in this experiment. Other more complex experiments reported by Madden support this conclusion as well.

Although age differences in selective attention are not well supported by evidence, age differences in divided attention have previously been suggested by several research findings (Craik, 1977). However, the evidence for age differences in divided attention processes have not gone unchallenged. Indeed, Somberg and Salthouse (1982) have recently developed a divided attention task in which performance differences between young and elderly adults are absent. This task is described in box 6.1.

What conclusions are warranted about divided attention abilities as related to age? Though the Somberg and Salthouse experiment is convincing, it may be too early to conclude that divided attention abilities are age invariant. Ruth Wright has argued that an age-related decrement in divided attention is present but also suggests that "it is not divided attention among stimuli, per se, which is responsible for the decrement but rather division of attention or capacity among competing mental operations" (Wright, 1981, p. 612). Her suggestion is supported by her research, which uses verbal and arithmetic tasks and which manipulates the difficulty of these tasks. The difficulty of these tasks presumably is related to the number of mental operations they involve. The results show that performance declines as difficulty increases and that the amount of decline is greater for elderly subjects than for young adults. This pattern is consistent with Wright's hypothesis.

Limited Attentional Capacity

Although there is controversy surrounding age differences in divided attention, the concept of **limited attentional capacity** (Hasher & Zacks, 1979; Kahneman, 1973) promises to clarify matters considerably. Attentional capacity is thought of as a type of psychological energy needed to perform mental work. The amount of this capacity can vary depending upon a person's level of arousal and other factors. Nonetheless, at any one moment, capacity is thought to be limited. Further, the amount of attentional capacity is thought to decline with age (Craik & Simon, 1980; Hasher & Zacks, 1979).

There are several sorts of evidence for a deficit in attentional capacity in late adulthood. Perhaps the strongest evidence comes from comparisons of **effortful information processing,** which is thought to draw on limited capacity, and **automatic information processing,** which presumably does not draw on limited capacity. In one of William Hoyer's experiments (Plude & Hoyer, 1981), young and elderly women searched for two or four target letters in displays of one, four, or nine letters. Half of the women in each age group were in the *varied mapping* condition; they looked for different target letters on different trials. The remaining women were in the *constant mapping* condition; they looked for the same letters on all trails. There is good evidence (Schneider & Shiffrin, 1977) that practice on the constant mapping procedure results in automatic processing, that is, processing that is independent of other demands on limited attentional capacity. Interestingly, Plude and Hoyer found only very small age differences in that condition. In contrast, the varied mapping condition produced a large deficit in the elderly group of women. The results support the contention that there are age differences in effortful processing (which draws on limited capacity). Age differences in processing, then, may result from limitations in capacity. These results have important practical implications: Though elderly people may suffer processing deficits, these deficits can be overcome, at least to some extent, if processing is automatized. Shortly, we will discuss the possibility that the distinction between effortful and automatic processing is important in long-term memory tasks, as well as in tasks more closely tied to perception.

In summary, there is very little support for the notion of deficits among elderly people in selective attention abilities, and there is controversy surrounding such deficits in divided attention abilities. However, available evidence does suggest that attentional capacity is limited and becomes more limited in old age. Although this interesting conclusion will doubtlessly be subject to additional testing by researchers, it appears for the present to be secure.

MEMORY

The experimental psychology of memory is approximately 100 years old, originating with the research of Herrmann Ebbinghaus (1885). However, the vast majority of this work has been carried out with young adults, usually college students, and has added little to our knowledge of adult development and aging. Recently, however, a growing number of researchers have examined memory performance in *late* adulthood as compared to performance in *young* adulthood (see Craik, 1977). A smaller number of researchers have examined memory in *middle* adulthood. The results that are emerging are far from simple, but they promise to tell us much about the nature of information processing across the life span.

Factors Involved in Memory Differences

Is memory better in young adults than in elderly individuals? As will soon become apparent, there is no simple yes or no answer. Rather, several factors are involved in answering this question: (1) the relative involvement of short-term versus long-term memory (see box 6.2), (2) the nature of the information-processing activities that are engaged in during learning, (3) the nature of the memory test (for example, recall versus recognition), (4) the nature of the to-be-remembered materials (for example, familiar versus unfamiliar, verbal versus nonverbal), and (5) the nature of the person—in particular, the repertoire of knowledge and skills he or she possesses and can bring to bear on the memory task. We will consider each factor in turn and then present a conceptual framework developed by James J. Jenkins (1978) that seems to fit the various findings.

Box 6.2
HOW SHORT-TERM AND LONG-TERM MEMORY WORK

Many years ago, the famous psychologist William James (1890) distinguished between **primary memory and secondary memory.** James identified primary memory with conscious awareness of recently perceived events and secondary memory with the recall of events that have left consciousness. James's distinction was based primarily on his own introspections, but today a similar distinction is supported by a great deal of experimental evidence. Further, we have today a host of *information-processing models* that incorporate the distinction between primary, or short-term memory, and secondary, or long-term memory, assigning the two types of memory to separate memory "stores."

A generalized three-stage model of memory (Murdock, 1967) is presented here. Note that it includes a system of sensory stores in addition to a short-term store and a long-term store. Note also that the model indicates processes that produce transfer of information from one store to another: transfer from sensory memory to short-term memory entails attention, and transfer from short-term memory to long-term memory requires rehearsal. Note finally that the model claims different laws of forgetting for the three memory stores. Forgetting from sensory stores is thought to result from an autonomous decay process; information is lost (within seconds or less) simply as a function of time. Forgetting from short-term memory generally results from **displacement;** new information bumps out old information. Forgetting from long-term memory is thought to result from **interference** between memory for a given piece of information and other information learned previously or subsequently. Interference in long-term memory is not equivalent to displacement. No one assumes that the learning of one fact causes a bumping out of another fact from long-term memory. Indeed, many investigators believe that interference does not destroy information *in* long-term memory but simply impairs the *retrievability* of information *from* long-term memory. A popular notion is that older individuals suffer in memory tasks because of greater interference from their greater store of past learning. However, there is no convincing evidence for this idea (Craik, 1977).

Early models of short-term and long-term memory were deficient in their treatment of "transfer" from short-term to long-term memory. Today it is recognized that simple rote rehearsal is not the only path, or even a very efficient

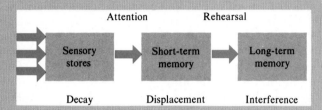

A generalized three-stage model of memory.

path, to learning. Processes of organization, semantic elaboration, and imagery can be highly effective for enhancing long-term memory. The importance of different *processes* in memory has led Fergus I. M. Craik and Robert S. Lockhart (1972) to question the view that separate "stores" exist for short-term and long-term memory. They prefer to describe short-term memory as a *process* that allows a person to hold material in conscious awareness for short periods of time. Craik and Lockhart argue that long-term retention also is based on processes. They claim that long-term retention is facilitated by "elaborate" semantic processing at the time of study (Craik & Tulving, 1975). Such retention also is facilitated by effective retrieval processes at the time of test (Lockhart, Craik, & Jacoby, 1976). A process view of memory has important implications for the psychology of aging because it suggests that age differences in memory can be understood (and perhaps removed) in terms of processing activities that people engage in when learning and remembering. Although Craik and his colleagues disagree with the notion of memory "stores," the distinction between some type of short-term memory (process or store) and some type of long-term memory (process or store) is widely accepted and well supported by evidence. Further, this distinction has proven invaluable for an understanding of age differences in human memory (Craik, 1977).

Table 6.1

MEMORY SPAN FOR LETTERS PRESENTED AUDITORILY

| | *Age (Years)* | | | | | |
	20s	*30s*	*40s*	*50s*	*60s*	*70s*
Span	6.7	6.2	6.5	6.5	5.5	5.4

Source: From Botwinick, Jack and Martha Storandt, *Memory Related Functions and Age,* 1974. Courtesy of Charles C Thomas, Publisher, Springfield, Illinois.

Short-Term Versus Long-Term Memory

Box 6.2 contains a discussion of the distinction between short- and long-term memory. This distinction is important for our current discussion because adult age differences appear stronger in tasks that depend upon long-term memory than in tasks that involve a substantial short-term memory component (Craik, 1977). Consider for example the task of memory span, a commonly used test involving short-term memory. A person's memory span is the number of digits or letters he or she can repeat in order without error. The results of a representative study of memory span for letters (Botwinick & Storandt, 1974) are shown in table 6.1. Note that the fifty-year-olds performed as well as the twenty-year-olds, and even the sixty- and seventy-year-olds performed almost at that level. Memory span is only approximately one letter shorter among elderly subjects than among young adults.

In contrast to tests that rely on short-term memory, tests that require long-term memory, or the recall of events that have left consciousness, often show substantial age-related differences. A good measure of long-term memory can be derived from the task of **free recall.** In this task, a list of items (usually common words) is presented to adults, who then attempt to recall as many items as possible, in any order. A classic experiment (Schonfield & Robertson, 1966) examined free recall by adults in five age groups. The lower line in figure 6.2 shows the free recall for each age group.

As you can see, a clear age-related decline occurred for free recall. This trend clearly differs from the information about the memory span shown in table 6.1. Such comparisons have led some experts on adult cognition, such as Craik (1977), to conclude that the accuracy of short-term memory is unimpaired by aging, while the accuracy of long-term memory shows age-related decline.

Although the *capacity* of short-term memory may be unimpaired or only slightly impaired in old age, evidence suggests losses in the *speed* with which short-term memory can be searched or scanned. Saul Sternberg (1969) has developed an ingenious procedure for measuring search speed, and his procedure has been used to test elderly individuals. In this procedure, subjects are presented with a list of items (usually digits, such as 6, 3, 9) to hold in their memory. Then they are presented another digit, and they have to decide as quickly

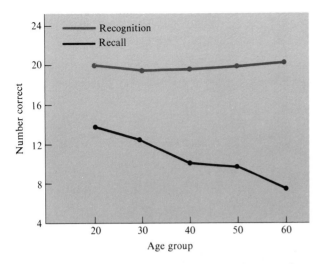

Figure 6.2   Recognition and recall scores as a function of age.

Are there differences in the memories of these early and middle-aged office workers?

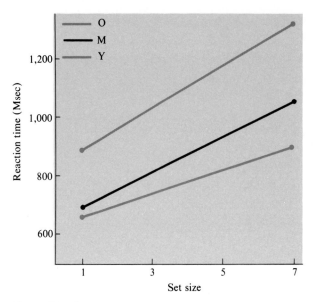

Figure 6.3   Mean response times as a function of age and set size.

as possible whether it matches one of the digits in memory. Lists of varying lengths are examined, and as you might expect, reaction times rise (answers are given more slowly) as the length of the list gets longer. Figure 6.3 shows the results from one study (Anders, Fozard, & Lillyquist, 1972) that compared the memory scanning ability of individuals in early, middle, and late adulthood. Note that longer lists produced longer reaction times, which is a typical finding. Note also that the slope of the reaction-time curve is greater for individuals in middle and late adulthood than for those in early adulthood. This difference in slope indicates that the two older adult groups scan through lists of items in short-term memory in a slower manner.

Scanning is not the only short-term memory process that may become slower with age. Evidence suggests that *spatial processing* in short-term memory also slows in older people. Spatial processing tasks reveal the functions of mental imagery and are extremely important for that reason.

The *mental rotation* task (Shepard & Metzler, 1971) is one of the best techniques available for exploring spatial processes involved in mental imagery. In one version of this task, a capital letter is presented on a screen, sometimes normally and sometimes reflected, that is, reversed from left to right. A subject in this task, decides, as quickly as possible, whether each letter presented is normal or reflected, and indicates his judgments by pressing one of two response keys

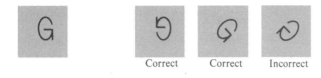

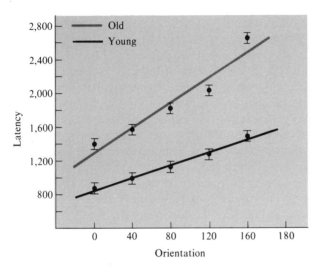

Figure 6.5 Mean decision latency for young and old subjects as a function of stimulus orientation.

in front of him. The latencies (how long it takes) of these responses are measured. All of this sounds simple enough, except that the letters are usually presented at a tilt rather than upright. The degree of tilt can range from 0° (upright) to 180° (upside down), with reference to the vertical. The key finding from such studies is that latencies get longer as the tilt gets greater. This effect of tilt on latency indicates that adults must imagine the tilted letters rotated to the upright, before making their "normal" versus "reflected" judgment (see figure 6.4 for examples of the way the letters may be presented).

One study of mental rotation (Cerella, Poon, & Fozard, 1981) was performed with young and elderly adults. The results are shown in figure 6.5. Note that the latencies grow longer with greater departures from vertical orientation—this is the phenomenon that supports mental rotation. But note also that the *slope* of the line relating orientation to latency is greater for older adults. This pattern suggests that mental rotation is slower in older adults than in younger adults.

Research on speed of scanning and mental rotation in short-term memory raises several interesting questions. One is whether the age-related losses in speed of scanning reflect the same underlying causes as the age-related losses in speed of mental rotation. Cerella and his colleagues (1981) point out that the degree of age-related slowing in rotation was quite close to the degree of age-related slowing in scanning observed by Anders, Fozard, and Lillyquist (1972). This may be a coincidence, but it may suggest a common factor that produces age-related slowing in many different processes (Birren, 1974). A second important question pertains to the role of life-style and educational factors in producing age-related slowing. A recent experiment on mental rotation (Jacewicz & Hartley, 1979) compared performance of young adults with that of elderly adults who currently were enrolled in college. No age differences in rotation rate were observed, suggesting that education and life-style may be critically important determinants of whether age differences in speed of rotation and other processes occur. A third question is whether simple practice can remove age differences in the speed of mental processes. The study discussed earlier by Timothy Salthouse and Benjamin Somberg (1982) included a Sternberg-type memory scanning task. Performance on this task was examined over fifty experimental sessions. The results suggested slower scanning rates among the elderly but only early in practice. After forty experimental sessions, the slope of the function relating reaction time and memory set size was equivalent in young and elderly adults.

In summary, available evidence suggests that the capacity of short-term memory declines only minimally with age. Although *processes* of short-term memory may show age-related slowing, factors such as education, life-style, and practice may determine the extent to which such slowing is present. Thus, among highly educated elderly who are well-practiced on a task, it is not yet clear that even speed of processing in short-term memory is impaired. Certainly the impression we get from reviewing this evidence is that short-term memory can be accurate and efficient into the sixth and seventh decades of life. The remainder of this section on memory focuses on long-term memory, for which evidence of age-related differences is stronger.

Information-Processing Activities at Input

Though age-related differences are common in long-term memory, the magnitude of these differences—indeed sometimes their presence or absence—depends upon the nature of information processing at input. Three types of input processing appear especially important: organization, semantic elaboration, and mental imagery. Recent research suggests that all three processes—the characteristics of which are summarized in table 6.2—might be less efficient or at least less likely to occur in old age as compared to young adulthood. However, this research also suggests that appropriate techniques can be employed to overcome or at least reduce this deficiency.

Table 6.2

INFORMATION-PROCESSING ACTIVITIES INVOLVED IN MEMORY

Process	Time of Occurrence in Memory Task	Description of Process
Organization	Learning of to-be-remembered material	The learner actively groups input items together into higher-order units or chunks. For example, in a long list of words, "raisin," "apple," and "pear" might be grouped together and treated as a single unit ("fruits") by the learner.
Semantic elaboration	Learning of to-be-remembered material	Involves contact between presented items and long-term memory representations, which give access to meaning. Is usually involved in organization as well as imagery, though it might occur without these processes.
Imagery	Learning of to-be-remembered material	Involves generation of a representation experienced as a mental image or "picture in the head," "tape recording in the head," etc.
Search or retrieval	Testing of previously learned material	Involves procedures for bringing long-term memory information into conscious awareness. Is thought to be facilitated if to-be-remembered information was well organized at input.

Note: While there are many different theories of how memory operates, the importance of these and other information-processing activities is widely acknowledged. Thus age-related differences in one or more of these processes would be expected to produce age-related differences in memory. By the same token, improving the utilization of these processes in individuals in middle or late adulthood may markedly improve the memory performance of these older people. We also note that these processes have been explored primarily in the domain of *verbal* memory; much less is known about their nature and importance for nonverbal memory (memory for faces, songs, etc.).

Evidence for the role of *organization* comes from George Mandler's (1967) sorting task. To do Mandler's task, one is asked to sort words into subjective groups or categories. One's subsequent recall of words is heavily influenced by the number of categories one created, the more (up to about seven) the better. David Hultsch (1971) compared individuals in early, middle, and late adulthood in a sorting condition and a nonsorting condition, in the latter of which individuals simply were told to study the words presented. The results are shown in figure 6.6. Young adults showed good recall regardless of whether they were told to sort or simply to learn the words. In contrast, recall by the two older-aged groups was improved by the sorting task. Thus the difference between the younger and older subjects was reduced when the sorting technique was used. The pattern suggests that older subjects may sometimes be deficient at organizing material for recall. However, the deficiency apparently can be reduced by a procedure—such as the sorting procedure—which ensures that organizational activities take place.

Related to effects of organization are those of *semantic or categorical elaboration* of to-be-remembered words. In one investigation (Smith, 1977), free recall of words under three study conditions was tested. Adults in the no-cue condition saw each word presented by itself. Those in the structural-cue condition saw each word accompanied by its first letter (that is, they might have

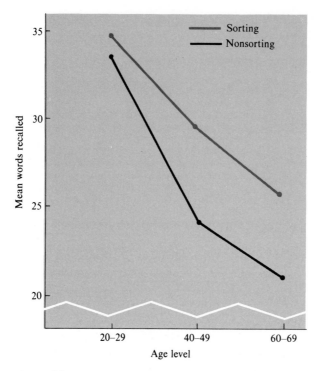

Figure 6.6   Mean number of words recalled as a function of age and experimental treatment.

seen "grape" accompanied by "G"). In the semantic-cue condition, adults saw each word presented along with the name of a superordinate category into which it fit (that is, they might have seen "grape" accompanied by "fruit"). In the first two conditions, age-related differences appeared. The young group (aged twenty to thirty-nine) had the best recall, the late adulthood group (aged sixty to eighty) showed the poorest recall, while the middle-aged group (aged forty to fifty-nine) was intermediate. In the third condition, which involved semantic-category cues, recall was approximately equal in all age groups with no noticeable evidence for older adults to recall more poorly. These findings suggest that an age-related decline in recall memory exists, a decline that begins by middle age. Again, however, it is suggested that this decline can be eliminated by procedures that ensure semantic elaboration of the words at the time of study.

Another process relevant to recall is **imagery,** which is known to improve memory in many different situations (Paivio, 1971). One study (Mason & Smith, 1977) focused on the recall of individuals in early, middle, and late adulthood. Those in the "imagery" condition were instructed to form mental images for each word, but those in the control condition heard no mention of imagery. Imagery instructions did not affect recall in the early and late adulthood groups but did improve recall in the middle adulthood groups. Indeed, middle-aged adults performed as well as young adults in the imagery condition, though they fell below young adults in the control condition. Again, these results suggest an age-related deficiency in recall memory that can be eliminated through appropriate learning procedures. In this case, however, the data suggest that a learning procedure can be effective with middle-aged adults but *not* with elderly adults. Indeed, a study by Michael Eysenck (1974) comparing young and elderly adults showed that age differences can be *greater* under imagery instructions than under other types of instruction. And Fergus Craik and Eileen Simon (1980) have described studies in which semantic categorization tasks (similar to the semantic categorization task of Smith, 1977) failed to reduce, or even increased, age-related deficits in recall memory. Thus we have evidence that appropriate learning procedures *sometimes* reduce age-related deficits in memory but that they *sometimes* do not.

Why might appropriate learning procedures sometimes fail to help memory in elderly people? One idea is that of a **processing deficit** in old age (Eysenck, 1974); elderly persons may simply be *less capable* of engaging in the organizational, semantic, and imagery processes that are helpful in memory tasks. Processing deficits might be explained by age-related declines in attentional capacity (Hasher & Zacks, 1979). That is, elderly people may show processing deficits because they have less of the capacity needed for processing. Another less pessimistic idea is that our manipulations of processing activity sometimes fail with the elderly learner. Because of low motivation, lack of practice on memory tasks, or other factors, simple instructions to use imagery, or semantic categorization, may be insufficient to influence what elderly people actually do. That is, the same instructions may produce different information-processing activity in elderly people than in young adults. Still a third explanation calls attention to possible *retrieval* problems in the elderly. Even if input processing is equivalent in young and elderly adults, the latter may have difficulty finding information in memory during the memory test. The experiments cited here all used *recall* tests, which may exacerbate problems of retrieval. The next section considers how procedures of recognition testing can affect age-related differences in memory.

The Nature of the Retention Test

We previously discussed age-related differences in free recall observed by Schonfield and Robertson (1966; see figure 6.2). Their experiment also included a recognition test. The test included previously studied words along with "new" words, and adults attempted to recognize the former. Performance on this recognition test is shown by the top line in figure 6.2. As can be seen, there obviously was no hint of an age-related deficit.

A strikingly similar pattern was observed in another investigation (Bahrick, Bahrick, & Wittlinger, 1975), involving a more natural memory task of remembering one's high school classmates. Face recognition, name recognition, and

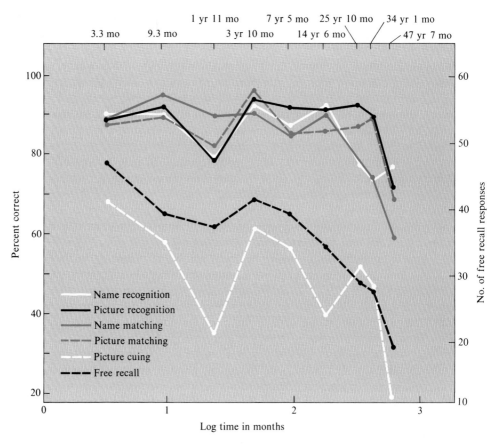

Figure 6.7   Recognition and recall of names and faces of high school colleagues.

name-face matching were assessed. And free recall of names and cued recall of names in response to faces were evaluated. The individuals ranged from early (three months since high school graduation) to late (forty-seven years since graduation) adulthood. As indicated in figure 6.7, time since high school was directly related to age in this study; older adults have experienced a longer interval of time since high school. It is clear from figure 6.7 that recognition and matching performance remained virtually constant (and nearly perfect) up to a retention interval of thirty-four years, which means that adults who were over fifty years old were performing about as well as eighteen-year-olds. This finding occurred in spite of the disadvantage older adults might have faced due to the time lag since high school (indeed, the time lag might have produced the drop in recognition and matching that finally occurred at the forty-seven-year lag). In contrast, the recall measures, particularly free recall, showed clear evidence of age-related decline. Note especially the steady drop in free recall from the three-year interval (adults about twenty-one years old) to the forty-seven-year interval (adults about sixty-five years old). This decline could reflect forgetting or it could reflect age-related changes in the efficiency of recall memory or both. In any event, we again have a case in which recall performance by older adults falls below that of younger adults, without a corresponding difference in recognition.

There is currently some controversy regarding just *why* recognition tests can remove age-related deficits. One possibility (Craik, 1977) is that recall tests place great demand upon effortful processes of search or retrieval from memory. Recognition tests may involve such processes to some degree but may also reflect what cognitive psychologists call less effortful *direct-access* mechanisms (Mandler, 1980). Note that in a recognition test previously presented items are actually presented to the adult; he or she only has to distinguish these items from "lures" that have not been previously presented. This procedure may lessen the need to search for items in memory. Students' often-stated preference for multiple-choice versus essay exams reflects in part our perception that the recall demanded by essay exams requires more work and effort than the recognition needed for multiple-choice tests. Thus the recall findings may in part be due to an age-related decline in effortful search and retrieval.

Another interpretation of the recognition results emphasizes processes that occur during the initial study of information. For example, it is possible that the effort of organizing material during learning is not needed when testing is by recognition (Smith, 1980). Thus age-related differences in organization may not be revealed with recognition testing.

Although we have described cases in which recognition testing removes age-related differences, it would be wrong to conclude that such testing *always* removes age-related differences. A better conclusion is that age-related deficits can be minimal or absent *if recognition testing is combined with controls over information processing at input*. One investigation that illustrates this point was conducted by Sharon White (described in Craik, 1977). White's subjects were given a long list of words. Some words were followed by questions to answer (for example, "Is the word a type of fruit?"). Other words were followed by the instruction "learn." After receiving the list, the subjects were given a recall test for all of the previously presented words. They were also tested for recognition. The results showed age differences in recall memory and no age differences in recognition memory, but only for words accompanied by questions. Elderly subjects did more poorly than young adults in remembering the "learn" words, even with recognition testing.

Studies such as White's (see also Craik & Simon, 1980; Perlmutter & Mitchell, 1982) suggest a complex interplay among the factors of age, processing activities at input, and type of test. When subjects are told to learn materials, age-related deficits are often found, *regardless of recall versus recognition testing*.

Apparently, younger people respond better to the learn instruction than elderly adults. This may be because young people are frequently still in school and well-practiced at the tasks of memorizing. When adults are *not* told to memorize but simply to process the materials in some way age differences in input processing are less likely to occur. And age differences in memory under these conditions are often small, if not absent altogether. An absence of age differences is especially likely with recognition-testing procedures, perhaps because these minimize demands for effortful processes of search or retrieval at test. As Perlmutter and Mitchell (1982) concluded, "when retrieval support has been provided, and encoding operations directed, age differences seem to vanish." Their interpretation of this conclusion is provocative: apparently *encoding abilities* of younger and older adults do not differ, although their *spontaneous use of encoding operations do* (Perlmutter & Mitchell, 1982).

Aside from the recall-recognition distinction, other aspects of memory testing may determine the presence or absence of differences in the memory of young and middle-aged adults. One such factor is the *pacing* of the test (that is, the time one is allowed to remember on the test). In one investigation (Monge & Hultsch, 1971), young and middle-aged adults were compared on a **paired-associates learning task.** If you took the paired-associates task you might study pairs of words (for example, radio-paper, book-fence) and then be tested on your ability to recall one member of the pair when you are presented with the second member (radio-_____; book-_____). The task is much like learning a foreign language vocabulary, or learning the names of people you meet at a party.

This task allowed the study of (a) the *inspection interval,* during which pairs are studied, and (b) the *anticipation interval,* during which adults try to recall one member of a pair given the other member as a cue. Young adults outperformed middle-aged adults, and both groups improved when the inspection (study) interval was lengthened. However, only middle-aged adults improved when the anticipation (recall) interval was lengthened. Indeed, with the longest anticipation interval (6.6 seconds for recall), the middle-aged adults performed as well as the young adults on the task. So when middle-aged adults were given more time to recall, they performed as efficiently as young adults.

The Nature of the Materials or Information

A fourth factor to consider in understanding age-related differences is the nature of the materials that adults are trying to remember. The vast majority of research on memory has tested recall and recognition of familiar verbal materials, especially words. At present, our knowledge is limited concerning memory for other types of information. However, one study (Riege & Inman, 1981) suggests that age-related differences in memory depend upon the type of information subjects are remembering. Recognition memory for three types of relatively unfamiliar, nonverbal information was examined: geometric art patterns (visual); bird songs

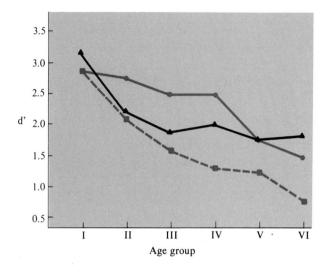

Figure 6.8 Average performance (d') of volunteers, divided on the basis of age decade (group I = twenty to twenty-nine years, etc.) into six groups, on the nonverbal recognition tests: visual (•), auditory (▲), and tactual (□) recurrent recognition.

(auditory); and wire shapes (tactual). As suggested by figure 6.8, clear age-related trends appeared, particularly with the tactually experienced wire shapes. The results with tactual stimuli stand in marked contrast to the absence of age effects in recognition memory for familiar words obtained by Schonfield and Robertson (figure 6.2), and in recognition memory for names and faces of high school classmates obtained by Bahrick et al., (figure 6.7). It is noteworthy that the tactual recognition task of Riege and Inman is perhaps even more unusual and unfamiliar than their visual and auditory recognition tasks. Possibly, then, memory for unfamiliar nonverbal information is especially susceptible to age-related deficits in the middle and elderly years.

An excellent demonstration of the power of the familiarity variable was provided in a study by Barrett and Wright (1981). These investigators have shown that manipulations of familiarity can eliminate and even reverse memory differences between the young and the elderly. Barrett and Wright examined recall memory for "young-familiar" words, such as bummer, narc, and pinball, and for "old-familiar" words, such as gooseberry, blotter, and bolster (see table 6.3 for a complete listing of these words). The former were more familiar to young adults than to elderly individuals, while the latter were more familiar to older people. The results were clear-cut: young adults outperformed elderly adults on recall of "young-familiar" words, but elderly adults outperformed young adults on recall of "old-familiar" words. Clearly, then, any comparison of memory in different age groups must consider the factor of familiarity and especially the possibility that to-be-remembered materials might be more familiar to one age group than to the other.

Table 6.3

THE YOUNG AND OLD WORD LISTS

Young List	*Old List*
afro	drugget
tweeter	poultice
bummer	gooseberry
ripoff	phaeton
gig	slate
spa	slacker
freon	crony
sunspot	counterpin
turntable	panteloons
terrarium	pompadour
denim	flitters
disco	settee
synthesizer	fedora
dude	petticoat
foreplay	blotter
cassette	parasol
communes	bungalow
narc	teacakes
readout	flivver
decoupage	gramophone
reefer	davenport
stereo	hollyhock
calculator	flapper
bellbottom	bolster
gauchos	bloomers
pinball	doily
frisbee	victrola
orgy	vamp

Source: Barrett & Wright, 1981, pp. 194–99. Reprinted by permission of the *Journal of Gerontology,* 36, pages 194–199, 1981.

Familiarity is not the only important dimension of information to be remembered. Recent research supports a crucial distinction between information that is learned through *automatic processes* and information that is learned through *controlled,* or *effortful, processes* (Hasher & Zacks, 1979). Earlier we distinguished between automatic and effortful processes in perceptual and attention tasks. The evidence supported large age differences in effortful processing but not in automatic processing. A similar conclusion is supported in memory research.

Most learning seems difficult. Thus it may sound silly to propose that some types of learning are automatic in that they do *not* require attentional capacity. However, research has supported automatic learning of certain aspects of a stimulus, such as how recently the stimulus occurred, how frequently it occurred, and where it occurred. Processing of such aspects of stimuli appears to occur without our intention or awareness, yet we are able to remember such aspects later. An example is our ability to remember where on a page we read certain information (on exams, it sometimes seems as if remembering *where* we read something can help us remember *what* we read). Recent experiments have compared young and elderly adults on memory for aspects of stimuli such as those just described (Attig & Hasher, 1980; McCormack, 1981, 1982). The result has been little or no difference between younger and older adults. This finding supports the conclusion of no age differences in memory for automatically learned information, and it is consistent with the view of age differences in information-processing capacity that we considered earlier. If elderly adults do have a reduction in processing capacity, they should not do as well on effortful memory tasks, such as free recall. However, they should not be hampered on automatic memory tasks, such as memory for spatial location.

Characteristics of the Learner

A fifth factor relevant to age-related declines concerns the learner. Apart from age, many characteristics of the person can determine the level of performance in memory tasks. These characteristics include attitudes, interests, health-related factors, and perhaps of greatest importance, previously acquired knowledge and skills. It now appears that individuals maintain their ability to use well-learned knowledge and skills throughout middle age and into old age. Tests of common, factual knowledge (for example, vocabulary, events in the news) typically show no decline from young adulthood up to old age (Perlmutter, 1980). This seems to be true even when factual knowledge is tested by recall (versus recognition).

Janet and Roy Lachman (1980) have developed a way to measure recall of previously learned facts while controlling for individual differences in the number of facts known. Using recognition tests to estimate the total amount of knowledge a person possesses, the Lachmans derived a formula for assessing the probability that a given piece of memory knowledge can be retrieved in a recall test. This retrieval measure showed no decline between early and middle adulthood, and no decline between middle and late adulthood as well. Other evidence suggests that familiar words produce "spreading activation" of semantic knowledge in long-term memory (Collins & Loftus, 1975). Available research indicates that this spreading activation occurs in adults of all ages (Howard, Lasaga, & McAndrews, 1980).

In reviewing the complex evidence on age differences in memory, Marion Perlmutter (1980) suggests that a distinction between **memory processing** and **memory knowledge** may be useful. Aging may be associated with a decline in the efficiency of memory processes but not with the amount of memory knowledge that is available for use in many different tasks. Thus age-related declines may be restricted to those tasks in which a person's prior knowledge is not useful. Memory tests for bird songs and abstract designs may be good examples of such tasks (see figure 6.8). Other tasks, which capitalize upon previously learned information, may show no age declines. Indeed, older subjects may outperform young adults. Perlmutter's distinction between memory processing and knowledge is similar to Horn and Donaldson's distinction between fluid and crystallized components of intelligence, indicating at least some convergence of psychometric and information-processing ideas.

It is encouraging, of course, that actualization of previously acquired knowledge is relatively invulnerable to age effects. But age-related deficits in new learning are distressing. Should we conclude that capacities for new learning decline with age, that you can't teach an old dog new tricks? An interesting study by Kathryn Waddell and Barbara Rogoff (1981) rules strongly against such a pessimistic claim. Middle-aged and elderly women were asked to remember the spatial locations of objects. In one condition, the objects were placed in a naturalistic "panorama," while in the other condition, the objects were simply placed arbitrarily in cubicles. Performance in the two conditions was equivalent among middle-aged women, but elderly women performed more poorly than middle-aged women in the cubicle condition. The authors concluded that "age differences in adult memory performance may be limited to tasks that remove previously learned relationships between items (as in recall of lists of unrelated words), requiring subjects to invent an organizational structure to facilitate recall" (Waddell & Rogoff, 1981, p. 878). In other words, elderly people are apparently quite good at new learning as long as the material to be learned and the learning task itself are compatible with previously acquired knowledge and skills.

One additional type of learner characteristic warrants our attention. The characteristic is that of **metamemory,** which can be defined as a learner's knowledge about his or her own memory (see Flavell & Wellman, 1977). If your metamemory were deficient, you might not know what memorization activities were appropriate to a given memory task. This could cause your performance on the task to suffer. Indeed, researchers have speculated that some age differences in memory performance actually are attributable to age differences in metamemory.

In fact, the empirical evidence for age differences in metamemory is at present rather weak. Some evidence that supports a metamemory deficit was found in a study by Jack Botwinick and his colleagues (Bruce, Coyne, & Botwinick, 1982). In this study, young and elderly subjects were asked to predict how many words from a twenty-word list they could recall given unlimited study time. Then they were presented with lists—with unlimited study time—so that actual recall performance could be examined. The elderly subjects tended to overestimate their actual recall abilities, suggesting a deficit in metamemory. In another study involving unlimited study time (Murphy, Sanders, Gabriesheski, & Schmitt, 1981), it was found that younger adults studied longer than elderly adults and also showed better recall. The suggestion was that younger adults had better knowledge of "readiness to recall" during learning—and recall readiness is a type of metamemory. Despite this evidence favoring age differences in metamemory, the majority of findings rule against such differences. In the first place,

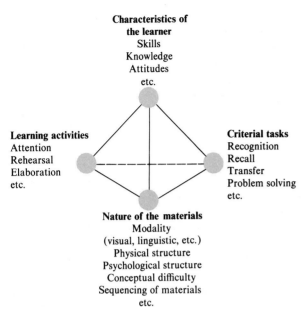

Figure 6.9 An organizational framework for exploring questions about learning, understanding, and remembering.

the finding that young adults use more study time (Murphy et al., 1981) was not replicated by Botwinick and his colleagues (Bruce, Coyne, & Botwinick, 1982). Further, other ways of assessing metamemory have failed to support age-related differences (Perlmutter, 1978; Rabinowitz, Ackerman, Craik, & Hinchley, 1982).

To summarize our discussion of factors that may influence memory decline, we present the tetrahedral model of James Jenkins (1978) in figure 6.9. The model emphasizes the importance for learning and memory of learning activities (e.g., organization, semantic elaboration), criterial tasks (e.g., recall and recognition), the to-be-learned materials (e.g., familiar words, unfamiliar bird songs), and the characteristics of the learner (e.g., knowledge and skills). The preceding discussion has touched on each of these factors, though we also have found it necessary to distinguish short-term memory (which generally shows minimal age-related declines) from long-term memory (which often does show declines, depending upon the other four factors). In general, the evidence reviewed suggests that age-related deficits in memory are most likely when (1) the task taps long-term memory, (2) effective learning strategies are not mentioned to the learner, (3) criterial tasks demand effortful "search" or "retrieval," (4) the materials are unfamiliar and difficult to verbalize, and/or (5) adults cannot perform well simply on the basis of previously acquired and well-learned knowledge and skills.

Conclusions About Age Differences in Memory

Having discussed age-related deficits in perception and attention, as well as in memory, the question arises—do the former help to explain the latter? The answer appears to be yes. Consider first the evidence for age-related slowing in perception (Salthouse & Somberg, 1982). Such slowing is also implicated in memory tasks. Short-term memory performance (at least by unpracticed subjects) suggests that scanning and rotation processes occur more slowly in older adults. Further, there are cases in which age differences in long-term memory are reduced—sometimes eliminated—when more time is allowed for recall (Monge & Hultsch, 1971).

Consider second the evidence from studies of searching for letters under constant mapping versus varied mapping conditions (Plude & Hoyer, 1981). Age differences are greater under varied mapping conditions, which apparently entail more effortful processing than under constant mapping conditions. The pattern can be interpreted with the notion of age-related declines in attentional capacity. And a great deal of memory research can also be explained with this notion. Indeed, a recent experiment suggests that memory by elderly subjects resembles memory by young-adult subjects whose attentional capacity is drained by performance of an interfering task during learning (Rabinowitz, Craik & Ackerman, 1982). Thus age-related slowing and age-related declines in attentional capacity are both implicated in memory deficits. Of course, there may be other contributing factors as well.

THOUGHT

At the outset of this chapter, we discussed the nonunitary nature of the major cognitive functions of perception, attention, memory, and thought. We stressed that each of these functions comprises many and varied elementary processes. However, it is safe to say that the function of thought is the most obviously nonunitary of them all. Under the heading of thought, we can discuss the evidence on age-related differences in the solving of problems, the acquisition of concepts, the comprehension of language, and even metacognition, that is, thought *about* thought and other cognitive functions. We will see that the complexity of thought is reflected in the tentative nature of the conclusions we can reach about it. Certainly, our conclusions about thought will be a good deal less firm than those we reached earlier about perception, attention, and memory. This is hardly surprising. The puzzle of thought is surely the deepest of all of the puzzles confronting cognitive psychologists today.

Problem Solving

In our discussion of memory, we learned that a variety of factors determine the magnitude of differences between young and elderly adults. A similar conclusion would seem appropriate for problem solving, though many potential factors have not yet been adequately explored. We can say at this point that the "practicality" of a problem has emerged as one important factor and that a problem's "demands" for specific strategies has emerged as another. Both of these factors derive from Nancy Denney's research, which we discussed in chapter 5.

Recall from chapter 5 some investigations of problem solving that Denney has conducted. In one of these investigations (Denney & Palmer, 1981), adults between twenty and seventy-nine attempted to solve traditional problem-solving tasks of the sort used in laboratory experiments, as well as practical problem-solving tasks similar to those faced in everyday life. Performance on the traditional tasks showed a linear decline with age, whereas performance on the practical tasks actually improved with age into the forties, declining only in the sixties and seventies. The study clearly suggests that the practicality of problems—their relevance to everyday life—can influence age-related differences in problem-solving performance.

Denney (1980) has explored a second factor that may influence problem-solving performance—task demands. Some problem-solving tasks can be approached in two or more different ways, all of which eventually will work. Other tasks, however, demand a single approach, as other approaches will certainly fail. A good example of the former is the traditional problem-solving task of twenty questions. If you were attempting to perform the twenty-questions task, the experimenter might show you a display containing pictures of forty-two different objects and tell you that he or she had one of these objects in mind. Your task would be to determine which object was critical, but you would only be allowed questions that have yes or no answers. The most efficient way to solve this task is to ask *constraint-seeking* questions, questions that allow you to eliminate an entire class of objects. For example, you might begin by asking whether the critical object was in rows 1 through 3 (versus rows 4 through 6). A less efficient strategy for solving the task is to ask *hypothesis-testing* questions, questions about individual objects (for example, "Is it the shoe in row 1?"). Though the hypothesis-testing strategy is inefficient, it will eventually produce the solution.

Denney and others have compared young and elderly adults on the twenty-questions task and have found that the elderly ask fewer constraint-seeking questions—and they solve the task more slowly as a result. However, the elderly increase their use of constraint-seeking questions when given a modified twenty-questions task, one designed to make the hypothesis-testing strategy virtually useless. In the modified task, the experimenter simply said that she was thinking of "an animal" or just "something," and subjects were to determine what it was.

Elderly subjects significantly increased their use of constraint-seeking questions when given this task, whereas younger subjects were unaffected. The pattern suggests that elderly people are able to use efficient problem-solving strategies, such as asking constraint-seeking questions, but they may fail to use such strategies unless the problem-solving task clearly requires them.

Other factors that may determine age differences in problem solving have been examined, but the evidence has been unclear or even negative. For example, the factor of training or experience with problem-solving tasks has been investigated, but it has *not* been shown to influence the size of age-related differences. In a review of research in this area, Denney (1982) has concluded that while training can influence problem-solving performance, it does so with young and middle-aged adults, as well as with elderly people. As Denney remarks, "Thus, the evidence that performance of elderly individuals can be facilitated through intervention should not be taken to mean that age differences can be eliminated with various intervention techniques or that elderly individuals are somehow more responsive than other age groups to the effects of training" (p. 817). Note that Denney's model, which we discussed in chapter 5, implies that training effects (differences between exercised and unexercised abilities) do not increase from young adulthood to old age—rather, they decline slightly.

Concept Acquisition

Concept acquisition is actually a particular type of problem-solving task; it probably is not fundamentally different from other types of problem solving that psychologists have studied. If you were a subject in a typical concept acquisition task, you might be presented with a large black triangle and asked to guess whether this stimulus was an example of a "concept" the experimenter had in mind. The experimenter would tell you whether your guess was correct or incorrect, and then another stimulus would be presented (say, a small white square). You would be asked to guess whether this second stimulus was a concept example, you would be told whether your guess was correct, then a third stimulus would be presented, and so on. The task would continue until you demonstrated by your answers that you had acquired the concept or until some time limit had been reached. The concept might be "all triangles," or "squares, but only if they are black," and so on. (Some concepts are much harder to acquire than others.) The task is entertaining for subjects and easy for an experimenter to set up (all you need is some paper and pencils). To get a feel for the task, you might try conducting a concept-acquisition experiment on yourself and a few friends.

A number of studies have compared concept acquisition by different-aged groups. The results have shown better performance by young than by elderly adults. For example, Bert Hayslip and Harvey Sterns (1979) investigated age differences in two versions of a concept-acquisition task, a standard version using geometric shapes and a more concrete version called the "poisoned foods task" (subjects heard descriptions of meals and had to judge whether the diner would live or die—the concept might have been "any meal with veal"). On both versions of the task, young adults made fewer errors and acquired the concept in fewer trials.

Unfortunately, research has not yet told us what factors are responsible for age-related differences in concept acquisition. Hayslip and Sterns (1979) used the poisoned foods task in order to examine the *concreteness* factor. Their results, however, failed to suggest that the concreteness of the task was critical. Within Denney's framework, we should expect that the practicality or relevance of the concept-acquisition task might be critical. Indeed, John Bransford (1979) has argued that most research on concept acquisition has really examined concept *identification,* the process of determining which of a number of *old* concepts (for example, triangles, white things) an experimenter currently has in mind. Bransford has distinguished concept identification from concept *formation,* which involves the acquisition of entirely *new* concepts. Perhaps concept formation is more relevant to everyday life, more compatible with currently exercised abilities, and therefore less likely to show differences between young and elderly adults.

Language Comprehension

Language comprehension can be analyzed into several component skills, including (a) the drawing of inferences from verbal messages, (b) the detection of anomalies or logical fallacies in verbal messages, and (c) the understanding of the gist of a story. Gillian Cohen (1979) has examined age-related differences in each of these components.

In order to study inferencing, Cohen had her subjects listen to short narratives such as the following:

> Mrs. Brown goes to sit in the park every afternoon if the weather is fine. She likes to watch the children playing, and she feeds the ducks with bread crusts. She enjoys the walk there and back. For the last three days it has been raining all the time although it's the middle of summer and the town is still full of people on holiday.

After listening to each narrative, the subjects were asked two questions, an *inference* question and a *verbatim* question. The verbatim question for the passage above was, "What does Mrs. Brown give the ducks to eat?" (The answer is bread crusts). The inference question was, "Did Mrs. Brown go to the park yesterday?" (The answer is no, because it was raining). Note that the inference question demands more than literal recall of the passage, it requires more complicated processes of comprehension.

A comparison of highly educated elderly (all university or professionally trained) with highly educated young adults (all university students) showed age-related deficits in answering the inference questions but not in answering the verbatim questions. The pattern suggests that the two age groups were equally able to remember the passages but that the younger group made more or better inferences.

In a second experiment, Cohen (1979) compared young and elderly groups on their ability to detect anomalies (contradictions) in verbal messages. Each subject heard sixteen verbal messages, eight of which contained no anomalies and eight of which contained something wrong. For example, one wrong message described the Jones family as living near an airport but went on to describe their home as very quiet and peaceful. The highly educated young adults exceeded the highly educated elderly at detecting the anomalous messages. Yet the groups did not differ in making factual errors when explaining why messages were wrong. Again, the pattern suggests that there were no age differences in verbatim memory but true age differences in comprehension.

Cohen's third experiment examined memory for a story. The story was 300 words long but could be analyzed into forty-eight separate facts or "propositions." However, the gist of the story could be reduced to six "summary propositions": "(1) Two tribes lived on an island. (2) The tribes had different ways of life. (3) The Dooni tribe had most power on the governing council. (4) The tribes disagreed about a plan to build a harbor. (5) The Dooni got their way. (6) Fighting between the tribes broke out" (Cohen, 1979, p. 424). The young adult subjects remembered more of these summary propositions than did the elderly subjects. Other analyses suggested that "old subjects were less well able to concentrate their recall on the gist information in the story" (Cohen, 1979, p. 426). Taken together, Cohen's experiments strongly suggest that language comprehension by elderly adults can be less efficient than that by young adults. Does this mean that the elderly lack the basic logical abilities to draw inferences, detect anomalies, and extract gist? Cohen does not think so. Rather, she argues that "in old age, comprehension of spoken language is handicapped by diminished ability to perform simultaneously the task of registering the surface meaning and also carrying out further processes involving integration, construction, or reorganization of different elements of the meaning" (p. 426). This diminished ability is "interpreted as reflecting a limitation in processing capacity in old age" (p. 412). Recall that age differences in memory performance have also been interpreted as reflecting capacity limitations.

Cohen's experiments on language comprehension are interesting and provocative, but they are not the last word. Other studies in the literature, using somewhat different methodologies, have sometimes found no differences between young and elderly adults in inferencing (Walsh & Baldwin, 1977) and story recall (Meyer, Rice, Knight, & Jensen, 1979a, 1979b). This should not surprise us; many factors probably determine the presence or absence of age differences in language processing. Cohen's studies remain provocative demonstrations of language-processing deficits that may *sometimes* occur in old age.

At the beginning of this chapter, we pointed out two important deficiencies of research on information processing across the life span. The first is that most existing work is cross-sectional in nature, and the second is that cognition in middle-age has not been extensively examined. Though these deficiencies are undeniable, they are beginning to be corrected, particularly in the area of memory. In the next two sections, we consider some of what has been learned from longitudinal analyses of information processing and from studies of information processing in middle age.

LONGITUDINAL STUDIES OF COGNITION ACROSS THE LIFE SPAN

The information-processing studies reviewed thus far have used cross-sectional designs, in which two or more groups of different-aged individuals are compared. Such designs are susceptible to the internal-validity threat of selection—especially cohort effects (see chapter 2). In such designs it is arguable that effects related to age are actually due to differences among generations with respect to education, diet, health, and so on, not to age, per se.

Obviously, the role of true age changes versus cohort effects would be clarified through longitudinal investigations. Unfortunately, most existing longitudinal work has been conducted within the psychometric framework (see chapter 5). Psychometric studies have limited relevance to the nature of information processing across the life span.

Fortunately, longitudinal studies of tasks more relevant to information processing are beginning to emerge. To date, David Arenberg's longitudinal analyses of memory across the life span are among the most thorough available. His analyses (see Arenberg, 1978; Arenberg & Robertson-Tchabo, 1977) were derived from the Baltimore Longitudinal Study and included subjects from six different cohorts, with mean ages ranging from approximately thirty to approximately seventy at the time of first testing. Many of these subjects were tested twice, at intervals six or more years apart. Thus Arenberg was able to make longitudinal comparisons of performance by the same subjects at two different times of testing. Further, independent samples from the same cohorts were initially tested at two different times (approximately seven years apart). Thus Arenberg could also make independent samples comparisons of performance by same-cohort subjects of different ages. (Recall from chapter 2 that independent samples comparisons solve the internal-validity threat of testing effects.) The data showed clear declines with age in memory performance, particularly for subjects who were in their sixties when they were initially tested. These declines were observed in a paired-associates learning task (similar to that of Monge & Hultsch, 1971, described earlier), a serial learning task (in which subjects attempt to learn to recall a list of items in order), and a memory-for-designs task (in which subjects view difficult-to-verbalize designs and then attempt to reproduce them from memory). Clearly, these findings support true age changes in memory and imply that the results of cross-sectional studies are not solely attributable to cohort differences.

Much work remains to be done, however. In the first place, we obviously need longitudinal data on other cognitive functions besides memory. An existing longitudinal analysis of problem solving (Arenberg, 1974) suggests no age changes until very late in life, that is, after age seventy. This result converges with psychometric data (see chapter 5), which has frequently failed to support clear longitudinal declines in intelligence. (But remember the problem of mortality in longitudinal research; this can threaten the generalizability of longitudinal comparisons.) In the second place, existing longitudinal data on cognitive functions derives largely from simple longitudinal designs. We need much more data from sequential designs, which will provide comparisons of developmental changes in different cohorts and at different times in history (see chapter 2). In the third place, we need a more analytical examination of the factors involved in developmental changes in cognition. If there is anything that the cross-sectional research has taught us, it is that age differences in cognition are not unitary but depend upon factors such as the processing activities of subjects, the familiarity of materials to subjects, and so forth. It is time to explore such factors longitudinally.

COGNITION IN MIDDLE AGE

There is actually little disagreement that the efficiency and quality of cognition declines at some point in adulthood. A more critical issue is when does this decline begin, and how early might it create difficulties for an adult? Horn and Donaldson (1980) and Denney (1981) argue that the decline begins early, in the late thirties or before, though it may cause problems only on certain types of tasks (tasks involving fluid abilities or tasks that are unpracticed). Baltes and Schaie (1976) disagree, stressing that general intellectual declines, except those due to health-related or emotional factors, are restricted to very old age, that is, the seventies or eighties. Most of the research that has fueled this debate has been conducted within the psychometric tradition. Does research on information processing help to clarify matters?

Actually, it does not, though the promise for future advances is great. Many of the studies reviewed in this chapter, particularly those on memory, included middle-aged groups in addition to young and elderly groups. Looking back over this material you will find that performance by middle-aged subjects often falls between that of young and elderly subjects. However, this is not always the case. Consider for example the interesting study of nonverbal memory by Riege and Inman (figure 6.8). They compared six age groups, with ages in the twenties, thirties, forties, fifties, sixties, and seventies. In comparing these groups, as you can do yourself by turning back to figure 6.8, Riege and Inman found three different patterns of age-related declines. Visual memory performance (as indicated by the circles on the graph) showed only minimal declines with age until the sixties, at which point a substantial drop occurred. Auditory memory (as indicated by the triangles) showed a drop from the twenties to the forties but no drop thereafter. Tactual memory (as indicated by the squares) appeared to show a gradual decline throughout the adult life span.

Why do some types of performance show early declines, whereas other types of performance show later declines? One answer is suggested by the Mason and Smith experiment described earlier. Recall that Mason and Smith (1977) tested recall memory in young, middle-aged, and elderly groups, giving imagery instructions to half of the subjects and standard learning instructions to the others. The results were that imagery instructions helped *only* the middle-aged subjects, who performed similarly to the young adults when given imagery instructions but similarly to the elderly when given standard instructions. The consequence was that recall memory showed an early decline (by middle age) in the standard condition but late decline (after middle age) in the imagery condition. The pattern suggests that appropriate learning activities can delay the appearance of age-related declines in memory.

Summary

The information-processing approach to cognition is unique in its focus on the elementary processes that underlie cognition and also in its reliance on behavioral data, that is, not simply introspection. The roots of information-processing theory lie in the fields of communication, computer science and artificial intelligence, and modern linguistics. The approach is generating a huge body of research and promises to tell us much about cognition across the life span.

Information-processing research can be organized under the four headings of perception, attention, memory, and thought. Though these headings are convenient, they do not represent unitary processes. Rather, they are best considered as functions or capacities, each of which comprises many and varied types of information processing.

Aspects of perception that appear to show deficits as people get older include the processing of relevant material amidst irrelevant material, processing of information out of context, and speed of processing. The evidence for age-related differences in speed of perceptual processing is especially strong and suggests that practice cannot eliminate these differences.

Discussion of attention focuses on the topics of selective attention, divided attention, and limited attentional capacity. Though there is some evidence for age differences in selective attention, at this point it is not convincing. The research on divided attention produces stronger support for age-related differences. However, the implications of this work have been questioned (Somberg & Salthouse, 1982). A growing body of research supports age-related differences in the capacity to process information. Some of this research has compared age differences in automatic processing versus effortful processing and suggests that age differences in the latter are stronger. This is consistent with the idea that processing capacity is limited and becomes more limited with age.

The research on memory is extensive and illuminates several factors that determine the magnitude of differences between young and elderly adults. Specifically, age differences appear to be greater when (a) the memory task taps long-term memory, (b) effective learning strategies are not enforced, (c) criterial tasks demand effortful search or retrieval, (d) the to-be-remembered materials are unfamiliar, and (e) the task is irrelevant to previously acquired knowledge and skills. The underlying causes of age differences in memory may include a slowing of information processing associated with age and also a lessening of information-processing capacity associated with age. Age differences in metamemory may also be involved, though the evidence in this case is weak.

A lesson from memory research is that age differences in cognition are not uniform but depend upon various factors. Research on thought supports a similar conclusion, though our knowledge of the relevant factors is much less complete. Nancy Denney's (1981) research on problem solving supports the practicality of the problem as a critical factor—age-related declines begin earlier on nonpractical tasks than on practical tasks. Other research by Denney suggests that the demands of the problem-solving task are important in that elderly people may use a maximally effective strategy but only if it is absolutely necessary to reach a solution.

The work on concept acquisition supports clear age-related differences, but the factors involved in these differences have not been clarified. One problem with this research is its somewhat artificial quality. The existing literature has focused on the laboratory task of concept identification (identifying which of several "old" concepts an experimenter has in mind) and ignoring the more practical task of concept formation (learning an entirely new concept). Future research will probably examine the issue of age-related declines in concept formation as well as concept identification.

Within the general domain of thought, research on language comprehension is among the most provocative and exciting. Gillian Cohen's (1979) research supports age-related deficits in (a) drawing inferences from verbal passages, (b) detecting anomalies in verbal passages, and (c) recalling the gist of stories. Although there is presently very little additional research on these functions, there already is evidence that the magnitude of age differences is not uniform but depends upon various factors. Cohen (1979) has suggested that the demand of a task on attentional capacity is one of these factors.

Research by David Arenberg supports true longitudinal declines in paired-associates learning, serial learning, and memory for visual designs. These declines seem particularly clear for people over sixty. Arenberg also has examined longitudinal data on a problem-solving task. In this case, however, the evidence for declines has been found only in subjects over seventy. Clearly, more data are needed. Particularly welcome would be studies using sequential designs to help establish the generality of longitudinal declines in cognition.

Review Questions

1. Describe the historical background of the information-processing perspective.
2. Evaluate the extent to which there is a decline in perception during late adulthood. Discuss the nature of research used to evaluate this issue.
3. How has attention been studied in late adulthood? What evidence is there for attentional decline through the adult years?
4. Discuss the nature of short-term and long-term memory and their development during adulthood.
5. How do information-processing activities at input, the nature of the retention task, the nature of the materials or information, and the characteristics of the learner influence the development of memory during the adult years?
6. What overall conclusions can be drawn about the development of memory during adulthood?
7. How has the development of thought been studied in adulthood? What developmental differences in thought during adulthood have been revealed?
8. Discuss the longitudinal studies of cognition across the life span and indicate what they reveal about the development of cognition.
9. What is cognition in middle adulthood like?

Further Readings

Denney, N. W. Aging and cognitive changes. (1982). In B. J. Wolman (Ed.), *Handbook of developmental psychology.* Englewood Cliffs, NJ: Prentice-Hall.
An excellent overview of cognitive activity in late adulthood. Moderately difficult reading.
Diamond, N. Cognitive theory. (1982). In B. J. Wolman (Ed.), *Handbook of developmental psychology.* Englewood Cliffs, NJ: Prentice-Hall.
An excellent introduction to cognitive psychology with implications for development. Moderately difficult reading.
Siegler, R. S. (1982). Information-processing approaches to development. In P. Mussen (Ed.), *Carmichael's manual of child psychology: History, theories, and methods.* New York: Wiley.
An authoritative overview of the basic ideas of information processing and their role in understanding development. Moderately difficult reading.

Section
IV

SOCIAL PROCESSES, CONTEXTS, AND DEVELOPMENT

PROFILE

At the age of twenty, Marsha Bliss has her entire adult life ahead of her. She has some important decisions to make. She is dating Frank Lefevre, a man she could get very serious about. Marsha is in her junior year of college, and Frank, age twenty-three, is in his first year of medical school. They share many similar ideas about life and have some dissimilar but complementary personality characteristics. They both like to go to cultural events, enjoy trying out different restaurants together, and enjoy studying with each other. Marsha is more of a social butterfly than Frank, who seems to be more serious about academic matters. Marsha admires Frank's achievement orientation, and Frank seems enchanted by Marsha's ability to get along with people.

During adolescence, Frank thought about a number of different careers, and in his first few years of college, he wondered whether he really wanted to be a doctor. One summer he even took a job in an architect's office to see what that occupation was like. Marsha is majoring in business, and she is eager to get out in the world of work and have an opportunity to use her social skills in some aspect of business. During the last several summers she has worked as a salesperson at a department store and as a lifeguard. She thinks her calling is sales, so she plans to interview with a number of different companies when she graduates next year.

Four years later Frank and Marsha get married. Marsha has a job as a salesperson with Xerox, and Frank has decided to do his internship in orthopedics. They decide to delay having any children for a couple of years because they need Marsha's income. Also, they feel very strongly about Marsha's being at home with their baby for the first few years.

In their late twenties, Frank finally finishes his internship, and he and Marsha have a child, whom they name Erik. Marsha does quit her job and stays home with Erik for eighteen months, but then she starts to feel restless. She misses the friendship network she had become involved with on her job, and as she says, "staying at home all day may be fine for some women, but it just isn't my bag." Frank likes his work—he has joined two other doctors and formed a professional corporation to specialize in sports injuries.

Marsha reenters the workplace. This time she gets a sales job with IBM. After several years, though, juggling her work and family responsibilities gradually starts to frustrate her. And her husband, while being a good father when he is with Erik, just doesn't spend very much time with the family. Conflict between Marsha and Frank begins to escalate and eventually leads to Marsha's filing for a divorce.

Divorce was not easy for Marsha or Frank in the first few years after their separation. Marsha felt waves of loneliness and feelings of emptiness. The time demands on her didn't end with the divorce; they seemed to increase. However, Marsha was lucky in the sense that financial matters were not as difficult for her as they are for most single mothers.

Five years after the divorce, Frank marries someone ten years younger than he. His new wife seems to have a stronger motivation than Marsha to stay at home and let Frank have the dominant occupational identity in the family. Ten years later, when Frank is asked about his second marriage, he responds: "We seem to get along better than Marsha and I did. Angela, my second wife, doesn't mind my working long hours and, indeed, seems to enjoy the prestige of my work."

Meanwhile, Marsha does not remarry, deciding to stay a single mother with a strong career orientation. Ten years later, at the age of forty, she has worked her way up to a management position with IBM and loves her work. Erik still demands a lot of her attention, but they have adapted well. Several times a month, Erik sees his father, who has been very supportive and plans on paying for Erik's college education.

Marsha is a very energetic woman. She has somehow managed to find time to get involved in community and neighborhood activities. She is even thinking about running for a seat on the city council in the suburb where she lives. Frank has continued his interest in golf and plays twice a week on a regular basis. Marsha hasn't found much time for leisure, although she does work out in a Jazzercise class a couple of times a week.

In middle adulthood, Marsha and Frank have found satisfaction through different life-styles. When we touch their lives again in late adulthood, we find that Erik has married and has a child of his own. Marsha and Frank are grandparents, and Marsha in particular enjoys spending time with Mark, her new grandchild. Marsha has continued to work. She is now sixty-three years old and will be facing retirement soon. She still has not remarried, but she says that after she retires it is not out of the question that she might find someone she would like to marry. Frank is still married and is looking forward to retirement. He and his wife have bought a condominium next to a golf course, which Frank hopes to use often.

At sixty-five, Frank retires and moves to Florida with his wife. He plays golf almost every day, and he soon develops a network of friends there. His wife also gets to know a number of women who have interests similar to hers. Marsha, meanwhile, also retires, but she hasn't remarried. She stays in the suburb where she has lived all of her life, and even into her seventies, she continues to be involved heavily in neighborhood groups and community politics.

7

FAMILIES AND THE DIVERSITY OF ADULT LIFE-STYLES

Imagine That You Were a Parent During the Depression

INTRODUCTION

FAMILIES

Strengths and Weaknesses of Different Family Forms

The Single-Career Family

The Dual-Career Family

The Single-Parent Family

The Remarried Nuclear Family

The Kin Family

The Experimental Family

The Development of Marital Relationships

Courtship

The Early Years of Marriage

The Childbearing and Childrearing Years

Postchildrearing Years/The Empty Nest

The Aging Couple

Widowhood

Marital Satisfaction and Conflict

Box 7.1 Marital Relations and Parenting

The Behavior Exchange View of Marital Satisfaction and Conflict

The Parental Role, Developmental Changes in Parenting, and Parenting Styles

The Parental Role

Developmental Changes in Parenting

The Beginnings of Parenthood

The Middle Childhood Years

The Adolescent Years

IMAGINE *that you were a parent during the depression.*
How would the depression have affected your behavior as a parent? How would it have influenced your marital relationship? And how would the depression have influenced your children?

Glenn Elder (1974, 1981) has written extensively about the Great Depression of the early 1930s. His interest focuses on how such historical events provide a context for studying lives and development. Elder (1981) reports that many mothers sought jobs despite a rather hostile climate toward women taking jobs away from men. Families drew on limited economic resources and borrowed from kin before taking public assistance as a last resort. For children, boys usually helped by obtaining paid jobs and girls did household chores. Family hardship seemed to strengthen initiative and independence among children and accelerated movement toward adult roles of work and independence.

However, during the height of the depression, its negative effects on families were often apparent. Economic deprivation seemed to heighten adult discontent, depression about living conditions, likelihood of marital conflict, inconsistencies in relations with children, and risk of the father's impairment—heavy drinking, demoralization, and health disabilities.

Thus the hard times of the 1930s brought some families together yet shattered others (Elder, 1980). From Elder's perspective, when parents were relatively close to each other *before* the loss of income, economic deprivation increased warm feelings toward both parents among children. However, when combined with marital discord, economic deprivation sharply increased hostility toward fathers among girls and particularly among boys but strengthened the relationships between girls and their mothers. Marital discord was the only context in which economic loss produced uniformly negative consequences for the development of boys (Elder, 1981).

It is important to study the adaptations families make over time, the timing and duration of events in an individual's life cycle, and the changing patterns of interdependence and synchronization among the life histories of family members. By applying a life-cycle perspective to marriage and the family unit, we can begin to see the interdependence of the life histories of the members (Elder, 1974).

Jo Ann Aldous (1978), an expert on family development, has lectured on family careers over time. Her comments accurately capture an emphasis on family history and the life cycle:

> The fact that trends in family careers over the last century suggest more people living long enough to marry and to have children as well as to divorce and to remarry demonstrates how the timing and sequencing of events in the life course and the family career are interlinked and in turn are affected by societal time. For families and their members, the time and sequence of family, educational, and work careers are of the essence, with societal events such as wars, depressions, and inflations also affecting family timetables.
>
> The interdependence of societal, family, and individual times are very clear. Take the healthiness of the economy as an example. Aside from war, the state of the economy is probably the most critical influence on the family timetable. It is no accident that our higher out-of-wedlock rates today are associated with high unemployment rates for youths sixteen to twenty-four years of age. This is the period of family formation, and high unemployment makes it harder for young people to form families. (pp. 10, 14)

In sum, it is important to study the family in concert with other aspects of the family members' life cycles, and it is necessary as well to be sensitive to the societal conditions that exist at a particular point in history. In these contexts the career orientation and success of marital partners are important, as are the appearance of such unanticipated events as depression or war. The fact that the Great Depression seemed to have some systematic effects on marital relations and parenting has important implications for the 1980s. The relatively high unemployment rate and uncertain economic conditions may start replaying some of the effects on marital relations and parenting that were observed in the early 1930s.

INTRODUCTION

In this chapter we discuss many different facets of the family, beginning with a description of the diversity of family forms and continuing with the development of marital relationships across the adult years. Next we consider what contributes to marital satisfaction and conflict, including information about the link between marital relations and parenting. We outline the developmental course of marital relationships and consider the parental role and developmental changes in parenting as well. Other aspects of families that require attention include parenting styles, sibling relationships, intergenerational relationships, and grandparenting. The last part of the chapter is devoted to the diversity of adult life-styles, including single adults, formerly married adults, divorced adults (including sex differences in divorce and the effects of divorce on children), marital separation in later life, and remarriage and the stepfamily.

FAMILIES

The American family is changing. To begin our discussion of families, we survey the strengths and weaknesses of different family forms in the United States and estimate the percentage of families in each.

Strengths and Weaknesses of Different Family Forms

Sussman (1968) has described the strengths and weaknesses of six different family forms: the single-career family, the dual-career family, the single-parent family, the remarried nuclear family, the kin family, and experimental families.

The Single-Career Family

The single-career family is the intact nuclear family comprised of a husband, wife, and children living in a common household in which one partner, usually the husband, is the breadwinner. It is estimated that approximately 13 percent of all households are of this type.

Among the strengths of this type of family are (1) it is the primary family structure for socializing members throughout the life cycle; (2) it is the main family structure involved in caring for disabled, deviant, and dependent members; and (3) it may be the best adapted family form for fitting the demands of the corporate economic structure.

However, the single-career family has weaknesses as well. First, this family form is easily broken. As a result, there is an increase in the intervention of organizations and the amount of money spent to maintain individuals of broken homes and new family forms. Second, the single provider in the working class is unable to provide adequately for the maintenance of the family; even in the middle class, the provider has difficulty in providing an expected quality of life.

There has been a tremendous increase in the number of single-parent families in our culture.

The Dual-Career Family

The dual-career family consists of a husband, wife, and children living in a home in which both adults work. It represents 16 percent of all households.

Two of the strengths of the dual-career family are (1) it is a competent family form for providing maximum income and achieving quality of life expectations and (2) it is a very adequate family for attaining gender equality and provides a form for sharing of household and marital responsibilities.

The dual-career family also has its weaknesses. Often it is necessary to depend on kin and institutional support systems (for example, day care) for effective functioning. Furthermore, this type of family often experiences difficulties in coordinating career and family responsibilities.

The Single-Parent Family

Approximately 16 percent of all households are headed by a single parent. In most cases the parent is single because of divorce, but in some instances the reason is never having married or because of the death of a spouse.

Single-parent families may have certain strengths. Often many adults are around and they can function as socialization models for children. In some instances, adults other than parents may be more effective socializers. If appropriate support systems are available, the single parent may be able to attain greater self-expression because accountability is limited to children, not to a marital partner as well. In some instances marital conflict may have reached a maladaptive point in a nuclear family and been harmful to the children involved. The removal or absence of one parent may lead to a more nurturant, liveable family.

But single-parent families have weaknesses, too. There is a need for support systems that assist the parent in parenting, economic matters, health maintenance, and social relationships, and sometimes such support systems are not available. Single-parent families are often characterized by insufficient income, an aspect of the weakness just mentioned but one so prevalent it requires special attention. A consequence of the need to obtain financial support is the pressure to remarry with the possibility that the previous marriage experience may be repeated. For some families in which the single parent is employed, too much of the socialization process may be left unsupervised by a parent and consequently there may be too much reliance on peer relations.

The Remarried Nuclear Family

The **remarried nuclear family** consists of a husband, wife, and children; one or both of the adults have previously been married and brought children with them from the previous marriage(s). Sometimes these families are referred to as blended families, and they represent approximately 11 percent of all households.

Among the strengths of remarried nuclear families are (1) prior marital experiences may lead to an increased stability in subsequent marriage and (2) parenting that formerly may have been the sole responsibility of a single adult can now be shared with the new spouse and his or her older children.

Some of the weaknesses in such families include the following: (1) There may be difficulties in blending two formerly independent households into one, and this may lead to stress for one or more family members. (2) Formations of two large families may require considerable economic resources, counseling, and other supports. (3) The economic and social commitments to individuals from previous marriages may constrict the development of adequate, stable relationships in the new family.

The Kin Family

The **kin family** is made up of bilateral or intergenerationally linked members who are living in the same household. Approximately 6 percent of all households are of this type. Its strengths include the maintenance of family values and transmission of knowledge and skill across generations and the fact that multiple adults are available for socialization and shared household and work tasks.

In terms of weaknesses in the kin family, demands for geographical mobility are not easily met and it may be that the resistance to change that threatens this family form can reduce the motivation of individuals to achieve in society.

The Experimental Family

The **experimental family** form consists of individuals in multiadult house-holds (communes) or cohabiting adults. Approximately 4 percent of house-holds are of this type.

In communal settings, large numbers of people are available to form a sup-port network to meet individual needs. For this reason, this family form may be particularly helpful to individuals in transition from one family form to another, such as a divorced mother with a small child. Furthermore, people who are not ready or are unwilling to make a commitment to long-term partnership may be able to experience economic and social sharing, psychological growth, and ex-panded interpersonal relationships and friendships in an experimental family.

Experimental families also have certain weaknesses. Few have well-mapped strategies, techniques, or financial bases to maintain their activities or attain their goals. Similarly, in many experimental families, role responsibilities are not clearly defined with the result being difficulty in implementing parenting and economic and household functions.

Some social scientists do not define the family as broadly as Sussman does. For example, Ethel Shanas (1979) refers to the more traditional definition of family in terms of a group of individuals related by blood or marriage. Indeed, Shanas takes issue with the commonly heard assumption that the contemporary family is losing its hold in society because it has become so complex, family members are living apart from one another, and other institutions are handling many of the functions formerly left to the family, such as caring for young chil-dren and the elderly. Shanas argues that the family is actually gaining more strength as the context in which a person can relax, be appreciated as a unique individual, and find support and nurturance in an increasingly complex and im-personal technological society.

In the 1980s the family is still extraordinarily important in the lives of in-dividuals throughout the life cycle, but the percentage of people living in family forms other than the single-career family has expanded tremendously. Next we look at the development of marital relationships across the life cycle.

The Development of Marital Relationships

Marital roles are often renegotiated over and over as each partner ages. For ex-ample, the traditional division of labor between husband and wife that places the wife in the childrearing role and the husband in the occupational career role requires many adjustments during the life cycle of a family. (See figure 7.1.)

From the time two people marry, an average of two years goes by before they have their first child, and the next twenty-five to thirty-five years are devoted to childrearing and launching. Although this represents a sizable segment of the life span, the typical married couple experience more than one half of their total

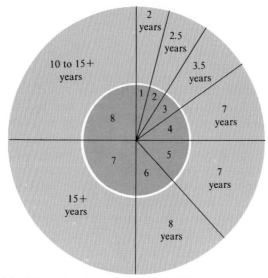

1. Married couples prior to the arrival of children.
2. Families bearing children (oldest child, two and a half or less).
3. Families with preschool children (oldest child six or less).
4. Families with schoolchildren (oldest child thirteen years or less).
5. Families with children in their teens (oldest thirteen to twenty years).
6. Families in launching-of-children stage (first child gone to last child leaving).
7. Parents in middle age (post-childrearing; empty nest to retirement).
8. Parents in old age (retirement to death of both spouses).

Figure 7.1   Eight stages of the family life cycle.

years together after their last child leaves home. This extended period of shared time is a recent occurrence. Since the turn of the century, as people have married earlier and stayed married longer, an average of ten years has been added to married life, assuming that divorce has not occurred. In the average family of 1900, the last child left home about two years after the death of one parent. Today both parents are usually alive when the youngest child departs. The husband will be working about fifteen more years, and often both marital partners now live long enough to go from a young-old (fifty-five to seventy-four) category to an old-old (seventy-five plus) category of the life cycle (Neugarten, 1975).

The developmental description of marriage and the family follows this seqence: courtship, the early years of a marriage, the childrearing years, the post-childrearing years, the aging couple, and widowhood.

Courtship

What causes us to choose a marriage partner? Some psychologists believe that the choice of a mate entails a selection process based on mutual qualities and interests (Murstein, 1970). Initially physical appearance is often an important factor. If after becoming acquainted two individuals discover that they share similar values, attitudes towards life, ideas about the roles of men and women, politics and religion, sex, and the role of men and women in society and marriage, then a closer relationship between the two is likely to develop. Once two people find that they have similar qualities and ideas about many areas of life, the couple may explore the possibility of marriage and how each would perform certain vital tasks in the marriage.

However, some sociologists (e.g., Winch, 1958) have argued that complementary needs play an important part in the mate selection process. For example, if one member tends to be introverted, a spouse who is socially outgoing may complement her or his marital partner. Not all role choices, of course, are made on the basis of such complementarity. A person will usually choose a mate who has some characteristics that are similar to his or her own and some that are not. Later in this chapter when we discuss marital satisfaction and conflict, we will see that a view called behavior exchange theory has implications for marital choice.

The Early Years of Marriage

The first few months of marriage are filled with exploration and evaluation. Gradually, a couple begin to adjust their expectations and fantasies about marriage with reality. For couples who have lived together before marriage, there may be fewer surprises, yet undoubtedly, as the two people explore their new roles, they will both negotiate a life-style based on each person's past experiences and present expectations.

Economic situations, as well as educational aspirations, may influence initial role delegation in the newly formed marriage. Traditional roles may be reversed in instances where the husband is still in college and has to depend on his wife for financial support.

Birth control now permits a couple to delay children until a time when both feel emotionally and financially prepared for this expense and personal commitment. Since most marriages are begun when people are in their twenties, most couples are not only involved in the marriage role but also in becoming established in an occupation (Levinson, 1977). As more women become involved in meaningful careers, decisions must be made as to when and if their careers will be interrupted to bear children.

Early communication patterns set the tone in a marital relationship. Research (e.g., Reedy, Birren, & Schaie, 1981) confirms that good communication is more characteristic of marital relationships in early adulthood than in middle or late adulthood. Passion and sexual intimacy also seem to be more important to young adults, whereas loyalty and sensitivity to feelings may be stressed more among middle-aged and older adults. During courtship and the early portion of a marriage an important issue to be resolved is the extent to which the relationship leads to intimacy rather than idealization or disillusionment (Rhodes, 1977). In building an intimate relationship, each partner needs to find ways of relating that are mutually rewarding. A constructive marital relationship also depends on each partner's assuming responsibility in the relationship, as well as their ability to negotiate differences and conflicts. During the early part of a marriage each partner also needs to relinquish unrealistic fantasies and idealizations because romantic ideas sooner or later clash with reality and produce disillusionment. Much more about the importance of intimacy in adult development appears in chapter 8, where we discuss relationships, and in chapter 10, where we discuss personality processes and development.

The beginning of the marital relationship involves the establishment of a family unit apart from the families of origin. A couple must independently reexamine their knowledge about roles involved in a marriage, much of which has been based on their experiences in their family of origin. Some previous family practices may be considered and accepted, others modified or rejected. The task at hand is to come to an agreement as to which roles each marriage partner will perform and how each can find a meaningful life-style within the institution of marriage.

The Childbearing and Childrearing Years

Of course, not all married couples plan to have children. However, for the majority who do, a number of concerns arise. Recall from our discussion of family history and the life cycle that early adulthood, the time when most women give birth to children, also is the time when many adults are busy trying to establish a career. It is not surprising, then, that it is during the early years of a child's life when parents report the greatest degree of dissatisfaction with marriage (Rollins & Feldman, 1970), possibly because of role conflict or overload. When the peaking of demands in family coincides with the peaking of demands in the occupational world, conflict may result. The childbearing and early childrearing stages of the family are the times when such peaking generally occurs.

During these periods married women tend to drop out of the labor market; three-fifths of women who have preschoolers are full-time homemakers. Costs go up with children and financial resources often go down. Conversations between husbands and wives change from general topics and couple interests to a focus on children, and there is less companionship between husbands and wives.

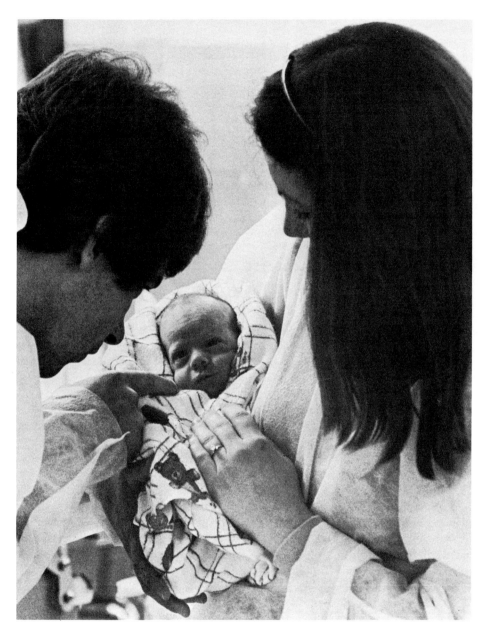

The birth of a child produces changes in adults, such that marital dissatisfaction often drops during the early childrearing years.

Wives may feel less able to share their problems with their husbands. Power may become more husband centered, and there is less sharing of tasks around the house. The demands on husband-fathers and wife-mothers to engage in child care, housework, and companion roles increase. And while parental and spousal role demands are up, occupational demands are also peaking.

Jo Ann Aldous (1978) goes on to discuss further ideas about the childrearing years and the adjustments adolescents require a family to make.

> Another stage of family conflict is the intersection of the adolescent's educational career and his parents' work careers. The discrepancy between parental income and the societal event of longer economic dependency of adolescents obtaining advanced education creates "life squeeze" stress.
>
> To pay a youth's college expenses, family expenditures must increase by between 10 and 25 percent with two or three children, and with more children, they go up even more. These financial demands peak at the same time in all families, but financial remuneration patterns from different occupations do not peak at the same time, and the amount of their increase also varies. (p. 9)

This financial squeeze in the family life cycle may lead many older women back into the working world.

Postchildrearing Years/The Empty Nest

A time comes in a couple's life when their children become independent and begin to provide for themselves and form friendships outside the family unit. Instead of a parent-child relationship at this time, the interaction gradually changes to that of one adult relating to another adult.

This period is a time of reorganization for the parents where the focus of family life again may be oriented toward relationships between marital partners. For couples who have learned to relate to each other through their children, they no longer have their children as props for their relationship. They must now rely more on their relationship with each other (Rhodes, 1977).

When their adolescents or youth leave home, some parents experience what has been called the **empty nest syndrome.** The relationship between strict role division and the empty nest syndrome has been identified through lengthy interviews with middle-aged women who were suffering from acute depression after their children had left home (Bart, 1973). The greater a mother's involvement with her children, the greater was her difficulty in living without them. Those women who defined themselves primarily in terms of their mother roles, whose entire lives had been wrapped up in their children, felt as though they had nothing to live for when offspring left the nest. They had dedicated themselves to the cultural mandate of living a selfless, nurturing life on behalf of spouse and children and expected some reward for this self-denial at the end of their childrearing years. What they expected was to share their adult children's lives, and when children failed to comply with this expectation, the women felt lost and suffered from depression. As one postparental woman put it, "I don't feel like I'm going anywhere. I feel just like I'm standing still, not getting anywhere" (Bart, 1973). All of these "supermothers," when asked what they were most proud of said, "My children." None mentioned an accomplishment of their own. Some fathers also experience difficulty with the empty nest syndrome.

The Aging Couple

The time from retirement until the death of a spouse signals the final stage of the marriage process. Retirement undoubtedly alters a couple's life-style and requires some adaptation in their relationship. The greatest changes may occur in the traditional family (in which the husband works and the wife is a homemaker). The husband may not know what to do with himself, and the wife may feel uneasy having him around the house all of the time. In such families, both spouses may need to move toward more expressive roles. The husband must adjust from being the good provider to helping around the house, whereas the wife must change from functioning only as a good homemaker to being even more loving and understanding (Troll, 1971). Marital happiness in late adulthood may also be influenced by each partner's ability to deal with personal conflicts, for example, aging, illness, and eventual death (Levinson, 1977).

Individuals who are married in late adulthood appear to be happier than those who are single (Lee, 1978). Such satisfaction seems to be greater for women than for men, possibly because women place more emphasis on attaining satisfaction through marriage than men do. However, as more women develop careers, the relationship between satisfaction and marriage may not hold.

Of course, there are many different types of adult life-styles. Not all individuals in late adulthood are married. At least 8 percent of people who reach the age of sixty-five have never been married. Contrary to the popular stereotype, those older people seem to have the least difficulty coping with loneliness in old age. Many of them long ago found how to live autonomously and developed self-reliance (Gubrium, 1975).

Eventually, for married couples, one spouse dies and the surviving spouse must adjust to being a widow or widower. As we see next, there are a number of age and sex differences among surviving spouses, and individuals vary extensively in their ability to cope with the death of a spouse.

Widowhood

When a spouse dies, the surviving marital partner goes through a period of grieving. Over the course of a year, most individuals come to accept the loss of a spouse and seem to adapt reasonably well. In one investigation, 83 percent of the subjects indicated that they still felt a great deal of distress over their spouse's death. Men seem to adjust better than women to the death of a spouse, and older people seem to adjust better than younger people (Carey, 1977).

Some researchers call the bereavement process that surviving spouses go through in the year after the death *grief work* (Parkes, 1972). The individual's working model of the world becomes disrupted because of the loss of a strong attachment (Bowlby, 1980). Grief work may lead to a new identity for the individual, an identity that can be healthy or unhealthy. Four stages that many people go through in the grief process are (1) numbness, (2) pining for the lost attachment figure, (3) depression, and (4) recovery. To successfully cope with the death of a spouse, many psychologists believe that it is important for the surviving spouse to go through these four stages (Rux, 1976).

The death of a husband may be particularly difficult for a wife who has not developed a separate identity of her own (for example, through a career). When identity as a wife is stripped away, such women may feel that there is no meaning left in their life. But even for women who have many interests outside of their husband's identity, his death will be a traumatic experience. Not having a husband in the provider role, the wife may have to live on public support or find a job. And she may experience social problems after having become accustomed to socializing with other couples or relying heavily on social interaction with her husband. She may also be criticized if she develops a relationship with another man too soon after the death of her husband. Feelings of loneliness and a range of emotions including grief, hostility, and ambivalence are likely to appear. Finally, for many widows, sexual needs will go unmet.

Men are not isolated from the trauma of a spouse's death either. They may have come to rely heavily on their wife for emotional support, intimacy, and sexual satisfaction, and her loss usually triggers a great deal of grief and stress. Support systems, such as a circle of friends, are usually more readily available to the wife whose husband has died than vice versa, particularly because there are many more older women in our society than older men. It appears that older people's children are more likely to allow a widow to move in with them than a widower. One advantage the widower in late adulthood has over the widow is that if he decides to date and/or remarry the available pool of women is large.

Even though loneliness is reported to be fairly high among widowed older people, the marriage rate for those in late adulthood is not very high. Among some older people, remarriage may be viewed as a betrayal of the deceased spouse. Some elderly people are limited by mobility, energy, or budget constraints in their efforts to meet new people, including potential mates. Such limitations suggest why the remarriages that do occur in late adulthood are often between people who have previously known each other.

In some marriages the partners get a great deal of enjoyment from each other and treasure their intimate moments, the feeling of love that comes from caring about someone else and sharing oneself with another person, and the satisfaction of having a stable partner in life. Yet other marriages are rife with conflict, tenseness, and unhappiness. Next we explore what factors seem to constitute "good" and "bad" marriages as we evaluate the topic of marital satisfaction and conflict.

Marital Satisfaction and Conflict

Family sociologists have been interested in documenting the factors that contribute to marital satisfaction for a number of years. Some years ago Blood and Wolfe (1960) interviewed 900 Detroit housewives to find out how the length of marriage and birth of children in the marriage are related to marital satisfaction. In general, they found that marital satisfaction declines in a linear fashion from the beginning of a marriage through thirty years of marriage. The researchers also found that it was not simply the addition of children that contributed to marital dissatisfaction because women in childless marriages reported the same decline in marital satisfaction over time. The drop in satisfaction for the childless wives was less than was the case for women who had children, but it was still a significant decline. The components of marital satisfaction in this investigation included love, companionship, children, understanding of mate, and standard of living. The decline in marital satisfaction was the same for all five components. Other research suggests that marital satisfaction peaks in the first five years of marriage and then declines through the period when the children are adolescents (Pineo, 1961). According to this investigation, after the youth left home, marital satisfaction increased but never reached the level of the first five years of marriage (Pineo, 1961). Support for this **upswing thesis** in marital satisfaction has been found in other studies as well (e.g., Glenn, 1975; Stinnett, Carter, & Montgomery, 1972). To a considerable degree, the issue of whether there is a continuing decline or an increase in marital satisfaction when adolescents leave home focuses on the concept of the empty nest syndrome described earlier. The two patterns of the empty nest syndrome and the upswing thesis are shown in figure 7.2.

Several reasons for the upswing thesis have been offered by David Gutmann (1975, 1977). He suggests that since the divorce rate has increased, divorced couples who earlier in history were likely to be represented in the married group as maritally dissatisfied are no longer in the middle-aged marital grouping. As men and women age from early adulthood to middle adulthood, aspects of their sex roles seem to reverse. Women appear to be more assertive later in their married life, whereas men seem to show more affiliative and sensitive tendencies as they age. More about changes in sex roles in adulthood will appear later in this chapter.

There is also some evidence that if individuals do not assume marital and family roles according to the standard age-graded system in a culture, greater marital dissatisfaction may result. For instance, in one investigation (Nydegger, 1973), middle-class women indicated that when they married either at a very young or old age they were more dissatisfied with their marriage. In a similar fashion, men who married very young reported a low level of marital satisfaction, but men who married when they were older, at age forty or beyond, indicated that they enjoyed their role as a parent and reported more marital satisfaction

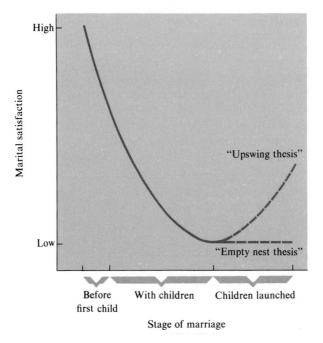

High ⊢

Marital satisfaction

"Upswing thesis"

Low ⊢

"Empty nest thesis"

Before   With children   Children launched
first child

Stage of marriage

Figure 7.2 Relationship between marital satisfaction and stage of marriage.

than men who married in their twenties and thirties. The increased marital satisfaction of the men who married later may have occurred because they were able to avoid the role conflict or overload created by the peaking of occupational and family demands in early adulthood. In addition, marital satisfaction is greater when a child is conceived after marriage than before (Russell, 1974).

One final note about marital satisfaction is important. Measuring marital satisfaction is not an easy task. Most of our information comes from self-reports by one or both partners. These self-reports may be contaminated by social desirability. That is, each partner may try to place him or herself in a more positive light than is really the case and characterize the marriage as more satisfactory than it truly is. People also vary in their willingness to disclose information about themselves, particularly on such sensitive issues as how satisfactory or conflicted their marriage is. There has been an almost complete absence of observational approaches in the study of marital satisfaction and marital relationships. Furthermore, some family sociologists believe that we should study marital adjustment more than satisfaction. In this case, marital adjustment is conceptualized in dyadic rather than individualistic terms (the strategy in much of the marital satisfaction literature).

Jay Belsky (1981) indicates that another strategy for assessing marital relationships would focus on marriage as a romance (emphasizing infatuation and sexuality) and as a friendship (emphasizing efficiency and mutuality). Belsky goes on to say that in the transition to parenthood, more stress may occur when the marriage is romance oriented than when it is partnership oriented.

For some years family sociologists have argued that marital satisfaction and family satisfaction are not the same thing (e.g., Reiss, 1971). In most cases, although not all, adults are not high on one of these factors and low on the other; often, however, an adult is high on one of the factors and moderate on the other. For example, a husband may have a very enjoyable relationship with his wife, a relationship that may include sexual satisfaction and companionship. By contrast, this same man may not enjoy being around a noisy, intrusive child who wants his attention when he comes home from work, not to mention the likelihood that the child also drains some of his wife's energy and attention. In such cases, the parenting role would be viewed by the husband with less satisfaction than the marital role and in all likelihood would lead this particular husband to report lower marital satisfaction than if the couple had not had children. Clearly, the link between marital and parenting roles is complex, and there are myriad combinations of events, attitudes, and situations that contribute to satisfaction in one or the other. In box 7.1, the link between marital relations and parenting is described in greater detail. Next we look more closely at the parental role itself.

The Behavior Exchange View of Marital Satisfaction and Conflict

One way to evaluate marital satisfaction and discord focuses on behavior exchange theory (Jacobson & Moore, in press). In contrast to psychoanalytic conceptions of marital conflict and satisfaction that stress the personality characteristics that individuals bring to a marriage, **behavior exchange theory** emphasizes the hedonism and competence involved in marital relationships. Hedonism is reflected in the belief that each partner's reinforcement value for the other determines their degree of satisfaction (Gottman, 1979). Competency is reflected in the mastery of specific relationship skills (Weiss, 1978).

Some evidence suggests that the reward-punishment ratio of social exchanges among marital partners is a good predictor of marital satisfaction and the successfulness of the marriage (e.g., Barnett & Nietzel, 1979; Vincent, Weiss, & Birchler, 1975). Basically, an attempt is made to assess one partner's tendency to direct rewarding (and punishing) behavior toward the other partner; it is argued that by assessing one's partner reward-punishment ratio a person can predict the extent to which such behavior will appear on the part of the other partner as well. However, virtually all of the data are cross-sectional in nature so it is impossible to determine if a cause-and-effect relationship exists between reward-punishment ratio and marital satisfaction. Nonetheless, in the only longitudinal test of the reward-punishment ratio (Markman, 1979), couples who were

Box 7.1
MARITAL RELATIONS AND PARENTING

Box 7.1
MARITAL RELATIONS AND PARENTING

Marital conflict can have an aversive effect on parenting.

Jay Belsky's (1981) model of direct and indirect effects in the family system has important implications for understanding the link between marital relations and parenting (see figure). Belsky's review of research on this link follows.

One investigation of families in the infant's first month of life indicates that tension and conflict between marital partners are associated with problems in the mother's ability to competently feed the infant. In this same study, the husband's esteem for his wife as a mother, by contrast, was positively related to her feeding skills (Pederson, Anderson, & Cain, 1977). Other information suggests that on the basis of investigating changes in mother-infant reciprocity across the first month of the baby's life, the mother's ability to enjoy and affectionately interact with her infant may in part be due to the quality of her relationship with her husband (Price, 1977).

The effects of marital relations on parenting are not all positive, of course. In one investigation, the more husbands criticized and blamed their wives for various problems, the more these mothers showed negative orientations toward their five-month-old offspring (Pederson, Anderson, & Cain, 1977). When marital relationships are not satisfactory, parents, particularly mothers, may make compensatory (sometimes of an overprotective nature toward the child) investments in the parenting role (Vincent, Cook, & Messerly, in press).

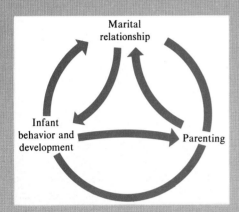

The possibility that the effect of the marital relationship on parenting may eventually touch the infant's development is indicated by recent research on child abuse and parental visiting patterns in neonatal intensive care nurseries. In one investigation, it was revealed that the quality of marriage predicted the frequency with which mothers visited their hospitalized premature infants (Minde, Marton, Manning, & Hines, 1980). In another study, infrequent visits to hospitalized infants were related to parenting disorders, such as child abuse (Faranoff, Kennell, & Klaus, 1972). It has also been discovered that divorce may be associated with prematurity and infant hospitalization. The possibility exists that this complex process could even be triggered by the infant who functions, inadvertently, as producer of his/her own development:

infant development → marital relations → parenting → infant development (Belsky & Tolan, 1981).

Repeatedly it has been argued by family sociologists that much of the difficulty that the birth of a first child creates is linked with the role strain experienced by spouses (e.g., Rollins & Galliger, 1978). With the arrival of the baby, husbands and wives must function not only as maintainers of a household, friends, and employees (at their places of work) but as parents as well (Nye & Berado, 1973). To the extent that the responsibilities of being a parent become a burden that overwhelms the mother and the father, it is likely that these other roles will be adversely affected. It has frequently been found that the degree of crisis experienced by a couple following the birth of a child is systematically tied to wives' physical exhaustion and lack of interest in sexual relations (Dyer, 1963; Hobbs, 1965; Hobbs & Wimbish, 1977; Le Masters, 1957).

Although it is doubtful that successful parenting turns poor marriages into good ones, there is reason to believe that the shared activities the care of a child creates (bathing, picture taking, playing, and so on) can provide the opportunity for enjoyable marital interaction. One possible pattern of events in Belsky's model that this occurrence may produce is as follows:

parenting → marital relations → infant development → spousal relations

planning to marry were followed for two and a half years. Support for the view was found in that the overall positive nature of couple communication, rated by the partners themselves, was highly predictive of marital satisfaction two and a half years later.

With regard to the competency-based model of marital satisfaction, it is argued that at some point in a marriage each spouse desires to make some change(s) in the partner. The question is how the partner goes about making the change. For example, distressed couples are often said to call on aversive control tactics to bring about changes, using punishment in many cases. The provisions of support and understanding are thought to be important communication skills in the competence model.

Not only do distressed couples seem to use punishment rather than understanding and support when they wish to make a change in their partner, but it appears that they also often link together negative chains of behavior in their attempt to change the partner (e.g., Gottman, 1979). Happy couples usually avoid the destructive effects of stringing together long chains of negative behavior and seem to develop neutralizing ways to deal with the impact when one partner starts acting in a negative way. However, much more work needs to be accomplished in the area of marital discord and satisfaction. We know that a marital partner is not a passive recipient of reward and punishment, so any effective model must include ideas about the reciprocal determinism of behavior and focus on cognitive determinants of behavior as well (Doherty & Jacobson, 1982).

In this section we have discussed the ties between marital relations and parenting. In the next section we will see that not only have developmental timetables been proposed for marital relations but so too have developmental views of parenting.

The Parental Role, Developmental Changes in Parenting, and Parenting Styles

In our culture it has been the standard to think that when one grows up one will get married and have children. Most parents still socialize their children in this manner, although in recent years, as divorce has become epidemic, an increasing number of parents are adaptively socializing their offspring for more flexible adult roles, which may involve marriage and children, unmarried single adulthood, or marriage without children.

The Parental Role

In discussing the parental role, William Van Hoose and Maureen Worth (1982) point out some basic ideas about parenthood, as well as some of the myths that enshroud it. For many adults the parental role is well planned and coordinated with other roles in life and is developed with the individual's economic situation in mind. For others the discovery that they are about to become a parent is a startling surprise. In either event, the prospective parents may have mixed emotions as well as romantic ideas and illusions about having a child. Parenting involves a number of interpersonal skills and emotional demands, yet there is often little formal education for this task. Most parents learn parenting practices from their own parents—some they accept, some they discard. Husbands and wives may bring divergent viewpoints of parenting practices to the marriage. Unfortunately, when methods of parenting are passed from one generation to the next, both desirable as well as detrimental practices are perpetuated.

The needs and expectations of parents have stimulated many myths about parenting (Okun & Rappaport, 1980): (1) the birth of a child will save a failing marriage; (2) as a possession or extension of the parent, the child will think, feel, and behave like the parents did in their childhood; (3) children will take care of parents in old age; (4) parents can expect respect and get obedience from their children; (5) having a child means that the parents will always have someone who loves them and be their best friend; (6) having a child gives the parents a "second chance" to achieve what they should have achieved; (7) if parents learn the right techniques they can mold their children to be what they want; (8) it's the parents' fault when children fail; (9) mothers are naturally better parents than fathers; and (10) parenting is an instinct and requires no training.

In earlier times, women considered being a mother a full-time occupation. Currently, there is a tendency to have fewer children, and as birth control has become common practice, many people choose the time for children and the number of children they will raise. The number of one-child families is also increasing. Advances in medical practices have decreased the risk of death and illness for both mother and child. Today, many women have never had to nurse their children through long bouts of serious illnesses, wondering if their child would live or die. Instead of endurance, patience, fortitude and tenderness— the traditional virtues of women in all previous historical periods—we now have contraception and penicillin (Binstock, 1972).

Giving birth to fewer children and the reduced demands of child care free up a significant portion of a woman's life span for other endeavors. Three accompanying changes are (1) as a result of the increase in working women, there is less maternal investment; (2) men are apt to invest a greater amount of time in fathering; and (3) parental care in the home is often supplemented by institutional care. As a result of these changes, questions of how to incorporate child care with other roles and responsibilities is frequently cited as an issue in the lives of many adults (Rossi, 1977).

The parenting role has other distinctions as well. Unlike most adult responsibilities the parenting role cannot be acceptably changed or discarded. We can quit one job and take another, or we can go through retraining for an entirely different job. We can also divorce and remarry. However, once children are born, they require a commitment over a period of time; we cannot acceptably revert to nonparent status. Ideally, potential parents would realistically assess whether they are willing to make the extensive investment in time, physical energy, and emotional involvement required to rear competent children.

The child's interaction and experiences with his or her mother, father, and siblings provide the beginnings of the lifelong process of socialization. However, fathers, siblings, other relatives, peers, and teachers generally have not been given the credit that mothers have for influencing the child's social development. Thus, if the son grows up to become a homosexual, it is often argued that the mother was overprotective, robbing him of his virility. If he develops schizophrenia, she probably did not give him enough love. If he fails in school, it is because she did not provide him with enough achievement-oriented experiences. In particular, the attachment bond between the mother and the infant is viewed as the basis for the development of a healthy personality later in life. Jerome Kagan (1979) believes this idea is one of the few sacred, transcendental themes in American ideology that remains unsullied. Emotions are aroused when discussion of surrogate care outside of the home begins. Kagan predicts that the major result of an emotionally close parent-child bond is a direction of the child toward acceptance of the family's values. If these values coincide with those of the popular culture, all is well. If not, a close mother-infant bond may not be an advantage. As Kagan points out, the mother who establishes a deep mutual attachment with her infant daughter but who promotes the once traditional female values of passivity, inhibition of intellectual curiosity, and anxiety over competence may be preparing her daughter for serious conflict in adolescence and young adulthood.

Today more infants than ever before in the United States are spending less time with their mothers; more than one out of every three mothers with a child under the age of three is employed, and almost 42 percent of the mothers of preschoolers work outside the home (U.S. Department of Commerce, 1979). Is this change good for children? A recent opinion poll indicates that a majority of the public thinks it harms the family, but research evidence suggests a different conclusion (Hoffman, 1979).

Developmental Changes in Parenting
We now look at some of the complex feelings and orientations of parents as they move through the parenting timetable.

The Beginnings of Parenthood When individuals become parents through pregnancy, adoption, or becoming a stepparent, they find themselves facing a disequilibrium in their lives that requires a great deal of adaptation. While the parents (or parent) want to develop a strong bond with their infant, they still want to maintain a healthy, intimate relationship and adult friendships and, possibly, to continue their careers. Prospective parents often ask themselves what they will be like as parents and examine their experiences as children to see if they want to adopt a different strategy in childrearing than their parents had. Parents also ask how this new being will change their life. A baby places new restrictions on partners—no longer will they be able to rush off to a movie on a moment's notice, and money will not likely be as readily available for trips, nights on the town, and so forth. If the mother has a career, she wonders how her infant will change her vocational life. She may ask, "Will it harm the baby to put her in a day-care center during the first year of her life? Will I be able to find responsible baby-sitters?"

More fathers have become sensitive to the important role they play during pregnancy as well as in childrearing. An increasing number of fathers have completed Lamaze training, in which the father assists his partner in the delivery of the baby. When the events surrounding the birth of the baby unfold in a smooth manner, with both man and woman feeling a strong sense of involvement, the parenting process is off to a positive start.

The excitation and joy that accompany the birth of a healthy baby are often followed by what are called *postpartum blues* in mothers, a depressive state that sometimes lasts as long as nine months into the infant's life. The early months of physical demands that a baby makes may bring not only rewarding intimacy but also exhaustion for the mother. Pregnancy and childbirth may be demanding physical events that require recovery time for the mother. As one mother tells it:

> When I was pregnant I felt more tired than ever before in my life. Since my baby was born I am one hundred percent more tired. It's not just physical exhaustion from the stress of childbirth and subsequent days of interrupted sleep, but I'm slowed down emotionally and intellectually as well. I'm too tired to make calls to find a babysitter. I see a scrap of paper on the floor and I'm too tired to pick it up. I want to be taken care of and have no demands made of me other than the baby's. (*Ourselves and Our Children*, 1978, pp. 42–43)

Many fathers are not aware of or sensitive to these extreme demands placed on the mother's body and mind. Busy trying to make enough money to pay the bills, the father may not be at home much of the time. His ability to sense and adapt to the stress placed on his wife during this first year of the child's life has important implications for the success of the marriage and family. In several research studies it was demonstrated that when fathers helped mothers more and gave them strong support, the mothers were more likely to show competent mother-infant interaction in which they were sensitive to the infant's needs (Feiring & Lewis, 1978; Pederson, Andersen, & Cain, 1977). Fortunately, many fathers are now more actively involved in the childrearing process. We will discuss this in more detail later in the chapter.

The two- and three-year-old is no longer the baby wrapped in sleeping clothes that people stop to admire in the supermarket. Active, curious, locomotive young children require parents to be more than holders, feeders, and comforters. Toddlers and preschoolers won't sit in carts, want to choose food for themselves, and ask difficult questions—behaviors that require adaptation on the part of the parents who find themselves thrown into new childrearing roles as limit setters, authority figures, teachers, and guides.

At some point during the early years of the child's life, parents need to recognize that they must learn how to successfully juggle their roles as parents and self-actualizing adults. Until recent years in our American culture, nurturing our children and carrying out a career were seen as incompatible. Fortunately, we have come to recognize that caring and achieving, nurturing and working—although difficult to mesh—can be successfully achieved and often represent competent and well-adjusted people and parents.

The Middle Childhood Years By the time children enter elementary school, they are capable of asking complex questions about themselves and their world. A parent needs to change from a model who knows everything to someone who doesn't know all the answers. During middle childhood, social agents outside the child's family take on more importance; peers, teachers, and other adults play increasingly important roles in the child's life. Two frequent questions parents are confronted with during the middle childhood years are: How much do our children need us? How much can they do without us? By the time the child enters elementary school, he can take care of himself for a large part of the day, and he feels good about being able to do this. Competent parents need to adjust their behavior and let go of children at this time so that they can explore the world more independently. Eight-year-olds don't seek the attention of either parent to the extent that toddlers do; sometimes this can be disturbing to parents who see their children growing away from their control and influence. Children in the middle years still are very much dependent on their parents and still require extensive guidance and monitoring, but parents need to operate more in the background at this time. Parents should recognize that while they still are the most important adults in the child's life, they are no longer the only significant adult figures.

Work and achievement are other themes of middle childhood that require adaptation and guidance on the part of parents. During the elementary school years, it is important that parents encourage children to develop a sense of industry and accomplishment, that is, to be able to work and to make things work. In our American culture, parents sometimes push too hard, too early, for achievement, shoving their children into tension-provoking comparisons with peers. The opposite extreme, that of lack of involvement and concern for the child's achievement and school success, can lead to difficulties as well. In the latter situation, children may feel that their parents do not value education and achievement, and consequently they will not be motivated to achieve.

The Adolescent Years Parents must adapt to a number of changes during their children's adolescent years, from the time they begin **puberty,** around the age of eleven to thirteen until they leave home—usually at about the age of seventeen to twenty. Adolescents undergo extremely difficult physical changes that focus on the development of their sexuality. Young adolescents' bodies become flooded with hormones and their minds become confused about the development of their breasts and pubic hair, and about ejaculation and menstruation. Many parents, too, are confused about how they should talk to their adolescents about sex.

Adolescents are often characterized by extreme mood changes—happy one moment, sad the next—without much clear explanation for them. Parents often report having an extremely difficult time figuring out their teenagers and feeling angry with them when they question parental values, want elaborate explanations of rules and regulations, and spend time with peers of whom the parents may disapprove. Parents of adolescents often need to be silent at the very time they want to yell. Parent-adolescent conflict seems to be greatest toward the end of the junior high school years and lessens by the time the adolescent finishes high school.

Another important aspect of adolescence that many parents do not handle well is help with career planning. Many parents leave career development to schools and guidance counselors, but there is evidence that high school students spend less than three hours per year with the guidance staff at their school (Super & Hall, 1978). Most high school students do not explore the world of work adequately and receive little direction in how to go about this. Unfortunately, some parents want to live vicariously through their son's or daughter's accomplishments. The father who did not get into medical school and the mother who did not make it in professional ice skating may pressure their adolescents in unrealistic ways to achieve occupational status beyond the youths' abilities or interests. It is important that adolescents be exposed to a variety of vocational opportunities and be allowed to make autonomous decisions about which career path to follow. The guidance that a parent gives a youth in choosing and preparing for a vocation can be an important factor in achieving self-identity in late adolescence.

This brief look at some of the important changes that occur simultaneously in parent and child during infancy, young childhood, middle childhood, and adolescence suggests that successful parents do not maintain a static orientation as their child develops. Successful parenting often involves adaptive responses to the changing needs and emerging themes of the child's development, and the complexity of this adaptation process has increased in recent years.

Parenting Styles

In this next section, we will look at some different styles of parenting and evaluate which is the most competent.

Control-Autonomy The control-autonomy dimension of parenting refers to the parents' establishment and enforcement of rules and to the techniques used to promote or hinder the child's development of independence. Control-autonomy actually can be subdivided into psychological control, psychological autonomy, firm control, and lax control. *Psychological control* consists of parental behavior that keeps the child closely tied to the parent, whereas *psychological autonomy* refers to parent behavior that allows the child to develop more independently. *Firm control* occurs when the parent sets rules and regulations and requires the child to abide by them, whereas *lax control* results when the parent establishes rules but does not enforce them or does not develop clear-cut standards for the child's behavior.

How do these parenting orientations influence the child's social behavior? A high degree of psychological control promotes dependent, regressive behavior—crying and thumb sucking, for example—and difficulty in establishing peer relationships (Armentrout & Burger, 1972; Schaefer, 1965). Also, extensive control of the child's activities and demands for obedience by parents may result in inhibited, shy behavior in children, whereas little or no parental control is often related to impulsive behavior in children (Armentrout & Burger, 1972; Baumrind, 1971; Kagan & Moss, 1962). Competent parenting is characterized, then, by behavior that is neither excessively high nor low in control. Diana Baumrind's (1971) research supports the belief that parents should be neither punitive toward their children nor aloof from them, but rather they should develop rules and regulations for their children and enforce them. She emphasizes three types of parenting that are associated with different aspects of the child's social behavior: authoritarian, authoritative, and laissez-faire (permissive).

Authoritarian parenting describes parents who are restrictive, have a punitive orientation, exhort the child to follow their directions, respect work and effort, and place limits and controls on the child, with little verbal give-and-take between parent and child. This type of parenting behavior is linked with the following social behaviors of the child: an anxiety about social comparison, failure to initiate activity, and ineffective social interaction.

Authoritative parenting encourages the child to be independent but still places limits, demands, and controls on his or her actions. There is extensive verbal give-and-take, and parents demonstrate a high degree of warmth and nurturance toward the child. This type of parenting behavior is associated with social competency, particularly self-reliance and social responsibility.

Laissez-faire (permissive) parenting places relatively low demands, limits, and controls on the child's behavior. The child is given considerable freedom to regulate his or her own behavior, with parents taking a nonpunitive stance. Parents are not very involved with their child. This type of parenting behavior is associated with the following social behaviors of the child: immature, regressive behavior, poor self-restraint, and inability to direct and assume leadership.

For many years arguments have been aired about the best way to rear children. Is an authoritarian style better than a permissive style? Or vice versa? Many parents have not been completely satisfied with either approach, believing that a controlling but warm approach (the authoritative) may be best.

Warmth-Hostility One component of competent parenting in Baumrind's research is warmth and verbal give-and-take between parent and child. Warmth-hostility (sometimes referred to as acceptance-rejection) in parenting is associated with predictable social behavior in children (Banister & Ravden, 1944; Goldfarb, 1945; McCord, McCord, & Howard, 1961). Overly hostile parents who show little affection toward their children have children who show patterns of hostile and aggressive behavior. Parents who show a high degree of warmth, nurturance, and acceptance toward their children have children who show high self-esteem (Coopersmith, 1967) and altruism (Zahn-Waxler, Radke-Yarrow, & King, 1979). It should also be mentioned that parents who show warmth toward their children are more likely to use reasoning and explanation in dealing with their children's transgressions than parents who are aloof and cold toward their children. The use of reasoning during discipline helps children to internalize rules and regulations and to understand the circumstances in which they can act in particular ways. The parent's nurturant orientation toward the child makes that parent someone the child wants to approach rather than avoid, increasing the likelihood of interaction between them. And parental warmth, rather than hostility and punitiveness, helps to reduce anxiety and make the parent-child relationship less fearful and power-oriented for the child.

Not only is it important to examine how parents interact with their children, but it is also important to consider another aspect of family ties in adulthood—the nature of sibling relationships.

Sibling Relationships

Although we have extensive information about siblings in childhood, we have very little knowledge about the nature of sibling relationships in adulthood (Lamb & Sutton-Smith, 1982). In one longitudinal study that focused on stress and adaptation at different points in the adult life cycle, it was concluded that sibling perceptions change very little during the adult years (Lowenthal, Thurnher, & Chiriboga, 1975). There is support for the belief that same-sex adult sibling relationships are characterized by more rivalry and ambivalence than opposite-sex adult sibling relationships (Lowenthal, Thurnher, & Chiriboga, 1975). One aspect of sibling relationships in adulthood that has captured the attention of researchers is feeling of affection or closeness toward a sibling (e.g., Allan, 1977;

Cicerelli, 1980). In one investigation of closeness in sibling relationships, sixty-five adults aged twenty-five to ninety-three were interviewed about their sibling relationships. Adults who felt close to their siblings placed emphasis on the family unit, revealed memories of shared experiences, and had frequent contact with their siblings (Ross & Dalton, 1981). Just as is true in childhood, there is evidence that siblings can be important socializing influences in adulthood and that such influences involve both rivalry and affection.

Next we see that family relationships become even more complex when we consider intergenerational relationships.

Intergenerational Relationships

Although **intergenerational relationships** can be comprised of many different age segments of child and adult development, the age period of the life cycle that has received the most attention is middle adulthood—a time when adults often have adolescent offspring and parents who have entered, or are beginning to enter, late adulthood. In discussing the role of middle-aged parents, Erik Erikson (1968) believes that it is important for parents at this point in the life cycle to assume some responsibility for the new generation of adults that is about to emerge. Although Erikson does not argue that the transmission of values and attitudes to the next generation has to occur through parent-child or parent-adolescent rearing, his major focus clearly is on the important role parents play in the generativity process.

At the same time that middle-aged parents may be working hard in trying to guide their adolescent offspring into mature youth or young adults capable of performing competently in a job and making autonomous decisions, they may also have to deal increasingly with the aging of their own parents. A symposium at the 1981 annual meeting of the American Psychological Association on "The older generation: What is due, what is owed?" focused on this set of intergenerational relationships. As part of the symposium, Louis Lowy described the nature of intergenerational relationships (1981a) and discussed the issue of conflict between parents and their children (1981b). His views are presented in box 7.2.

A recent overview by Lilian Troll and Vern Bengston (1982) of what we know about the nature of intergenerational relations throughout the life span arrived at the following conclusions:

1. There is substantial but selective intergenerational continuity within the family. Parent-child similarity is most noticeable in religious and political areas, least in sex roles, life-style, and work orientation.
2. Social and historical forces—cohort or period effects—serve as moderator variables in family-lineage transmission. Transmission is enhanced in areas where social forces encourage particular values or behavior. It is reduced where social forces discourage them, as where particular characteristics become "keynotes" of a new rising generational unit.

Box 7.2
INTERGENERATIONAL RELATIONSHIPS AND CONFLICT

In discussing the nature of intergenerational relationships, Louis Lowy (1981a) has this to say:

> The adult at the chronological age of around forty or forty-five or fifty reaches what can be called a filial crisis. This is a time when parents can no longer be looked upon as a rock of support in times of emotional trouble or economic stress, but when they themselves may, and often do, need comfort, support, and affection from their offspring. Or to put it differently, when their offspring need to be depended upon in times of stress or trouble, or for advice, nurturance, or tangible financial or other type of assistance. In a filial crisis, adult sons or daughters do not take on a parental role vis á vis their aging parent; rather they take on a filial role (Lowy, 1977). In other words, they can be depended upon and therefore are dependable as far as the parent is concerned. A healthy resolution of this "filial crisis" leaves behind the rebellion against one's parents initiated during adolescence and quite often unresolved long after. One sees the parents now as more mature adults would see them. One sees them in a new perspective, as individuals with their own foibles, strengths and weaknesses, needs and rights, with a life history all of their own, that made them the persons they are now and were before their own children were born. If the filial crisis is resolved successfully, the person has achieved filial maturity and the process of crisis resolution now provides an opportunity to adult children to prepare themselves eventually for their own aging, to cope with their own developmental tasks as they are getting older, and to cope with the demands of their later years. Naturally this is not a smooth process.

Lowy (1981b) also discusses the issue of conflict between parents and their children.

> It is my thesis that intergenerational conflict is essential for a healthy discharge of the normal tensions that exist among family members. It has been said that only in the cemetery is there absence of any conflict. But we want to engender a continuing sense of life and vitality among members of different generations, when grand- or great-grandchildren will be growing up with grand- or great-grandparents in their eighties and nineties and can enjoy each others' company in a give-and-take relationship. Therefore, there must be opportunity for ventilation and expression and handling of conflict. When conflict becomes overwhelming or when it ceases to be manageable by the families themselves and becomes destructive, a "third party" is needed to which families can turn in order to get help.

Lowy believes that the resolution of conflict is even more of an issue now that families span three and often four generations.

3. At the present time we cannot conclude that gender is an important variable in transmission. While some studies support the common assumption that fathers are more influential than are mothers, other studies do not. Sex of child does not appear to be a relevant variable in parent-child similarity.

4. Friends or peers may serve as a moderating influence on family transmission in some areas, such as sexual behavior or use of marijuana, which are prominent issues for their cohort. Parental influences seem strong in achievement, work, and educational orientations, however. In general peer and parent influences appear complementary rather than oppositional.

5. Qualitative aspects of family relationships, such as "closeness," do not seem to affect lineage transmission.

6. The effect of variation in individual life-span developmental levels (aging or maturation) upon lineage transmission is neither general nor obvious. It is a prime example of "selective continuity" and cannot at present be separated from period effects.

7. Parent-child "attachments" are perceived as exceptionally strong interpersonal bonds throughout the life course. Where variations in perceived level of affect appear, they may be related to the ontogenetic status of generation members involved.

8. Gender differences are apparent in research on cross-sectional family relationships. Parents feel differently about daughters and sons; daughters and sons relate differently to mothers and fathers. In general females have stronger kinship ties, and more affection is reported for female family members than for males.

9. In the absence of extreme social discontinuity, value congruence does *not* seem to be related to degree of parent-child attachments. Ties tend to remain close even where there is little consensus.

10. Relationships with friends or peers are more likely to be complementary than in opposition to relationships with family members of other generations. Age peers or friends are not substitutes for family-lineage relations.

Two general conclusions stand out. First, it is noteworthy that so many studies show a high degree of intergenerational attachment or cohesion. Despite differentials in maturational levels, geographic propinquity, gender, and socioeconomic mobility, as well as possibly confounding effects of cultural change and peer interaction, *parent-child solidarity appears to represent consistently an important interpersonal bond in contemporary American culture.* This appears true at all stages of the life course and among individuals from varying locations in the social structure.

Second, it is of interest that *high levels of intergenerational cohesion do not necessarily reflect high levels of similarity* in general orientations or specific opinions. This generalization must, of course, continue to be tested in empirical work specifying arenas of similarity (transmission) as well as various aspects of parent-child cohesion, but if this proposition remains substantiated, its implication for theory are significant. (Lillian E. Troll, Vern L. Bengtson, "Intergenerational Relations throughout the Life Span" in *Handbook of Developmental Psychology,* edited by B. J. Wolman, © 1982, pp. 907–908. Reprinted by permission of Prentice-Hall, Inc., Englewood Cliffs, N.J.)

Many individuals in late adulthood can be evaluated in terms of their role in intergenerational relationships in general. More specifically, they can be studied in terms of their role as grandparents.

The relationship between grandparents and grandchildren often is one of mutual satisfaction.

Grandparenting

Think for a moment about your ideas, images, and memories of grandparents. Although the grandparenting role is a prevalent one in our society, it still is not well understood. We generally think of grandparents as old people, but there are many middle-aged grandparents as well. In one investigation (Neugarten & Weinstein, 1964), seventy pairs of grandparents were interviewed about their relationship with their grandchildren. Emphasis was placed on the degree of comfort the grandparents felt in their role, the significance of the role, and the style in which they carried out the role. At least one third of the grandparents said that they had some difficulties with the grandparent role, both in terms of thinking of themselves as grandparents and how they should act and in terms of conflicts with their own children over how to rear the grandchildren.

Three prevalent meanings were given to the grandparenting role. For some individuals being a grandparent was a source of biological renewal and/or continuity. In such cases, feelings of renewal (youth) or extensions of the self and family into the future (continuity) appeared. For others, being a grandparent was a source of emotional self-fulfillment, generating feelings of companionship and satisfaction from the development of a relationship between adult and child that was often missing in earlier parent-child relationships. For still others, the grandparent role was seen as *remote,* indicating that the role had little importance in their lives.

In addition to evaluating the meaning of grandparenting, the styles of interaction exhibited by the grandparents were assessed. Three styles were dominant: formal, fun seeking, and distant figure. The *formal style* involved performing what was considered to be a proper and prescribed role. Although people who assumed this style showed a strong interest in their grandchildren, they left parenting to the parents and were careful not to offer childrearing advice. The *fun seeking style* was typified by informality and playfulness. Grandchildren were seen as a source of leisure activity, and mutual satisfaction was emphasized. The *distant figure style* was characterized by benevolence but infrequent contact between grandparent and grandchild. In the study a substantial portion of grandparents were distant figures. Among the others, grandparents who were over the age of sixty-five were more likely to display a formal style of interaction, whereas those under sixty-five were more often fun seeking.

Grandparents often do play a significant role in the lives of their grandchildren. In one investigation (Robertson, 1976), young adult grandchildren showed highly favorable attitudes toward their grandparents. A full 92 percent indicated that they would miss some important things in life if there had been no grandparents present when they were growing up, and 70 percent said that teenagers do not see grandparents as boring. Such information suggests that the grandparent-grandchild relationship is reciprocal.

The grandparent role may be particularly significant in the lives of older adults because it is one of the few social roles potentially available to them. Participation can occur either as a biological or a foster grandparent, giving many older adults the sense that they have an important social function in our society.

THE DIVERSITY OF ADULT LIFE-STYLES

A greater proportion of the adult population is now single than in the past. William Van Hoose and Maureen Worth (1982) describe the nature of single adulthood and some of the stereotypes about single adults.

Single Adults

In contrast to 4 to 5 percent of fifty-year-old adults who never marry, 8 to 9 percent of twenty-year-olds will never marry (Glick, 1979). For some, being single is a preferred life-style. For others, however, being single did not occur because of their own choosing but because of the death of a spouse, divorce, personal characteristics, or other circumstances that have hindered them in the selection of a mate. In fact at any given time, about 30 percent of all adult males and 37 percent of adult females are unmarried (Macklin, 1980). One circumstance that has caused more women to remain single has been called the "marriage squeeze" (Glick & Carter, 1976). In the 1940s and 1950s a postwar baby boom occurred. Because of the custom of females' marrying males who are older, a shortage of

Personal freedom is often cited as one of the major advantages of being a single adult.

males of desirable age developed in the 1970s. However, this discrepancy should slacken in the 1980s. Nonetheless, in the 1980s there seems to be an increasing number of women who have difficulty finding a desirable mate.

Common issues of single adults center around intimate relationships with other adults, confronting loneliness, and finding a place in a society that is marriage oriented. While some adults are legally single, they are involved in an intimate living arrangement with another person. The focus here, however, is on those adults who are not currently married or living with someone else.

A history of myths and stereotypes encompasses being single, ranging from "the swinging single" to the "desperately lonely, suicidal single" (Libby & Whitehurst, 1978). Most singles, of course, are somewhere in the middle of such extremes. Singles are often challenged by others to get married so they no longer will be selfish, irresponsible, impotent, frigid, and immature (Edwards, 1977). Clearly, though, there are advantages to being single—time to make decisions about the course of life one wants to follow, time to develop the personal resources to meet goals, freedom to make autonomous decisions and pursue one's own schedule and interests, opportunity to explore new places and try out new things, and availability of privacy (Edwards, 1977).

Today there is more flexibility to choose a particular life-style. This freedom partially explains why some adults choose to marry later in life and why the number of people aged thirty-five and under who are single is rapidly growing. One factor in this choice is the changing attitudes of many women toward careers and personal fulfillment. Some women choose to develop a career before assuming marriage responsibilities. Some men also use their early adult years for pursuits other than marriage. Birth control devices and changing attitudes about premarital sex make it possible for single adults to explore their sexuality outside the bounds of marriage.

Many single adults cite personal freedom as one of the major advantages of being single. One woman who never married commented, "I enjoy knowing that I can satisfy my own whims without someone else's interferences. If I want to wash my hair at two o'clock in the morning, no one complains. I can eat when I'm hungry and watch my favorite television shows without contradictions from anyone. I enjoy these freedoms. I would feel very confined if I had to adjust to another person's schedule."

Some adults never marry. Initially, they are perceived as living glamorous, exciting lives. However, once a young woman reaches her late twenties and a young man his early thirties, there is increasing societal pressure on them to "settle down." If a woman wants to bear children, she may feel a sense of urgency to marry before her childbearing days diminish. This is the period when many single adults make a decision to marry or to remain single.

Formerly Married Adults

William Van Hoose and Maureen Worth (1982) continue their description of single adults by evaluating the lives of the formerly married. Each year through divorce, separation, desertion, or the death of a spouse, many adults become single.

The transition from being married to being single is often marked by grieving that is focused on the former relationship. This is true even when the marriage ends in divorce. Holidays may be a particularly difficult time for those individuals who are separated from their children or for those who remember previous times when a spouse was present.

Divorced Adults

In many respects divorced and widowed adults experience the same emotions. In both instances the individuals experience the death of a relationship and next to a death of a spouse, a divorce causes the most trauma in the lives of individuals (Krantzler, 1974). Whether an adult initiates the divorce or is divorced by a spouse seems to have little impact on the grieving process. However, factors related to emotional problems and poor adjustment include a sudden or unexpected separation, and an unwanted divorce (Spanier & Castro, 1979; Weiss, 1975).

At present, divorce is increasing annually by 10 percent, and one out of every three families is affected. Because the median age for divorce is thirty-eight, many divorced people must rear dependent children (Messinger, Walker, & Freeman, 1978). Although divorce has increased for all socioeconomic groups, those in disadvantaged groups have a higher incidence of divorce (Norton & Glick, 1976). Youthful marriage, low educational level, and low income are linked with an increased divorce rate. So too is premarital pregnancy. In one investigation, half of the women who were pregnant before marriage failed to live with their husband for more than five years (Sauber & Corrigan, 1970).

For those who do divorce, the process of separation and divorce is usually complex and emotionally charged. Yet despite such emotional turmoil, Mavis Hetherington (Hetherington, Cox, & Cox, 1978) reports that of forty-eight divorced couples observed, six of these couples had sexual intercourse during the first two months after separation. Prior social scripts and patterns of interaction are hard to break. Robert Weiss (1975) suggests that although divorce is a marker event in the relationship between spouses, it often does not signal the end of the relationship. He believes that the attachment to each other endures regardless of whether the former couple respects, likes, or is satisfied with the present relationship.

Further information about the divorce/separation process suggests that former spouses often alternate between feelings of seductiveness and hostility (Hunt & Hunt, 1977). They also may have thoughts of reconciliation. And while at times they may express love toward their former mate, the majority of feelings are negative and include anger and hate. Divorce, then, is a complex emotional process for adults, as well as children.

Sex Differences in Divorce

Divorce may have a different effect on a woman than on a man. For example, one investigation has found that divorce is more traumatic for women than for men, whereas the majority of both sexes indicate that the period before the decision to divorce is the most stressful (Albrecht, 1980). Women who have gained much of their identity through the role of wife and mother are particularly vulnerable after divorce. Many divorced women need to work outside the home and may not be adequately prepared for managing a new job and home responsibility. Four out of five divorced women have school-aged children (Women's Bureau, U.S. Bureau of the Census, 1979). Women, more often than men, must also cope with less income (Santrock & Warshak, 1979).

The term *displaced homemaker* describes the dilemma of many divorced or widowed women. These women always assumed that their work would be in the home. Although their expertise at managing a home may be considerable, future employers do not recognize this experience as work experience. Donna is typical of this type of woman. She married young, and at eighteen she had her first child. Her work experience consisted of a part-time job as a waitress while in high school. Now Donna is thirty-two and has three children ages fourteen, twelve, and six. Her husband divorced her and married again. The child support payments are enough for food, but little is left for rent, clothing, and other necessities. Without any marketable skills, Donna is working as a sales clerk in a local department store. She cannot afford a housekeeper and worries about the children being unsupervised while she works, particularly on Saturdays and summer vacations. Creating a positive single identity is essential for such divorced adults so that they can come to grips with their loneliness, lack of autonomy, and financial hardship (Carter, 1977; Hancock, 1980).

Men, however, do not go through a divorce unscathed. They usually have fewer rights to their children, experience a decline in income, and receive less emotional support. The separation/divorce process also may have negative effects on a man's career (Hetherington, Cox, & Cox, 1978).

Effects of Divorce on Children

Both the absence of the father from the home and the divorce of parents are global in magnitude. Their effects on the child are mediated by a host of other factors, including the relationship of the child to the custodial parent; the availability of and reliance on family support systems, such as friends, relatives, and other adults; peer support; whether there is an ongoing, positive relationship with the noncustodial parent; and so forth. Many generalizations about the effects of divorce of parents on adolescents are stereotypical and do not take into account the uniqueness of many single-parent family structures.

Divorce may be a positive solution for a family functioning in a destructive way, but for most children the separation of parents, the divorce, and the first year after the divorce cause difficult times. Children show a strong desire to live in two-parent rather than one-parent homes (Santrock, Warshak, & Eliot, 1982; Wallerstein & Kelly, 1980). In one of the most comprehensive studies of the effects of divorce on children, Mavis Hetherington (Hetherington, Cox, & Cox, 1978) followed the families of preschool children from the time of divorce until two years later. A great deal of upheaval in family functioning occurred in the divorced families, producing a state of disequilibrium. During the first year after the divorce, the families experimented with a number of coping mechanisms, some successful and some not so, as they tried to deal with their new situation. This period of disequilibrium was followed by an equilibrium that seemed to stabilize by the end of the second year after the divorce.

Divorce affects the financial structure of families and influences parent-child relations. Some of its most negative effects on children may be associated with economic problems. The problems for the divorced mother are exacerbated because only one of every three ex-husbands contributes to the support of his family (Winston & Forsher, 1971). And many divorced women do not have the training and skills to obtain a job that will provide economic support for their families. The downward turn in economic standards for the family that is headed by a divorced mother often produces a lower standard of living and possible relocation to a poorer neighborhood, which may mean that children have to change schools and lose friends. At a time when children need some continuity and support, such events may provide an even further confusion in their lives (Tessman, 1978).

Family Conflict   Many separations and divorces are highly charged emotional affairs that enmesh the child in conflict. The child may hear parents yelling and crying. Statements may be made that place the child in a position of competing loyalties, with one parent trying to persuade the child that the conflict is the other parent's fault. The mutual demeaning may be depressing to children and cause them to "deidealize" their parents (Hetherington, 1979).

Conflict is a critical aspect of family functioning, so critical that it appears to outweigh the influence of family structure on the child's behavior. Children in single-parent families function better than those in conflict-ridden nuclear families (Hetherington, Cox, & Cox, 1978; Rutter, in press). Escape from conflict may be a positive benefit of divorce for children, but unfortunately, in the year immediately following the divorce, conflict does not decline but rather increases (Hetherington et al., 1978). At this time, children—particularly boys—in divorced families show more adjustment problems than in homes in which both parents are present.

The Father's Role   At one time, studies of the role of the father in single-parent families were confined to looking simply at the link between the absence of the father and the child's personality development, but now more attention is being given to the role that the father plays in the newly divorced family. For example, to what extent is there a continuing, ongoing positive relationship between the ex-spouses? To what extent do they deal consistently with the child's behavior? In many instances, the role of the father is indirect and merely supportive of the main caregiver, the mother. In other situations, his role may be more direct, through discipline, direct instruction, and modeling when he visits with the child; in particular, his role as a disciplinarian and authority figure may continue to serve an important function in a divorced family by helping the mother control the child.

The child's relationship with both parents after the divorce influences his or her ability to cope with stress (Hetherington et al., 1978; Kelly, 1978). During the first year after the divorce, the quality of parenting the child experiences is often very poor; parents seem to be preoccupied with their own needs and adjustment, experiencing anger, depression, confusion, and emotional instability that inhibit their ability to respond sensitively to the child's needs. During this period, parents tend to discipline the child inconsistently, be less affectionate, and be ineffective in controlling the child. But during the second year after the divorce, parents are more effective at these important childrearing duties (Hetherington et al., 1978).

The custodial parent has a strong influence on the child's behavior in divorced families. The psychological well-being and childrearing capabilities of the father or the mother are central to the child's ability to cope with the stress of divorce. It appears that divorced mothers have more difficulty with sons than they do with daughters. Hetherington (1979) believes that divorced mothers and their sons often get involved in what she calls a cycle of coercive interaction. But what about boys growing up in homes in which the father has custody—is there the same coercive cycle? In one investigation, sons showed more competent social behavior when their fathers had custody, whereas girls were better adjusted when their mothers had custody (Santrock & Warshak, 1979).

Support Systems   The majority of information we have about divorced families emphasizes the absent father or the relationship between the custodial parent and the child, but child psychologists have become increasingly interested in the role of support systems available to the child and the family. Support systems for divorced families seem more important for low-income than middle-income families (Colletta, 1978; Spicer & Hampe, 1975). The extended family and community services played a more critical role in family functioning of low-income families in these two investigations. Competent support systems may be particularly important for divorced parents with infant and preschool children because the majority of these parents must work full time to make ends meet.

Age of the Child   A final issue involving children of divorce focuses on the age of the child at the time of the divorce. Preschool children are not as accurate as elementary school children and adolescents in evaluating the cause of divorce, their own role in the divorce, and possible outcomes. Consequently, young children may blame themselves more for the divorce and distort the feelings and behavior of their parents, including hopes for their reconciliation (Wallerstein & Kelly, 1975, 1980). Even adolescents experience a great deal of conflict and pain over their parents' divorce; but after the immediate impact of the divorce, they seem to be better than younger children at assigning responsibility for the divorce, resolving loyalty conflicts, and understanding the divorce process (Wallerstein & Kelly, 1974, 1975, 1980).

Marital Separation in Later Life

Although research on divorce has increased tremendously in recent years, little attention has been paid to how this critical life event may influence the long-term married. Recently, David Chiriboga (1982) evaluated the psychosocial functioning of 310 recently separated men and women ranging in age from twenty to the seventies. Included in the analyses were measures of morale, psychiatric symptoms, time perspective, self-reported physical health, social disruption, and divorce-induced upset. The older adults showed more distress than did younger adults, and the sex differences suggested that men and women may have different vulnerabilities.

People in their fifties stood out as being the most maladapted in the face of divorce, whereas those in their forties functioned more like young adults. This developmental finding may have occurred because of greater commitment to the former married life and therefore more difficulties in letting go. It could also suggest that older adults have fewer options and a general uncertainty about what to do next. Many older people were unable to project even one year into the future, with men over fifty being the most vulnerable.

What accounts for the increased divorce rate in the United States? Aside from the social sanctioning of divorce, it appears that the major causes of divorce are intrinsically bound in what our American society expects of marriage, which we discussed earlier in this chapter. When such unrealistic demands fall short, adults assume that the solution is to divorce.

Remarriage and the Stepfamily

The number of remarriages in which children are involved has been steadily growing. Now about 10 to 15 percent of all households in the United States are comprised of stepfamilies (Espinoza & Newman, 1979). Projections into the 1990s estimate that approximately 25 to 30 percent of all children will be part of a stepfamily before their eighteenth birthday (Glick, 1980). Remarried families are usually referred to as stepfamilies, blended families, or reconstituted families.

Unfortunately, much of our stepparenting knowledge is not empirically based. Childhood stories of such characters as Cinderella and Hansel and Gretel have portrayed the stepmother as a wicked witch. Although the stepfather has not been stereotyped as negatively in children's literature, he is often regarded as taking on the responsibility of stepchildren only out of love for his new spouse.

The word *stepparent* itself is ambiguous; its definitions include "parent" and "nonparent" (Fast & Cain, 1966). In American culture the stepparent is encouraged to accept the role of parent; however, stepparents cannot totally assume this role; they are also nonparents. With regard to three important parental functions—biological-reproductive, financial, and socialization—a stepparent cannot assume the biological role, financial obligations for a child are often shared with the natural parent, and the socialization process often has to be shared with the natural parent.

Virtually any review of the stepparent literature indicates mixed findings. Some researchers have found no differences between stepparent and intact families (e.g., Duberman, 1973), whereas others have found significant differences (Bowerman & Irish, 1962). Nevertheless, members of a stepparent family must cope with certain difficulties.

When a remarriage occurs, adjustment to the new family may be overwhelming. The mother who remarries not only has to adjust to having another father for her children but also to being a wife again. There may not be much time for the husband-wife relationship to develop in stepfamilies. The children are a part of this new family from the beginning, a situation that leaves little time for the couple to spend time alone and to grow with each other (Visher & Visher, 1978).

As single parents, many women find that their self-image improves because they discover that they can support themselves and their family. The divorced woman's independence and performance in both the maternal and paternal role may be difficult to relinquish when she remarries (Westoff, 1977).

The stepfather also has many stressful situations to deal with when he becomes a husband and father simultaneously. He must remember that he is following a preceding parent, who may still be around to see his children from time to time. The stepparent should be a supplement, then, rather than a replacement for the natural father. The stepfather may feel that the nuclear family still exists somehow, and the stepfamily, in which he is a major cog, is an appendage. Family sociologists point out that the relationship in a first marriage often does continue in some way when children are involved (e.g., Stinnett & Walters, 1977). Children often continue to see their natural father. When this happens regularly, the stepfather is confronted with his nonparent role. It is fairly difficult to assume the parental role when in reality the nonparent role is a big part of his life. The stepfather needs time to develop rapport, trust, and love with his stepchildren and wife. During this developing phase, problems may arise. When the remarriage is in its infancy, the stepfather may encounter difficulty in disciplining his stepchildren. If he left his own children, he may feel guilty and resent caring for his stepchildren. The mother also may feel that punishment is dealt out in a seemingly undemocratic way to her own children by the stepfather. Blood ties run deep and favoritism may occur; whether it does or not, the members of a stepparent family often think it exists.

In one investigation it was found that the relationship between stepchildren and stepfathers was more negative when the stepfather had been married previously (Duberman, 1973). Such fathers may move too quickly into the prerogatives and authority of a parent without making allowance for their stepchildren's initial suspiciousness and resistance (Wallerstein & Kelly, 1980).

After a divorce and remarriage, the newly formed couple may begin to feel hemmed in; after all, the divorce was the result of failing to make a relationship work. This may create a distancing in the remarriage in order to protect oneself from getting hurt (Stinnett & Walters, 1977). Such fears do not create a harmonious marriage and may interact with any parent-child difficulties that may arise.

In a remarriage, names can create difficulties. What does the stepchild call his or her stepfather, for example? There is something of a double bind here. What may please the stepfather and make him feel accepted may be very disturbing to the natural father. The child's last name may also create problems. A child with a different last name from the other members of the family may cause embarrassment to all members. Approximately one third of the adoptions in this country include a stepchild and a stepfather, so many stepfather families are making the name change.

Recurrent in the remarriage literature are references to money problems (Roosevelt & Lofas, 1977). Although the divorced mother may bring some financial support to the newly formed stepparent family, the stepfather usually is saddled with the major financial burden. Not only does he have to support his new family, but he often has to pay alimony and child support to his ex-wife. The reality of child support either coming into or going out of the stepfamily can produce worry and resentment. It can be a burden that is next to impossible to carry. The current wife may resent the stepfather's payments to the former wife, and the former wife may resent what he gives to his present wife. Money may become a symbol of love, used as a weapon in a remarriage. For example, the child may be denied something until the natural father increases child support, even when the stepfather is able to make the purchase. This is another instance in which the stepfather encounters the reality of the nonparent role.

Remarriages may suffer from some of the same problems that a first marriage encountered but in even more intense and extensive ways since more individuals are involved. One of the pluses the remarriage may have is the maturity of the adults involved. The growth and psychological changes that a person undergoes between twenty and thirty years of age may help the success of a remarriage. The mother who has been divorced once usually does not want to go through it again. She may still vividly remember the pain and hurt of the first marriage and the ensuing divorce. Such bad memories and subsequent motivation for success may help cement the stepparent family together when strains occur.

Summary

There are a number of varied family forms: the single-career family, the dual-career family, the single-parent family, the remarried nuclear family, the kin family, and experimental families. All of the forms possess both strengths and weaknesses.

The developmental course of marriage follows the sequence of courtship, the early years of marriage, the childrearing years, the postchildrearing years, the aging couple, and widowhood. Marital choice may be influenced by similarities, complementary needs, and the hedonism and competence of behavioral exchange. Early communication patterns set the tone in a marital relationship, and there is evidence of greater marital satisfaction in early rather than in middle and late adulthood. Although not all couples have children, for those who do, increased demands are placed on them. A particularly difficult task is the ability to successfully juggle career and family pressures. The time comes in a couple's life when their children become independent and leave home. Debate focuses on whether this time, sometimes referred to as "the empty nest," is characterized by an increase or decrease in happiness. The time of retirement until the death of a spouse is the final stage of the marriage process with considerable adjustment being required at this point in development. Eventually, one spouse dies and the surviving spouse must adjust to being a widow or widower. The initial process usually consists of a period of grieving.

Some marriages are robust and others are destructive. What contributes to these outcomes? One view has emphasized the importance of the time when children leave home; more recently, social scientists have argued that an upswing in mood occurs at this time—this is referred to as the upswing thesis. Further, there is some evidence that if individuals assume marital and family roles in a standard age-graded fashion, greater marital satisfaction will result. It is also important to consider the link between marital relations, parenting, and the child's behavior, which can have direct and indirect effects on one another. The behavior exchange view suggests that we need to examine more closely the hedonism and competence of marital interaction in order to understand the degree to which a marriage is characterized by satisfaction or conflict.

Parenting involves a number of interpersonal skills and emotional demands, yet there is little formal education for this task. Many parents have mixed emotions and romantic ideas or illusions about having a child. The developmental course of parenting includes the beginnings of parenthood, the middle childhood years, and the adolescent years. Successful parenting often involves adaptive responses to the changing needs and emerging themes of the child's development. Among the various parenting styles, a warm but controlling approach, sometimes called authoritative parenting, seems to promote social competence in children better than authoritarian or permissive strategies.

Most individuals grow up with one or more siblings. Studies of adult sibling relationships suggest that sibling relationships do not often change very much in the adult years, that same-sex rivalry seems greater than opposite-sex rivalry, and that sibling relationships consist of attachment and closeness as well as conflict.

One of the most important aspects of studying families from a developmental perspective involves the nature of intergenerational relationships. Middle age may be a particularly important point for considering the impact of intergenerational relationships on development. Many middle-aged parents are sandwiched between the needs of their adolescents and their elderly parents. A recent overview of what we know about intergenerational relations suggests that there is parent-child similarity across generations in religious and political areas but less similarity in sex roles, life-style, and work orientation. Even among generations who do not seem to share the same values, there is a strong degree of commitment to intergenerational ties. Peer and friendship relations often complement rather than contradict intergenerational relationships. Further, peers and friendships do not seem to be able to replace the attachment bonds between family members across generations. An important aspect of intergenerational relations for many elderly people is grandparenting. Various meanings have been attributed to the grandparenting role, and the styles of interaction of grandparents have been documented.

Just as there has been an increase in the diversity of family forms, so too has there been an increase in the number of single adults. About 10 percent of all adults who are now twenty years old will never marry. Common issues of single adults center around intimate relationships with other adults, confronting loneliness, and finding a place in a society that is marriage oriented. There has also been an increase in the number of formerly married adults. For those who divorce, the process is unusually complex and emotionally charged. The most stressful impact seems to be the period just after the separation, but over the course of several years the divorced adult seems to adjust better to being a single adult. Divorced mothers may be particularly vulnerable to stress because of increased economic and childrearing responsibilities. Many divorced mothers report that they just don't seem to have enough time to do all of the things required of them. The effects of divorce on children are mediated by a host of factors including postdivorce family functioning and the availability of support systems. Marital separation in later life may be more traumatic than earlier in life because of greater commitment to marriage and uncertainty about the future. The number of stepfamilies is increasing; it is estimated that in the 1990s one fourth to one third of all children under the age of eighteen will have lived in a stepfamily at some point. Difficulties in stepfamilies may arise because so many attachments and loyalty bonds are involved, and with large stepfamilies, money problems may be acute.

Review Questions

1. Describe the strengths and weaknesses of each of the six major family forms.
2. Outline the developmental course of marital relations, at each point suggesting some of the major issues involved and adaptations that have to be made.
3. What contributes to marital satisfaction and conflict? What is the interrelationship of parenting, marital relations, and the child's behavior?
4. Discuss the different aspects of the parental role and the developmental changes in parenting. What kind of parenting style seems to be better than others?
5. What is the nature of sibling relationships in adulthood?
6. Why is midlife such an important and often conflicting time in intergenerational relations? What can we conclude about the nature of intergenerational relations?
7. What are the different meanings of the grandparent role?
8. What are some of the myths that surround single adults?
9. What is the life of divorced adults like, and what are the effects of divorce on children?
10. What is the adjustment process like when separation occurs in later life?
11. What is the nature of life in stepparent families?

Further Readings

Doherty, W. J., & Jacobson, N. S. (1982). Marriage and the family. In B. J. Wolman (Ed.), *Handbook of developmental psychology.* Englewood Cliffs, NJ: Prentice-Hall.

An excellent overview of different theories of marital choice and satisfaction, including recent information about behavioral exchange theory. Easy to medium difficult reading.

Kelly, J. B. (1982). Divorce: The adult perspective. In B. J. Wolman (Ed.), *Handbook of developmental psychology.* Englewood Cliffs, NJ: Prentice-Hall.

Joan Kelly's research (in collaboration with Judith Wallerstein) is recognized as among the most important contributions to our knowledge about divorce. Reasonably easy to read.

Murstein, B. I. (Ed.). (1978). *Exploring intimate life styles.* New York: Springer.

Includes a number of articles written by different individuals on alternative life-styles in adulthood. Reasonably easy to read.

Troll, L. E., & Bengston, V. L. (1982). Intergenerational relations throughout the life span. In B. J. Wolman (Ed.), *Handbook of developmental psychology.* Englewood Cliffs, NJ: Prentice-Hall.

A superb, well-written overview of the many complex aspects of intergenerational relations.

8

ADULT RELATIONSHIPS AND THE CULTURAL AND SOCIAL SETTING

IMAGINE *what it would be like to have no friends and to be lonely.* Indeed, imagine what life would be like with no other people—no one to compare ourselves with, no one to be our companion. Imagine what it would be like not to have someone who makes us feel secure and gives us support when we need it.

Some people lack an emotional attachment or a social network, and this is likely to result in a feeling of loneliness. Robert Weiss (1973) believes that there are two kinds of loneliness: **emotional isolation,** which results from the loss or absence of an emotional attachment, and **social isolation,** which occurs through the loss or absence of social ties. Either type of loneliness is likely to make an individual feel restless and depressed. Weiss also believes that one type of relationship cannot easily be substituted for another in order to diminish the feeling of loneliness. Consequently, an adult grieving over the loss of a love relationship is likely to still feel very lonely even though he or she may have friends to spend time with.

Divorce or the death of a spouse inevitably produces feelings of loss and loneliness for many people. One divorced woman commented that you get the feeling that the whole world has just come to an end and that you are completely alone. From Weiss's perspective, a support network of friends and relatives may help the divorced woman adapt, but she is still likely to experience emotional isolation.

Similarly, people who have close emotional attachments may still feel a great deal of loneliness if they do not have social ties as well. Weiss described one woman who had a happy marriage but whose husband had to take a job in another state where they had no friends. In their new location she listened to her husband describing all of the new friends he was developing on his new job while she was sitting home taking care of the kids. She was bored and miserable and finally convinced her husband to move to a suburb where she would have a better opportunity to develop friendships.

It is important to distinguish being alone from being lonely. Most of us cherish the moments when we can be alone for awhile, away from the hectic pace of our lives. Zick Rubin (1979) has commented that for people in high-pressure jobs, aloneness may heal whereas loneliness can hurt. In our society we have been conditioned to believe that aloneness is to be dreaded, so we develop expectations that solitude may bring sadness. However, it has been revealed that people who choose to live alone are no more lonely than people who live with others (Rubenstein & Shaver, 1981).

Perhaps more important than the actual physical presence of someone else, such as a spouse, lover, or friend, is the knowledge that someone else will be there when we need him or her. Although loneliness seems to be more prevalent among unmarried, divorced, and widowed people, none of us is assured of protection from loneliness. In one national survey, 26 percent of those interviewed said that they had felt very lonely or remote from other people during the last few weeks (Bradburn, 1969).

It has been argued that friendship contacts are more frequent among the elderly of higher socioeconomic status. However, the more numerous friendships among middle-class elderly may be offset by more intensity and greater involvement in the friendships of working-class older people. Because those of the working class have less geographic mobility, they may enter each new phase of adult life with the same friendships in tow.

Intimacy, love, attachment, and friendship are among the most cherished aspects of adult life. If we do not have an intimate relationship with someone, we may spend endless hours thinking about how to develop such a relationship. And if we don't have any friends, most of us spend time and effort trying to develop friendships. Very few of us want to go through the world alone for very long—feelings of loneliness, when they persist for a long time, can be debilitating and lead to some form of mental disturbance.

INTRODUCTION

Social processes and contexts other than those related to the family also influence our development as adults. Extrafamilial influences include social relationships with friends and acquaintances. We may develop attachments to people other than our parents, children, and spouse. In this chapter we look at the concepts of attachment and love, as well as intimacy, in an effort to explore the nature of relationships in adulthood. We will see that intimacy and similarity are important aspects of friendships.

In considering the contexts in which we live and whom we relate with as adults, it is important to evaluate our culture. Therefore, we describe the nature of the cultural process, social class, the history of how society has viewed and treated the elderly, and cross-cultural comparisons, particularly of how aging is viewed. Finally, we present the major theories that have been crafted to explain the social basis of aging.

RELATIONSHIPS

In chapter 7 we talked a lot about relationships. We looked at factors that influence marital choice, marital relationships through the adult years, factors that contribute to marital satisfaction and conflict, the relationships between parents and children, within and across generations, as well as some central aspects in the lives of single adults, many of which involve relationships.

What do relationships give us? Not only are we motivated to seek the company of other people in general, but most of us would like to form close and prolonged relationships with specific people. We have found that adults usually seek two kinds of relationships with others, one an emotional attachment to one other person (usually a lover or spouse), the other social ties to a number of friends. The two sets of relationships serve different needs: emotional attachments stimulate a sense of comfort and security, whereas social ties create a sense of group identity and integration.

Attachment and Love

Many researchers and theoreticians have emphasized that the concept of attachment should be used only during the period of infancy. One recent effort, however, suggests that it may be fruitful not to limit the concept of attachment to the caretaker-infant relationship and that the concept may be successfully used to study other aspects of the life cycle as well.

Toni Antonucci (1981) studied the social interactive/social supportive behaviors of adolescents and considered them in relation to the adolescents' own attitudes about future social interaction (specifically, age at marriage) and their own actual behaviors (reported eleven years after high school graduation). The data used in this investigation came from Project Talent, an enormous effort to study the personal, educational, and experiential factors that promote or inhibit the development of human talent. Of the original sample of 400,000 ninth to twelfth graders in Project Talent, 4,000 subjects were selected for study by Antonucci. High school students were asked several questions that could be considered to reflect attachment to family and peers. The high school attachment measures included discussion of future plans with father and with mother; age at which marriage is intended; and activity level in affiliative high school activities, such as groups and clubs. The age at which the respondent first married was assessed. And in adulthood, questions focused on such factors as marital satisfaction, parenting satisfaction, and happiness in social life.

What were labeled attachment behaviors in adolescence were linked with social behavior and interaction in adulthood. Some of the findings indicate that what has been described as insecure attachment in infancy may have some applicability to later social interactions. For example, adolescents who date very early and often and who marry early may be showing a form of insecure attachment, according to Antonucci. Adolescents who engage in appropriate and varied sex-typed behaviors, such as affiliative behaviors for boys and achievement/vocational related behaviors for girls may be expressing a more secure attachment. Indeed, these latter adolescents were more likely to report high levels of marital satisfaction and life satisfaction and a happier social life some eleven years after their high school graduation.

Love has been the domain of poets and novelists more than it has been the province of scientific psychology. Though not easily defined and measured, love, nevertheless, is a pervasive aspect of interpersonal relationships in adulthood. Many adults spend hour after hour thinking about love, anticipating a romantic love relationship, watching themes of love on soap operas, reading about such themes in magazines or books, and listening to music filled with references to love. One psychologist, Zick Rubin (1970, 1973) has attempted to measure one type of love, romantic love. He developed two scales, one for liking and one for loving. Rubin believes that **liking** refers to the sense that someone is similar to us and involves our positive evaluation of that person; **loving,** on the other hand, indexes being close to someone and includes dependency, a more selfless orientation to help the other person, and qualities of exclusiveness and absorption. The qualities of exclusiveness and absorption seem to differentiate liking from loving more than the others. If you just like someone, that individual probably does not preoccupy your thoughts and you are not likely to be overly concerned if that person likes someone else. By contrast, love stimulates a great deal of preoccupation with another person, including feelings of possessiveness. Rubin's ideas of loving and liking seem to correspond to Weiss's beliefs about emotional attachment and social ties, respectively.

Attachment and love seem to be important to our survival and well-being throughout life (e.g., Bowlby, 1969; Reedy, Birren, & Schaie, 1981; Spitz, 1945). Recall that the data on marital satisfaction suggest that love does not increase as marriages age but instead often decreases. We know little about what keeps love alive and well as lovers grow older, but there is increased interest in studying various dimensions of attachment across the life span (e.g., Antonucci, 1981; Hartup & Lempers, 1973; Troll & Smith, 1976; Weinraub, Brooks, & Lewis, 1977). Recently, Margaret Reedy, James Birren, and K. Warner Schaie (1981) examined the theoretical and research literature on the developmental nature of attachment in adult love relationships and found two themes. The first indicates that relationships move toward deeper levels of intimacy over time and that the passionate fires of youthful love are somehow transformed into the deeper, more serene and tender love of advanced age (e.g., Levinger, 1974). From this perspective, physical attraction, perceived similarity of the loved one, self-disclosure, romance, and passion are important in new relationships, whereas security, loyalty, and mutual emotional interest in the relationship sustain love relationships over long periods of time. According to George Levinger (1974), "mutuality" supports love relationships over time and occurs when partners share knowledge with each other, assume responsibility for each other's satisfaction, and share private information that governs their relationship.

The second theme in the literature on the development of love relationships suggests two basic marital types, institutional and companionship (Hicks & Platt, 1970). The **institutional relationship** is oriented toward tradition; loyalty and security are primary aspects of the relationship, and normative rules for behavior are sex-differentiated along traditional lines. The husband's role is more instrumental, whereas the wife's role is more expressive. By contrast, the **companionship relationship** stresses the importance of the affective interaction, including passion, expressions of love, rapport, communication, and respect. Investigators have found that over time tradition may replace companionship as the primary bonding force in love relationships. For example, in a twenty-year longitudinal study, it was found that decline in marital satisfaction from youth to middle adulthood was associated with decline in companionship, demonstration of affection and passion, common interests, and communication (Pineo, 1961).

In order to further explore the nature of age and sex differences in the characteristics of satisfying love relationships, Reedy, Birren, and Schaie (1981) studied 102 happily married couples in early (average age twenty-eight), middle (average age forty-five), and late adulthood (average age sixty-five). As can be seen in figure 8.1, age differences in the nature of satisfying love relationships were found. The idea that passion and sexual intimacy are relatively more important in early adulthood and tender feelings of affection and loyalty are relatively more important to later-life love relationships was supported. It was also indicated that young adult lovers rate communication as more characteristic of their love relationships than do their counterparts in middle and late adulthood.

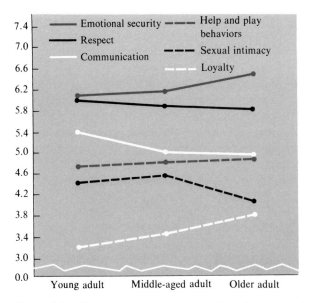

Figure 8.1   Changes in the components of satisfying love relationships across the life span.

This finding, combined with the data about emotional security and loyalty being more important in later life, supports the second major theme of the development of love relationships—that of distinguishing between institutional and companionship aspects of love.

Aside from the age differences, however, there were some striking similarities in the nature of satisfying love relationships in the Reedy, Birren, and Schaie study. At all ages, emotional security was ranked as the most important factor in love, followed by respect, communication, help and play behaviors, sexual intimacy, and loyalty. Clearly, then, there is a great deal more to love than sex. These findings indicate that a new historical trend in the quality of relationships may be emerging. In the last decade there was extensive interest in individual freedom and independence, but the data suggest a historical shift toward security, fidelity, trust, and commitment in relationships. This historical trend mirrors the theme of Daniel Yankelovich's popular book *New Rules in American Life: Searching for Self-Fulfillment in a World Turned Upside Down* (1981), in which he elaborates on the changing orientation of adults away from self-interest toward an ethic of commitment to others.

The findings of Reedy, Birren, and Schaie (1981) also suggest that the nature of love in satisfying relationships is different for men than for women. Women rated emotional security as more important in love than men did. No sex differences were found for communication and sexual intimacy, and somewhat surprisingly, men more than women rated loyalty as more characteristic of their love relationship.

Though this research suggests that intimacy is a more central factor in a satisfying love relationship as marriages age, life-span theorist Erik Erikson believes that early adulthood is the period in which the development of intimacy becomes a crisis.

Intimacy is a very important ingredient in our close relationships with others, whether those relationships involve an emotional attachment to a spouse or lover or a social tie to a friend. Next we look at the concept of intimacy in greater detail, beginning with some comments about Erikson's view of intimacy versus isolation, followed by a description of styles of intimate interaction, and concluding with a discussion of intimacy in late adulthood.

Intimacy

Erik Erikson (1968) believes that intimacy should come after individuals are well on their way to achieving a stable and successful identity. The development of intimacy, in Erikson's view, is another life crisis—if intimacy is not developed in early adulthood, the person may be left with what Erikson refers to as isolation.

Erikson refers to **intimacy** in terms of both sexual relationships and friendships. He comments:

> As the young individual seeks at least tentative forms of playful intimacy in friendship and competition, in sex play and love, in argument and gossip, he is apt to experience a peculiar strain, as if such tentative engagement might turn into an interpersonal fusion amounting to a loss of identity and requiring, therefore, a tense inner reservation, a caution in commitment. Where a youth does not resolve such a commitment, he may isolate himself and enter, at best, only stereotyped and formalized interpersonal relations; or he may, in repeated hectic attempts and dismal failures, seek intimacy with the most improbable of partners. For where an assured sense of identity is missing, even friendships and affairs become desperate attempts at delineating the fuzzy outlines of identity by mutual narcissistic mirroring; to fall in love means to fall in love with one's mirror image, hurting oneself and damaging the mirror. (p. 167)

An inability to develop meaningful relationships with others during young adulthood can be harmful to an individual's personality. It may lead him to repudiate, ignore, or attack those who appear frustrating to him. Erikson (1968) asserts that such situations can account for the shallow, almost pathetic attempts of youth to merge themselves with a leader. Many youth want to be apprentices or disciples of leaders and adults who will shelter them from the harm of an "outgroup" world. If this fails, and Erikson believes that it must, then sooner or later the individual will recoil into a self-search to discover where he or she went wrong. Such introspection sometimes leads to painful feelings of isolation and depression and may contribute to mistrust of others and restrict the individual's willingness to act on his or her own initiative. Next we see that there are a number of different styles of intimacy that can be followed.

Styles of Intimate Interaction

One classification of intimacy suggests five styles of interaction: intimate, preintimate, stereotyped, pseudointimate, and isolated (Orlofsky, Marcia, & Lesser, 1973). The **intimate** individual forms and maintains one or more deep and long-lasting love relationships. The **preintimate** individual has mixed emotions about commitment; this ambivalence is reflected in her or his strategy of offering love without any obligations or long-lasting bonds. In most instances, the **stereotyped** individual has superficial relationships that tend to be dominated by friendship ties with same-sex rather than opposite-sex individuals. The **pseudointimate** individual appears to be maintaining a long-lasting heterosexual attachment, but the relationship has little or no depth or closeness. Finally, the **isolated** individual withdraws from social encounters and has little or no intimate attachment to same- or opposite-sex individuals. Occasionally the isolate shows signs of developing interpersonal relations, but usually such interactions are anxiety provoking. One investigation indicated that intimate and preintimate individuals are more sensitive to their partners' needs, as well as more open in their friendships, than individuals characterized by the other three intimacy statuses (Orlofsky, 1976).

Research with both college males and females has indicated that individuals who attain a stable sense of identity are more likely to attain intimacy than to remain at one of the other four intimacy stages. By contrast, students who are characterized by foreclosure, moratorium, and diffusion identities show more variable levels of intimacy (Kacerguis & Adams, 1978). This work supports Erikson's belief that identity development is closely linked (and perhaps even an important precursor) to intimacy.

How do researchers investigate intimacy? The strategy is usually the same as in the search for pinning down identity; often, a questionnaire is developed that focuses on various aspects of intimacy. One such instrument is the Yufit Intimacy-Isolation Questionnaire, which has twenty intimacy questions (for example, "Do you lead an active social life? talk with people about their innermost problems? Are you consistent in giving affection?") and twenty isolation questions (for example, "Do you avoid excitement or emotional tension? Do you often feel unnoticed in a group?").

Bernice Neugarten (1980) argues that intimacy is not a critical issue only in early adulthood. Next we see that intimacy is an important concern of individuals in middle and late adulthood as well.

Intimacy in Middle and Late Adulthood

Intimacy is a multidimensional concept that includes mutual trust, support, understanding, and the sharing of confidences. There seems to be an important relationship between intimacy and psychological well-being. The work of Marjorie Lowenthal and her colleagues suggests that the presence of a confidant is a critical aspect of psychological adaptation to aging as measured by morale, avoidance of psychosomatic symptoms, and the ability to cope with stress (Lowenthal,

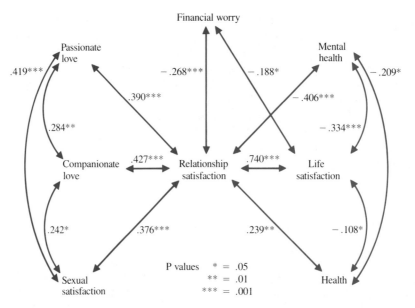

Figure 8.2   Relationship between intimacy and three measures of satisfaction with life.

Thurnher, & Chiriboga, 1975). By contrast, extreme social isolation is associated with psychiatric illness (Lowenthal, 1964).

Indeed, being embedded in a network of close interpersonal ties seems to be associated with general life satisfaction and a sense of belonging, worth, and identity. In one recent investigation of intimacy in the lives of 240 women in middle and late adulthood, the level of satisfaction and happiness experienced by women in their intimate relationships was strongly linked with overall life satisfaction and well-being. The quality of intimacy was also a significant factor in the older women's physical health (Traupmann, Eckels, & Hatfield, 1982). A more complete accounting of the link between factors involved in intimacy and life satisfaction is presented in figure 8.2.

Friendships

In our discussion of relationships and intimacy we have seen that close social ties with peers—friendships—are very important to us as adults. In this section we look further at the nature of friendships in adulthood.

Intimacy and Similarity in Friendships

Intimacy in friendship may be defined in different ways. It has been broadly defined to include everything in a relationship that makes it seem close or intense (Huston & Burgess, 1979). However, in some investigations friendship has been defined more narrowly in terms of intimate self-disclosure and the sharing of

Intimacy seems to characterize the friendships of female adults more than male adults.

private thoughts. Reference also has been made to private and personal knowledge about a friend (Sullivan, 1953). It has been suggested that the friendships
of females are characterized more by intimacy than is the case for males (Berndt,
1982). Indeed in cross-sex dating relationships and marital relationships, females are much more likely to disclose themselves to males than vice versa and
are much more prone to mutual self-exploration than males are (e.g., Douvan &
Adelson, 1966). It also appears that females bring the capacity for intimacy to
courtship and train males to be intimate (e.g., Simon & Gagnon, 1969). In other
words, women are more oriented toward revealing sensitive, intimate feelings
than men are.

Does intimate friendship have an effect on personality or life satisfaction? We have seen that intimacy is linked to life satisfaction, and there is evidence that having a close and stable best friend is associated with self-esteem (Mannarino, 1979), but we do not know whether the differences are caused by life satisfaction and self-esteem or by intimacy. In other words, adults with high self-esteem and life satisfaction may be more likely to be able to develop a close, intimate friendship, just as having a close friend may promote self-esteem and life satisfaction.

Similarity is also an important aspect of friendship. Friends are usually similar in terms of age, sex, and race (Hallihan, 1979). Friends usually have similar attitudes toward politics and achievement orientations (Ball, 1981). Friends often like the same kinds of music and clothes and like to engage in the same kinds of leisure activities (Ball, 1981). For the most part we meet our friends through our activities at school or college, at work, in our neighborhood, or in community activities.

Friendships Across the Adult Years

During the course of adult development people come into contact with many adults other than their marital partner. In one investigation of friendships in early adulthood, the close acquaintances of 275 women, whose average age was twenty-nine years, were likely to be next-door neighbors (Athanasion & Yoshioka, 1973). The friendships of their children increased the likelihood that the mothers would be friends. These women tended to affiliate with other women whose marital status was similar to their own, who were close to their own age, had about the same number of children, and were at about the same level of family income. When women lived farther away from each other, the fact that they were friends was more likely to be related to occupation and education.

One life-span developmental study of friendships found that the newly married have more friends than adolescents, middle-aged adults, or the elderly (Weiss & Lowenthal, 1975). During early adulthood, friendships that were established earlier may dissipate, particularly in the case of young adults who get married. Decisions must be made about whether the couple will see such friends separately or whether they will put up with their spouse's friends, some of whom they may detest. Often friendships develop that are based on a four-party relationship (two couples) rather than a two-party relationship (one couple); the two couples may go out to dinner together, play bridge together, and so forth.

In middle adulthood many friends are old friends. Still, new acquaintances may develop, often through formal organizations, which middle-aged adults participate in at a fairly high rate (Troll, 1975). During middle adulthood, closeness and convenience seem to be less salient in the nature of friendships than is true in early adulthood. In one investigation of 150 middle-aged adults who had moved within the last five years, a majority of the individuals named as their best friend someone from the locale where they had lived before (Hess, 1971).

There is evidence that married middle-aged men often allocate more of their time to friendships than to their family and may rely on the suggestions of friends more than the advice of their spouse. However, throughout the adult years women seem to maintain their friendships longer than men do (Maas & Kuypers, 1974; Riley, Johnson, & Foner, 1972).

In late adulthood death of a spouse may narrow the circle of friends for men, whereas it may expand the circle for women. Women who have had sustained career commitment may show a more restricted social network in old age because they have not had much time to devote to the nurturance of friendships (Troll, 1971). Finally, some researchers have suggested that the cohesiveness found in many retirement communities may reflect a loosening of kin relationships (Lowenthal & Robinson, 1976).

Next we look at the cultural and social settings in which adults live.

CULTURE AND SOCIETY

The cultural milieu—that is, the physical and social settings in which adults live—has many aspects. We have already examined some important aspects of our culture, including family and social networks, and in the next chapter we will look at other important features of our culture. Here, however, we look at how the cultural process works, the nature of social class, and societal and cross-cultural views of aging.

The Cultural Process

The term *culture* as used here refers to the existing cluster of behaviors, attitudes, values, and products of a particular group of people. Thus we can refer to the culture of the United States, the culture of China, the culture of the Soviet Union, and so forth. It is important to recognize that the culture of any nation or group cannot be defined as a single strand. Within each culture there are many subcultures that have their own sets of behaviors and values.

To get a sense of the importance of the cultural process in understanding adult development, we look at the culture of the Ik in Uganda, as described by anthropologist Colin Turnbull (1972). For about 2,000 years the Ik lived as nomadic hunters. But some forty years ago, their livelihood was destroyed when the government of Uganda turned their hunting grounds into a national park. Since hunting was forbidden in the park, the Ik were forced to try to farm the steep, barren mountain areas of the park.

Famine, crowding, and drought led to tremendous upheavals in family orientation and moral values. Children were sent out on their own with no life supports supplied by parents. Interestingly, when the children eventually had children of their own they, in turn, put them out on their own at a very young age, as young as three years old.

The principle of individual survival became far and away the most important motive in the life of the Ik. Turnbull describes the Ik as having no love at all. Imagine yourself on a barren mountainside away from civilization in the country of Uganda. Your way of life has been disrupted. You no longer have food. Would you act like the adults in the Ik culture?

Think about the community you grew up in. Was it rural or urban? What was the moral climate—conservative or liberal? How strong was the role of religion? How much community organization and interest was there? Were there town celebrations? Was it a young community with few old people, were there lots of old people, or was there a mixture of adult age groups? Were most of the townspeople white- or blue-collar workers? Did most people have two cars and send their children off to summer camp? What kind of support systems were available for the elderly? By thinking about questions such as these, you can get a sense of varying community subcultures—all of which are starkly different from the cultural milieu of the Ik in Uganda.

Social Class

Subcultural comparisons of individuals from different socioeconomic backgrounds provide further evidence of the role of culture in adult development. You probably have some idea of what is meant by *social class*. We talk about it all the time: "He is not making much money and doesn't live in a nice house because he comes from a lower-class background." "She is achievement oriented because she comes from a middle-class family." "He's lower class." "She's middle class." In such ways we express our perceptions of people's socioeconomic status.

Social stratification in the United States carries with it certain inequalities. It is generally acknowledged that members of society (1) have occupations that vary in prestige, (2) have different levels of power to influence the institutions of a community, (3) have different economic resources, and (4) have different educational and occupational opportunities. These differences in ability to control resources and to participate in the rewards of society produce unequal opportunities for individuals (Hess, 1970).

Poverty

One of the socioeconomic concerns of individuals in late adulthood is the decrease in income they likely are to experience. A classic complaint of the aged and aggrieved parent is that a mother can care for five young children more readily than five adult children can care for one mother. In most families, though, children do not neglect an elderly relative out of heartlessness but out of helplessness. Aiding someone who is growing frail and infirm can be frustrating and difficult.

The elderly have a higher poverty rate than any other adult age category.

The elderly have a higher poverty rate than any other adult age category. For example, in the United States in 1977 of the 22 million people aged sixty-five and over, 3.2 million or 14 percent were classified as poor by the federal government. In 1977 the federal poverty line for a nonfarm family of four was $6,200. For an elderly couple it was $3,700 and for an elderly person living alone it was $2,900. The number of elderly poor probably would be much greater if it included the "hidden poor," those individuals who would be classified as poor on the basis of their own income but who have been taken in by relatives who are

Table 8.1

POVERTY RATES[a] AMONG AGED PERSONS[b] BY RACE AND SEX OF HEAD, 1959 AND 1977

	1977	*1959*
Male Head		
Whites	7%	28%
Blacks	28%	59%
Female Head		
Whites	21%	47%
Blacks	48%	70%

[a]Percent poor.
[b]Head age sixty-five or older.

Source: Table 16, *U.S. Bureau of the Census (1978b).*

not poor. Some estimates place the number of hidden poor at 5 million people (U.S. Senate, Special Committee on Aging, 1977).

Although many elderly people are poor, table 8.1 shows that there has been a marked improvement in the economic status of the elderly in recent years. It also is evident from the table that there is a higher rate of poverty for elderly women than men and a higher rate among elderly blacks than whites.

Housing

John Williamson, Anne Munley, and Linda Evans (1980) describe the housing problems that many elderly people face:

> In the motion picture *Harry and Tonto,* Harry is a retired teacher living with his cat, Tonto, in a condemned apartment building within one of New York City's deteriorating slum neighborhoods. Despite confrontations with muggers and the area's other undesirable characteristics, Harry insists on remaining and must be removed bodily by police when the wrecking crew arrives. Harry moves in with his son's family because they live sufficiently near his former neighborhood for Harry to visit his best friends frequently; and, as Harry tells Tonto, "When you have friends, that's home." In his new household, Harry puts up with constant bickering. As soon as his friend dies, Harry and Tonto leave the unhappy environment and embark on a series of adventures in search of a living situation they can tolerate.
>
> Though presented in a humorous vein, Harry's quest for satisfying housing demonstrates that living situations can be an important concern for the aging person. Harry's need is not just for housing. He is seeking an environment which is suited to his physical, psychological, and social needs. . . .
>
> Ironically the bulk of research concerned with the living environments of the elderly has focused on special situations such as nursing homes, public housing, mobile home parks, welfare hotels, or retirement communities. In reality, however, these living conditions account for less than 10 percent of this country's elderly population. Approximately 90 percent live in age-integrated settings, but relatively little is

known about their environmental circumstances (Carp, 1976). Although the percentage of older persons who own their dwelling units is high, data concerned with housing quality are less optimistic. The U.S. Senate Special Committee on Aging (1976) estimates that 30 percent of the elderly occupy housing which is deteriorating or substandard [and] one in five lives in a housing unit which lacks basic plumbing facilities (Carp, 1976). (pp. 256, 257, 259)

An example of the haphazard matching of life-style and environment is the mode of urban living referred to as SRO (single room occupancy), which is described in box 8.1. Social isolation and lack of socially desirable activity often characterize such settings.

Income plays an important role in the living conditions of the elderly. Only about 1 percent of aged families and one tenth of 1 percent of unrelated elderly people have incomes of $50,000 or more. For such individuals, housing options are virtually unlimited. At the other extreme are individuals who live in places like the slum hotel described in box 8.1. Of course, most of the elderly fall between these two extremes. Typically, their number one expense is housing. For people aged seventy-five and over, housing accounts for almost one half of their budget (Harris, 1978).

Fortunately, more help than ever is now available in the form of improving institutions and expanding in-home services. Candace Trunzo (1982) describes these improvements, as she gives advice to adults on how to help their elderly parents live more comfortable lives:

> The growing numbers of home healthcare workers now permit more old people to live on their own. There are agencies that help the elderly find roommates—young or old—to share quarters, costs and companionship. Special geriatric day-care centers make it possible for old people—who might otherwise have to go to nursing homes—to live with relatives who work. And for those who do require institutionalization, there's a much wider choice of facilities.
>
> It is usually up to the family to weave through the maze of available government, community and commercial services. You'll probably have an easier time than your ailing father, say, finding out what the alternatives are, doing the necessary paperwork and checking the suitability of facilities. The elderly, even the most vital, independent ones, sometimes won't take the initiative, points out Michael Smyer, associate chairman of the gerontology center at Pennsylvania State University. "They are not a 'gimme' group," he explains. "The psychology of entitlement didn't saturate their generation the way it has ours."
>
> Most people want to live at home; getting old or sick doesn't change that. While you may think your relative requires the kind of care only a nursing home can provide, there may be an alternative that will satisfy both of you. Says Jean Kinnard of the American Association of Homes for the Aging: "If there is any trend in care for the elderly, it's a tendency to reach out more with meals on wheels, adult day care and other services. The concept is called homes without walls, and the idea is to help the elderly who can still live independently."

Box 8.1
LIFE IN THE SLUM HOTEL

An estimated 146,000 poor older persons reside in run-down hotels or rooming houses in the blighted sections of cities (Carp, 1976). Though SROs house a very small percentage of all older persons, residents' life-styles reflect the same staunch desire for privacy, independence, and autonomy that is also manifested by elderly residing in "more desirable" homes.

An ethnography of a slum hotel in a "large Western city" (Stephens, 1976) shows how the elderly who are near the bottom of the economic ladder live. Approximately 30 percent of the occupants of this particular hotel were elderly. . . .

Isolation in one form or another was the hallmark of this social environment. For the most part, the ninety-seven elderly males avoided not only the eleven elderly females but each other as well. These people were virtually required to relinquish their needs for intimacy to survive in the hotel. The two principal reasons for developing or maintaining relationships were common economic interests or shared leisure activities. Relationships among residents seemed to require some justification; simple social interaction never seemed to be enough.

The prime source of income for many older residents involved "hustling"— scavenging, peddling, pushing drugs, or shoplifting. In some cases, two or more residents developed relationships which facilitated hustling schemes. It was also necessary for a "hustler" to let others know of hustling successes since hustling was a key determinant of social status along three dimensions: its profitability, its dependability as a source of income, and the degree of autonomy it provided. Besides socializing over successful hustling feats, residents also related to one another through drinking or betting activities.

Only minimal social activity took place at the hotel, and it served as the focal point for little physical activity other than sleep. Most residents had to go outside the hotel for food and routine health needs. Some took meals at the least expensive places in the neighborhood where muggings were frequent. The rooms had no cooking or refrigeration facilities, but some residents cooked using a hot iron braced by two bibles as a hot plate. . . .

Locked into this situation by poverty, ill health, and a desire to maintain independence, many older residents of this hotel planned to die there. (Williamson, Munley, & Evans, pp. 259–260).

Nursing homes may be the only alternative for some families. About 5 percent of those over sixty-five are institutionalized. Sadly, not all nursing homes offer competent care, but in general they have come a long way from the mid-1970s, when charges of patient neglect and abuse were common, according to Edward Kuriansky, the special state prosecutor in New York who is in charge of nursing home investigations. The best facilities tend to be nonprofit institutions sponsored by religious, union, or fraternal organizations. At the better facilities, rehabilitation is the byword regardless of the patient's age. The Wesley Woods Health Center in Atlanta, for example, features an extensive rehabilitation program, including occupational, physical, and speech therapy as well as psychotherapy to motivate patients to improve their health. Approximately 40 percent of its patients are able to return to their homes. (pp. 71, 72, 74, 76)

Cross-Cultural and Societal Views of Aging

The United States is a youth-oriented culture, one that places a premium on being young rather than old. As a result many of our elderly live an age-segregated life. This perspective stands in contrast to the lofty status of the elderly in some cultures, particularly certain peasant and primitive cultures. First, we look in greater detail at how we view the elderly in the United States; then we examine the perception and treatment of the elderly in different cultures.

Aging in the United States

One of the biggest problems facing the elderly in the United States may be the negative stereotypes that many people have about older people. Too often we view the elderly as useless and inadequate. Evidence suggests that elementary school children already have unrealistic perceptions of the elderly, viewing them in one of two extremes—very kind or very mean. Children also perceive many of the elderly as lonely, bored, and inactive and as having time hanging over their heads (Hickey, Hickey, & Kalish, 1968). In one investigation (Kastenbaum & Durkee, 1964), adolescents and young adults tended to view old age as risky, unpleasant, and without any significant positive values.

Gerald Gruman (1978) has traced the historical background of attitudes toward the elderly, concluding that the origin of current negative stereotypes seems to have first appeared at the end of the Western frontier in the 1890s. Then America was striving to become a strong nation, acquiring new territory in the process. Young people were seen as a vital resource for this task, whereas the elderly were seen as weak and inadequate. At this time it was standard practice for industries to make anyone over the age of forty quit working.

The Great Depression of the 1930s eliminated any savings that most elderly people might have had. This period may have been the lowest period that the elderly in America have experienced. Poverty was often severe, savings were gone, and younger men needed work. Retirement was established, one of the reasons

Table 8.2

**RESPONSES TO TRUTH OF MYTH-STEREOTYPE STATEMENTS
AND MEANS OF PERCENT EXCEPTIONS**

Statements	Respondents who initially considered statement true (%)	Exceptions to statement considered:	
		True (M %)	False (M %)
1. As people grow older, they become more alike.	37		
2. If people live long enough, they will become senile.	25	22	25
3. Old age is generally a time of serenity.	52	28	24
4. Older people tend to show little interest in sex.	47	26	22
5. Old people tend to be inflexible.	65	22	27
6. Most older people lack creativity and are unproductive.	20	23	25
7. Older people have great difficulty learning new skills.	46	24	24
8. When people grow old, they generally become "cranky."	22	18	24
9. Most older people are lonely and isolated.	66	26	27
10. As people become older, they are likely to become more religious.	77	18	24

Source: Schonfield, 1982. Reprinted by permission of *The Gerontologist, 22,* pages 267–272, 1982.

possibly being to make room for younger workers who were felt to have more strength, skill, and vigorous new ideas. Many of the elderly lived with their children because they had no other option. The aged were viewed as a social problem—what should be done with them?

As the number of elderly people dramatically increased, social programs began to be developed to meet their needs. In the 1960s and 1970s greater social concern was directed toward the elderly. Some social scientists, while recognizing that much more needs to be accomplished, nonetheless believe that there has been a gradual improvement in the quality of life and status of elderly people since World War II (Tibbitts, 1979). In the United States today the increasing population of older people who are healthy, productive, and intelligent suggests that stereotypes of the elderly as sick, inadequate, and worthless need to be discarded.

Interestingly, David Schonfield (1982) has found that when adults of varying ages are allowed to tell about exceptions to their generalizations about the elderly, less negative stereotyping seems to be the case. (See table 8.2.) As you can see from the first column, 20 to 77 percent initially said that one or another generalization was true. But a different picture emerged when participants were asked about exceptions to the generalization.

Table 8.3

AGE DISTRIBUTION OF RESPONDENTS WHO AT LEAST ONCE OPTED FOR 50% EXCEPTIONS AFTER SAYING A MYTH-STEREOTYPE STATEMENT WAS TRUE OR FALSE

Age group (years)	Total respondents	Respondents using "50% Exceptions" (%)
Under 25	46	26
25–44	36	39
45–64	48	38
65–74	33	45
75+	26	58

Source: Schonfield, 1982. Reprinted by permission of *The Gerontologist, 22,* page 279, 1982.

Most people believe that there are invariably exceptions to statements about the elderly. And as you can see from table 8.3, older respondents were more likely to see exceptions to generalizations about the elderly than were younger respondents.

Next we see that there are some cultures in which the elderly are given a higher status than they are in the United States.

Aging in Other Cultures

In China and Japan the elderly are often given a higher status than in the United States. Intergenerational relations are reciprocal rather than linear. Filial piety runs high in China—respect and homage to family and community elders is a way of life. In Japan the elderly are more integrated into their families than the elderly in most industrialized countries. More than 75 percent live with their children, and very few single older adults live alone. Respect for the elderly in Japan is evidenced in a variety of everyday encounters: the best seats are usually given to the elderly, cooking caters to the tastes of the elderly, and people bow to the elderly. However, such respect appears to be more prevalent among rural than urban Japanese and more frequent among middle-aged than young adult Japanese (Palmore, 1975). Although retirees in Japan are often rehired, this typically involves lower status, lower pay, loss of fringe benefits, and loss of union membership.

Respect for the elderly is pervasive among Muslim families as well. It is thought that the blessings of the elders, whether they are dead or alive, is necessary to avoid disaster and problems.

It is possible that the elderly attain high status in many primitive and peasant cultures because so few individuals live to be old. Because there are so few old people in such cultures, the younger members may believe that the few surviving elders are imbued with special powers and wisdom. However, in most industrialized societies like Japan and the United States, where the aged now

The elderly often have been given a high status in China and Japan.

constitute a sizeable proportion of the population, it is no longer a special feat to live to an old age.

Next we see that three major theories have been developed to try to explain the social basis of aging.

Social Theories of Aging

For some years two perspectives dominated thinking about the social basis of aging: disengagement theory and activity theory. A third view, of more recent vintage, is called social breakdown theory.

Disengagement Theory

For a number of years **disengagement theory** was believed to represent the best social explanation of aging. Developed by Cumming and Henry (1961), disengagement theory argues that as older people slow down they gradually withdraw from society. Disengagement is viewed as a mutual activity in which the individual not only disengages himself or herself from society, but society as well disengages from the individual. According to the theory, the older individual develops an increasing self-preoccupation, lessens emotional ties with others, and shows a decreasing interest in the affairs of the world. Such reduction of social interaction and increased self-preoccupation was thought to be necessary to maintain life satisfaction in late adulthood.

Disengagement theory has been criticized by a number of prominent theorists and researchers. For example, disengagement theory predicts that low morale would accompany high activity and further that disengagement is inevitable and is sought out by the elderly. A series of research studies have failed to support these beliefs (e.g., Maddox, 1968; Reichard, Livson, & Peterson, 1962). For example, in one investigation (Maddox, 1964), when age was held constant, there was substantial variation in the indicators of disengagement displayed. As suggested next, when individuals continue to maintain very active lives in late adulthood they do not show a decrease in life satisfaction.

Activity Theory

In a well-known investigation of engagement and disengagement, Bernice Neugarten and her colleagues (Neugarten, Havighurst, & Tobin, 1968) found that activity and involvement are often associated with life satisfaction. They categorized individuals in late adulthood into four different types of personality styles: integrated (engaged, involved people); armored-defended (holding on types, particularly to middle adulthood roles); passive-dependent (medium to low activity level, sometimes passive and apathetic); and unintegrated (disorganized, deteriorated cognitive processes, weak emotional control). The life satisfaction of the integrated and armored-defended personality types, who were more active and involved, was greater than the passive-dependent and unintegrated types, who were less active and involved.

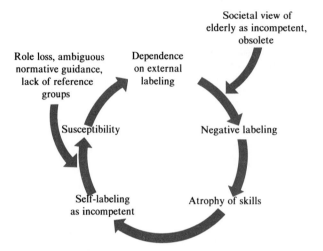

Figure 8.3   The social breakdown syndrome.

According to **activity theory,** then, the more active and involved older people are, the less likely they are to age and the more likely they are to show life satisfaction. Activity theory suggests that it is often healthy for individuals to continue their middle adulthood roles through late adulthood and that if these roles are taken away (for example, through retirement), it is important for people to find substitute roles that keep them active and involved in the world.

Social Breakdown Theory

A third, more recently developed social theory of aging is called **social breakdown theory,** or social breakdown/social reconstruction theory (Kuypers & Bengston, 1973). This theory suggests that aging is promoted through negative psychological functioning that involves a poor self-concept, negative feedback from others and society, and a lack of skills to deal with the world. As suggested in figure 8.3, social breakdown occurs in a sequence that begins with susceptibility and ends with identifying and labeling oneself as incompetent.

In order to prevent the social breakdown syndrome from developing, these researchers believe that we need to reorganize our social system so that individuals in late adulthood will be treated in more respectful ways and will develop better self-images and feel more competent about their role in society. Figure 8.4 shows how social reconstruction could reverse the social breakdown syndrome.

Because of the tremendous variation in cultural-ethnic background among the aged in the United States, social integration must be considered within the context of cultural value systems. One life-style and set of activities may suit

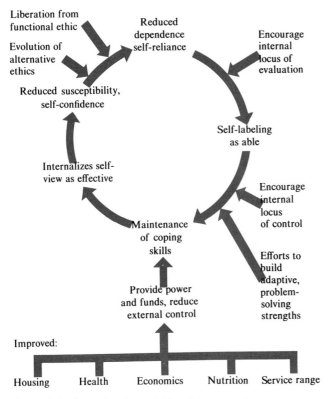

Figure 8.4   Reversing the social breakdown syndrome.

people from one ethnic background better than another. For example, social interaction with family members tends to be more frequent and important for older people of French-American background than their Scandinavian counterparts. The Scandinavian elderly have adapted to an individualized life-style and may seek social integration through organizational participation.

Summary

Our relationships with other people are extraordinarily important to us as adults. For those who do not have emotional attachments or social ties, the result too often is loneliness. Indeed, it may be important to develop not only an emotional attachment but also to have a network of social ties to adequately round out one's life as an adult, although social ties often cannot completely replace the loss of an emotional attachment. Emotional attachments give us comfort and security, and social ties provide us with a sense of group identity and integration. It has been found that physical attraction, perceived similarity of the loved one, self-disclosure, romance, and passion may be more important in new relationships but that security, loyalty, and mutual emotional interest are more germane to enduring relationships.

Intimacy is a very important ingredient in close relationships with others, whether they be spouse, lover, or close friend. Erik Erikson believes that people should develop intimacy after they are well on the way to developing a stable and successful identity. However, debate focuses on just how necessary it is to experience and resolve the intimacy crisis in the order suggested by Erikson. For example, women often show a stronger interest in the intimacy stage before the identity stage, a sequence that is not always maladaptive. It is also important to recognize that there are different styles of intimacy—intimate, preintimate, stereotyped, pseudointimate, and isolated. Intimacy is a theme of development in middle and late adulthood as well as early adulthood. Indeed being embedded in a network of close interpersonal ties appears to be closely linked with life satisfaction. Friendships seem to be characterized by intimacy and similarity, and female friendships seem to involve more intimacy than male friendships. In cross-sex relationships, women often bring the capacity for intimacy to courtship and train males to be intimate. Friendships clearly are an important aspect of our social relationships throughout the adult years.

An important aspect of a culture is social class. One of the major concerns of individuals in late adulthood is the decrease in income that they are likely to experience. The elderly have a higher poverty rate than any other age group. Fortunately, more help than ever is available in the form of improving institutions and expanding in-home services. Trying to wade through the complex aspects of cultural effects on the elderly is difficult. One concept that may help is a distinction between social integration and social isolation. Social integration of the aged has been defined in terms of organizational participation, social activity, social networks, residential integration, and friendship patterns.

Aging in our culture unfortunately still carries with it a number of negative stereotypes, and these stereotypes seem to appear early with evidence that elementary school children often view the elderly as inactive, lonely, and bored. It appears that negative stereotypes about the elderly in America began in the late 1800s. The Great Depression contributed to the poverty of the elderly, and it wasn't until after World War II that greater social concern was directed at the elderly. Indeed, while much more needs to be done, the quality of life of the elderly in the United States seems to have improved in recent years. Nevertheless, some cultures may be better to age in than ours—Japan and China, for example.

Three major theories have been developed to explain the social basis of aging: disengagement, activity, social breakdown. Little support has been found for the disengagement theory. Because of the tremendous variation in cultural-ethnic background of the aged in the United States, social integration must be considered in the context of cultural value systems.

Review Questions

1. Describe the two kinds of relationships most people need, including the functions that each serves.
2. What is the nature of intimate relationships, attachment, and love across the adult years?
3. Describe Erikson's ideas about intimacy and discuss the extent to which we must go through the intimacy stage in the order he prescribes.
4. Name and explain the five styles of intimate interaction.

5. How can we improve the quality of life of the elderly in terms of their living environment?
6. Trace the historical background of attitudes toward the elderly in the United States.
7. How do attitudes toward the elderly in the United States differ from attitudes in other cultures?
8. Identify and describe three theories about the social basis of aging.

Further Readings

Huston, T. L. (Ed.). (1974). *Foundations of interpersonal attraction.* New York: Academic Press.
   A book of readings focused on what attracts people to one another, with extensive information about the formation, maintenance, and termination of relationships, as well as valuable ideas about what makes relationships enjoyable experiences for the parties involved. Reading level is of medium difficulty.
Kahana, B. (1982). Social behavior and aging. In B. J. Wolman (Ed.), *Handbook of developmental psychology.* Englewood Cliffs, NJ: Prentice-Hall.
   An up-to-date overview of information about the concept of social integration. Includes material about attitudes toward the aged, planning services for the aged, and contributions to society during later life. Reasonably easy reading.
Libby, R. W., & Whitehurst, R. N. (1977). *Marriage and alternatives: Exploring intimate relationships.* Glenview, IL: Scott Foresman.
   Selected readings about the variety of adult life-styles that exist in our contemporary society, including information about the many life-style options married adults have available to them. Easy and entertaining reading.
Meacham, J. A., & Santilli, N. R. (1982). Interstage relationships in Erikson's theory: Identity and intimacy. *Child Development, 53,* 1461–1467.
   Focuses on the nature of sequencing of Erikson's stages of identity and intimacy. Promotes critical thinking about Erikson's ideas about the intimacy stage of development. Moderately difficult reading.
Reedy, M. N., Birren, J. E., & Schaie, K. W. (1981). Age and sex differences in satisfying love relationships across the adult life span. *Human Development, 24,* 52–66.
   Describes the authors' work on six components of a love relationship: emotional security, respect, help and play behaviors, communication, sexual intimacy, and loyalty. Outlines differences in intimate love relationships in early, middle, and late adulthood. Easy-to-medium reading difficulty.
Rubin, Z. (1973). *Liking and loving.* New York: Holt, Rinehart & Winston.
   Provides detailed information about interpersonal attraction. Deals with distinctions between loving and liking. Easy to read.
Yankelovich, D. (1981, April). New rules in American life: Searching for self-fulfillment in a world turned upside down. *Psychology Today,* pp. 35–91.
   Yankelovich is a social scientist viewed as an expert at conducting national surveys of trends in America life. The material in *Psychology Today* is adapted from his book, *New Rules,* a best-seller, in which he attempts to show how we are becoming a nation concerned more with commitment to others in the 1980s. Easy and very interesting reading.

9

WORK, LEISURE, AND RETIREMENT

Imagine That You Have Inherited So Much Money
That You Do Not Have to Work

INTRODUCTION

THE SOCIAL, HISTORICAL CONTEXT OF WORK

WORK OVER THE LIFE CYCLE

Occupational Exploration, Planning, and Decision Making
Exploration
Planning and Decision Making
Entering an Occupation
Adjustment
Reaching and Maintaining Occupational Satisfaction and Mid-Life
Career Change
Psychological Factors in Mid-Life Career Change
Box 9.1 The Relationship of Personality Attributes in Adolescence and Mid-Life to Upward
Occupational Mobility
Work in Late Adulthood
Characteristics of Seventy-year-old Workers in the United States

IMAGINE *that you have inherited so much money that you do not have to work.*

Would you stop working? Would you go out and buy a Rolls Royce, a yacht, a mansion? Would you travel around the world? After a year or two, after you had had your fling, what would you do?

In one investigation workers were asked what they would do if they inherited enough money to allow them to stop working (Morse & Weiss, 1968). Only 20 percent said that they would quit working. Approximately one third of the workers said that joblessness would make them feel lost, useless, and ineffective in deciding what to do with their time. It seems that work is a vital part of our identity as adults and often becomes the organizing center of our lives. Indeed, one of the first things that one is asked on meeting someone else is "What do you do?" a question that invariably is interpreted by the respondent as meaning what kind of occupation he or she has rather than what kind of personality or life-style. A person's occupation may, of course, index information about his or her intellectual level, pattern of motivation, life-style, type of neighborhood, and socioeconomic relationships. The world of work may become a central focus for many people because it represents a primary basis for time scheduling on a daily, monthly, yearly, and life-span basis.

Most American adults spend at least one of every three waking hours working. In our culture, we have been reared to think that we can go from rags to riches if we work hard enough. Compared to other cultures, ours is an extraordinarily achievement-oriented setting for development. Indeed, early in development, we become more competitive and individually oriented and less cooperative and family oriented than our Mexican neighbors, for example (Holtzmann, 1981; Kagan & Madsen, 1972). We are taught as we grow up that through imagination, energy, self-denial, and persistence we will become a success in life. And a focal point in our culture is that we can find pleasure in work. In the 1980s Americans still seem to abide by the words of Thomas Carlyle, who in 1843 declared, "Work, and therein have well-being."

How is work likely to promote a sense of satisfaction and well-being in life? The answer to this question provides some clues to the complex puzzle of human motivation. For one, work helps to satisfy our basic needs. It helps us to buy food, shelter, and clothing, and it can help us to support a family. But work can contribute to psychological satisfaction as well. Work is the primary setting in adulthood in which we develop skills and show competence; this in turn can increase our self-esteem. Other motives that may undergird an adult's strong interest in working include the inherent interest of the work, the chance to learn or use new ideas, and the opportunity to socialize and develop relationships with other people.

Because work is such an important aspect of our culture, unemployment can be a tragic experience. Not long ago unemployment reached the highest point since the depression, with about 10 percent of Americans who wanted to work out of work. Unemployment can be a difficult experience, not just because of loss of income but because of the sense of purpose one may lose as well. As one unemployed woman commented, "Working on the job gave my time value. It gave my body value. It gave *me* value" (Maurer, 1979, p. 290).

INTRODUCTION

In this chapter we explore one of the most important contexts of adult development—work. Initially, we look at the social, historical context of work, then spend considerable time outlining the changes in work that take place across the adult years. Such changes include occupational choice, finding a place in the world of work, adjustment to work, reaching and maintaining occupational satisfaction, and work in late adulthood. We further evaluate the meanings of work, looking in detail at the achievement motive, intrinsic motivation, and the work ethic. We also look further at the impact of unemployment on adults. Then we outline what is perhaps the greatest change in the labor force in the last thirty-five years: the increasing number of women who are working outside the home. Special attention is given to the achievement orientation and career development of females in early adulthood. Not only do people need to learn how to work well, but they also need to develop leisure activities. We discuss the nature of leisure activities, leisure at mid-life, and leisure in retirement. In the last part of the chapter, we provide information about factors related to retirement, along with a description of the phases of retirement.

THE SOCIAL, HISTORICAL CONTEXT OF WORK

Robert J. Havighurst (1982) has described the importance of work in all cultures and its evolution in the United States. All societies have had their own ways of earning a living, that is, of getting food, clothing, and shelter. Cave men and women had their own peculiar technology; so did the Hebrews of biblical times and so have the Native Americans (Indians and Eskimos).

The society of the United States in the nineteenth century was a **preindustrial society.** The majority of families farmed land, the family members worked together, and the family was spoken of as the unit of production. Some townspeople worked as family units, with one or more sons learning from their fathers to be blacksmiths or carpenters, for example. In many parts of the world today—much of Africa, Latin America, and Asia—such work conditions still prevail. But by the end of the nineteenth century, the United States was becoming urbanized and industrialized. By 1910 only one third of the men were farmers or farm laborers.

The year 1910 is often given as the date for the beginning of the **industrial revolution** in the United States. Factories multiplied, and the labor force changed so dramatically that by 1950 half of all male workers were involved in some form of manufacturing or construction. In an industrial society, machines that operate with mechanical energy substantially increase productivity. Coal, petroleum, and natural gas have been the fuels of the twentieth century, and with cheap fuel, worker productivity has risen substantially, as has real income and the profits of industrial owners.

At the present time we are in the middle of making a transition to a post-industrial society. Approximately 65 to 70 percent of all workers are engaged in services. It has been predicted that by the year 2000 only 10 percent of the labor force will be involved in manufacturing, producing goods for the other 90 percent.

The term *services* can refer to many different activities. In earlier times, the common services focused on domestic work, transportation, and the distribution of goods, whereas in the postindustrial society we are witnessing a significant increase in jobs related to human services—education and health—and professional and technical services—research, data processing, and communication, for example. There has been healthy growth in many middle-class occupations to the extent that education and professional training have provided access to high status and income.

Havighurst (1982) has speculated about what work will be like in the year 2000. He believes that significant attention needs to be directed to the cost of energy and its effects on work life. The cost of energy may control the socioeconomic structure of the twenty-first century. It may determine the numbers and age structure of the labor force, and it will surely influence the distribution of the population between large and small cities. It will also affect the size of housing units. A major increase in the cost of energy is likely to lower the material standard of living. People may respond by working longer hours and/or more years to increase production of goods and services so that they can maintain their standard of living. This would mean that the elderly would be encouraged to stay in the labor force as long as they are reasonably productive. It might even mean that retirement at a fixed age would be abolished, and the average age of retirement could go to seventy or older. We could also expect considerable part-time employment in the elderly population.

Next we look at work over the life cycle. We have just seen that earlier in American history many adolescents engaged in work experiences with their family but with the appearance of the industrial revolution schooling began to replace family apprenticeships to capitalize on newly created jobs. During the twentieth century vocational choices have broadened considerably.

WORK OVER THE LIFE CYCLE

During adolescence, career orientation and vocational choice become more serious matters than they were in childhood. In this section we explore the roles of exploration, planning, and decision making in vocational choices. Then we discuss entry into an occupation as individuals attempt to find their place in the world of work. Subsequently, we evaluate the flexibility of careers in middle adulthood, along with ideas about reaching and maintaining occupational satisfaction. The section concludes with a description of conditions that facilitate work in late adulthood and the characteristics of seventy-year-old workers in the United States.

Occupational Exploration, Planning, and Decision Making

At some point toward the end of adolescence or the beginning of early adult-hood, most individuals enter an occupation. Most career choice theorists and counselors believe that before deciding upon a particular career, it is wise to explore a wide number of occupational alternatives. Donald Super believes that exploration of alternative career paths is the most important aspect of career development.

Exploration

Donald Super and Douglas Hall (1978) believe that in countries where equal employment opportunities have developed—such as the United States, Great Britain, and France—exploration of various career paths is critical in career development. The role of the school is especially important in career exploration because families and friends tend to be from the same social class and often know little about educational opportunities and occupations other than their own (e.g., Reynolds & Shister, 1949).

Individuals often approach career exploration and decision making with a great deal of ambiguity, uncertainty, and stress (e.g., Jordaan, 1963; Jordaan & Heyde, 1978). In one investigation Super and his colleagues (Super, Kowalski, & Gotkin, 1967) studied young adults after they left high school. The investigators found that over half of the position changes (such as student to student, student to job, job to job) made between leaving school and the age of twenty-five involved floundering and unplanned changes. In other words, the young adults were neither systematic nor intentional in their exploration and decision making about careers.

Several recent efforts have been made to increase career exploration among high school students. In one investigation (Hamdani, 1974), a career education and guidance course was developed for disadvantaged inner-city high school students. A regular teacher, who was not especially motivated or competent, was the instructor, with Hamdani acting as a consultant. The semester-long course did produce an increase in the disadvantaged students' career planning, as well as their use of resources for exploration and decision making.

The nature of the career exploration is important in determining whether a positive effect on individuals will accrue. Some counseling programs that have been self-oriented (that is, in which students are left to their own devices rather than in the more directive environmental approach of Hamdani) do not show positive effects on students' career exploration and decision making (Corbin, 1974; Hammer, 1974). In many cases these programs fail to involve the students in enough exploration for changes to occur. When self-directed student programs are instituted, some instruction, monitoring, and discussion with a counselor seems necessary for the student to benefit from the program. It is not enough for the high school or college student to engage in career exploration without any guidance.

Most high school and college students do not explore the world of work adequately on their own and receive very little direction from high school and college counselors about how to do so. According to the National Assessment of Educational Progress report (1976), students not only do not know what information to seek about careers, they do not know how to seek it. Just as discouraging is the fact that, on the average, high school students spend less than three hours per year with the guidance counselors at their schools (Super & Hall, 1978).

Planning and Decision Making

The first step in making a decision about a career, according to Super and Hall (1978), is to recognize that a problem actually exists. After people become aware that a vocation problem exists, they can seek and weigh various pieces of information about the problem, make and test various plans, and then, if necessary, revise the plans.

In a study of career decision making developed by Super and Overstreet (1960), a large number of ninth-grade boys were asked about their career decision n...king. Vocational maturity was evident in terms of the boys' ability to engage in planning for short- and long-term career goals. The ability of vocationally mature adolescents to develop a structured time perspective about their future career also emerged in the work of Jepsen (1974) with high school juniors.

Exploration, planning, and decision making about careers, then, are important cognitive activities that need to be encouraged in adolescents and young adults.

Entering an Occupation

The long period of preparation required for many middle-class occupations means that schooling in the form of either college or vocational training will continue in the twenties. But at some point during the late teens or twenties one usually enters an occupation. The beginning years of an occupation may take an inordinate amount of a person's time, such that other aspects of life like marriage and the development of a family become secondary. Havighurst (1982) believes that the task of getting started in an occupation is more difficult for middle-class than lower-class people because success in an occupation is essential to maintaining a middle-class status. Many women find that the task of entering an occupation conflicts with the tasks of finding a marital partner and starting a family.

Entering an occupation signals the beginning of new roles and responsibilities. The career role is somewhat different from the roles that a person may have had as a temporary or part-time worker during adolescence. In the adult career role, expectations for competence are high and the demands are real. When a

Entering the occupational world, the young person finds adult career role expectations for competence are high and the demands are real.

person enters a job for the first time he or she may be confronted by unanticipated problems and conditions. Transitions will be required as the person attempts to adjust to the new role. Meeting the expectations of a career and adjusting to a new role are crucial for the individual, not only during this era but for other periods of life as well.

Adjustment

Some career development experts suggest that the second stage in the occupational cycle should be labeled the **adjustment stage.** This is the period that Daniel Levinson (1978) describes as "age thirty transition." According to Levinson, once a person has entered an occupation, he must develop a distinct occupational identity and establish himself in the occupational world. Along the way, he may fail, drop out, or begin on a new path. He may stay narrowly on a single track or try several directions before settling firmly on one. This adjustment phase lasts several years. A professional may spend several years in academic study, whereas an executive may spend his early years in lower- or middle-management jobs. Hourly workers typically need several years to explore the work world, become familiar with the industry and a labor union, and move beyond the apprentice status to a permanent occupational role.

The level of attainment a person reaches by the early thirties also varies. A professional may just be getting started or may have already become well established and widely known in his or her profession. One executive may be on the first rung of the corporate ladder or a few may be near the top. An hourly worker may be an unskilled laborer without job security or a highly skilled craftsperson earning more than some executives or professionals.

Reaching and Maintaining Occupational Satisfaction and Mid-Life Career Change

In middle adulthood most men reach the highest status and income in their careers; women, if they have been employed most of their adult lives, do likewise. But there are some interesting exceptions of people in middle adulthood who start over and select a new career.

Many men and women who have had relatively routine jobs deliberately make a change in search of work that is more interesting and rewarding. Presently approximately 53 percent of women aged forty to fifty-nine are in the work force, many of them having obtained jobs after raising a family. Approximately 10 percent of men change the nature of their work between the ages of forty and sixty, either because of their own motivation or because they lose their job (Havighurst, 1982). And some people change jobs because they are not physically fit for the work after a certain age (for example, professional athletes, police officers, and some army personnel).

Mid-life is often a time of career reassessment.

Psychological Factors in Mid-Life Career Change

For the 10 percent of Americans who change jobs in mid-life, what are some of the psychological reasons behind this dramatic life change?

The mid-life career experience has been described as a major turning point in adulthood by Daniel Levinson (1978). One aspect of the mid-life phase involves adjusting idealistic hopes to realistic possibilities in light of how much time is left in an occupation. Middle-aged adults often focus on how much time they have left before retirement and the speed with which they are reaching their occupational goals. If individuals are behind schedule, or if their goals are now viewed as unrealistic, reassessment and readjustment are necessary. Levinson (1978) comments that for many middle-aged men there is a sense of sadness over unfulfilled dreams. Levinson and his colleagues found that many middle-aged men feel constrained by their bosses, wives, and children. Such feelings may lead to rebellion, which can take several forms—extramarital affairs, divorce, alcoholism, suicide, or career change.

It is important to consider the deeper meanings of career change during the middle years. Mid-life career changes are often linked to changes in attitudes, goals, and values (Thomas, 1977). Divorce can be used as an analogy in describing the relationship between changes in life-style and career change. A change in career, in and of itself, provides only a rough indicator of what is going on with a person psychologically just as divorce is a gross indicator of the quality of a marital relationship. Some marriages remain intact despite prolonged conflict, whereas others are terminated with only slight signs of deterioration. Likewise, some people hang onto their jobs despite intense dislike for their work, whereas others change careers even when their jobs are still satisfactory.

Levinson notes that a person of middle age wants desperately to be affirmed in the roles that he or she values most. At about age forty Levinson's subjects fixed on some key event in their careers as carrying the ultimate message of their affirmation or devaluation by society. This might be a promotion or a new job or a symbolic form of success, like writing a best-seller. Levinson concludes that the inevitable result of changes and pressures in mid-life is alteration. Even if nothing in the individual's external life changes, the individual does. The person simply does not remain in the earlier life structure. Even if the structure stays relatively intact externally, inevitable internal changes give it a different meaning.

Two additional career-related changes in mid-life must be noted. Mid-life is often accompanied by fiscal events that influence career decisions. For example, in some families mid-life is accompanied by a severe strain on financial resources caused by children in college. In other families there is a reorientation toward retirement and concerns begin to mount about financial resources for retirement (Heald, 1977).

Another problem of this era may result from role changes brought on by fiscal conditions. The wife may assume a working role, or resume such a role, to help with college expenses or to pursue her own vocational interests after children have left the house. In either case the husband must adapt to the competition for the breadwinning role. This adaptation may prove especially difficult if the wife's career outranks the husband's either in status or in salary (Heald, 1977).

Of particular interest are the factors related to occupational mobility in adulthood. What factors contribute to the likelihood that an individual from a working-class background will be in a middle-class occupation in adulthood? Data reported from the California Longitudinal Study (Clausen, 1981) allow us to address this question. See box 9.1 for information about the relationship between personality attributes in adolescence and mid-life and occupational status at mid-life.

Box 9.1
THE RELATIONSHIP OF PERSONALITY ATTRIBUTES IN ADOLESCENCE AND MID-LIFE TO UPWARD OCCUPATIONAL MOBILITY

In the California Longitudinal Study, data collected on the personality attributes of individuals when they were in junior high and at mid-life (forties) were compared with the degree to which the individuals were likely to show upward occupational mobility by the time they had reached mid-life. That is, some of the individuals who came from working-class backgrounds ended up with middle-class occupations at mid-life. Were there any clues from the personality characteristics of these individuals that were associated with upward occupational mobility?

John Clausen (1981) found that men who moved up occupationally from working-class backgrounds into middle-class occupations exceeded their nonmobile peers from comparable backgrounds in dependability, productivity, personal effectiveness, aspiration level, and intellectual capacities and interests in the junior high school years. The picture that emerged for the working-class mobiles was that of pleasant, dependable, conventional working-class boys who worked productively to get ahead as contrasted with more rebellious, self-defensive, less conventional middle-class boys who were seen as less pleasant and less dependable. The upwardly mobile working-class boys were also more nurturant and secured more education than their peers who remained in the working class. Further, the upwardly mobile boys continued to increase their intellectual skills and interests as they moved up the occupational ladder. In general, at mid-life they more closely resembled men who came from middle-class families than they did their former working-class peers who were employed in blue-collar jobs. Thus a combination of personal characteristics, the socializing influence of higher education, and the requirements of white-collar jobs served to increasingly differentiate these boys from their peers. And it was these upwardly mobile men who were the most satisfied with their occupational success.

In Berkeley and Oakland, America was still the land of opportunity in the years of the study. Over the twenty to thirty years of working, the original 40 percent of subjects with working-class status dropped to 10 percent. It would be interesting to see information about the remainder of the country, where it is likely that the pick and shovel also gave way to the backhoe (Sears, 1982).

Many boys from working class families in the 1930s were upwardly mobile and moved into middle class occupations.

Work in Late Adulthood

Productivity in old age seems to be the rule rather than the exception. People who have worked hard throughout their life often continue to do so until their death. Some keep a schedule that exhausts the young worker, and some elderly people continue to demonstrate highly creative skills, often outperforming their early and middle adulthood counterparts. In business and industry, there is a positive relationship between age and productivity that favors the older worker. And older workers have a 20 percent better absenteeism record than younger workers. Somewhat surprisingly, older workers also have fewer disabling injuries and their frequency of accidents is lower than that for young adults (Comfort, 1976). It appears, then, that the recent changes in federal laws allowing many people over sixty-five to continue productive work were a wise and humane decision.

Characteristics of Seventy-year-old Workers in the United States

John Flanagan (1981) has reported the results of a national survey of individuals in late adulthood that focused on the characteristics of people who work. The age range of the people studied was sixty-eight to seventy-three, but for convenience, Flanagan refers to the sample as the "seventy-year-olds." The 500 men and 500 women in the sample participated in an extensive four- to five-hour interview that included questions about their education, family history, and employment. Each individual also reported on his or her overall quality of life. These elderly adults further indicated whether they were currently employed and, if so, the importance to them of eighteen different aspects of a job.

The first question evaluated by Flanagan was "How many of these individuals are working and what are they doing?" Only 4 percent of the men were working full time, but an additional 12 percent were working part time. The same percentage of women were working full time but only 8 percent more were working part time. Most of the men had jobs that did not require professional training. About 41 percent had general labor and service type jobs requiring no special skills. Nearly 14 percent more were in mechanical, technical, or construction trades, and 33 percent were in sales and clerical positions. Only about 12 percent were in jobs requiring college training. However, more of the women (about 29 percent) were in jobs requiring college training, with teachers accounting for many of these jobs. Unskilled labor jobs accounted for about 31 percent of the women who worked, and sales and clerical jobs represented 39 percent of women who worked either full or part time.

The total group of seventy-year-old men and women who were working either full or part time were asked to report what they saw as the most important aspects of a job. The seven characteristics reported to be either important or very important to 80 percent or more of the seventy-year-old workers included

1. Work that I feel I do well (listed by almost everyone)
2. Work that I feel is important or worthwhile
3. Friendly, likable coworkers
4. Work in pleasant surroundings
5. Interesting work
6. Work that is challenging and permits me to use my abilities fully
7. A supervisor who is pleasant and interested in my welfare

In comparing the life satisfaction of the seventy-year-old workers with those who did not work, it was found that the overall quality of life was much the same for seventy-year-olds who worked and those who did not. These findings suggest that many elderly people can make valuable contributions in the world of work with no loss in the overall quality of life. Indeed, working in late adulthood may prove beneficial to many individuals, not just in terms of life satisfaction but in terms of longevity as well.

In addition to exploring the developmental course of work in the adult years, it also is important to examine the meanings of work for adults.

THE MEANINGS OF WORK, THE ACHIEVEMENT MOTIVE, AND UNEMPLOYMENT

Virtually all workers see their job as a way of earning a living, but as we see next, work has other meanings as well. In this section we examine these meanings as well as the achievement motive, and the implications of unemployment.

The Meanings of Work

Recall from the Imagine section at the beginning of the chapter that a large majority of individuals would continue working even if they inherited enough money to live without having to work. Some people view their job in terms of its prestige, or the lack of prestige, whereas for others a job may be their prime contact with the outside world, and for still others a job may be the primary setting for the development of social relationships outside the family. The functions of work may vary from some jobs to others. The salesperson worries about cracking a tough customer; the assembly-line worker complains about the monotony of his job yet brags that he is the best at his job in the plant; the executive discusses her immense responsibilities in the corporation. But there are some common threads that even run through jobs with diverse functions.

Table 9.1

THE RELATION BETWEEN THE FUNCTIONS AND MEANINGS OF WORK

Work Function	*Work Meaning*
Income	Maintaining a minimum sustenance level of existence
	Achieving some higher level or group standard
Expenditure of time and energy	Something to do
	A way of filling the day or passing time
Identification and status	Source of self-respect
	Way of achieving recognition or respect from others
	Definition of role
Association	Friendship relations
	Peer-group relations
	Subordinate-superordinate relations
Source of meaningful life experience	Gives purpose to life
	Creativity, self-expression
	New experience
	Service to others

Source: Friedmann & Havighurst, 1954, p. 7. Reprinted by permission of the University of Chicago Press.

Table 9.1 provides an illustrative list of the meanings individuals assign to their own work and how these meanings may be linked with more universal functions of work.

In table 9.2 the data from two studies conducted by Robert Havighurst (Friedmann & Havighurst, 1954; Havighurst, McDonald, Perun, & Snow, 1976) reveal that skilled craft and white-collar groups stress the extra-financial meanings of work to a much greater degree than do workers in heavy industry. It may be that the meanings of work described in table 9.1 become more relevant as we go up the occupational and skill ladders.

Next we look at what many psychologists consider to be an important motive in our culture—achievement—and evaluate its relationship to work.

The Achievement Motive and Work

The **achievement motive** refers to the need to maintain or increase one's competence in activities in which a standard of excellence is involved. If a person is strongly motivated to achieve, he or she will show considerable effort and persistance in succeeding. There is some controversy about how effectively we can measure achievement motivation. The most common strategy has been to use a personality test that requires the individual to tell a story about some pictures likely to elicit achievement themes. It turns out that the person's story responses about achievement may not correspond closely with actual achievement behavior. Nonetheless, the concept of achievement motivation is thought to be an important part of our achievement orientation and work.

Table 9.2

MEANINGS OF WORK[a]

Meanings	Category of Worker (Percent Choosing)						Social Scientists	
	Steel Workers	Miners	PhotoEngravers over 65	Salespersons	Senior Physicians	College Administrators	Male	Female
1. Income, for my needs	28	18	11	0	0	4	6	5
2. Routine: Makes time pass	28	19	15	21	15	1	1	1
3a. Brings self-respect				12	7	14	12	8
3b. Brings prestige 3a + 3b	16	18	24	11	13	11	14	5
4. Association with fellows	15	19	20	20	19	11	10	17
5. Self-expression; new experience; creativity	13	11	30	26	15	27	39	41
6. Service to others; useful	N.D.[b]	16	N.D.	10	32	31	17	22

[a]The interview or questionnaire format varied from one group to another, making strict comparisons questionable. The data are reported in percentages within groups; assuming each respondent to have given his/her favored response.
[b]N.D. = No data

Source: Friedmann & Havighurst, 1954 (table 26); Havighurst, McDonald, Perun, & Snow, 1976 (table 7.2). In R. J. Havighurst, 1982, p. 782.

As a rule, the higher the adult's achievement motivation, the more likely she or he is to choose work and an occupation that is characterized by risk and challenge. Starting one's own business would be one example. David McClelland, the architect of much of the early interest in the achievement motive (e.g., McClelland, Atkinson, Clark, & Lowell, 1953), more recently (McClelland, Constanian, Regaldo, & Stone, 1978) has called on achievement-motivation training to improve the performance of small businesses and to increase the employment of minorities.

What kind of psychological profile do highly achievement-oriented adults reveal? One recent effort to investigate this question focused on the interrelationship of work orientation, mastery, and competitiveness (Spence & Helmreich, 1978). Instead of relying on story completions, self-report measures were developed to separate these motives: (1) work orientation, which is the desire to work hard and do a good job; (2) mastery, the preference for difficult and challenging activities; and (3) competitiveness, the motivation to beat other people. The highest achieving adults are consistently high on work and mastery motives but low on the competitive motive. Such a pattern was revealed among college students who made the highest grades, business executives with the highest salaries, and scientists who made the most significant contributions (Spence, 1979). Why? Possibly because competitiveness can impede achievement since it is related to extrinsic motivation (for example, wanting to outperform one's peers). Some psychologists believe that extrinsic motives can decrease an individual's interest in the activity she or he is working on and consequently can reduce success (Deci, 1975; Lepper & Greene, 1975). By contrast, *intrinsic motivation* (doing something for the pleasure in the activity itself rather than for external reasons such as money or rewarding comments from others, which is described as *extrinsic motivation*) is thought to be an important aspect of work.

Currently, the Japanese are outperforming Americans in the production of automobiles, steel, appliances, computer chips, and even subway cars. Two reasons have been offered for this fact: First, U.S. productivity has become stagnant; second, the U.S. work ethic has deteriorated badly. The first reason is true—our country's productivity has improved at very small increments, recently has shown no growth at all, and may be decreasing. In box 9.2 we look at the second reason in greater detail.

However, many adults would simply like to be working. Unemployment has become a major problem not only in the United States but in many other countries as well.

Unemployment

Unemployed workers face stress whether the job loss is temporary, cyclical, or permanent. The psychological meaning of job loss may depend on a number of factors, including the individual's personality, social status, and resources. This was the conclusion of an investigation by Terry Buss and F. Stevens Redburn (1983) that focused on how the shutdown of a steel plant in Youngstown, Ohio, affected workers. For example, a fifty-year-old married worker with two adolescents, a limited education, no transferable job skills, and no pension would not react the same way as a twenty-year-old apprentice electrician.

It is well documented that professional, semiskilled, and unskilled workers experience stress from losing their jobs, but is there any evidence that one set of workers suffers more than the others? In one investigation (Brenner, 1973), married men between the ages of thirty and sixty-five who were earning good salaries and were well-educated were studied. White-collar workers were the most sensitive to economic downturn and had the most to lose when income and self-image were considered.

In the Buss-Redburn study managers and steelworkers were compared in 1978 and 1979. Managers were less affected one year after the plant closing. The steelworkers felt more helpless, victimized, and distrustful, tended to avoid social interaction, and were more aggressive. They were also more depressed and

Box 9.2
INTRINSIC MOTIVATION, THE WORK ETHIC, AND WORKER PRODUCTIVITY

Sometimes it is argued that people don't work as hard today as they did in the past. But if by the work ethic we mean the intrinsic worth involved in doing the best possible job regardless of financial reward, recent survey research suggests that the work ethic in the United States is very strong and may be growing even stronger. In a 1980 Gallup poll, though fewer Americans said that they enjoy their work now than was true in the past, an overwhelming 88 percent of all working Americans said that it is personally important for them to work hard and do their best on the job (Yankelovich, 1982).

The argument is that a faulty work ethic is not responsible for our productivity decline. However, at the same time a 1981 Harris study suggests that Americans also believe that people are working less. Sixty-nine percent of a national sample of adults feel that workmanship is worse than it was a decade ago, and 63 percent feel that most people do not work as hard today as they did ten years ago. Such opinion polls do not prove that we are actually working less effectively than in the past, but it is difficult to ignore such widespread impressions. For example, for a number of years the University of Michigan asked a sample of workers to keep a diary of job activities. Analysis of these diaries suggested that between 1965 and 1975 the amount of time spent working actually declined by more than 10 percent (Yankelovich, 1982).

Why this discrepancy between the work ethic and worker productivity? According to Daniel Yankelovich (1982) the answer is very clear. When Gallup's 1980 poll asked workers who they thought would benefit the most from improvement in their productivity, only 9 percent felt that they, the workers, would. A large majority felt that others would benefit the most—management, stockholders, or consumers, for example.

In a review of 103 investigations that focused on whether an improved incentive system in American industry—including both money and greater control over one's work—would increase an individual's productivity, eighty-five of the investigations found that it would.

The Japanese seem to understand this important point better than Americans. The former distinguish between the soft factors of production—such as the dedication of the work force—and hard factors—such as technology, capital investment, and development. The Japanese believe that the soft factors are just as important as the hard ones. Yankelovich argues that American business leaders do not have a good understanding of how the soft and hard factors are interrelated.

showed a greater degree of perceived immobility. Over time, the steelworkers were less trustful and continued to feel immobile, helpless, and stressed. Further, they reported more health problems and increased their intake of alcohol. In contrast, the managers were coping much better than the steelworkers. Except for a lack of trust, their psychological profile either continued to improve or remained the same. However, in the second wave of interviews conducted in 1979, the managers began to report more family problems and a higher tendency to consume over-the-counter drugs. Nevertheless, the steelworkers were still more severely affected by the plant closing, indicating more aggression, victimization, distrust, and helplessness.

Being unemployed in the 1980s may be as bad or in some cases even worse than was true in the 1930s. The unemployed in the 1930s had a strong feeling that their jobs would return; because many of today's workers are being replaced by technology, expectations that their jobs will reappear are less encouraging.

Next we consider the most dramatic change in the world of work: the increasing participation of women.

WOMEN AND WORK

The greatest change in labor force participation has consisted of greater employment of women between the ages of twenty and sixty-five and of married women with children. By 1980, 51 percent of females twenty years of age and older were in the labor force, a figure that has increased approximately 14 percent since 1960.

However, although some women are entering previously all-male occupations, the majority of women still have not achieved parity with men in the occupational marketplace. The difference between the average salaries for women and men is still huge—less than $10,000 per year for women and almost $17,000 per year for men in 1980. While women have entered the work force in greater numbers than ever before, many of the jobs they have taken have been low-paying, low-status positions such as clerical jobs (Wright, 1982).

Aletha Huston-Stein and Ann Higgens-Trenk (1978) have discussed some of the sociocultural factors that have affected the increasing numbers of women in colleges and jobs outside the home. The demand for female employees increased significantly after World War II because the number of job openings in traditionally female occupations (for example, nurse, teacher, clerical worker) increased at a more rapid pace than job availability in male occupations. Many married women were induced to enter the labor market for the first time. More recently, the number of traditionally female professional jobs, particularly in teaching, has declined, so the greatest demand for female employment is in low-status positions (Van Dusen & Sheldon, 1976).

Another factor affecting the increasing numbers of working women involves divorce. The divorce rate has been increasing exponentially in recent years; this might be viewed either as a *reason* more women are working or as a *consequence* of the economic independence women are gaining. The woman who works and knows she can support herself may be more likely to end an unhappy marriage. On the other hand, divorce often forces a woman to work to support herself and her children.

Many barriers still prevent women from entering occupations that are intellectually and financially rewarding. While discrimination in education and employment has been reduced, it has not been eliminated (e.g., Astin & Bayer, 1975; Harway & Astin, 1977).

Because of the structure and demands of many occupations, many women may not be able to enter them as easily as men can. Particular difficulties arise for the woman who feels committed to being a homemaker and mother. Many professional and managerial positions require extensive amounts of time and travel. Such jobs virtually require that the female have a helpmate to fulfill home responsibilities (Papanek, 1973). Perhaps one reason so many women select teaching as a profession is that the time schedule permits them to be home reasonably early so that they can cook dinner and take care of their children. Some social scientists (for example, Gronseth, 1972) suggest that as long as the male is viewed as the primary economic provider in a culture, the career plans and achievements of women will continue to be underdeveloped and subordinate.

The Achievement Orientation and Career Development of Females in Early Adulthood

Although many of the factors influencing young women's decisions about careers and families occur in childhood, early adulthood is a critical period (Huston-Stein & Higgens-Trenk, 1978). The timing of marriage, childbearing, education, and work has long-term implications for the life patterns of women. Once a choice is made, particularly having a child, a woman's range of options becomes more limited, or at least more difficult to pursue.

Although the majority of college women anticipate both a career and marriage, many are unrealistic about the difficulties of this combination (Shields, 1973). The dissatisfaction and conflict in combining a family and career seems to result more from role overload than role conflict. Women who cope with time pressures and conflicts by redefining their own and their families' responsibilities are more satisfied than those who attempt to meet all demands alone.

Women who return to higher education or careers after marrying and having children show high levels of commitment. Women who are employed have higher levels of life satisfaction and feelings of adequacy and self-esteem than full-time homemakers. However, the psychological benefits of employment are greater for the educated middle-class and the liabilities are greater for lower-class women.

These findings suggest that future research should focus on the developmental changes in women caused by home and work roles. Effective coping techniques could help women deal with these rapidly changing life patterns.

We have discussed a number of aspects of work, but as adults, we must not only learn how to work well. We also need to learn how to relax and develop leisure activities. Throughout the history of our country many people have believed Henry Ford, who emphasized that our salvation rests in our work. Few people are aware of Ford's frequent trips to his mansion in Dearborn, Michigan, where he relaxed and participated extensively in leisure activities. Similarly, Ronald Reagan seems to have found a better balance between work and leisure than many of us.

With the kind of work ethic on which our country has been based, it is not surprising to find that many adults view leisure as boring and unnecessary. During the later years of life when elderly people find it necessary to reduce their work load or to retire, they often find themselves with more free time than they know how to handle. Next we look at the nature of leisure in adulthood.

LEISURE

Aristotle recognized the importance of leisure in life, stressing that we should not only work well but use leisure well. He even thought that leisure was better because it is the end of work. What is *leisure?* The word is usually used to indicate the pleasant times after work when people are free to pursue activities and interests of their own choosing, such as hobbies, sports, and reading.

The Nature of Leisure Activities

Eighty years ago the average work week was seventy-one hours. Only in the last several decades has it averaged forty hours. What do most of us do now that we have more free time than cohorts in previous generations did?

Only within the last fifteen to twenty years have social scientists devoted much time to investigating areas such as leisure and recreation. One of the basic themes relating to leisure and the use of time is the increasing reliance on television over other forms of mass media as a key form of entertainment. Overall, television viewing has partially displaced other leisure activities.

Though television viewing time has increased dramatically in recent years, since the mid-1970s there has been a leveling off or slight drop in television viewing (Social Indicators III, 1980). There has also been a steady decrease in the proportion of people who read a newspaper daily, falling from 69 to 58 percent during the six years ending in 1978. College-educated adults are more likely to read a newspaper daily and to watch television fewer hours than the population as a whole (Social Indicators III, 1980).

National statistical data (Social Indicators III, 1980) also suggest that sports are an extremely important part of the leisure activities of Americans, either directly through participation or vicariously through in-person viewing, television watching, newspaper or magazine reading, discussion with friends, and so forth. The diversity of sports activities allows many people to escape the rigors and pressures of everyday life, even if it is only for a few hours per week. The power of sports in our lives was nowhere more vividly captured than when the Washington Redskins won the Super Bowl in 1983, the first time that they had won a professional football championship in forty years. During their championship run, the city of Washington, D.C., was consumed by its interest in pro football to the point where at times the running of the United States government seemed trivial to many inhabitants of the city.

Leisure at Mid-Life

When Mark became forty years old he decided that he needed to develop some leisure activities and interests. He bought a personal computer and joined a computer club. Mark now looks forward to coming home from work and "playing" with his "toy." At the age of forty-three Barbara sent her last child off to college and told her husband that she was going to spend the next several years reading the many books she had bought but had not found time to read.

Mark and Barbara have chosen different leisure activities, but their actions suggest that middle age is a time when leisure activities take on added importance. Roger Gould (1978) believes that the middle-age years are a time of questioning how time should be spent and of reassessing priorities. Mid-life seems to be a time when adults want more freedom and the opportunity to express their individuality.

Leisure may be a particularly important aspect of middle adulthood because of the changes many people experience at this point in development. Such changes include physical changes, changes in relationships with spouse and children, and career change. By middle adulthood more money is available to many people, and there may be more free time and paid vacations. Such mid-life changes may lead to expanded opportunities for leisure activities. For many people, mid-life is the first time in their adult lives that they have the opportunity to diversify their interests.

Adults at mid-life need to start preparing both financially and psychologically for retirement. Constructive and fulfilling leisure activities in middle adulthood are very important in this preparation. If an adult develops leisure activities that can be continued into retirement, then the transition from work to retirement may be less traumatic.

Table 9.3

A SYNTHESIS OF RESEARCH ON LEISURE PARTICIPATION

Activities	*A*	*B*	*C*	*D*	*E*
Reading/writing	37	36	55	67	51
Television	28	36	89	69	78
Arts/crafts, etc.	26	26	40	46	37
Cards/games	23	–	56	29	16
Walking	16	25	–	31	47
Visiting family/friends	19	47	63	75	56
Physical activity	10	3	–	–	–
Gardening	9	39	40	49	27
Travel/camping	19	–	–	–	29
Organizations/clubs	2	17	51	29	8
Outings/driving	9	–	66	32	29
N	245	2797	65	540	?

A data from Table 5 of this study
B Harris, 1976
C Nystrom, 1974
D McAvoy, 1979
E Schmitz-Secherzer, 1979

Source: Roadburg, 1981. Reprinted by permission of *The Gerontologist, 21,* #2, pages 142–145, 1981.

Leisure Activities in Retirement

What do people do with their time when they retire? According to table 9.3, which synthesizes information collected in five different investigations of leisure activities in retirement (Harris, 1976; McAvoy, 1979; Nystrom, 1974; Roadburg, 1981; Schmitz-Secherzer, 1979), reading/writing, television, arts/crafts, games, walking, visiting family and friends, physical activity, gardening, travel/camping, organization and club activity, and outings are among the most popular leisure activities among the elderly.

Sometime between the ages of sixty and seventy, most people must give up their occupation, whether they are professional or manual workers. For people whose job is the central focus of their life, retirement can be a difficult and unwelcome experience. Others relish the new freedom they have and fill their lives with enjoyable leisure activities. An important goal for our society is to make the retirement process flexible enough to meet the needs of people with a variety of attitudes toward work (Havighurst, 1982).

Gardening is one of the leisure activities often chosen by retired individuals.

RETIREMENT

Until recently, many individuals did not have a choice between work and retirement. The Social Security system provided benefits at the age of sixty-five, and most private pension plans mandated retirement at sixty-five. In 1978, however, Congress extended the mandatory retirement age from sixty-five to seventy in business and industry and removed the age limit completely for federal employees. A best guess is that the future will see even further lessening of regulation on mandatory retirement, and we can expect more individuals to be confronted with the decision of when to retire rather than being forced into retirement.

In this section we look at the factors related to retirement and the possible different phases that people go through when they retire.

Factors Related to Retirement

A number of factors influence retirement decisions. Financial security, health status, attitudes toward work, job satisfaction, and personal interests contribute to an individual's decision of whether to retire or continue working. It is not uncommon for people to retire from one job, become restless, and then pursue another job. For example, Frank Baird, a seventy-two-year-old motel manager found that he could not tolerate the inactivity of retirement:

> "They gave me a gold watch—a beautiful thing—six months' pay, a new car, and a fabulous pension," Baird explained. "We spent three months traveling, playing golf, fishing, and getting lazy. At first, I thought it was great. You know, for years you look forward to the freedom, the leisure time, the no hassles. But let me tell you, friend, it gets old. After six months I was bored stiff, and my wife, she was getting fed up too. You know, she had her friends and her activities and didn't need me under foot. Then I found this job, and it's great. I love it! New people, people from all over, and I am able to make their stay a little more pleasant. Don't ever retire, friend, if you've got a job, stick with it. Retirement is for the birds. Unless you're a lazy bird." (Van Hoose & Worth, 1982, p. 317)

Though disillusionment with retirement and financial problems seem to be the major reasons individuals continue to work after a conventional retirement age, in the case of Frank Baird the major factors in his decision to return to work seemed to be his feelings of uselessness and isolation.

Still there are many individuals who look forward to retirement and relish the time when they will not have to work long hours. The feelings of Katy Adams, a retired teacher, express this sentiment:

> "I don't feel any great loss at all. No, no. I taught math and science for thirty-one years, and if I hadn't taken time out to raise two daughters, I would have made it forty. I loved every minute of it, but now it is time to take a rest. After all that time I have earned it, don't you think? Why would I want to go on teaching? I have my retirement, my insurance, and my health. Now I just want to enjoy it." (Van Hoose & Worth, 1982, p. 317)

Although more people now have the option of working until seventy and many will continue to work beyond the mandatory retirement age, there appears to be no major trend in that direction. In fact, the number of males aged sixty-five and over in the labor force is dropping. One of the reasons may be that the U.S. Civil Service Commission has encouraged earlier retirement through rules that allow employees to retire after twenty-five years of service. Some industrial firms and labor organizations have also cooperated and developed programs that allow some individuals to retire in their mid-fifties.

A recent analysis of predictors of retirement (Palmore, George, & Fillen-baum, 1982), included data from the two largest national studies of retirement. The Retirement History Study (RHS) was conducted by the Social Security Administration from 1969 to 1979. At the time of analysis, data through 1975 were included on a sample of 11,153 men aged fifty-eight to sixty-three. To reduce computer costs, most analyses were conducted on a random one third of the sample. The RHS includes detailed information about demographic and economic factors, work history, health, and limited social-psychological characteristics. The National Longitudinal Survey (NLS) was conducted for the Department of Labor by the Center for Human Resources Research at Ohio State University between 1966 and 1976. Initially the NLS was a national sample of 5,020 men aged forty-five to fifty-nine. The NLS contains detailed demographic, economic, and work history information, moderate health information, and limited social-psychological information.

Four measures of retirement were studied: (1) *Objective retirement* (ages sixty-five and over)—people were defined as objectively retired if employed less than thirty-five hours per week and received a retirement pension, either public or private. In the national studies approximately 85 percent of the men working at least sixteen hours per week at the beginning and aged sixty-six to sixty-nine at the end of the studies had retired. (2) *Early retirement* (ages under sixty-five)—a person was defined as retiring early if he had retired before age sixty-five. About half of the retirees in the national studies had retired early. (3) *Age at retirement*—this variable allowed finer distinctions than the gross dichotomy of retired or not retired. In the NLS about 15 percent retired before age sixty-two, about a third retired at ages sixty-two to sixty-four, about 17 percent retired at sixty-five, and about a third retired after sixty-five. (4) *Amount of employment*—to some extent this is a reverse measure of amount of retirement; no employment means maximum retirement, part-time employment means partial retirement, and full-time employment means minimal retirement. Slightly more than half of the men employed at the beginning of the studies were not working at all by the end, less than a third were working part time, and less than a fifth were working full time.

Analyses revealed that structural factors, such as socioeconomic status and job characteristics that increased the incentives or necessity of retirement, were stronger predictors of objective retirement (among all those over sixty-five) than were the subjective characteristics of health self-rating and retirement attitudes.

In terms of predicting early retirement, health factors became more important predictors and job characteristics became relatively less important than in the case of objective retirement. Thus in comparison with normal retirement, early retirement seems to be linked more with the subjective factors of self-rated health and attitudes.

To predict age at retirement, socioeconomic factors (annual wages and occupation) were strong positive predictors of late age at retirement, which reflects greater opportunities and incentives to continue working for higher socioeconomic groups. Health limitations again were a reasonably strong predictor of earlier retirement, as was the job characteristic of mandatory retirement. Both job attitudes and retirement attitudes were important predictors of age at retirement. Thus age at retirement, which includes both early and late retirement, was predicted by a balanced mixture of socioeconomic, health, job, and attitude factors.

In terms of projecting the amount of employment in late adulthood, the amount worked at the end of the studies was predicted mainly by job characteristics, such as being self-employed, not subject to mandatory retirement, and not being employed in a core industry. In the national studies, demographic, socioeconomic, health, and attitude predictors all together were less effective predictors than job characteristics. This finding suggests that structural factors were more important predictors of amount worked (or retired) than all of the individual and subjective factors put together.

According to Erdman Palmore and his associates (Palmore, George, & Fillenbaum, 1982), at ages under sixty-five, retirement is neither expected nor forced. Thus early retirement is influenced more by subjective factors such as self-perceptions of health, attitudes toward work and retirement, and the perception of how adequate one's retirement income is. However, at ages over sixty-five, most workers are pushed into retirement by mandatory retirement policies and expectations of employers, fellow workers, friends, and family. Therefore, only the few who are self-employed or in jobs not related to mandatory retirement (structural factors) continue to work.

The theoretical model shown in figure 9.1 reflects the findings of the analysis of the national studies of retirement. However, compared to prior studies of retirement and its related factors, most of which were cross-sectional in nature, health was relatively less important in the current longitudinal analysis for men over the age of sixty-five.

In sum, in the United States there is considerable variability in the age at which people retire and in the reasons why they retire. Further, the reasons may vary depending on how retirement is defined. In Japan, most companies force their workers to retire at the age of fifty-five. However, many fifty-five-year-old Japanese want to continue to work. At least 25 percent of these individuals find other full-time employment after they have been released by their companies.

Some social scientists believe that many people go through a series of phases before and during retirement. One such perspective has been developed by Robert Atchley (1976).

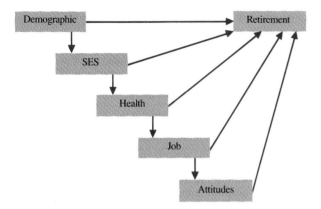

Figure 9.1   Theoretical model of factors predicting retirement.

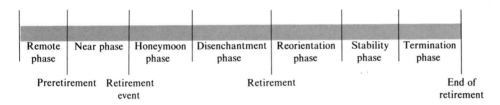

Figure 9.2   Seven phases of retirement.

Phases of Retirement

Atchley (1977) suggests that many people go through seven phases of retirement: remote, near, honeymoon, disenchantment, reorientation, stability, and termination. The sequence of these phases is shown in figure 9.2.

Most individuals begin work with the vague belief that they will not die on the job and that they will enjoy the fruits of their labor at some point in the distant future. In this **remote phase** of retirement, most people do virtually nothing to prepare themselves for retirement. As they age toward possible retirement, they often deny the fact that the event will eventually happen.

Only when workers reach the **near phase** do they sometimes participate in preretirement programs. Such programs, which could significantly help workers make the transition to retirement, are not that pervasive. Preretirement programs, when they do exist, usually either help individuals to decide when they should retire by familiarizing them with the benefits and pensions they can expect to receive or involve discussion of more comprehensive issues, such as physical and mental health. Only about 10 percent of the labor force is involved in such preretirement programs, and most are of the first type mentioned. In one investigation (Atchley, 1976), individuals who had been exposed to a retirement preparation program had higher retirement incomes, engaged in more activities after retirement, and held fewer stereotyped beliefs about retirement than their counterparts who were not exposed to a preretirement program.

As indicated in figure 9.2, after retirement has occurred, there are five remaining phases in this model of the retirement process. Of course, many people do not go through all of these phases, and many others do not go through them in the manner indicated in the figure. How significant each phase will be in the adjustment of the retired person depends upon such factors as his or her preretirement expectations and the reality of retirement in terms of money, available options, and the ability to make decisions (Williamson, Munley, & Evans, 1980).

It is not unusual for people initially to feel euphoric in the period just after their retirement. Individuals may be able to do all of the things they never had time to do before, and they may derive considerable pleasure from leisure activities. People who are forced to retire, or who retire because they are angry about their job, however, are less likely to experience the positive aspects of this phase of retirement, which is called the **honeymoon phase.** This phase eventually gives way to a routine. If the routine is satisfying, adjustment to retirement is usually successful. Those whose life-styles did not entirely revolve around their jobs before retirement are usually able to make the retirement adjustment and develop a satisfying routine more easily than those who did not develop leisure habits during their working years.

Even individuals who initially experience retirement as a honeymoon usually feel some form of letdown or, in some cases, serious depression. Preretirement fantasies about the retirement years may be unrealistic in such cases. Atchley calls this the **disenchantment phase.**

At some point, though, individuals who become disenchanted with retirement come to grips with the issue and reorient themselves to the reality of their retirement and begin to reason about how to cope with it successfully. The major purpose of this **reorientation phase** is to explore, evaluate, and make some decisions about the type of life-style that will likely lead to life satisfaction during retirement.

The **stability phase** of retirement is attained when individuals have decided upon a set of criteria for evaluating choices in retirement and how they will perform once they have made these choices. For some this phase may occur after the honeymoon phase, whereas for others the transition is slower and more difficult.

According to Atchley (1977), at some point the retirement role loses its significance and relevance in the eyes of the older person. Some older people go to work again, often accepting a job that is totally unrelated to what they did before retirement. Full-time leisure may become boring to them or they may need money to support themselves. Sickness or disability, of course, can alter the retirement process as well. The autonomy and sufficiency that was developed in the stable phase may begin to give way to dependency on others, both physically and economically. This final phase of retirement is called the **termination phase** by Atchley.

Because people retire at different ages and for a variety of reasons, there is no immutable timing or sequencing to the seven phases of the retirement process described by Atchley. Nonetheless, these phases help us to understand what some of the most important adjustments to retirement are.

Summary

Work has been an important part of all cultures throughout history. In the last 100 years substantial changes in the nature of work have taken place, initially as part of the industrial revolution and subsequently in postindustrial society. In the postindustrial society we have witnessed a significant increase in jobs related to human services, jobs that usually require extensive training and education. In the future, changes in the nature of work are likely to be influenced by the cost of energy.

Virtually all vocational theories stress the importance of the exploration of a wide array of career alternatives. Other cognitive activities thought to be important in occupational choice are planning and decision making. At some point in the late teens or twenties, individuals enter an occupation. Doing so signals the beginning of new roles and responsibilities. Career expectations for competence are high and the demands are real. Some career development experts believe that people enter an adjustment stage, which Levinson calls "age thirty transition." In middle adulthood most men attain the highest status and income in their careers, and women, if they have been employed most of their adult years, do likewise. But there are some interesting exceptions of people in middle adulthood who start over and select a new career for various reasons. One aspect of mid-life career change involves adjusting idealistic hopes to realistic possibilities in light of how much time is left in an occupation. Of particular interest are the factors related to occupational mobility in adulthood. In the California Longitudinal Study data collected on the personality attributes of individuals when they were in junior high and at mid-life suggest that upwardly mobile boys from working-class backgrounds who subsequently achieved middle-class occupational status were pleasant, dependable, conventional, and worked hard to get ahead. Many individuals continue their work into late adulthood, and productivity in old age is often the rule rather than the exception. Data collected on seventy-year-old workers suggest that compared to retired individuals, the elderly workers show no loss in life satisfaction.

Almost all workers see their job as a way of earning a living. But work also has other meanings for most workers—prestige, contact with the outside world, and social relationships. White-collar jobs seem to have extra-financial meaning more than blue-collar jobs. The achievement motive is one of the most important human motives involved in work. As a rule, the higher the adult's achievement motivation, the more likely he or she will choose work characterized by risk and challenge. Our work ethic—the intrinsic worth involved in doing the best possible job regardless of financial reward—seems currently to be very strong. Nonetheless, worker productivity is either stagnant or decreasing. One explanation suggests that workers believe that they are the least likely to benefit from increased productivity. Instead, workers say that consumers and management would benefit most from increased worker productivity.

No change in the labor force has been as great as the increased participation of women. Though discrimination has been reduced, it has not been eliminated. Early adulthood is a critical time in a woman's decision about work. The timing of marriage, childrearing, education, and work has long-term implications for the life patterns of women.

We not only need to learn how to work well, but we need to learn how to relax and participate in leisure activities as well. Prominent leisure activities in adulthood include reading a newspaper, magazine, or book; watching television; and visiting with friends and family. Overall, television viewing has increased substantially in the last fifteen years, although in the last several years this trend has leveled out. Sports, experienced either directly or vicariously, are also an important aspect of the leisure activities of many adults. Constructive leisure activities in mid-life may be helpful in making the transition from work to retirement. In retirement reading/writing and watching television continue to be frequently chosen leisure activities.

Sometimes between the ages of sixty and seventy, most people must give up their occupation. For people whose job is the central focus of their life, retirement can be a difficult experience. In a recent analysis of predictors of retirement, early retirement (before sixty-five) occurred because of subjective factors such as health, attitudes toward work and retirement, and how adequate the person's current finances were. But for people over sixty-five, most workers are pushed into retirement by mandatory retirement policies and expectations of others. Some social scientists believe that we go through a series of phases before and after retirement—remote, near, honeymoon, disenchantment, reorientation, stability, and termination. Because individuals retire at different ages and for different reasons, there is no set timing or sequencing to the phases, although they can help us to understand some of the important adjustments to retirement.

Review Questions

1. Describe the social, historical context of work.
2. What are the main theories of occupational choice? Describe the roles of exploration, planning, and decision making in occupational choice.
3. Discuss the developmental course of work once one enters an occupation.
4. What are some of the meanings of work?
5. Discuss the achievement motive and work.
6. What factors influence the psychological meaning of job loss? How?
7. What is the nature of the changing role of women in the labor force? Discuss the achievement orientation and career development of females in early adulthood.
8. Describe the importance of leisure in adult life, in particular during the middle adult years, and outline the kinds of leisure activities adults engage in after they retire.
9. Are we in need of revised social policy about work and retirement? Explain.

Further Readings

Atchley, R. C. (1975). Adjustment to loss of job at retirement. *International Journal of Aging and Human Development, 6,* 17–27.

Describes the important adjustments that one needs to make when one retires. Describes the salience of work in the hierarchy of the adult's interests. Easy to read.

Farrell, M. P., & Rosenberg, S. D. (1981). *Men at mid-life.* Boston: Auburn House.

An excellent source of information about mid-life career change in men as well as vocational development in men. Reading level is of medium difficulty.

Huston-Stein, A., & Higgens-Trenk, A. (1978). Development of females from childhood through adulthood: Career and feminine role orientations. In P. Baltes (Ed.), *Life-span development and behavior* (vol. 1). New York: Academic Press.

An excellent overview of the achievement and career orientations of females, with particular concern for socializing influences that have led to different achievement and career paths for young adults. Reasonably easy reading.

Levinson, D. J. (1978). *The seasons of a man's life.* New York: Knopf.

The full account of Levinson's information on which he has based his view of the many transitions people make in the adult years; heavy focus on the vocational role as a central component of transitions in the lives of men. Easy reading.

Smelser, N. J., & Erikson, E. H. (1980). *Themes of work and love in adulthood.* Cambridge, MA: Harvard University Press.

An edited volume of essays all focused on the themes of work and love in adulthood, written by experts such as Erik Erikson, Neal Smelser, Robert LeVine, Melvin Kohn, Marjorie Fiske, Roger Gould, and Daniel Levinson. Easy to read.

Van Dusen, R. A., & Sheldon, E. B. (1976). The changing status of American women. *American Psychologist, 31,* 106–116.

Provides an overview of the substantial increase in the number of women in the labor force, examining obstacles and psychological ramifications in the transition from a more traditional sex-role model to the more androgynous model that seems to be developing today. Reasonably easy reading.

PERSONALITY PROCESSES
AND DEVELOPMENT

PROFILE

At the age of nineteen, Angela Porter is a university sophomore and has not yet decided what occupation she wants to pursue. She has given some thought to getting married and letting her husband support her. Angela is not sure exactly what she wants from life, but she spends a lot of time thinking about it. Her identity has not yet crystallized, and she feels no particular need to commit herself to a husband or to some type of work at this point in her life. Angela is very feminine and doesn't really like the new look in sex roles; she likes being a female and feels secure in her feminine role. She also shows some concern about morals—it bothered her when she found out that her roommate cheated on an examination last week. Angela shows a conventional orientation toward rules and regulations and believes that they should be abided by. She also believes that there are important morals in relationships. Indeed, for Angela probably the most important aspect of morality is the interdependence that two people develop and the commitment they give to each other. She says that the most stressful experiences she has on a day-to-day basis are wasting her time, meeting high standards, and feeling lonely sometimes. Her most uplifting experiences occur when she and some of her friends get together and laugh and have a good time.

Angela seems to be more serious now than she was in high school, however, and she doesn't show quite as much self-preoccupation with her body as she did during her adolescent years. When asked if her personality has changed very much since junior high, she responds that she is basically the same old Angela but that in some ways her personality has gradually changed. She feels that she is more mature now—she thinks twice about doing something wild, and she is more conscientious about her study habits. She also feels a bit more outgoing now than when she was in junior high, but how extraverted she is often depends on the situation and whom she is with.

As we follow Angela through her college years, we find that by the end of her senior year she has fallen in love with Jack Harmon. According to Angela, Jack is a "pretty cocky guy, but maybe he deserves to be a little conceited because he really is smart, gets along well with people, and is a good athlete." Still, Angela is trying to make Jack a little more humble. So far she has only been modestly successful. Jack has a traditionally masculine sex-role orientation and likes the fact that Angela has a traditional female sex-role orientation. In talking about marriage, they have discussed what roles they feel a man and a woman should play in a marriage, and they agree on most points.

After they both graduate from college, Jack and Angela get married. Jack initially takes a job with an electronics firm, but his goal is to own his own business by the time he is thirty-five. When we look at Jack and Angela at the ages of forty and thirty-nine, respectively, they are both giving some consideration to their roles in the world—their commitment seems to be changing somewhat in that they are showing a stronger orientation toward contributing something to the next generation. Nonetheless, Jack has still maintained his strong achievement orientation and his business is doing well. Angela is still staying at home and maintaining the major responsibility for their two children, who are now fourteen and sixteen years old. Angela has begun to think more about what she will do to fill her time once the children have left, but she hasn't come to any firm conclusions yet. Jack seems to be more hurried than he was even when he was working hard in his twenties. He thinks more about how much time he has left in life and what he is going to do with that time, although he feels confident that he will continue to do well in the world of work.

When Angela is fifty-two years old, her mother, with whom she has been very close, dies of an irreversible form of dementia. It has been an arduous several years for Angela because early in the illness her mother stayed at Jack and Angela's house; then during the gradual deterioration of her mother's mind, Angela visited her every day in a nearby nursing home. Jack has been very supportive and has helped Angela cope with this stressful situation. Angela is a strong person, though, and she has adapted by filling her time with several new activities—she has joined a garden club and has become more active as a volunteer helper at the local hospital.

Jack, at the age of fifty-three, is earning as much money as he thought he would, although he is a little less cocky than he used to be. Maybe Angela has subtly been able to tone down his ego over the course of living with him for thirty years. He is still very self-confident and sociable, but he doesn't come across as being as brash and conceited as he was during early adulthood. Jack actually seems gradually to be becoming softer, more sensitive, and warmer in his relationship with Angela and with other people as well. Angela does not seem to be showing any signs of traditional masculine sex-role characteristics. She feels satisfied with her life and is very happy that she has been able to competently rear her children and provide a good family life for them and her husband.

When we look at Angela and Jack at the ages of seventy-two and seventy-three, they have been married almost fifty years. They spend quite a bit of time looking back and reminiscing about their earlier years, recalling events and circumstances, happy and sad moments, conflicts and reconciliations, missed and captured opportunities, sometimes questioning whether they did things right. But by and large they feel satisfied with their lives, sensing an integrity about their personalities that seems to let them live the last years of their lives peacefully. Although they have maintained a fairly active life since Jack's retirement, they do not show as much active mastery toward their world as they did in their early and middle adult years, and they also seem to be more introspective.

10

VIEWS AND THEORIES OF PERSONALITY DEVELOPMENT

I MAGINE *that you have developed a major theory of adult personality development.*

What would influence someone like you to develop a theory about personality development and aging and how would he or she go about it? A person usually goes through a long university training program that is likely to culminate in a doctoral degree. As part of the training, the person is exposed to many ideas about a particular topic such as personality, clinical psychological, or adult development and aging. Another factor that could help explain why an individual develops a particular theory focuses on the kind of life experiences that the theorist had during his or her childhood and adult years.

One of the influential theories of adult personality development is Erik Erikson's eight-stage theory. Erikson believes that resolving an identity crisis is central to healthy personality development in adulthood. Let's see how Erikson's youth might have influenced his belief that searching for an identity is an important aspect of adult personality development. He studied art and a number of languages rather than scientific courses like biology and chemistry. He did not like the formal atmosphere of his school, and this was reflected in his grades. At age eighteen, rather than going to college the adolescent Erikson wandered across Europe, keeping notes about his experiences in a personal diary. After a year of travel, he returned to Germany and enrolled in an art school, became dissatisfied, and enrolled in another. Then he began to give up his sketching and eventually traveled to Florence, Italy. Robert Coles (1970) vividly describes Erikson at this time:

> To the Italians he was not an unfamiliar sight, the young, tall, thin Nordic expatriate with long, blond hair. He wore a corduroy suit and was seen by his family and friends as not odd or "sick" but as a wandering artist who was trying to come to grips with himself, not an unnatural or unusual struggle, particularly in Germany. (p. 15)

Interestingly, some well-known personality theorists who were initially interested in the early years of development turned their attention to development in adulthood as they themselves aged through the adult years. In his early writings, psychoanalyst Erikson focused mainly on the first twenty years of life (e.g., *Childhood and Society,* 1952), only later showing strong curiosity about age-related changes in adulthood (e.g., *Ghandi's Truth,* 1969). Erikson's ideas about the eight stages of development throughout the life cycle represent one of the most widely discussed views of life-span development.

Charlotte Buhler (1933, 1968) is another individual whose initial interest in childhood later changed to focus on life-span development. She divided the life span into the following five periods: (1) childhood—birth to fourteen; (2) youth—fourteen to twenty-five; (3) adult I—twenty-five to between forty-five and fifty; (4) adult II—between forty-five and fifty to between sixty-five and seventy; (5) aging—seventy and up. Buhler believes that self-fulfillment is the key to successful development and says that individuals are motivated to attain personal goals throughout the life cycle. Her five goal-related phases to self-fulfillment are described here:

Childhood—children have not yet set their life goals, but they may think about them in somewhat vague ways.
Youth—at this point in development, individuals first discover the concept that their lives are their own, and they begin to think about their potential.
Adult I—individuals develop more specific goals at this time.
Adult II—individuals look back on their past, evaluating their lives in the process, and revise their planning for the future.
Aging—individuals relax their concentration on achieving goals.

Robert R. Sears is yet another individual who initially studied on the early years of development. Sears was one of the architects of social learning theory in the late 1930s and early 1940s. At that time he focused on early learning experiences as guides to personality development. However, in 1973 he wrote: "But the next five or six decades are every bit as important, not only to those adults who are passing through them but to their children, who must live with and understand parents and grandparents" (p. v). Sears, now in his seventies, has been interested in the early adult precursors and current predictors of life satisfaction in late adulthood (e.g., Sears & Barbee, 1977).

As we age through the adult years, not only theorists but each of us may examine his or her life and ask why our personality has developed the way it has and speculate about what future development is likely to hold for us.

You probably have some ideas about the nature of adult personality development. Do you feel that personality develops in a stagelike manner, or do you believe that personality development in adults is smoother? Do you feel that biological maturation plays a more important role in one's personality development as an adult, or is one's personality the way it is mainly because of one's social experiences? As you will soon see, these are some of the concerns of theorists who attempt to describe and explain adult personality development.

INTRODUCTION

In this chapter we will attempt to define personality and survey a number of theoretical perspectives on adult personality change and development. Our discussion is essentially divided into theories that emphasize stages of personality development and those that do not. We present Erik Erikson's life-span developmental view of personality stages, along with Robert Peck and George Vaillant's revisions of Erikson's theory, and Roger Gould and Daniel Levinson's views of stages of adult personality development. The major nonstage theories of adult personality that we emphasize are cognitive social learning theory and the life-events framework, including Albert Bandura and Walter Mischel's cognitive social learning views and ideas about the importance of viewing personality in terms of person × situation interaction. We also describe the life events views of Bernice Neugarten and discuss the importance of considering individual variation in personality development.

WHAT IS PERSONALITY?

First of all, what is personality? It is hard to get agreement on an answer to this question because the answer often hinges on the theoretical view one adopts. Personality is sometimes thought of as a person's most revealing or dominant characteristic. In this regard we might say that Ellen has a "shy personality" and Arlene has a "neurotic personality." Here are three, more formal, definitions of personality:

> . . . the dynamic organization within the individual of those psychophysical systems that determine his characteristic behavior and thought (Allport, 1961, p. 28)

> . . . a person's unique pattern of traits (Guilford, 1959, p. 5)

> . . . the most adequate conceptualization of a person's behavior in all its detail (McClelland, 1951, p. 69)

As Walter Mischel (1981) concludes, there is a common theme running through these somewhat diverse definitions of personality, namely, that **personality** refers to distinctive patterns of behavior, thought, and emotion that characterize each person's adaptation to the situations of his or her life.

Personality study has traditionally focused on generating theories about human nature and individuality and about the causes and meanings of important psychological differences among people. In this effort, personality psychologists have sought to find the most enduring and stable human attributes. In so doing, they have studied how people develop and change, as well as how people achieve stability throughout the course of life.

Personality psychologists often differ substantially in regard to their view of human behavior. Sigmund Freud's view emphasized the importance of unconscious motives whose true nature is outside the adult's awareness and whose sources lie deeply buried in the distant past. John Watson and B. F. Skinner, by contrast, have stressed the importance of learned behavior in understanding personality, a view that emphasizes recent and current experience, as well as the belief that the things a person does—his or her overt behaviors—not his or her unobservable unconscious wishes, are the source of information about personality. Clearly, there is great variability in the way personality theorists view personality.

There is also disagreement about how effectively we can measure personality. To convert personality theories from speculations into ideas that can be studied scientifically, we have to state the theories in testable terms. Behavioral theories are stated in perhaps the most testable terms, whereas psychoanalytic theories are stated in the least testable terms—more on this later in the chapter. To behaviorists, personality is behavior that is observable. Many personality theorists, however, believe that the behavioral view leaves out much of the richness and complexity of personality. Psychoanalytic theorists, for example, believe that behavior is merely a sign of the internal workings of personality and that the internal dynamics of a person's mind, not observable behavior, constitute the core of personality. But it is not easy to measure the internal dynamics of personality. And how do we measure something so global and with so many components and rich diversity as an adult's personality? Many personality psychologists believe that we should ask the person about his or her personality, but people do not always perceive themselves in objective terms. Even within the field of personality, for every personality psychologist who believes that we must study people under carefully controlled experimental conditions, there is one who argues that we can only understand individuals by studying them under naturalistic, lifelike conditions. One astute observer of personality in adulthood, George Vaillant (1977), stressed that lives are "too human for science, too beautiful for numbers, too sad for diagnosis, and too immortal for bound journals" (p. 11).

As you can see, there is a great deal of lively debate about how personality should be conceptualized as well as how it should be studied. Personality theory and research can be applied to help improve the psychological quality of our lives. Even adults with few problems may benefit from examining what we know about personality development. Indeed, one of the topics of this chapter is life satisfaction, an aspect of personality that has received considerable attention in regard to the late adult years.

The field of personality is beginning to move away from global theorizing about human nature, and many personality psychologists are trying to cast their questions in a form that allows for scientific study. Much contemporary personality research focuses on the role of specific social experiences and events in personality development and everyday adaptation (Mischel, 1981).

In chapter 1 you read about the distinction between stage and nonstage theories of development. This distinction provides a useful way to organize our discussion of views and theories of personality development.

STAGE VIEWS AND THEORIES

Recall that one of the major issues in our study of adult lives is the extent to which development should be described in a stage or nonstage manner. A number of personality stage theories have emphasized stages of child development but described few or no stages of adult development. The assumption in such theories—the most prominent being Freud's psychoanalytic theory—is that the major changes in development occur during childhood, not adulthood. Freud's theory, for example, stresses that the final stage of development is entered during adolescence.

In addition to theories that place a premium on childhood stages of development, other theories emphasize a series of stages that unfold throughout the life cycle. The most prominent of these views is the psychoanalytic theory of Erik Erikson, who has described life-span personality development in terms of eight stages. There have also been a number of stage theories that describe stages of adult personality development with little or no mention of childhood stages or antecedents.

Erik Erikson's Life-Span Developmental View of Personality

One serious misgiving of contemporary psychoanalytic thinkers arises from the fact that Freud short-changed the importance of culture. He failed to see that each society handles children and adults in very different ways. As a result, the stages of development only loosely describe the pattern of change for all individuals. That culture exerts a strong influence on the timing and dynamics of each stage is a theme reflected in the work of Erik Erikson, a German psychologist born in 1902.

Although Erikson accepts the basic outline of Freud's theory, he places more emphasis on the influence of culture and society as a shaper of the individual's destiny. Much of Erikson's own professional work was with children and adults in different cultures, which reflects his anthropological approach to the study of individual development. Erikson's theory is particularly important because it stresses rational, or ego, processes and because it casts a life-span frame of reference on development.

Erikson postulates eight stages of development—sometimes called the **eight ages of man.** Each one centers around a salient and distinct emotional concern stemming from biological pressures from within and sociocultural expectations from outside the person. These concerns, or conflicts, may be resolved in a positive and healthy manner or in a pessimistic and unhealthy way. Each conflict has a unique time period during which it ascends and overshadows all the others. In order for later stages of development to proceed smoothly, each earlier stage conflict must be resolved satisfactorily. These stages of development are represented in figure 10.1. In the left-hand column are the major phases of life-span

Phases of the life cycle							
Infancy	Early childhood	Middle and late childhood	Adolescence	Young adulthood	Middle adulthood	Late adulthood	

	Infancy	Early childhood	Middle and late childhood	Adolescence	Young adulthood	Middle adulthood	Late adulthood
1	Basic trust vs. mistrust						
2		Autonomy vs. shame, doubt					
3			Initiative vs. guilt				
4				Industry vs. inferiority			
5					Identity vs. role confusion		
6						Intimacy vs. isolation	
7							Generativity vs. stagnation
8							Ego integrity vs. despair

Figure 10.1 Erikson's eight stages of development.

development. The eight conflicts are listed diagonally, in order of their ascendancy.

The first stage, **trust versus mistrust,** corresponds to the oral stage in Freudian theory. An infant is almost entirely dependent upon his or her mother for food, sustenance, and comfort. The mother is the primary representative of society to the child. If she discharges her infant-related duties with warmth, regularity, and affection, the infant will develop a feeling of trust toward the world. The infant's trust is a comfortable feeling that someone will always be around to care for his or her needs even though the mother occasionally disappears. Alternatively, a sense of mistrust or fearful uncertainty can develop if the mother fails to provide these needs in the caretaking setting. According to Erikson, she is setting up a distrusting attitude that will follow the child through life.

Autonomy versus shame and doubt is the second stage and corresponds to the anal stage in Freudian theory. The infant begins to gain control over the bowels and bladder. Parents begin imposing demands on the child to conform to socially acceptable forms and occasions for eliminating wastes. The child may develop the healthy attitude of being capable of independent or autonomous control of his or her own actions or may develop the unhealthy attitude of shame or doubt because he or she is incapable of control.

Initiative versus guilt corresponds to the phallic period in Freudian theory. The child is caught in the midst of the Oedipal or Electra conflict, with its alternating love-hate feelings for the parent of the opposite sex and with fear of fulfilling the sexual fantasies that abound. The child may discover ways to overcome feelings of powerlessness by engaging in various activities. If this is done, then the basic healthy attitude of being the initiator of action will result. Alternatively, the child may fail to discover such outlets and feel guilt at being dominated by the environment.

Industry versus inferiority, coinciding with the Freudian period of latency, covers the years of middle childhood when the child is involved in expansive absorption of knowledge and the development of intellectual and physical skills. As the child is drawn into the social culture of peers, it is natural to evaluate accomplishments by comparing himself or herself with others. If the child views himself or herself as basically competent in these activities, feelings of productiveness and industriousness will result. On the other hand, if the child views himself or herself as incompetent, particularly in comparison with peers, then he or she will feel unproductive and inferior. This unhealthy attitude may negatively color the child's whole approach to life and learning, producing a tendency to withdraw from new and challenging situations rather than meet them with confidence and enthusiasm.

Identity versus role confusion is roughly associated with Freud's genital stage, centering on the establishment of a stable personal identity. Whereas for Freud the important part of identity formation resides in the adolescent's resolution of sexual conflicts, for Erikson the central ingredient is the establishment of a clear path toward a vocation—selection of a job or an occupational role to aspire to. This allows the adolescent an objective that he or she and other members of society simultaneously acknowledge. If the adolescent comes through this period with a clearly selected role and the knowledge that others in society can clearly identify this role, feelings of confidence and purposefulness emerge. If not, the child may feel confused and troubled.

Erikson introduced the first of the post-Freudian stages, **intimacy versus isolation.** Early adulthood brings with it a job and the opportunity to form an intimate relationship with a member of the opposite sex. If the young adult forms friendships with others and a significant, intimate relationship with one individual in particular, then a basic feeling of closeness with others will result. A feeling of isolation may result from an inability to form friendships and an intimate relationship.

A chief concern of adults is to assist the younger generation in developing and leading useful lives. **Generativity versus stagnation** centers on successful rearing of children. Childless adults often need to find substitute young people through adoption, guardianship, or a close relationship with the children of friends and relatives. Generativity, or the feeling of helping to shape the next generation, is the positive outcome that may emerge. Stagnation, or the feeling of having done nothing for the next generation, is the unhealthy outcome.

In the later years adults enter the period of **ego integrity versus despair**, a time for looking back at what they have done with their lives. Through many different routes, the older person may have developed a positive outlook in each of the preceding periods of emotional crises. If so, the retrospective glances will reveal a picture of life well spent, and the person will be satisfied (ego integrity). However, the older person may have resolved one or more of the crises in a negative way. If so, the retrospective glances will yield doubt, gloom, and despair over the worth of one's life.

It should be noted that Erikson does not believe the proper solution to a stage crisis is always completely positive in nature. Some exposure and/or commitment to the negative end of the individual's bipolar conflict often is inevitable (for example, the individual cannot trust all people under all circumstances and survive). However, in a healthy solution to a stage crisis, the positive resolution of the conflict is dominant.

Erikson's theory, like all psychoanalytic theories, is difficult to verify through empirical research (Langer, 1969). How does one find out how an individual has experienced Erikson's stages of development? You might follow Erikson's pattern of probing the depths of an individual's personality by conducting a number of open-ended interviews. Or you might decide to develop a questionnaire or survey to give to an adult, a questionnaire or survey that asks how he really feels about himself. But neither of these methods is really adequate for fully and accurately evaluating the adult's ability to resolve the eight crises. The problem becomes particularly acute when one is faced with the necessity of having to investigate such crises in large numbers of adults. While experts in adult development recognize the importance of Erikson's theory as an integrative framework, they point out that aside from clinical studies and psychobiographies, there is very little empirical information that would help in the evaluation of the theory. There is even some debate about whether the stages and concepts are spelled out in adequate detail to allow empirical studies of hypotheses that might be derived from Erikson's explanations. At present, the number of such attempts is small, and the theory has not been examined in longitudinal fashion. Further, it is not clear how one would go about making operational the motivational, behavioral, and cognitive components of Erikson's theory (Hill, 1973).

In addition to theories that emphasize childhood and life-span stages of development and adult cognitive stages, a number of theories have focused almost exclusively on adult stages of personality development.

Theories Emphasizing Adult Personality Stages

Four theories stand out as examples that have focused exclusively on adult stages of personality development: Robert Peck's expansion of Erikson's adult stages, Roger Gould's transformations, Daniel Levinson's seasons of a man's life, and George Vaillant's expansion of Erikson's adult stages.

Robert Peck's Expansion of Erikson's Adult Stages

Robert Peck (1968) has attempted to refine Erikson's stages of generativity and integrity. Peck believes that Erikson's descriptions of middle and late adulthood may be too general, so he has attempted to define those years more precisely. In the middle adult years, Peck argues that one faces four challenges:

1. *Valuing wisdom versus valuing physical powers.* This challenge occurs when people in their forties cling to physical powers that are diminishing. Peck stresses that adults at this age who shift their focus to cognitive abilities from physical prowess are likely to adapt better to their world.

2. *Socializing versus sexualizing in human relationships.* Peck emphasizes that during middle age it is important for adults to relate to each other more on the basis of people than of sex. If this is accomplished, then marital relationships in particular are likely to prosper after children leave home.

3. *Cathectic flexibility versus cathectic impoverishment.* It is important for middle-aged adults to widen their circles of social involvement so that as their own parents die and their children leave home they will not feel as much loneliness, and losses of attachment figures will be softened. The label *cathectic* is used to refer to emotional bonds with people.

4. *Mental flexibility versus mental rigidity.* The person in middle age who keeps dwelling on the past will not get along as well in the world as the person who is open to new experiences and interpretations.

Peck believes that one must face three challenges in late adulthood:

1. *Ego differentiation versus work-role preoccupation.* It is important for older people to establish a varied set of valued activities so that time spent and interest in occupation and with children can be filled.

2. *Body transcendence versus body preoccupation.* Although most elderly people encounter illnesses, some seem to be able to enjoy life through creative activities and human interactions that allow them to go beyond their aging body.

3. *Ego transcendence versus ego preoccupation.* Although death is inevitable and not likely to be too far away, many elderly people feel very much at ease with themselves by realizing that they have contributed to the future through competent rearing of their children or through their vocation and ideas.

Roger Gould's Transformations

A well-known perspective on adult development that has linked stage and crisis with development is Roger Gould's view (1975, 1978, 1980), which emphasizes that mid-life is every bit as turbulent as adolescence, except that during middle adulthood striving to handle crisis is likely to lead to a healthier, happier life. Gould first explained his view in the book *Transformations* (1975).

Gould's study of 524 men and women led him to propose seven developmental stages of adult life:

Stage	Approximate age	Development(s)
1	16–18	Desire to escape parental control
2	18–22	Leaving the family: peer group orientation
3	22–28	Developing independence: commitment to a career and to children
4	29–34	Questioning self: role confusion; marriage and career vulnerable to dissatisfaction
5	35–43	Urgency to attain life's goals: awareness of time limitation; realignment of life's goals.
6	43–53	Settling down: acceptance of one's life.
7	53–60	More tolerance: acceptance of past; less negativism; general mellowing

Gould believes that in our twenties we assume new roles; in our thirties we begin to feel stuck with our responsibilities; and in our forties we begin to feel a sense of urgency when we realize that our lives are speeding by. When we realize that each step is a natural one, Gould believes that we are on the path to adult maturity.

One of the shortcomings of Gould's theory is that it is based on clinical observations and questionnaire data. Gould used two different techniques to obtain information about adult development. First, eight medical students listened to tape recordings of patient sessions. The medical students were asked to note the personal feelings of the patients that stood out. Second, a questionnaire was developed and given to a "normal, nonclinical" sample of 524 white, middle-class adults. The clinical nature of ratings by medical students is a questionable strategy, the middle-class bias of both the clinical and the nonclinical sample leads to problems of generalization to a lower-class sample, and in neither the clinical observations nor the questionnaire was there any attempt to measure the reliability of the information obtained. In the clinical part of the study, we need to know if two individuals listen to the same tapes whether they will agree that what they are hearing suggests a particular problem or not. In regard to the questionnaire, we need to know whether the respondents consistently responded to the items in a particular way. Finally, no statistical analysis was conducted in Gould's work.

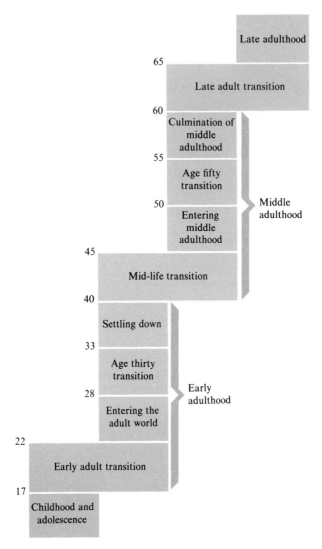

Figure 10.2   Development periods in the eras of early and middle adulthood.

Daniel Levinson's The Seasons of a Man's Life

Daniel Levinson's (1978, 1980) work on adult development is set out in his well-known book *The Seasons of a Man's Life* (1978), which grew out of his research on the personality development of forty middle-aged men. Levinson uses biographical case material to illustrate the stages of personality people go through. His interviews were conducted with hourly workers, business executives, academic biologists, and novelists. Though Levinson's major interest has focused on mid-life transition, he has described a number of phases, stages, and transitions in the life cycle, as indicated in figure 10.2.

Daniel Levinson, the architect of Seasons of a Man's Life.

Like Robert Havighurst, Levinson emphasizes that developmental tasks must be mastered at each of these stages. In early adulthood, the two major tasks to be mastered are exploring the possibilities for adult living and developing a stable life structure. Levinson sees the twenties as a novice phase of adult personality development. At the end of one's teens, a transition from dependence to independence should occur. This transition is marked by the formation of a dream—an image of the kind of life the youth wants to have, particularly in relation to marriage and career development. The novice phase is a time of reasonably free experimentation and of testing the dream in the real world.

From about the ages of twenty-eight to thirty-three, the individual goes through a transition period in which he must face the more serious question of determining his goals. During the thirties, a person usually focuses on and works toward family and career development. In the later years of this period, the person enters a phase of *b*ecoming *o*ne's *o*wn *m*an (or BOOM, as Levinson calls it). By age forty the individual has reached a stable location in his career, has outgrown his earlier, more tenuous attempts at learning to become an adult, and now must look forward to the kind of life he will lead as a middle-aged adult.

According to Levinson, the change into middle adulthood lasts about five years and requires the adult to come to grips with four major conflicts that have existed in his life since adolescence. These four conflicts include (1) *being young versus being old;* (2) *being destructive versus being constructive;* (3) *being masculine versus being feminine;* (4) *being attached to others or separated from them.* The success of the mid-life transition depends on how effectively the individual is able to reduce these polarities and accept each of them as integral parts of his being.

Because Levinson interviewed middle-aged adult males, we can consider the data about middle adulthood more valid than the information about early adulthood. When people are asked to remember information about earlier parts of their lives, they may distort and forget important things. Further, the Levinson interview data included no females. *The Seasons of A Man's Life,* like Gould's *Transformations,* is not a research report in any conventional sense. There are no statistics to speak of and no quantified results. However, the data reported by Levinson are characteristic of the clinical tradition, and the quality and quantity of the biographies are outstanding.

George Vaillant's Expansion of Erikson's Adult Stages

George Vaillant argues that two additional stages should be added to Erikson's adult stages. One of these, called *career consolidation,* occurs from approximately twenty-three to thirty-five years of age. The second stage, *keeping the meaning versus rigidity,* occurs from about forty-five to fifty-five. This is a time of relaxation for many adults, a time at which goals have either been attained or if they have not, this fact is accepted. In this period, adults show concern about extracting some meaning from their lives and fight against falling into a rigid orientation.

When these two stages are added to Erikson's stages, there is at least reasonable agreement among Gould, Levinson, and Vaillant about the nature of stages in adulthood. All would concur with a general outline of adult development that begins with the change from identity to intimacy, then from career consolidation to generativity, and finally from searching for meaning to some final integration. Thus, although the labels are different, the underlying themes of adult development are remarkably similar (see figure 10.3).

The adult development perspectives of Gould, Levinson, and Vaillant emphasize the importance of phases or stages of development in the life cycle. Though information about phases and stages in the life cycle can be helpful in pointing out dominant themes that characterize many people at particular points in adult development, there are several important ideas to keep in mind when considering these theoretical perspectives as viable models of adult development. First, the research on which they are based often is not empirically sound. Second, there has been a tendency of many of the perspectives to focus too extensively on stages as crises in development, particularly in the case of the mid-life crisis. Third, there is an increasing tendency of theory and research on adult development to emphasize the importance of life events rather than stages or phases of development. Fourth, there is often a great deal of individual and contextual variation in the manner in which the themes, stages, phases, or life events in adult development characterize particular individuals. In box 10.1 further critical evaluation of popular stage-crisis theories suggests why many scientists are highly skeptical about such views.

Next we see that some prominent personality theorists do not believe we should conceptualize personality change during adulthood in terms of stages. Biology and maturation are less prominent in the nonstage views of personality.

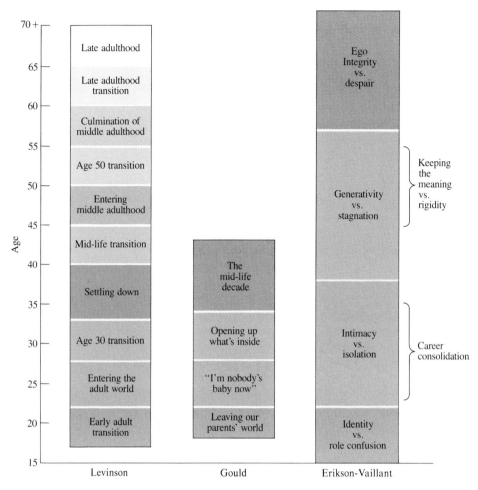

Figure 10.3   A comparison of the adult stages of Levinson, Gould, and Erikson-Vaillant.

The social learning perspective stresses that human development is void of abrupt transitions but still places a premium on change in personality during the adult years. A second view of adult personality development that plays down the importance of stages is the life-events framework. However, in contrast to social learning theory, which places a low level of emphasis on abrupt change, some life-events views emphasize abrupt change in personality. Nonetheless, both social learning theory and the life-events framework stress the importance of the environment and context in which a person lives as the most important influences on personality change in adulthood.

Box 10.1
WHY SHEEHY'S *PASSAGES* IS NOT
ACCEPTED BY SCIENTISTS

Gail Sheehy's *Passages* (1976) was so popular that it topped the *New York Times* best-seller list for twenty-seven weeks. Sheehy's goal in *Passages* is to describe adult development. She cites discussions with Daniel Levinson and Roger Gould and case study information based on 115 interviews with men and women as the main sources of her view.

Sheehy argues that we all go through developmental stages roughly bound by chronological age. Each stage contains problems that we must solve before we can progress to the next stage. The periods between stages are labeled *passages*. Sheehy uses catchy phrases to describe each stage: the trying twenties, catch-30, the deadline decade (between thirty-five and forty-five), and finally the age-forty crucible. Sheehy's advice never wavers, no matter which stage is involved. Adults in transition may feel miserable, but those who face up to agonizing self-evaluation, who appraise their weaknesses as well as their strengths, who try to set goals for the future, and who try to become as independent as possible will be happier than those who do not fully experience and benefit from these trials.

Sheehy believes that by means of these passages, individuals earn an *authentic identity*. This identity is not based on the authority of one's parents or on cultural prescriptions. Instead, it is constructed through the adult's own strenuous efforts. Sheehy says that the adults who allow themselves to be halted and seized by issues and then shaken into reexamination are the people who find their identity and thrive.

Unfortunately, Sheehy does not disclose such elementary information as the sex and racial composition of her sample of 115 adults, how the sample was selected, what questions were asked in the interview and by whom, and for what length of time the interviews lasted. Furthermore, the data may be biased toward stress because a disproportionate number of divorced adults were in the sample. When the author describes cases, she does so to buttress the concept of a developmental theme, with no indication of the representativeness of the incidents reported. Finally, Sheehy conducted no statistical analyses.

The Social Learning Perspective

Social learning theorists believe that to understand personality change in adulthood we need to focus on overt, directly observable behavior. However, though social learning theorists stress the role of environment in determining personality, recently many of them have veered away from B. F. Skinner's belief that personality and behavior can best be understood solely by examining the external consequences of one's actions. Indeed, the label **cognitive social learning theory** best describes the views of Albert Bandura and Walter Mischel.

Albert Bandura.

Albert Bandura's Reciprocal Determinism

From Albert Bandura's perspective, the statement that behavior is determined by its consequences refers to the self-produced consequences of one's own actions as well as to consequences of the actions of others. In other words, self-reinforcement is often just as important as reinforcement from others.

Consider the achievement behavior of a woman who is required to perform certain duties on her job. Although she cannot ignore her desire for a salary increase, her own need for excellence will just as likely motivate her to improve and do a better job on her work assignment. Substandard performance, on the other hand, might lead her to self-criticism. In this sense, the woman's achievement behavior is as much a function of her reaction to herself as to the reactions of others. This concept differs from Skinner's theory, which argues that behavior is determined only by external consequences.

The existence of self-produced consequences and personal performance standards suggests that using reinforcement to control someone else's behavior will not always be successsful. As Bandura (1977) has pointed out, if external reinforcement was always effective, we would behave like weather vanes—in the presence of a John Bircher we would act like a John Bircher, and in the presence of a Communist we would behave like a Communist. Instead, behavior develops through the process of reciprocal control. Consider the following conversation between two twenty-year-olds:

BOB Come on, Nancy, will you please clean up the house?
NANCY (Looks away as if she doesn't hear him)
BOB Look, Nancy, I'm talking to you! Don't ignore me.
NANCY What, Bob?

BOB I said, clean up this trashy place!

NANCY Bob, how come you haven't fixed the screen door?

BOB (Yelling) Screen door? That's not nearly as important as keeping the house clean.

NANCY Aw, okay; I'll clean the house later.

What has been learned in this interchange? Nancy has learned that she can control Bob's criticism by criticizing him in return and by making a vague promise. Bob has learned that if he gets upset and amplifies his feelings, he can at least get Nancy to make some kind of promise. This type of interchange occurs all of the time in relationships throughout the life span. It is a coercive process in which two people attempt to control each other's behavior. Indeed, whenever one person is trying to control another, the second person is usually resisting control or attempting to control in return. In this sense, Bandura (1971) asserts that the manipulation and control of people suggested by Skinner in *Walden Two* could never evolve.

Bandura refers to this concept of behavior as **reciprocal determinism** (Bandura, 1977). The individual is not completely driven by inner forces or manipulated helplessly by environmental factors; rather, the person's psychological makeup is best understood by analyzing the continuous reciprocal interaction between behavior and its controlling conditions. In other words, behavior partly constructs the environment, and the resulting environment, in turn, affects behavior.

Bandura (1971, 1977) also believes that individuals learn extensively by example. Much of what we learn involves observing the behavior of parents, peers, teachers, and others. This form of social learning is called **imitation, modeling,** or **vicarious learning.** For example, the woman who watches another woman get a salary increase may be motivated to begin behaving like the other woman.

Bandura believes that if learning proceeded in the trial-and-error fashion advocated by Skinner, it would be very laborious and even hazardous. For example, to put a woman, who had never driven before, in a car, have her drive down the road, and reward the positive responses she makes would be senseless. Instead, many of the complex educational and cultural practices of individuals are learned through their exposure to competent models who display appropriate ways to solve problems and cope with the world.

Sometimes it is said that social learning theorists take a mechanical view of development. Jonas Langer (1969) has even labeled the social learning view as **a mechanical mirror theory.** The label suggests that individuals do not control their own destiny but instead are controlled and manipulated by environmental influences until they mirror their environments in mechanical fashion. On the other hand, the psychoanalytic view of development emphasizes the internal forces that control the individual's growth. In the psychoanalytic view, the forces are the relationships of the three personality structures to one another.

Walter Mischel, noted personality researcher, is the architect of cognitive social learning theory.

Certainly it is valid to say that social learning adherents believe that behavior is influenced by the individual's response to the environment. To this extent, the social learning model indicates that an individual's behavior is controlled by the external environment. However, as we have just seen, many social learning thinkers, such as Bandura, stress that the individual controls and even constructs his or her own environment. Recall the example of the man trying to get the woman to clean up the house. Not only was he controlling her behavior, but she was controlling his. Many contemporary social learning theorists stress this type of bidirectional stimulus control (e.g., Bijou, 1976).

Walter Mischel's Cognitive Social Learning Theory

In addition to Albert Bandura, another individual whose thinking has been important in the development of cognitive social learning theory is Walter Mischel (1973, 1977, 1981). Indeed, it was Mischel who first described this perspective in a 1973 paper that focused on the development of a cognitive social learning theory. Mischel has discussed a number of specific cognitive concepts that he feels are central to understanding adult lives. These include expectancies, plans, encoding strategies, personal constructs, and subjective stimulus values.

The expectancies we have for our own behavior as well as for the behavior of others are important determinants of social behavior. An adult's history provides him or her with an array of expectations. For example, a man may have been "burned" in a previous marriage by a wife who was short and had red hair, so in the future he may be very wary of dating anyone with similar characteristics. We use innumerable descriptions to categorize people, and those descriptions lead us to entertain certain expectations about how people are likely to act. You may have heard that your boss is tough, and even though she hasn't treated you that way, you may be just waiting for the time that she really cracks down on you.

We also have the capability of generating complex plans. Once we develop a plan, it can guide our conduct for months and even years. For example, suppose that during college you decide to become a doctor. This decision has important implications for your study habits, choice of courses, the way you spend many of your weekends, and how you will spend some five to ten years of your life after college. By contrast, you may plan to get married just after you get out of high school and to settle down and have a family. Such decisions have important implications for the nature of your adult life for many years to come.

Person × Situation Interaction

The emphasis on the importance of the social context in determining behavior that characterizes the social learning approach has important implications for our understanding of adult development.

In cognitive social learning theory, the emphasis on studying both the characteristics of the person and the contexts in which he or she lives is described by the equation: personality = person × situation interaction. More is said about this important approach to personality in box 10.2.

In the next perspective, there also is a strong emphasis on the social context in which development occurs. Though not focusing as strongly on behavior as the social learning approach does, the life-events framework places a premium on the social-historical context in understanding adult personality development.

The Life-Events Framework

There has been considerable interest in determining the importance of life events in the personality development of adults (e.g., Dohrenwend, Krasnof, Askenasy, & Dohrenwend, 1978; Holmes & Rahe, 1967; Hultsch & Plemons, 1979; Neugarten & Datan, 1973). In the earlier versions of the **life-events framework** (e.g., Holmes & Rahe, 1967), it was suggested that life events produce taxing circumstances for individuals, thus forcing them to change their personality. In this manner, such events as the death of a spouse, divorce, marriage, and so forth were thought to involve varying degrees of stress and therefore were likely to have an important influence on the individual's personality.

However, modified, more sophisticated versions of the life-events framework, though recognizing that life events need to be considered in understanding the nature of personality development, nonetheless have argued that it is important to consider the sociohistorical circumstances in which life events are occurring (e.g., Neugarten & Datan, 1973). Indeed, Bernice Neugarten believes that to understand adult development we need to focus on the intertwining of three kinds of time: life time, social time, and historical time. (See box 10.3 for Neugarten's comments about age-related stereotypes.)

Box 10.2
MORE ABOUT THE PERSON $\times$ SITUATION VIEW OF PERSONALITY

Walter Mischel's (1981) cognitive social learning perspective has much in common with the adult contextual view of development. He believes that adults are sensitive to the situations and contexts in which behavior occurs, such sensitivity reflecting the adaptiveness of individuals. This adaptiveness helps people to cope with a changing world. Mischel agrees that there are extensive individual differences in reactions to the same situation or treatment and there are some consistent differences in how adults behave in particular classes of situations; for example, stability over time has been adequately demonstrated for individual differences in ego strength and aggression.

But it is important to recognize that person-environment interactions are never static. The fact that the major longitudinal studies of personality development have included substantial information about living environment and life-styles as well as personality characteristics suggests the importance of searching for the predictors of adult personality development in person $\times$ situation interaction rather than in the stability of personality characteristics alone. For example, in recent data from the California Longitudinal Study reported by Paul Mussen and his colleagues, a wife's emotional stability along with her husband's health in early adulthood were linked with the husband's life satisfaction in late adulthood. The wife's emotional well-being would be described as a situation variable—it reflects an important aspect of the context in the husband's life. His health would be an important person variable.

Mischel stresses that individual differences have typically been studied by holding the situation constant and observing the differences in the way adults react to the same situation. Yet one of the most important differences among people is the way in which *they* select, influence, and change the situations of their lives. The interpersonal relationships that comprise much of our daily lives are constantly selected and modified by us in accord with our competencies, constructs, expectancies, values, and plans. Thus in the California Longitudinal Study, it may be that healthy men did not randomly select wives with just any personality characteristics or life-style, or put the other way, it may have been that emotionally stable women did not just pick any males for husbands. Healthy men and emotionally stable women probably made some competent choices about whom they wanted to spend the rest of their lives with. As Mischel (1981) stresses, "Each person generates many of the very conditions to which he or she then reacts in a series of continuous interactions between behavior and conditions" (p. 535).

This image of adults is one of active, aware problem solvers who can benefit from an enormous range of experiences and cognitive activities. In this view the self is synonymous with the person who influences his or her world but is also influenced by it. Adults are viewed as so complex and multifaceted that they resist easy classifications. It is an image that has moved a great distance away from models of adults' being driven by instinctual forces, characterized by static traits, and controlled helplessly by external rewards and punishments.

Box 10.3
ARE MANY AGE-RELATED THEMES OF DEVELOPMENT STEREOTYPES?

Bernice Neugarten (1980a) says that "we are already familiar with the twenty-eight-year-old mayor, the thirty-year-old college president, the thirty-five-year-old grandmother, the fifty-year-old retiree, the sixty-five-year-old father of a preschooler, the fifty-five-year-old widow who starts a business, and the seventy-year-old student. 'Act your age' is an admonition that has little meaning for adults these days."

Yet an increasing number of popular books suggest very common patterns for our complex lives, such as the "Trying Twenties" and "Passage to the Thirties" in Gail Sheehy's widely read *Passages* (1976). People who read such books worry about their mid-life crises, apologize if they don't seem to be coping with them properly, and seem dismayed if they aren't having one. Such transformations or crises, though, may not define what is normal or off the track. It is not that adults are changeless but rather that adults change far more, and far less predictably, than many oversimplified stage theories suggest. Neugarten continues:

My students and I have studied what happens to people over the life cycle. . . . We have found great trouble clustering people into age brackets that are characterized by particular conflicts; the conflicts won't stay put, and neither will the people. Choices and dilemmas do not sprout forth at ten-year intervals, and decisions are not made and then left behind as if they were merely beads on a chain.

It was reasonable to describe life as a set of discrete stages when most people followed the same rules, when major events occurred at predictable ages. People have long been able to tell the "right age" for marriage, the first child, the last child, career achievement, retirement, death. In the last two decades, however, chronological age has moved out of sync with these marking events. Our biological time clocks have changed: the onset of puberty for both sexes is earlier than it used to be just a generation ago; menopause comes later for women; most significantly, more people than ever now live into old age.

And our social time clocks have changed too. New trends in work, family size, health, and education have produced phenomena that are unprecedented in our history: for example, a long "empty nest" period when the children have left home and the parents are together again; a growing prevalence of great-grandparenthood; an enormous number of people who are starting new families, new jobs, and new avocations when they are forty, fifty, or sixty years old.

Most of the themes of adulthood appear and reappear in new forms over long periods of time. Issues of intimacy and freedom, for example, which are supposed to concern young adults just starting out in marriage and careers, are never settled once and for all. They haunt many couples continuously; compromises are found for a while, then renegotiated. Similarly, feeling the pressure of time, reformulating goals, coming to grips with success (and failure)—these are not the exclusive property of the forty-eight to fifty-two-year olds, by any means. (Neugarten, 1980b, pp. 289–90)

Chronological age sometimes is not a good prediction of behavior in adulthood.

Neugarten and Nancy Datan (1973) have illustrated how the social-historical context influences the timing of important life events. For example, whereas for a number of years the age at which individuals got married was occurring earlier, in the last several decades it has been occurring later, as more women choose to go to college and begin a career before marrying and having children. Early in this century, marriage corresponded to the man's being ready to be a breadwinner. Changing sociohistorical circumstances have complicated the timing of such life events. Changing sociohistorical circumstances can have important influences on the adult's personality development. Consider the likelihood that through a combination of education, work, and changing societal sex-role standards, many women now show more independence and assertiveness than was true in past decades. More women are searching for an identity outside of the traditional homemaker role. More about sex roles appears in chapter 12.

Although Neugarten includes the concept of life time in her view of personality development, her emphasis is on the manner in which social and historical time can modify life time. Some of Neugarten's comments (1980) suggest that many age-related themes of personality development are stereotypes.

Other life-events views, though, include age, or life stage, in the formula for understanding personality development, while still placing the most emphasis on sociohistorical contexts (e.g., Hultsch & Plemons, 1979). For example, stage theories of development such as Erikson's have contributed to the belief that mid-life is a crisis. However, the life-events framework views mid-life as more of a transition than a crisis. When mid-life becomes a crisis, in most cases it is because of some unanticipated change in the rhythm of the life cycle, some highly stressful life event, such as divorce or the death of one's spouse.

Thus many theorists and researchers who study adult personality development have not been satisfied with the stage-crisis approaches that have been proposed. To obtain a more integrated view of adult personality development, they believe that the study of life events adds valuable information (e.g., Datan & Ginsburg, 1975; Hultsch & Plemons, 1979; Neugarten, 1980; Riegel, 1975; Riley, 1979).

Klaus Riegel (1975) argues that our lives are characterized by many life events—getting married, having children, getting divorced, the death of a spouse, losing a job, and so forth. When Riegel asked adults to recall their past, he found that they were more likely to emphasize periods of transition related to life events rather than periods of stability. Table 10.1 shows a list of life events and the approximate points in adulthood at which they are likely to occur.

Applying a Life-Course Perspective to Life Events

It is important to make connections among age or life stage, the probability of certain events taking place, and the power of the event as a stressor (Brim & Ryff, 1980). Some events, such as an accident or disfigurement, are not necessarily age linked and have a low probability of occurring. Therefore, we seldom prepare for such events psychologically. However, other events, such as menopause,

Table 10.1

LEVELS AND EVENTS IN ADULT LIFE

Level (years)	Gradual changes				Sudden changes
	Males		Females		
	Psychosocial	Biophysical	Psychosocial	Biophysical	
I (20–25)	college/first job 　　marriage first child		first job/college 　　marriage	first child	
II (25–30)	second job other children children in preschool		loss of job children in preschool	other children	
III (30–35)	move 　　promotion children in school		move 　　without job children in school		
IV (35–50)	second home 　　promotion departure of children		second home 　　second career departure of children		
V (50–65)	unemployment isolation 　　grandfather 　　head of kin	incapacitation	unemployment 　　grandmother 　　head of kin	menopause	loss of job loss of parents loss of friends illness
VI (65+)	deprivation	sensorimotor deficiencies		widowhood incapacitation	retirement loss of partner death

Source: Riegel, 1975, p. 107. Reprinted by permission.

the empty nest, and retirement, have strong ties with age and consequently allow us to anticipate the development of coping strategies that may help alleviate some of the stress that they are likely to engender (Neugarten, 1980; Pearlin & Lieberman, 1977). Figure 10.4 shows how a life-course perspective can be applied to life events (Hultsch & Plemons, 1979). Variations with age in the probability of certain events, the timing and sequencing of the events, the motivational factors stimulated by the events, the coping resources available for dealing with the events, and adaptational outcomes are considered. Still, we have very little research data with which to evaluate such promising models of life events, which go beyond the simplistic notion that we can understand adult development by merely charting which life events are more stressful than others and whether individuals have been exposed to them (Lazarus & DeLongis, 1981).

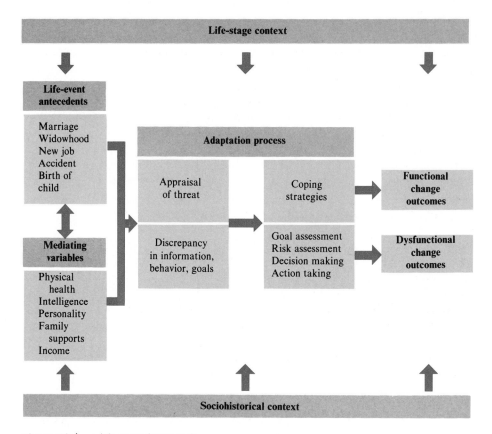

Figure 10.4   A life-event framework.

The life events framework described in figure 10.4 has four main components: antecedent life-event stressors, mediating factors, a social psychological adaptation process, and consequent adaptive or maladaptive outcomes. From this perspective, all life events are potentially stressful. Events typically thought of as positive, such as marriage and being promoted at work, as well as those usually perceived as negative, such as divorce and the death of a spouse, are all viewed as potentially stressful. Factors that may mediate the effects of life events on the individual can be categorized as internal (physical health, intelligence) or external (salary, social support network). *Social-psychological* adaptation refers to the individual's coping strategies, which may produce either a positive or negative outcome.

It is important to consider both the life stage and the sociohistorical context in which a life event occurs, as indicated in figure 10.4. Two time lines that are important in the course of our lives, then, are individual time and historical time.

The same event (such as the death of a spouse) occurring at age thirty may have a different impact on the individual than at age seventy-three. And the same event (such as a woman rather than a man being promoted at work) occurring in 1932 may not have the same influence in 1982.

Though the life events framework has provided valuable information about adult development, like other theories described in this chapter, it is not without problems (Dohrenwend & Dohrenwend, 1978; Lazarus & DeLongis, 1981; Rabkin & Struening, 1976). One of the most significant drawbacks of the life-events framework is that it may place too much emphasis on change, not adequately recognizing the important personal characteristics an individual brings to the situation in which a life event is experienced. A second shortcoming is the lack of importance attached to the personal significance of an event and the possible changes in coping resources and practices of individuals facing a particular life event.

In studying stress in adulthood, Richard Lazarus (Lazarus & DeLongis, 1981) has found that in people between forty-five and sixty-four, there is an inverse relationship between life events and age; that is, the frequency of major life changes decreases with age. However, it cannot be concluded that older people have less stress because life-events lists exclude many events that may be significant in the aging process. In most instances, the meaningfulness of the stress to the individual is not assessed. Further, such important factors as infirmity, limited energy, loneliness, and hostile or unresponsive environments are not included in the investigation of the stress associated with life events.

Lists of life events are typically limited to the range of events covered. However, many life events of considerable importance may be unnamed and not even perceived by the adult being questioned. Some of these might even be appropriately labeled "nonevents," such as the leveling out of a career, being passed over for a promotion, male menopause, and hostility shown by children (Brim & Ryff, 1980).

In addition to the stage and nonstage views of development that we have just examined, it could be argued that there are also two other major ways in which adult personality development can be conceptualized.

INDIVIDUAL DIFFERENCES IN STAGES, THEMES, AND LIFE EVENTS DURING ADULTHOOD

Broadly speaking, there are two theoretical approaches to the study of personality development—one focuses on similarities, the other on differences. The stage theories of Sheehy, Gould, Levinson, Freud, and Erikson all attempt to describe the universals—not the individual variation—in development. It may be helpful to recall the earlier comments of Bernice Neugarten: "We have found great trouble clustering people into age brackets that are characterized by particular conflicts; the conflicts won't stay put, and neither will the people."

Table 10.2

STRESS TYPE BY SEX

Stress Type	Men	Women	Total
Considerable presumed stress			
Challenged	23	14	19
Overwhelmed	28	34	31
Light presumed stress			
Lucky	32	26	29
Self-defeating	17	26	21
Total	100	100	100

Source: Adapted from Lowenthal, Thurnher, & Chiriboga, 1975. By permission of Jossey-Bass Publishers, Inc., San Francisco.

And in a recent extensive investigation of a random sample of 500 men at mid-life, Michael Farrell and Stanley Rosenberg (1981) concluded:

While some studies have found middle age to be the apex of satisfaction and effectiveness, others found it to be a period of identity crisis and discontent. . . . Both our research design and our findings suggest a more complex model [than the universal stage model], one anchored in the idea that the individual is an active agent in interpreting, shaping, and altering his own reality. He not only experiences internal and external changes, he gives meaning to them. The meaning given shows a wide range of variation. (p. 2)

Think about yourself and other people you know. There are certain things that you have in common with others, yet there are many ways in which you differ. Individual variation, then, is an important aspect of any viable model of adult development.

We have emphasized that not all people go through stages, themes, or life events in exactly the same way. That is, there is a great deal of individual variation in the way people handle the transition from early adulthood to middle adulthood and from middle adulthood to late adulthood. At one level there is evidence that men and women may experience stressful life events differently (Lowenthal, Thurnher, & Chiriboga, 1975). For example, table 10.2 shows that the type of stress experienced by men and women differs.

Irwin Sarason (1980), an expert on anxiety and stress, has called attention to the wide array of individual differences in the frequency and preoccupying characteristics of stress-related cognitions. Whereas the most adaptive response to stress is a task orientation that directs a person's attention to the task at hand rather than to emotional reactions, some individuals are task oriented and others are not. The adaptive value of being able to set aside temporarily strong emotions in order to deal with a problematic situation is reflected in George Vaillant's

Grant study (1974, 1977). In reporting college students' adjustments over a thirty-year-period after leaving school, Vaillant found that pervasive personal preoccupations are maladaptive in both work and marriage. Some individuals in the Grant study showed strong personal preoccupations, others did not.

Sarason (1980) emphasizes that the ability to set aside unproductive worries and preoccupations is crucial to functioning under stress. How stress is handled depends on both the individual and the situation, so an interactional approach is required that incorporates both individual differences and situational factors (Lazarus & Launier, 1978). Both of these are part of what is going on in an individual's life when stress appears. What is going on includes available social supports and what the person brings to the situation and such tendencies as the ability to anticipate stress, to feel secure, and to feel competent. At least five factors influence how an individual will respond to life stress, according to Sarason:

1. The nature of the task, or stress
2. The skills available to perform the task or handle the stress
3. Personality characteristics
4. Social supports available to the person experiencing stress
5. The person's history of stress-arousing experiences and events

In this chapter we have seen that a major focus of personality theory is the nature of personality change and stability. All of the theories we have described view personality change in adulthood as possible, but they vary in how they believe that change comes about and in how extensive they believe the change is. In the next chapter, we look further at change and stability in adult personality development as we examine some major longitudinal studies.

Summary

Though there are diverse definitions of personality and diverse theoretical views of how personality is defined and measured, most agree that personality refers to distinctive patterns of behavior, thought, and emotion that characterize each person's adaptation to the situations in his or her life. However, there is a diversity of opinion on how personality should be assessed.

Personality theories and views usually focus on stage and nonstage perspectives. Among the stage theorists, Freud believed that there is little or no personality change during the adult years, whereas Erikson, still approaching personality development from a psychoanalytic perspective, stresses personality change throughout the life cycle. Erikson has also placed more emphasis on the importance of culture in determining personality than Freud did. Four of Erikson's eight stages are particularly important in terms of personality development in adulthood—identity versus role confusion, intimacy versus isolation, generativity versus stagnation, and ego integrity versus despair. Erikson's theory has stimulated a great deal of interest in themes of personality at different points in adulthood, but the empirical data to support his theory have been hard to develop.

Several other views emphasize stages of adult personality development. Robert Peck has attempted to refine Erikson's stages of generativity and integrity, arguing that in middle adulthood we face the challenges of valuing wisdom versus physical powers, socializing versus sexualizing, widening versus narrowing our social network, and being mentally flexible versus mentally rigid. According to Peck, challenges in late adulthood include filling our time with meaningful activities, going beyond our aging body for enjoyment, and accepting and realizing that we have contributed to the future. Roger Gould believes that mid-life is every bit as turbulent as adolescence. He argues that in our twenties we assume new roles, in our thirties we begin to feel stuck with our responsibilities, and in our forties we begin to sense an urgency when we see our lives speeding by. When we realize that these steps are natural ones, we are on the path to adult maturity, according to Gould. Daniel Levinson's work has appeared in the well-known book, *The Seasons of a Man's Life.* According to Levinson, the middle-aged adult faces four conflicts: being young versus being old, masculine versus feminine, destructive versus constructive, and attached to others versus separated from them. The success of the mid-life transition depends on how effectively individuals are able to reduce these polarities. George Vaillant argues that two additional stages should be added to Erikson's eight stages: (1) career consolidation, occurring at approximately twenty-three to thirty-five years of age, and (2) a time of relaxation when goals have been attained or if not, that fact has been accepted, occurring between ages forty-five and fifty-five. Unfortunately, there are a number of methodological shortcomings in the data on which these theories are based.

Nonstage theorists believe that adult personality development occurs more gradually and is influenced more by the situations, settings, or contexts in which an individual lives. The social learning perspective emphasizes that personality often varies from one situation to the next, being influenced by the people in each situation and the extent to which they reward or punish the individual. A variation of social learning theory called cognitive social learning theory, while still emphasizing the importance of context in personality, believes that it is important to study a person's cognitive activity as well. Albert Bandura and Walter Mischel have been the major cognitive social learning theorists. They believe that human beings construct their environments just as their environments influence them. Mischel, in particular, has stressed the importance of understanding personality development in terms of the person $\times$ situation interaction, arguing that we cannot appropriately understand personality unless we study it in the many contexts in which it occurs. The image of adult personality development is one of a person being an active, aware problem solver who can benefit from an enormous range of experiences and cognitive activities. It is an image of adult personality that has moved a great distance away from models of adults being driven by instinctual forces and static traits and controlled helplessly by external rewards and punishments.

The life-events framework, like social learning theory, has given context an important role in the determination of personality. Life-events theorists believe that personality often changes because of the life events one experiences and that some life events carry more stress and require more coping and adaptation than others. In more sophisticated versions of the life-events framework, Neugarten and others have argued that we need to consider the sociohistorical circumstances in which life events occur. To this end, she believes personality development can best be understood through the interaction of life time, social time, and historical time. Nonetheless, Neugarten leaves the impression that social time and historical time are more important in the personality equation than life time, or at least they have not been given adequate attention. A number of nonstage theorists believe that too much emphasis has been placed on adult development's unfolding in a stagelike manner in which people are confronted by crises at various points in their adult life. In particular, they attack the mid-life crisis theorists, arguing that mid-life is usually a transition rather than a crisis, unless nonnormative life events occur. While the more sophisticated versions of the life-events view include age, it is the sociohistorical context and the experience of life events that form the crucible of personality development in this view.

In addition to dividing adult personality theories into stage and nonstage, we can consider adult personality in terms of individual differences, the extent to which adults are similar to others versus the degree to which they are different. Not all people go through stages, themes, or life events in the same way, so it is important to recognize that there is a great deal of individual variation in adult personality development.

Each of the theories described has contributed important information to our understanding of adult personality development, but adopting a single, grand theory to explain the complexity of personality is probably a mistake.

Review Questions

1. What are some of the different ways in which personality has been defined? What are the commonalities in these definitions?
2. Briefly describe Erik Erikson's eight stages of development. What are some drawbacks to his view?
3. Outline Peck, Gould, and Levinson's adult stages. What are some drawbacks to these perspectives?
4. Why is Gail Sheehy's view not accepted by scientists?
5. Discuss Bandura's ideas about reciprocal determinism.
6. What are Mischel's views on cognitive social learning theory? What is meant by viewing personality in terms of person $\times$ situation interaction?
7. Outline the different versions of the life-events view of personality. What are some of the strengths and weaknesses of the life-events view?
8. Describe the importance of individual differences in personality development during the adult years.
9. Which of the personality theories do you feel offers the best description and explanation of personality development during the adult years? Why?

Further Readings

Erikson, E. H. (1968). *Identity: Youth and Crisis.* New York: Norton.
This book represents Erikson's most detailed work on adolescents and includes a full description of his eight stages of the life cycle. Easy reading.

Hultsch, D. F., & Plemons, J. K. (1979). Life events and life-span development. In P. B. Baltes and O. G. Brim, Jr. (Eds.), *Life-span development* (Vol. 2). New York: Academic Press.
A detailed life-events model of personality development emphasizing the sociohistorical context of life events and the individual's adaptation to these events. Moderately difficult reading level.

Levinson, D. (1978). *The seasons of a man's life.* New York: Ballantine.
Levinson's national best-seller that describes his theory of adult personality development. Also includes substantial case study material. Easy reading.

Mischel, W. (1981). *Introduction to personality* (3rd ed.). New York: Holt, Rinehart & Winston.
The leading introductory college text on personality. Provides detailed overview of theories, methods, and research on the nature of adult personality. Moderately easy reading level.

Neugarten, B. L., & Datan, N. Sociological perspectives on the life cycle. In P. B. Baltes & K. W. Schaie (Eds.), *Life-span developmental psychology.* New York: Academic Press, pp. 53–71.
A view of personality in terms of multiple time perspectives and the changing rhythm of the life cycle. Reasonably easy to read.

11

STABILITY AND CHANGE AND THE DEVELOPMENT OF PERSONALITY THROUGH THE ADULT YEARS

IMAGINE *that you are seventy years old and thought of as more*
helpless than helpful.

How do you think you would feel? Probably not very good. It is not unusual to think of the elderly as helpless beings, incapable of contributing to their world. Indeed, some researchers have found that many elderly people often do feel helpless (e.g., Cohn, 1981). The elderly often feel that they do not have control over their environment, a finding assessed most often through the use of a locus of control measure (e.g., Lawton, Nahemow, Yaffe, & Feldman, 1976). However, recent research on locus of control suggests that individuals in late adulthood do not necessarily show more external than internal control (e.g., Midlarsky & Kahana, 1981).

The fact that the elderly have generally been viewed as more helpless than helpful can be found in the literature on altruism. In the few investigations of altruism that have included older people, they have been studied as recipients rather than givers. However, elderly individuals are often competent people who provide help to others. Indeed, in one investigation of the service needs of urban people (Kahana & Felton, 1977), it was found that elderly people living in the community provided more services than they received.

Elizabeth Midlarsky and Eva Kahana (1981) recently summarized the ways in which altruism and helping can contribute to life satisfaction among the elderly. They indicate that being useful to the community is considerably more meaningful to those above the age of sixty-five than to younger age groups. The elderly have also been found to be useful service providers for one another through neighborhood support services, civic activities, group activities, and dyadic helping situations (Ehrlich, 1979). Types of help given included providing telephone reassurance, performing chores, giving emergency assistance, and providing empathetic interactions. In another investigation of altruism among the elderly, helping behavior was positively related to self-esteem (Trimakas & Nicolay, 1974).

Whereas being a resource to others is likely to enhance self-esteem, being a recipient of help can lead to a decrease in other people's positive regard for the recipient. The reluctance of older people to seek and accept assistance has been well documented (e.g., Butler & Lewis, 1977). It is clearly possible that such reluctance is motivated by the need to preserve one's self-esteem. It has been suggested that the current attempts to raise the public's consciousness about the elderly should not lead to thoughtless "helping" (Rodin & Langer, 1980). Instead, we may benefit many

Claude Pepper has been a leader in getting the government to recognize the needs of the elderly in the United States.

elderly individuals by providing them with increased opportunities to be of help to others. Such opportunities are likely to increase elderly people's feelings of self-worth, contribute to the belief that their lives still have meaning, and enhance the likelihood that they will feel like they are contributing members of their family and community.

The fact that the elderly are not helpless is evident in the increased political voice they have in our country. Led by Representative Claude Pepper, Chairman of the House of Representatives Committee on Aging, many older people are arguing vociferously for a greater say in determining the factors that have pronounced consequences for their lives—factors such as the abolishment of mandatory retirement, improved health benefits, and better living conditions. As more of our population becomes made up of older people, we can expect the elderly to have an even greater voice in determining the standards of our culture.

An increasing number of individuals in late adulthood have joined forces to organize groups on their behalf. The California Legislative Council for Older Americans and national groups such as the National Retired Teachers Association/American Association of Retired Persons, the National Council of Senior Citizens, and the National Association of Retired Federal Employees now seem to include more assertive members than they did in the past. One example of the effectiveness such organized groups have had as lobbyists is the extension of the mandatory retirement age to seventy.

Many individuals who are now in late adulthood are products of the Victorian era—they believe strongly in working from dawn to dusk and in paying their own way, and they feel embarrassed if they don't. They not only have been silent but have been reluctant to receive charity or welfare of any type. However, they are beginning to make demands on government agencies as it becomes clear that many who worked from dawn to dusk are not protected from the spirals of inflation. One elderly suburbanite said that old people may be an outgrowth of the Victorian Era, brought up to speak only when spoken to, but now they're getting mad. And they're going to yell real loud when somebody steps on their toes (Williamson, Munley, & Evans, 1980).

INTRODUCTION

In this chapter we discuss the issue of stability and change in personality, in the process describing the major longitudinal studies of personality development in adulthood. In our description of personality development through the adult years, we begin with Erik Erikson's belief that identity is a central issue in personality during adolescence and early adulthood. We also suggest that identity is an important aspect of personality *throughout* the adult years. We comment on the delicate balance between intimacy/commitment and independence/freedom and focus on how these aspects of personality develop in the contexts of work and relationships. Our focus on developmental changes in middle adulthood involves revisiting the issue of mid-life crisis and the changing time perspective of individuals. In our discussion of personality development in late adulthood, we further investigate several major perspectives described in chapter 10 and present detailed information about the importance of the life review and reminiscence in late adulthood, as well as the significance of life satisfaction as an integrative concept in personality.

STABILITY AND CHANGE

The degree to which personality is stable or changes is a major issue in adult development. The issue may be approached in many different ways. We may wish to evaluate the extent to which childhood personality characteristics predict adulthood personality characteristics. For example, is the introverted child also the introverted adult? Is the neurotic adolescent also the neurotic adult at mid-life? We can ask whether the achievement-oriented woman in early adulthood is still striving hard to be successful at the age of fifty. Or to what extent is the thirty-year-old who is depressed still that way at the age of seventy? Further, rather than looking only at the stability of a single personality characteristic, such as introversion, we may evaluate how one or several characteristics at one point in life predict another or several other characteristics at a later point in life. Or we may be interested in how social experiences, such as peer relationships, family experiences, and work experiences, can predict personality characteristics later in life. And we may be concerned about whether such prediction is possible over a short period of time, say one to five years, or over a longer period of time, even as long as forty or fifty years.

To the extent that there is consistency or continuity from one period of time to another in some attribute of personality, we usually describe personality as being *stable*. In contrast, to the extent that there is little consistency from one period of time to another, we refer to *change* or discontinuity in personality.

Personality theorists are often categorized on the basis of whether they stress stability and consistency in personality across time as well as across situations. Personality theorists called *personologists* or *traditional trait theorists* argue for consistency and stability, whereas *contextual, situational theorists* believe that there is little consistency and stability in personality but rather a great deal of change. The latter heavily stress the importance of studying the context in which behavior occurs because they believe that behavior often changes according to the context or situation in which the person is.

We will discover the importance of studying the contextual aspects of personality in combination with the characteristics a person brings to a situation as we survey some of the major efforts to evaluate the extent to which personality remains stable from childhood through the adulthood years and the extent to which personality changes in the adult years.

Predicting Adult Personality from Childhood and Adolescent Personality Characteristics and Experiences

It is a common finding in the study of continuity and discontinuity in personality development that the closer in time we measure personality characteristics, the more similar a person will look. Thus, if we measure a person's self-concept at the age of thirty and then again at the age of forty, we are likely to find more stability than we would if we measured the person's self-concept at ten and then again at forty. As was suggested in chapter 10, we no longer believe in the infant determinism suggested by Freud's psychosexual theory, which argued that our personality as adults is virtually cast in stone by the time we are five years of age. Clearly, if we attempt to measure a specific personality characteristic such as dependency, it is hard to find evidence of stability from early childhood to mid-life. For one thing, it is very difficult to come up with comparable measures of dependency, which during the early childhood years is directed at parents but which during mid-life may be transferred to a spouse or lover or a mix of marital partner, parents, and friends. We might measure dependency in the early childhood years by observing the young child's attempts to seek the proximity of its mother, but how would we do this in adulthood? We might try to get a measure of how far away he moved from his parents and how much he clings to his wife and friends for security and support. The task of evaluating continuity over long periods of time is a difficult one. If we are to come up with even reasonable ideas about this issue, we need to follow individuals longitudinally rather than assessing their lives in a cross-sectional manner.

The California Longitudinal Study: Early Adolescence Through Mid-Life

Perhaps the most important data that bear on the issue of stability and change from childhood and adolescence through middle adulthood have been collected as part of the California Longitudinal Study. The data actually represent three longitudinal studies, two of which were begun in 1928–1929 (Macfarlane's Guidance Study and Bayley's Berkeley Growth Study), the other in 1931 (Stolz and the Jones's Oakland Growth Study). Although the three projects initially had different intents, they were subsequently merged into a single sample with two cohorts that differ by approximately eight years.

Many, but by no means all, of the methods and procedures used with the groups were the same. Initially, the total of the three samples reached 521 subjects, but because of death, withdrawal, or the lack of comparable measures among the groups, the data analyses are often conducted on fewer adults. Most of the analyses are on subgroups of fewer than a hundred subjects for each sex. The data reported in *Present and Past in Middle Life* (Eichorn, Clausen, Haan, Honzik, & Mussen, 1981), the most recent profile of information, traces the lives of these individuals from early adolescence to mid-life. Q-sorts were used in this latest investigation. The **Q-sort technique** is a method of obtaining trait ratings, consisting of many cards, on each of which is printed a trait description. The rater groups the cards in a series of piles ranging from those that are least characteristic to those that are most characteristic of the rated person.

In commenting on issues of consistency, stability, discontinuity, and change, Dorothy Eichorn and her colleagues concluded that their results from early adolescence to mid-life on a host of personality characteristics and life-styles do not support either extreme in the debate over whether adult personality development is characterized by stability or change. In all domains of personality assessed in the California Longitudinal Study, some evidence for individual consistency was found, but as we would expect, some characteristics were more stable across time than others and some individuals changed markedly even on characteristics for which the group as a whole was consistent.

Dimensions more directly concerned with the self (cognitively invested, self-confident, and open or closed self) showed greater consistency from early adolescence to mid-life than did dimensions more reflective of the quality of interpersonal interactions (nurturant or hostile and undercontrolled or overcontrolled).

The authors of *Present and Past in Middle Life* (Eichorn, Clausen, Haan, Honzik, & Mussen, 1981) concluded that the pervasive influence of personality was evident in every domain of life examined. Two of the most influential personality dimensions were cognitive investment and emotional control, as reflected both on the Q-sort and the California Psychological Inventory measures. Emotional control, for instance, appears to influence the overall course of lives, for it predicts adult health status, early death, problem drinking, and even IQ. People with poor impulse control may take more risks in their lives and may find it more difficult to break maladaptive habits.

The Fels Longitudinal Study: Infancy Through Early Adulthood
In another well-known study, the Fels Longitudinal Study, it was found that sex-typed characteristics tended to show some stability from the elementary school years through the first part of early adulthood (Kagan & Moss, 1962).

Investigating ratings of behavior in age periods birth to three, three to six, six to ten, ten to fourteen, and adulthood, Jerome Kagan and Howard Moss (1962) found that the stability of the behaviors is linked to cultural sex-role standards.

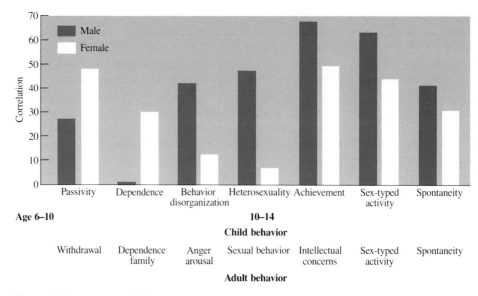

Figure 11.1   Summary of relations between selected child behaviors and phenotypically similar adult behaviors.

Mastery of intellectual tasks and sex-typed interests, which are reinforced for both boys and girls in our culture, were very consistent for both boys and girls from the ages of six to ten through early adulthood (age range nineteen to twenty-nine, mean twenty-four years)—see figure 11.1. However, because in our culture males are more frequently rewarded for being aggressive and girls for being dependent, the Kagan and Moss study revealed consistency across these time periods for boys' aggressive behavior and for girls' dependency behavior.

The Kagan and Moss study, which was completed in the late 1950s, may not reflect our society's changing sex-role standards, when adolescence and adulthood may lead to more upheaval in commitment to sex-typed behaviors. Recall from chapter 10 our discussion of the critical role early adulthood may play in the female's work orientation. Because distinctions in cultural standards for males and females are becoming more blurred, it is now easier for a female at eighteen to thirty years of age to choose a career once labeled "masculine" and not to show as much dependent behavior as was necessary at an earlier point in our history. Some would argue, however, that sex roles are more clearly defined for men than they are for women in our society. More will be said about changing sex roles in the next chapter.

The New York Longitudinal Study: Infancy to Early Adulthood

An extensive longitudinal study conducted with a group of boys and girls in New York City provided some answers to the question of how various dimensions of personality change or remain stable (Thomas, Chess, & Birch, 1970). The study was begun in 1956, so the children are now adults. However because of the inevitable lag between research and the public reports on it, information is available only from the subjects' birth to the beginning of their adult years.

Alexander Thomas and his associates set out to describe temperament as broadly as possible and to obtain as much information as they could. To this end, they interviewed the parents of 138 subjects from middle-class homes four times a year during the first year of life, twice a year for the next four years, and once a year after that. Interviews ranged over a wide variety of topics (eating, sleeping, playing, meeting new people, interacting with parents and siblings, and the like), with the goal of understanding the style of each individual's behavior across many situations.

The identification of temperament becomes more difficult as a child enters the adolescent period. Behavioral characteristics become increasingly influenced by the interaction of temperament, motivation, capability, and special events in life.

The only predictable aspect of the period from infancy through adolescence is that the individual will experience person-environment interaction. Consistency in development comes from continuity over time in both the person and important aspects of his or her environment. Changes in development are produced by major changes in the person or in his or her environment.

In sum, the first twenty years of life are not meaningless in predicting an adult's personality, but neither are the first five years of life as important as Freud believed them to be in revealing what a person will be like as an adult. There is every reason to believe that later experiences in the adolescent years may be as important in determining what a person will be like in young adulthood as experiences earlier in life. But just as early adult personality characteristics build on adolescent characteristics, so too do adolescent characteristics build on childhood characteristics. Thus, in trying to understand personality in adulthood, it would be misleading to look only at the adult's life in the present tense, ignoring the developmental unfolding of personality. So too would we be far off target if we only searched through a thirty-three-year-old's first five to ten years of life in trying to predict why he or she is now having difficulty coping with a problem. The truth about personality, then, lies somewhere between the infant determinism of Freud and a contextual approach that ignores the antecedents of the adult years completely.

Bernice Neugarten, a pioneer in research on adulthood and aging.

Stability and Change in the Adult Years

Let's look at some of the major studies of personality development that shed light on the stability-change issue, particularly as it pertains to personality in the adult years.

Neugarten's Kansas City Study

One of the earliest longitudinal studies of personality in adulthood was conducted by Bernice Neugarten on a large sample of people aged forty to eighty over a ten-year period in Kansas City (Neugarten, 1964). Projective tests, questionnaires, and several forms of interviews were used. Neugarten concluded that personality is continuous in a number of respects but that some age-related changes occur as well. The most stable characteristics were adaptive characteristics, such as styles of coping, attaining life satisfaction, and strength of goal-directed behavior. Some consistent age differences occurred in intrapsychic dimensions of personality—inner versus outer orientation and active versus passive mastery. For example, forty-year-olds felt that they had control over their environment and risk taking didn't bother them very much. However sixty-year-olds were more likely to perceive the environment as threatening and sometimes dangerous, and they had a more passive view of the self. This personality change in adulthood was described by Neugarten as going from **active to passive mastery.**

Movement from active mastery in mid-life to a more passive orientation in late adulthood has been discovered in a number of people other than the Kansas City adults. Groups of people as diverse as the Navajo Indians, isolated groups in Israel, and the Mayans of Mexico also seem to move from an active, controlling belief about their interaction with the world to a more passive, receptive, less controlling orientation as they age (Guttmann, 1977).

According to Neugarten, there also seems to be an increased concern about inner life among older adults as compared to middle-aged adults. Older people in the study were more introspective and self-reflecting than younger adults. Neugarten refers to this change in the personality of older people as *interiority* (Rosen & Neugarten, 1964).

In addition to passive mastery and interiority, a shift in sex-role preoccupation seemed to occur in late adulthood in the Kansas City adults. It was found that some role reversal begins to take place as people grow older—men become more tolerant of their nurturant impulses, and females become more tolerant of their aggressive tendencies.

Costa and McCrae's Boston Study

Another major longitudinal study was conducted by Paul Costa and R. R. McCrae at the Veterans Administration Outpatient Clinic in Boston; it involved approximately 2,000 men in their twenties through eighties. Measures included assessments of personality, attitudes, and values (Costa & McCrae, 1976, 1977, 1978, 1980). Costa and McCrae believe that personality can be understood in terms of three major dimensions: neuroticism, extraversion, and openness to experience. Each of these three dimensions in turn reflects a number of related traits. For example, neuroticism is said to include anxiety, low stability, depression, self-consciousness, impulsivity, and vulnerability; extraversion includes attachment, gregariousness, assertiveness, activity, excitement seeking, and positive emotions; and openness to experience reflects openness to fantasy, esthetics, feelings, actions, ideas, and values.

In their longitudinal analysis, Costa and McCrae report that continuity in these three main dimensions of personality is the rule rather than the exception in the adult years. Ten-year retest correlations for neuroticism were in the .60 range, for extraversion approximately .75, and for openness to experience about .50. Costa and McCrae, then, are proponents of the belief that there is considerable stability in personality during the adult years.

The California Longitudinal Study: Early Adulthood Through Late Adulthood

By far the longest longitudinal study and the one with perhaps the most diverse data base is the California Longitudinal Study. We have already commented on certain aspects of this gigantic data-gathering effort that has now spanned almost fifty years. The data have far-reaching implications for our understanding of development.

In recent years a number of reports have emanated from the California Longitudinal Study. In one of the earlier reports (Block, 1971), stability seemed to characterize the personalities of individuals in their twenties. However, as new data on these same individuals continued to be analyzed, more evidence of change in their personalities seemed apparent (Haan, 1976). Our description of these individuals as they aged through early and middle adulthood was presented earlier, and we found that there were some complex continuities as well as some discontinuity between early adolescence and mid-life.

Not only did the researchers in the California Longitudinal Study initially investigate more than 500 children, but they had the foresight to evaluate the parents of these children as well. Most of the parents were in their late twenties or early thirties when they first were assessed in the late 1920s and early 1930s. Two relatively recent reports have assessed these adults in late adulthood.

In the first report, Maas and Kuypers (1974) found that some personality types and some life-style clusters were more stable over the adult years than others. For instance, the life-style indicators for women changed more than those for men, with the greatest changes occurring for work-oriented mothers. Lifestyle indicators included satisfaction and involvement in the areas of home, work, leisure, marriage, parenting, grandparenting, family of origin, and friendships. Personality typologies ranged across many dimensions, such as dependability, cheerfulness, behavioral tempo, and intellectual capacity.

As an example of the changes that took place, consider the fathers Maas and Kuypers studied. The greatest change happened for those called the conservative-ordering fathers. In early adulthood they were withdrawn, shy, distant, and conflicted. In their thirties they indicated considerable marital conflict. But at age seventy marital problems had diminished and they had become conventional, controlling, and even more distant.

In early adulthood the active-competent fathers had been demonstrative and extraverted and showed a strong sense of personal adequacy. However, they were often described as tense and nervous. As older men, these active-competent fathers were conforming, direct, charming, and capable, although they often criticized others and were sometimes distant in their relationships. They had been successful in their careers and indicated a strong friendship network, even though they still spent a lot of time in solitary leisure. Maas and Kuypers suggested that the personal and economic rewards of a successful career permitted the active-competent fathers to develop the somewhat desirable personalities that were reflected in later adulthood.

The mothers in the California Longitudinal Study were described as work centered, group centered, or uncentered. At the age of thirty the work-centered mothers said they were dissatisfied with their marriage and seemed to be experiencing economic problems. As they grew older, though, they seemed to become happier. In the middle years they still centered their life around their employment, showing some independence from their marital life. Their economic situation seemed to have improved, and they had developed a network of friends. The group-centered mothers also showed some positive changes in lifestyle. However, uncentered mothers (those not focused on either a spouse or a particular activity other than being a mother), while seeming to be happy at age thirty, had the lowest SES standing at age seventy and were in poorer health than their counterparts.

In the second study of the California parents, Paul Mussen, Marjorie Honzik, and Dorothy Eichorn (1982) investigated the association between life satisfaction ratings at approximately the age of seventy and cognitive, personality, interpersonal, and family characteristics in early adulthood, using data from the Guidance Study of the California Longitudinal Study. When the parents of the participants in the study were in their early thirties, the mothers were rated on fifteen cognitive and personality characteristics and both parents were rated on personal, interpersonal, and family variables. About forty years later, the surviving parents were interviewed intensively and given life-satisfaction ratings.

A number of personal characteristics and qualities of the home and of the marital relationship in early adulthood predicted men's and women's life satisfactions some forty years later. It was found that mothers who had been seen as cheerful, mentally alert, satisfied with their lot, self-assured, and neither worrisome nor fatigued at age thirty were more likley to be satisfied with their lives at age seventy. For the early family ratings, the mothers' own health and self-confidence and their husband's concern about health were predictors of life satisfaction at age seventy. The women's satisfaction in later life was more strongly influenced, however, by qualities of the early marital relationship and other life circumstances, such as adequacy of income and leisure time, than by their own or their husband's personality traits. In contrast, for men, the best predictors of life satisfaction at age seventy were their own and their wives' traits that reflected a relaxed, emotionally stable personality supported, at least for the men themselves, by good physical condition.

The differences between roles, interests, and activities of American men and women in the generations in which they were studied may account for some of these sex differences in antecedents of life satisfaction at age seventy. For the women, living in accordance with traditional standards of feminine behavior when they were in their early thirties, the roles of wife, mother, and homemaker were dominant, whereas roles outside the home were of diminished importance. Thus the qualities of early marital and family relationships were the foundations of these women's later life satisfaction. Yet the women's life satisfaction was more difficult to predict than the men's, which may be associated with greater historical discontinuity in the roles and functions of women in our society. The same discontinuity for women was found in the larger sample studied by Maas and Kuypers (1974).

Emotional well-being during the early years of marriage was a reasonably good predictor of life satisfaction at age seventy for both sexes. For men the emotional well-being was reflected in freedom from worry and tension, and for women it was a buoyant, positive, responsive attitude toward life. Bernice Neugarten (1977) has also suggested that adults who were emotionally stable in middle adulthood seem to function adequately in late adulthood as well.

Next we outline some of the reasons why stability may occur in personality development and some of the reasons why change may result. These reasons were initially presented in chapter 1, where we first discussed the important issue of stability and change. They bear repeating here because they accurately summarize the belief that we need to view adult development as neither extraordinarily stable nor totally changeable. Further, this summary suggests why we find more stability in some people's lives and more change in others'.

The Reasons Behind Stability and Change in Personality Development

What are some of the factors that may lead to change in adult development? Five such factors follow (Bee & Mitchell, 1980):

1. *Changes in broad expectations at different historical eras.* For instance, men may be more nurturant and women more assertive because of changes in sex roles linked with the women's movement. Further, historical changes in an individual's lifetime may produce discontinuous changes in personality, cognition, or even health (for example, exercise).

2. *Changes in specific life experiences of the individual.* Social learning and contextual theorists argue that changes in behavior will occur whenever an adult's environment changes significantly.

3. *Regular changes in life tasks at different ages, consisting of different demands.* Erikson's stages belong in this category and so do Levinson's ideas about transition points in adult development.

4. *Biological changes, such as hormone changes, that affect both behavior and attitudes.* The hormone alterations that are related to menopause exemplify this kind of change.

5. *Hierarchical development.* An example of this type of change is Roger Gould's belief that it is important for adults to shed their childhood consciousness. For adults who cast off such consciousness through successive transformations, change rather than consistency is to be expected. From this perspective an introverted fifteen-year-old may become an extraverted thirty-eight-year-old by coming to understand herself.

In contrast, there are reasons why stability, or consistency, in adult development or between childhood and adulthood could occur:

1. *Biological processes.* An adult may inherit certain tendencies and characteristics. There is some indication, for example, that some forms of mental

illness, such as schizophrenia, are strongly influenced by inheritance. And intelligence, as well as certain aspects of personality, such as introversion/extraversion, have genetic ties.

2. *The continuing influence of early experiences.* If early experience is more important in development than later experience, then the tendencies and characteristics we develop in childhood and adolescence may persist through adulthood. Both Freud and Piaget have taken this position.

3. *Early experience plus consistent adult experience.* Many of us choose life courses that are compatible with the way we think about ourselves. Consequently, we may continue to show consistency over our life course not necessarily because early experience predominates but because the early patterns continue to be rewarded in the circumstances we choose as adults. Social learning theory accepts this scenario as a major reason why some individuals show stability and consistency in their lives.

Next we look at some of the major aspects of personality that may appear at a particular point in adult development and evaluate the extent to which such characteristics may represent themes of personality throughout the adult years.

PERSONALITY DEVELOPMENT THROUGH THE ADULT YEARS

What is your personality likely to be like as you proceed through the adult years? What is the main theme of your personality now? Is it establishing an identity, intimacy, freedom and independence, a time perspective, sensing a need to contribute to the next generation, or reviewing your life and trying to make sense out of it? These are some of the themes of adult personality development that we will evaluate.

Early Adulthood

We have seen that early adulthood is a time of vocational orientation and expanding relationships with others. Themes of personality development that seem particularly important in early adulthood are identity, intimacy/commitment, and independence/freedom. Work and relationships are important contexts for the development of these themes.

Identity

One of the governing themes of self-evaluation during adolescence and young adulthood is identity—Who am I? Where am I going? What kind of career will I pursue? How well do I relate to females, to males? Am I able to make it on my own? These are questions that clamor for solutions in the young adulthood years. However, identity is an issue throughout the adult years as well.

Relationships are important contexts for the development of identity.

The term *identity* is virtually inseparable from the self. Identity is an integrative concept that is used to capture the diverse, complex components of the adolescent and young adult's personality development. The description of identity development can be traced directly to the thinking and writing of Erik Erikson (1963, 1968). As you may recall, identity development represents the fifth stage in Erikson's model and occurs at about the same time as adolescence and early adulthood. If postadolescents and individuals near the end of early adulthood have not developed a positive sense of identity, they are described as having identity diffusion or confusion. More about Erikson's view of identity and how he attempts to weave together the pieces of the lives of famous individuals in order to understand how their struggle with identity influenced their personality development in adulthood is described in box 11.1.

It is important to recognize that identity may be an important integrative concept throughout the adult years, not just in adolescence and early adulthood. Erikson argues that the extent to which we develop intimacy, generativity, and integrity depends on whether we have achieved a strong sense of identity. Themes of intimacy, generativity, and integrity are crises that Erikson believes are experienced and resolved as we go through early, middle, and late adulthood, respectively. Knowing who you are and what you are going to do with your life is a concern for most people at any age.

Intimacy/Commitment and Independence/Freedom

The early adult years are a time when people often develop an intimate relationship with another person. An important aspect of this relationship is the commitment of the individuals to each other. At the same time many people show a strong interest in independence and freedom. Personality development in early adulthood, as well as in middle and late adulthood, often involves an intricate relationship of intimacy/commitment and independence/freedom.

Recall that intimacy is the aspect of development that follows identity in Erikson's eight stages of development.

A related aspect of developing an identity in adolescence and early adulthood is independence. At the same time that individuals are trying to establish an identity, they face the difficulty of having to cope with increasing their independence from their parents, developing an intimate relationship with another individual, and increasing their friendship commitments, while also being able to think for themselves and do things without always relying on what others say or do.

The extent to which the young adult has begun to develop autonomy clearly has important implications for adaptation in the early adult years. The young adult who has not sufficiently moved away from parental ties may have difficulty in both interpersonal and vocational matters. Consider the mother who overprotects her daughter, continues to support her, and doesn't want to "let go" of her. In early adulthood, the daughter may have difficulty developing a mature intimate relationship, and she may have problems in the world of work as well. When a promotion comes up that involves more responsibility and possibly more stress, she may turn it down. When things don't go well in her relationship with a young man, she may go crying to her mother.

Commitment and freedom are important themes of personality in the middle and late adult years as well. Many middle-aged people take a serious look at vocational roles in life and at the extent to which they want to retain a strong commitment to another individual. For married individuals, mid-life is a time when adolescents leave home. Spouses who have had to spend long hours taking care of children now have much more time on their hands. At this point, there may be a reexamination of commitment to one's spouse and of what one is going to do with one's life. Again, we see the way in which changing circumstances can alter an individual's personality. In the late adulthood years, many people do not want to have to be taken care of, but at the same time they want to establish ties to others.

There is a delicate balance between intimacy/commitment and independence/freedom in an individual's personality and in relationships with others. These are not necessarily opposite ends of a continuum—some individuals are able to experience a healthy independence and freedom in their personality along with an intimate relationship with another individual. Intimacy/commitment and

Box 11.1
ERIK ERIKSON'S ANALYSIS OF THE IDENTITY DEVELOPMENT OF ADOLF HITLER, MARTIN LUTHER, AND MAHATMA GANDHI

Erik Erikson is a master at using the psychoanalytic method to uncover historical clues about identity formation. Erikson has used the psychoanalytic method both with the youth he treats in psychotherapy sessions and in the analysis of the lives of famous individuals. Erikson (1963) believes that the psychoanalytic technique sheds light on human psychological evolution. He also believes that the history of the world is a composite of individual life cycles.

In the following excerpts from Erikson's writings, the psychoanalytic method is used to analyze the youths of Adolf Hitler, Martin Luther, and Mahatma Gandhi.

In one passage, Erikson (1962) describes the youth of Adolf Hitler:

> I will not go into the symbolism of Hitler's urge to build except to say that his shiftless and brutal father had consistently denied the mother a steady residence; one must read how Adolf took care of his mother when she wasted away from breast cancer to get an inkling of this young man's desperate urge to cure. But it would take a very extensive analysis, indeed, to indicate in what way a single boy can daydream his way into history and emerge a sinister genius, and how a whole nation becomes ready to accept the emotive power of that genius as a hope of fulfillment for its national aspirations and as a warrant for national criminality. . . .
>
> The memoirs of young Hitler's friend indicate an almost pitiful fear on the part of the future dictator that he might be nothing. He had to challenge this possibility by being deliberately and totally anonymous; and only out of this self-chosen nothingness could he become everything. (Erikson, 1962, pp. 108–109)

But while the identity crisis of Adolf Hitler led him to turn toward politics in a pathological effort to create a world order, the identity crisis of Martin Luther in a different era led him to turn toward theology in an attempt to deal systematically with human nothingness or lack of identity:

independence/freedom are global concepts, and in research on adult development it is important that they be well defined and measured. The interrelation of intimacy/commitment and independence/freedom may vary according to the sociohistorical context in which it is studied. As we have seen, changing sex-role standards have undoubtedly increased the extent to which many women in our society reveal strong desires for independence. Finally, we must emphasize that intimacy/commitment and independence/freedom are not just concerns of early

> In confession, for example, he was so meticulous in the attempt to be truthful that he spelled out every intention as well as every deed; he splintered relatively acceptable purities into smaller and smaller impurities; he reported temptations in historical sequence, starting back in childhood; and after having confessed for hours, would ask for special appointments in order to correct previous statements. In doing this he was obviously both exceedingly compulsive and, at least unconsciously, rebellious. . . .
>
> At this point we must note a characteristic of great young rebels: their inner split between the temptation to surrender and the need to dominate. A great young rebel is torn between, on the one hand, tendencies to give in and fantasies of defeat (Luther used to resign himself to an early death at times of impending success), and the absolute need, on the other hand, to take the lead, not only over himself but over all the forces and people who impinge on him. (Erikson, 1968, pp. 155–157)

And in his Pulitzer Prize winning novel on Mahatma Gandhi's life, Erikson (1969) describes the personality formation of Gandhi during his youth:

> Straight and yet not stiff; shy and yet not withdrawn; intelligent and yet not bookish; willful and yet not stubborn; sensual and yet not soft. . . . We must try to reflect on the relation of such a youth to his father, because the Mahatma places service to the father and the crushing guilt of failing in such service in the center of his adolescent turbulence. Some historians and political scientists seem to find it easy to interpret this account in psychoanalytic terms; I do not. For the question is not how a particular version of the Oedipal Complex "causes" a man to be both great and neurotic in a particular way, but rather how such a young person . . . manages the complexes which constrict other men. (Erikson, 1969, p. 113)

In these passages, the workings of an insightful, sensitive mind is shown looking for a historical perspective on matters. Through analysis of the lives of famous individuals such as Hitler, Luther, and Gandhi, and through the thousands of youth he has talked with in person, Erikson has pieced together a descriptive picture of identity development.

adulthood but are important themes of personality that are worked and reworked throughout adulthood.

Next we examine personality development through the middle adult years.

Middle Adulthood

In this section we further explore the question of whether mid-life is actually a period of crisis and discuss the idea that mid-life is a period of transition in which the middle-aged adult shifts his or her sense of timing and time perspective.

The Question of Crisis

Daniel Levinson emphasizes changes in personality that involve the individual's concept of self and stresses the importance of understanding the interrelated processes of separation and individuation that characterize developmental transitions in adulthood. He believes these transitions require the adult to review and evaluate the past to determine which aspects to retain and which to reject as he or she moves into the future. Levinson sees the middle-aged adult as suspended between the past and the future, trying to cope with this gap that may threaten the continuity of the adult's life.

George Vaillant (1977) has reached a conclusion very similar to Levinson's about mid-life. Vaillant's data involve a follow-up of ninety-four out of an original sample of 268 Harvard University men who originally were interviewed while they were undergraduates. The ninety-four were again interviewed in their early thirties and late forties. Vaillant says that just as adolescence is a time for detecting parental flaws and finding out the truth about childhood, the forties is a decade of reassessing and recording the truth about the adolescent and early adulthood years.

However, whereas Levinson believes that mid-life is very likely to involve a crisis—he suggested that about 80 percent of the adult males in his study experienced either a moderate or severe crisis—Vaillant believes that only a minority of adults experience mid-life as a crisis:

> Just as pop psychologists have reveled in the not-so-common high drama of adolescent turmoil, just so the popular press, sensing good copy, had made all too much of the mid-life crisis. The term *mid-life crisis* brings to mind some variation of the renegade minister who leaves behind four children and the congregation that loved him in order to drive off in a magenta Porsche with a twenty-five-year-old striptease artiste. Like all tabloid fables, there is much to be learned from such stories, but such aberrations are rare, albeit memorable, caricatures of more mundane issues of development. As with adolescent turmoil, mid-life crises are much rarer in community samples than in clinical samples. The high drama in Gail Sheehy's best-selling *Passages* was rarely observed in the lives of the Grant Study men. (pp. 222–223)

Experts on adult development who follow a life-events framework believe that the question of whether mid-life is a crisis or not is the wrong question to ask. Rather, they emphasize that attention should be focused on how various events that are likely to occur in middle adulthood influence the individual. Further, they believe that many complex factors mediate the effects of life events on the individual (Hultsch & Plemons, 1979; Neugarten, 1980; Riegel, 1975). Whether mid-life precipitates a crisis is likely to depend on the extent to which life events are likely to trigger it.

Timing and Time Perspective

Bernice Neugarten (1970) believes that a main theme of adult life is developing a sense of timing of events in the life cycle. She also believes that although we may experience periods of crisis, they do not dramatically change our sense of self or alter our life course. Neugarten believes that too much emphasis has been placed on crises in adulthood and not enough attention has been given to a psychology of timing in adulthood. From her perspective only a minority of adults experience a mid-life crisis and for those who do it is because of some interruption in the rhythm of adult development. Data on the degree of stress that people experience at different points in development are also unsupportive of a crisis view of the middle adult years (Brim, 1976; Lazarus & DeLongis, 1981).

Although middle adulthood is perhaps inappropriately labeled as a period of crisis, just as adolescence is inappropriately described as a period of storm and stress, it is a time of transition. At mid-life, people tend to show more concern about physical competency and appearance even though they often perceive greater alterations in their physical appearance than actually do occur (Gould, 1978). Whether actual physical decline occurs or not during mid-life, many people often expect it to occur, an expectation that may influence what they feel is happening to them personally. As Neugarten has suggested, people seem to experience a transition in their perspective on time during the middle adult years. Prior to middle adulthood, people do not often count years in terms of how many are left. Because of a shift in time perspective, people in middle adulthood may begin to see limitations to their being able to change their lives. And in every culture there comes a time when the ruling generation must relinquish some of its power and status to the younger generation. In our culture much of this shift occurs during middle adulthood. At work, new and upwardly mobile employees may threaten the middle-aged adult's security and sense of competence. New styles and fads reinforce the middle-aged adult's sense that a younger generation is moving into a position of dominance. In the community, ideas of younger people are often seen as fresh and new while those of older adults are viewed as outdated (Steinberg, 1980). Individuals vary, of course, in the manner in which such changes affect their lives and the degree to which such changes meet with their satisfaction.

The middle adult years, then, are transition years, years in which people seem to vary their perspective on time and think more about their contribution to those who will succeed them in the next generation of adults. Next we look at the continuing development of personality in late adulthood.

Late Adulthood

In this section we look at the last stage of Erikson's eight stages of development, ego integrity versus despair, as well as at other major perspectives on personality development, and further explore the criteria most likely to contribute to life satisfaction in late adulthood.

Some Major Perspectives

Psychoanalytic theorists Sigmund Freud and Carl Jung viewed old age as a period similar to childhood. Freud, for example, believed that in old age people return to the narcissism that characterizes the unconscious thought of early childhood. Jung believed that in old age thought is submerged in the unconscious, gradually sinking so deeply into the unconscious that little touch with reality is possible. Charlotte Buhler (1968) believed that late adulthood is a time when an individual adds up his or her life. Buhler viewed nearness to death as the motivating force behind a person's interest in reviewing his or her life. As noted in chapter 10, Robert Peck (1968) believes that three issues must be confronted in late adulthood—work roles, body perception, and reality. And as noted in chapter 8, one of the influential social theories of aging, activity theory, argues that psychological well-being in late adulthood is related to the degree to which older people remain active and involved in their world.

Earlier in this chapter in our discussion of continuity/discontinuity and the major longitudinal studies of aging, we also concluded that in late adulthood individuals move from more active to more passive mastery of their environment and become more inner than outer oriented (Neugarten, 1964). However, in the longitudinal analysis by Maas and Kuypers (1974), it was concluded that no simple generalizations of all adults could be made as they age from thirty to seventy. In contrast, by focusing on subgroups of adults and their life-styles some perceptible changes can be detected in late adulthood.

The theorist who has had the most impact on our thinking about personality development in late adulthood is Erik Erikson. Erikson believes that late adulthood is characterized by the last of eight stages of development, ego integrity versus despair. From Erikson's perspective, the later years of life are a time for looking back at what we have done with our lives. Through many different routes the older person may have developed a positive outlook in each of the preceding periods of emotional crises. If so, the retrospective glances and reminiscence will reveal a picture of a life well spent and the person will be satisfied (ego integrity). However, the older person may have resolved one or more of the earlier crises in a negative way. If so, the retrospective glances will yield doubt, gloom, and despair over the total worth of his or her life. Erikson's own words capture the richness of his thought about personality development in late adulthood:

> A meaningful old age, then . . . serves the need for that integrated heritage which gives indispensable perspective to the life cycle. Strength here takes the form of that detached yet active concern with life bounded by death, which we call *wisdom* in its many connotations from ripened "wits" to accumulated knowledge, mature judgment, and inclusive understanding. Not that each man can evolve wisdom for himself. For most, a living *tradition* provides the essence of it. But the end of the cycle

also evokes "ultimate concerns" for what change may have to transcend the limitations of his identity and his often tragic or bitterly tragic comic engagement in his one and only life cycle within the sequence of generations . . . a civilization can be measured by the meaning which it gives to the full cycle of life, for such meaning, or the lack of it, cannot fail to reach into the beginnings of the next generation and push into the changes of others to meet ultimate questions with some clarity and strength.

To whatever abyss ultimate concerns may lead individual men, man as a psychosocial creature will face, toward the end of his life, a new edition of an identity crisis which we may state in the words, "I am what survives of me." (1968, pp. 140–141)

Erikson's emphasis that the development of integrity depends upon a positive review of one's life has been discussed extensively by Robert Butler (1975) in an article entitled "The Life Review: An Interpretation of Reminiscence in the Aged," a portion of which is excerpted in box 11.2.

We have seen that a positive review of one's life contributes to life satisfaction in late adulthood. Next we look at other factors that influence life satisfaction.

Life Satisfaction

Life satisfaction is an important integrative concept in late adulthood. We already have seen that it has been a major focus of several important longitudinal studies of aging. There has been increased interest in discovering the specific aspects of an elderly person's life that contribute to life satisfaction. In one study of 141 lower-class men and women (Markides & Martin, 1979), health and income were the two factors most likely to be associated with life satisfaction. This research also indicated that elderly people who were active—going to church, to meetings, on trips, and so on—were happier than those who tended to stay at home. These results coincide with the data collected in Erdman Palmore's longitudinal study of aging described in chapters 5 and 8, suggesting that health is a primary indicator of life satisfaction in late adulthood, as are various aspects of activity.

In one of the most well-known studies of life satisfaction, Robert R. Sears (1977) conducted a follow-up of the Terman gifted men when their average age was sixty-two. Just after World War I, Lewis Terman began his famous longitudinal study of gifted children. He later realized that if this group of children were followed into later maturity valuable information could be collected about the experiences that contribute to ultimate satisfaction with life and to different styles of coping with important life problems.

Satisfaction is a global term, and so is coping with life problems. In the Terman follow-up investigation, satisfaction focused on two aspects of life: occupation and family life. The specific coping styles for the areas of occupation and

Box 11.2
THE LIFE REVIEW: AN INTERPRETATION
OF REMINISCENCE IN THE AGED

Robert Butler

The **life review** as a looking-back process that has been set in motion by looking forward to death, potentially proceeds toward personality reorganization. Thus, the life review is not synonymous with, but includes reminiscence; it is not alone either the unbidden return of memories, or the purposive seeking of them, although both may occur.

The life review sometimes proceeds silently, without obvious manifestations. Many elderly persons, before inquiry, may be only vaguely aware of the experience as a function of their defensive structure. But alterations in defensive operations do occur. Speaking broadly, the more intense the unresolved life conflicts, the more work remains to be accomplished toward reintegration. Although the process is active, not static, the content of one's life usually unfolds slowly; the process may not be completed prior to death. In its mild form, the life review is reflected in increased reminiscence, mild nostalgia, mild regret; in severe form, in anxiety, guilt, despair, and depression. In the extreme, it may involve the obsessive preoccupation of the older person with his past, and may proceed to a state approximating terror and result in suicide. Thus, although I consider it to be a universal and normative process, its varied manifestations and outcomes may include psychopathological ones.

The life review may be first observed in stray and seemingly insignificant thoughts about oneself and one's life history. These thoughts may continue to emerge in brief intermittent spurts or become essentially continuous, and they may undergo constant reintegration and reorganization at various levels of awareness. A seventy-six-year-old man said:

My life is in the background of my mind much of the time; it cannot be any other way. Thoughts of the past play upon me; sometimes I play with them, encourage and savor them; at other times I dismiss them.

family life, respectively, were work persistence into the sixties and unbroken marriage versus divorce. The recorded events and expressions of feelings were recorded every ten years. Both occupational satisfaction and work persistence were best predicted by feelings of satisfaction, ambition, and good health, expressed as early as age thirty. Family-life satisfaction and success in marriage were predicted by good childhood social adjustment, good mental health in later years, retrospective (age forty) positive attitudes toward parents, and best of all, by the Terman Marital Happiness Test (taken at age thirty). Sears's findings on life satisfaction lend credence to the belief that there is constancy as well as change in

Adaptive and Constructive Manifestations

As the past marches in review, it is surveyed, observed, and reflected upon by the ego. Reconsideration of previous experiences and their meanings occurs, often with concomitant revised or expanded understanding. Such reorganization of past experience may provide a more valid picture, giving new and significant meanings to one's life; it may also prepare one for death, mitigating one's fears.

The occasions on which the life review has obviously been creative, having positive, constructive effects, are most impressive. For example:

> A seventy-eight-year-old man, optimistic, reflective, and resourceful, who had had significantly impairing egocentric tendencies, became increasingly responsive in his relationships to his wife, children, and grandchildren. These changes corresponded with his purchase of a tape recorder. Upon my request he sent me the tapes he had made, and wrote: "There is the first reel of tape on which I recorded my memory of my life story. To give this some additional interest I am expecting that my children and grandchildren and great-grandchildren will listen to it after I am gone. I pretended that I was telling the story directly to them."

Ingmar Bergman's very fine, remarkable Swedish motion picture, *Wild Strawberries,* provides a beautiful example of the constructive aspects of the life review. Envisioning and dreaming of his past and his death, the protagonist-physician realizes the nonaffectionate and withholding qualities of his life; as the feeling of love reenters his life, the doctor changes even as death hovers upon him.

In the course of the life review the older person may reveal to his wife, children, and other intimates, unknown qualities of his character and unstated actions of his past; in return, they may reveal heretofore undisclosed or unknown truths. Hidden themes of great vintage may emerge, changing the quality of a lifelong relationship. Revelations of the past may forge a new intimacy, render a deceit honest; they may sever peculiar bonds and free tongues; or they may sculpture terrifying hatreds out of fluid, fitful antagonisms. (1975, pp. 331, 332, 338, Copyright 1975 by Robert N. Butler, M.D. By permission of Harper & Row, Publishers, Inc.)

adult development. In the longitudinal study of the Terman gifted men there was a high consistency of expressive feelings about work, health, and self-worth over the three decades from ages thirty to sixty. Interestingly, in spite of the men's autonomy and great average success in their occupations, they placed greater importance on achieving satisfaction in their family life than in their work.

In a follow-up study of the Terman gifted women (Sears & Barbee, 1977), somewhat fewer than half of the women worked, and most of those who did work had professional careers. The working women reported more satisfaction

People who are active in late adulthood show more life satisfaction than those who are passive.

with their lives in general than those who did not work. Nonworking women were less satisfied with their family lives than the working women were and less satisfied than the men were. Many of these nonworking women would now opt for a career if they could relive their lives.

In another large-scale investigation of life satisfaction and the quality of life in late adulthood, John Flanagan (1981) obtained life histories of 1,000 people aged sixty-eight to seventy-two from many different backgrounds and geographical areas of the United States. The histories were obtained by trained interviewers who used a structured interview booklet. The components used to study the quality of life in late adulthood focused on physical and material well-being; relations with other people; social, community, and civic activities; personal development and fulfillment; and recreation. It appears that health problems and lack of money are the most significant factors that interfere with a good quality of life. Fortunately, only 30 percent of the older people reported that their health was fair or poor, with only 6 percent in the poor category. Slightly more than half of the men but nearly three fourths of the women reported total family incomes of less than $8,000 per year—almost two thirds of these women were living alone. About one sixth of the men and more than one third of the women had total family incomes of less than $4,000 per year. Clearly the lack of money is a major contributor to reducing the quality of life.

There also seems to be little doubt that over the life span, marital relationships and childrearing make important contributions to the quality of one's life. However, at age seventy, there also are many immediate problems and situations that have a compelling effect on the current quality of life.

Seventy-year-olds' need for rewards from personal activity are clearly shown in reports on the contributions of work and active recreation to the elderly's present quality of life in the California Longitudinal Study. Other factors of special value to women are close friends and helping others. These factors tend to be especially important for many widows at this age level. Still other factors that are important include socializing and recreation. A factor that was reported by many seventy-year-olds as a negative contributor to their quality of life was lack of learning and education. About one third of the sample studied never entered high school and one half of the total group did not graduate from high school.

It is important to reemphasize that life satisfaction is a very broad concept. It is defined in different ways and measured in different ways. One of the most influential views of life satisfaction was developed by Bernice Neugarten and her associates (Neugarten, Havighurst, & Tobin, 1968). Their intent was to develop a multidimensional measure that would reflect the complexity of psychological well-being. To this end, they identified five components of life satisfaction:

1. *Zest versus apathy*—degree of involvement in activities, with other people or with ideas.
2. *Resolution and fortitude*—extent to which adults take responsibility for their own lives.
3. *Congruence*—degree to which goals are achieved.
4. *Self-concept*—adults' perception of self, physically, psychologically, and socially.
5. *Mood tone*—extent to which adults have optimistic attitudes and feel happy.

In a recent reevaluation of the Life Satisfaction Index (LSI) with a large, heterogeneous national sample (Hoyt & Creech, 1983), the most consistent structure was comprised of three factors: satisfaction with the past, satisfaction with the present, and future orientation/optimism. There was some support, though weaker, for a fourth factor called negative mood tone. In sum, although life satisfaction seems to be an important integrative concept in understanding personality development in late adulthood, further work needs to be done to develop more precise measures of life satisfaction.

In the next chapter we look at two important aspects of personality—sex roles and moral development and values—and give attention to the topics of stress and coping and mental health.

Summary

There are many complex aspects to the question of how stable or changeable personality is in adulthood, and simple answers do not emerge. Some overall themes do appear, however, in the longitudinal studies of personality development. We cannot completely ignore the childhood and adolescent antecedents of adult development, because what goes on in the first twenty years of life does have implications for personality development in the adult years. However, such influences are nowhere near as strong as infant determinists like Freud thought. The longitudinal data on adult personality development suggest both continuity and discontinuity, and when continuity occurs it is often complex. When we begin looking at a combination of information about environmental conditions—such as the contexts of family, peers, and work—along with knowledge of the individual's personality characteristics, our ability to predict what an individual will be like at a later point in adulthood may be more accurate than when predictions are made on information about personality characteristics alone or environmental experiences alone. The true nature of personality lies somewhere between the traditional view of personality that has emphasized the stability of individual personality characteristics and the contextual perspective that fails to recognize the personality characteristics an individual brings to a context or setting. Predicting personality from one point in adulthood to another is very difficult, and some people show more stability than others. The closer in time we make various personality assessments, the more likely we are to find continuity; when we evaluate individuals at longer intervals, the less likely we are to find continuity. Personality development in adulthood should not be viewed as extraordinarily stable or completely changeable.

Identity is a central theme of personality development, but identity is not solely the property of adolescence and early adulthood. It is also an important influence throughout the adult years. Themes of intimacy/commitment and independence/freedom are also important aspects of personality development in early adulthood, although they too are significant throughout the adult years. Much of personality development in early adulthood focuses on social processes: intimacy, interpersonal relationships, and the context of work, particularly getting started in an occupation and getting adjusted to the role of work in one's life.

In middle adulthood some individuals do experience a mid-life crisis, particularly those who are confronted with nonnormative life events. The majority of adults, however, experience middle adulthood as a transition period rather than a crisis. One change at mid-life that seems to characterize many people is a modification in time perspective, such that many begin to think more about how much time is left rather than what has gone before.

A number of prominent theorists, including Erik Erikson, believe that late adulthood is a time of life review and reminiscence. Data from longitudinal studies of adult personality suggest some changes in personality in late adulthood. Bernice Neugarten believes that older people show less active and more passive mastery over their environment and have more of an inner than an outer orientation to their world. Data collected by Maas and Kuypers suggest that one cannot simply look at all people and generalize about what important changes take place through the adult years. These researchers identified different types of mothers and fathers and found differing patterns of change depending on a variety of circumstances.

Life satisfaction in late adulthood is a complex issue that is related to a number of antecedents in earlier adulthood, a number of current personal characteristics, and environmental conditions. Health, activity, family life, and occupation are often linked with life satisfaction. It is important to realize, however, that because life satisfaction is such a broad concept it is difficult to measure. One recent investigation found that the factors used to reflect life satisfaction in the most widely used index of life satisfaction—the Life Satisfaction Index (LSI)—may not be appropriate. Analyses suggest that we need to develop more precise measures of life satisfaction.

Review Questions

1. Differentiate the views of personologists, or traditional trait theorists, from the views of contextual, situational theorists.
2. What are the findings of the major longitudinal studies of personality development in terms of predicting adult personality from its childhood and adolescent antecedents?
3. What do the major longitudinal studies of personality development tell us about stability and change in the adult years?
4. Describe the development of identity in early adulthood.
5. Discuss the concept of mid-life crisis. How valid is the concept?
6. Explain some of the personality changes that seem to characterize late adulthood.
7. What seem to be important predictors of life satisfaction in late adulthood?

Further Readings

Brim, O. G., Jr., & Kagan, J. (Eds.). (1980). *Constancy and change in human development*. Cambridge, MA: Harvard University Press.
   Includes detailed information about many different aspects of life, including physical, cognitive, and personality development. Provides insight into some of the difficulties in measuring constancy and change over long time periods. Moderately difficult reading level.
Eichorn, D. H., Clausen, J. A., Haan, N., Honzik, M. P., & Mussen, P. H. (1981). *Present and past in middle life*. New York: Academic Press.
   Must reading. Described by Robert Sears as the most important contribution to adult personality study in the last thirty years. Reveals the complexities of predicting personality over long numbers of years. Medium difficult reading level.
Neugarten, B. L. (Ed.). (1968). *Middle age and aging: A reader in social psychology*. Chicago, IL: University of Chicago Press.
   One of the leading thinkers in adult development and aging describes some of the important considerations of change during middle and late adulthood. Medium difficult reading level.

12

SEX ROLES, MORAL DEVELOPMENT, STRESS AND COPING, AND MENTAL HEALTH

Imagine That Over Several Years You Have Married, Been Fired from Your Job, and Separated from and Then Reconciled with Your Spouse

I MAGINE *that over several years you have married, been fired from your job, and separated from and then reconciled with your spouse.*

From knowledge of these events could we tell how stressful your life is? One model of stress suggests that life events produce taxing circumstances that increase the stress in one's life. For example, table 12.1 presents one way in which the stressfulness of life events has been described. People are characteristically asked to rate how stressful various life events are (e.g., Dohrenwend, Krasnof, Askenasy, and Dohrenwend, 1978). Holmes and Rahe's Social Readjustment Rating Scale has often been used for this purpose.

How do researchers arrive at the stress values of various life events? An event such as marriage is taken as an anchor point and assigned a value. In the case of the Social Readjustment Rating Scale, marriage was assigned the value of 50. A sample of adults was then asked how much readjustment would be required if they experienced each of the other events listed in the table. This question was asked in relation to the event of marriage. For example, would being fired at work require more or less readjustment than marriage? And how about sex difficulties, divorce, and death of a close friend? Do they require more or less readjustment than marriage? The average score for an event was then divided by 10 to arrive at the number you see beside each life event in the table. Look at the life events and their readjustment scores and rankings. Do you agree with their ordering?

Generally, a significant but modest relationship has been found between degree of stress and physical illness. Many individuals who have experienced more stressful life events seem to show more physical and health-related problems—but not all (Rabkin & Struening, 1976). Some people psychologically handle stress better than others, resisting illness even in the face of highly stressful life events. For example, when business executives have vigorous attitudes toward challenging situations, they experience fewer physical problems and less illness than their counterparts with opposite attitudes who are in the same stressful circumstances (Kobasa, 1979). People who face stress but retain their health probably perceive change as a challenging opportunity, not a threat.

One of the major topics of this chapter focuses on stress and coping. An important theme in our discussion of this topic is that there is much more to understanding stress than merely cataloging how stressful life events are.

Table 12.1

SOCIAL READJUSTMENT RATING SCALE

Rank	Life event	Mean value	Rank	Life event	Mean value
1	Death of spouse	100	31	Change in work hours or conditions	20
2	Divorce	73	32	Change in residence	20
3	Marital separation	65	33	Change in schools	20
4	Jail term	63	34	Change in recreation	19
5	Death of close family member	63	35	Change in church activities	19
6	Personal injury or illness	53	36	Change in social activities	18
7	Marriage	50	37	Mortgage or loan less than $10,000	17
8	Fired at work	47	38	Change in sleeping habits	16
9	Marital reconciliation	45	39	Change in number of family get-togethers	15
10	Retirement	45	40	Change in eating habits	15
11	Change in health of family member	44	41	Vacation	13
12	Pregnancy	40	42	Christmas	12
13	Sex difficulties	39	43	Minor violations of the law	11
14	Gain of new family member	39			
15	Business readjustment	39			
16	Change in financial state	38			
17	Death of close friend	37			
18	Change to different line of work	36			
19	Change in number of arguments with spouse	35			
20	Mortgage over $10,000	31			
21	Foreclosure of mortgage or loan	30			
22	Change in responsibilities at work	29			
23	Son or daughter leaving home	29			
24	Trouble with in-laws	29			
25	Outstanding personal achievement	28			
26	Wife begin or stop work	26			
27	Begin or end school	26			
28	Change in living condition	25			
29	Revision of personal habits	24			
30	Trouble with boss	23			

Source: Holmes & Rahe, 1967. Reprinted with permission.

INTRODUCTION

In this chapter we explore four important aspects of personality processes and development during the adult years. To begin, we explore the intriguing topic of sex roles. In previous chapters (8, 9, and 10) we commented on sex differences and sex-role orientation. Here we describe the nature of sex roles and how they develop during the adult years. Another important aspect of personality involves our thoughts, feelings, and actions pertaining to standards of right and wrong—the subject matter of moral development. We outline and evaluate Lawrence Kohlberg's theory, and examine the cognitive social learning theory of morality. Then we discuss different models of stress and the importance of coping resources in handling stress. Finally we address the topic of mental health in late adulthood by considering the categorization of mental health problems, the dementia syndrome, depression, and how we can best meet the mental health needs of the elderly.

SEX ROLES

All of us are curious about our gender. In this section we explore the nature of sex roles and the extent to which they are changing. We also look at sex differences and sex roles across the adult years.

The Nature of Sex Roles

The label **sex role** has been used to describe the different characteristics individuals display because of their sex. However, some experts (e.g., Spence & Helmreich, 1978) define sex role as the behaviors that are expected of individuals because they are either male or female. An important aspect of sexual makeup is what is referred to as **sexual, or gender, identity.** We can define this as the extent to which individuals actually take on as part of their personalities the behaviors and attitudes associated with either the male or female role. In the United States and in most other countries, the well-adjusted individual has traditionally been one who has developed a sex-appropriate sex role. That is, males are supposed to be "masculine" and females are supposed to be "feminine." In past years researchers assessed the concept of sex roles as a bipolar construct, with masculinity and femininity at opposite poles. Recently an alternative view of sex roles has been developed, and it is based on the concept of androgyny.

The belief that masculinity and femininity are opposites was refuted by psychologists in the mid-1970s when they began to suggest not only that masculinity and femininity are independent of one another but also that the healthiest way to conceive of sex roles may be to view all individuals as having both masculine and feminine characteristics. **Androgyny** has become a byword in research on sex roles in the late 1970s and early 1980s. What do we mean when we say thirty-five-year-old Bob is androgynous? We mean that his psychological

Our psychological makeup includes both masculine and feminine characteristics.

makeup includes both male and female aspects of behavior; sometimes it is said that people like Bob have an androgynous sex-role orientation. Sandra Bem (1974, 1977) and Janet Spence (Spence & Helmreich, 1978; Spence, Helmreich, & Stapp, 1974) pioneered the notion that sex roles should not be looked at as bipolar sexual extremes but rather as dualistic dimensions within each sex. In other words every male has and should have some feminine attributes, and every female has and should have some masculine attributes. Furthermore, both Bem and Spence believe that androgyny is not only natural but allows the individual to adapt more competently to a wide variety of situations.

Bem created the Bem Sex-Role Inventory (BSRI), and Spence developed the Personality Attributes Questionnaire (PAQ), both of which measure androgyny. The types of sex-role attributes that are tapped by these two increasingly used sex-role measures include dominance, independence, passivity, competitiveness, loyalty, aggressiveness, and forcefulness, among others. See table 12.2 for a list of items from Bem's inventory.

Table 12.2

EXAMPLES OF MASCULINE AND FEMININE ITEMS FROM BEM'S SEX-ROLE INVENTORY

Masculine Items	*Feminine Items*
Acts as a leader	Affectionate
Analytical	Compassionate
Competitive	Feminine
Forceful	Gullible
Individualistic	Sensitive to the needs of others
Self-reliant	Sympathetic
Willing to take a stand	Warm

Source: Bem, 1974. Reproduced by special permission of the publisher, Consulting Psychologists Press, Inc. from the Bem Sex Role Inventory by Sandra Bem, PhD., copyright 1978.

The PAQ includes such positively valued "masculine" traits as independence, competitiveness, ability to make decisions easily, unwillingness to give up easily, self-confidence, and a sense of superiority; positive "feminine" characteristics include gentleness, helpfulness, kindness, and awareness of others' feelings. While androgyny has been scored in different ways by researchers, Spence and her colleagues (Spence, Helmreich, & Stapp, 1975) advocate classifying those who score high on both the feminine and masculine scales as androgynous. Individuals who score low on both the masculine and feminine scales are labeled undifferentiated; and individuals who score high on one scale and low on the other are categorized as masculine or feminine.

Androgynous individuals are viewed positively for two reasons. First, the classification of a person as androgynous is based on the appearance of both masculine and feminine characteristics rather than the absence of both. Second, and more important, the attributes that comprise androgyny are those aspects of masculinity and femininity that are valued by our culture. The androgynous person is achievement oriented, shows high self-esteem, is a warm individual, and so on (Babladelis, 1979).

Not everyone agrees with Spence and Bem's belief that we ought to be developing androgynous individuals. For example, the culmination of Phyllis Katz's (1979) developmental view is conformity to socially prescribed sex roles. She believes that sex-role socialization is a lifelong process and that socialization agents outside of the family play more important roles than was previously thought. The first developmental period in her theory is infancy-puberty, at which time children learn appropriate child sex roles. During adolescence, a second developmental period appears in the form of preparation for adult sex roles. Sexual maturation, heterosexual relationships, and career goals represent areas of sexual change in adolescence. The third developmental level refers to adult sex-role development, involving adjustment to changing family structure and occupational roles. In box 12.1, we further explore some ideas suggesting that androgynous people may not be the best-adjusted adults.

Box 12.1
BEYOND ANDROGYNY?

Though androgyny has many appealing qualities, some psychologists do not believe that it provides the solution to determining individuals who have the best-adjusted personality (Locksley & Colten, 1979). Consider the belief that androgynous adults are better adjusted because they are more flexible and are not confined by sex-role stereotypes. In one investigation (Jones, Chernovetz, & Hansson, 1978), Bem's androgyny test was given to evaluate the degree to which adults showed traditional masculine or feminine versus an androgynous orientation. The adults were also given a number of other measures: self-esteem, helplessness, sexual maturity, and personal adjustment. The androgynous adults were not better adjusted. Indeed, for both sexes a masculine orientation rather than androgyny tended to predict better flexibility and adjustment.

Furthermore, serious conceptual criticisms have been leveled at androgyny. The argument is that in a society where sex has such a pervasive role in everyday life, it structures the way in which people experience life. Critics stress that the concept of androgyny is not justified since it implies autonomy from sex-linked social and biological foundations of personality. They point out that such biological and social differences in the sexes are everywhere because sex is a structural feature of contexts and the ongoing organization of life experiences (Locksley & Colten, 1979).

Thus the critics of the androgyny concept believe that our sex—being male or female—invariably affects how people see us, what they expect us to be like and to do, as well as what we expect ourselves to be like.

Where do you stand on this controversial issue? Who do you believe are better adjusted—androgynous, traditional female-oriented, or traditional male-oriented adults? It may be that for some people better adjustment is determined by the sociocultural-historical context in which they live. Some women who are married, stay home most of the day, take care of their children, and have a traditionally oriented husband may be better adjusted having a traditional female orientation. Other individuals who believe in change, who believe that both males and females should be characterized by personality characteristics of both sexes, may be better adjusted with an androgynous sex-role orientation. None of the three sex-role orientations—masculine, feminine, or androgynous—has exclusive rights to better adjustment as an adult.

Sex Roles and Sex Differences in Adult Development

In writing about sex-role development in adulthood, Sharon Nash and S. Shirley Feldman (1981) indicate that we do not have good empirical data about the nature of change in most of the grand theories of adult development (for example, the theories of Erikson, Havighurst, Levinson, and Neugarten) and that the same situation exists for most of the various strands of adult personality development, one in particular being sex-role development. To help provide some information about the development of sex roles across the life cycle, Nash and Feldman (Feldman, Biringen, & Nash, in press) designed a study to systematically assess the development of sex-related aspects of self-concepts from adolescence through grandparenthood. They theorized that changes in the demand characteristics of family-related life circumstances would be related to fluctuations in sex-related self-perceptions during adulthood.

The Bem Sex-Role Inventory (Bem, 1974) was used to assess sex-related personality attributes of 804 people who were classified according to stage in the family life cycle. Eight groups were assessed, including one of adolescents, three of preparenting adults (singles, married-childless, and expectants), two active parenting groups (parents whose youngest child was less than ten years old, hereafter called young parents, and those whose youngest child was fourteen to seventeen years old, hereafter called mature parents), and two postparenting groups (empty nesters whose grown children no longer lived at home and grandparents). Four factors were derived from responses to the twenty "masculine" and twenty "feminine" items: leadership (acts as a leader, is dominant, competitive, ambitious); autonomy (self-reliant, self-sufficient, independent, individualistic); compassion (understanding, sensitive, sympathetic); and tenderness (affectionate, warm, gentle, cheerful, loves children).

Because the researchers expected sex differences to wax and wane across the life cycle, they examined sex effects separately for each stage of life. The results indicated that men and women were similar in instrumental qualities in the young adult years, when typically both sexes are involved in salaried work. By contrast, expectancy and the early years of parenthood were marked by sex differences in both autonomy and leadership. By the height of the mature parenting years, only the sex difference in leadership remained, possibly because the roles of both father and mother require a considerable amount of autonomy, although in different domains: men make career-related choices, and women resolve family-oriented issues. The sex difference in autonomy was ephemeral, emerging only during expectancy and young parenthood, a period of time marked by the woman's withdrawal from the role of wage earner and the presence of dependent children.

More women than ever before are entering traditionally male occupations.

On the expressive factors, compassion and tenderness, women surpassed men at most stages of life. Sex differences in tenderness were absent at two stages as a result of men's elevated stress. The first was among married-childless adults, whose developmental task is to establish intimacy. The second was among grandparents. Without the responsibility and demands of daily interactions with children and with the reduction of both work pressures and the need to provide for an expanding family, grandfathers seemed more comfortable than younger men in being emotionally demonstrative or tender.

Nash and Feldman (1981) concluded:

> By studying sex-role behaviors and related self-attributions across the life span, it becomes clear that sex roles do not merely define a catalogue of traits that consistently differentiate males and females. The psychological study of sex roles must include a consideration of social context, from the subtle to the more pervasive situational constraints. In particular, the performance of sex-role behaviors is affected by the presence of other people and may vary as a function of the age or sex or role status of these people (Berman, Sloan, & Goodman, 1979; Feldman & Nash, 1979; Fullard & Reiling, 1976). (p. 31)

Are Sex Differences in Personality More Prominent in Early Adulthood Than in Middle and Late Adulthood?

Several lines of evidence suggest that traditionally sex-typed characteristics are more pronounced in early than late adulthood (e.g., Douvan & Adelson, 1977; Livson, 1976) and that as adults age from middle to late adulthood they become progressively more androgynous (e.g., Gutmann, 1975, 1977; Livson, 1976; Lowenthal, Thurnher, & Chiriboga, 1975; Neugarten, 1964).

For example, in the Kansas City Longitudinal Study (Neugarten, 1964, 1973), adults aged forty to ninety were followed from 1953 to 1962. (These adults were born during the last part of the nineteenth century and the beginning of the twentieth century.) Neugarten (1973) concluded that differences between the sexes appear with age. The older men were more receptive to their own affiliative and nurturant behavior than the younger men, and the older women were more receptive than younger women to their own aggressive and egocentric behavior. However, in both sexes, older people were perceived to move more toward eccentric, self-preoccupied behavior and to show greater concern about satisfying their personal needs.

Several other longitudinal studies have also included comparisons of the personal ties of males and females as they age (e.g., Chiriboga & Pierce, 1978; Eichorn, Clausen, Haan, Honzick, & Mussen, 1981; Livson, 1976; Lowenthal, Thurnher, & Chiriboga, 1975; Maas & Kuypers, 1974; Mussen, Honzik, & Eichorn, 1982). In summarizing information collected from the various longitudinal comparisons of the personality development of males and females, Barbara Turner (1982) concluded that despite the rich data, the findings cannot be generalized to larger populations or to other cohorts. Sex-role research is strongly influenced by the historical-cultural context in which people live. Several pieces of research, however, do characterize the young adult as emotionally inexpressive (Douglas & Arenberg, 1978; Gutmann, 1977; Livson, 1976; Vaillant, 1977), which is consistent with sex-role expectations for achievement males. However, there may be some subcultural variations in this developmental theme. For example, young black men in the United States often show more warmth and expressiveness than their white counterparts (Turner & Turner, 1974). It is important to note that for the most part the samples in the longitudinal studies of personality are small, predominantly middle class, white, well educated, and generally have very supportive environments. Furthermore, adults born in the 1920s and who have lived in California are overrepresented.

Nevertheless, regardless of the data source, some patterns of personality appear to differ for adult men and women. Little or no change in sex-related differences in personality seems to appear when we only assess adults over a short number of years (e.g., Schaie & Parham, 1976; Siegler, George, & Okun, 1979). In investigations using personality Q-sort ratings based on clinical interviews (e.g., the California Longitudinal Studies), the general trend of personality for both genders reflects an increase in adaptive traits and a corresponding decrease in maladaptive traits, in that psychologically healthy women and men resemble each other far more at age fifty than at age eighteen. However, increasing similarity in personality does not describe women and men who are less well adapted in middle adulthood.

There is a continuing debate over whether personality change in late life is characterized by sex-related differences, the question being whether there is decreasing "femininity" in women and decreasing "masculinity" in men. The data on this issue come primarily from projective tests (Gutmann, 1975) and self-reports of self-concept (Chiriboga & Pierce, 1978; Thurnher, 1979). However, when all of the findings are pieced together it does seem that there is an increase in sex-typed feminine traits in the personality profiles of older men (e.g., Hyde & Phillis, 1969; Livson, 1976) or a decrease in sex-typed masculine traits (Chiriboga & Pierce, 1978; Douglas & Arenberg, 1978). But there does not seem to be as strong a tendency for the personality profiles of older women to be characterized by an increase in sex-typed masculine traits (Chiriboga & Pierce, 1978; Hyde & Phillis, 1979; Livson, 1976).

Barbara Turner (1982) concluded that it is premature to believe that there is continuity over the adult years in the personality of men and women. Often the men who have been studied have stable and advantageous circumstances—for example, few are widowed or divorced, and few have incomes even near the poverty line. Women are far more likely to experience normative role discontinuities that may interact with personality development. Furthermore, the developmental tasks of women in later life may vary more than those of men.

In summary, it is important to remember the comments of Barbara Nash and Shirley Feldman (1981) mentioned earlier, namely that sex-role behaviors and related self-attributions do not merely reflect a catalogue of traits that consistently differentiate males and females. The psychological study of sex roles should focus on the social contexts in which individuals live and their changing life circumstances. Again, we find the importance of conceptualizing personality in terms of person × situation interaction.

Next we look at another important aspect of personality in adulthood—moral development. Some experts believe that there may be sex differences in the way men and women reason about moral dilemmas.

MORAL DEVELOPMENT

In a sense the study of moral development is one of the oldest topics of interest to those who are curious about human nature. In prescientific periods philosophers and theologians heatedly debated the moral status of humans. Today we still debate the nature of moral development; most of us have strong opinions about acceptable and unacceptable behavior, ethical and unethical conduct, and the ways in which acceptable and ethical behavior are to be fostered in our culture.

Moral development concerns rules and conventions about acceptable behavior—often in relation to a person's interactions with other people. In studying these rules, psychologists examine three different aspects of moral development. First, how do people reason or think about rules of ethical conduct? For example, cheating is generally considered unacceptable behavior. The individual can be presented with a story in which someone must choose whether to cheat in a specific situation. When the individual is asked to decide what is appropriate for the character to do and why, focus is placed on the individual's rationale, or the type of reasoning he or she uses to justify the moral decision. A second issue in moral development entails the actual behavior of people in the face of rules for ethical conduct. Here, for example, the concern is whether the individual himself actually cheats in different situations and what factors influence this behavior. A third domain of moral development concerns how the individual feels after making a moral decision, particularly when he or she has chosen to do something that he or she considers unethical. Here the concern is whether the individual feels guilty about doing something unethical. Next we describe Lawrence Kohlberg's theory of moral thought, a theory that has been given considerable attention.

Kohlberg's Theory

The core of Kohlberg's theory of moral development is the cognitive development of the individual. Kohlberg (1976) believes that six distinct stages of moral development are associated with changes in the individual's thought structure. The stages begin around the age of six and continue well into adulthood.

Kohlberg arrived at his view after twenty years of interviewing children, adolescents, and adults. In Kohlberg's method the subject is presented with a series of stories about characters who face moral dilemmas. The subject is then asked a series of questions about each of the dilemmas.

Kohlberg (1976) believes that most children under age nine are at the **preconventional level** of moral development (stages 1 and 2). Interestingly, some adolescents, particularly those who are delinquent, also score at this level. Most adolescents and adults think at the **conventional level** (stages 3 and 4) when they are faced with moral dilemmas. A small percentage of adults may reach the **postconventional level** (stages 5 and 6). The label *conventional* means that adults conform to and uphold the laws and conventions of society simply because they are the laws and conventions of the society. The adult who reaches postconventional thinking understands, and for the most part accepts, society's rules and regulations, but her or his reasoning goes deeper than that of the adult who thinks in a conventional manner. For an adult at the postconventional level, the rules of the society have to mesh with her or his own underlying moral principles. In cases in which the rules of the society come into conflict with the adult's principles, the individual will follow her or his own principles rather than the conventions of society.

What causes a person to move from one stage to the next? Kohlberg believes that the individual's moral orientation unfolds as a consequence of cognitive development. Cognitive development is dependent upon the interaction of genetic endowment and social experiences. The individual passes through the six stages in an invariant sequence, from less to more advanced. He or she acts constructively on the world in proceeding from one stage to the next rather than passively accepting a cultural norm of morality.

Kohlberg and his associates (Colby, Kohlberg, Gibbs, & Lieberman, 1980) conducted a twenty-year longitudinal study of the subjects who were in Kohlberg's original sample in 1956. The data allowed Kohlberg to chart the developmental course of moral judgments from early adolescence through the latter part of early adulthood. The mean percentage of reasoning about moral dilemmas at each of the first five stages in Kohlberg's theory across the twenty years of the subjects' lives is shown in figure 12.1. The data show a clear relation between age and moral judgment stage. Over the twenty-year period, reasoning at stages 1 and 2 decreased, and reasoning at stage 4, which did not appear at all in the ten-year-olds, was reflected in 62 percent of the thirty-six-year-olds. Moral reasoning at stage 5 did not appear until the age of twenty to twenty-two, but it never rose above 10 percent of the subjects interviewed. Thus, just as formal operational thought does not always emerge in adolescence, neither do the higher stages in Kohlberg's theory of moral development. Reasoning about moral dilemmas does seem to change in adulthood, however. Adults in their thirties reason at more advanced levels than adolescents or children.

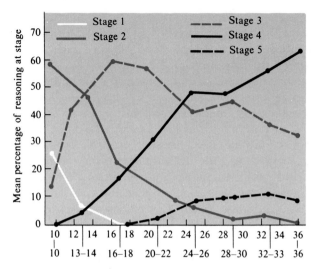

Figure 12.1   Mean percentage of reasoning at each stage for each age group.

Moral Development in Middle and Late Adulthood

Longitudinal studies of moral development suggest that unconventional adolescents often do not become more conventional with time (Haan & Day, 1974). However, when older adults (mean age of sixty-nine) were evaluated, some interesting results appeared (Haan, 1976): the older men differed from older women and from themselves when they were younger by thinking in more conventional ways.

The Cognitive Social Learning View

In keeping with our theme that person × situation interaction is an important way to conceptualize personality, we present the ideas of Walter and Harriet Mischel (1975), which focus on a cognitive social learning view of morality.

Combining elements of cognitive development with elements of the behavioral learning process highlights the cognitive social learning view of Walter and Harriet Mischel (1975). They distinguish between a person's moral competence, or ability to produce moral behaviors, and his or her moral performance of those behaviors in specific situations. In their view competence or acquisition depends primarily on cognitive-sensory processes; it is an outgrowth of these processes. The competencies include what people are able to do, what they know, their skills, their awareness of moral rules and regulations, their cognitive ability to construct behaviors. Their moral performance, or behavior, however, is determined by their motivation and the rewards and incentives to act in a specific moral way.

In general, social learning theorists have been critical of Kohlberg's view. Among other reasons, they believe that he places too little emphasis on moral behavior and the situational determinants of morality. However, while Kohlberg argues that moral judgment is an important determinant of moral behavior, he, like the Mischels, stresses that people's interpretation of both the moral and factual aspects of a situation lead them to a moral decision (Kohlberg & Candee, 1979). For example, Kohlberg mentions that "extramoral" factors, like the desire to avoid embarrassment, may cause people to avoid doing what they believe to be morally right. In sum, both the Mischels and Kohlberg believe that moral action is influenced by a complex of factors.

The ability to cope and adapt to one's environment is an important feature of personality in adulthood. During the course of adult life people experience stressful circumstances, some of which are major life events and others of which are day-to-day hassles. In the next section we look at the nature of stress and coping in adulthood.

STRESS AND COPING

Psychologists have been interested in stress for many years. Each of us has at least some concern about stress. We would all like to be able to cope adaptively to stress, and if we don't do a very good job of handling stress, most of us would like to learn better ways of dealing with it. Adult developmentalists have been interested in how stress should be conceptualized, how it should be measured, and whether people experience more stress at one point in adulthood than another. Too often simple notions about stress can lead to erroneous conclusions about its nature during the adult years. Richard Lazarus and Anita DeLongis (in press) believe that to better understand psychological stress and coping in aging we should distinguish between two models of stress. They further believe that to delineate more effective ways to cope with stress we should study adults' cognitive appraisal, sources of personal meaning that underlie stress and coping through the adult years, themes of commitment, and beliefs about the self and the environment.

Two Models of Stress

Essentially, there are two models in the study of life stress, and they have yielded different measurement strategies. The most frequently adopted model emphasizes that life events produce change and further that such change will lead to some form of adaptation. Indeed, one of the most prominent features of stress research is its focus on dramatic events and taxing circumstances. Recall our discussion in the Imagine section where we described the Social Readjustment Rating Scale, which was devised to measure the stress of experiencing various life events.

Some experts on adult development and stress believe that this approach places too much emphasis on change and too often ignores important mediating processes such as the personal importance of the events as well as the coping resources and strategies of the person facing stress (Lazarus & DeLongis, in press; Sarason & Spielberger, 1980).

In research on stress across the adulthood years, Richard Lazarus and his colleagues (DeLongis, Coyne, Dakof, Folkman, & Lazarus, 1982) have found that in adults aged forty-five to sixty-four an inverse relationship between life events and age exists, suggesting that there are fewer significant life events as people age. But we cannot conclude that just because the frequency of significant life events decreases with age that older people experience less stress. Such a strategy does not take into account the meaning of stress or the chronic nature of infirmity, limited energy, loneliness, and unresponsive environments that may characterize many individuals in late adulthood.

Some of the more insightful approaches to life events and stress have focused on variations with age in the probability of certain events, the timing and sequencing of these events, the motivational factors involved with them, the coping resources that can be called on to manage them, cognitive assessment of their significance, and their adaptational outcomes (Hultsch & Plemons, 1979).

However, an intriguing alternative approach to conceptualizing and assessing stress has been developed by Lazarus and his associates (e.g., DeLongis, Coyne, Dakof, Folkman, & Lazarus, 1982). This approach should be viewed as a supplement to the life-events view; it emphasizes the importance of *daily hassles,* meaning the irritating, frustrating, stressful pressures that accompany our day-to-day existence. Some hassles are transient, and others may be chronic. Lazarus has developed a hassles scale that evaluates the frequency and intensity of such stressful circumstances as misplacing or losing things, not having enough time for family, filling out forms, being concerned about one's weight, and being involved in unchallenging work.

In their own research, Lazarus and his colleagues have found the strategy of measuring daily hassles to be a better predictor of adaptation in terms of morale, psychological symptoms, and somatic illness than knowledge of life-events scores (DeLongis, Coyne, Dakof, Folkman, & Lazarus, 1982; Kanner, Coyne, Schaefer,

& Lazarus, 1981). Why might this be so? Daily hassles may have a stronger link with health outcomes because they evaluate proximal aspects of stress, whereas life-events scores measure distal aspects. **Proximal** refers to an adult's immediate perception or experience of the environment, whereas **distal** refers to a more removed perception that is more macro in nature and may not have common meaning for people.

However, in many instances life events may increase daily hassles. Divorce, death of a spouse, and retirement are likely to increase day-to-day stress. Still, many hassles are not related to life events.

In studying the daily hassles of college students and middle-aged adults, Lazarus and his colleagues found that the older adults often reported economic concerns—rising prices, taxes, and so on—while the students were coping with academic and social problems—wasting time, meeting high standards, being lonely. It is important to remember that Lazarus's sample was essentially white, middle class, and well educated. The daily hassles of other types of adults probably vary. The important issue here, however, is the provision of a supplement to life-events scores in our effort to evaluate stress.

The significance of an illness can vary according to the time frame of a person's life. For example, in one study (Mages & Mendelsohn, 1979), older people who discovered that they had cancer often accelerated such important aspects of life as disengagement from external commitments, increased dependency, and the life review process. However, older adults may be more likely to confront cancer with less anger than younger adults, who have not had the opportunity to live as much of their adult lives. Such findings emphasize the importance of the personal meaning of diverse stressful events at different points in adult development (Hultsch & Plemons, 1979; Lazarus & DeLongis, in press).

It is important to recognize that a combination of life events and daily hassles will not provide us with all of the information we need to know about stress in adult lives. Expectations are also an important aspect of the cognitive appraisal of stress. As Lazarus and DeLongis (in press) comment:

> Thus, in what seems like a paradox, chronically ill people can be expected even more readily than chronically well people to endorse as uplifts experiences such as getting a good night's sleep or feeling energetic. In aging, it makes sense that there will be a *downward* spiral of expectations about health and financial condition with each passing year. Thus, it is not surprising that within our middle-aged sample we found a positive relationship between age and the number of uplifts experienced, with this effect being strongest for experiences concerned with finances, energy, and health. In the context of negative expectations, positive occasions take on more salience as uplifts. This line of reasoning is consistent with Costa and McCrae's (1980) application of Helson's (1959) adaptation level theory in handling similar paradoxes in measurement and research on life satisfaction. Without background data on a person or group, the significance of an endorsement of a hassle or uplift will remain obscure. (p. 11)

Daily hassles and uplifts may be a better predictor of stress than major life events.

Coping

Our coping resources and coping strategies are important ingredients in influencing our adaptation to stress and the ability to live a psychologically healthy life. We rarely respond passively to stress. We attempt to change matters when it is possible, and when it is not, we often invoke cognitive strategies to alter the meaning of stressful circumstances.

Measuring coping resources and strategies has not been an easy task. Too often coping has been assessed as a trait or style using a single measure at one point in time. Such measurement has not allowed us to do a very good job of predicting how adults will react across time and in various situations. In keeping with an emphasis on person × situation interaction in understanding personality, Lazarus and his associates (e.g., Folkman & Lazarus, 1980) have constructed a checklist on ways of coping. This checklist focuses on what adults thought, felt, and did in a number of specific stressful circumstances. Using this measure, the researchers found that two basic strategies of coping are often used: problem solving and the regulation of emotion. Most people use both of these strategies rather than relying solely on one or the other. When coping patterns were charted according to the age of the subjects, there were no effects, although it should be noted that the oldest adults were sixty-four years old and still in the mainstream of life. Though some experts have argued that a decrease in coping occurs as we grow through the latter part of life (e.g., Gutmann, 1974; Jung, 1933), the evidence for such change is not strong and there is always substantial individual variation (Lazarus & DeLongis, in press).

Certain major sources of stress seem to characterize older adults more than their younger counterparts (e.g., Brim & Ryff, 1980; Hultsch & Plemons, 1979), but it does not follow that these stressful events and circumstances will be coped with in a distinctive manner. Within each age group, there are probably major differences in coping, and one way of coping may work better for some adults than for others. For example, of the one hundred middle-aged adults studied by Lazarus and his associates, fifteen were experiencing stress in caring for an ill parent. The experience of providing such care produced a strong feeling of obligation, frequent guilt and resentment, and an approaching sense of loss of the relationship. But in analyzing a number of interviews over a number of months, it was discovered that these middle-aged adults used three styles of coping with an ailing parent: *confrontational* (focusing on dealing with anger, guilt, and sadness, and involving efforts to bring stressful encounters with parent to an end); *denial* (suppression and eventual repression of negative feelings); and *avoidant* (consistent suppression rather than denial or repression of negative emotions).

A basic underlying theme of stress and coping is that throughout our adult lives we struggle to make sense out of what is happening to us. The struggle consists of thoughts and feelings and divergent beliefs and commitments. The attempt to make sense out of what is happening to us shapes our cognitive appraisal of stressful encounters and our coping strategies. The cognitive-affective struggle we go through has important implications for our health, psychological functioning, competence at work, and success in interpersonal relationships. According to Lazarus and DeLongis (in press), the significance of such a process-oriented perspective

> may be even greater in the study of aging than in mid-life because of the presence of widespread losses of roles and relationships. But whether viewed in the context of the entire life course or more narrowly in aging, we must see people as engaged in a life drama with a continuous story line that is best grasped not as a still photo but as a moving picture with a beginning, middle, and end. (p. 24)

As we have seen, adaptation and coping are important ingredients in understanding the adult's experience of stressful events and circumstances. Next we see that the personality profiles of adults who seem to have the best coping abilities include both resources and deficits.

Resources and Deficits in the Personality Profiles of Adults Who Effectively Cope with Stress

Marjorie Fiske (1980) indicates that virtually every individual harbors both deficits and resources within her or his psychic makeup. Some degree of psychopathology exists, for example, in most seemingly well-adapted people (Barron, 1963; Singer, 1963). And age has a great deal to do with how symptoms are diagnosed. At twenty-two, a woman may be having a postpartum depression; at forty-four, a menopausal one. But at sixty-six, the same symptoms are frequently (and erroneously) diagnosed as senile brain damage.

Fiske believes that we must learn more about the adapative coexistence of both deficits and resources because one "strong" resource may offset or counterbalance several deficits. In an ongoing longitudinal study, Fiske is attempting to assess the balance between inner resources and deficits among men and women at different stages of the life course and the relationship between these dimensions and the individual's sense of well-being. Looked at separately, the two dimensions are related to life satisfaction in an entirely expectable fashion. People with the most resources (such as the capacity for mutuality, growth, competence, hope, and insight) tend to be satisfied with themselves and their lives; those with deficits (psychological symptoms, including anxiety, hostility, and self-hatred) are the least satisfied. But these expected results are found among fewer than one-third of the people being studied. Among the other two-thirds, a combination of many "positive" and many "negative" attributes seems to increase people's sense of well-being.

Such findings suggest that it may be misleading to look only at the degree of impairment in a particular individual, because when we look closely at people who are the most satisfied with their lives, they harbor an array of both "positive" and "negative" attributes, are deeply involved in their worlds, and cope well with the diversity of stress that in-depth encounters with work and with people involve (Chiriboga & Lowenthal, 1975).

MENTAL HEALTH IN LATE ADULTHOOD

In his foreword to *Handbook of Mental Health and Aging* (1980), Seymour Kety commented:

> A national health problem that is most severe in terms of its prevalence and cost is a group of mental disorders and dysfunctions which are associated with aging. Either because somatic mechanisms are more robust or, being simpler and easier to comprehend, are more readily preserved or restored as the result of progress in medical science, a substantial segment of the population can now look forward to a longer life, but one which may unfortunately be hampered by mental disability. This is a prospect that is both troubling to the individual and costly to society. Since mental handicap makes an individual increasingly dependent on the help and care of others, the cost of these services and perquisites to other members of the family and to the whole of society as well represents a burden which has been estimated at 36.78 billions of dollars per year in the United States. More important, perhaps, is a cost that cannot be measured or tabulated: the loss of human potential and of the affected person's capacity for adaptation and ability to contribute to human welfare. (p. xi)

Defining *mental health* is not an easy task, although the term has become commonplace in our society. The term presumably not only embraces the absence of mental illness, difficulties, and frustrations but also reflects one's abilities or capacity to deal with the issues of life in an effective if not pleasurable or satisfying manner. Because older adults are more likely than younger adults to have some type of physical illness, the interweaving of physical and mental problems is more likely to occur in later than in younger adulthood (Birren & Sloane, 1981).

Although categorizing adults according to a particular type of mental illness has been criticized by some mental health experts, particularly behaviorists, we present some of the most important categories of mental health problems that many psychologists and psychiatrists use.

Categorizing the Mental Health Problems of the Elderly

In attempts to categorize mental health problems a distinction between organic and functional disorders is usually made. *Organic disorders* are sometimes referred to as organic brain syndromes and are associated with some physical cause, such as brain damage. By contrast, *functional disorders* are thought to be unrelated to physiological problems and to be caused by personality or environmental factors. Two forms of organic disorders that have been studied are **acute**

brain syndromes, which are reversible, and **chronic brain syndromes,** which are not reversible. Treatment for acute brain syndrome is usually aimed at the cause of the disorder, such as malnutrition, drug reaction, or infection. Chronic brain syndromes are usually permanent and involve brain damage, which may produce a variety of symptoms, such as confusion, suspiciousness, lack of concern for amenities, and loss of control over bodily functions. Although some clinicians continue to use the organic-functional dichotomy, recent knowledge about such disorders as schizophrenia, which is usually classified as a functional disorder, suggest that the organic-functional categorization may be misleading because a large number of experts now believe that there is a genetic component to many incidences of schizophrenia. Other than the acute and chronic brain syndromes, some of the mental disturbances that have been identified in late adulthood are schizophrenia and paranoid psychoses, affective psychoses, neuroses and personality disorders, and alcoholism. However, there is disagreement about appropriate categorization here as well. For example, how can we distinguish between an affective psychosis and a depressive neurosis? Both often show the same symptoms (for example, lethargy, depression). A **psychosis** is considered to be a more severe form of mental disorder, one that keeps the individual from maintaining contact with reality, whereas a **neurosis** is viewed as a less debilitating form of mental disorder in which the person, while usually showing a high level of anxiety, can generally function in the everyday world. However, psychologists often have a difficult time agreeing on a person's symptoms as well as in which category of mental illness to place the person. The problem is complicated in late adulthood because physical deterioration of a person's body may cause him or her to be diagnosed as having a mental problem when in reality the problem is a physical one.

It is difficult to estimate the number of people over the age of sixty-five who suffer from a given mental disorder. There have been numerous surveys of mental illness in late adulthood, but only those cases that come to medical attention through admissions to mental hospitals, psychiatric visits, and so on are counted. Further, many elderly people suffer from multiple problems, making a single classification difficult. In a review of the major surveys of the incidence of various categories of mental illness in late adulthood, David Kay and Klaus Bergmann (1980) concluded that the most consistent finding to emerge is the prevalence of chronic brain syndrome in people aged sixty-five and over. Of these individuals, 1 to 2 percent are severely impaired, and 3 to 4 percent are moderately impaired, the proportions increasing with age. At any one time the majority are living at home rather than in institutions and are being cared for by relatives and neighbors. Another consistent finding from community surveys is the very large number of old people with neuroses, especially depressive neuroses. Most of these people are not receiving any formal psychological treatment. The causes of such neuroses in late adulthood have not been adequately studied although the factors we described earlier as contributors to life satisfaction and quality of life in late adulthood (health, income, personal review of one's life, relationships with spouse and/or children, friendships, isolation, and work and vocation) are probably contributors here.

Perhaps the most controversial and confounding set of disturbances pertain to individuals who have been classified as senile or as having some type of dementia. **Dementia** is often considered to be a chronic, irreversible condition, but in reality it may involve potentially treatable functional and organic illnesses (Small & Jarvik, 1982).

The Dementia Syndrome

Dementia is estimated to affect 5 percent of people over the age of sixty-five and 20 percent or more over the age of eighty (Garland & Cross, 1982). It is characterized by deterioration of intelligence and behavior. In a recent overview of the causes and treatments of dementia, Gary Small and Lissy Jarvik (1982) concluded that dementia may be better understood by considering it to be a *clinical syndrome*—a cluster of symptoms and signs that should lead to a search for the cause of the disorder. A sampling of the most prevalent forms of dementia follows.

Dementia Caused by Disorders Lacking Specific Treatments

Alzheimer's disease, described initially in chapter 4, falls into this classification; it is estimated that 50 percent of the dementias in the elderly consist of this disorder (Tomlinson, Blessed, & Roth, 1970). Although there are clues to its origins, no specific treatment is yet available. The illness is likely a heterogeneous disorder involving any of several causes: chromosomal abnormalities, immune changes, slow viruses, and neurotransmitter defects.

Dementia Caused by Psychiatric Disorders

The clinical picture of depression in the elderly often mimics dementia—some classifiers have even labled it **depressive pseudodementia** (Kiloh, 1961). The reported frequency of mistaking depressed for demented elderly people ranges from 8 to 15 percent (Ron, Toone, & Garralda, 1979). Such characteristics as apathy, psychomotor retardation, impaired concentration, delusions, and confusion in the depressed elderly person may be easily mistaken as dementia, particularly when they are accompanied by complaints of memory loss.

The dementia syndrome may be caused by drugs and toxins and physical illness as well. The sedative effects of some drugs and drug combinations may contribute to memory impairment. Alcohol abuse can also be associated with dementia (Schuckitt, Morrissey, & O'Leary, 1979). In terms of physical illness, the disorder of thyroid metabolism may impair cognitive ability, and hyperthyroidism is a reversible cause of the dementia syndrome. And almost any intracranial lesion may produce memory loss or dementia.

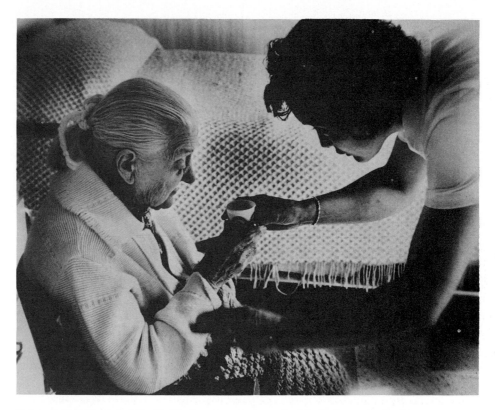

It is very important that the ill elderly person be treated with dignity and affection.

Seeking the particular cause of dementia is extremely important because in at least 10 to 30 percent of dementia cases treatment has been at least somewhat successful (Smith & Kiloh, 1981). The data from a number of studies suggest that we would be wise to discard the labels *senile* and *dementia,* which may have a pejorative, negative effect. It may be helpful instead to think in terms of a clinical syndrome of thoughts and behaviors that in many cases can be treated. Next we look at depression in late adulthood.

Depression

Depression is probably the most common psychiatric complaint among older adults (Butler & Lewis, 1977). Margaret Gatz, Michael Smyer, and Powell Lawton (1980) describe further the problem of depression in late adulthood:

> The importance of attending to depressive symptoms among the elderly is underscored by the high rate of suicide among older adults, particularly white males. Miller (1979) suggested that the actual number of geriatric suicides, including those not reported, may be at least 10,000 each year. Two aspects of depression in older adults

make it particularly troublesome to treat. The first is that there are often real reasons for feeling depressed, for instance, personal losses that may trigger existential questions. Reflecting this aspect, Gurland (1976), in a review of several epidemiological studies, noted that the highest rates of depressive *symptoms* are found in persons above age sixty-five. In contrast, the prevalence of depressive *disorders,* as diagnosed by psychiatrists, is highest between the ages of twenty-five and sixty-five and not among the older group. The second difficult aspect of depression is that family and friends do not enjoy being around depressed people. The depressed person tends to be dependent and demanding, thereby discouraging the very people who might be supportive. Thus, the families and caretakers need assistance, and the depressed older adults need interventions that will mobilize their resources while recognizing their concerns as valid. (pp. 11–12)

Meeting the Mental Health Needs of the Elderly

How are we going to meet the mental health needs of the elderly? First, psychologists must be encouraged to do more work with the elderly, and the elderly must be convinced that they can benefit from therapy. Second, we must make mental health care affordable. (Medicare currently pays lower percentages for mental care than for physical care.)

In addition we must find answers to several pressing questions. Reveron (1982) suggests what some of these questions are and reports on one researcher's idea on increasing the number of geropsychologists:

What professionals provide what kind of services to which groups of senior citizens? Does the therapy work? Which old people benefit from what kinds of therapy and in what ways? Who doesn't benefit and why? How often do the aged use mental health services and why? How frequently and in what settings do they come in contact with what kinds of mental health professionals? . . .

To increase the number of geropsychologists [Gatz, Smyer, & Lawton, 1980] some study of aging should be built into undergraduate programs of psychology and related areas such as sociology. If students are exposed earlier to study of the aged, she says, more of them may become interested in working with the elderly. Also, Gatz says, retraining and continuing education of psychologists is necessary to equip them to better help older clients. (p. 9)

Summary

The nature of sex roles is highly complex, involving biological gender, activities and interests, personal-social attributes, gender-based social relationships, and stylistic and symbolic content. Recently much attention has been given to the concept of androgyny—the belief that every individual's personality has masculine and feminine dimensions and that adults who portray positive aspects of both traditional male and female roles may be the most flexible and best adjusted. However, the critics of androgyny argue that our sex—being male or female—invariably affects how other people see us, what they expect us to be like and do, and what we expect ourselves to be like. The degree to which an adult with a masculine, feminine, or androgynous sex-role orientation shows better adjustment probably depends on the sociohistorial context in which he or she lives. In considering the development of sex-role orientation through the adult years, there appears to be an increase in sex-typed feminine traits in the personality profiles of older men or a decrease in sex-typed masculine traits. However, there does not seem to be as strong a tendency for older women to be characterized by an increase in sex-typed masculine traits. It always is important to keep in mind that sex-role behaviors and attributes do not merely reflect a catalogue of traits that consistently differentiate males and females. The psychological study of sex roles should focus on the social contexts in which people live and their changing life circumstances.

Moral development concerns rules and conventions about acceptable behavior. Psychologists often study three aspects of moral development—reasoning, behavior, and feeling. The core of Kohlberg's major theory of moral development is cognitive development. Kohlberg has modified his views over the years, more recently acknowledging that he initially was more optimistic than he should have been about adults' abilities to reach the highest stages of his model—self-principled reasoning. The majority of adults reason at the conventional level in Kohlberg's scheme, and moral reasoning is heavily influenced by people's education and intelligence. Cognitive social learning theorists believe that more focus needs to be given to the contexts and situations in which morality is displayed but agree with Kohlberg that there are some important cognitive ingredients of morality.

One's ability to cope and adapt to life is an important feature of personality. During the life course people experience many stressful circumstances. One view of stress focuses on the stressful nature of life events, the other on the daily hassles and uplifts that people experience. There seems to be converging agreement that knowledge of the stress involved in significant life events by themselves is not a good predictor of adaptation and adjustment. The nature of coping and stress is far too complex for such a simple explanation of adjustment. Expectations are an important part of cognitively appraising stress-related circumstances. So too are coping resources and coping strategies. People rarely respond passively to stress; they attempt to change matters when possible, and if that is not possible, they cognitively alter the meaning of the situation. While coping is an important aspect of understanding adaptation to stress, too often it has been construed as a trait or style and been assessed with a single measure. It is important to assess what people do think and feel in a number of stressful situations. Adults usually cope with stress by either calling on problem-solving strategies or regulating their emotions—most adults use both strategies. Certain major sources of stress seem to characterize older adults more than their younger counterparts, but it does not follow that these stressful events and circumstances will be coped with in a distinctive way. Within each phase of adulthood there are many different ways in which people cope with stress, and some strategies may be adaptive for some adults while other strategies may prove more efficient for other adults. Throughout the adult years people struggle to make sense out of what is happening to them. The struggle consists of thoughts and feelings and divergent beliefs and commitments. The attempt to make sense out of what is happening to us shapes our cognitive appraisal of stressful encounters and coping strategies. In detailed studies of adult lives there is evidence that the adults who cope most adaptively to stress have a personality profile that includes both deficits and resources.

The importance of viewing stress from such a process-oriented perspective may be particularly important in the late adulthood years because of the presence or absence of widespread losses of roles and relationships. Indeed, the mental health of older people has captured considerable attention in recent years. Defining mental health is not an easy task and there is disagreement on the categorization of mental illnesses at all age levels of adulthood. A distinction has been made between acute brain syndromes, which are reversible, and chronic ones, which are not reversible. Perhaps the most controversial and confounding set of disturbances pertain to individuals who are classified as "senile" or as having some form of dementia. In recent years health professionals have recognized that many elderly people who were classified as having a chronic, irreversible form of dementia in reality had a potentially treatable disorder. Approximately 50 percent of the dementias are comprised of Alzheimer's disease, which at this time has no effective treatment. Depression is another mental health problem in late adulthood, which comprises the most frequent complaint among the elderly with mental health problems.

A number of questions must be answered before we can meet the mental health needs of older people. For many years senior citizens have been an underserved group in the mental health profession. Mental health experts, such as Margaret Gatz, believe that mental health programs will have to spur an enormous amount of attention among psychologists if they are going to meet the increasing need for services among the aged.

Review Questions

1. Describe the different components of sex roles.
2. How certain are we that androgynous adults are more flexible and better adjusted? Explain.
3. What are some ways in which sex roles may change in the late adulthood years?
4. Outline Kohlberg's theory of moral development.
5. What is the nature of moral development during the adulthood years?
6. What are some criticisms of Kohlberg's view?
7. Discuss the two main models of stress.
8. Outline Richard Lazarus's ideas about stress and coping.
9. Explain Marjorie Fiske's ideas about how both resources and deficits characterize adults who cope with stress effectively.
10. What is dementia? Elaborate on how some forms of mental illness have been misdiagnosed in terms of irreversible dementia.
11. Explain two aspects of depression in elderly adults that make it difficult to treat.
12. What needs to be done to help meet the mental health needs of the elderly?

Further Readings

Birren, J. E., & Sloane, R. B. (Eds.). (1980). *Handbook of mental health and aging.* Englewood Cliffs, NJ: Prentice-Hall.
Includes some forty-one chapters, most of which are directly related to the mental health concerns of adults, particularly older adults. Surveys a wide variety of mental health concerns, including prevention, diagnosis, and treatment. Medium reading difficulty.

Lazarus, R. S., & DeLongis, A. (In press). Psychological stress and coping in aging. *American Psychologist.*
A full overview of Lazarus's stimulating ideas about the nature of stress and coping. Well written.

Lickona, T. (Ed.). (1976). *Moral development and behavior.* New York: Holt, Rinehart & Winston.
Includes a number of different views on various aspects of moral development. Medium reading difficulty.

Turner, B. F. (1982). Sex-related differences in aging. In B. J. Wolman (Ed.), *Handbook of developmental psychology.* Englewood Cliffs. NJ: Prentice-Hall.
A sophisticated overview of sex differences in adulthood and aging. Carefully points out the many limitations and complexities of research on sex-role development. Medium reading difficulty.

DEATH AND THE DYING PROCESS

PROFILE

When David Martin was five years old his grandfather died, and David thought that his grandfather could be brought back to life. However, when David was nine years old his grandmother died, and he realized that her death was final. When David was fourteen his uncle was killed in an automobile crash, and though David showed some concern, his thoughts about his uncle's death did not last very long. On the other hand, his mother showed a great deal of grief over the loss of her brother; indeed, at the age of forty-two David's mother seemed to show a greater interest in matters related to death than she had in her early adult years.

Death and the dying process are topics that have never been discussed very much in the Martin family, even though a number of relatives died during David's childhood and adolescence. All of the relatives were mourned at funerals, and the bodies of many were buried in the area of a large cemetery where family members from a number of previous generations are also buried.

As we follow David into early and middle adulthood, we find that he has married and has two children. However, at the age of forty-three, David begins to have some trouble breathing. He goes to see a physician, who discovers that David has lung cancer. The doctor openly discusses the likelihood that David has somewhere between one and five years to live. At first David is shocked. He says to himself, "This can't be happening to me. What am I going to do?" Over the course of the next several months he receives treatment for lung cancer and goes through a series of interchangeable moods—anger, disbelief and hope—as he attempts to make sense out of what is happening to him. After his attempts to cope with the stress of impending death through heavy emotional expression, he decides that it is best to go ahead and do what he can in the time he has left, to finish what he considers to be some important projects. David begins to feel better about himself because he hasn't given up; rather he has decided to take some control over his life and focus on his strengths rather than think about dying.

David's wife, Gretchen, has been an important support for him since he found out about his approaching death. She has been a good listener and has helped to look for strengths in his personality, but when he has let go emotionally, she has understood that he may need to do this as part of coping with the dying process. One of Gretchen's closest friends died several years ago, and that experience seems to help her sense some of what her husband is going through.

David was able to hang onto his life for seven years. Gretchen feels that his attitude was an important part of his ability to live longer than his doctor thought was possible. David continued his work for six years after he found out that he had cancer, and it was only in the last six months of his life that his body deteriorated to the point at which he could not work any longer

David's death has been very difficult for Gretchen. She loved him very much, and she feels a great deal of emptiness now that he is gone. It is now one year since David's death, and she still feels some grief for him. After his death, she thought a lot about why it occurred, and this has caused her to try harder to make sense out of the world. In the past year Gretchen has felt a drain of energy and has frequently been ill. She has not even considered going out with any other men since David's death. She has devoted her time to her children, to the church she attends, and to some community activities she has been involved in.

As we follow Gretchen further into middle adulthood, we find that at the age of fifty-eight her children have long since left home and both are married themselves now. Five years ago Gretchen met a man at her church whose wife had died of a heart attack several years before. After knowing each other for almost a year, he asked Gretchen if she would like to go out to dinner with him. She told him she would have to think about it. She talked to some of her friends, and they agreed that she should go. Her doubts about going reflected the continuing attachment she felt to her husband who had died some fifteen years earlier. Gretchen did go out to dinner with Tom, and they were eventually married. Although Gretchen is very happy in her current marriage with Tom, there are still times when she reflects on her life with David and occasionally feels pangs of grief over his loss.

13

DEATH AND THE DYING PROCESS

Imagine That You Just Found Out Your Best Friend Has Cancer and Does Not Have Very Long to Live

INTRODUCTION

DEFINITIONS OF DEATH AND THE SOCIOHISTORICAL CONTEXT OF DEATH

Definitions of Death

Box 13.1 Euthanasia

The Sociohistorical Context of Death

ATTITUDES TOWARD DEATH AT DIFFERENT POINTS IN THE LIFE CYCLE

FACING ONE'S OWN DEATH

Kübler-Ross's Psychological Stages of Dying

First Stage: Denial and Isolation

Second Stage: Anger

Third Stage: Bargaining

Fourth Stage: Depression

Fifth Stage: Acceptance

Pattison's Phases of the Living-Dying Interval

More About Coping with the Stress of Facing Death

Box 13.2 The Denial of Dying

I MAGINE *that you just found out your best friend has cancer and does not have very long to live.*
How would you feel? How would you react? What would you say to your friend? What could you do to help?

It is important to remember in relating to a dying person that he or she is still living. Your friend still has value as a human being and still has mental and physical needs. It is important to recognize that a dying person experiences many different emotions and goes through many different strategies trying to make sense out of what has happened and how he or she can face impending death. His or her emotions may include anger, hope, fear, curiosity, envy, apathy, relief, even anticipation; these emotions may move back and forth from mood to mood, and the dying person may experience several emotions simultaneously.

For some dying people, external accomplishments are not possible. In such instances, it may be important to focus your conversation more on internal and personal growth. Dying and death are scary matters, so don't be afraid to admit that you are afraid too. However, grief therapists always suggest that it is important to maintain hope for the dying person. Assure him that everything medically possible is being done to give him a chance to live longer. Assure him that you are there as long as he needs you. You can show such assurance by holding and touching him, by mourning and weeping with him, and by recognizing how hard it is for him to die.

Ask if there is anything you can do to make his life comfortable. Let him decide for himself, even for what seem to be very small choices, what he wants. You might offer to help get things in final order, such as helping him write messages and giving directions. If you are willing and able, offer to help survivors cope with their problems after the person has died. You can listen while they reminisce about happy times and fond feelings.

Many grief therapists suggest that if dying people show rage, do not make them ashamed of their anger. If they are severely depressed, it may not always be in their best interest to try to act cheerful around them. Above all else, do not make them feel guilty about anything. Be willing to share their feelings with them as openly and honestly as you can.

Avery Weisman's (1972) primary concern is that those who are close to dying people should not deal with them according to stereotypes about dying or aging people. When we categorize people, they become less than what they are or could be. The alternative is to look for the exceptions and treat every dying person as a unique individual. James Peterson (1980), commenting on the mental health of dying people, suggests:

> One must have looked into the greyness of the night that every man passes through and not flinch in order to hold the hands of those who are making the great transition. All of the defenses and denials we ascribe to others may in reality be projections of our own extinction. When one has achieved some composure about his own death, he may finally be able to listen creatively with responses and silences that help others have an appropriate death. (p. 941)

Later in the chapter we will comment further on counseling and communication with a dying person, including the extent to which the person should be told that he or she is going to die.

INTRODUCTION

The process of dying and the event of death are integral parts of the human life cycle. In this chapter we evaluate different ways in which death is defined, survey the sociohistorical context of death, and comment on the practice of euthanasia. In focusing on one's own death, we describe attitudes toward death at different points in the life cycle, noting in particular attitudes toward death and the dying process in the adult years. In our discussion of facing death, we present and critically evaluate Elisabeth Kübler-Ross's stages of dying, and then outline phases of dying suggested by E. Mansell Pattison. In regard to the important process of coping with impending death, we describe learned helplessness, perceived control, and denial. We continue to discuss communication with the dying patient, evaluating whether open communication about the person's death status should be the norm. Next we turn to the contexts in which people die—hospitals, hospices, and at home—and then discuss coping with the death of someone else, focusing heavily on the process of grief, including stages of grief, making sense out of the world, widows and widowers, and the impediments to successful grieving. Finally, we detail various forms of mourning and take a critical look at the funeral industry.

DEFINITIONS OF DEATH AND THE SOCIOHISTORICAL CONTEXT OF DEATH

How do we define death? When can we declare that someone is dead? And do we view death the same way at different points in history and in different cultures?

Definitions of Death

Ten years ago a person was considered dead when breathing stopped and no heartbeat could be heard. Rigor mortis, dilation of the pupils, and a relaxation of the sphincter muscle were labeled as other signs of death. In the 1980s, however, determining and defining death are not as simple. Modern medicine has contributed a neurological definition of death—**brain death**—in which all electrical activity of the brain has ceased for a specified period of time as determined by an electroencephalogram (EEG). A flat recording by an EEG suggests death, regardless of how vital other organs may seem under resuscitation (Aiken, 1978; Demsey, 1975). When a person is dying, the cells of the higher portion of the brain, which is the area of the brain most affected by oxygen deprivation, die within five to ten minutes. The lower brain centers, such as those that monitor heartbeat and respiration, die next. When the person's heart stops beating but is restored by resuscitation, a person who technically has died may be revived. Unfortunately, if the higher brain centers have been affected by oxygen deprivation, the individual is unlikely to recover his or her mental and motor capabilities, or if the individual does recover them, the impairment will be severe.

The ability of modern medicine to resuscitate a dying person complicates the definition of death. A heart that has stopped can be massaged or stimulated

Box 13.1
EUTHANASIA

The term **euthanasia** is mainly used to refer to the act of painlessly putting to death people who are suffering from incurable disease or severe disability—in this sense, it often is referred to as *mercy killing*. In debates concerning euthanasia, a distinction is often made between **active euthanasia,** in which death is induced by some positive action, such as the injection of a lethal dose of a drug, and **passive euthanasia,** in which death is induced by the withdrawal of some life-sustaining therapeutic effort, as when a respirator or heart-lung machine is turned off. Some experts argue that passive euthanasia is not a form of euthanasia at all but simply the process of letting nature take its course.

In most definitions of euthanasia reference is made to putting to death a person who is suffering a painful and incurable disease. However, the pain criterion is not always met. Consider for example the euthanasia conducted with severely deformed infants. In many instances these infants are not experiencing any pain at all. Adults who are in an irreversible coma are rarely in pain either. The case of Karen Quinlan has received a great deal of attention in recent years—despite being in an irreversible coma she was not experiencing a great deal of pain.

The President's Commission for the Study of Ethical Problems in Medicine and Biomedical and Behavioral Research has been holding hearings on the moral dilemmas posed by treating severely ill and handicapped patients. Mary Anne Warren, a philosopher, recently testified before the committee. She argued that where a child is not expected to live long, where that life would be unbearable, or where caring for the child would mean enormous personal and financial costs to the family or society, active euthanasia should be practiced.

Although there is now greater support for the legalization of euthanasia than there was in the past (Gallup, 1972), it is possible that no such legislation will be enacted in the foreseeable future.

electrically and can continue pumping indefinitely while the brain remains irreparably damaged. Numerous people with irreversible brain damage have been kept alive for years by intravenous feeding and artificial breathing devices. Such cases illustrate some of the ethical and legal questions posed as a result of our ability to resuscitate and prolong life. Some of the most common issues are among the following: Is a person dead when the brain dies but the heart is stimulated and continues pumping blood? Should people who are unconscious and have no chance for recovery be permitted to die—that is, should their treatment be terminated? Under what circumstances, if any, should euthanasia be practiced? Does a person have a right to die? Does a person have the right to take his or her own life? And who should be making such decisions? See box 13.1 for further discussion of euthanasia. Some adults make out a living will (see figure 13.1), which

To My Family, My Physician, My Lawyer and All Others Whom It May Concern

Death is as much a reality as birth, growth, maturity and old age—it is the one certainty of life. If the time comes when I can no longer take part in decisions for my own future, let this statement stand as an expression of my wishes and directions, while I am still of sound mind.

If at such a time the situation should arise in which there is no reasonable expectation of my recovery from extreme physical or mental disability, I direct that I be allowed to die and not be kept alive by medications, artificial means or "heroic measures". I do, however, ask that medication be mercifully administered to me to alleviate suffering even though this may shorten my remaining life.

This statement is made after careful consideration and is in accordance with my strong convictions and beliefs. I want the wishes and directions here expressed carried out to the extent permitted by law. Insofar as they are not legally enforceable, I hope that those to whom this Will is addressed will regard themselves as morally bound by these provisions.

(Optional specific provisions to be made in this space — see other side)

Optional proxy statement: I hereby designate _____
to make treatment decisions for me in the event I am comatose or otherwise unable to make such decisions for myself.

Optional Notarization: Signed_____

"Sworn and subscribed to   Date _____

before me this _____ day
                                                            Witness_____
of _____, 19_____."
                                                            Witness_____

_____
Notary Public
(seal)

Copies of this request have been given to _____

_____   _____

(Optional)   My Living Will is registered with Concern for Dying (No. _____)

Distributed by Concern for Dying, 250 West 57th Street, New York, NY 10107 (212) 246-6962

Figure 13.1   A living will.

specifies the conditions under which they wish to be considered biologically dead.

Not only has there been variation in the definition of death, but death may also be viewed differently depending upon the sociohistorical context.

The Sociohistorical Context of Death

In some cultures old people are killed or allowed to die when they are no longer productive. In many cultures—China and Japan, for example—the elderly are treated with great respect. There seems to have been an increased respect for the elderly in the United States since World War II (Tibbits, 1979). The ancient Greeks faced death as they faced life—openly and directly. To live a full life and die with glory was the prevailing attitude of the Greeks. People are more likely to be conscious of death in times of war, famine, and plague. While Americans are conditioned from early in life to live as though they were immortal, in much of the world this fiction cannot be maintained. Death crowds the streets of Calcutta in daily overdisplay, as it does the scrubby villages of Africa's Sahel. Children live with the ultimate toll of malnutrition and disease, mothers lose as many babies as survive into adulthood, and it is the rare family that remains intact for many years. Even in peasant areas where life is better and health and maturity may be reasonable expectations, the presence of dying people in the house, the large attendance at funerals, and the daily contact with aging people prepare the young for the fact of death and provide them with information about how to die. By contrast, in the United States it is not uncommon to reach maturity without ever having seen someone die (Foster & Anderson, 1978).

Most societies throughout history, and most cultures today, have some philosophical or religious belief system or ritual that deals with death. For example, elderly Eskimos in Greenland who no longer can contribute to their society may walk off alone never to be seen again or they may be given a departure ceremony at which they are honored, then ritually killed. Following is a description of such a ceremony (Freuchen, 1961):

> In some tribes, an old man wants his oldest son or favorite daughter to be the one to put the string around his neck and hoist him to his death. This was always done at the height of the party where good things were being eaten, where everyone—including the one who was about to die—felt happy and gay, and which would end with the angakok conjuring and dancing to chase out the evil spirits. At the end of his performance, he would give a special rope made of seal and walrus skin to the "executioner" who then placed it over the beam of the roof of the house and fastened it around the neck of the old man. Then the two rubbed noses, and the young man pulled the rope. Everybody in the house either helped or sat on the rope so as to have the honor of bringing the old suffering one to the Happy Hunting Grounds where there would always be light and plenty of game of all kinds. (pp. 194–195)

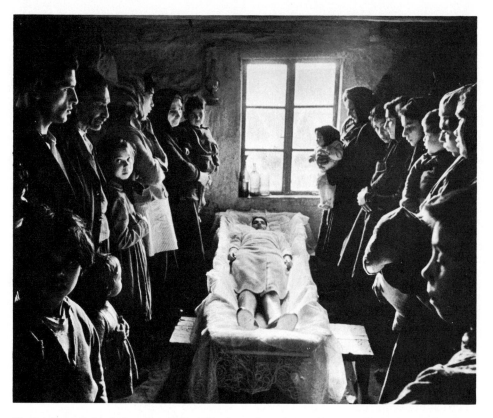

Most cultures today have some philosophical or religious belief system that deals with death.

In most societies death is not viewed as the end of existence—though the physical body has died, the spiritual body is believed to live on. This religious perspective is also favored by more Americans than a view suggesting that there is no continuing spiritual existence (Kalish & Reynolds, 1976).

Cultural variations in perceptions of and reactions to death include those of the Gond culture in India and the Tanala culture of Madagascar. The Gond believe that death is caused by magic and demons, and the Tanala think that death occurs for natural reasons. Possibly because of their beliefs about death, the Gond show a much angrier and less peaceful orientation toward the death of one of their members than the Tanala do. Other cultural variations in attitudes toward death include beliefs about reincarnation, which is an important aspect of the religions of Hinduism and Buddhism.

Perceptions of death vary and reflect diverse values and philosophies. Death may be seen as a punishment for one's sins, an act of atonement, or a judgment of a just God. For some, death means loneliness; for others, death is a cruel interruption of the quest for happiness. For still others, death represents redemption, a relief from the trials and tribulations of the earthly world. Some embrace death and welcome it; others abhor and fear it. For those who welcome it, death may be seen as the fitting end to a fulfilled life. From this perspective, how we depart from earth is influenced by how we have lived. In the words of Leonardo da Vinci, death should come to a person after a full life just as sleep comes after a hard day's work.

Generally speaking, people in the United States often react to death with denial and avoidance. Such denial can take various forms:

The tendency of the funeral industry to gloss over death and fashion greater life-like qualities in the dead.

The adoption of euphemistic language for death, such as *exiting, passing on, never say die,* and *good for life,* which implies forever.

The persistent search for the fountain of youth.

The rejection and isolation of the aged who may remind us of death.

The adoption of the concept of a pleasant and rewarding afterlife, thus suggesting that we are immortal.

Emphasis of the medical community on the prolongation of biological life rather than on the diminishment of human suffering.

Our failure to discuss death with our children.

In many ways, then, we are deathavoiders and deathdeniers. But ultimately we do face death—others' and our own. Next, we review attitudes toward death across the life cycle.

ATTITUDES TOWARD DEATH AT DIFFERENT POINTS IN THE LIFE CYCLE

Children who are two or three years of age rarely get upset by the sight of a dead animal or by being told that a person has died. Children at this age generally have no idea what death really means. They often confuse death with sleep, or they ask in a puzzled way, "Why doesn't it move?"

Though children vary somewhat in the age at which they begin to understand death, the limitations of preoperational thought often make it difficult for a child to comprehend the meaning of death before the age of seven or eight. Young children, unfortunately, may blame themselves for events such as divorce and death, illogically reasoning that the event may have developed because they disobeyed the person who died. Furthermore, children under the age of six rarely perceive that death is universal, inevitable, and final. Instead, young children usually think that only people who want to die, or who are bad or careless, actually do die. Children at this age believe that the dead can be returned to life. Sometime between the ages of five and seven, however, these ideas give way to a more realistic perception of death.

Maria Nagy (1948) conducted the first investigation of children's attitudes toward death. She found that most children aged three to five denied the existence of death, most between the ages of six and nine believed that death exists but only happens to some people, and most children nine years or older recognized the finality and universality of death. In discussing death with children, most psychologists recognize that honesty is the best strategy rather than treating the concept as unmentionable. However, many of us have grown up in a society where death is rarely discussed. In one investigation that surveyed the attitudes of 30,000 young adults, more than 30 percent said they could not recall any discussion of death during their childhoods; and an equal number said that while death was discussed, the discussion took place in an uncomfortable atmosphere (Shneidman, 1973). In this investigation the majority of young people reported that they initially became aware of death sometime between the ages of five and ten. Almost one of every two respondents said that the death of a grandparent represented their first personal confrontation with death.

During adolescence, the prospect of death, like the prospect of aging, is often regarded as a notion that is so remote that it doesn't have much relevance. Death is often avoided, glossed over, kidded about, neutralized, and controlled by a cool, spectator-like orientation. Such a perspective is typical of the self-conscious thought of the adolescent. Some adolescents, though, do show a concern about death, both in the sense of trying to fathom its meaning and nature and in the sense of confronting the actual prospect of their own demise (Kastenbaum, 1969).

Our discussion of middle adulthood indicated that middle age is a time when people often begin to think about how much time is left in their life rather than what has gone before. As a result, they are more likely than their young adult counterparts to begin thinking about the finality of their own life. In one national survey middle-aged adults had more fear of death and were more likely than individuals in early or late adulthood to believe that death always comes too soon (Riley, 1970). In the same survey people in late adulthood were generally less frightened by death, thought about it more, and talked with others about it more than did other aged adults.

What are your feelings about your own death? Does it interest you? Does it scare you? Next we explore the topic of facing one's own death.

FACING ONE'S OWN DEATH

In his book *The Sane Society,* Erich Fromm comments, "Man is the only animal that finds his own existence a problem which he has to solve and from which he cannot escape. In the same sense man is the only animal who knows he must die" (p. 23). Over the centuries philosophers, theologians, poets, and psychologists have attempted to explain the phenomenon of death and have theorized about why all people must die and whether death is the end or there is yet another life after the one on earth.

We may never know the answers to many questions about death, but several investigations shed some light on our attitudes toward our own death. Most dying people want an opportunity to make some decisions regarding their own life and death. Some people want to complete unfinished business; they want time to resolve problems and conflicts and to put their affairs in order (Kübler-Ross, 1974).

In this section we look at the well-known psychological stages of dying developed by Elisabeth Kübler-Ross and then see what dying phases are. Because facing death is stressful, we also evaluate the nature of several coping devices.

Kübler-Ross's Psychological Stages of Dying

Elisabeth Kübler-Ross (1969) has divided the behavior of dying patients into five stages. It should be emphasized that these stages do not always follow one another in the precise order listed and the stages often overlap. Furthermore, patients sometimes go back and forth from one stage to another.

First Stage: Denial and Isolation
The most common initial reaction to terminal illness is one of **denial and isolation.** Often the dying person responds with such thoughts as, "No, it can't be me. It's not possible." However, denial is usually only a temporary defense and is eventually replaced with acceptance when the person is confronted with such matters as financial considerations, unfinished business, and worry about surviving family members.

Second Stage: Anger
When the dying person recognizes that denial can no longer be maintained, it often gives way to feelings of **anger,** resentment, rage, and envy. Now the person's question becomes, "Why me?" At this point, the individual becomes increasingly difficult to care for as anger often becomes displaced and projected onto physicians, nurses, hospital staff, family members, and even God. The realization of loss is great, and those who symbolize life, energy, and competent functioning are particularly salient targets of the terminally ill person's resentment and jealousy.

Third Stage: Bargaining
According to Kübler-Ross, in the third stage the dying person develops the hope that death can somehow be postponed or delayed. Some people enter into a brief period of **bargaining** or negotiation—often with God—as they try to delay their death. Psychologically, these people are now saying, "Yes, me, but . . ." In exchange for a few more days, weeks, months of life, they promise to lead a reformed life dedicated to God or to the service of others.

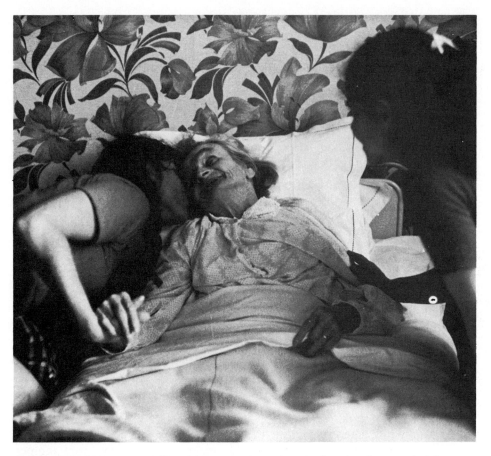

Most dying persons want to talk with someone about their death and make some decisions regarding it.

Fourth Stage: Depression

As the dying person comes to accept the certainty of death, she or he often enters a period of **depression** or preparatory grief, becoming very silent, refusing visitors, and spending much of the time crying or grieving. Such behavior should be viewed as normal in this circumstance and is actually an effort to disconnect the self from all love objects. Attempts to cheer up the individual at this stage should be discouraged, according to Kübler-Ross, because the dying person has a real need to contemplate her or his impending death.

Fifth Stage: Acceptance

If the individual has progressed through the first four stages, she or he usually experiences a final stage, which is characterized by a sense of peace, a unique acceptance of one's fate, and a desire to be left alone. This fifth, **acceptance** stage of the dying process is often devoid of feelings—physical pain and discomfort are often absent. Kübler-Ross describes this period as the end of the struggle, the final resting stage before undertaking a long journey.

It is important to point out that no one has been able to confirm that people indeed go through the stages in the order that Kübler-Ross has suggested (e.g., Schulz & Alderman, 1974; Shneidman, 1973). Kübler-Ross herself feels that she has been misread, saying that she never intended the stages to be an invariant set of steps toward death. Even though Kübler-Ross (1974) recognizes the importance of individual variation in how people face death, she still believes that the optimal way to face it is in the sequence she has proposed.

Some people struggle to the very end, desperately trying to hang onto their lives. In these cases acceptance of death never comes. Some psychologists believe that the harder people fight to avoid the inevitable death they face and the more they deny it, the more difficulty they will have in dying peacefully and in a dignified way; other psychologists argue that not confronting death until the very end may be adaptive for some people (Lifton, 1977; Shneidman, 1973). According to Richard Kalish (1981),

> Different people die in different ways and experience a variety of feelings and emotions during the process: hope, fear, curiosity, envy, apathy, relief, even anticipation. And they appear to move back and forth from mood to mood; sometimes the moods follow each other in short order; other times two moods are present in the dying person simultaneously. (p. 186)

Pattison's Phases of the Living-Dying Interval

The *trajectory of life* is defined by E. Mansell Pattison (1977) as our anticipated life span and the plan we make for the way we will live out our life. When a circumstance develops through the course of injury or illness, a disruption in our life trajectory occurs because we perceive that we are likely to die much sooner than we had anticipated. Pattison says that between the time we discover that we will die sooner than we had thought and the time we actually die we are in what he calls the **living-dying interval,** which is characterized by three phases of development: acute, chronic, and terminal. The goal of those who treat individuals in the living-dying interval is to assist them in coping with the first, or acute, phase, help them to live as reasonably as possible through the second, or chronic, phase, and move them into the third, or terminal, phase. (See figure 13.2.)

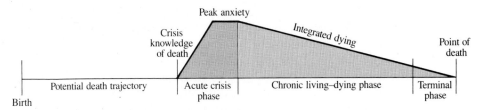

Figure 13.2   Acute, chronic, and terminal phases of the dying process. (From the book *The Experience of Dying* by E. Mansell Pattison. © 1977 by Prentice-Hall, Inc. Published by Prentice-Hall, Inc., Englewood Cliffs, N.J. 07632)

In the **acute phase,** individuals face probably the most severe crisis in their lives—the fact that they will die sooner than they had thought and will not get to accomplish everything they had hoped to. People often feel immobilized, have very high levels of anxiety, and call into play a number of defense mechanisms to deal with the acute fear and stress that they are undergoing. In this phase people need a great deal of emotional support from others and need to be helped to deal rationally with the fact that they are going to die.

In the **chronic phase,** Pattison believes that individuals begin to confront their fear of dying. Such fears as loneliness, suffering, and the unknown often surface and must be dealt with. Health professionals can assist dying people by helping them put life in perspective and working through some of the defense mechanisms that surfaced earlier.

In the **terminal phase,** individuals begin to withdraw as their hope for getting better gives way to the realization that they are probably going to get worse. At this point they recognize and accept the finality of approaching death.

Just as Kübler-Ross's stages are not fixed and invariant, Pattison's dying phases do not represent the trajectory every individual goes through. Next we focus more extensively on the nature of the coping process when we face death, including a discussion of the concepts of learned helplessness, perceived control, and denial.

More About Coping with the Stress of Facing Death

Even though the theories of Kübler-Ross and Pattison sensitize us to some of the important aspects of the dying process, there is much more to consider in understanding the complex way in which people cope effectively or ineffectively with the stress of facing death. As Edwin Shneidman (1973) has commented, at any one moment there are a number of emotions that may wax and wane; hope, disbelief, bewilderment, anger, and acceptance may come and go as people attempt to make sense out of what is happening to them.

One concept that may contribute to our understanding of how some people face death is **learned helplessness.** People faced with the threat of pain naturally act to avoid or escape the aversive circumstances. But what happens when people are forced to face uncontrollable events, like death? When they learn that a negative or traumatic outcome is beyond their control, a state of learned helplessness may develop. In this situation, people may stop responding altogether, give up, and become apathetic, despondent, and depressed.

Learned helplessness was initially documented in experimentation with animals (e.g., Seligman, 1975), but it has been observed in humans as well (Abramson, Seligman, & Teasdale, 1978). The overall results indicate that after people experience uncontrollable negative events they may stop future efforts to cope and show helplessness. When such circumstances continue they sense virtually the opposite of mastery and efficacy that come from experiences in which they are confident that they can cope with the problems in their lives. Thus as result of learned helplessness, the person who faces death may become apathetic; sometimes this is referred to as the *giving-up syndrome.*

By contrast, when people are led to believe that they *can* influence and control events—such as prolonging their lives—they often become more alert and sometimes more cheerful. Such **perceived control** may even prolong a person's life. In one demonstration of the importance of perceived control, a group of institutionalized elderly adults were provided with the opportunities to make decisions actively and to be personally responsible for something outside of themselves (a plant). The elderly adults soon began to act more competently and to feel better than those in groups who were left in the usual passive institutional routine and for whom all of the decisions were made by the staff. Eighteen months later a follow-up revealed that only half as many of the elderly had died in the active mastery group as in the passive mastery groups (Rodin & Langer, 1977). The time of death, then, may be influenced by the extent to which the dying individual is given choices and perceives that he or she has some control over the environment (Seligman, 1975).

It may be that denial of approaching death may work together with perceived control over one's environment to represent one of the most adaptive coping strategies. In one investigation, most patients went on denying death at least part of the time right up until the time that they died (Hinton, 1967). Life without hope represents learned helplessness in its most extreme form. Denial, when combined with efforts at developing perceived control over life and death, may be an adaptive process. More about the denial process appears in box 13.2.

Next we look at the important topic of counseling and communication with a dying person and at some of the contexts in which people die, including hospitals, hospices, and at home.

Box 13.2
THE DENIAL OF DYING

Denial can be a very important protective mechanism that enables people to cope with the torturous feeling that they are going to die. People who are dying can either deny the existence of information about their impending death or they can reinterpret the meaning of the information to avoid its negative implications. There may be three forms of denial (Weisman, 1972). The first involves the denial of *facts.* For example, a woman who has been told by her physician that a scheduled operation is for cancer, subsequently believes that the operation is for a benign tumor. The second form of denial involves *implications.* A man accepts the fact that he has a disease but denies that it will end in death. A third form of denial involves *extinction,* which is limited to people who accept a diagnosis and its implications but still act as if they were going to live through the ordeal. This last form of denial does not apply to people whose deep religious convictions include some form of belief in immortality.

Another classification of denial includes the categories brittle and adaptive. *Brittle* denial involves observed anxiety and agitation. The individual will often reject attempts to improve his or her psychological adaptation to impending death. However, *adaptive* denial occurs when the individual decides not to dwell on this aspect of his or her life but emphasizes his or her strengths and opportunities. Adaptive deniers want help and support. Such adaptive denial fits well with the ideas of perceived control and the elimination of learned helplessness.

In discussing the role of denial Richard Kalish (1981) concluded that denial can be adaptive, maladaptive, or even both at the same time. One can call on denial to avoid the destructive impact of shock by delaying the necessity of dealing with one's death. Further, denial can function to insulate a person from coping with intense feelings of anger and hurt, emotions that may intrude on other behaviors and feelings because they are so intense. Denial is not good or bad. An evaluation of its adaptive qualities needs to be made on an individual basis.

COMMUNICATING WITH THE DYING PERSON AND THE CONTEXTS IN WHICH PEOPLE DIE

In efforts to help the dying person increasing emphasis is being placed on effective communication and the context in which the person will die.

Open awareness with friends and relatives may benefit the dying person.

Communicating with the Dying Person

It is generally agreed that the situation is optimal when the dying person knows he is dying, significant others in his world know that he is dying, and they can interact with each other on the basis of this mutual knowledge. Research has consistently revealed that people believe a dying person has the right to know (Kalish & Reynolds, 1976).

Richard Kalish (1981) describes the advantages of an open-awareness context for the dying person:

He can close his life in accord with his own ideas about proper dying.

He often can complete some plans and projects, can make arrangements for survivors, and can participate in decisions about a funeral and burial.

He has the opportunity to reminisce, to converse with others who have been important in his life, and to end life conscious of what life has been like.

He has more understanding of what is happening within his body and of what the medical staff are doing to him.

It may be easier to die when people we love and like can converse freely with us about what is happening to us, even if it entails considerable sadness. Kalish (1981) describes a circumstance in which open communication with a dying person seemed beneficial:

> My eighty-one-year-old aunt was extremely ill and had been for two years; the indications were that she would probably not live for many more weeks. My home was eight hundred miles away, but I was able to get to visit her and my uncle for a couple of days. It bothered me to see her hooked into a machine that held her life; the ugly wig she had worn during the past couple of years had been discarded, and there were only a few wisps of hair left, but at least they were hers, her teeth had been placed in the drawer by her bed since she couldn't take solid food and at this point she was not concerned about how she looked.
>
> My uncle and I were in her room talking with her as she moved in and out of awareness. He was standing at the foot of the bed and I was sitting next to her, holding her hand. He began to talk to her about coming to visit me as soon as she could get up and around again, probably next summer. I noticed that she tuned his comments out. Then I found a pretext to get him out of the room.
>
> When we were alone, I stood up and kissed her. I'd like to say that it was easy, but it really wasn't. I told her that I loved her, and I realized that I had never said that to her before, hadn't even thought about it, hadn't even consciously thought that I loved her. I just . . . loved her.
>
> Then I said, "Bea I have to leave now. I may never see you again, and I want you to know how much I love you." Her eyes were closed and she was breathing strangely, but she winced at my words, and I became frightened that I'd said too much, so I hesitated. "Well, I hope that I'll see you again, but I might not." And I left.
>
> She died before I could visit again, and I always wondered whether I should have said what I did, but it seemed important to say it. Even if it pained her to hear me, she knew it was true, and she had not shrunk from painful situations before. It had been easy for me over many years to talk and write about death and dying, but it was very difficult for me to be in the situation where someone I loved was dying. I did what I have told other people to do, and it wasn't at all natural—I had to force myself. But when I heard, three weeks later, that she had died, I considered myself fortunate to have had the chance to be with her before she died and to have been both caring and honest. (p. 172)

In addition to considering the nature of communication about the dying process to the person who is dying, it also is important to look at other aspects of communicating with and counseling the dying person. Some experts believe that therapy and communication with dying people should not focus on mental pathology or preparation for death but should instead emphasize areas of the person's strengths and preparation for the remainder of his or her life (LeShan, 1969).

For the dying person, external accomplishments often are not possible. In these instances, the focus of communication should be directed more at internal and personal growth. It is important to recognize that a caring relationship is a very important aspect of the dying person's life and that such caring does not have to come from a mental health professional; a concerned nurse, an attentive physician, an interested chaplain, a sensitive spouse or friend, all provide an important resource for the dying person.

Not only are people important to the dying person, but the context in which the person dies can contribute to making the remainder of his or her life as humane, peaceful, and enjoyable as possible.

Hospitals, Hospices, and Dying at Home

Most deaths in the United States occur in a hospital; a smaller number occur in other institutions such as nursing homes and board-and-care centers (Hinton, 1979). Hospitals offer a number of advantages to the dying person: professional staff members are readily available, medical equipment is present, and the technology of medicine is likely to be the best available. Yet a hospital may not be the most efficient location for the dying person to enjoy intimate relationships or retain autonomy. As a consequence, most people say that they would rather die at home (Kalish & Reynolds, 1976). However, many people feel that they will be a burden at home, that there is limited space there, and that dying at home may alter previous role relationships, such as being cared for by one's children. People who are facing death also worry about the competency and availability of emergency medical treatment if they remain at home.

In considering the relative strengths and weaknesses of hospital versus home care for the dying, it is important to recognize that there is often a third context in which the dying person can live the remainder of his or her life—the **hospice,** which combines institutional care and home care and adds something of its own as well. Many experts on the care of the dying view the hospice as an innovative and humanistic program for the care of the terminally ill.

The hospice is a humanized institution with a commitment to making the end of life as free from pain, anxiety, and depression as possible as opposed to a hospital where the goals are to cure illness and prolong life. The hospice movement began in the late 1960s in London when a new kind of medical institution, St. Christopher's Hospice, opened. Little effort is made to prolong life at St. Christopher's—there are no heart-lung machines and intensive care unit, for example. A primary goal is to bring pain under control and to help the dying patient face death in a psychologically healthy way. One aspect of the hospice orientation toward the dying patient is to keep the person an important part of his or her family. Every effort is made to make the members of the family welcome at the hospice. It is believed that such a strategy is not only beneficial to the dying patient but that it also helps the family to feel less guilt after the death of a family member (Hinton, 1972).

The hospice movement is growing rapidly in the United States. By 1978 there were a dozen hospice operations and 170 hospice groups in various stages of development (Lack & Buckingham, 1978). Hospice advocates point out that it is possible to control terminal pain for almost everyone and that it is possible to create an environment for the patient far superior to that found in most hospitals.

The dying process and death affect others as well. Next we look at the effects of death and dying on significant others.

COPING WITH THE DEATH OF SOMEONE ELSE

Loss can come in many forms in our lives—divorce, the death of a pet, a job, for example—but no loss is greater than the loss that comes through the death of someone we love and care for, such as a parent, sibling, spouse, child, relative, or friend. In the life stress ratings developed by Holmes & Rahe (1967), death of a spouse is given the highest number.

Loss can lead to bereavement, grief, and mourning. **Bereavement** is a state that involves loss and occurs when something or someone we care about is taken away from us. **Grief** indicates the sorrow, anger, guilt, and confusion that often accompany a loss or bereavement. It is generally accepted that the process of grieving is necessary for full recovery from the loss of a significant person in our life, although grieving involves pain and suffering. **Mourning** is the overt, behavioral expression of grief and bereavement. Mourning is heavily influenced by cultural standards—the nature of the funeral, how we dress, whether we say prayers or not, and so forth.

Grief

Just as stages of dying have been proposed, so have several stages of grieving been suggested. One view indicates that we go through three stages of grief after we lose someone we love and care about very much: shock, despair, and recovery (Averill, 1968). Another perspective argues that we go through four stages: numbness, pining, depression, and recovery (Parkes, 1972).

In the first view of grief, at stage one the survivor feels shock, disbelief, and numbness and often weeps or becomes easily agitated. This stage often occurs soon after the death and usually lasts from one to three days. It is not unlike the denial and anger stages the dying person goes through according to Kübler-Ross.

At stage two there is painful longing for the dead, memories and visual images of the deceased, sadness, insomnia, irritability, and restlessness. Beginning not long after the death, this stage often peaks in the second to fourth weeks following the death and may subside after several months but can persist for one or two years. Elements of bargaining for the return of the deceased person as well as depression may be detected, again corresponding to one of Kübler-Ross's stages of dying.

Stage three usually appears within a year after the death. Analogous to the acceptance stage of dying, this grief-resolution phase is marked by a resumption of ordinary activities, a greater likelihood that the deceased will be recalled with pleasant memories, and the establishment of new relationships with others.

However, just as we found that Kübler-Ross's stages of dying are not invariant and that people do not have to go through them in the order she suggests to adapt effectively, the same can be said for the stages of grief. It may be more facilitative to conceive of grief as a process and to recognize that what is observed early in the process may differ substantially from what is seen later (Parkes, 1972). Furthermore, most people underestimate the time it takes to move from the shock of death to full recovery. Though many people return to what may seem to be normal functioning in the course of several days or several weeks, grieving may go on for months, although over time its intensity usually diminishes. A reminder of the dead person or a stressful time later in life may produce feelings of grief even several years later. Some experts on grief believe that reasonable recovery from the loss of an attachment figure takes at least one year, and two years is not unusual (Kalish, 1981).

Grief can be felt in many ways. One of the most common is called grief pangs, which include somatic distress that occurs in waves lasting from twenty minutes to an hour, such as a tight feeling in the throat, choking with shortness of breath, need to sigh, empty feeling in the stomach, lack of physical strength, tension, sobbing, and crying (Lindemann, 1944; Parkes, 1964). The sadness and sorrow that people experience as part of the grieving process can be intense enough to classify the grieving individual as in a state of depression.

Not only is denial a part of the dying process for the person who is dying, but those who are attached to a dead person often engage in a process of denial as well. Searching also seems to be part of the grief process. Some widows say that they "search" for their dead husbands everywhere, which is a normal part of the pining process. It is a restless kind of searching that involves preoccupation of thought about the deceased. Among the other emotional reactions in the grieving process are relief, guilt, and anger.

Making Sense Out of the World
One of the most important aspects of grieving is that it stimulates many people to strive to make sense of their world. This process is described by Richard Kalish (1981):

> A common occurrence during the grieving period is to go over again and again, all the events that led up to the death. This can become a virtual preoccupation with some individuals, but almost all of us partake of it to some extent. In the days and weeks after the death, the closest family members will share experiences with each other—sometimes providing new information and insights into the person who died, sometimes reminiscing over familiar experiences.

Each person offers his or her own piece of the puzzle of death. "When I saw him last Saturday, he looked as though he were rallying." "Yes, but the next morning, the nurse told me he had had a bad night." "Do you think it might have had something to do with his sister's illness?" "I doubt it, but I heard from an aide that he fell going to the bathroom that morning." "That explains that bruise on his elbow." "No wonder he told me that he was angry because he couldn't seem to do anything right." And so it goes, the attempt to understand why someone who was rallying on Saturday was dead on Wednesday.

When a death is caused by an accident or a disaster, the effort to make sense of it is pursued more vigorously. As added pieces of news come trickling in, they are integrated into the puzzle. The bereaved want to put the death into a perspective that they can understand—divine intervention, a curse from a neighboring tribe, or a logical sequence of cause and effect, or whatever it may be.

In no case has this effort been more evident than in the constant review of the death of President John F. Kennedy. Although some two decades have passed since his assassination, the events leading up to the killing are regularly dragged into public view. The presumed issues—whether or not there was a conspiracy and, if so, whether it was from the political left or the political right—strike me as of little importance today. Rather, we are still trying to make sense of the entire event. That the death was the act of one unstable man working alone strikes many people as impossible. How could such an absurd set of circumstances destroy such a powerful man? It is easier to believe that an intricate conspiracy by the CIA or by the Communist Party was the basis for the killing.

Eventually each of us finds an adequate "story of the dying and death"—of John Kennedy or of our father or of a friend. Versions of the death may differ—whether the physician really did all she could to save the patient, whether Aunt Bella showed up frequently at the hospital or not, whether the operation succeeded or didn't quite succeed, whether father was ready to die or would have lived longer if possible— but each person's version satisfies him, and that version, with slight modifications, becomes the official version for the teller.

The vestiges of grief, however, remain much longer than a few years, probably forever. A fifty-year-old biologist came in for therapy following a very upsetting divorce proceeding. During the fourteenth session, she began to speak for the first time about her father, who had died nearly thirty years earlier; within a few minutes, the client was sobbing deeply, as she recalled the pain of losing her father. It wasn't that she had refrained from appropriate grieving at the time her father had died; rather the grief was so great that there was still more that needed expression.

The stages of dying eventually end, but the stages of grieving do not. Even full recovery does not mean that all sense of loss, all sense of sadness and deprivation, all sense of anger and guilt have ended. Nor, as Victor Marshall has pointed out, should we wish this to be the case. (personal communication, 1979, p. 227–228)

Widows and Widowers

The death of a spouse is among the most intense losses that one can experience. One investigation of 4,500 widowers over the age of fifty-four revealed a major increase in their death rate in the six months following bereavement. Later the death rate returned to normal (Young, Benjamin, & Wallis, 1963). Other researchers have documented that widowed individuals experience more psychological and physical symptoms than married individuals—persisting fears, insomnia, dizziness, chest pains, fainting spells, and so forth (e.g., Maddison & Viola, 1968; Parkes, 1964). These effects may be caused by fatigue, poor diet, and social restrictions, or they may be due to the depression that often accompanies bereavement, causing a lowering of resistance to disease (Schulz, 1978).

Kinds of Death That Make It Difficult for the Bereaved to Resolve Their Grief

Following are some kinds of death that make it difficult for people to resolve their grief (Kalish, 1981):

Suicides or deaths due to self-neglect and carelessness

Untimely deaths, such as deaths of young people, people just married, or people about to achieve something significant

Deaths that required the bereaved person to care for the dying person in a manner that proved to be distressing

Deaths that the bereaved person has some reason to believe he or she was partly or fully responsible for, such as a child's drowning in a swimming pool

Homicides

Unconfirmed death with no body found

Other sudden and unexpected deaths

Deaths so drawn out over time that the survivors become impatient for death to occur

Next we look at different forms of mourning and the nature of the funeral in our society.

Forms of Mourning and the Funeral

There are many cultural differences in mourning. For example, **suttee** is the optional Hindu practice of burning a dead man's widow to increase his family's prestige and firmly establish an image of her in his memory (Kroeber, 1948). In some cultures a ceremonial meal is held, and in others a black armband is worn for one year following a death. According to Kalish and Reynolds (1976), there is also evidence that in the United States certain aspects of mourning vary from one ethnic group to another (see table 13.1).

Table 13.1

RESPONSES OF 434 PERSONS IN THE GREATER LOS ANGELES AREA REGARDING THE LENGTH OF TIME FOLLOWING THE DEATH OF SPOUSE BEFORE IT WOULD BE APPROPRIATE FOR A PERSON OF RESPONDENT'S AGE, SEX, AND ETHNICITY TO DO EACH OF THE INDICATED ACTIONS

	Percent of Black Americans	*Percent of Japanese Americans*	*Percent of Mexican Americans*	*Percent of "Anglo" Americans*
To remarry				
Unimportant to wait	34	14	22	26
1 week–6 months	15	3	1	23
1 year	25	30	38	34
2 years	11	26	20	11
Other (including never; depends)	16	28	19	7
To stop wearing black				
Unimportant to wait	62	42	52	53
1 day–4 months	24	26	11	31
6 months +	11	21	35	6
Other/depends	4	11	3	11
To return to his/her place of employment				
Unimportant to wait	39	22	27	47
1 day–1 week	39	28	37	35
1 month +	17	35	27	9
Other/depends	6	16	9	10
To start going out with other men/women				
Unimportant to wait	30	17	17	25
1 week–1 month	14	8	4	9
6 months	24	22	22	29
1 year +	11	34	40	21
Other/depends	21	19	18	17
What do you feel is the fewest number of times he/she would visit his/her spouse's grave during the first year—not counting the burial service?				
Unimportant to do	39	7	11	35
1–2 times	32	18	19	11
3–5 times	16	18	12	18
6 + times	13	58	59	35
(Don't know, etc.)	(11)	(6)	(3)	(19)
What do you feel is the fewest number of times he/she should visit his/her spouse's grave during the fifth year after the death?				
Unimportant to do	52	8	20	43
1–2 times	30	17	39	35
3–5 times	9	16	22	15
6 + times	10	30	18	6
(Don't know, etc.)	(14)	(6)	(4)	(22)

Source: Kalish & Reynolds, 1976.

The funeral is an important aspect of the mourning process in many cultures. One consideration has to do with what happens to the body. In the United States most bodies are placed in caskets under the earth or in mausoleums. Approximately 9 percent are cremated (Kalish, 1981). Most people who are cremated are content with having their ashes spread in the garden of a crematorium, but some wish their ashes to be taken to specific locations. A viewing of the body occurs following approximately 75 percent of the deaths in the United States (Raether & Slater, 1974).

Some controversy has developed with regard to funerals in recent years. Funeral directors and their supporters argue that the funeral provides a form of closure to the relationship with the deceased, especially when there is an open casket. Their dissenters, however, stress that funeral directors are just trying to make money and, further, that the art of embalming is grotesque.

One way to avoid the exploitation that may occur because bereavement may make one vulnerable to more expensive funeral arrangements is to purchase them in advance. However, many of us do not follow this procedure. In one survey only 24 percent of those over the age of sixty had made any funeral arrangements (Kalish & Reynolds, 1976). Therefore, most Americans face the expenses of a funeral and body disposition only after a family member has died. The time directly after the death is usually marked by many pressures, emotional distress, diluted bargaining power, and lack of experience in making informed and rational decisions. Unfortunately, a sense of guilt on the part of some survivors, their reluctance to ask about various options, and their desire to bury their loved one in style often increase the likelihood of purchasing unnecessary services and merchandise. It has been argued by some federal officials that the funeral industry has shrouded its business in secrecy and that it is therefore very important for consumers to aggressively seek out information, especially price information, in order to make an informed decision (Federal Trade Commission, 1975).

Summary

Although death is inevitable, it has often been a taboo topic in our culture. It may seem simple to determine when an individual has died, but recent medical advances have complicated the determination. For example, brain death can occur even though critical organs like the heart and lungs continue functioning. This complication has led to ethical questions of whether we ought to practice euthanasia and whether we should prolong people's lives. It is important to consider the sociohistorical context of death. Our culture shows more avoidance and denial of death than do most cultures.

Because of the limitation of preoperational thought, it is difficult for the preschool child to comprehend death. Early in the elementary school years children may still not understand the universality of death, although they do begin to understand its permanence. At some point before adolescence, most children do understand both the finality and universality of death. Adolescents often react to death in a superficial way, possibly because of the self-preoccupation that characterizes many adolescents. Young adults also show little concern about death, but during middle adulthood people begin to show considerably more interest in it, often being as concerned, or in some cases more concerned, about death than people in late adulthood.

Elisabeth Kübler-Ross has suggested five psychological stages of dying: denial and isolation, anger, bargaining, depression, and acceptance. Researchers have been unable to verify that dying people go through the stages in the sequence prescribed, however, Kübler-Ross's main contribution involves her humanization of the dying process. E. Mansell Pattison has suggested three phases of what he calls the living-dying interval: acute, chronic, and terminal. However, the dying process involves much more than stages or phases. Learned helplessness, perceived control, and denial are important aspects of the coping process for the dying person. If learned helplessness is detected, perceived control should be encouraged. Denial is not good or bad; for many dying people adaptive denial may be helpful.

An open system of communication with the dying is often the best strategy. Above all we should avoid stereotypes about dying and the aged and consider the dying person as a unique individual, focusing on his or her strengths and opportunities rather than death. For dying people with limited ability to participate in their environment, it may be best to stress inner and personal growth. The contexts in which people die are also important. Hospitals have medical expertise and equipment, but more intimacy and autonomy is usually possible at home. An alternative is the hospice, a humanized institution that many experts believe offers the best of home and hospital benefits. The hospice movement began in the 1960s and continues to expand.

The loss of someone we are attached to is among the most stressful life events. Coping with someone else's death has been described in terms of bereavement—the state of loss—and mourning—the overt, behavioral expression of bereavement and grief. Just as stages of dying have been proposed, so have stages of grief been set forth—shock, despair, and recovery being one set of stages. However, people do not have to go through the stages in order to adaptively cope with grief. One of the most common ways of experiencing grief is through grief pangs. Denial is a part of the grief process, just as it is a part of the dying process. One aspect of the grief process involves making sense out of the world and trying to solve the puzzle of death. One of the most severe grieving processes occurs when a spouse dies. Widowed individuals may incur illness and even have an increased likelihood of dying themselves.

Mourning takes many forms, depending on the culture and subculture. In the United States the mourning process usually involves a funeral, which is followed by burial or cremation. In recent years controversy about the funeral industry has increased. One way to avoid irrational decisions in a time of stress is to make funeral arrangements in advance. However, even after the age of sixty, a majority of people do not do this.

Review Questions

1. Do you believe that euthanasia should be practiced? Explain.
2. Discuss the sociohistorical contexts of death.
3. What are common attitudes about death in young childhood, adolescence, and early, middle, and late adulthood?
4. Describe and critically evaluate Kübler-Ross's five psychological stages of dying.
5. Describe how learned helplessness, perceived control, and denial can affect dying people.
6. What are some of the best strategies for communicating with a dying person?
7. Describe the contexts in which people die—hospitals, hospices, and at home—including the pluses and minuses of each.
8. Outline the stages of grief that people may go through, how they may try to make sense out of the world when someone close to them dies, and how grief may be particularly intense in the case of a widow or widower.
9. What kinds of death may make it difficult to resolve the grief process?
10. Discuss various forms of mourning and the controversy over the funeral industry.

Further Readings

Kalish, R. A. (1981). *Death, grief, and caring relationships*. Monterey, CA: Brooks/Cole.
An excellent, detailed overview of many facets of death and the dying process. One of the most thorough, comprehensive sources available. Well written.

Peterson, J. A. (1980). Social-psychological aspects of death and dying and mental health. In J. E. Birren & R. B. Sloane (Eds.), *Handbook of mental health and aging*. Englewood Cliffs, NJ: Prentice-Hall.
An excellent survey of the role of the mental health profession in dealing with dying people and those attached to them. Medium reading level.

Shneidman, E. S. (1973). *Deaths of man*. New York: Quadrangle.
Comprehensive overview of issues and data from the author's national survey of death attitudes. Easy reading.

Siegel, R. K. (1980). The psychology of life after death. *American Psychologist, 35,* 911–931.
The full text of Siegel's critical evaluation of the psychology of near-death experiences. Reasonably easy reading.

Wilcox, S. G., & Sutton, M. (Eds.). (1981). *Understanding death and dying* (2nd ed.). Sherman Oaks, CA: Alfred Publishing.
Edited readings cover a wide range of subjects from the study of death from a new vantage point to death and the child, including Maria Nagy's ideas about the child's theories of death. Reasonably easy reading.

GLOSSARY

A

ABSTRACT MAPPING Level 8 of Fischer's cognitive structural view which involves one's ability to relate one's own abstract identity to that of another person in a rudimentary way.

ABSTRACT SYSTEM Level 9 of Fischer's cognitive structural view which entails the reciprocal coordination of one's own various identities with the identities of significant others and with social expectations.

ACCEPTANCE The fifth and final stage of Elisabeth Kübler-Ross's psychological stages of dying. In this stage, which is characterized by peace, acceptance of fate, and desire to be left alone, dying patients end their struggle against death.

ACCOMMODATION The eye's ability to focus and maintain an image on the retina.

ACHIEVEMENT MOTIVE The need to maintain or increase one's competence in activities in which a standard of excellence is involved.

ACHIEVING STAGE A stage of young adulthood in which the goal is the achievement of potential.

ACQUISITIVE STAGE A stage of childhood and adolescence in which the individual functions in a protected environment and the goal is the acquisition of knowledge.

ACTIVE EUTHANASIA Inducing death in an incurably ill person by some positive action, such as injecting a lethal dose of a drug.

ACTIVE TO PASSIVE MASTERY Bernice Neugarten's view that adults move from active mastery of their lives in mid-life to a more passive orientation in late adulthood.

ACTIVITY THEORY The theory of aging which states that activity and involvement in late adulthood are often associated with life satisfaction and can be categorized into four different types (integrated, armored defended, passive-dependent, and unintegrated).

ACUTE BRAIN SYNDROMES Forms of organic disorders that are reversible, with treatment aimed at the cause of the disorder.

ACUTE PHASE The first phase of the living-dying interval in which individuals face the fact that they will die sooner than they thought and probably not be able to accomplish their goals.

ADJUSTMENT STAGE The second stage in the occupational cycle that is described as the transition from apprentice to skilled craftsperson or executive.

ADULT CONTEXTUAL MODEL A model that suggests a form of adaptive growth in adult development in which formal logic diminishes and more pragmatic, reality-oriented thought increases.

AGE-GRADED FACTORS Influences on development that are closely tied to time since birth.

AGING Processes of change that occur after maturity, including biological, psychological, and social processes.

ALPHA RHYTHM The dominant rhythm displayed by the brain and linked with relaxed yet awake behavior.

471

ALZHEIMER'S DISEASE A disease that usually begins in the fifth or sixth decade of life and is sometimes thought of as a presenile dementia, often with speech disturbance and a problem in gait and with atrophy of all areas of the brain.

ANDROGYNY Having the characteristics or nature of both male and female.

ANGER The second of Elisabeth Kübler-Ross's psychological stages of dying. In this stage dying patients realize that denial of death cannot be maintained, causing them to become angry, resentful, and envious.

ANIMAL MODELS Animals used in research in order to control the factors that cannot be controlled in humans, such as diet and environmental factors.

ATTENTION A function that is based on many processes and that controls what and how much information is encoded.

AUTHORITARIAN PARENTING A style of parenting in which the parent is restrictive and punitive in orientation, exhorts the child to follow directions, respects work and effort, and places limits on the child.

AUTHORITATIVE PARENTING A style of parenting in which the parent encourages the child to be independent within limits, shows warmth, and sets rules in a context of verbal give and take.

AUTOIMMUNITY A condition that is caused by failure of the immune mechanisms to detect normal cells or by mistakes in the formation of antibodies that make them react to normal cells as well as foreign ones.

AUTOMATIC INFORMATION PROCESSING Attention processing that presumably does not draw on limited capacity.

AUTONOMY VERSUS SHAME AND DOUBT The second stage in Erikson's eight-stage theory of development in which the child develops the healthy attitude that he or she is capable of independent control of actions or the unhealthy attitude of shame and doubt that he or she is incapable of such control.

B

BARGAINING The third of Elisabeth Kübler-Ross's psychological stages of dying. In this stage dying patients hope that death may be postponed by negotiating—often with God.

BASAL METABOLISM RATE (BMR) A biological mechanism defined as the minimum amount of energy a person uses in a state of rest.

BEHAVIOR EXCHANGE THEORY A theory that emphasizes the hedonism and competence involved in marital relationships.

BEHAVIORIST APPROACH An approach to perception that is consistent with the mechanistic metamodel, which emphasizes environmental control of behavior.

BEREAVEMENT The process through which people review their memories of loss.

BETA RHYTHM A fast brain rhythm that characterizes an attentive, alert state.

BETWEEN-SUBJECTS MANIPULATIONS Manipulations of subjects by random assignment to groups.

BRAIN DEATH A neurological definition of death which states that death occurs when all electrical activity of the brain has ceased for a specified period of time as determined by an electroencephalogram.

C

CENTRAL TENDENCY The manipulation of a given set of *n* scores to determine the mean, median, or mode.

CHANNEL A mechanism over which information is transmitted.

CHOREA A disease that usually occurs in middle adulthood and involves involuntary movements, change in personality, irresponsibility, and dementia; also known as Huntington's disease and Woody Guthrie's disease.

CHRONIC BRAIN SYNDROMES Forms of organic disorders that are not reversible and that may produce a variety of symptoms, such as confusion or suspicion.

CHRONIC PHASE The second phase of the living-dying interval in which individuals begin to confront their fear of dying.

CLIMACTERIC The loss of the ability to reproduce, which occurs over a prolonged period of time.

COGNITIVE SOCIAL LEARNING THEORY A theory that combines what is known about learning processes and thinking patterns to explain social behavior.

COHORTS Individuals born at approximately the same time.

COHORT-SEQUENTIAL DESIGN An alternative to simple longitudinal design that entails two or more longitudinal studies, each covering the same range, conducted over differing spans of time.

COMMUNICATION The transmission of a message by a sender to a receiver over a channel.

COMPANIONSHIP RELATIONSHIP A marital type of relationship that stresses the importance of affective interaction, including passion, expressions of love, rapport, communication, and respect.

CONCRETE-INDIVIDUALISTIC PERSPECTIVE A general cognitive structural view of child development which reasons that the world young children see revolves around themselves. The reasoning focuses on preserving the social order and fitting each member of society into it.

CONCRETE THINKING A type of thinking that is limited to concrete ideas and experiences and represents a less extensive thinking process than formal thinking. It leaves an individual less open to disenchantment from practical experience and with difficulty in understanding metaphors.

CONSANGUINITY Related pairs, such as fathers and sons, siblings, or cousins, are compared with randomly paired individuals who are unrelated.

CONSTRUCTS Abstract entities that cannot be directly observed but are presumed to influence observable aspects of cognition and personality, such as memory, intelligence, and creativity.

CONSTRUCT VALIDITY The observed phenomena actually do reflect the construct.

CONTEXTUAL METAMODEL An interactive view of the individual, both passive and active, which applies to different levels of analysis, these being environmental, biological, social, and historical.

CONTINUITY Development contingent on the incorporation of a previous behavior to construct a new level of behavior that is attributable to biological processes and the continuing influence of childhood and consistent adult experiences.

CONVENTIONAL LEVEL The third and fourth stages in Kohlberg's theory of moral development in which moral thought is based on the desire to preserve good interpersonal relations (stage 3) and to comply with formalized rules that exist in society (stage 4).

CONVERGENT THINKING A type of thinking that moves toward one correct answer.

CORRELATION A relationship or association between two variables that can be either positive or negative and vary from weak to strong.

CORTI The organ in the inner ear that transforms the vibrations picked up by the outer ear into nerve impulses.

COUNTERBALANCING Controlling for order effects when variables are manipulated within subjects.

CROSS-LINKAGE THEORY The theory that aging occurs because of the formation of bonds between various parts of the cell.

CROSS-SECTIONAL STUDY A study that examines effects by comparing groups that differ in the range of each effect.

CROSS-SEQUENTIAL DESIGNS Designs that examine two or more cohorts, covering different ranges, at each of two testing times in order to separate cohort and time-of-measurement effects.

CRYSTALLIZED INTELLIGENCE The type of intelligence that involves skills, abilities, and understanding gained through instruction and observation.

CT SCAN A tracing of a computer and an X ray that reveals brain anatomy.

CURVILINEAR The reflection of associations between variables that represent a curved line when plotted.

D

DEMENTIA A disorder of late adulthood that is estimated to affect 5 percent of people over the age of sixty-five and 20 percent or more over the age of eighty. It is characterized by a deterioration of intelligence and behavior.

DENIAL An important defense mechanism that may enable an individual to cope with the hopeless feeling of impending death.

DENIAL AND ISOLATION The first of Elisabeth Kübler-Ross's psychological stages of dying. In this stage dying patients react to terminal illness with shock, denial, and withdrawal. This is usually only a temporary defense.

DEPENDENT VARIABLES The values that are measured as a result of manipulation.

DEPRESSION The fourth of Elisabeth Kübler-Ross's psychological stages of dying. In this stage dying patients become silent, spend much time crying, and want to be alone in an effort to disconnect themselves from objects of love.

DEPRESSIVE PSEUDODEMENTIA Depression that mimics dementia.

DIALECTICAL VIEW A view that balance and equilibrium are never attained; therefore, a better understanding of adults will come about by studying disequilibrium and change.

DISCONTINUITY OF CHANGE Appearance, disappearance, or replacement of a previous behavior because of changes in the environment, life tasks, biology, and hierarchical development.

DISENCHANTMENT PHASE A phase of retirement during which the individual experiences a letdown about retirement because of unrealistic expectations; this phase requires a reorientation to reality.

DISENGAGEMENT THEORY The theory of aging which argues that as older people slow down, they gradually withdraw from society.

DISPLACEMENT The forgetting from short-term memory that generally results from new information's bumping out old information.

DISTAL An individual's perception or experience of the environment that is macro in nature and may not have common meaning.

DIVERGENT THINKING A type of thinking closely related to creativity that produces many different answers to a single question.

DIVIDED ATTENTION A type of attention in which we attempt to process all of the information that is present in a situation. (for example, watching a film and listening to an instructor's comments at the same time).

DUAL-CAREER FAMILY A family consisting of a husband, wife, and children who live in a home in which both adults work.

DUAL-TASK PERFORMANCE Performance that entails dividing one's attention between two tasks.

E

EARLY ADULTHOOD Time frame from the late teens or early twenties through the thirties during which personal and economic independence is often attained.

ECOLOGICAL APPROACH Ulric Neisser's approach to perception that is consistent with the organismic metamodel, which emphasizes the interactions between information in the environment and the processes of perception.

EFFORTFUL INFORMATION PROCESSING Attention processing that is thought to draw on limited capacity.

EGO INTEGRITY VERSUS DESPAIR The last stage in Erikson's eight-stage theory of development in which older adults look back at what they have done with their life. If they feel that their life has been well spent, they will be satisfied. If not, they will experience doubt and gloom.

EIGHT AGES OF MAN Term used to describe Erikson's eight-stage theory of development.

ELECTROENCEPHALOGRAM (EEG) A tracing that can measure the four different patterns of electrical activity detected in the brain.

EMOTIONAL ISOLATION Loneliness that results from the loss or absence of an emotional attachment, resulting in depression and restlessness.

EMPTY NEST SYNDROME The experience of some parents when their children leave home. The syndrome is experienced mainly by parents who have devoted their lives to nurturing their children rather than by those who have developed wider interests and realistic attitudes about parental responsibilities.

ERROR CATASTROPHE THEORY The theory that errors occur in the RNA responsible for the production of enzymes that are essential to metabolism and result in a reduction of cell functioning and possibly death.

EUTHANASIA The act of painlessly putting to death people who are suffering from incurable diseases or severe disability.

EVENT-RELATED RESPONSES (ERPs) OR EVOKED POTENTIALS (EPs) Electrophysiological responses that are linked with the processing of specific stimuli and are thought to represent a limited set of cognitive operations, usually sensory discrimination and decision making.

EXPERIMENTAL FAMILY A family form consisting of individuals in multiadult households (communes) or cohabitating adults.

EXPERIMENTAL MORTALITY The dropping out of subjects in a longitudinal study before all of the testings are complete.

EXTRANEOUS VARIABLES Values that are not measured or manipulated but are suspected to be important.

EXTRAVERSION A characteristic possessed by sociable, outgoing individuals who, when stress appears, lose themselves in people.

F

FACTOR ANALYSIS A technique that produces a summary of many correlations reduced to a small number of factors that provides *loadings* of each original variable upon each factor for interpretation.

FAMILY-OF-TWINS DESIGN A strategy that consists of adult monozygotic twins, siblings, half-siblings and parent-offspring to estimate the heritability of intelligence.

FLUID INTELLIGENCE The type of intelligence that focuses on the individual's adaptability and capacity to perceive things and integrate them mentally.

FORMAL OPERATIONAL THINKING A type of thinking in which one uses abstract thoughts to make judgments or solve problems dealing with hypothetical situations. This type of thinking also includes the ability to understand metaphorical meaning.

FREE-RADICAL THEORY A special application of the cross-linkage theory. Chemical components of the cells are claimed to exist only for a second or less before they damage cells through their reactions with substances that cause chromosome damage.

FREE RECALL A test of long-term memory in which the individual is asked to recall as many items as possible from a given list.

G

GENERATIVITY VERSUS STAGNATION The seventh stage of Erikson's eight-stage theory of development in which the adult either does or does not assist the younger generation in developing and leading useful lives.

GENETIC ERROR THEORIES Theories which indicate that aging is caused by damage to the genetic information contained in the formation of cellular protein.

GENETIC SWITCHING THEORY The theory that, as the result of genetical programming, certain genes switch off, causing information needed to produce DNA not to be available, which leads to cell death and the loss of organ functioning.

GENOTYPE The special arrangement of chromosomes and genes each person inherits that makes him or her unique.

GRIEF The sorrow, anger, guilt, and confusion that usually accompany a significant loss or bereavement.

H

HARDWARE The physical machinery of a computer; the brain and sensory systems of a human.

HERITABILITY A mathematical estimate of ranges of genetic and environmental parameters that is often computed with a standard heritability quotient with similarity measured by the correlation coefficient *r*.

HISTORICAL TIME The variable dimension that controls the social system, which creates a set of age norms and an age-grade system that are both changing to shape the individual life cycle.

HOMEOSTATIC IMBALANCE THEORY The theory that aging is the result of the almost linear decline of the body's organ reserves and their ability to maintain homeostasis.

HONEYMOON PHASE A phase of retirement during which the individual experiences initial euphoria just after retirement that may give pleasure from leisure activities.

HORMONAL THEORY The theory that aging pacemakers in control centers of the brain stimulate a series of neurological and hormonal changes that cause one to age.

HOSPICE An institution committed to making the end of life as free from pain and depression as possible and to keep the dying patient an important part of his or her family.

HOT FLASH A feeling of extreme heat that is usually confined to the upper part of the body and is often accompanied by a drenching sweat. The most commonly experienced symptom of menopause, which diminishes gradually and disappears completely.

I

ICONIC A kind of sensory image that lasts up to at least one-half second after the initial experience has stopped.

IDENTITY VERSUS ROLE CONFUSION The fifth stage of Erikson's eight-stage theory of development in which the adolescent becomes confident and purposeful or confused and troubled.

IMAGERY The formation of picture-like representations, a process relevant to recall that is known to improve memory.

IMITATION (MODELING OR VICARIOUS LEARNING) A form of social learning that involves learning from observed examples of behavior.

INBREEDING The mating of animals of the same parent.

INDEPENDENT-SAMPLES DESIGN A modification of procedure in a longitudinal study of randomly assigning subjects to two or more groups and testing these groups at different times.

INDEPENDENT VARIABLES The values that are manipulated in order to measure other values.

INDUSTRIAL REVOLUTION The period that began in 1910 in the United States when factories multiplied, the labor force changed dramatically, and machines that operated with mechanical energy were used to substantially increase productivity and income.

INDUSTRY VERSUS INFERIORITY The fourth stage of Erikson's eight-stage theory of development in which the school-aged child develops a capacity for productivity and competence or views himself or herself as inadequate.

INFORMATION-PROCESSING APPROACH An approach to perception that emphasizes the importance of active processing of information through such processes as attention, memory, and reasoning.

INITIATIVE VERSUS GUILT The third stage of Erikson's eight-stage theory of development in which the preschool child either develops a desire for achievement or is held back by feelings of guilt at being dominated.

INSTITUTIONAL RELATIONSHIP A marital type of relationship oriented toward tradition, loyalty, and security, with traditional sex-differentiated rules for behavior.

INTERFERENCE The forgetting from long-term memory that is thought to result from impaired retrievability because of other information learned previously or subsequently.

INTERGENERATIONAL
RELATIONSHIPS Relationships comprised of many different age segments of child and adult development.

INTER-ITEM RELIABILITY The extent to which measurements on one half of the items in a test are predictable from the measurements on the other half.

INTERNAL VALIDITY An experiment's independent variables reflect what they are intended to reflect.

INTER-RATER RELIABILITY The assessed amount of agreement between two or more observers who make independent observations in studies of social behavior.

INTERVIEW A set of structured or unstructured questions put to someone and that person's responses.

INTIMACY An individual's seeking at least tentative forms of commitment in friendship, sex, and love, particularly in early adulthood.

INTIMACY VERSUS ISOLATION The sixth stage in Erikson's eight-stage theory of development in which the young adult achieves a capacity for honest, close relationships or is unable to do so.

INTIMATE INTERACTION An interaction that forms and maintains one or more deep and long-lasting love relationships.

INTRAINDIVIDUAL CHANGE Individual differences in the course of adult development that are important in understanding intellectual, personality, and biological functioning in adulthood.

ISOLATED INTERACTION An interaction of withdrawal from social encounters that has little or no intimate attachment.

K

KIN FAMILY A family comprised of bilateral or intergenerationally linked members living in the same household.

L

LAISSEZ-FAIRE (PERMISSIVE) PARENTING A style of parenting in which the parent places low demands, limits, and controls on the child.

LATE ADULTHOOD The period from approximately sixty-five until death, which involves adjusting to retirement, reduced income, and many times, to decreasing health and strength.

LEARNED HELPLESSNESS The attitude of people to give up when they believe that rewards are beyond their personal control and that personal behavior will not affect the outcome of a situation.

LIFE-EVENTS FRAMEWORK A view which suggests that life events produce taxing circumstances for individuals, forcing them to change their personality; it is important to consider the sociohistorical circumstances in which those events are occurring.

LIFE REVIEW A looking-back process that is set in motion by looking forward to death and that potentially proceeds toward personality reorganization.

LIFE SATISFACTION An important integrative concept in late adulthood that determines an elderly person's level of satisfaction with the sum total of his or her life.

LIFE TIME The biological timetable that governs the chronological sequence of changes in the life cycle.

LIKING The feeling that someone is similar to us and our positive evaluation of that person.

LIMITED ATTENTIONAL CAPACITY A type of psychological energy that is needed to perform mental work and the capacity of which varies depending on one's level of arousal, age, and other factors.

LINEAR The measure of correlation between variables that reflects the relative strength of an association by a straight line when plotted.

LIVING-DYING INTERVAL The span between the time we discover we will die sooner than expected and the time we actually die. According to E. Mansell Pattison this span is characterized by three phases of development: acute, chronic, and terminal.

LONGITUDINAL DESIGN A test designed to be administered to the same individual at certain intervals over a period of time.

LONGITUDINAL STUDY A study that examines an effect on a single group of approximately the same value of the measured effect by testing and retesting on one or more occasions in the future.

LOSS A situation in life that comes in many forms, such as divorce or death of a spouse or other loved one, and that leads to bereavement, grief, and mourning.

LOVING A pervasive aspect of interpersonal relationship in adulthood that involves being close to someone in a selfless way and includes qualities of exclusiveness and absorption.

M

MALE CLIMACTERIC The decline of sexual potency that usually begins when men are in their sixties and seventies and progresses at a much slower rate than female menopause.

MASKING A technique in which a visual stimulus is given briefly after an initial visual presentation and impairs perception of the initial stimulus.

MEAN The procedure of averaging a given set of *n* scores by adding their values and dividing by *n*.

MECHANICAL MIRROR THEORY Jonas Langer's label for social learning theory; the label suggests that individuals do not control their own destiny but instead are controlled and manipulated by environmental influences until they mirror their environments in mechanical fashion.

MECHANISTIC METAMODEL The grand model that assumes a vision of the adult as a passive machine that reacts to events but does not actively anticipate, formulate, or engage in complex internal activity.

MEDIAN A value in the middle of the distribution of scores where as many scores fall above that value as fall below it.

MEMORY A function that is based on many different processes and allows access to the knowledge needed for encoding and also stores the products of encoding for later use.

MEMORY KNOWLEDGE The amount of information that is available for recall.

MEMORY PROCESSING The efficient storage of information that has been received.

MENOPAUSE The onset of irregular menses and their eventual total cessation as a result of ovarian degeneration and a decline of estrogen secretion that signals the cessation of childbearing capacity.

METAMEMORY Knowledge about one's own memory and how it works.

METAMODEL A grand model that transcends more specific, concrete, testable models as the foundation for research in selected areas.

MIDDLE ADULTHOOD The phase of the life cycle that approximately spans the years thirty-five to sixty-five and is characterized by expanding responsibilities, reaching career satisfaction, and adjusting to the physiological changes of middle age.

MODE The most frequent score in a set of scores.

MORAL DEVELOPMENT Development involving rules and conventions about acceptable behavior—often in relation to a person's interactions with others.

''MOST EFFICIENT'' DESIGN A design in which individuals in different cohorts are examined with further measurements made at different times; data are collected from new, independent samples of cohorts at the second time of testing.

MOTOR PATHWAYS. The mechanisms used to transmit signals for motor performance from the brain and spinal cord to various parts of the body.

MOURNING The overt, behavioral expression of grief and bereavement that is heavily influenced by cultural standards.

MULTIDIRECTIONALITY OF CHANGE Nonlinear view that implies developmental changes in a given type of functioning may decline, stabilize, or improve within or among individuals.

MUTATION THEORY The theory that aging is due to changes in the DNA of the cells in vital organs of the body.

N

NEAR PHASE A retirement-related phase during which workers may participate in preretirement programs that can help them to make the eventual transition to retirement. Unfortunately, such programs involve only about 10 percent of the work force.

NEUROSIS A form of mental disorder in which the individual, while usually showing a high level of anxiety, can generally function.

NEUROTICISM The opposite of emotional stability.

NONNORMATIVE A type of adult development that is experienced by only a small portion of same-aged individuals.

NONNORMATIVE LIFE-EVENTS FACTORS Influences on development that are related to chance encounters.

NORMATIVE A type of development in children that is similar across individuals and even cultures.

NORMATIVE HISTORY-GRADED FACTORS Influences on development that are related to historical time.

NORMS A pattern or representative values for a group.

O

OBESITY A condition in which a person weighs more than 20 percent over normal skeletal and physical requirements.

OPTIMALLY EXERCISED ABILITY Level of performance expected if optimal exercise and/or training has occurred.

ORGANISMIC METAMODEL The grand model that assumes the adult is active, with goals, plans, and complex strategies to attain ends.

P

PAIRED-ASSOCIATES LEARNING TASK A process of learning pairs of words and then being tested on the ability to recall one member of the pair when presented with the other.

PARADIGMS Foundations that cannot be proved or disproved on the basis of previous achievements for the purpose of conducting and interpreting research.

PASSIVE EUTHANASIA Inducing a natural death by withdrawing some life-sustaining therapeutic effort, such as turning off a respirator or heart-lung machine.

PEARSON PRODUCT MOMENT CORRELATION COEFFICIENT Abbreviated as r this computes the quantitative strength of a correlation on a scale of -1.0 to $+1.0$.

PERCEIVED CONTROL A way of handling stress in which people believe that they can control events—such as prolonging their lives.

PERCEPTION A function that is based on many different processes and is conceptualized as the encoding of information.

PERSONALITY The distinctive patterns of behavior, thought, and emotion that characterize each person's adaptation to the situations of his or her life.

PERSON × ENVIRONMENT INTERACTION Emphasis is placed on the importance of both individual differences and situational factors in determining personality.

PETT SCAN Computer technology tracing that records the actual metabolism of the brain by measuring radioactive emissions.

PHENOTYPE All of the observed and measurable characteristics of an individual.

POPULATION All of the individuals in a certain class.

POSTCONVENTIONAL LEVEL The final two stages of Kohlberg's theory of moral development in which moral thought is based upon the application of laws through appeal to their purpose (stage 5) and by appeal to universal principles of ethics (stage 6).

PRECONVENTIONAL LEVEL The first two stages of Kohlberg's theory of moral development in which moral thought is based on fear of punishment (stage 1) and naive instrumental hedonism (stage 2).

PREINDUSTRIAL SOCIETY The nineteenth century United States society comprised mainly of families who farmed land, worked together, and were thought of as a unit of production.

PREINTIMATE INTERACTION An interaction of mixed emotions about commitment that is reflected in a strategy of offering love without obligations.

PRIMARY MEMORY The conscious awareness of recently perceived events.

PRIOR-TO-SOCIETY PERSPECTIVE An adult stage of reasoning that involves being a member of many different social units, with arbitrary membership determined by uncontrollable factors. These social units are viewed as convenient and imperfect systems developed by people to assist in getting along with one another.

PROCESSING DEFICIT The failure to use appropriate learning procedures, such as organizational, semantic, and imagery processes, which leads to inefficient memory.

PROXIMAL An individual's immediate perception or experience of the environment.

PSEUDOINTIMATE INTERACTION An interaction that maintains a long-lasting heterosexual attachment but that has little or no closeness.

PSYCHOMETRIC APPROACH An approach in the study of development that emphasizes measurement-based tests.

PSYCHOSIS A severe form of mental disorder that keeps the individual from maintaining contact with reality.

Q

Q-SORT TECHNIQUE A method of obtaining trait ratings, consisting of many cards, on each of which is printed a trait description. They are grouped by a rater into piles ranging from those that are least characteristic to those that are most characteristic of the person being rated.

QUALITATIVE CHANGE The quality or kind of change upon which the organismic metamodel puts great emphasis.

QUASI EXPERIMENTS Studies that resemble true experiments in design and analysis but contain an independent variable that cannot be manipulated.

QUESTIONNAIRE A carefully constructed set of written questions that respondents read and answer in writing.

R

RANDOM ASSIGNMENT The powerful technique of assigning individuals to exposure conditions on a random basis in order to distribute extraneous factors evenly.

RANGE The simplest measure of variability, which is given by the lowest and highest scores in a set.

REACTION TIME TASKS Tests that measure the time elapsed between the appearance of a signal and a person's responding movement.

REACTIVITY The way in which an individual reacts to being tested. A person's behavior in a research project may not be the same as in everyday life.

RECEIVER A mechanism that picks up information.

RECIPROCAL DETERMINISM Albert Bandura's concept that a person's psychological makeup is best understood by analyzing the continuous reciprocal interaction between behavior and its controlling conditions.

REINTEGRATIVE STAGE A stage that corresponds with late adulthood during which the individual focuses on simplification and cognitive activity is more influenced by motivational factors.

RELIABILITY The consistency of the results of a test; the answers must be consistent if an individual is tested more than once.

REMARRIED NUCLEAR FAMILY A family consisting of a husband, wife, and children in which one or both of the adults have been previously married and brought children with them from the previous marriage(s).

REMOTE PHASE A retirement-related phase during which most individuals do virtually nothing to prepare for retirement because they deny that it is an eventual possibility or because it is in the distant future.

REORIENTATION PHASE A retirement phase during which people may explore, evaluate, and make some decisions about the type of life-style that will likely lead to satisfaction during retirement.

REPRESENTATIVE SAMPLE A sample of a population that has the same characteristics as the entire population.

RESOURCE ALLOCATION STRATEGIES Ways in which people trade off one task against another.

RESPONSIBLE STAGE A stage that corresponds with middle adulthood during which the individual has attained competence and independence and now has to assume responsibility for others.

REVERSIBILITY Removal of certain age-related deficits through appropriate intervention.

S

SAMPLE A portion of a population.

SCHEMA An organized internal structure of knowledge, which is the part of Urlic Neisser's model.

SCHIZOPHRENIA A psychological disorder that involves disturbed, unrealistic thought processes and is not believed to be homogeneous.

SECONDARY MEMORY The recall of events that have left consciousness.

SELECTIVE ATTENTION A type of attention in which we attempt to ignore irrelevant information while focusing on relevant information (for example, ignoring a television program while listening to a friend).

SELECTIVE BREEDING The mating of animals over successive generations on the basis of their similarities in a specific characteristic.

SENILE DEMENTIA A progressive disorganization of virtually all aspects of the mind, with personality being affected as much as memory, intelligence and judgment.

SENSORY PATHWAYS The mechanisms used to transmit incoming sensory information to the brain.

SEX ROLE The behaviors that are expected of individuals because they are either male or female.

SEXUAL, OR GENDER, IDENTITY The extent to which individuals actually take on as part of their personalities the behaviors and attitudes associated with either the male or female role.

SINGLE-CAREER FAMILY The intact nuclear family comprised of a husband, wife, and children living in a common household in which one partner is the breadwinner.

SINGLE-PARENT FAMILY A family comprised of a child or children and only one parent; the one parent may be divorced, widowed, or never have married.

SINGLE-TASK PERFORMANCE Performance that does not entail dividing one's attention.

SOCIAL BREAKDOWN THEORY The theory which suggests that aging is promoted through negative psychological functioning (poor self-concept, negative feedback, and a lack of skills to deal with the world).

SOCIAL COGNITION Cognitive development that is focused on the individual's reasoning about social matters.

SOCIAL ISOLATION Loneliness that occurs through the loss or absence of social ties, resulting in a restless feeling and depression.

SOCIAL TIME The variable dimension that underlies the age-grade system of a particular society. Time based on societal and cultural factors.

SOFTWARE The programming for a computer; learning and development for a human.

STABILITY PHASE A phase of retirement during which individuals decide upon a set of criteria for evaluating retirement and how they will perform once they make their choices.

STAGES Abrupt and sequential developmental categories of qualitative behavioral change.

STANDARD DEVIATION A common measure of variability that is equal to the square root of the variance of a set of scores.

STANDARDIZATION The establishment of fixed procedures for administration, scoring, and norms for age, grade, race, sex, and so on.

STANDARDIZED TESTS Questionnaires, structured interviews, or behavioral tests developed to identify characteristics or abilities of individuals relative to those of a large group of similar individuals.

STEREOTYPED INTERACTION An interaction of superficial relationships that tend to be dominated by friendship ties with the same sex.

SUTTEE The Hindu practice of burning a dead man's widow to increase his family's prestige and establish her image in his memory.

SYSTEM OF ABSTRACT SYSTEMS The most advanced level of Fischer's cognitive structural view which involves the coordination of one's identities over the life cycle so that a meaningful whole can be achieved.

T

TERMINAL PHASE The last phase of the living-dying interval in which individuals withdraw their hope for recovery and accept the finality of approaching death.

TERMINATION PHASE The final phase of retirement during which the retirement role loses its significance and relevance.

TEST-RETEST RELIABILITY The degree of predictability that measurements taken on one test on one occasion will be similar to those taken on another occasion.

THINKING A function that involves complex processes of organizing information, combining different types of information, and selecting strategies for perceiving, remembering, and attending to information.

TIME-SEQUENTIAL DESIGNS Designs that involve two or more cross-sectional studies, each covering the same range, conducted at different times.

TRUST VERSUS MISTRUST The first stage in Erikson's eight-stage theory of development in which the infant develops either the comfortable feeling that those around him care for his needs or the worry that his needs will not be taken care of.

TYPE A A person who is excessively competitive, has an accelerated pace of ordinary activities, is impatient with the rate at which most events occur, often thinks about doing several things at the same time, shows hostility, and cannot hide the fact that time is a struggle in his or her life.

TYPE B A person who is typified by the absence of Type A behavioral tendencies.

U

UNEXERCISED ABILITY Level of performance that can be expected if an individual has had no exercise or training in a particular ability.

UPSWING THESIS The contention that there is an increase in marital satisfaction when children leave home.

V

VALIDITY The soundness of measurements in terms of reflecting what they are intended to reflect.

VARIABILITY The manipulation of the differences of a given set of n scores to determine the range, variance, or standard deviation.

VARIABLE Something that can take on at least two different levels or values.

VARIANCE A common measure of variability that is measured by computing the difference between each score in a set and the mean, squaring the differences, and taking the mean of the squared differences.

W

WITHIN-SUBJECT MANIPULATIONS Manipulations of the independent variable through examination of each subject in an experiment under two or more conditions.

REFERENCES

A

Abramson, L. Y., Seligman, M. E. P., & Teasdale, J. D. (1978). Learned helplessness in humans: Critique and reformulation. *Journal of Abnormal Psychology, 87,* 49–74.

Adams, G. M., & de Vries, H. A. (1973). Physiological effects of an exercise training regimen among women aged 52 to 79. *Journal of Gerontology, 20,* 50–55.

Aiken, L. R. (1978). *The psychology of later life.* Philadelphia: Saunders.

Albrecht, S. L. (1980). Reactions and adjustment to divorce: Differences in experiences of males and females. *Family Relations, 29,* 59–68.

Aldous, J. (1978, September 22). *Family careers over time.* Address given at Department of Sociology, University of Notre Dame, Notre Dame, IN.

Allan, G. (1977). Sibling solidarity. *Journal of Marriage and the Family, 39,* 177–184.

Allport, G. W. (1961). *Pattern and growth in personality.* New York: Holt, Rinehart & Winston.

Alpaugh, P., & Birren, J. (1977). Variables affecting creative contributions across the adult life span. *Human Development, 20,* 240–248.

Anders, T. R., Fozard, J. L., & Lillyquist, T. D. (1972). The effects of age upon retrieval from short-term memory. *Developmental Psychology, 6,* 214–217.

Anderson, B., Jr., & Palmore, E. (1974). Longitudinal evaluation of ocular function. In E. Palmore (Ed.), *Normal aging II: Reports from the Duke longitudinal studies, 1970–1973.* Durham, NC: Duke University Press.

Anderson, J. R. (1980). *Cognitive psychology and its implications.* San Francisco: W. H. Freeman.

Anderson, R., & Darkenwald, G. (1979). *Participation and persistence in American adult education.* New York: College Entrance Examination Board.

Antonucci, T. (1981, August). *Attachment from adolescence to adulthood.* Paper presented at the meeting of the American Psychological Association, Los Angeles, CA.

Arenberg, D. (1974). A longitudinal study of problem solving in adults. *Journal of Gerontology, 29,* 650–658.

Arenberg, D. (1978). Differences and changes with age on the Benton Visual Retention Test. *Journal of Gerontology, 33,* 534–540.

Arenberg, D., & Robertson-Tchabo, E. A. (1977). Learning and aging. In J. E. Birren & K. W. Schaie (Eds.), *Handbook of the psychology of aging.* New York: Van Nostrand Reinhold.

Armentrout, J. A., & Burger, G. K. (1972). Children's report of parental child-rearing behavior at five grade levels. *Developmental Psychology, 7,* 44–48.

Asch, S. E. (1936). A study of change in mental organization. *Archives of Psychology, 28,* (Whole No. 195).

Aslanian, C. B., & Brickell, H. M. (1980). *Americans in transition: Life changes as reasons for adult learning.* Princeton, NJ: College Board Publications.

Astin, H. S., & Bayer, A. E. (1975). Sex discrimination in academe. In M. T. S. Mednick, S. S. Tangri, & I. W. Hoffman (Eds.), *Women and achievement.* New York: John Wiley.

Atchley, R. C. (1976). *The sociology of retirement.* Cambridge, MA: Schenkman.

Atchley, R. C. (1977). *The social forces in later life: An introduction to social gerontology* (2nd ed.). Belmont, CA: Wadsworth.

Athanasion, R., & Yushioka, G. A. (1973). The spatial character of friendship formation. *Environment and Behavior, 5,* 143–165.

Attig, M., & Hasher, L. (1980). The processing of frequency of occurrence information. *Journal of Gerontology, 35,* 66–69.

Ausubel, D. P. (1968). *Educational psychology.* New York: Holt, Rinehart & Winston.

Ausubel, D. P., Sullivan, E. V., and Ives, S. W. (1979). *Theory and problems of child development* (3rd ed.). New York: Grune & Stratton.

Averill, J. R. (1968). Grief: Its nature and significance. *Psychological Bulletin, 70,* 721–748.

B

Babladelis, G. (1979). Accentuate the positive. *Contemporary Psychology, 24,* 3–4.

Bachman, J., O'Malley, P., & Johnson, J. (1978). *Youth in transition (Vol. VI). Adolescence to adulthood—Change and stability of the lives of young men.* Ann Arbor: Institute for Social Research, University of Michigan.

Baer, D. M. (1970). An age-irrelevant concept of development. *Merrill-Palmer Quarterly, 16,* 238–245.

Bahrick, H. P., Bahrick, P. O., & Wittlinger, R. P. (1975). Fifty years of memory for names and faces: A cross-sectional approach. *Journal of Experimental Psychology: General, 104,* 54–75.

Balinsky, B. (1941). An analysis of the mental factors of various age groups from nine to sixty. *Genetic Psychology Monographs, 23,* 191–234.

Ball, S. J. (1981). *Beachside comprehensive.* Cambridge: Cambridge University Press.

Baltes, P. B. (1973). Prototypical paradigms and questions in life-span research on development and aging. *The Gerontologist, 13,* 458–467.

Baltes, P. B., & Goulet, L. R. (1971). Exploration of the developmental parameters by manipulation and simulation of age differences in behavior. *Human Development, 14,* 149–170.

Baltes, P. B., & Labouvie, G. V. (1973). Adult development of intellectual performance: Description, explanation, and modification. In C. Eisdorfer & M. P. Lawton (Eds.), *The psychology of adult development and aging.* Washington, DC: American Psychological Association.

Baltes, P. B., Reese, H. W., & Lipsitt, L. P. (1980). Life-span developmental psychology. *Annual Review of Psychology, 31,* 65–110.

Baltes, P. B., & Schaie, K. W. (1976). On the plasticity of intelligence in adulthood and old age: Where Horn and Donaldson fail. *American Psychologist, 31,* 720–725.

Baltes, P. B., & Willis, S. L. (1978). Cognitive development and intervention in later adulthood. *The Penn State Adult Development and Enrichment Program (ADEPT).* Unpublished symposium manuscript, College of Human Development, Pennsylvania State University, University Park.

Bandura, A. (1971). *Social learning theory.* New York: General Learning Press.

Bandura, A. (1977). *Social learning theory.* Englewood Cliffs, NJ: Prentice-Hall.

Bandura, A. (1982). The psychology of chance encounters and life paths. *American Psychologist, 37,* 747–755.

Banister, H., & Ravden, M. (1944). The problem child and his environment. *British Journal of Psychology, 34,* 60–65.

Bardwick, J. (1971). *Psychology of women: A study of biocultural conflicts.* New York: Harper & Row.

Barnett, L. R., & Nietzel, M. T. (1979). Relationship of instrumental and affection behaviors and self-esteem to marital satisfaction in distressed and nondistressed couples. *Journal of Consulting and Clinical Psychology, 47,* 946–954.

Barrett, T. R., & Wright, M. (1981). Age-related facilitation in recall following verrantic processing. *Journal of Gerontology, 36,* 194–199.

Barron, F. (1963). *Creativity and psychological health.* New York: Van Nostrand Reinhold.

Barron, S. A., Jacobs, L., & Kirkei, W. R. (1976). Changes in size of normal lateral ventricles during aging determined by computerized tomography. *Neurology, 26,* 1011–1013.

Bart, P. (1973). Portnoy's mother's complaint. In H. Z. Lopata (Ed.), *Marriages and families.* New York: Van Nostrand Reinhold.

Bartell, G. (1972). *Group sex.* New York: Peter H. Wyden.

Bartlett, F. C. (1932). *Remembering.* Cambridge: Cambridge University Press.

Basen, M. M. (1977). The elderly and drugs—Problem overview and program strategy. *Public Health Reports, 92,* 43–48.

Baumrind, D. (1971). Current patterns of parental authority. *Developmental Psychology Monographs, 4*(1, Pt. 2).

Bee, H. L., & Mitchell, S. K. (1980). *The developing person.* San Francisco: Harper & Row.

Behrman, J. R., Hrubec, Z., Taubman, P., & Wales, T. J. (1980). *Contributions to economic analysis.* Amsterdam: North Holland.

Bell, R. R., & Bell, P. L. (1972). Sexual satisfaction among married women. *Medical Aspects of Human Sexuality, 6,* 136–144.

Bell, R. R., & Lobsenz, N. (1979, September). Married sex: How uninhibited can a woman dare to be? *Redbook,* pp. 75–78.

Bell, R. R., & Peltz, O. (1974). Extramarital sex among women. *Medical Aspects of Human Sexuality, 8,* 10–31.

Belloc, N. B., & Breslow, L. (1972). Relationship of physical health status and health practices. *Preventive Medicine, 1,* 409–421.

Belmont, J. M., & Butterfield, E. S. (1971). Learning strategies as determinants of memory deficiencies. *Cognitive Psychology, 2,* 411–420.

Belsky, J. (1981). Early human experience: A family perspective. *Developmental Psychology, 17,* 3–23.

Belsky, J., & Tolan, W. (1981). The infant as producer of his development: An ecological analysis. In R. Lerner & N. Busch-Rossnagel (Eds.), *The child as producer of its own development.* New York: Academic Press.

Bem, S. L. (1974). The measurement of psychological androgyny. *Journal of Consulting and Clinical Psychology, 42,* 155–162.

Bem, S. L. (1977). On the utility of alternative procedures for assessing psychological androgyny. *Journal of Consulting and Clinical Psychology, 45,* 196–205.

Benet, S. (1976). *How to live to be 100.* New York: The Dial Press.

Berman, P. W., Sloan, V. L., & Goodman, V. (1979). *Development of sex differences in preschool children's interactions with an infant: Spontaneous behavior and response to a caretaking assignment.* Paper presented at the meeting of the Society for Research in Child Development, San Francisco.

Berndt, T. J. (1982). The features and effects of friendship in early adolescence. *Child Development, 53,* 1447–1460.

Bever, T. G. (1970). The cognitive basis for linguistic structures. In J. R. Hayes (Ed.), *Cognition and the development of language.* New York: John Wiley.

Bijou, S. W. (1976). *The basic stage of early childhood development.* Englewood Cliffs, NJ: Prentice-Hall.

Binstock, J. (1972, June). Motherhood: An occupation facing decline. *The Futurist,* pp. 99–102.

Birren, J. E. (1974). Translations in gerontology—from lab to life. Psychophysiology and speed of response. *American Psychologist, 29,* 808–815.

Birren, J. E., Butler, R. N., Greenhouse, S. W., Sokoloff, L., & Yarrow, M. R. (Eds.). (1963). *Human aging: A biological and behavioral study.* Washington, DC: U.S. Government Printing Office.

Birren, J. E., & Renner, J. (1980). Concepts and issues of mental health and aging. In J. E. Birren & R. B. Sloane (Eds.), *Handbook of mental health and aging.* Englewood Cliffs, NJ: Prentice-Hall.

Birren, J. E., & Sloane, R. B. (Eds.). (1980). *Handbook of mental health and aging.* Englewood Cliffs, NJ: Prentice-Hall.

Bjorksten, J. (1968). The cross-linkage theory of aging. *Journal of the American Geriatrics Society, 16,* 408–427.

Bjorksten, J. (1974). Cross-linkage and the aging process. In M. Rockstein, M. Sussman, & J. Chesley (Eds.), *Theoretical aspects of aging.* New York: Academic Press.

Block, J. (1971). *Lives through time.* Berkeley, CA: Bancroft.

Block, M. R., Davidson, J. L., Grambs, J. D. (1981). *Women over forty.* New York: Springer.

Blood, R. O., & Wolfe, D. M. (1969). *Husbands and wives, the dynamics of married living.* New York: The Free Press.

Bondareff, W. (1977). The neural basis of aging. In J. E. Birren & K. W. Schaie (Eds.), *Handbook of the psychology of aging.* New York: Van Nostrand Reinhold.

Boston Women's Health Book Collective (1976). *Our Bodies, Ourselves* (2nd ed.). New York: Simon & Schuster. Reprinted by permission of Simon & Schuster.

Botwinick, J. (1978). *Aging and behavior* (2nd ed.). Copyright © 1978 by Springer Publishing Company, Inc., New York. Used by permission.

Botwinick, J., & Storandt, M. (1974). *Memory, related functions and age.* Springfield, IL: Charles C. Thomas.

Bowerman, C. E., & Irish, D. P. (1962). Some relationships of stepchildren to their parents. *Marriage and Family Living, 24,* 113–121.

Bowlby, J. (1969). *Attachment and loss* (Vol. 1). London: Hogarth (New York: Basic Books).

Bowlby, J. (1980). *Loss: Sadness and depression. Attachment and loss* (Vol. III). New York: Basic Books.

Bradburn, N. (1969). *The structure of psychological well-being.* Chicago: Aldine.

Bransford, J. D. (1979). *Human cognition: Learning, understanding, and remembering.* Belmont, CA: Wadsworth.

Brenner, M. H. (1973). *Mental illness and the economy.* Cambridge, MA: Harvard University Press.

Brent, G., Smith, D., Michaelewski, H., & Thompson, L. (1976). Differences in evoked potentials in young and old subjects during habituation and dishabituation procedures. *Psychophysiology, 14,* 96–97.

Brickell, H. M. (1979). *A study of the tuition refund plan at Mack Trucks, Inc., Hagerstown, Md.* New York: College Entrance Examination Board.

Brim, O. G. (1976). Theories of the male mid-life crisis. *Counseling Psychologist, 6,* 2–9.

Brim, O. G., & Ryff, C. D. (1980). On the properties of life events. In P. B. Baltes & O. G. Brim (Eds.), *Life-span development and behavior* (Vol. 3). New York: Academic Press.

Broadbent, D. E. (1958). *Perception and communication.* London: Pergamon Press.

Broadbent, D. E., & Heron, A. (1962). Effects of a subsidiary task on performance involving immediate memory in younger and older men. *British Journal of Psychology, 53,* 189–198.

Broderick, C. (1982). Adult sexual development. In B. J. Wolman (Ed.), *Handbook of developmental psychology.* Englewood Cliffs, NJ: Prentice-Hall.

Bruce, P. R., Coyne, A. C., & Botwinick, J. (1982). Adult age differences in metamemory. *Journal of Gerontology, 37,* 354–367.

Bruckner, R. (1967). Longitudinal research on the eye. *Clinical Gerontology, 9,* 87–95.

Bruner, J. S. (1966). *Toward a theory of instruction.* Cambridge, MA: Harvard University Press.

Buhler, C. (1933). *Der menschliche, Lebenslauf al pscbologishes problem.* Leipzig: Verlag von S. Herzel.

Buhler, C. (1968). The course of human life as a psychological problem. *Human Development, 11,* 184–200.

Burnet, S. F. M. (1974). *Intrinsic mutagenesis: A genetic approach to aging.* New York: John Wiley.

Buss, T., & Redburn, F. S. (1983). Untitled and unpublished manuscript. Center for Urban Studies, Youngstown State University, Youngstown, OH.

Butler, R. N. (1975). *Why survive? Being old in America.* New York: Harper & Row.

Butler, R. N., & Lewis, M. (1977). *Aging and mental health.* St. Louis: Mosby.

C

Campbell, D. T., & Stanley, J. C. (1963). *Experimental and quasi-experimental designs for research.* Chicago: Rand McNally.

Carey, R. G. (1977). The widowed: A year later. *Journal of Counseling Psychology, 24,* 125–131.

Carp, F. M. (1976). Housing and living environments of older people. In R. H. Binstock & E. Shanas (Eds.), *Handbook of aging and the social sciences.* New York: Van Nostrand Reinhold.

Carroll, C., & Miller, D. (1982). *Health.* Dubuque, IA: Wm. C. Brown.

Carter, D. K. (1977). Counseling divorced women. *The Personnel and Guidance Journal, 55,* 537–541.

Cerella, J., Poon, L. W., & Fozard, J. L. (1981). Mental rotation and age reconsidered. *Journal of Gerontology, 36,* 604–624.

Chernin, K. (1981, November 22). Women and weight consciousness. *New York Times News Service.*

Chiriboga, D. A. (1982). An examination of life events as possible antecedents to change. *Journal of Gerontology, 5,* 595–601.

Chiriboga, D. A., & Lowenthal, M. F. (1975). Complexities of adaptation. In M. F. Lowenthal & D. A. Chiriboga (Eds.), *Four stages of life.* San Francisco: Jossey-Bass.

Chiriboga, D. A., & Pierce, R. (1978). Of time and transitions. Unpublished manuscript, University of California, San Francisco.

Chomsky, N. (1965). *Aspects of the theory of syntax.* Cambridge, MA: MIT Press.

Cicirelli, V. G. (1980). Sibling relationships in adulthood. In L. W. Poon (Ed.), *Aging in the 1980s: Psychological issues.* Washington, DC: American Psychological Association.

Clausen, J. A. (1981). Men's occupational careers in the middle years. In D. H. Eichorn, J. A. Clausen, N. Haan, M. Honzik, & P. Mussen (Eds.), *Present and past in middle life.* New York: Academic Press.

Cohen, G. (1979). Language comprehension in old age. *Cognitive Psychology, 11,* 412–429.

Cohn, E. S. (1981, August). *Loss of control and fear of victimization in the elderly.* Paper presented at the meeting of the American Psychological Association, Los Angeles, CA.

Colby, A., Kohlberg, L., Gibbs, J., & Lieberman, M. (1980). A longitudinal study of moral judgment. Unpublished manuscript, Harvard University, Cambridge, MA.

Coles, R. (1970). *Erik H. Erikson: The growth of his work.* Boston: Little, Brown.

Colletta, N. D. (1978). *Divorced mothers at two income levels: Stress, support, and childrearing practices.* Unpublished thesis, Cornell University, Ithaca, NY.

Collins, A. M., & Loftus, E. F. (1975). A spreading activation theory of semantic processing. *Psychological Review, 82,* 407–429.

Comfort, A. (1976). *A good age.* New York: Crown.

Comfort, A. (1980). Sexuality in later life. In J. E. Birren & R. B. Sloane (Eds.), *Handbook of mental health and aging.* Englewood Cliffs, NJ: Prentice-Hall.

Corbin, J. N. (1974). *The effects of counselor-assisted exploratory activity on career development.* Unpublished doctoral dissertation, Columbia University, New York.

Corso, J. (1977). Auditory perception and communication. In J. E. Birren & K. W. Schaie (Eds.), *Handbook of the psychology of aging.* New York: Van Nostrand Reinhold.

Costa, P. T., & McCrae, R. R. (1976). Age differences in personality structure: A cluster analytic approach. *Journal of Gerontology, 31,* 564–570.

Costa, P. T., & McCrae, R. R. (1980). Still stable after all these years: Personality as a key to some issues in aging. In P. B. Baltes & O. G. Brim (Eds.), *Life-span development and behavior* (Vol. 3). New York: Academic Press.

Craik, F. I. M. (1977). Age differences in human memory. In J. E. Birren & K. W. Schaie (Eds.), *Handbook of the psychology of aging*. New York: Van Nostrand Reinhold.

Craik, F. I. M., & Lockhart, R. S. (1972). Levels of processing: A framework for memory research. *Journal of Verbal Learning and Verbal Behavior, 11,* 671–684.

Craik, F. I. M., & Simon, E. (1980). Age differences in memory: The roles of attention and depth of processing. In L. W. Poon, J. L. Fozard, L. S. Cermak, D. Arenberg, & L. W. Thompson (Eds.), *New directions in memory and aging.* Hillsdale, NJ: Erlbaum.

Craik, F. I. M., & Tulving, E. (1975). Depth of processing and the retention of words in episodic memory. *Journal of Experimental Psychology: General, 104,* 268–294.

Crook, M. N., Alexander, E. A., Anderson, E. M. S., Coules, J., Hanson, J. A., & Jeffries, N. T. (1962). *Age and form perception.* U.S. Air Force School of Aviation Medicine Report, No. 57–124.

Cross, K. P. (1978). A critical review of state and national studies of the needs and interests of adult learners. In C. B. Stalford (Ed.), *Conference report: Adult learning needs and the demand for life-long learning.* Washington, DC: National Institute of Education, U.S. Department of Health, Education, and Welfare.

Cumming, E., & Henry, W. (1961). *Growing old.* New York: Basic Books.

D

Datan, N., & Ginsberg, L. H. (Eds.). (1975). *Life-span developmental psychology. Normative life crises.* New York: Academic Press.

Deci, E. (1975). *Intrinsic motivation.* New York: Plenum.

DeLongis, A., Coyne, J. C., Dakof, G., Folkman, S., & Lazarus, R. S. (1982). Relationship of daily hassles, uplifts, and major life events to health status. *Health Psychology, 1,* 119–136.

Demsey, D. (1975). *The way we die.* New York: McGraw-Hill.

Denckla, W. D. (1974). Role of the pituitary and thyroid glands in the decline of minimal O_2 consumption with age. *Journal of Clinical Investigation, 53,* 572–581.

Denney, N. W. (1980). The effect of the manipulation of peripheral, noncognitive variables on problem-solving performance among the elderly. *Human Development, 23,* 268–277.

Denney, N. W. (1981, August). *A model of cognitive development across the life span.* Paper presented at the meeting of the American Psychological Association, Los Angeles, CA.

Denney, N. W., & Palmer, A. M. (in press). Adult age differences in traditional and practical problem-solving measures. *Journal of Gerontology.*

Denney, N. W., & Pearce, K. A. (1981). *A developmental study of adults' performance on traditional and practical problem solving tasks.* Unpublished manuscript, University of Kansas, Lawrence.

Dennis, W. (1966). Creative productivity between the ages of 20 and 80 years. *Journal of Gerontology, 21,* 1–18.

deVries, H. A. (1970). Physiological effects of an exercise training regimen upon men aged 52 to 88. *Journal of Gerontology, 25,* 325–336.

Diamond, M. C. (1978). Aging and cell loss: Calling for an honest count. *Psychology Today.* September 1978, p. 126.

Doherty, W. S., & Jacobson, N. S. (1982). Marriage and the family. In B. J. Wolman (Ed.), *Handbook of developmental psychology.* Englewood Cliffs, NJ: Prentice-Hall.

Dohrenwend, B. S., & Dohrenwend, B. P. (1978). Some issues in research on stressful life events. *Journal of Nervous and Mental Disease, 166,* 7–15.

Dohrenwend, B. S., Krasnoff, L., Askenasy, A., & Dohrenwend, B. P. (1978). Exemplification of a method for scaling life events: The PERI life-events scale. *Journal of Health and Social Behavior, 19,* 205–229.

Dolen, L. S., & Bearison, D. J. (1982). Social interaction and social cognition in aging. *Human Development, 25,* 430–442.

Douglas, K., & Arenberg, D. (1978). Age changes, cohort differences, and cultural change on the Guilford-Zimmerman Temperament Survey. *Journal of Gerontology, 33,* 737–747.

Douvan, E., & Adelson, J. (1966). *The adolescent experience.* New York: John Wiley.

Duberman, L. (1973). Step-kin relationships. *Journal of Marriage and the Family, 35,* 282–292.

Durio, H. F. (1975). Mental imagery and creativity. *Journal of Creative Behavior, 9,* 233–244.

Dyer, E. (1963). Parenthood as crisis: A restudy. *Marriage and Family Living, 25,* 488–496.

E

Eaves, L. J. (1978). Twins as a basis for the causal analysis of human personality. In W. E. Nance (Ed.), *Twin research proceedings.* New York: Liss.

Ebbinghaus, H. (1885). *Uber das gedachtris: Untersuchungen Zue experimentellen psychologie.* Leipzig: Duncker & Humbolt. (Translated by H. A. Ruger & C. E. Bussenius, 1913, and reissued by Dover, 1964.)

Edwards, J. N., & Booth, A. (1976). The cessation of marital intercourse. *American Journal of Psychiatry, 133,* 1333–1336.

Edwards, M. (1977). Coupling and re-coupling vs. the challenge of being single. *Personnel and Guidance Journal, 55,* 542–545.

Ehrlich, P. (1979). Mutual help for community elderly. Unpublished manuscript, Southern Illinois University, Carbondale, IL.

Eichorn, D., Clausen, J., Haan, N., Honzik, M., & Mussen, P. (1981). *Present and past in middle life.* New York: Academic Press.

Eichorn, D. M., Hunt, J. V., & Honzik, M. P. (1981). Experience, personality, and I.Q.: Adolescence to middle age. In D. Eichorn, J. Clausen, N. Haan, M. Honzik, & P. Mussen (Eds.), *Present and past in middle life.* New York: Academic Press.

Eisdorfer, C., Nowlin, J., & Wilkie, F. (1970). Improvement of learning in the aged by modification of autonomic nervous system activity. *Science, 170,* 1327–1329.

Eisdorfer, C., & Wilkie, F. (1973). Intellectual changes with advancing age. In L. F. Jarvik, C. Eisdorfer, & J. E. Blum (Eds.), *Intellectual functioning in adults.* New York: Springer.

Elder, G. H. (1974). *Children of the Great Depression: Social change in life perspective.* Chicago: University of Chicago Press.

Elder, G. H. (1980). Adolescence in historical perspective. In J. Adelson (Ed.), *Handbook of adolescent psychology.* New York: John Wiley.

Elder, G. H. (1981). Social history and life experience. In D. Eichorn, J. Clausen, N. Haan, M. Honzik, & P. Mussen (Eds.), *Present and past in middle life.* New York: Academic Press.

Elkind, D. (1961). Quantity conceptions in junior and senior high school students. *Child Development, 32,* 551–560.

Elkind, D. (1969). Piagetian and psychometric conceptions of intelligence. *Harvard Educational Review, 39,* 319–337.

Elkind, D. (1976). *Child development and education: A Piagetian perspective.* New York: Oxford University Press.

Engen, T. (1977). Taste and smell. In J. E. Birren & K. W. Schaie (Eds.), *Handbook of the psychology of aging.* New York: Van Nostrand Reinhold.

Ericsson, K. A., & Simon, H. A. (1978). Retrospective verbal reports as data. Unpublished manuscript, Carnegie-Mellon University, Pittsburgh.

Erikson, E. H. (1952). *Childhood and society.* New York: Norton.

Erikson, E. H. (1962). *Young Man Luther.* New York: Norton.

Erikson, E. H. (1968). *Identity: Youth and crisis.* New York: Norton.

Erikson, E. H. (1969). *Gandhi's Truth*. New York: Norton.

Espinoza, R., & Newman, Y. (1979). *Stepparenting*. DHEW Publication N (ADM) 78–579. Washington, DC: U.S. Government Printing Office.

Eysenck, M. W. (1974). Age differences in incidental learning. *Developmental Psychology, 10,* 936–941.

F

Faranoff, A., Kennell, J., & Klaus, M. (1972). Follow-up of low birth weight infants: The predictive value of maternal visiting programs. *Pediatrics, 49,* 287–290.

Farnsworth, P. R., McNemar, O., & McNemar, Q. (Eds.). (1965). *Annual Review of Psychology* (Vol. 16). Palo Alto, CA: Annual Reviews.

Farrell, M. P., & Rosenberg, S. D. (1981). *Men at midlife*. Boston: Auburn House.

Fast, I., & Cain, A. (1966). The stepparent role: Potential for disturbance in family functioning. *American Journal of Orthopsychiatry, 36,* 485–491.

Federal Trade Commission, Bureau of Consumer Protection. (1978). *Funeral industry practices*. Washington, DC: Author.

Feffer, M. (1959). The cognitive implications of role-taking behavior. *Journal of Personality, 27,* 152–168.

Feiring, C., & Lewis, M. (1978). The child as a member of the family system. *Behavioral Science, 23,* 225–233.

Feldman, S. S., Biringen, Z. C., & Nash, S. C. (in press). Fluctuations of sex-related self-attributions as a function of stage of family life cycle. *Developmental Psychology*.

Feldman, S. S., & Nash, S. C. (1979). Changes in responsiveness to babies during adolescence. *Child Development, 50,* 942–949.

Finch, C. E. (1976). The regulation of physiological changes during mammalian aging. *The Quarterly Review of Biology, 51,* 49–83.

Fischer, K. W. (1980). A theory of cognitive development: The control and construction of hierarchies of skills. *Psychological Review, 87,* 477–531.

Fischer, K. W., & Lazerson, A. (in press). *Human development*. New York: Worth.

Fiske, M. (1980). Tasks and crises of the second half of life: The interrelationship of commitment, coping, and adaptation. In J. E. Birren & R. B. Sloane (Eds.), *Handbook of mental health and aging*. Englewood Cliffs, NJ: Prentice-Hall.

Flanagan, J. (1981, August). *Some characteristics of 70-year-old workers*. Paper presented at the meeting of the American Psychological Association, Los Angeles, CA.

Flavell, J. H. (1977). *Cognitive development*. Englewood Cliffs, NJ: Prentice-Hall.

Flavell, J. H. (1979). Metacognition and cognitive monitoring: A new area of psychological inquiry. *American Psychologist, 34,* 906–911.

Flavell, J. H. (in press). Structures, stages, and sequences in cognitive development. In W. A. Collins (Ed.), *The concept of development: The Minnesota symposia on child psychology*. Hillsdale, NJ: Erlbaum.

Flavell, J. H., & Wellman, H. M. (1977). Metamemory. In R. V. Kail, Jr. & J. W. Hagen (Eds.), *Perspectives on the development of memory and cognition*. Hillsdale, NJ: Erlbaum.

Floderus-Myrhed, B., Pedersen, N., & Rasmussen, I. (1980). Assessment of heritability for personality, based on a short form of the Eysenck Personality Inventory: A study of 12,898 twin pairs. *Behavior Genetics, 10,* 153–163.

Folkman, S., & Lazarus, R. S. (1980). An analysis of coping in a middle-aged community sample. *Journal of Health and Social Behavior, 21,* 219–239.

Ford, J. M., Hink, R. F., Hopkins, W. F., Roth, W. T., Pfefferbaum, A., & Kopell, B. S. (1979). Age effects on event-related potentials in a selective attention task. *Journal of Gerontology, 34,* 388–395.

Foster, G. M., & Anderson, B. G. (1961). *Medical anthropology*. New York: John Wiley.

Fozard, J. L., Wolf, E., Bell, B., McFarland, R. A., & Podolsky, S. (1977). Visual perception and communication. In J. E. Birren & K. W. Schaie (Eds.), *Handbook of the psychology of aging*. New York: Van Nostrand Reinhold.

Freeman, J. (1982). The old, old, very old Charlie Smith. *The Gerontologist, 22,* 532.

Freuchen, P. (1961). *Book of the Eskimos.* Cleveland: World Press.

Friedman, M., & Rosenman, R. M. (1974). *Type A behavior and your heart.* New York: Knopf.

Friedmann, E., & Havighurst, R. J. (1954). *The meaning of work and retirement.* Chicago: University of Chicago Press.

Fries, J. F. (1980). Aging, natural death, and the compression of morbidity. *The New England Journal of Medicine, 303,* 130–135.

Fromm, E. (1955). *The sane society.* New York: Fawcett Books.

Fullard, W., & Reiling, A. M. (1976). An investigation of Lorenz's "babyness." *Child Development, 47,* 1191–1193.

G

Gallup, G. R. (1972). *The Gallup poll: Public opinion 1935–1971.* New York: Random House.

Garland, B. J., & Cross, P. S. (1982). Epidemiology of psychopathology in old age: Some implications for clinical services. *Psychiatric Clinician of North America, 5,* 11–26.

Garrett, H. E. (1946). A developmental theory of intelligence. *American Psychologist, 1,* 372–378.

Gatz, M. (1980). Introduction, Section on Clinical Issues. In L. W. Poon (Ed.), *Aging in the 1980s: Psychological issues.* Washington, DC: American Psychological Association.

Gatz, M., Smyer, M. A., & Lawton, M. P. (1980). The mental health system and the older adult. In L. W. Poon (Ed.), *Aging in the 1980s: Psychological issues.* Washington, DC: American Psychological Association.

Getzel, J. W. (1975). Problem finding and inventiveness of solutions. *Journal of Creative Behavior, 9,* 12–18.

Gibson, J. J. (1979). *The ecological approach to visual perception.* Boston: Houghton-Mifflin.

Gilligan, C. (1982). *In a different voice.* Cambridge, MA: Harvard University Press.

Glaser, B. G., & Strauss, A. L. (1965). *Awareness of dying.* Chicago: Aldine.

Glenn, N. (1975). Psychological well-being in the post-parental stage: Some evidence from national surveys. *Journal of Marriage and the Family, 37,* 105–111.

Glick, P. C. (1979, Summer/Fall). *Future American families.* The Washington COFO MEMO 2.

Glick, P. C., & Carter, H. (1976). *Marriage and divorce. A social and economic study* (2nd ed.). Cambridge, MA: Harvard University Press.

Goldfarb, W. (1945). Psychological privation in infancy and subsequent adjustment. *American Journal of Orthopsychiatry, 15,* 247–255.

Gondonneau, J., Mironer, L., Dourlin-Rollier, A. M., & Simon, P. (1972). *Rapport sur le comportement sexuel des Francais.* Paris: Pierre Charron et Rene Julliard.

Gottesman, I. I., & Shields, J. (1982). *The schizophrenic puzzle.* New York: Cambridge University Press.

Gottman, J. M. (1979). *Marital interaction: Experimental investigations.* New York: Academic Press.

Gould, R. L. (1975). Adult life stages: Growth toward self-tolerance. *Psychology Today, 8,* 74–78.

Gould, R. L. (1978). *Transformations: Growth and change in adult life.* New York: Simon & Schuster.

Gould, R. L. (1980). Transformations during early and middle adult years. In N. J. Smelser & E. H. Erikson (Eds.), *Themes of work and love in adulthood.* Cambridge, MA: Harvard University Press.

Green, R. F., & Berkowitz, B. (1964). Changes in intellect with age: II. Factorial analyses of Wechsler-Bellevue scores. *The Journal of Genetic Psychology, 104,* 3–18.

Gronseth, H. (1972). The family in capitalist society and the dysfunctionality of the husband-provider role. In J. M. Henslin & I. L. Reynolds (Eds.), *Social institutions as appendages to market society.* New York: McKay.

Gruman, G. (1978). Cultural origins of present day "ageism": The modernization of the life cycle. In S. F. Spicker, K. M. Woodward, & D. D. Van Tassel (Eds.), *Aging and the elderly: Human perspectiveness in gerontology*. Atlantic Highlands, N.J.: Humanities Press.

Gubrium, J. F. (1975). *Living and dying at Murray Manor*. New York: St. Martin's.

Guilford, J. P. (1959). *Personality*. New York: McGraw-Hill.

Guilford, J. P. (1967). *The nature of human intelligence*. New York: McGraw-Hill.

Gutmann, D. L. (1975). Parenthood: A key to the comparative psychology of the life cycle. In N. Datan & L. Ginsberg (Eds.), *Life-span developmental psychology: Normative life crises*. New York: Academic Press.

Gutmann, D. L. (1977). The cross-cultural perspective: Notes toward a comparative psychology of aging. In J. E. Birren & K. W. Schaie (Eds.), *Handbook of the psychology of aging*. New York: Van Nostrand Reinhold.

H

Haan, N. (1976). ". . . change and sameness . . ." reconsidered. *International Journal of Aging and Human Development, 7,* 59–65.

Haan, N. (1981). Common dimensions of personality development: Early adolescence to middle life. In D. M. Eichorn, J. Clausen, N. Haan, M. Honzik, & P. Mussen (Eds.), *Present and past in middle life*. New York: Academic Press.

Haan, N., & Day, D. (1974). A longitudinal study of change and sameness in personality development, adolescence to later adulthood. *Aging and Human Development, 5,* 11–39.

Hallihan, M. T. (1979). Structural effects on children's friendships and cliques. *Social Psychology Quarterly, 42,* 43–54.

Hamdani, R. J. (1974). *Exploratory behavior and vocational development among disadvantaged inner-city adolescents*. Unpublished doctoral dissertation, Columbia University, New York.

Hammer, B. B. (1974). *The effects of two treatments designed to foster vocational development in disadvantaged inner-city adolescents*. Unpublished doctoral dissertation, Columbia University, New York.

Hancock, E. (1980). The dimensions of meaning and belonging in the process of divorce. *American Journal of Orthopsychiatry, 59,* 18–27.

Harkins, S. W., & Chapman, R. (1976). Detection and decision factors in pain perception in young and elderly men. *Pain, 2,* 253–264.

Harris, C. S. (1978). *Fact book on aging: A profile of America's older population*. Washington, DC: National Council on Aging.

Harris, L. (1975). *The myth and reality of aging in America*. Washington, DC: National Council on Aging.

Hartup, W. W., & Lempers, J. (1973). A problem in life-span development. The interactional analysis of family attachment. In P. B. Baltes & K. W. Schaie (Eds.), *Life-span developmental psychology*. New York: Academic Press.

Harway, M., & Astin, H. S. (1977). *Sex discrimination in career counseling and education*. New York: Praeger.

Hasher, L., & Zacks, R. T. (1979). Automatic and effortful processes in memory. *Journal of Experimental Psychology: General, 108,* 356–388.

Havighurst, R. J. (1973). History of development psychology: Socialization and personality development through the life span. In P. B. Baltes & K. W. Schaie (Eds.), *Life-span developmental psychology*. New York: Academic Press.

Havighurst, R. J. (1982). The world of work. In B. J. Wolman (Ed.), *Handbook of developmental psychology*. Englewood Cliffs, NJ: Prentice-Hall.

Havighurst, R. J., McDonald, W. J., Perun, P. J., & Snow, R. B. (1976). *Social scientists and educators: Lives after sixty*. Chicago: Committee on Human Development, University of Chicago.

Hayflick, L. (1965). The limited *in vitro* lifetime of human diploid cell strains. *Experimental Cell Research, 47,* 614–636.

Hayflick, L. (1975; September). Why grow old? *Stanford Magazine,* pp. 36–43.

Hayflick, L. (1977). The cellular basis for biological aging. In C. E. Finch & L. Hayflick (Eds.), *Handbook of the biology of aging.* New York: Van Nostrand Reinhold.

Hayslip, B., & Sterns, H. L. (1979). Age differences in relationships between crystallized and fluid intelligences and problem solving. *Journal of Gerontology, 34,* 404–414.

Heald, J. E. (1977). Mid-life career influence. *Vocational Guidance Quarterly, 25,* 309–312.

Hebb, D. O. (1978, November). On watching myself get old. *Psychology Today,* pp. 15–23.

Helson, H. (1959). Adaptation level theory. In S. Koch (Ed.), *Psychology: A study of a science* (Vol. I). New York: McGraw-Hill.

Henderson, N. D. (1982). Human behavior genetics. *Annual Review of Psychology, 33,* 403–440.

Hepworth, S. (1980). Untitled and unpublished manuscript, University of Sheffield, Sheffield, England.

Hess, B. (1971). *Amicability.* Unpublished doctoral dissertation, Rutgers University, New Brunswick, NJ.

Hetherington, E. M. (1979). Divorce: A child's perspective. *American Psychologist, 34,* 851–858.

Hetherington, E. M., Cox, M., & Cox, R. (1978). The aftermath of divorce. In J. H. Stevens & M. Mathews (Eds.), *Mother-child/father-child relations.* Washington, DC: National Association for the Education of Young Children.

Hickey, T. L., Hickey, L. A., & Kalish, R. A. (1968). Children's perceptions of the elderly. *Journal of Genetic Psychology, 112,* 227–235.

Hicks, M. W., & Platt, M. (1970). Marital happiness and stability: A review of the research in the sixties. *Journal of Marriage and the Family, 27,* 677–699.

Hill, J. P. (1973). *Some perspectives on adolescence in American society.* Paper prepared for the Office of Child Development of the U.S. Department of Health, Education, and Welfare, Washington, DC.

Hinton, J. (1972). *Dying* (2nd ed.). New York: Penguin.

Hobbs, D. (1965). Parenthood as crisis: A third study. *Journal of Marriage and the Family, 27,* 677–689.

Hobbs, D., & Wimbish, J. (1977). Transition to parenthood by black couples. *Journal of Marriage and the Family, 39,* 677–689.

Hodgkins, J. (1962). Influence of age on the speed of reaction and movement in females. *Journal of Gerontology, 17,* 385–389.

Hoffman, M. L. (1979). Development of moral thought, feeling, and behavior. *American Psychologist, 34,* 958–966.

Holden, C. (1980, November). Twins: Reunited. *Science, 80.*

Holmes, T. H., & Rahe, R. H. (1967). The social readjustment rating scale. *Journal of Psychosomatic Research, 11,* 213–218. Pergamon Press, Ltd.

Holtzmann, W. H. (1981). Cross-cultural comparisons of personality development in Mexico and the United States. In D. A. Wagner & H. W. Stevenson (Eds.), *Cultural perspectives on child development.* San Francisco: Jossey-Bass.

Horn, J. L., & Cattell, R. B. (1966). Age difference in primary mental ability factors. *Journal of Gerontology, 21,* 210–220.

Horn, J. L., & Cattell, R. B. (1967). Age difference in fluid and crystallized intelligence. *Acta Psychologica, 16,* 107–129.

Horn, J. L., & Donaldson, G. (1980). Cognitive development II: Adulthood development of human abilities. In O. G. Brim & J. Kagan (Eds.), *Constancy and change in human development.* Cambridge, MA: Harvard University Press.

Hornblum, W., & Overton, W. (1976). Area and volume conservation among the elderly: Assessment and training. *Developmental Psychology, 12,* 68–74.

Houle, C. O. (1961). *The inquiring mind.* Madison: University of Wisconsin Press.

Howard, D. V., Lasaga, M. I., & McAndrews, M. P. (1980). Semantic activation during memory encoding across the adult life span. *Journal of Gerontology, 35,* 885–890.

Hoyer, W. J., & Plude, D. J. (1980). Attentional and perceptual processes in the study of cognitive aging. In L. W. Poon (Ed.), *Aging in the 1980s: Psychological issues.* Washington, DC: American Psychological Association.

Hoyt, D. R., & Creech, J. C. (1983). The life satisfaction index: A methodological and theoretical critique. *Journal of Gerontology, 38,* 111–116.

Hultsch, D. F. (1971). Adult age differences in free classification and free recall. *Developmental Psychology, 4,* 338–342.

Hultsch, D. F., & Deutsch, F. (1981). *Adult development and aging.* New York: McGraw-Hill.

Hultsch, D. F., & Pentz, C. A. (1980). Encoding, storage, and retrieval in adult memory: The role of model assumptions. In L. W. Poon, J. L. Fozard, L. S. Cermak, D. Arenberg, & L. W. Thompson (Eds.), *New directions in memory and aging.* Hillsdale, NJ: Erlbaum.

Hultsch, D. F., & Plemons, J. K. (1979). Life events and life-span development. In P. B. Baltes & O. G. Brim (Eds.), *Life-span development and behavior.* New York: Academic Press.

Hunt, E. (1971). What kind of a computer is man? *Cognitive Psychology, 2,* 57–98.

Hunt, M. (1974). *Sexual behavior in the 1970s.* Chicago: Playboy Press.

Hunt, M., & Hunt, B. (1977). *The divorce experience.* New York: McGraw-Hill.

Huston, T. L., & Burgess, R. L. (1979). Social exchange in developing relationships. An overview. In T. L. Huston & R. L. Burgess (Eds.), *Social exchange in developing relationships.* New York: Academic Press.

Huston-Stein, A., & Higgins-Trenk, A. (1978). Development of females from childhood through adulthood: Career and feminine role orientations. In P. Baltes (Ed.), *Life-span development and behavior* (Vol. 1). New York: Academic Press.

Hyde, J. S., & Phillis, D. E. (1979). Androgyny across the life span. *Developmental Psychology, 15,* 334–336.

Hyde, J. S., & Rosenberg, B. G. (1976). *Half the human experience: The psychology of women.* Lexington, MA: Heath.

J

Jacewicz, M. M., & Hartley, A. A. (1979). Rotation of mental images by young and old college students: The effects of familiarity. *Journal of Gerontology, 34,* 396–403.

Jacobson, N. S., & Moore, D. (in press). Behavior exchange theory of marriage: Reconnaissance and reconsideration. In J. P. Vincent (Ed.), *Annual review of family therapy* (Vol. 2), Greenwich, CT: J.A.I. Press.

James, W. (1890). *The principles of psychology* (Vol. 1). New York: Holt, Rinehart & Winston.

Jaquish, G. A., & Ripple, R. E. (1981). Cognitive creative abilities and self-esteem across the adult life span. *Human Development, 24,* 110–119. Reprinted by permission of S. Karger, Ag, Basel.

Jenkins, J. J. (1979). Four points to remember: A tetrahedral model of memory experiments. In L. S. Cermak & F. I. M. Craik (Eds.), *Levels of processing in human memory.* Hillsdale, NJ: Erlbaum.

Jepsen, D. A. (1974). Vocational decision-making strategy types. *Vocational Guidance Quarterly, 23,* 12–23.

John, E. R., Karmel, B. Z., Corning, W. C., Easton, P., Brown, D., Ahn, H., John, M., Harmoney, T., Prichep, L., Toro, A., Gerson, I., Bartlett, F., Thatcher, R., Kaye, H., Valdes, P., & Schwartz, E. (1977). Neurometrics. *Science, 196,* 1393–1409.

Jones, W., Chernovetz, M. E., & Hansson, R. O. (1978). The enigma of androgyny: Differential implications for males and females? *Journal of Consulting and Clinical Psychology, 46,* 298–313.

Jordaan, J. P. (1963). Exploratory behavior. In D. E. Super, R. Statishersky, N. Mattin, & J. P. Jordaan (Eds.), *Career development: Self-concept theory.* New York: College Entrance Examination Board.

Jordaan, J. P., & Heyde, M. B. (1978). *Vocational development during the high school years.* New York: Teachers College Press.

Jung, C. G. (1933). *Modern man in search of a soul.* New York: Harcourt.

K

Kacerguis, M. A., & Adams, G. R. (1978). *Erikson stage resolution: The relationship between identity and intimacy.* Unpublished manuscript, Utah State University, Provo.

Kagan, J. (1979). Family experience and the child's development. *American Psychologist, 34,* 886–891.

Kagan, J. (1980). Perspectives on continuity. In O. G. Brim & J. Kagan (Eds.), *Constancy and change in human development.* Cambridge, MA: Harvard University Press.

Kagan, J., & Moss, H. A. (1962). *Birth to maturity.* New York: John Wiley.

Kagan, S., & Madsen, M. C. (1972). Experimental analysis of cooperation and competition of Anglo-American and Mexican children. *Developmental Psychology, 6,* 49–59.

Kahana, B. (1982). Social behavior and aging. In B. J. Wolman (Ed.), *Handbook of developmental psychology.* Englewood Cliffs, NJ: Prentice-Hall.

Kahana, E., & Felton, B. (1977). Social context and personal needs—A study of Polish and Jewish aged. *Journal of Social Issues, 33,* 56–74.

Kahneman, D. (1973). *Attention and effort.* Englewood Cliffs, NJ: Prentice-Hall.

Kalish, R. A. (1981). *Death, grief, and caring relationships.* Copyright © 1981 by Wadsworth, Inc. Reprinted by permission of the publishers, Brooks/Cole Publishing Company, Monterey, California.

Kalish, R. A., & Reynolds, D. K. (1976). An overview of death and ethnicity. *Death and Ethnicity: A Psychocultural Study.* Copyright Baywood Publishing Company, Inc., Farmingdale, N.Y. All Rights Reserved. Reprinted by permission of the publisher and the authors.

Kanner, A. D., Coyne, J. C., Schaefer, C., & Lazarus, R. S. (1981). Comparison of two modes of stress measurement: Daily hassles and uplifts versus life events. *Journal of Behavioral Medicine, 4,* 1–39.

Kaplan, H. S. (1974). *The new sex therapy.* New York: Brunner/Mazel.

Kastenbaum, R. J. (1969). Death and bereavement in later life. In A. H. Kutscher (Ed.), *Death and bereavement.* Springfield, IL: Chas. C. Thomas.

Kastenbaum, R., & Durkee, N. (1964). Young people view old age. In R. Kastenbaum (Ed.), *New thoughts on old age.* New York: Springer.

Katz, P. A. (1979). The development of female identity. *Sex Roles, 5,* 155–178.

Kay, D. W. K., & Bergmann, K. (1980). Epidemiology of mental disorders among the aged in the community. In J. E. Birren & R. B. Sloane (Eds.), *Handbook of mental health and aging.* Englewood Cliffs, NJ: Prentice-Hall.

Keating, D. (1980). Thinking processes in adolescence. In J. Adelson (Ed.), *Handbook of adolescent psychology.* New York: John Wiley.

Kelly, J. B. (1978, February). *Children and parents in the midst of divorce: Major factors contributing to differential response.* Paper presented at the National Institute of Mental Health Conference on Divorce, Washington, DC.

Kenniston, K. (1970). Youth: A "new" stage of life. *The American Scholar, 39,* 631–654.

Kenshalo, D. R. (1977). Age changes in touch, vibration, temperature, kinesthesis, and pain sensitivity. In J. E. Birren & K. W. Schaie (Eds.), *Handbook of the psychology of aging.* New York: Van Nostrand Reinhold.

Kety, S. (1980). Foreword: Bringing knowledge to bear on the mental dysfunctions associated with aging. In J. E. Birren & R. B. Sloane (Eds.), *Handbook of mental health and aging.* Englewood Cliffs, NJ: Prentice-Hall.

Kiloh, L. G. (1961). Pseudo-dementia. *Acta Psychiatry Scandinavia, 37,* 336.

Kinsey, A. C., Pomeroy, W. B., & Martin, C. E. (1948). *Sexual behavior in the human male.* Philadelphia: Saunders.

Kinsey, A. C., Pomeroy, W. B., & Martin, C. (1953). *Sexual behavior in the human female.* Philadelphia: Saunders.

Klahr, D., & Wallace, J. G. (1975). *Cognitive development: An information-processing view.* Hillsdale, NJ: Erlbaum.

Kline, D. W., & Szafran, J. (1975). Age differences in backward monoptic visual noise making. *Journal of Gerontology, 30,* 307–311, 949–974.

Kobasa, S. (1979). Stressful life events, personality, and health: An inquiry into hardiness. *Journal of Personality and Social Psychology, 37,* 1–11.

Kohlberg, L. (1976). Moral stages and moralization. In T. Lickona (Ed.), *Moral development and behavior.* New York: Holt, Rinehart & Winston. Copyright 1976 by Holt, Rinehart & Winston. Reprinted by permission of Holt, Rinehart & Winston, CBS College Publishing.

Kohlberg, L., & Candee, D. (1979). *Relationships between moral judgment and moral action.* Unpublished manuscript, Harvard University, Cambridge, MA.

Koskenvuo, M., Langinvainia, H., Kaprio, J., Rantasalo, I., & Sama, S. (1979). *The Finnish twin registry: Baseline characteristics III. Occupational and social factors.* Helsinki: Department of Public Health and Science, University of Helsinki.

Krantzler, M. (1974). *Creative divorce.* New York: M. Evans.

Kroeber, A. L. (1948). *Anthropology* (2nd ed.). New York: Harcourt.

Kübler-Ross, E. (1969). *On death and dying.* New York: Macmillan.

Kübler-Ross, E. (1974). *Questions and answers on death and dying.* New York: Macmillan.

Kuhn, T. S. (1962). *The structure of scientific revolutions.* Chicago: University of Chicago Press.

L

Labouvie-Vief, G. (1980). Beyond formal operations: Uses and limits of pure logic in life-span development. *Human Development, 23,* 141–161.

Labouvie-Vief, G. (1982). Dynamic development and mature autonomy: A theoretical prologue. *Human Development, 25,* 161–191.

Lachman, J. L., & Lachman, R. (1980). Age and the actualization of world knowledge. In L. W. Poon, J. L. Fozard, L. S. Cermak, D. Arenberg, & L. W. Thompson (Eds.), *New directions in memory and aging: Proceedings of the George A. Talland memorial conference.* Hillsdale, NJ: Erlbaum.

Lack, S., & Buckingham, R. W. (1978). *First American hospice: Three years of home care.* New Haven, CT: Hospice, Inc.

Lamb, M. E., & Sutton-Smith, B. (1982). *Sibling relationships: Their nature and significance across the life span.* Hillsdale NJ: Erlbaum.

Langer, J. (1969). *Theories of development.* New York: Holt, Rinehart & Winston.

Larson, M. E. (1973). Humbling cases for career counselors. *Phi Delta Kappan, 54,* 374.

Larsson, T., Sjogren, T., & Jacobson, G. (1963). Senile dementia. *Acta Psychiatrica Scandanavia,* Supplement 167.

LaRue, A., & Jarvik, L. F. (1982). Old age and biobehavioral changes. In B. J. Wolman (Ed.), *Handbook of developmental psychology.* Englewood Cliffs, NJ: Prentice-Hall.

Lawton, M. P., Nahemow, W., Yaffe, S., & Feldman, S. (1976). Psychological aspects of crime and fear of crime. In J. Goldsmith & S. Goldsmith (Eds.), *Crime and the elderly.* Lexington, MA: Lexington Books.

Lazarus, R. S., & DeLongis, A. (1981, August). *Psychological stress and coping in aging.* Paper presented at the meeting of the American Psychological Association, Los Angeles, CA.

Lazarus, R. S., & DeLongis, A. (1983). Psychological stress and coping in aging. *American Psychologist, 38,* 245–254.

Lazarus, R. S., & Launier, R. (1978). Stress-related transactions between person and environment. In L. A. Pervin & M. Lewis (Eds.), *Perspectives in interactional psychology.* New York: Plenum.

Leaf, A. (1973, September). Getting old. *Scientific American,* pp. 44–53.

Lee, G. R. (1978). Marriage and morale in late life. *Journal of Marriage and the Family, 40,* 131–139.

Lehman, H. C. (1953). *Age and achievement.* Princeton, NJ: Princeton University Press.

Lehman, H. C. (1960). The age decrement in outstanding scientific creativity. *American Psychologist, 15,* 128–134.

LeMasters, E. E. (1957). Parenthood as crisis. *Journal of Marriage and the Family, 27,* 267–379.

Lepper, M. R., & Greene, D. (1975). Turning play into work: Effects of adult surveillance and extrinsic rewards on children's intrinsic motivation. *Journal of Personality and Social Psychology, 31,* 479–486.

Lerbinger, O. (1972). *Designs for persuasive interaction.* Englewood Cliffs, NJ: Prentice-Hall.

LeShan, L. (1969). Psychotherapy and the dying patient. In L. Pearson (Ed.), *Death and dying.* Cleveland: Case Western Reserve University Press.

LeVine, R. A. (1973). *Culture, behavior, and personality.* Chicago: Aldine.

Levinger, G. (1970). Husbands' and wives' estimates of coital frequency. *Medical Aspects of Human Sexuality, 4,* 42–57.

Levinson, D. J. (1977). The mid-life transition: A period in adult psychosocial development. *Psychiatry, 40,* 99–112.

Levinson, D. J. (1978). *The seasons of a man's life.* New York: Knopf.

Levinson, D. J. (1980). Toward a conception of the adult life course. In N. J. Smelser & E. H. Erikson (Eds.), *Themes of work and love in adulthood.* Cambridge, MA: Harvard University Press.

Libby, R. W., & Whitehurst, R. N. (1977). *Marriage and alternatives: Exploring intimate relationships.* Glenview, IL: Scott, Foresman.

Lifton, R. J. (1977). The sense of immortality: On death and the continuity of life. In H. Feifel (Ed.), *New meanings of death.* New York: McGraw-Hill.

Lindemann, E. (1944). Symptomatology and management of acute grief. *American Journal of Psychiatry, 101,* 141–148.

Lindsay, P. H., & Norman, D. A. (1977). *Human information processing* (2nd ed.). New York: Academic Press.

Livson, F. B. (1976). Patterns of personality development in middle-aged women: A longitudinal study. *International Journal of Aging and Human Development, 7,* 107–115.

Livson, N., & Peskin, H. (1981). Psychological health at age 40: Prediction from adolescent personality. In D. M. Eichorn, J. Clausen, N. Haan, M. Honzik, & P. Mussen (Eds.), *Present and past in middle life.* New York: Academic Press.

Lockhart, R. S., Craik, F. I. M., & Jacoby, L. L. (1976). Depth of processing in recognition and recall: Some aspects of a general memory system. In J. Brown (Ed.), *Recall and recognition.* New York: John Wiley.

Locksley, A., & Colten, M. E. (1979). Psychological androgyny: A case of mistaken identity? *Journal of Personality and Social Psychology, 37,* 1017–1031.

Loehlin, J. C., & Nicholes, R. C. (1976). *Heredity, environment, and personality: A study of 850 sets of twins.* Austin: University of Texas Press.

Lowenthal, M. (1964). *Lives in distress.* New York: Basic Books.

Lowenthal, M. F., & Robinson, B. (1976). Social networks and isolation. In R. H. Binstock & E. Shanas (Eds.), *Handbook of aging and the social sciences.* New York: Van Nostrand Reinhold.

Lowenthal, M. F., Thurnher, M., & Chiriboga, D. (1975). *Four stages of life. A comparative study of women and men facing transitions.* San Francisco: Jossey-Bass.

Lowy, L. (1977, Fall). Adult children and their parents: Dependency or dependability? *Long Term Care and Health Service Administration Quarterly.*

Lowy, L. (1981, August-a). *The older generation: What is due, what is owed?* Paper presented at the meeting of the American Psychological Association, Los Angeles, CA.

Lowy, L. (1981, August-b). *Prevention of intergenerational conflict in the family.* Paper presented at the meeting of the American Psychological Association, Los Angeles, CA.

Luria, Z., & Rose, M. D. (1981). *Psychology of human sexuality.* New York: John Wiley.

M

Maas, H. S., & Kuypers, J. A. (1974). *From thirty to seventy.* San Francisco: Jossey-Bass.

Macklin, E. D. (1980). Nontraditional family forms: A decade of research. *Journal of Marriage and the Family, 42,* 905–922.

Madden, D. J., & Nebes, R. D. (1981, November). *Age effects in selective attention during visual search.* Paper presented at the meeting of the Gerontological Society of America, Toronto.

Maddison, D., & Viola, A. (1968). The health of widows in the year following bereavement. *Journal of Psychosomatic Research, 12,* 297–306.

Maddox, G. L. (1964). Disengagement theory: A critical evaluation. *The Gerontologist, 4,* 80–83.

Maddox, G. L. (1968). Persistence of life-style among the elderly. In B. Neugarten (Ed.), *Middle age and aging.* Chicago: University of Chicago Press.

Mages, N. L., & Mendelsohn, G. A. (1979). Effects of cancer on patients' lives: A personalogical approach. In G. C. Stone, F. Cohen, & N. E. Adler (Eds.), *Health psychology.* San Francisco: Jossey-Bass.

Mancini, J. A., & Orthner, D. K. (1978). Recreational sexuality preference among middle-class husbands and wives. *The Journal of Sex Research, 14,* 96–106.

Mandler, G. (1967). Organization and memory. In K. W. Spence & J. T. Spence (Eds.), *The psychology of learning and motivation 1.* New York: Academic Press.

Mandler, G. (1980). Recognizing: The judgment of previous occurrence. *Psychological Review, 87,* 252–271.

Mannarino, A. P. (1979). The relationship between friendship and altruism in preadolescent girls. *Psychiatry, 42,* 280–284.

Markides, K., & Martin, H. A. (1979). A causal model of life satisfaction among the elderly. *Journal of Gerontology, 34,* 86–93.

Markman, H. J. (1979). Application of a behavioral model of marriage in predicting relationship satisfaction of couples planning marriage. *Journal of Consulting and Clinical Psychology, 47,* 743–749.

Marshall, W. A. (1973). The body. In R. R. Sears & S. S. Feldman (Eds.), *The seven ages of man.* Los Altos, CA: William Kaufman.

Mason, S. E., & Smith, A. D. (1977). Imagery in the aged. *Experimental Aging Research, 3,* 17–32.

Masters, W. H., & Johnson, V. E. (1966). *Human sexual response.* Boston: Little, Brown.

Masters, W. H., & Johnson, V. E. (1970). *Human sexual inadequacy.* Boston: Little, Brown.

Matthysse, S. W., & Kidd, K. K. (1976). Estimating the genetic contribution to schizophrenia. *American Journal of Psychiatry, 133,* 185–191.

Maurer, H. (1979). *Not working: An oral history of the unemployed.* New York: Holt, Rinehart & Winston.

McAvoy, L. L. (1979). The leisure preferences, problems, and needs of the elderly. *Journal of Leisure Research, 11,* 40–47.

McClelland, D. C. (1951). *Personality.* New York: Holt-Dryden.

McClelland, D. C., Atkinson, J. W., Clark, R. A., & Lowell, E. L. (1953). *The achievement motive.* New York: Appleton.

McCord, W., McCord, J., & Howard, A. (1961). Familial correlates of aggression in nondelinquent male children. *Journal of Abnormal and Social Psychology, 62,* 79–83.

McCormack, P. D. (1981). Temporal coding by young and elderly adults: A test of the Hasher-Zacks model. *Developmental Psychology, 17,* 509–515.

McFarland, R. A., Domey, R. G., Warren, A. B., & Ward, D. C. (1960). Daily adaptation as a function of age: I. A statistical analysis. *Journal of Gerontology, 15,* 149–154.

Meacham, J. A., & Santilli, N. R. (1982). Interstage relationships in Erikson's theory: Identity and intimacy. *Child Development, 53,* 1461–1467.

Medvedev, Z. A. (1974). The nucleic acids in development and aging. In B. L. Strehler (Ed.), *Advances in gerontological research* (Vol. I). New York: Academic Press.

Messinger, L., Walker, K., & Freeman, J. (1978). Preparation for remarriage following divorce: The use of group techniques. *American Journal of Orthopsychiatry, 48,* 264–272.

Meyer, B. J. F., Rice, G. E., Knight, C. C., & Jensen, J. L. (1979, Summer-a). *Differences in the type of information remembered from prose by young, middle-aged, and old adults* (Research Report No. 5, Prose Learning Series). Tempe: Arizona State University, Department of Educational Psychology, College of Education.

Meyer, B. J. F., Rice, G. E., Knight, C. C., & Jensen, J. L. (1979, Summer-b). *Effects of comparative and descriptive discourse types on the reading performance of young, middle-aged, and old adults* (Research Report No. 7, Prose Learning Series). Tempe: Arizona State University, Department of Educational Psychology, College of Education.

Midlarsky, E., & Kahana, E. (1981, August). *Altruism and helping among the elderly: An alternative to helplessness?* Paper presented at the meeting of the American Psychological Association, Los Angeles, CA.

Minde, K., Marton, P., Manning, D., & Hines, B. (1980). Some determinants of mother-infant interaction in the premature nursery. *Journal of the American Academy of Child Psychiatry, 19,* 1–21.

Mischel, W. (1973). Toward a cognitive social learning reconceptualization of personality. *Psychological Review, 80,* 252–283.

Mischel, W. (1977). On the future of personality measurement. *American Psychologist, 32,* 246–264.

Mischel, W. (1981). *Introduction to personality* (3rd ed.). New York: Holt, Rinehart & Winston.

Mischel, W., & Mischel, H. (1975). *A cognitive social learning analysis of moral development.* Paper presented at the meeting of the Society for Research in Child Development, Denver, CO.

Monge, R. H., & Hultsch, D. F. (1971). Paired-associate learning as a function of adult age and the length of the anticipation and inspection intervals. *Journal of Gerontology, 26,* 157–162.

Morgan, S. (1978). *Hysterectomy.* New York: Healthright.

Morse, W. C., & Weiss, R. S. (1968). The function and meaning of work and the job. In D. G. Zytowski (Ed.), *Vocational behavior.* New York: Holt, Rinehart & Winston.

Morstain, B. R., & Smart, J. C. (1977). A motivational typology of adult learners. *Journal of Higher Education, 48,* 665–679.

Murdock, B. B. (1967). Recent developments in short-term memory. *British Journal of Psychology, 58,* 421–433.

Murphy, M. D., Sanders, R. E., Gabriesheski, A. S., & Schmitt, F. A. (1981). Metamemory in the aged. *Journal of Gerontology, 26,* 185–193.

Murstein, B. I. (1970). Stimulus-value-role: A theory of marital choice. *Journal of Marriage and the Family, 32,* 465–481.

Mussen, P., Honzik, M., & Eichorn, D. (1982). Early adult antecedents of life satisfaction at age 70. *Journal of Gerontology, 37,* 316–322.

N

Nagy, M. (1948). The child's theories concerning death. *Journal of Genetic Psychology, 73,* 3–27.

Nash, S. C., & Feldman, S. S. (1981). Sex-role and sex-related attributions: Constancy and change across the family life cycle. In M. E. Lamb & A. L. Brown (Eds.), *Advances in developmental psychology* (Vol. 1). Hillsdale, NJ: Erlbaum.

National Assessment of Educational Progress. (1976). Adult work skills and knowledge. Report No. 35–COD–01. Denver, CO: Author.

Neisser, U. (1976). *Cognition and reality: Principles and implications of cognitive psychology.* San Francisco: W. H. Freeman.

Nesselroade, J. R., Schaie, K. W., & Baltes, P. B. (1972). Ontogenetic and generational components of structural and quantitative change in adult behavior. *Journal of Gerontology, 27,* 222–228.

Neugarten, B. L. (1968). *Personality in middle and late life.* New York: Atherton Press.

Neugarten, B. L. (1973). Personality change in later life: A developmental perspective. In C. Eisdorfer & M. P. Lawton (Eds.), *The psychology of adult development and aging*. Washington, DC: American Psychological Association.

Neugarten, B. L. (1975). The future and the young-old. *Gerontologist, 15,* 4–9.

Neugarten, B. L. (1977). Personality and aging. In J. E. Birren & K. W. Schaie (Eds.), *Handbook of the psychology of aging*. New York: Van Nostrand Reinhold.

Neugarten, B. L. (1980) *Annual Editions, Human Development* 80181. Guilford, Conn.: Duskin Publishing, pp. 289–290.

Neugarten, B. L. (1980, February). Must everything be a mid-life crisis? *Prime Time.*

Neugarten, B. L., & Datan, N. (1973). Sociological perspectives on the life cycle. In P. B. Baltes & K. W. Schaie (Eds.), *Life-span developmental psychology.* New York: Academic Press.

Neugarten, B. L., Havighurst, R. J., & Tobin, S. S. (1968). Personality and patterns of aging. In B. L. Neugarten (Ed.), *Middle age and aging*. Chicago: University of Chicago Press.

Neugarten, B. L., & Weinstein, K. K. (1964). The changing American grandparent. *Journal of Marriage and the Family, 26,* 199–204.

Newell, A., & Simon, H. A. (1972). *Human problem solving*. Englewood Cliffs, NJ: Prentice-Hall.

Norton, A. J., & Glick, P. C. (1976). Marital instability: Past, present, and future. *Journal of Social Issues, 32,* 5–20.

Nowak, C. A. (1977). Does youthfulness equal attractiveness? In L. E. Troll, J. Israel, & K. Israel (Eds.), *Looking ahead: A women's guide to the problems and joys of growing older*. Englewood Cliffs, NJ: Prentice-Hall.

Nydegger, C. N. (1973, November). *Late and early fathers*. Paper presented at the meeting of the Gerontological Society, Miami Beach, FL.

Nye, I., & Berado, F. (1973). *The family: Its structure and interaction*. New York: Macmillan.

Nystrom, E. P. (1974). Activity patterns and leisure concepts among the elderly. *The American Journal of Occupational Therapy, 28,* 337–345.

O

Obrist, W. D. (1972). Cerebral physiology of the aged: Influence of circulatory disorder. In C. M. Gaitz (Ed.), *Aging and the brain*. New York: Plenum.

Obrist, W. D. (1980). Cerebral blood flow and EEG changes associated with aging and dementia. In E. W. Busse & D. G. Blazer (Eds.), *Handbook of geriatric psychiatry*. New York: Van Nostrand Reinhold.

Obrist, W. D., & Bissell, L. F. (1955). The electroencephalogram of aged patients with cardiac and cerebral vascular disease. *Journal of Gerontology, 10,* 315–330.

Okun, B. F., & Rappaport, L. J. (1980). *Working with families: An introduction to family therapy*. North Scituate, MA: Duxbury.

Omenn, G. S. (1978). Psychopharmacogenetics: An overview and new approaches. *Human Genetics Supplement, 1,* 83–90.

Orgel, L. E. (1973). Aging of clones of mammalian cells. *Nature, 243,* 441–445.

Orlofsky, J., Marcia, J., & Lesser, I. (1973). Ego identity status and the intimacy vs. isolation crisis of young adulthood. *Journal of Personality and Social Psychology, 27,* 211–219.

Ourselves and Our Children. (1978). New York: Random House. From the Boston Women's Health Collective. Copyright 1978 by Random House. Reprinted by permission.

P

Paivio, A. (1979). *Imagery and verbal processes*. Hillsdale, NJ: Erlbaum. (Original work published 1971).

Palmore, E. (1969). Predicting longevity: A follow-up controlling for age. *The Gerontologist,* 247–250. Vol. 9.

Palmore, E. (1975). *The honorable elders: A cross-cultural analysis of aging in Japan*. Durham, NC: Duke University Press.

Palmore, E. (1980). Predictors of longevity. In S. Haynes & M. Feinleib (Eds.), *Epidemiology of aging.* Washington, DC: U.S. Government Printing Office.

Palmore, E. B. (1982). Predictors of the longevity difference: A 25-year follow-up. *The Gerontologist, 22,* 513–518.

Palmore, E. B., George, L. K., & Fillenbaum, G. G. (1982). Predictors of retirement. *Journal of Gerontology, 37,* no. 6, 733–742. Reprinted by permission of the *Journal of Gerontology.*

Palmore, E. B., & Jeffers, F. C. (1971). *Prediction of the life span.* Lexington, MA: Heath.

Papalia, D., & Bielby, D. (1974). Cognitive functioning in middle and old age adults. A review of research on Piaget's theory. *Human Development, 17,* 424–443.

Papanek, H. (1973). Men, women, and work: Reflections on the two-person career. In J. Huber (Ed.), *Changing women in a changing society.* Chicago: University of Chicago Press.

Parkes, C. M. (1964). The effects of bereavement on physical and mental health—A study of the medical records of widows. *British Medical Journal, 2,* 274–279.

Parkes, C. M. (1972). *Bereavement: Studies of grief in adult life.* New York: International Universities Press.

Pattison, E. M. (Ed.). (1977). *The experience of dying.* Englewood Cliffs, NJ: Prentice-Hall.

Pearlin, L. I., & Lieberman, M. A. (1977). Social sources of emotional distress. In R. Simmons (Ed.), *Research in community mental health.* Greenwich, CT: J.A.I. Press.

Peck, R. C. (1968). Psychological developments in the second half of life. In B. L. Neugarten (Ed.), *Middle age and aging.* Chicago: University of Chicago Press.

Pedersen, F. A., Anderson, B. J., & Cain, R. L. (1977, March). *An approach to understanding linkages between the parent-infant and spouse relationships.* Paper presented at the meeting of the Society for Research in Child Development, New Orleans, LA.

Peevers, B. H., & Secord, P. F. (1973). Developmental changes in attribution of descriptive concepts to persons. *Journal of Personality and Social Psychology, 27,* 120–128.

Perlmutter, M. (1978). What is memory aging the aging of? *Developmental Psychology, 14,* 330–345.

Perlmutter, M. (1980). An apparent paradox about memory aging. In L. W. Poon, J. L. Fozard, L. S. Cermak, D. Arenberg, & L. W. Thompson (Eds.), *New directions in memory and aging: Proceedings of the George A. Talland memorial conference.* Hillsdale, NJ: Erlbaum.

Perlmutter, M., Metzger, R., Nezworski, T., & Miller, K. (1981). Spatial and temporal memory in 20- and 60-year-olds. *Journal of Gerontology, 36,* 59–65.

Perlmutter, M., & Mitchell, D. B. (1982). The appearance and disappearance of age differences in adult memory. In F. I. M. Craik & S. Trehub (Eds.), *Aging and cognitive processes.* New York: Plenum.

Perry, L. C., Brown, R. M., & Perry, D. G. (1979). Interactive effects of cognitive involvement and response topography upon differential eyelid conditioning to conceptual discriminada. *American Journal of Psychology, 92,* 401–412.

Peskin, H., & Livson, N. (1981). Uses of the past in adult psychological health. In D. M. Eichorn, J. Clausen, N. Haan, M. Honzik, & P. Mussen (Eds.), *Present and past in middle life.* New York: Academic Press.

Peterson, J. A. (1980). Social-psychological aspects of death and dying and mental health. In J. E. Birren & R. B. Sloane (Eds.), *Handbook of mental health and aging.* Englewood Cliffs, NJ: Prentice-Hall.

Pfeiffer, E., & Davis, G. (1974). Determinants of sexual behavior in middle and old age. In E. Palmore (Ed.), *Normal aging II.* Durham, NC: Duke University Press.

Pfeiffer, E., Verwoerdt, A., & David, G. C. (1974). Sexual behavior in middle life. In E. Palmore (Ed.), *Normal aging II: Reports from the Duke longitudinal studies, 1970–1973.* Durham, NC: Duke University Press.

Piaget, J. (1967). *Six psychological studies.* New York: Random House.

Piaget, J. (1971). *Biology and knowledge* (Beatrix Walsh, Trans.). Chicago: University of Chicago Press.

Pineo, P. C. (1961). Disenchantment in the later years of marriage. *Marriage and Family Living, 23,* 3–11.

Platt, J. J., & Spivack, G. (1975). *Manual for the means-end problem solving procedure (MEPS): A measure of interpersonal cognitive problem solving skill.* Philadelphia: Hahnemann Medical College and Hospital.

Plude, D. J., & Hoyer, W. J. (1981). Adult age differences in visual search as a function of stimulus mapping and processing load. *Journal of Gerontology, 36,* 598–604.

Powell, A. H., Eisdorfer, C., & Bogdonoff, M. D. (1964). Physiological response patterns observed in a learning task. *Archives of General Psychiatry, 10,* 192–195.

Protinsky, H., & Hughston, G. (1978). Conservation in elderly males: An empirical investigation. *Developmental Psychology, 14,* 114.

R

Rabinowitz, J. C., Ackerman, B. P., Craik, F. I. M., & Hinchley, J. K. (1982). A processing resource account of age differences in recall. *Canadian Journal of Psychology, 36,* 325–355.

Rabkin, J. G., & Struening, E. L. (1976). Life events, stress, and illness. *Science, 194,* 1013–1020.

Raether, H. C., & Slater, R. C. (1974). *The funeral: Facing death as an experience of life.* Milwaukee: National Funeral Directors Association.

Rao, D. C., Morton, N. E., Gottesman, I. I., & Sew, R. (1981). Path analysis of qualitative data on pairs of relatives: Applications to schizophrenia. *Human Heredity.*

Reedy, M. N., Birren, J. E., & Schaie, K. W. (1981). Age and sex differences in satisfying love relationships across the adult life span. *Human Development, 24,* 52–66.

Reese, H. W. (1973). Models of memory and models of development. *Human Development, 16,* 397–416.

Regan, D. (1979). Electrical responses evolved from the human brain. *Scientific American, 241,* 134–146.

Reichard, S., Livson, F., & Peterson, P. (1962). *Aging and personality: A study of 87 older men.* New York: John Wiley.

Reiss, I. L. (1971). *The family system in America.* New York: Holt, Rinehart & Winston.

Retherford, R. D. (1975). *The changing sex differential in mortality.* Westport, CT: Greenwood Press.

Reveron, (1982, February). *APA Monitor,* p. 9. Copyright 1982 by the American Psychological Association. Reprinted by permission of the publisher.

Reynolds, L. G., & Shister, J. (1949). *Job horizons.* New York: Harper & Row.

Rhodes, S. L. (1977). A developmental approach to the life cycle of the family. *Social Casework, 58,* 301–311.

Richards, R. A. (1976). A comparison of selected Guilford and Wallach-Kogan creative thinking tests in conjunction with measures of intelligence. *Journal of Creative Behavior, 10*(3), 151–164.

Riege, W. H., & Inman, V. (1981). Age differences in nonverbal memory tasks. *Journal of Gerontology, 36,* 51–58.

Riegel, K. F. (1973). Dialectic operations: The final period of cognitive development. *Human Development, 16,* 346–370.

Riegel, K. F. (1975). Adult life crises: A dialectic interpretation of development. In N. Datan & L. H. Ginsberg (Eds.), *Life-span developmental psychology.* New York: Academic Press.

Riegel, K. F., & Riegel, R. M. (1972). Development, drop, and death. *Developmental Psychology, 6,* 306–319.

Riley, M. W. (1970). What people think about death. In O. G. Brim, H. E. Freeman, S. Levine, & N. A. Scotch (Eds.), *The dying patient.* New York: Russell Sage Foundation.

Riley, M. W. (Ed.). (1979). *Aging from birth to death: Interdisciplinary perspectives.* Boulder, CO: Westview Press.

Riley, M. W., & Foner, A. (1968). *Aging and society (Vol. 1). An inventory of research findings.* New York: Russell Sage Foundation.

Riley, M. W., Johnson, M. E., & Foner, A. (Eds.). (1972). *Aging and society: A sociology of age stratification.* New York: Russell Sage Foundation.

Roadberg, A. (1981). Perceptions of work and leisure among the elderly. *The Gerontologist, 21,* 142–145.

Robertson, J. F. (1976). Significance of grandparents; Perceptions of young adult grandchildren. *The Gerontologist, 16,* 137–140.

Rodin, J., & Langer, E. (1980). Aging labels: The decline and fall of self-esteem. *Journal of Social Issues, 36,* 12–29.

Rollins, B. C., & Feldman, H. (1970). Marital satisfaction over the family life cycle. *Journal of Marriage and the Family, 32,* 20–28.

Rollins, B. C., & Galliger, R. (1978). The developing child and marital satisfaction. In R. Lerner & G. Spanier (Eds.), *Child influences on marital interaction: A life-span perspective.* New York: Academic Press.

Ron, M. A., Toone, B. K., & Garralda, M. E. (1979). Diagnostic accuracy in presenile dementia. *British Medical Journal, 134,* 161–168.

Rose, C., & Bell, B. (1971). *Predicting longevity.* Lexington, MA: D. C. Heath.

Rose, R. J., Harris, E. L., & Christian, J. C. (1979). Genetic variance in nonverbal intelligence: Data from kinships of identical twins. *Science, 205,* 1153–1155.

Rosen, J. L., & Neugarten, B. L. (1964). Ego functions in the middle and later years: A thematic apperception study. In B. L. Neugarten (Ed.), *Personality in middle and late life.* New York: Atherton.

Rosenfeld, A. (1976). *Prolongevity.* New York: Avon.

Rosenman, R. H., Friedman, M., Strauss, R., Jenkins, C. D., Zyanskiv, S., Wurm, M., Kositcheck, R., Hah, W., & Werthessen, N. T. (1970). Coronary heart disease in the western collaborative study: A follow-up experience of 4½ yrs. *Journal of Chronic Diseases, 23,* 173–190.

Ross, I. G., & Dalton, M. J. (1981, August). *Perceived determinants of closeness in adult sibling relationships.* Paper presented at the meeting of the American Psychological Association, Los Angeles, CA.

Rossi, A. S. (1977). A biosocial perspective on parenting. *Daedalus, 106,* L–31.

Rubenstein, C., & Shaver, P. (1981). The experience of loneliness. In L. A. Peplau & D. Perlman (Eds.), *Loneliness: A source book of current theory, research, and therapy.* New York: Wiley-Interscience.

Rubin, Z. (1970). Measurement of romantic love. *Journal of Personality and Social Psychology, 16,* 265–273.

Rubin, Z. (1973). *Liking and loving: An invitation to social psychology.* New York: Holt, Rinehart & Winston.

Rubin, Z. (1979, October). Seeking a cure for loneliness. *Psychology Today.* pp. 82–91.

Rumaniuk, J. G., & Romaniuk, M. (1981). Creativity across the life span: A measurement perspective. *Human Development, 24,* 366–381.

Rutter, M. (in press). Maternal deprivation 1972–1978. New findings, new concepts, new approaches. *Child Development.*

Rux, J. M. (1976). *Widows and widowers: Instrumental skills, socioeconomic status, and life satisfaction.* Unpublished doctoral dissertation, Pennsylvania State University, University Park.

S

Salthouse, T. A., & Somberg, B. L. (1982). Skilled performance: Effects of adult age and experience on elementary processes. *Journal of Experimental Psychology: General, 111,* 176–207.

Sanders, R. E., & Sanders, J. C. (1978). Long-term durability and transfer of enhanced conceptual performance in the elderly. *Journal of Gerontology, 33,* 408–412.

Santrock, J. W., & Warshak, R. A. (1979). Father custody and social development in boys and girls. *Journal of Social Issues, 35,* 112–125.

Santrock, J. W., Warshak, R. A., & Eliot, G. (1982). Social development and parent-child interaction in father custody and stepmother families. In M. E. Lamb (Ed.), *Nontraditional families.* Hillsdale, NJ: Erlbaum.

Sarason, I. G. (1980). Life stress, self-preoccupation, and social supports. In I. G. Sarason & C. D. Spielberger (Eds.), *Stress and anxiety* (Vol. 7). Washington, DC: Hemisphere.

Sarrell, L., & Sarrell, P. (1974). The college subculture. In M. S. Calderone (Ed.), *Sexuality and human values*. New York: Association Press.

Sauber, M., & Corrigan, E. M. (1970). *The six-year experience of unwed mothers as parents*. New York: Community Council of Greater New York.

Schaefer, E. S. (1965). A configurational analysis of children's reports of parent behavior. *Journal of Consulting Psychology, 20,* 552–557.

Schaie, K. W. (1965). A general model for the study of developmental problems. *Psychological Bulletin, 64,* 92–107.

Schaie, K. W. (1970). A reinterpretation of age-related changes in cognitive structures and functioning. In L. R. Goulet & P. B. Baltes (Eds.), *Life-span developmental psychology: Research and theory*. New York: Academic Press.

Schaie, K. W. (1973). Methodological problems in descriptive developmental research on adulthood and aging. In J. R. Nesselroade & H. W. Reese (Eds.), *Life-span developmental psychology: Methodological issues*. New York: Academic Press.

Schaie, K. W. (1977a). Quasi-experimental research designs in the psychology of aging. In J. E. Birren & K. W. Schaie (Eds.), *Handbook of the psychology of aging*. New York: Van Nostrand Reinhold.

Schaie, K. W. (1977b). Toward a stage theory of adult cognitive development. *International Journal of Aging and Human Development, 8,* 129–138.

Schaie, K. W. (1979). The primary mental abilities in adulthood: An exploration in the development of psychometric intelligence. In P. B. Baltes & O. G. Brim (Eds.), *Life-span development and behavior* (Vol. 2). New York: Academic Press.

Schaie, K. W., & Geiwitz, J. (1982). *Adult development and aging*. Boston: Little, Brown.

Schaie, K. W., & Parham, I. A. (1976). Stability of adult personality: Fact or babble? *Journal of Personality and Social Psychology, 34,* 146–158.

Schank, R. C., & Abelson, R. P. (1977). *Scripts, plans, goals, and understanding*. Hillsdale, NJ: Erlbaum.

Schiffman, S. (1977). Food recognition by the elderly. *Journal of Gerontology, 32,* 586–592.

Schiffman, S., & Pasternak, M. (1979). Decreased discrimination of food odors in the elderly. *Journal of Gerontology, 34,* 73–79.

Schmitz-Secherzer, R. (1979). Aging and leisure. *Society and Leisure, 2,* 377–396.

Schneider, W., & Shiffrin, R. M. (1977). Controlled and automatic human information processing: I. Detection, search and attention. *Psychological Review, 84,* 1–66.

Schonfield, D. (1982). Who is stereotyping whom and why? *The Gerontologist, 22,* 267–272.

Schonfield, D., & Robertson, B. A. (1966). Memory storage and aging. *Canadian Journal of Psychology, 20,* 228–236.

Schukitt, M. A., Morrissey, E. R., & O'Leary, M. R. (1979). Alcohol problems in elderly men and women. In D. M. Peterson (Ed.), *Drug use among the aged*. New York: Spectrum.

Schultz, W. R., & Hoyer, W. J. (1976). Feedback effects on spatial egocentrism in old age. *Journal of Gerontology, 31,* 72–75.

Schulz, R. (1978). *The psychology of death, dying, and bereavement*. Reading, MA: Addison-Wesley.

Schulz, R., & Alderman, D. (1974). Clinical research and the stages of dying. *Omega, 5,* 137–143.

Sears, R. R. (1977). Sources of life satisfaction of the Terman gifted men. *American Psychologist, 32,* 119–128.

Sears, R. R. (1982). Review of present and past middle life. *Contemporary Psychology, 27,* 925–926.

Sears, R. R., & Barbee, A. H. (1977). Care and life satisfaction among Terman's gifted women. In J. C. Stanley, W. C. George, & C. H. Solano (Eds.), *The gifted and the creative: A fifty-year perspective*. Baltimore: Johns Hopkins University Press.

Segerberg, O. (1982). *Living to be 100: 1200 who did and how they did it*. New York: Charles Scribner's Sons.

Seligman, M. E. P. (1975). *Helplessness*. San Francisco: W. H. Freeman.

Shanas, E. (1979). Social myth as hypothesis: The case of the family relations of old people. *The Gerontologist, 19,* 3–9.

Sheehy, G. (1976). *Passages.* New York: Dutton.

Shepard, R. N., & Metzler, J. (1971). Mental rotation of three-dimensional objects. *Science, 171,* 701–703.

Shields, S. A. (1973). *Personality trait attribution and reproductive role.* Unpublished master's thesis, Pennsylvania State University, University Park.

Shneidman, E. S. (1973). *Deaths of man.* New York: Quadrangle/New York Times.

Shock, N. W. (1960). Mortality and measurement of aging. In B. L. Strehler, J. D. Ebert, H. B. Glass, & N. W. Shock (Eds.), *The biology of aging.* Washington, DC: American Institute of Biological Sciences.

Shock, N. W. (1977). Biological theories of aging. In J. E. Birren & K. W. Schaie (Eds.), *Handbook of the psychology of aging.* New York: Van Nostrand Reinhold.

Siegler, I. C., George, L. K., & Okun, M. A. (1979). Cross-sequential analysis of adult personality. *Developmental Psychology, 15,* 350–351.

Siegler, R. S. (1982). Information-processing approaches to development. In W. Kessen (Ed.), *Carmichael's manual of child psychology* (Vol. 1). (4th ed.). New York: John Wiley.

Sigusch, V., & Schmidt, G. (1973). Teenage boys and girls in West Germany. *Journal of Sex Research, 9,* 107–123.

Simon, H. A. (1980). Information-processing explanations of understanding. In T. W. Jusczyk & R. M. Klein (Eds.), *The nature of thought: Essays in honor of D. O. Hebb.* Hillsdale, NJ: Erlbaum.

Simon, W., & Gagnon, J. H. (1969). On psychosexual development. In D. Goslin (Ed.), *Handbook of socialization theory and research.* Chicago: Rand McNally.

Singer, M. T. (1963). Personality measurements in the aged. In J. E. Birren, R. N. Butler, S. W. Greenhouse, L. Sokoloff, & M. R. Yarrow (Eds.), *Human aging.* Washington, DC: U.S. Government Printing Office.

Sinnott, J. D. (1975). Everyday thinking and Piagetian operativity in adults. *Human Development, 18,* 430–443.

Small, G. W., & Jarvik, L. F. (1982, December). The dementia syndrome. *The Lancet,* pp. 1443–1446.

Smith, A. D. (1977). Adult age differences in cued recall. *Developmental Psychology. 13,* 326–331.

Smith, A. D. (1980). Age differences in encoding, storage, and retrieval. In L. W. Poon, J. L. Fozard, L. S. Cermak, D. Arenberg, & L. W. Thompson (Eds.), *New directions in memory and aging: Proceedings of the George A. Talland memorial conference.* Hillsdale, NJ: Erlbaum.

Smith, J. S., & Kiloh, G. G. (1981). The investigation of dementia: Results in 200 consecutive admissions. *The Lancet,* pp. 824–827.

Social Indicators III. (1980). Washington, DC: U.S. Department of Commerce, Bureau of the Census.

Somberg, B. L., & Salthouse, T. A. (1982). Divided attention abilities in young and old adults. *Journal of Experimental Psychology: Human Perception and Performance, 8,* 651–663.

Spanier, G. G., & Castro, R. (1979). Adjustment to separation and divorce: An analysis of 50 case studies. *Journal of Divorce, 2,* 241–253.

Spence, J. T. (1979). *Achievement and achievement-related motives.* Paper presented at the meeting of the American Psychological Association, New York.

Spence, J. T., & Helmreich, R. L. (1978). *Masculinity and femininity: Their psychological dimensions.* Austin: University of Texas Press.

Spence, J. T., Helmreich, R. L., & Stapp, J. (1974). The personal attributes questionnaire: A measure of sex-role stereotypes and masculinity-femininity. *JSAS Catalog of Selective Documents in Psychology, 4,* 43.

Spicer, J., & Hampe, G. (1975). Kinship interaction after divorce. *Journal of Marriage and the Family, 28,* 113–119.

Spiegel, P. M. (1977). Theories of aging. In P. S. Timiras (Ed.), *Developmental physiology and aging.* New York: Macmillan.

Spieth, W. (1965). Slowness of task performance and cardiovascular diseases. In A. T. Wilford & J. E. Birren (Eds.), *Behavior, aging, and the nervous system.* Springfield, IL: Charles C. Thomas.

Spitz, R. A. (1945). Hospitalism: An inquiry into the genesis of psychiatric conditioning in early childhood. In D. Fenschel (Ed.), *Psychoanalytic study of the child* (Vol. 1). New York: International Universities Press.

Stein, N. L., & Glenn, C. G. (1979). An analysis of story comprehension in elementary school children. In R. O. Greedle (Ed.), *Discourse processing: Multidisciplinary perspectives.* Norwood, NJ: Ablex.

Steinberg, L. (1980). *Understanding families with young adolescents.* Carroboro, NC: Center for Early Adolescence.

Stephens, J. (1976). *Loners, losers, and lovers: Elderly tenants in a slum hotel.* Seattle: University of Washington Press.

Sternberg, S. (1969). High-speed scanning in human memory. *Science, 153,* 652–654.

Sterns, H. L., & Sanders, R. E. (1980). Training and education of the elderly. In R. R. Turner & H. W. Reese (Eds.), *Life-span developmental psychology: Intervention.* New York: Academic Press.

Stinnett, N., Carter, L. M., & Montgomery, J. E. (1972). Older persons' perceptions of their marriages. *Journal of Marriage and the Family, 34,* 665–670.

Stinnett, N., & Walters, J. (1977). *Relationships in marriage and family.* New York: Macmillan.

Storck, P. A., Looft, W. R., & Hooper, F. H. (1972). Interrelationships among Piagetian tasks and traditional measures of cognitive abilities in mature and aged adults. *Journal of Gerontology, 27,* 461–465.

Strehler, B. L. (1973, February). A new age of aging. *Natural History.* pp. 8–19.

Stroud, J. G. (1981). Women's careers: Work, family, and personality. In D. Eichorn, J. Clausen, N. Haan, M. Honzik, & P. Mussen (Eds.), *Present and past in middle life.* New York: Academic Press.

Super, D. E., & Hall, D. T. (1978). Career development: Exploration and planning. *Annual Review of Psychology, 20,* 333–372.

Super, D. E., Kowalski, R., & Gotkin, E. (1967). *Floundering and trial after high school.* Unpublished manuscript, Columbia University, New York.

Super, D. E., & Overstreet, P. (1960). *Vocational maturity of ninth-grade boys.* New York: Teachers College Press.

Surwielo, W. W. (1963). The relation of simple response time to brain wave frequency and the effects of age. *Electroencephalography and Clinical Neurophysiology, 15,* 105–114.

Sussman, M. B. (1978, March–April). The family today—Is it an endangered species? *Children Today,* pp. 32–37, 45.

T

Tanner, J. M. (1966). Growth and physique in different populations of mankind. In P. T. Baker & J. S. Weiner (Eds.), *The biology of human adaptability.* Oxford: Clarendon.

Taylor, E. (1974). Creativity and aging. In E. Pfeiffer (Ed.), *Successful aging.* Durham, NC: Center for the Study of Aging and Human Development.

Tessman, L. H. (1978). *Children of parting parents.* New York: Aronson.

Thomas, L. E. (1977). Mid-life career changes: Self-selected or externally mandated? *Vocational Guidance Quarterly, 25,* 320–328.

Thurnher, M. (1979, November). *Turning points across the life course: Subjective perspectives.* Paper presented at the meeting of the Gerontological Society, New York.

Tibbits, C. (1979). Can we invalidate negative stereotypes of aging? *The Gerontologist, 19,* 10–20.

Tomlinson, B. E., Blessed, G., & Roth, M. (1979). Observations on the brains of demented old people. *Journal of Neurological Science, 11,* 205–242.

Tomlinson-Keasey, C. (1972). Formal operations in females from eleven to fifty-four years of age. *Developmental Psychology, 6,* 364.

Torrance, E. P. (1966). *Torrance tests of creative thinking.* Lexington, MA: Personnel Press.

Traupmann, J., Eckels, E., & Hatfield, E. (1982). Intimacy in older women's lives. *The Gerontologist, 22,* 493–498.

Trimakas, K. A., & Nicolay, R. C. (1974). Self-concept and altruism in old age. *Journal of Gerontology, 29,* 434–439.

Troll, L. E. (1971). The family of later life: A decade review. *Journal of Marriage and the Family, 33,* 263–290.

Troll, L. E. (1975). *Early and middle adulthood.* Monterey, CA: Brooks/Cole.

Troll, L. E., & Bengston, V. L. (1982). Intergenerational relations throughout the life span. In B. J. Wolman (Ed.), *Handbook of developmental psychology.* Englewood Cliffs, NJ: Prentice-Hall.

Troll, L. E., & Smith, J. (1976). Attachment through the life span: Some questions about dyadic bonds among adults. *Human Development, 19,* 156–170.

Trunzo, C. E. (1982). Solving the age-old problem. *Money, 11,* 70–80. Excerpted from the November 1982 issue of *Money* magazine by special permission; © 1982, Time, Inc. All rights reserved.

Turnbull, C. M. (1972). *The mountain people.* New York: Simon & Schuster.

Turner, B. F. (1982). Sex-related differences in aging. In B. J. Wolman (Ed.), *Handbook of developmental psychology.* Englewood Cliffs, NJ: Prentice-Hall.

Turner, B. F., & Turner, C. B. (1974). Evaluations of women and men among black and white college students. *Sociological Quarterly, 15,* 442–456.

U

Udry, J. R. (1974). *The social context of marriage.* Philadelphia: Lippincott.

U.S. Bureau of the Census. (1977, March). *Household and family characteristics* (Current Population Reports, Special Studies, Series P-20, No. 326). Washington, DC: U.S. Government Printing Office.

U.S. Department of Commerce, Bureau of the Census. (1979, April). *Population profile of the United States: 1978, population characteristics* (Current Population Reports, Series P-20, No. 336). Washington, DC: U.S. Government Printing Office.

U.S. Department of Health, Education, and Welfare. (1976). *The condition of education in the United States.* Washington, DC: U.S. Government Printing Office.

U.S. Department of Health, Education, and Welfare. (1979). *Monthly vital statistics report. Advance report, final mortality, 1977.* Hyattsville, MD: National Center for Health Statistics.

U.S. Senate, Special Committee on Aging. (1977). *Developments in aging: L976.* Washington, DC: U.S. Government Printing Office.

Upton, A. C. (1977). Pathology. In L. E. Finch & L. Hayflick (Eds.), *Handbook of the biology of aging.* New York: Van Nostrand Reinhold.

V

Vaillant, G. E. (1977). *Adaptation to life.* Boston: Little, Brown.

Van Dusen, R. A., & Sheldon, E. B. (1976). The changing status of American women: A life-cycle perspective. *American Psychologist, 31,* 106–116.

Van Gennep, A. (1960). *The rites of passage.* Chicago: University of Chicago Press.

Van Hoose, W. H., & Worth, M. (1982). *Adulthood in the life cycle.* Dubuque, IA: Wm. C. Brown.

Verwoerdt, A., Pfeiffer, E., & Wang, H. S. (1969). Sexual behavior in senescence—Changes in sexual activity and interest of aging men and women. *Journal of Geriatric Psychiatry, 2,* 163–180.

Vincent, J., Cook, N., & Messerly, N. (in press). A social learning analysis of couples during the second postnatal month. *American Journal of Family Therapy.*

Vincent, J. P., Weiss, R. L., & Birchler, G. R. (1975). A behavioral analysis of problem-solving in distressed and nondistressed married and stranger dyads. *Behavior Therapy, 6,* 475–487.

Visher, E., & Visher, J. (1978). Common problems of stepparents and their spouses. *American Journal of Orthopsychiatry, 48,* 252–262.

W

Waddell, K. J., & Rogoff, B. (1981). Effect of contextual organization on spatial memory of middle-aged and older women. *Developmental Psychology, 17,* 878–885.

Wagenwoord, J., & Bailey. (1978). *Men: A book for women.* New York: Avon Books.

Waldron, I. (1976). Why do women live longer than men? *Social Science and Medicine, 10,* 349–362.

Walford, R. L. (1969). *The immunologic theory of aging.* Baltimore: Williams & Wilkins.

Walkup, L. E. (1965). Creativity in science through visualization. *Perceptual and Motor Skills, 21,* 35–41.

Wallace, J. G. (1977). The course of cognitive growth. In V. P. Varma & P. Williams (Eds.), *Piaget, psychology and education.* Itasca, IL: Peacock.

Wallach, M. A. (1973). Ideology, evidence, and creative research. *Contemporary Psychology, 18,* 162–164.

Wallach, M. A., & Kogan, N. (1965). *Modes of thinking in young children.* New York: Holt, Rinehart & Winston.

Wallerstein, J. S., & Kelly, J. B. (1974). The effects of parental divorce: The adolescent experience. In E. J. Anthony & C. Koupernik (Eds.), *The child in his family: Children of psychiatric risk* (Vol. 3). New York: John Wiley.

Wallerstein, J. S., & Kelly, J. B. (1975). The effects of parental divorce: Experiences of the preschool child. *Journal of the American Academy of Child Psychiatry, 14,* 600–616.

Wallerstein, J. S., & Kelly, J. B. (1980). *Surviving the break-up: How children actually cope with divorce.* New York: Basic Books.

Walsh, D. (1976). Age differences in central perceptual processing: A dichotic backward masking investigation. *Journal of Gerontology, 31,* 178–185.

Walsh, D., & Baldwin, M. (1977). Age differences in integrated semantic memory. *Developmental Psychology, 13,* 509–514.

Wang, H. S. (1973). Cerebral correlates of intellectual function in senescence. In L. F. Jarvaik, C. Eisdorfer, & J. E. Blum (Eds.), *Intellectual functioning in adults: Psychological and biological influences.* New York: Springer.

Wang, H. S., & Busse, E. W. (1969). EEG of healthy old persons—A longitudinal study. I: Dominant background activity and occipital rhythm. *Journal of Gerontology, 24,* 419–426.

Wechsler, D. (1958). *The measurement and appraisal of adult intelligence* (4th ed.). Baltimore: Williams & Wilkins.

Weinraub, M., Brooks, J., & Lewis, M. (1977). The social network: A reconsideration of the concept of attachment. *Human Development, 20,* 31–47.

Weisman, A. D. (1972). *On dying and denying.* New York: Behavioral Publications.

Weiss, L., & Lowenthal, M. (1975). Life-course perspectives on friendship. In M. Lowenthal, M. Thurnher, & D. Chiriboga (Eds.), *Four stages of life.* San Francisco: Jossey-Bass.

Weiss, R. S. (1973). *Loneliness: The experience of emotional and social isolation.* Cambridge, MA: M.I.T. Press.

Weiss, R. S. (1975). *Marital separation.* New York: Basic Books.

Weiss, R. S. (1978). The conceptualization of marriage from a behavioral perspective. In T. J. Paolino & B. S. McGrady (Eds.), *Marriage and family therapy.* New York: Brunner Mazel.

Welford, A. T. (1980). Sensory, perceptual, and motor processes in older adults. In J. E. Birren & R. B. Sloane (Eds.), *Handbook of mental health and aging.* Englewood Cliffs, NJ: Prentice-Hall.

Westoff, L. (1977). *The second time around.* New York: Penguin.

Westoff, L. A., & Westoff, C. F. (1971). *From non to zero.* Boston: Little, Brown.

White, C. B. (1981, August). *Sexual interest, attitudes, knowledge and sexual history in relation to sexual behavior in the institutionalized aged.* Paper presented at the meeting of the American Psychological Association, Los Angeles, CA.

White, C. B., & Catania, J. (1981). Psychoeducational intervention for sexuality with aged, family members of the aged, and people who work with the aged. *International Journal of Aging and Human Development.*

Wilkie, F., & Eisdorfer, C. (1971). Intelligence and blood pressure in the aged. *Science, 172,* 959–962.

Wilkie, F., & Eisdorfer, C. (1973). *Intellectual changes: A 15-year follow-up of the Duke sample.* Unpublished manuscript presented at the meeting of the Gerontological Society, Miami, FL.

Williamson, J. B., Munley, A., & Evans, I. (1980). *Aging and society: An introduction to social gerontology.* New York: Holt, Rinehart & Winston. Copyright © 1980 by Holt, Rinehart & Winston, CBS College Publishing.

Wilson, R. W., & White, E. L. (1977). Changes in morbidity, disability, and utilization differentials between the poor and the non-poor, data from the Health Interview Survey, 1964 and 1973. *Medical Care, 15,* 636–646.

Winch, R. F. (1958). *Mate selection.* New York: Harper & Row.

Winston, M. P., & Forsher, T. (1971). *Nonsupport of legitimate children by affluent fathers as a cause of poverty and welfare dependence.* New York: Rand Corp.

Wiswell, R. A. (1980). Relaxation, exercise, and aging. In J. E. Birren & R. B. Sloane (Eds.), *Handbook of mental health and aging.* Englewood Cliffs, NJ: Prentice-Hall.

Wohlwill, J. F. (1973). *The study of behavioral development.* New York: Academic Press.

Women's Bureau, U.S. Bureau of the Census. (1979). *Marital status and living arrangements: March 1978* (Current Population Reports, Series P-20, No. 338). Washington, DC: U.S. Government Printing Office.

Women's Medical Center. (1977). *Menopause.* Washington, DC: Author.

Woodruff, D. S. (1978). *Can you live to be 100?* New York: New American Library.

Woodruff, D. S. (1979). Brain electrical activity and behavior relationships over the life span. In P. B. Baltes (Ed.), *Life-span development and behavior* (Vol. 1). New York: Academic Press.

Wright, J. W. (1982). *The American almanac of jobs and salaries.* New York: Avon.

Wright, R. E. (1981). Aging, divided attention, and processing capacity. *Journal of Gerontology, 36,* 605–614.

Y

Yankelovich, D. (1981, April). New rules in American life: Searching for self-fulfillment in a world turned upside down. *Psychology Today,* pp. 35–91.

Young, M., Benjamin, B., & Wallis, C. (1963). The mortality of widowers. *The Lancet, 2,* 454–456.

Yussen, S. R., & Santrock, J. W. (1982). *Child development: An introduction* (2nd ed.). Dubuque, IA: Wm. C. Brown.

Z

Zahn-Waxler, C., Radke-Yarrow, M., & King, R. M. (1979). Childrearing and children's prosocial initiations towards victims of distress. *Child Development, 50,* 319–330.

Zaks, P. M., & Labouvie-Vief, G. (1980). Spatial perspective taking and referential communication skills in the elderly: A training study. *Journal of Gerontology, 35,* 217–224.

PHOTO CREDITS

CHAPTER 11

381   UPI
388   Donald Rocker
394   Jean-Claude Lejeune
404   Jim Shaffer

CHAPTER 12

413   Michael Siluk
417   Robert Eckert/EKM-Nepenthe
432   N. R. Rowan

SECTION VI

left   Cathy Cheney/EKM-Nepenthe
middle   Kent Reno/Jeroboam
right   Eve Arnold/Magnum

CHAPTER 13

450   Josef Koudelka/Magnum
454   Martine Franck/Magnum
459   Tom Ballard/EKM-Nepenthe

FIGURE CREDITS

CHAPTER 1

Page 29 Ulric Neisser, *Cognitive Psychology,* © 1967, pp. 17, 112. Adapted by permission of Prentice-Hall, Inc., Englewood Cliffs, New Jersey.

CHAPTER 2

Figure 2.1 From Birren, J. E., and K. W. Schaie (editors). *Handbook of the Psychology of Aging.* Copyright © 1977 Van Nostrand Reinhold Company, New York.

CHAPTER 3

Figure 3.1 Bureau of the Census, National Center for Health Statistics, Washington, D.C., 1977.
Page 95 Courtesy of Dr. Thomas Bouchard.

CHAPTER 4

Figure 4.1 A figure of corrected best distance vision in the better eye, page 27 in ''Longitudinal evaluation of ocular function,'' by Banks Anderson, Jr., and Erdman Palmore, in *Normal Aging II: Reports from the Duke Longitudinal Studies,* 1970–1973, edited by Erdman Palmore. Copyright 1974 by Duke University Press.
Figure 4.2 From Langley, L. L. *Physiology of Man.* Copyright © 1971 Van Nostrand Reinhold Company, New York.
Figure 4.3 From *From Now to Zero: Fertility, Contraception and Abortion in America.* Copyright © 1968, 1971 by Charles F. Westoff and Leslie Aldridge Westoff. By permission of Little, Brown and Company.

CHAPTER 5

Figures 5.1 and 5.2 From Santrock, John W. *Life-Span Development.* Copyright © 1983 William C. Brown Publishers, Dubuque, Iowa. All Rights Reserved. Reprinted by permission.
Figures 5.4 and 5.5 Botwinick, 1967, Figures 20 and 21. Reprinted by permission of Jack Botwinick from *Cognitive Process in Maturity and Old Age.* Published 1967 by Springer Publishing Company, Inc. Copyright Jack Botwinick.

Figure 5.6 Reprinted with permission from *Americans in Transition: Life Changes as Reasons for Adult Learning,* by Carol B. Aslanian and Henry M. Brickell, © 1983 by the College Entrance Examination Board, New York.

CHAPTER 6

Figure 6.1 Salthouse, T. A. & Somberg, B. L. Skilled performance: Effects of adult age & experiences on elementary processes. *Journal of Experimental Psychology: General,* 1982, III, 176–207. Copyright 1982 by the American Psychological Association. Reprinted by permission of the authors.
Figure 6.2 Copyright (1966) Canadian Psychological Association. Reprinted by permission.
Figure 6.3 Anders, T. R., Fozard, J. L. & Lillyquist, T. D. The effects of age upon retrieval from short-term memory. *Developmental Psychology,* 1972, 6:214–217. Copyright 1972 by the American Psychological Association. Reprinted by permission of the authors.
Page 205 Murdock, G. G., Jr., Recent developments in short-term memory. *British Journal of Psychology,* 1967, 58, 421–433. Reprinted by permission.
Figure 6.5 Reprinted by permission of the *Journal of Gerontology,* 36, pages 620–624, 1981.
Figure 6.6 Hultsch, D. F. Adult age differences in free classification & free recall. *Developmental Psychology* 4:338–342, 1971. Copyright 1971 by the American Psychological Association. Reprinted by permission of the author.
Figure 6.7 Bahrick, H. P., Bahrick, P. O. & Wittlinger, R. P. Fifty years of memory for names and faces: A cross-sectional approach. *Journal of Experimental Psychology, 104*:54–75, 1975. Copyright 1975 by the American Psychological Association. Reprinted by permission of the author.
Figure 6.8 Reprinted by permission of the *Journal of Gerontology,* 36, pages 51–58, 1981.
Figure 6.9 From Jenkins, J. J. Four points to remember: A tetradchedral model of memory experiments. In L. S. Cermak and F. I. M. Craik (eds.) *Levels of Processing Memory.* Copyright © 1978 Lawrence Erlbaum Associates, Inc., Hillsdale, NJ. Reprinted by permission.

CHAPTER 7

Figure 7.1   After Fig. 7–2 The Family Life Cycle by Length of Time in Each of Eight Stages (p. 148) in *Marriage and Family Development,* 5th edition by Evelyn Millis Duvall (J. P. Lippincott Co.) Copyrighted © 1957, 1962, 1967, 1971, 1977 by Harper & Row Publishers, Inc. By permission of Harper & Row, Publishers, Inc.
Figure 7.2   From Santrock, John W. *Life-Span Development.* Copyright © 1983 William C. Brown Publishers, Dubuque, Iowa. All Rights Reserved. Reprinted by permission.
Page 255   Belsky, J. Early Human Experience: A Family Perspective. *Developmental Psychology,* 1981, *17:*3–23. Copyright 1981 by the American Psychological Association. Reprinted by permission of the author.

CHAPTER 8

Figure 8.1   Reedy, M. N., Birren, J. E. & Schaie, K. W. Age & Sex Differences in the Life-Span. *Human Development,* 1981, *24:*52–66. Reprinted by permission of S. Karger, Ag, Basel.
Figure 8.2   Reprinted by permission of *The Gerontologist,* 22, #6, pages 493–498, 1982.
Figures 8.3 and 8.4   J. A. Kuypers & V. L. Bengstrom, Social breakdown & competence: A model of normal aging. *Human Development,* 1973, *16:*181–201. Reprinted by permission of S. Karger, Ag., Basel.

CHAPTER 9

Figure 9.1   Reprinted by permission of the *Journal of Gerontology,* 37, #6, pages 773–742, 1982.
Figure 9.2   From *The Social Forces in Later Life: An Introduction to Social Gerontology,* 2nd Edition, by Robert C. Atchley. © 1977 by Wadsworth Publishing Company, Inc. Reprinted by permission of Wadsworth Publishing Company, Belmont, California 94002.

CHAPTER 10

Figure 10.1   Reproduced from *Childhood and Society,* 2nd edition, by Erik H. Erikson, by permission of W. W. Norton & Company, Inc. Copyright 1950, © 1963 by W. W. Norton & Company, Inc., and the Hogarth Press, London.
Figure 10.2   Levinson, D. J. Toward a conception of the adult life course. In N. J. Smelser & E. H. Erikson (eds.) *Themes of Work and Love in Adulthood.* Harvard University Press. Reprinted by permission.
Figure 10.4   From Hultsch, D. F. & J. K. Plemons, Life events and life span development. In P. B. Baltes & O. G. Brim, Jr. (Eds.) *Life-Span Development and Behavior.* Copyright © 1979 Academic Press. Reprinted by permission.

CHAPTER 11

Figure 11.1   From Kagan, J. and M. Moss. From *Birth to Maturity.* Copyright © 1960, John Wiley and Sons, Inc. Reprinted by permission of the authors.

CHAPTER 13

Figure 13.1   Reprinted with permission of Concern for Dying, 250 West 57 Street, New York, N.Y. 10107

NAME INDEX

515

U

Udry, J. R., 142
Upton, A. C., 109

V

Vaillant, G. E., 347, 350, 351, 356, 360, 361, 374, 375, 398, 419
Valdes, P., 124
Van Dusen, R. A., 328, 341
Van Gennep, A., 24
Van Hoose, W. H., 256, 268, 270, 334
Verwoerdt, A., 144, 145, 147
Vincent, J., 254
Vincent, J. P., 253, 254
Viola, A., 465
Visher, E., 276
Visher, J., 276

W

Waddell, K. J., 220
Wagenwood, J., 140
Waldron, I., 105
Wales, T. J., 91
Walford, R. L., 108
Walker, K., 271
Walkup, L. E., 180
Wallace, J. G., 195
Wallach, M. A., 179, 180
Wallerstein, J. S., 272, 274, 276
Wallis, C., 465
Walsh, D., 196, 226
Walters, J., 276
Wang, H. S., 123, 147, 178
Ward, D. C., 117
Warren, A. B., 117
Warren, M. A., 447
Warshak, R. A., 271, 272, 274
Watson, J., 350
Weiner, 92
Weinraub, M., 286
Weinstein, K. K., 267
Weisman, A. D., 445, 458
Weiss, L., 292
Weiss, R. L., 253
Weiss, R. S., 270, 271, 282, 285, 310
Welford, A. T., 117, 119, 196

Wellman, H. M., 220
Werthessen, N. T., 132
Westoff, L., 276
White, C. B., 146
White, E. L., 133
White, F., 114
White, S., 215
Whitehurst, R. N., 269, 307
Wilcox, S. G., 469
Wilkie, F., 50, 74, 178
Williamson, J. B., 107, 136, 296, 298, 338, 382
Willis, S. L., 156, 190
Wilson, R. W., 133
Wimbish, J., 255
Winch, R. F., 245
Winston, M. P., 272
Wiswell, R. A., 114, 115, 134, 149
Wittlinger, R. P., 213, 217
Wohlwill, J. F., 13
Wolf, E., 196
Wolfe, D. M., 251
Wolman, B. J., 231, 280, 307, 436
Woodruff, D. S., 123, 124
Worth, M., 256, 268, 270, 334
Wright, J. W., 328
Wright, M., 217, 218
Wright, R., 202
Wurm, M., 132

Y

Yaffe, S., 380
Yankelovich, D., 144, 287, 307, 327
Yarrow, M. R., 178
Yoshioka, 292
Young, M., 465
Yussen, S. R., 196

Z

Zacks, R. T., 202, 213, 218
Zahn-Waxler, C., 263
Zaks, P. M., 157
Zyanskiv, S., 132

SUBJECT INDEX

525

S